The Linguistic Structure of  English

The Linguistic Structure of Modern English

Laurel J. Brinton

University of British Columbia

Donna M. Brinton

University of Southern California

John Benjamins Publishing Company

Amsterdam / Philadelphia

TM The paper used in this publication meets the minimum requirements of American National Standard for Information Sciences — Permanence of Paper for Printed Library Materials, ANSI Z39.48-1984.

Library of Congress Cataloging-in-Publication Data

Brinton, Laurel J.
  The linguistic structure of modern English / Laurel J. Brinton, Donna M. Brinton. -- Rev. ed.
    p.   cm.
  Previously published as: The structure of modern English : a linguistic introduction, c2000.
  Includes bibliographical references and index.
    1. English language--Grammar. 2. English language--Phonology. 3. English language--Syntax.
    I. Brinton, Donna. II. Brinton, Laurel J. Structure of modern English. III. Title.
PE1106.B73   2010
425--dc22   2010007276

ISBN 978 90 272 1171 2   (Hb; alk. paper)
ISBN 978 90 272 1172 9   (Pb; alk. paper)
ISBN 978 90 272 8824 0   (Eb)

John Benjamins Publishing Company • P.O. Box 36224 • 1020 ME Amsterdam • The Netherlands
John Benjamins North America • P.O. Box 27519 • Philadelphia PA 19118-0519 • USA

Table of contents

The workbook can be found at http://dx.doi.org/10.1075/z.156.workbook

List of tables

List of figures

Acknowledgments

We would like to acknowledge the Office of Learning Technology, Distance Education, University of British Columbia for permission to use materials which were originally prepared by Laurel Brinton for a distance education course as the basis of this text and accompanying workbook.

We are grateful to colleagues in the English Department of the University of British Columbia: Lilita Rodman, Leslie Arnovick, Barbara Dancygier, Jessica de Villiers, and Ina Biermann. Sarah Bowers of Langara College offered invaluable feedback in her role as instructor for the distance education version of English 329. Thanks are due to the research assistant for the first edition, Patte Rockett, who assisted at various stages in the production of the manuscript. Also to be acknowledged are the many students in English 329 at the University of British Columbia, who have offered critiques and corrections of the material over the years.

Alan Doree, formerly of the University of British Columbia, did the painstaking work of preparing the numerous tree diagrams for the first edition; we are appreciative of the diligence and care he took with them. Barry D. Griner of the University of Southern California assisted in the proofreading of the second edition.

We are immensely grateful to Mark Davies of Brigham Young University, who generously allowed us permission to use examples from the Corpus of Contermporary American English (COCA) for the second edition of this text.

Howard Williams, of Teachers College, Columbia University, contributed not only the final chapter on pedagogy but also critiqued the entire first edition manuscript.

Finally, at John Benjamins Publishing we would like to thank Pieter Lamers for his work on the website, Patricia Leplae for her careful attention to the production of the text book, and Kees Vaes, who is the type of editor that every author hopes to have.

Preface to the second edition

The following text gives a full introduction to English sounds, grammar, and vocabulary. It begins with a study of the distinctive sounds of English (*phonology*). It turns next to an analysis of the structure of English words and their classification (*morphology*) as well as the classification of English words and their grammatical modification. This is followed by an exploration of the meaning of English words (*lexical semantics*). The next section is taken up with a detailed analysis of English sentence structure (*syntax*) from a generative perspective. The text then looks at the interaction of syntax and semantics (*sentence semantics*) and considers the functions and contexts of language use (*pragmatics*). Finally, it outlines the role of linguistics in first- and second-language teaching and learning (*pedagogy*).

This textbook is addressed to advanced undergraduate (and graduate) students interested in contemporary English, including those whose primary area of interest is English as a second language, primary- or secondary-school English education, English literature, theoretical and applied linguistics, or speech pathology. For this reason, this textbook, unlike many other introductory linguistics textbooks, emphasizes the empirical facts of English rather than any particular theory of linguistics. Furthermore, the text does not assume any background in language or linguistics. Students are required to learn the International Phonetic Alphabet as well as the technical vocabulary of grammar and linguistics, but all necessary terms and concepts are presented in the text.

New to the 2nd edition are the following:

1. the use of authentic spoken and written English examples taken from the Corpus of Contemporary American English (COCA) to exemplify features under discussion;
2. a full glossary of keys terms used in the text (indicated in text by bold-faced text);
3. an additional chapter (included in the first edition on the CD-ROM) on pedagogy;
4. new sections on cognitive semantics (Chapter 6) and politeness (Chapter 11);
5. completely updated print references;
6. web links to sites of special interest and relevance (given on the website); and
7. revised, more reader-friendly layout (including "hint" boxes and expanded "notes" on specific points)

Upon completion of this textbook and accompanying workbook, students will have acquired the following:

1. a knowledge of the sound system of contemporary English;
2. an understanding of the formation of English words and of their grammatical modification;

3.   a comprehension of the structure of both simple and complex sentences in English;
4.   a recognition of complexities in the expression of meaning, on both the word and sentence level;
5.   an understanding of the effects of context and function of use upon the structure of the language; and
6.   an appreciation of the importance of linguistic knowledge to the teaching of English to first- and second-language learners.

The textbook is divided into twelve chapters. Chapter 1 briefly examines the discipline of linguistics and the nature of human language and grammar. After a consideration of the means of production of human speech sounds, Chapter 2 studies the consonant and vowel sounds of English and methods of their phonetic transcription. Chapter 3 continues discussion of the English sound system, considering sound combinations, stress, intonation, and syllable structure; it also examines phonological rules in English and the concept of the *phoneme* (distinctive sound of a language). Chapter 4 explores the internal structure of words, the concept of the *morpheme* (meaningful unit of a language), and the varied processes of word formation in English. Chapter 5 begins by defining the grammatical categories and looking at the grammatical modification of English words and ends with a study of the means of word classification in the language. Chapter 6 surveys a number of traditional and structural approaches to word meaning and includes a discussion of figurative language and cognitive approaches to meaning. Chapter 7 treats the syntax of the simple sentence, looking at the internal structure of the noun, adjective, adverb, and prepositional phrase, complement structures in the verb phrase, verb types, and grammatical functions. Chapter 8 continues to treat the syntax of the simple sentence, including adverbial modifiers and verb specifiers, and then examines the structure of passive, interrogative, negative, and imperative sentences. The syntax of the complex sentence is dealt with in Chapter 9, including *that*-clauses, *wh*-clauses (*wh*-questions, relative clauses, and indirect clauses), and nonfinite clauses (infinitival and participial clauses). Chapter 10 turns to the question of sentence meaning, understood in terms of thematic roles and predication analysis. Chapter 11 looks at two quite different approaches to the question of the function of language in context: information structuring and speech act theory. Chapter 12 examines the pedagogical applications of the material presented in the textbook, including the changing role of linguistics in the teaching of English; it reviews arguments both in favor and opposed to explicit grammatical instruction for native and nonnative speakers and considers the importance of grammatical knowledge for both the teacher and the learner. At the end of each chapter, students are also directed to readings that provide more detailed or enriched content on certain topics or supplemental help in understanding the content of the chapter.

A website accompanies this textbook. It includes:

1.   a complete workbook with self-testing exercises. Answers for all of the self-testing exercises are provided. At relevant points in each chapter in the text, students are directed

to complete specific exercises and are advised to do so before continuing with the chapter. The exercises should provide a check on students' understanding and progress.
2. a comprehensive list of web links that expand on the information presented in the text and allow students to explore the topics more broadly on their own.

The website can be found at the following address: http://dx.doi.org/10.1075/z.156.workbook

1. A note to the student on punctuation

Various punctuation conventions are used in this textbook with which you may not be familiar.

It is the practice to distinguish between words (or parts of words) which are "mentioned" rather than used. Using words is what we do whenever we speak, but mentioning words is what we do when we refer to words as words or to the forms of words, rather than evoking their meanings. For example, try reading the following sentences:

> The word paper has five letters. Court has several different meanings. The feminine suffix -rix is almost obsolete. The clause whatever you do is an indefinite relative clause.

You may have had some difficulty reading these sentences. The reason for your difficulties is that these sentences contain word forms which are mentioned rather than used. The convention in printed texts is to italicize these mentioned forms, as follows:

> The word *paper* has five letters. *Court* has several different meanings. The feminine suffix -*rix* is almost obsolete. The clause *whatever you do* is an indefinite relative clause.

Note that this convention makes these sentences much easier to read. (In handwriting, mentioned forms are underlined.) Italics also denote all linguistic forms which are set off as example sentences. For example, below are two structurally ambiguous sentences:

> *Visiting relatives can be tiresome.*
> *Flying planes can be dangerous.*

This use of italics differs from the use of quotation marks to repeat the exact words of a spoken or written text, e.g. "convention" occurs two times in the previous paragraph.

Single quotation marks are used to give the meaning or gloss for a word; e.g. the word *garrulous* means 'tiresomely talkative'.

When the actual sound of the word is being referred to, the International Phonetic Alphabet is used. To distinguish such representations from regular writing, they are enclosed in slashes (in the case of phonemes) or square brackets (in the case of allophones), e.g.:

> The word *read* is pronounced /rɛd/ or /rid/.
> The "t" sound in *top* is pronounced [tʰ].

Another convention in linguistic works is the use of capitals to denote all the forms of a single word, thus WORK stands for *works, work, working, worked*. Capitals are also used for phonological and semantic features. These usages will be explained in more detail within the text.

2.   A note on the use of corpus examples

This text makes use of authentic examples from the Corpus of Contemporary American English (COCA): http://www.americancorpus.org/, the largest freely-available corpus of English containing over 400 million words and updated every 6–9 months. Examples in COCA come from a large variety of spoken and written text, equally divided among spoken texts (such as television), fiction, popular magazines, newspapers, and academic works. The corpus is easily searched electronically in a variety of ways, e.g. by individual words, phrases, or collocations or by genre (e.g. fiction, academic text). This corpus was compiled by Mark Davies of Brigham Young University, who designed its search engine and maintains the site.

A corpus lists all possible examples or "tokens" of a word as it occurs in source texts. For example, when searching for the term *linguistics*, one finds over 600 examples, including the following:

> *A month ago, he'd been finishing up his Ph.D. in <u>Linguistics</u>*   (COCA:FIC)
> *at UC Berkeley.*
>
> *With the waning of Noam Chomsky's long dominance in <u>linguistics</u>,*   (COCA:NEWS)
> *other scholars are increasingly applying the principles of evolution*
> *to the field.*
>
> *This is why researchers in applied <u>linguistics</u> are recommending*   (COCA:ACAD)
> *new strategies to fill the gaps in vocabulary – for instance, massive*
> *rote word learning, guessing word meanings by context, and using*
> *graded textbooks.*
>
> *They're using lot more with the Internet, they're bringing in visiting*   (COCA:SPOK)
> *instructors, and they're using professors from other fields like*
> *political science or history or <u>linguistics</u> who can also teach language*
> *courses.*

Note that the source of each citation is designated by the name of the corpus and the genre in which it occurs (e.g. COCA:FIC designates an example taken from a fictional text in COCA). Students are encouraged to explore the corpus on their own, which requires free registration. A tutorial on its use is included on the COCA website.

Chapter 1

The nature of language and linguistics

1. The nature of human language
2. The nature of grammar
3. Linguistics and the components of language
4. Organization of the book

Chapter preview

The chapter begins by looking at the nature of human language, starting from certain fundamental beliefs concerning the naturalness, power, and function of language and moving towards a more scientific analysis of human language as a system of arbitrary vocal signs, having the qualities of universality, innateness, and creativity. Particular attention is given to the rule-governed nature of language. Language is also seen as uniquely human. The ambiguous term *grammar* is then defined and a number of fallacies concerning grammar are disputed, for example, that one type of grammar is simpler than another, or that changes in grammar involve deterioration in a language. Finally, the discipline of linguistics is examined, with its division in five components, corresponding to the levels of language: phonology, morphology, syntax, semantics, and pragmatics.

Commentary

1. The nature of human language

Linguists understand language as a system of arbitrary vocal signs. Language is rule-governed, creative, universal, innate, and learned, all at the same time. It is also distinctly human. We will look at what is meant by each of these terms in some detail, but before doing so, let's briefly examine some preconceptions about language that a student might bring to the study of language.

1.1   Fundamental beliefs about language

As speakers of language, we all have certain deep-seated notions concerning the nature of language. Like all such fundamental beliefs, these are often wrong, though they may contain a germ of truth. For example, as literate beings, we tend to equate language with writing. But there are significant differences, not only between oral sounds and written symbols, but also between spoken and written syntax or vocabulary. More importantly, we assume that there is some necessary, inevitable, or motivated connection between a word and the thing it names. This assumption lies behind the belief that names tell us something about the bearer of that name (for example, when one utters a statement such as "She doesn't look like a Penelope!") or that a change in status must entail a change in name (for example, the custom – now changing, of course – for a woman to adopt her husband's surname upon marriage). It also lies behind the thought, which we may all probably be guilty of having at times, that a foreign language is somehow perverse and idiotic, while our own language is natural and sensible.

Because we believe that there is an inevitable connection between a word and the thing it represents, the word is very powerful: names are extremely important (as we see in the Old Testament Genesis) and the possession of language can be very dangerous (as we see in the Old Testament story of the Tower of Babel). We avoid naming certain taboo objects explicitly because doing so might invoke the object named; in addition, we may avoid directly naming things which we fear or stand in awe of, such as God, our parents, or dangerous animals, and things which are unpleasant or unclean, such as birth, death, bodily parts and functions, or disease. Instead, we substitute euphemisms. Even if we recognize that names do not, in fact, invoke the objects they name, there is a sense in which language has the effect of action. That is, by means of language alone we can perform an action, as for example when we say, "I nominate Alex". We will examine this phenomenon in Chapter 11.

Finally, we think of language in terms of its various functions, for example:

- language gives expression to our thoughts;
- language is used to transmit information, also known as its "communicative function";
- language is used to maintain social intercourse (as in greetings or talk about the weather) – often referred to as its "phatic" function; and
- language provides the raw material for works of literature.

But language has many more functions, for example, to get others to do things, to express emotions or feelings, to make promises, to ask questions, to bring about states of affairs, to talk to oneself, and even to talk about language itself, or what is known as "metalanguage".[1]

---

1.   Note that this function is common in everyday life, not just among linguists.

The misleading idea that language simply expresses thought is a result of the philosophical and logical tradition, which treats language as a collection of propositions consisting of referent(s) and a predication which have "truth-value" (are true or false). However, in normal language use, speakers are not always committing themselves to the truth of a proposition; in fact, they do so only in the case of assertions or statements. Likewise, the idea that language has a communicative function, that it conveys new information, derives from its use in fairly restricted contexts, such as in the classroom or the newspaper, or when gossiping. In fact, the most important and frequent function of language is its phatic function.

1.2 Linguistic signs

In the view of linguists, human language consists of **signs**, which are defined as things that stand for or represent something else. Linguistic signs involve sequences of sounds which represent concrete objects and events as well as abstractions. Signs may be related to the things they represent in a number of ways. The philosopher C. S. Peirce recognized three types of signs:

1. **iconic**, which resemble the things they represent (as do, for example, photographs, diagrams, star charts, or chemical models);
2. **indexical**, which point to or have a necessary connection with the things they represent (as do, for example, smoke to fire, a weathercock to the direction of the wind, a symptom to an illness, a smile to happiness, or a frown to anger); and
3. **symbolic**, which are only conventionally related to the thing they represent (as do, for example, a flag to a nation, a rose to love, a wedding ring to marriage).

It turns out that there is very little in language which is iconic. Onomatopoeic words, which resemble the natural sounds they represent, are a likely candidate. However, while *bow-wow* might represent the sound of a dog in English, for example, other languages represent the sound quite differently (for example, *guau* in Spanish or *amh-amh* in Irish). So even such words seem to be highly conventionalized. Certain aspects of word order are indeed iconic. In the following sentences, we would normally assume that the words, phrases, or clauses represent the temporal and/or causal order in which the events took place:

> *Susie went to New York, Montreal, and Toronto.*
> *Sybil became ill and left the party.*
> *She ate dinner, read the newspaper, and watched TV.*

For example, in the second sentence, we assume that Sybil became ill before she left the party and/or she left the party because she became ill. Note the very different interpretation we give to *Sybil left the party and became ill*. Or in the sentence *If you do well on this exam, you will get a good grade in the course*, we know that the condition precedes the consequence, both in the sentence and in real life. Iteration can also sometimes be iconic, as in *The car repairs became more and more expensive*, where the repetition of *more* has an intensifying effect.

A few aspects of language are indexical, such as the demonstrative pronouns *this* or *that*, which point to the things they represent as close to or far away from the speaker, or adverbs such as *now* and *then*, which denote the moment of speaking or after (or before) the moment of speaking, respectively.

Most language, however, is symbolic. Ferdinand de Saussure – a Swiss scholar whose work is often said to have been the beginning of modern linguistics – stated that the relation between the linguistic sign and what it signifies is conventional or **arbitrary**. By an arbitrary connection, he meant that the sequence of sounds constituting a word bears no natural, necessary, logical, or inevitable connection to the thing in the real world which it names. Speakers must agree that it names that thing. Speakers of English, for example, have entered into a social agreement that the word *apple* stands for a particular fruit; there is no resemblance between the sound of the word and the appearance or taste of the fruit. Since there is no motivation for the connection between the word and the fruit, speakers must simply learn it. However, like all social agreements, such as those concerning dress or manners, linguistic agreements can be changed. As an example, note that over time, as the invention originally known as a *grammaphone* evolved, it came to be referred to as a *record player* and later as a *turntable*. Similarly, reference to the *cellular* or *mobile phone* was quickly shortened to *cell phone* or *mobile* and as it acquired more features, to *smart phone*.

> **HINT:** To understand how linguistic agreements are changed, consider how societal conventions dictate the replacement of words that are felt to have acquired derogatory or negative connotations: previous reference to individuals as *Oriental* has been replaced by the term *Asian*; *crippled* individuals are now referred to as *handicapped* or *disabled*; and the term *manic-depressive* has been replaced by *bipolar disorder*, etc.

Self-Testing Exercise: Do Exercise 1.1.

1.3   The rule-governed nature of language

Language consists of signs occurring not in a random collection, but in a system. A system consists of smaller units which stand in relation to each other and perform particular functions. These smaller units are organized on certain principles, or rules. For this reason, language is said to be rule-governed. The rules of a language, or its underlying system, are inferable from the observable patterns of the language. This underlying system constitutes what is called grammatical **competence**, which is part of native speakers' implicit knowledge, their "internalized grammar"; while grammatical competence is complete and perfect, it should be remembered that speakers' actual use of language, what is called **performance**, may be quite incomplete and imperfect.[2]

> **HINT:** A helpful analogy that might be made is to the score of a symphony which, like competence, is perfect and unchanging – and to the orchestra's playing of the symphony – which, like linguistic performance, may be inexact or contain errors and which changes on each occasion of playing.

The rules of language act as a kind of constraint on what is possible in a language. For example, in the area of syntax, the rules of English permit *I like soap operas* or *Soap operas I like*, but not **Like soap operas I* (* means ungrammatical, not permitted by the rules of the language). In respect to word formation, *overnight* is a possible verb expressing a length of time (as in *The climbers overnighted on a rock ledge*), but *midnight*, since it expresses a point in time, is not a possible verb (as in **The revelers midnighted in the streets*). The phonological rules of English would permit the word *prace* (though it does not exist), but would not generate the word **psabr*. Furthermore, we know from the morphological rules of the language that if *prace* were a verb, the past tense would be *praced*, pronounced with a final "t" sound (not the "d" or "ed" sound that is found in other past tense forms), and if *prace* were a noun, the plural would be *praces*, pronounced with a final "ez" sound (not the "s" or "z" sound that is found in other plural forms).

1.4 Language universals, innateness, and creativity

A more general set of constraints on language is known as language **universals**. These are features of language which are not language-specific; that is, they would be found in all languages of the world. Because of the surface diversity of languages, however, the search for language universals has proceeded slowly. We do know, for example, that, if one considers the order of the three main sentence elements, the subject (Su), the verb (V), and the object (O), there are only three basic word orders that occur with any frequency among world languages, namely, SuVO, SuOV, and VSuO, even though logically three other orders would be possible (VOSu, OVSu, OSuV). It may turn out to be the case that certain grammatical categories (such as number), functions (such as subject), and processes (such as passive) are universal. One consequence of the notion of universals is that language appears to be more motivated (that is, iconic) than previously assumed.

To understand better what is universal in language, we can look at the notion of *principles* and *parameters*, as proposed by many linguists today. In terms of the syntax of a language, all languages vary significantly. However, at a deeper or more fundamental level

---

2. The distinction between competence and performance corresponds roughly to what Ferdinand de Saussure (c. 1906) called *langue* and *parole* (see Saussure, 1986).

they share certain universals. The shared elements of language are referred to as their principles, while the differences that are displayed in their syntax are known as their parameters. For example, we know that in the syntax of all languages, a sentence has a subject (a principle). However, not all languages express this language universal in the same way. In some languages (e.g. English, German), the subject must be overtly expressed whereas in others (e.g. Japanese, Chinese), it is generally omitted and in yet other languages (e.g. Spanish, Italian, Portuguese, but not French), pronoun subjects tend to be omitted. The latter languages are known as "pro-drop" languages. Compare:

English	*Lili's going to the beach.*	*She's going to the beach.*	**Going to the beach.*
German	*Lili geht zum Strand.*	*Sie geht zum Strand.*	**Geht zum Strand.*
Spanish	*Lili va a la playa.*	*Ella va a la playa.*	*Va a la playa.*
French	*Lili va á la plage.*	*Elle va á la plage.*	**Va á la plage.*

This parameter specifies whether in a given language the subject can be omitted or not. Universal grammar thus encompasses both principles and parameters, which together explain the features that all language share and the syntactic differences which make each language unique.

Inherent in the notion of universals is the belief that human language is **innate**, that we are born with an inborn capacity for language acquisition and are genetically equipped to learn a language (not a specific language, but human language in general). This "genetic predisposition" to learn a language is thought to account for the speed and ease with which children learn their first language during a crucial period of language acquisition (birth to age four), despite the fact that the linguistic data that they hear is incomplete, that they receive no negative evidence, and that they are seldom explicitly "taught" or corrected. Of course, children must be exposed to a language in order to acquire it, so language is in part learned as well as innate. Universals are clearly a consequence of the genetic endowment of human beings for language. A child acquiring a language is innately equipped with both principles and parameters, but the parameters become "set" as language learning progresses. A current scholarly debate is whether this innate capacity for language is part of more general cognitive strategies, such as spatial perception, or is contained in a separate language faculty, or "module"; the answer is not yet in. (On the usefulness of speakers' innate knowledge in the teaching of English, see Chapter 12.)

Despite the general and language-specific constraints on the form of language, we also consider language to be **creative**, or infinite. Creativity in language has two aspects:

– The first aspect is that human beings can produce and understand novel sentences and sometimes even new words. In fact, it is likely that no sentence that you have read so far in this text is one that you have encountered before.
– The second aspect is that we can create sentences of (theoretically) infinite length (as in the nursery rhyme *This is the dog that worried the cat that killed the rat that ate the malt that lay in the house that Jack built*), although there are obviously practical limits on length.

Self-Testing Exercise: Do Exercise 1.2.

1.5   Animal communication codes

Finally, human language is uniquely human. Language is what distinguishes human beings from other animals. While many animals have codes of communication, these differ in important ways from human language. Most animal language is indexical and "stimulus-bound", depending on the necessary presence of concrete stimuli. The topic of conversation must be present in the immediate environment; it cannot be displaced in time or space. Animal communication codes may also be iconic and natural, but they are not symbolic.[3] Furthermore, although the codes may be structurally quite complex, they are finite, not infinite or creative; there is a closed repertory of utterances. The codes are acquired exclusively through genetic transmission, not learned, whereas, as we have seen, human language is both innate and learned. Animals always give primary responses, while human beings often give secondary responses, reacting to how something is said rather than what is said. Human beings may also use language to refer to abstractions or nonexistent entities; they can use language to lie, exaggerate, or mislead; and they can even use it to reflect about language itself (i.e. metalinguistically). None of these is possible within an animal communication code.

2.   The nature of grammar

As well as having a number of misconceptions about the nature of language, students coming to the study of language for the first time often have a different definition of the term *grammar* than linguists do.

2.1   Definitions of grammar

It is important at the outset to be clear about the meaning of the ambiguous term *grammar*. In linguistics, the term is used to refer to the rules or principles by which a language works, that is, its system or structure. Speakers of a language all have an internalized grammar (their competence), whether they can articulate the rules of the language or not. And unless they have studied their language in a formal context, they probably can't. Throughout the ages, grammarians and linguists have been attempting to formulate the speakers' grammar in a set of rules, though it is probably fair to say that they have not yet been able to do so completely for any language. This sense of grammar is known as **descriptive grammar**.

---

3.   Although some chimpanzees have been observed to use American Sign Language creatively, this may have been merely accidental.

You have probably been exposed to a different sense of grammar known as **prescriptive grammar**, which involves attempts to establish and maintain a standard of correctness in the language, to "prescribe" (dictate) and "proscribe" (forbid) certain ways of speaking; but this has little to do with the actual working of the language. It is only in a prescriptive sense that we can talk about "good" grammar or "bad" grammar; prescriptive grammar involves value judgments based on factors external to language – such as social class or level of education (a topic discussed in more detail in Chapter 12).

> HINT: A prescriptive approach to language is not restricted to grammar, but also extends to spelling, punctuation, written style, and even what is considered socially correct or acceptable. Thus being told by your writing teacher "Never use the first person pronoun 'I' when writing an academic essay" could be considered prescriptive just as could being advised that *isn't* is the grammatically correct form of *ain't* or that *any* should be substituted for *no* in the sentence *We don't need no education*. Other examples of prescriptive rules in writing include avoiding the passive voice, never ending a sentence with a preposition (*To whom were you talking?*, not *Who were you talking to?*), and not splitting infinitives (*to comprehend fully*, not *to fully comprehend*).

The difference between descriptive grammar and prescriptive grammar is comparable to the difference between **constitutive rules**, which determine how something works (such as the rules for the game of chess), and **regulatory rules**, which control behavior (such as the rules of etiquette). If the former are violated, the thing cannot work, but if the latter are violated, the thing works, but crudely, awkwardly, or rudely.

> HINT: To understand the difference between constitutive and regulatory rules, consider what happens if in a game of chess you move a pawn three spaces in a single move. In this case, you are violating the constitutive rules of chess and are therefore not considered to be playing the game. But if on the other hand you eat peas off your knife at dinner, you are violating regulatory rules of eating etiquette and may be considered rude or vulgar. Yet you nonetheless can manage to eat the peas (perhaps somewhat awkwardly).

If you say, for example, *Cat the the dog chased* you are not speaking English; the sentence violates the constitutive rules of the language and is thus considered ungrammatical. Hearers might well have trouble understanding you (Is the dog chasing the cat or the cat chasing the dog?). However, if you say *He did good on the exam*, your sentence is grammatical and would be understood by all, but many people would find your sentence unacceptable; they would consider it "bad", "nonstandard", or "incorrect" English. This sentence violates the regulatory rules of English but not its constitutive rules.

On the role of prescriptivism in language teaching, see Chapter 12.

2.2   Fallacies concerning grammar

There are some fallacies concerning the nature of grammar which are widely believed. One fallacy is that there are languages that have "no" grammar or "little" grammar. If grammar is defined as the principles by which a language operates, it must be recognized that every language has a grammar and that each language's grammar is completely adequate. It is certainly true that there are different types of grammars – such as the widely divergent grammars of Chinese, German, Turkish, or Cree – but these are all equally operative.

A related fallacy is that certain types of grammars are simpler and hence more "primitive" than others, while other grammars (particularly grammars which make use of inflections, or word endings, to express distinctions) are more complex and hence more advanced. This view was widely held in the eighteenth and nineteenth centuries, but was dispelled by the discovery that supposedly primitive languages (for example the American Indian languages) had extremely complex grammars and that the earliest form of the Indo-European languages, which has been reconstructed, probably had a more elaborate inflectional system than classical languages such as Greek, Latin, and Sanskrit.

In fact, it is unclear how a concept such as grammatical "simplicity" would be defined: is it, for example, simpler to add an inflection to a word or to express the same concept with a separate word, as English often does? That is, is *the dog's tail* or *the tail of the dog* simpler? It also seems to be the case that if one area of the grammar of a language is "simple", other areas are usually more "complex" in compensation. The number of variant forms of the English verb, for instance, is quite small, usually only four (e.g. *work, works, worked, working*). Compared even with another so-called analytic language (one which has few inflections) such as French, then, the English verb is inflectionally very simple. But the auxiliary phrase in English balances matters out by being very complex: there may be as many as four auxiliaries preceding the main verb, and these must occur in a certain order and form (e.g. English can produce phrases as complex as *might have been being built*). Moreover, if one language makes a grammatical distinction that another language appears not to, further examination of the second language often reveals that it makes the same distinction, but in a different way. English native speakers learning Chinese, for example, are often initially confused by its lack of tense marking on the verb. Instead, they learn, Chinese indicates time quite differently from English, e.g. via the use of adverbials.

Another fallacy about the form of grammars, which was also current in the eighteenth and nineteenth centuries, was that grammars should be logical and "analogical" (that is, regular). So strong was this belief that there were a number of attempts to eliminate supposedly illogical features of English grammar, such as the use of two or more negatives for emphasis, which was common prior to the eighteenth century, but was then judged by principles of logic to make a positive. While some of this language engineering was successful, grammars do not naturally follow logical principles. There is some drive towards regularity in language, causing certain irregularities to be smoothed out over time, (as when *bōc* 'book' /*bēc* 'books' in Old English was replaced by *book/books* in Modern English).[4]

---

4. This phenomenon of attempting to smooth out irregularities also occurs in child language acquisition (for example, a child using the regular past tense form *taked* for the verb *take* instead of the correct, irregular past tense form *took*).

However, other irregularities, for quite unpredictable reasons, have been retained (as in the irregular plural forms *goose/geese* or *mouse/mice*). And in some cases, especially in the area of pronunciation, new irregular forms are even introduced into the language, as in the change of vowels in *five* versus *fifteen* – a historical change introduced in Middle English in the fourteenth century.[5] This opposing drive, which serves to keep language irregular, helps to explain why no perfectly regular language exists.

A fallacy about changes in grammar is that they result in deterioration, or, alternatively, evolution. Again, it would be difficult to define what is meant by grammatical "evolution" or "deterioration". There is no doubt that languages change over time, sometimes in quite radical ways, but the changes do not seem to entail an advancement or a loss of any kind; the status quo is maintained. Furthermore, changes in language are not entirely random, but often proceed in certain predictable ways (known as "drift") and by a number of quite well-understood mechanisms.

It is often believed that people are taught the grammar of their native language, but in fact little conscious teaching of grammar occurs in the critical period of language learning, apart from rather sporadic corrections of wrong forms (as in, "it's not *tooken* but *taken*"). Children learn the language by hearing instances of it, and, it is now believed, constructing their own "internalized" grammar.

Three further fallacies concerning grammar which have already been touched on are that there are completely random differences among the languages of the world (the notion of language universals calls this view into question), that the sentences a person produces directly reflect his or her grammatical knowledge (the distinction between competence and performance underlines the incorrectness of this view), and that there is only one sense of the term *grammar* (we saw above that we need to recognize both prescriptive and descriptive grammars as well as the linguist's as opposed to the speaker's grammar).

A final fallacy involves equating the grammar of the spoken language with that of the written language. In fact, research into the grammar of these two distinct modes of language reveals that in a sense, they have entirely different "grammars". The grammar of written English tends to be more embedded (e.g. containing appositives or dependent clauses), with the independent clause often in second position. The grammar of spoken English is more fragmented, with phrases or clauses often "strung together" with conjunctions. Spoken language is also typically more disfluent, with false starts, repetitions, conversational fillers (e.g. *um, er, you know*), and abandoned thought units. The following transcript of a college composition instructor explaining the importance of class participation on the first day of class illustrates this very different grammar of the spoken language:

> *Don't come to class and keep your mouth shut. Come to class and participate. People that participate end up getting better grades in this class. I don't you know I ... it just works*

---

5.   Note that the vowels in *four/fourteen, six/sixteen, seven/seventeen, eight/eighteen*, and *nine/nineteen* remain the same.

out that way. It has a way of kind of generating its own energy. I really um suggest … I know that some people are more shy than others. But do what you can to um engage first in your group and eventually um in class, because by articulating your own ideas they become, doing it in public, they become more clear to you and you're better able to write about them later. So don't be afraid to speak up.

Self-Testing Exercise: Do Exercise 1.3.

3. Linguistics and the components of language

Linguistics is defined as the study of language systems. For the purposes of study, language is divided into levels, or components. These components are conventional and, to some extent, arbitrary divisions of linguistic investigation, and although they are interrelated in complex ways in the system of language, we treat them more or less separately. They constitute the framework which organizes this textbook.

The first component is **phonology** (from the Greek word *phōnē* meaning 'sound, voice'), the study of the speech sounds of a particular language. A subdivision of phonology is **phonetics**, the study of the speech sounds of human language in general, either from the perspective of their production ("articulatory phonetics"), their perception ("auditory phonetics"), or their physical properties ("acoustic phonetics"). Although speech is a continuum of sound, it is possible to break it into different types of sounds, known as consonants, vowels, and glides or semivowels; we will study how these different sounds are articulated, as well as how other features of sound, including stress and pitch, are superimposed over these sounds. Since the repertory of human speech sounds is quite large (but not unlimited – there are physical constraints on the sounds human beings are capable of producing), no language makes use of all possible speech sounds, but instead selects a limited set. Furthermore, within this limited set of sounds, certain sounds will be distinctive, that is, make a difference in meaning (such as the "t" and "k" sounds in *tap* and *cap*), while others will be nondistinctive and predictable variants (such as the slightly different "t" sounds in *stop* and *top*).

Since the writing system of English does not provide us with a one-to-one correspondence between oral sound and written symbol, we need a tool for representing human sounds in an regular way when studying phonology; the International Phonetic Alphabet (the IPA) has been invented for this purpose. In it, each written symbol represents one, and only one, speech sound, while each speech sound is represented by one, and only one, written symbol. We will begin by learning this special alphabet.

The second component of language is **morphology** (from Greek *morphē* 'form'). Morphology is the study of the structure or form of words in a particular language, and of their classification. While the concept of a word is intuitively clear, it is not easy to define it objectively (is *ice cream* one word or two?), and morphology must begin by trying to formulate such a definition. Morphology then considers principles of word formation in a language:

- how sounds combine into meaningful units such as prefixes, suffixes, and roots (as in *re-mind-er*),
- which of these units are distinctive and which are predictable variants (such as the different forms of the indefinite article, *a* and *an*), and
- what processes of word formation a language characteristically uses, such as compounding (as in *road-way*) or suffixing (as in *pave-ment*).

Morphology then considers how words can be grouped into classes, what are traditionally called "parts of speech", again seeking some objective criteria – either of form or of meaning – for sorting the words of a language into categories. We will study all of these questions in respect to the form of words in English.

The third component of language is **syntax** (from Greek *suntassein* 'to put in order'). Syntax is the study of the order and arrangement of words into larger units, as well as the relationships holding between elements in these hierarchical units. It studies the structure and types of sentences (such as questions or commands), of clauses (such as relative or adverbial clauses), and of phrases (such as prepositional or verbal phrases). Syntax is an extensive and complex area of language, and nearly one-third of the textbook is devoted to the study of English syntax. The two components of morphology and syntax are sometimes classified together as "grammar".

The fourth component of language is **semantics** (from Greek *sēmainein* 'to signify, show, signal'). Semantics is the study of how meaning is conveyed in words, phrases, or clauses. The study of semantics focuses either on meanings related to the outside world ("lexical meaning") or meanings related to the grammar of the sentence ("grammatical meaning"). In studying meaning, we consider both the meaning of individual words ("lexical semantics") and the meaning which results from the interaction of elements in a sentence ("sentence semantics"). Lexical semantics often involves the meaning relationships between words, such as the synonymity ('sameness of meaning') of *smart* and *intelligent* or the antonymity ('opposite of meaning') of *rough* and *smooth*. Sentence semantics involves the relationship between syntax and semantics, as in the different meanings of the subject of a sentence (as the agent of a change in the sentence *Jill closed the door* or the entity undergoing a change in the sentence *The door closed*). A further area of study, which is also treated here, is the meaning relationships holding among parts in an extended discourse ("discourse semantics").

A fifth component of language, not part of the traditional subdivision but added in recent years, is **pragmatics** (from Greek *pragma* 'deed, affair', from *prassein* 'to do'). Pragmatics is the study of the functions of language and its use in context. For example, in the context of a driver and a passenger in a car stopped at a traffic light, the phrase *The light is green* uttered by the passenger is not simply a description but performs the pragmatic function of advising the driver to step on the gas pedal and move into the intersection.

As was pointed out above, language, in addition to serving to communicate information, actually has a variety of functions, including the expression of emotion, the maintenance of social ties, and even the performance of action (a statement such as *I declare you guilty* uttere'd by a judge). Furthermore, in any context, a variety of factors, such as the age, sex, and social class of the interlocutors and their relationships of intimacy and power, influence the form of language used. We will consider this fairly wide-open field from two different perspectives.

4.   Organization of the book

This book examines the linguistic structure of Modern English starting with the smallest units and working toward larger units. Thus, we begin with the phonological level (individual sounds), move to the morphological level (sounds combined into words and meaningful parts of words), and then to the syntactic level (words combined into phrases, clauses, and sentences). The relation of sentences within the larger discourse is the subject matter of pragmatics. Since meaning derives from aspects of phonological structure, from words and clauses, and from larger textual structures, we consider aspects of the semantic component as it relates to all of the levels. However, since meaning is most strongly associated with lexical items and syntactic structures, a section on word semantics follows the morphological section, and a section on sentence semantics follows the syntax section. This approach may be schematized as in Figure 1.1.

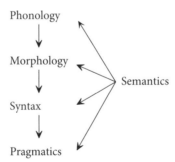

Figure 1.1. Organization of the Text

There are many different ways to study language, or different approaches, which can be termed "schools of linguistics". Each school has certain characteristics and certain strengths. In studying the different linguistic components, we use methods of analysis formulated within different schools of linguistics. Such an eclectic approach seems desirable because some theories are better suited to deal with certain areas than others. Traditional grammar (an approach to the study of language dating from Greek times) underlies much of our treatment, but our approach to both phonology and morphology will be primarily structuralist (an approach to the study of language dating from the 1930s to the 1950s), and our approach to syntax will be overtly generative (an approach to the study of language dating from the late 1950s to the present).

Chapter summary

Now that you have completed this chapter, you should be able to:

1. describe the characteristics of human language;
2. differentiate between iconic, indexical, and symbolic signs;
3. distinguish between different senses of the word *grammar*;
4. describe common fallacies about language and grammar; and
5. define the study of linguistics and its subparts.

Recommended additional reading

The topics discussed in this chapter are generally addressed in introductory linguistics textbooks, such as O'Grady and Archibald (2009, Chapter 1), Fromkin, Rodman, and Hyams (2007, Chapter 1), or in treatments of English linguistics, such as Curzan and Adams (2009, Chapter 1), Klammer, Schulz, and Della Volpe (2010, Chapter 1), Leech, Deuchar, and Hoogenraad (2006, Chapter 1), and Finegan (2008, Chapter 1). For a wide-ranging discussion of language, see Crystal (2010).

You may find a dictionary of linguistics, such as Crystal (2008) or Trask (1993), a very useful reference while reading this textbook. Hurford (1994) is a dictionary/grammar, with extensive examples from English as well as exercises and answers.

A comprehensive resource on animal communication is Hillix and Rumbaugh (2004). For a more abbreviated treatment of chimpanzee language, see Fromkin, Rodman, and Hyams (2007, Chapter 8) and Crystal (2010).

The most complete contemporary grammars of English are Quirk, Greenbaum, Leech, and Svartvik (1985), Biber, Johansson, Leech, Conrad, and Finegan (1999) (this grammar pays particular attention to written vs. spoken English), and Huddleston and Pullum (with Bauer et al.) (2002). All three also exist in shorter students' forms: Greenbaum and Quirk (1990), Biber, Conrad, and Leech (2002), and Huddleston and Pullum (2005).

Older traditional grammars of English based on historical principles are those by Curme (1931, 1935; and a shorter form, 1947), Jespersen (1909–49; and a shorter form, 1933), and Poutsma (1904–26).

Very useful grammars of English that are primarily traditional in orientation are those intended for teachers of English as a second language, such as Celce-Murcia and Larsen-Freeman (1999) or Larsen-Freeman (2007).

A prescriptive (but very intelligent) approach to English usage can be found in Fowler (1965 [1926]). (For a humorous take-off on Fowler, see Thurber (1931).) For an amusing treatment of the prescriptive approach to punctuation, see Truss (2003). Two contemporary guides are Swan (2005) and Peters (2004); the latter is based on actual usage.

Structural accounts of English include Fries (1952), Francis (1958), and Strang (1968). Bloomfield (1933) and Sapir (1921) are classic – and very readable – structural accounts of language in general.

References to generative accounts of English may be found in later chapters on phonology and syntax.

If you would like to read the writings of Ferdinand de Saussure, they can be found in a modern translation (1986 [1983]). Very readable discussions of the human language capacity are Davis (1994) and Pinker (1994, 2007).

Chapter 2

Consonants and vowels

1. The spoken versus the written form of language
2. The production of speech sounds
3. Consonant sounds
4. Vowel sounds
5. The function of vowels and consonants

Chapter preview

This chapter begins with a discussion of some of the differences between writing and speech, including what each medium can and cannot express. It then examines the production of human speech sounds. The criteria for analyzing consonant sounds are explained. An inventory of the consonant sounds in English and explication of the method of their phonetic transcription follows. Vowels sounds are next classified, with a description of which vowel sounds English has and how they are transcribed. The chapter ends with discussion of formal versus functional means of distinguishing vowels and consonants.

Commentary

As defined in Chapter 1, phonetics is the study of speech sounds in general. It has three subdivisions:

1. the study of how sounds are made or the mechanics of their production by human beings ("articulatory phonetics");
2. the study of how sounds are heard or the mechanics of their perception ("auditory phonetics"); and
3. the study of the physical properties of the speech waves which constitute speech sound ("acoustic phonetics").

In this chapter, after briefly examining how speech sounds are made, we will turn to phonology, the study of the speech sounds in a particular language, in our case, the inventory
of sounds constituting the sound system of English, including consonants, vowels, and
glides. Our study of English phonology will continue in the next chapter with a consideration of the distinctive and nondistinctive sounds in English as well as of sound combinations and syllable structure in the language.

1.   The spoken versus the written form of language

The initial step in the study of the sound system of a language is to distinguish between
speech and writing. This is often a difficult distinction for literate people to make since we are
tempted to consider the written form as equivalent to language. But speech and writing are,
in fact, two quite distinct media of language. Speech is temporally prior, both in the history
of humankind and in the history of the individual. Languages existed for millennia before
writing systems were invented. We learn to speak effortlessly, but must struggle to learn to
write; many, in fact, do not learn to write yet are fluent speakers of the language. It is salutary
to remember that even in Shakespeare's day the majority of English speakers were illiterate,
yet verbally proficient enough to understand Shakespeare's word plays. Some languages have
no written form, but all languages have spoken forms. Moreover, a variety of writing systems
are used to record the languages of the world, some languages have more than one writing
system, and even very closely-related languages may use very different writing systems.

1.1   English spelling

That writing is often an imperfect means of representing speech is perhaps most obvious
in the well-known inadequacies of English spelling. If we compare the actual sounds of
English with the **orthography**, the graphic symbols or letters used in writing, we find the
following discrepancies:

- one sound can be represented by a variety of **graphemes** (alphabet letters), as with
  the vowel sound in *meat*, *meet*, *machine*, *city*, *key*, *ceiling*, *people*, *niece*, *evil*, *Caesar*,
  amoeba, and *quay*;
- one grapheme can represent a variety of sounds, as with *d* in *damage*, *educate*, *picked*;
- one or more graphemes may represent no sound at all, as in *knee*, *gnat*, *lamb*, *receipt*,
  right, *honor*, *rhyme*, *psalm*, and *salmon*;
- two or more graphemes may represent a single sound, as in *throne*, *chain*, *edge*, *shore*,
  nation, *itch*, *inn*, *school*, *eat*, *friend*, *too*, *leopard*, *cause*, *blood*, or *lieutenant*;
- a grapheme may simply indicate the quality of a neighboring sound, as in *dinner* vs. *diner*
  (where a double or single *n* indicates the quality of the preceding vowel) or *dine* vs. *din*
  (where the presence or absence of final *e* indicates the quality of the preceding vowel);

–   a single grapheme may represent two or more sounds, as in *box*, where the letter *x* represents the sound sequence "ks"; and

–   some sounds have no graphic representation, as with the initial sounds in <u>u</u>*niverse* and <u>o</u>*ne*.

> *Self-Testing Exercise 2.1:* Examining the reasons for the marked incongruity between sound and spelling in English makes for a fascinating historical study. Read the brief discussion and do the self-testing exercise on the website.

For the study of speech sounds, therefore, orthographic systems are clearly inadequate. We need a system of recording sounds in which a single written symbol represents one and only one speech sound and in which a single sound is represented by one and only one written symbol. For this reason, the **International Phonetic Alphabet (IPA)** was invented in 1888 (and revised in 1989). It is based on the Roman alphabet primarily, with some symbols from other writing systems, as well as some invented symbols and **diacritics** (marks added to symbols). The recording of the sounds of a language in the IPA is called "transcription". Much of this chapter will be concerned with the transcription of English using the IPA.

1.2   The advantages of speech and writing

It is important to keep in mind, however, that each medium of language – speech and writing – fulfills different functions and has certain advantages. On one hand, the oral medium expresses certain meaning features that cannot always be recorded in the written medium:

1.   emphasis: indicated by syllable stress in speech and very inexactly by underlining in writing, as in *I want <u>thát</u> one, not <u>thís</u> one*;

2.   sentence type: indicated by **intonation** (the rising and falling contours of the voice) in speech and very crudely by end punctuation in writing, as in the difference between *He said he would help.* and *He said he would help?* (though often different word orders distinguish different sentence types such as questions or commands);

3.   homographs: words that are spelled the same but pronounced differently, for example, *sewer* 'one who sews'/'a conduit for sewage' or *hót dòg* 'a sausage'/*hót dóg* 'an overheated canine';

4.   paralanguage: tones of voice and vocal qualifiers, indicated by shouting, growling, whispering, drawling, and so on;

5.   variations in pronunciation resulting from dialect or idiolect (an individual's unique dialect);

6.   kinesics: indicated by body movement, facial expressions, and gestures;

7.   performance errors, slips, or hesitations; and

8. features of the speech situation, such as the relation of the speaker and the hearer or intimacy and personal contact.

In reading over the above list, you might have thought of dialogue in novels or plays as an exception. However, dialogue is always very stylized and conventionalized. For example, tones of voice, kinesics, contextual features, and many performance errors must be explicitly described. If dialogue were faithfully to represent the performance errors of real conversation, it would be nearly incomprehensible; the transcribed conversation would be quite incoherent. Features of regional or social dialect are also imperfectly represented (as in the use of unconventional spelling *Ah'm tahrd* for a Southern US pronunciation of *I'm tired* or the use of spellings which approximate the actual pronunciation of words such as *bekuz, nite, wuz,* and *sez* (for the conventionalized spellings *because, night, was,* and *says*).

On the other hand, there are aspects of language which writing expresses but speech cannot:

1. historical changes: older pronunciations preserved in the spelling, such as *comb, gnat,* or *taught*;
2. words: indicated by spaces, sometimes disambiguating ambiguous phonological sequences such as *nitrate/night rate, syntax/sin tax,* or *homemade/home aid*;
3. homophones: words which are pronounced the same but spelled differently, such as *bear/bare, meat/meet,* or *maid/made*;
4. related words or affixes which sound different, such as *photograph, photography, photographic* or the past tense affix *-ed* in *rated, walked, robbed*;
5. a greater range of vocabulary, more complex syntax, and greater refinement of style, resulting in part from the planning permitted by the situation of writing;
6. language free of performance errors (which, in fact, we often are not consciously aware of in the spoken form);
7. a standard language without dialectal differences, allowing easier communication among diverse groups;
8. permanency: permitting the keeping of historical annals, the recording of laws, and the writing of other permanent records.

Incidentally, it is because of points (1) and (7) above that the many attempts at spelling reform in the history of the English language have been unsuccessful. For example, we will see below that certain modern dialects of English do not pronounce the "r" in words such as *part* or *par*, while others do. Such instances of dialectal variation in pronunciation seriously impede decisions about standardizing English spelling: If English spelling were to represent pronunciation more closely, which dialect's pronunciation should become fixed in its orthography?

2. The production of speech sounds

Keeping in mind the primacy of speech, we will now consider how we make speech sounds. Speech sounds are produced using, but modifying, the respiratory system. When speaking, the number of breaths per minute increases. The intake of air (inspiration) becomes shorter while the period of exhalation (expiration) increases. A greater amount of air is expelled, with a gradual decrease in the volume of air and fairly constant pressure. Importantly for the production of sound, the air is often blocked or impeded at some point or points on its way out.

English and most languages of the world use the **egressive pulmonic system** to generate speech sounds. The term "egressive" refers to the fact that sound is produced when air is exiting, not entering, the lungs. "Pulmonic" refers to the use of the lungs as the power source. In speaking, air is expelled from the lungs by a downward movement of the ribs and upward movement of the diaphragm. The air travels up the bronchial tubes to the trachea, or "wind pipe", and through the larynx, or "Adam's apple". The larynx contains a valve which functions to close off the trachea while you are eating. This valve has been adapted for the purposes of speech; it is known as the **vocal cords**. The vocal cords are two muscles stretching horizontally across the larynx, attached to cartilage at either end that controls their movement. The vocal cords are relatively open during normal breathing, but closed during eating. The space between the cords when they are open is known as the **glottis**. The vocal cords of men and of women are of different lengths: 1.7 cm for women, 2.3 for men. This, as we will see later, accounts in part for the different vocal qualities of men and women. Air continues past the larynx into the pharynx, whose only real function is as a connector and resonator.

The air then moves into the vocal tract (see Figure 2.1), consisting of the **oral** and **nasal cavities**. The oral cavity, that is, the mouth, is a resonator and a generator of speech sounds via the articulators, which may be active (moving) or passive (stationary). The **active articulators** include the following:

–   the tongue, divided into (1) the front (consisting of the tip or "apex" and the blade or "lamina"), (2) the back (or "dorsum"), and (3) the root: the tongue modifies the shape of the cavity, acts as a valve by touching parts of the mouth to stop the flow of air, and is shaped in various ways to direct the flow of air.
–   the lower lip: the lip may be placed against the upper teeth or, together with the upper lip, may be closed or opened, rounded or spread.

The **passive articulators** include the following:

–   the teeth, both upper and lower.
–   the roof of the mouth, which is divided into (1) the **alveolar ridge**, which is 1 cm behind the upper teeth, (2) the hard **palate**, which is the domed, bony plate, (3) the soft palate, or **velum**, which is the muscular flap at the rear, and (4) the uvula, which is the tip of the velum.

– the pharynx, or back of the throat, which is used by some languages (but not English) in producing speech sounds.

> **HINT:** If you run your tongue back along the top of your mouth from your teeth, you should be able to feel your alveolar ridge just behind the upper teeth and to distinguish your palate from your velum. As your tongue travels backwards towards the velum, you should feel the membrane covering the roof of the mouth become softer.

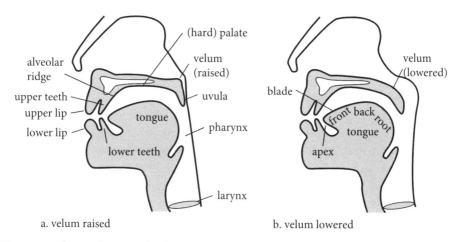

a. velum raised   b. velum lowered

Figure 2.1. The Vocal Tract with (a) Velum Raised and (b) Velum Lowered

A useful feature of the velum is that it is movable. If it is raised against the back of the pharynx (called "velic closure") blocking the entrance to the nasal passageway, then air passes out only through the oral cavity (see Figure 2.1a). The result is known as an **oral sound**. If the velum is lowered (called "velic opening"), then air can pass out through the other cavity, the nasal cavity, that is the nose (see Figure 2.1b). If air passes out of the nose exclusively, a **nasal sound** is produced, but if air passes out of both the nose and the mouth, a **nasalized sound** is produced. People who have a "nasal quality" to their voice probably have incomplete closure of the velum at all times, so that a little air is always able to escape through the nose. Also, when you have a cold and your velum is swollen, you will have imperfect velic closure and hence a nasal voice; you will also not be able to produce exclusively nasal sounds since your nose is blocked and will substitute oral sounds (e.g. the sound "b" for "m").

Let us return, briefly, to the larynx and the vocal cords to see how they function in producing sounds. When the cords are widely separated and fairly taut, no noise is produced. This is known as an "open glottis" and produces a **voiceless** sound (see Figure 2.2a). However, the vocal cords may also be set in vibration ("phonation"), and this produces a **voiced** sound (see Figure 2.2b). They vibrate open and shut as air passes through. Vibration is begun by initially closing the vocal cords completely, but with the cords fairly relaxed. Air pressure builds up below the cords and blows them apart. Then the pressure decreases and the cords close again; these events occur in rapid succession. Women's vocal cords, being smaller, vibrate more rapidly, normally 190–250 Hz (times/second), while men's larger vocal cords vibrate 100–150 Hz. When the vocal cords are vibrating, you can feel a vibration and hear a buzzing.

> **HINT:** To feel the vibration, place your fingers on your larynx or cup your hands over your ears and say *sa-za-sa-za*. You should sense the vibration of the cords with the "z" sound but not the "s" sound.

A "closed glottis" occurs when the vocal cords are brought completely together once and the air stream is interrupted. This produces a speech sound we will consider later called a "glottal stop".[1]

Whispering involves bringing the vocal cords close together, keeping them fairly taut but not vibrating them. Air is restricted through a small triangular passage between the arytenoid cartilages, and this produces a hissing sound (see Figure 2.2c). To produce a breathy voice, the vocal cords never close completely but are in vibration; hence, there is a murmuring sound. A creaky voice results from voicing with slow, regular vibration, whereas a harsh voice results from excessive tension in the vocal cords and irregular vibration. A hoarse voice usually results from swelling of the vocal cords producing irregular vibration and incomplete closure.

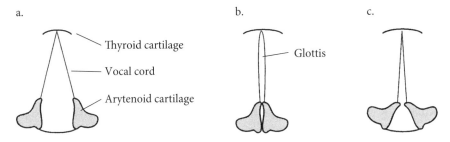

Figure 2.2. Configurations of the Larynx: (a) Voiceless (Exhalation), (b) Voiced, and (c) Whispered

---

1.   Two other air stream mechanisms may be used in producing certain sounds in other languages, the "glottalic" system and the "velaric" system. In the latter, for example, the tongue is raised against the velum and simultaneously at a point further forward in the mouth, trapping air. Moving the tongue downward rarefies the air, and when the tongue is released, air rushes in to produce an ingressive sound. There are three types of such sounds, called "clicks", in the Bantu (e.g. Xhosa, Zulu) and Khoisan languages of southern Africa. These include the bilabial click (the "kissing" sound), the alveolar click (the "tut-tut" or "tsk-tsk" sound of disapproval), and the lateral click (the sound made to spur a horse on). Although we use these sounds, of course, they are not regular speech sounds.

Two other features of sound are **loudness** and **pitch**. Loudness is related to the pressure and volume of air expelled; as these increase, the sound becomes louder. Pitch is a matter of the quality of the sound, which is a consequence of the frequency of the sound wave emitted. Every person has a natural frequency and range. Men's voices tend to have a lower pitch than women's due to the larger size of their vocal cords, which vibrate more slowly. Pitch can be modulated by altering the tension on the vocal cords and changing their length. Pitch decreases when the vocal cords are elongated and tensed and increases when they are relaxed, hence shorter. Most human voices have a range of about two octaves.

3.   Consonant sounds

Speech is a phonetic continuum, a continuous, smoothly flowing set of movements, not a set of discrete and isolated movements. It is convenient, however, to segment the speech chain into syllables, and to divide these in turn into consonants and vowels. A syllable consists necessarily of a vowel; optionally, it may begin and/or end with a consonant. A vowel is the nucleus or acoustic high point of a syllable; it is articulated for a longer time than surrounding consonants. While vowels tend to continue the airstream, consonants tend to break it. We begin our study of speech sounds with consonants, since they are somewhat easier to describe. We will look first – in abstract – at how consonants are articulated before examining in detail the specific consonants of English.

3.1   Classification of consonants

A **consonant** is defined as a speech sound which is articulated with some kind of stricture, or closure, of the air stream.

Consonants are classified according to four features:

1.   the state of the glottis: in vibration (voiced) or open (voiceless);
2.   the state of the velum: lowered (nasal) or raised (oral);
3.   the **place of articulation**: the location where the stricture or place of maximum interference occurs and what articulators are involved; and
4.   the **manner of articulation**: the amount of stricture, whether it is complete, partial (called "close approximation"), or relatively open ("open approximation").

The term "approximation" refers to the two articulators approaching (or approximating) one another.

In describing the place of articulation for consonants, it is traditional to list the active and then the passive articulator. Consonants involve a rather large number of discrete places of articulation (see Figure 2.3):

1. **bilabial**: the lips are brought together (the lower lip is active); the tongue is not involved but remains in the "rest position" (its position when you say *ah* for the doctor) – e.g. the sound of "b" in English;
2. **labiodental**: the lower lip is brought up against the upper front teeth; again the tongue is in rest position – e.g. the sound of "f" in English;
3. **dental**: the tip of the tongue (or apex) protrudes between the teeth or touches the back of the upper teeth – e.g. the sound of "t" in Spanish or "th" in English;
4. **alveolar**: the tip of the tongue makes contact with or is in close approximation to the alveolar ridge – e.g. the sound of "d" in English;
5. **alveolopalatal**: the front, or blade, of the tongue is raised to an area between the alveolar ridge and the palate – e.g. the sound of "sh" in English;
6. **palatal**: the front of the tongue is brought up against the palate – e.g. the sound of "y" in English;
7. **velar**: the back, or dorsum, of the tongue is brought into contact with the velum – e.g. the sound of "g" in English;
8. uvular: the back of the tongue touches the uvula;
9. pharyngeal: the root of the tongue (specifically, the epiglottis) is moved backwards against the wall of the pharynx; and
10. **glottal**: the vocal cords, functioning as articulators, make a brief closure.

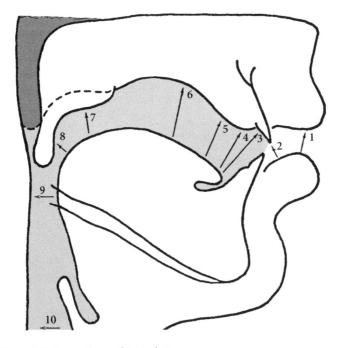

1. bilabial
2. labiodental
3. dental
4. alveolar
5. alveolopalatal
6. palatal
7. velar
8. uvular
9. pharyngeal
10. glottal

Figure 2.3. Some Places of Articulation

While the uvular and pharyngeal places are not used for the articulation of English consonants, they are used in other languages: e.g. the uvular for German "r" and a French fricative and the pharyngeal for a fricative in Arabic.[2]

Each of the various places of articulation just examined may combine with a number of different manners of articulation to produce consonant sounds:

1. **stop**: ("oral stop") involving complete closure of two articulators with the velum raised (velic closure) – e.g. the sound of "p" in English;
2. **nasal**: ("nasal stop") involving complete closure of two articulators with the velum lowered ("velic opening") – e.g. the sound of "n" in English; for every stop position in English, there is a nasal articulated in the same position (**homorganic**);
3. **fricative**: (or "spirant") involving close approximation of two articulators; the air stream is partially obstructed so that a turbulent airflow is produced, resulting in a hissing or rubbing sound – e.g. the sound of "s" in English;
4. **affricate**: consisting of a stop released into a homorganic fricative – e.g. the sound of "ch" in English; this sound is analyzed either as a complex or a simple sound;
5. **trill**: (or "roll") involving complete closure alternating intermittently with open approximation, that is, a rapid vibration of the active articulator against the passive articulator (this sound in not common in English except for the Scottish "r" made with an apical trill);
6. **flap**: (or "tap") involving momentary complete closure in which the active articulator strikes the passive articulator only once; it is one strike of a trill and similar to a stop except that the tongue is more tense and controlled than in a stop; and
7. **approximant**: one articulator approaches another but generally not to the extent that a turbulent air stream is produced; there is usually open approximation in the three different types of approximants:

    a. **lateral**: involving complete closure of the central portion of the vocal tract, with the lateral passage of air; the air may pass around the sides with no stricture (open approximation) – e.g. the sound of "l" in English – or, in languages other than English, with some stricture (close approximation);
    b. **retroflex**: involving the underside of the tongue curling back behind the alveolar ridge towards the palate – e.g. the sound of "r" in English; laterals and retroflexes are called "liquids";

---

2. Two places of articulation may also be used at the same time – what is called "coarticulation" – as in the case of labiovelars, which involve the lips, on one hand, and the tongue and velum, on the other.

c.   **glide** (or **semivowel**): involving a glide to or from a vowel; this sound is articulated like a vowel (with no stricture) but functions as a consonant to begin or end syllables – e.g. the sound of "w" in English.

3.2   Consonants of English and their phonetic notation

We will now consider what combinations of voicing, place of articulation, and manner of articulation are utilized in the articulation of consonants in English. Remember that not all possible combinations are used in all languages, though certain combinations (such as, perhaps, a velar trill) might be physiologically impossible.

As you read the following section, you should consult the consonant chart in Table 2.1. On the consonant chart, following common practice, the places of articulation are listed across the horizontal axis (roughly corresponding to a cross-section of the mouth viewed from the left, with the front of the mouth on the left and the back of the mouth on the right); the manners of articulation are listed along the vertical axis, moving in a rough way from greatest stricture at the top to lesser amounts of stricture as one moves down. Voiceless consonant are listed above voiced ones, where applicable. It is not necessary to specify the state of the velum since all consonants are oral except the nasals. Note that in giving a technical description of a consonant sound, it is traditional to list voicing, then place, then manner; get into the habit of describing the consonants in this order from the very beginning.

> **HINT:** In learning the sounds of English and, especially, in transcribing English words, you must not allow yourself to be influenced by the written form. Because of the imperfect correspondence between sound and spelling in English mentioned above, the spelling will often lead you astray or confuse you. You must try to function entirely in an oral context. You must also try to say words with a natural and relaxed pronunciation. There is a strong tendency when reading words or saying them in isolation to give them an overly formal and even distorted pronunciation. Try to speak as you do naturally in casual conversation. Do not whisper the words, either, as you cannot distinguish between voiced and voiceless sounds when whispering.

This section, in addition to surveying the consonant inventory of English, will teach you the phonetic alphabet symbol used to transcribe each of the consonants. We will use the modified version of the IPA used in North America. For the most part, you will be asked to give what is called **broad transcription** rather than **narrow transcription**. As the names imply, broad transcription merely records the grosser features of sound, whereas narrow transcription records all the nuances and finer aspects of sound, though not performance factors such as drunken slurs, loudness, and so on. The convention is to enclose broad transcription between slashes, such as /kæt/ for *cat*, and to use square brackets for narrow transcription, such as [kʰætˀ].

Table 2.1. The Consonants of English

					Place of Articulation				
Manner of Articulation		Bilabial	Labio-dental	Dental	Alveolar	Alveolo-palatal	Palatal	Velar	Glottal
Stop	voiceless	p			t			k	ʔ
	voiced	b			d			g	
Nasal		m			n			ŋ	
Flap					ⓡ tt				
Fricative	voiceless		f	θ	s	ʃ			h
	voiced		v	ð	z	ʒ			
Affricate	voiceless					tʃ			
	voiced					dʒ			
Approximant	lateral				l				
	retroflex				r				
	glide or semivowel						ɥ̈ j	w	h

In the stop series of English, there are paired voiced and voiceless stops produced in three locations:

1. bilabial: the voiced bilabial stop /b/ (as in band, ember, mob) and the voiceless bilabial stop /p/ (as in pound, open, coop);
2. alveolar: the voiced alveolar stop /d/ (as in danger, eddy, loud) and the voiceless alveolar stop /t/ (as in tangle, otter, moat); and
3. velar: the voiced velar stop /g/ (as in grass, rugged, rug) and the voiceless velar stop /k/ (as in carrot, election, luck).

As you can see, all stop sounds are represented in the IPA with Roman alphabet symbols. The bilabial stop is made by bringing the lips together, the alveolar by bringing the tip of the tongue up against the alveolar ridge, and the velar by bringing the back of the tongue up against the soft palate. Because the air stream is completely blocked, you cannot actually hear stops until you open your mouth to release them into a vowel. Released stops are called "plosives". Furthermore, the articulation of stops cannot be maintained; their articulation is instantaneous. Practice saying all of these sounds.

The stops share certain features. First, the voiced stops are articulated for a shorter period than the corresponding voiceless stops. Compare the final voiced stops in Column 1 with the voiceless stops in Column 2:[3]

---

3. Conversely, as we shall see later, vowels that precede voiced consonants are slightly longer than those that precede voiceless consonants.

Column 1	Column 2
cab /b/	cap /p/
cad /d/	cat /t/
rag /g/	rack /k/

You should find that the final consonants in Column 1 take less time to pronounce than those in Column 2.

Second, the three voiceless stops have two variants each. Note the following underlined sounds:

Column 1	Column 2
spot	pot
steam	team
scud	cud

Column 2 lists **aspirated** versions of the stops in Column 1; "aspiration" means that you release a small puff of air after articulating these sounds. If you hold your fingers or a small piece of paper in front of your mouth, you should be able to feel, or see, the puff of air. As we will learn in the next chapter, the occurrence of aspiration is entirely predictable, with the aspirated versions occurring word or syllable initially before a stressed vowel.[4] In narrow transcription, aspiration is indicated with a diacritic or mark added to the letter, in this case a superscript "h", hence [pʰ, tʰ, kʰ].

Third, voiced stops may be partially "devoiced" at the end of words; anticipating the following silence, we stop voicing part way through the sound. Devoicing is indicated with a diacritic called an "under-ring" [̥]; thus the "b" in *rub* could be represented [b̥]. Or we may simply not release the stop at the end of a word. Try saying *rap, rat,* and *rack* without releasing the stops; the words should still be distinctive even though the initial consonant and vowel are the same. Unreleased stops in narrow transcription are indicated with a superscript "corner" [̚]. Stops are also unreleased frequently before other stops, as in *apt, captain, rubbed, rubdown, necktie, act,* and *mugged.* Note that you don't actually release the [p̚, b̚, k̚, g̚] here but move directly to the next stop.

The alveolar stops also behave in several distinctive ways. First, when /t/ occurs between two vowels (in the "intervocalic" position), as in *pity, Betty, little, latter, better, writer, city,* or *pretty,* it is normally voiced in both American and Canadian English, though not in British English. Say the following words and note whether they are homophones for you:

bitter – bidder	atom – Adam
latter – ladder	shutter – shudder

---

4.   Another place in which aspiration may occur is in final position following /s/ or /f/, as in *soft, clasp, risk.* We will not be concerned with this environment for aspiration.

metal – medal   *petal – pedal/peddle*
litre – leader   *coated – coded*
wetting – wedding   *conceited – conceded*

If you have the same sound in both, you likely have either a /d/ sound or a sound called an alveolar flap. This is represented by a "fish hook r" [ɾ]. It is voiced and sounds very much like a /d/, but is more rapid and has more force since the tongue is tapped against the alveolar ridge once rapidly and forcefully. As we shall see below, flapping does not occur when the /t/ or /d/ precedes -*en* and perhaps not before -*el/-le*.

Second, when /d/ precedes the "th" sound, it is often made as a dental stop (with the tongue against the back of the teeth) rather than as an alveolar sound (with the tongue against the alveolar ridge). We do so because we are anticipating the following dental sound (discussed below). Note the different position of your tongue when you say the "d's" in the following words:

Column 1   **Column 2**
wide /d/   *width* [d̪]
bread /d/   *breadth* [d̪]

The "d" sounds in *width* and *breadth* are much like the dental sounds of Spanish or French. They are represented in narrow transcription with a subscript under the phonetic symbol which looks very much like a tooth, called a "subscript bridge" [d̪].

The velar place of articulation for /k/ and /g/ in fact ranges over quite a large area of the mouth. We anticipate the vowel that follows and articulate the velar stop either further forward towards the palatal region (as in the first two columns below) or further back in the velar region (as in the second two columns):

Column 1   **Column 2**   **Column 3**   **Column 4**
gill   *kill*   *cool*   *goof*
game   *came*   *cull*   *good*
gad   *cat*   *coat*   *goat*

A final stop, which is unpaired, is the glottal stop. It is a stop produced by bringing the vocal cords together and blocking the air stream at this point. A glottal stop is by definition voiceless and is represented by /ʔ/. You will articulate two glottal stops when you say *uh-uh* meaning 'no', transcribed /ʌʔəʔ/, but none when the word means 'yes', transcribed /əhʌ/. A glottal stop quite often precedes a final voiceless stop, so that *trip* would be pronounced /trɪʔp/. Some speakers of North American English and British English produce /ʔt/ or /ʔ/ instead of /t/ before -*en* or -*el/le* in words such as *beaten, fatten, battle,* or *bottle.* Cockney speakers produce /ʔ/ alone in final position instead of an unreleased stop after a vowel in words such as *rap, rat,* or *rack* and intervocalically where others have a flap in words such as *city* or *pretty.*

The nasal series consists of three nasal consonants articulated in the same positions as the three sets of oral stops. In fact, the only difference between stops and nasals is that in producing the nasals, the velum is lowered so that air is released through the nose. The nasals in English are all voiced (though other languages have voiceless nasals):

1. the bilabial nasal /m/ as in *mad*, *omen*, *room*;
2. the alveolar nasal /n/ as in *nose*, *onerous*, *loan*; and
3. the velar nasal /ŋ/ as in *singer*, *ring* (or the Chinese surname *Ng*).

To produce the bilabial nasal, your lips are brought together, as for /b/, but air is allowed to escape through the nose. Note that with the nasals you can maintain their articulation (as long as you have air). The alveolar nasal /n/ is articulated with the tongue in the same position as for /d/. The velar nasal is a bit more difficult to produce in isolation since in English it never begins a word. Put your tongue in position to articulate /g/, but then release air through your nose. In the case of the velar nasal, we encounter our first phonetic symbol not borrowed from the Roman alphabet; it is represented by an "n" with a tail called an "eng" /ŋ/. Another thing to note about the velar nasal is that it is always found before the graphemes *k* or *g*, though the "g" sound is usually not pronounced in final position (e.g. *anger*, *sinking*, *sink*, *sing*).

As with the alveolar stop, the alveolar nasal may have a dental variant when it occurs before the dental sound "th". Contrast the "n" sounds in the columns below:

Column 1	Column 2
ten [n]	*tenth* [n̪]
moon [n]	*month* [n̪]

The alveolar nasal [n] in Column 1 is articulated with the tongue against the alveolar ridge, the dental variant [n̪] in Column 2 with the tongue against the back of the upper teeth.

Another feature of the alveolar nasals is called "nasal release". This occurs when the nasal follows a homorganic stop (a stop produced in the same place of articulation), hence the sequences /tn/ and /dn/. In nasal release the stop is released directly into the nasal; that is, the tongue is kept against the alveolar ridge and the velum is lowered. There is no separate release of the stop. Say the following words and note how you move from the stop to the nasal: *fitness*, *catnip* *kidney*, *goodnight*. In narrow transcription, nasal release is represented with a superscript "n": [tⁿ] and [dⁿ].

The next set of sounds is the fricative series. English is unusual among the languages of the world in having a very large and diverse class of fricatives. There are voiced and voiceless fricatives produced in four positions:

1. the voiced labiodental fricative /v/ (as in *virtue*, *oven*, *love*) and the voiceless labiodental fricative /f/ (as in *fool*, *offer*, *rough*).
2. the voiced dental fricative /ð/ (as in *then*, *lather*, *lathe*) and the voiceless dental fricative /θ/ (as in *thigh*, *author*, *froth*). The voiced version is represented with an Irish

symbol (adopted by the Anglo-Saxons) called an "eth" or barred "d" and the voiceless version is represented with the Greek letter *theta*.[5]

3. the voiced alveolar fricative /z/ (as in *zero*, *ozone*, *ooze*) and the voiceless alveolar fricative /s/ (as in *sorry*, *passive*, *rice*).

4. the voiced alveolopalatal fricative /ʒ/ (as in *equation*, *rouge*) and the voiceless alveolopalatal fricative /ʃ/ (as in *shirt*, *marshal*, *rush*). These sounds are represented by the /ʃ/ "esh" (long "s") for the voiceless fricative and /ʒ/ "yogh" for the voiced fricative.[6]

The labiodental fricatives /v/ and /f/ are made by bringing the lower lip up against the upper teeth, the dental fricatives /ð/ and /θ/ by placing the tip of the tongue near the inner surface of the upper teeth. Dental fricatives are quite uncommon among the European languages and often cause difficulty for nonnative speakers. Even for native speakers, it may be difficult to distinguish between the voiced and voiceless variants. Listen carefully to the contrast in the following words:

Voiced		Voiceless
bathe /ð/	~	*bath* /θ/
either /ð/	~	*ether* /θ/
then /ð/	~	*thin* /θ/

> **HINT:** One rule of English which may help you in distinguishing these sounds is that the voiced dental fricative is found at the beginnings (word initial) of only certain types of words, namely articles, demonstratives, pronouns, adverbs, and conjunctions, such as *the, that, they, there, though*, but never nouns, adjectives, or verbs. The sound is found in the middle and at the end (word medial and word final) of all words. There are no restrictions on the occurrence of the voiceless dental fricative.

The alveolar fricatives /z/ and /s/ are made by bringing the tip of the tongue up towards the alveolar ridge, as with /t, d, n/, but not closing off the flow of air entirely. The alveolopalatal fricatives /ʒ/ and /ʃ/ are made by bringing the tongue up towards the region between the alveolar ridge and palate.

> **HINT:** To feel the difference in tongue position between the alveolar and the alveolopalatal fricatives, say /s/–/ʃ/ and /z/–/ʒ/ in sequence. You should feel your tongue moving back slightly; it is also flattening out a bit. But you should also note a further difference: the alveolopalatal sounds involve quite marked rounding of the lips.

---

5.   In some analyses, /θ/ and /ð/ are considered as interdental rather than dental. We have opted to classify them as dental since the tip of the tongue typically makes contact near the inner surface of the upper teeth rather than protrudes between the upper and lower teeth.

6.   Note that in some transcription systems these two fricative sounds are represented by the Roman alphabet symbols with a diacritic called a "hachek", a Czech word meaning 'little hook'; the symbol for the voiceless sound /š/ is called an "s-wedge" and for the voiced sound /ž/ is called a "z-wedge".

While /s/, /ʃ/, and /z/ are found in all positions in words, /ʒ/ is restricted in its occurrence: it is never found in initial position in English words, only in French words used in English such as *genre*.

As with alveolar /t/ and /n/, the alveolar fricatives may be dentalized before a dental. Note the position of your tongue when you say *esthetic* or *is this*; you are likely articulating /s̪/ or /z̪/.

While English has quite an elaborate set of fricatives, there are some possible fricatives that it does not make use of, such as the bilabial fricatives /φ/ or /β/ (you can make these by putting your mouth in position to say /p/ or /b/ but allowing some air to escape – you will feel a slight tingling in your lips) and the velar fricatives. The voiceless velar fricative /x/ is found in some dialects of English, for example, in the Scottish pronunciation of *loch*, also in the proper pronunciation of German *Bach*. English speakers usually substitute their closest sound, /k/, for the latter.

Fricatives can be divided into two subclasses based on the amount of acoustic energy released in articulating them.

1. One subclass, the **sibilants**, is produced by constricting the air and then directing it over a sharp edge, namely the teeth. This yields a sound with more acoustic energy, hence louder and higher in pitch than other fricatives; sibilants are perceived as loud hissing sounds. Sibilants include /s, z, ʃ, ʒ/ as well as the affricates (see below).
2. The nonsibilants involve constriction of the air but no sharp edge; they are consequently much quieter with less hissing. They include /f, v, θ, ð/.

Say these different sounds and note the acoustic difference. Sibilants are also differentiated from nonsibilants in that they are made with a groove or slight trough along the center line of the tongue.

The affricate series consists of only two sounds in English:

1. the voiced alveolopalatal affricate /dʒ/ (as in *jury*, *lodger*, *barge*); and
2. the voiceless alveolopalatal affricate /tʃ/ (as in *chin*, *pitcher*, *itch*).

As defined earlier, affricates are produced by articulating a stop and then releasing it into a fricative: you can produce the English affricates by saying the alveolar stops and releasing them immediately into the corresponding alveolopalatal fricative – /d/ then /ʒ/, /t/ then /ʃ/.[7] This suggests that they are complex sounds. We are interpreting them as single sounds, not clusters, however.[8]

---

7. Note that in some transcription systems /tʃ/ and /dʒ/ are represented by Roman alphabet symbols with hachek diacritics /č/ and /ǰ/, called a "c-wedge" and "j-wedge", respectively.

8. The affricates are treated as single sounds rather than as consonant clusters because they are the only sequences that can occur both word initially and word finally, and they are the only sequence of stop + fricative that can occur word initially (see the next chapter on "Phonotactics").

Affricates, fricatives, and stops all belong to a larger class of sounds called **obstruents** – so called because their production obstructs the flow of air through the oral cavity. They are grouped together because they behave similarly. For example, as mentioned in the case of stops, voiced obstruents are articulated for a shorter time than voiceless obstruents, and voiced obstruents at the end of words are partially devoiced.

The approximant series in English includes three sets of quite different sounds all articulated with open approximation (no real restriction on the airflow). English approximants are generally voiced, so it is not necessary to specify this feature in their description. The alveolar lateral, the sound in _lick_, _alloy_, _mall_, is represented by /l/. To feel what the tongue is doing when you articulate this sound, say /d/ and then /l/; you should feel the sides of your tongue drop, allowing air to pass around the sides. There is actually quite a lot of variability in the place of articulation of /l/, that is, in the place in the central portion of the mouth where the air is blocked, ranging from the alveolar to the palatal region. Note the position of your tongue when you pronounce the "l's" in the following columns of words:

Column 1	Column 2	Column 3
leaf	_loom_	_kiln_
late	_loan_	_cool_
lack	_lawn_	_felt_

> **HINT:** Say the words in the three columns above, concentrating on the position of your tongue when you produce the lateral sound. The laterals in Column 1 are produced the furthest forward in the mouth because you are adjusting to the "front" vowel which follows (see the next section on vowels). The laterals in Column 2 are produced further back in the mouth since they precede "back" vowels. Finally, the laterals in Column 3 are produced even further back in the mouth, in the velar region since they follow rather than precede a vowel.

The words in Column 3 contain what is called a "dark l" or "velarized l", represented with a superimposed tilde [ɫ]. Another feature of "l" is lateral release, which like nasal release (see above) occurs when the lateral follows a homorganic stop, namely /d/ or /t/. The stop is released directly into the lateral, as in _sadly_, _fiddler_, _butler_, _cutlass_, _atlas_; this phenomenon is represented in narrow transcription with a superscript l, [dˡ] and [tˡ].

The second type of approximant is the glide, or semivowel. There are two glides in English; they occur only at the beginning of syllables. The palatal glide /j/ is the sound in _yes_, _canyon_.[9] It is produced by raising the tongue in the palatal region. The velar glide is

---

9. In some transcription systems this sound is represented by /y/.

the sound in <u>wi</u>ll, a<u>w</u>are; it is represented by /w/. Note that when you say this sound, your tongue is raised in the velar region, but you also have strong **labialization**, or lip-rounding. For this reason, /w/ is sometimes described as labiovelar rather than simply as velar.

Now say the following sets of words:

Column 1 /ʍ/	Column 2 /w/
which	witch
where	wear
whale	wail

Do you have different sounds at the beginning of the words in the two columns? If not, you are using the sound /w/ in both. But if you do, you are using the sound /w/ for Column 2 but the sound /ʍ/ (or "inverted w"), a voiceless labiovelar fricative, for Column 1. That is, your mouth is in roughly the same configuration as for /w/ but with no voicing or with the air slightly constricted at the glottis.[10]

The third kind of approximant is the retroflex. The description of the English retroflex is rather difficult, and there is no completely satisfactory treatment. It is probably best to call it an alveolar retroflex: the tongue curls back somewhat, and there is also some amount of labialization. It is the sound in <u>r</u>iver, a<u>r</u>ea, mea<u>s</u>ure. We will represent it with /r/, though the IPA symbol for this sound is a "turned r" /ɹ/.[11] A number of dialects of English are what are called "nonrhotic", or r-less dialects (including standard British English and the dialects of North American English spoken in New York, the Southern US, and parts of New England). In these dialects, /r/ is omitted preconsonantally and word finally, as in *part* or *far*. Such dialects often have a "linking r", /r/ inserted before a vowel in the next or the same word, as in *the idea(r) is*. They may also have an "intrusive r", /r/ inserted preconsonantally after a vowel, as in *wa(r)sh*. Most dialects of English spoken in the US and Canada, however, consistently retain /r/; they are "rhotic" dialects.

The last consonant sound is the "h" sound found in <u>h</u>ard, a<u>h</u>ead. It also poses some difficulty for description. It is often described as a voiceless glottal fricative, since the air is partially obstructed by bringing the vocal cords together producing a kind of rough breathing; this is the analysis of the IPA, and hence /h/ is included on your consonant chart in the appropriate box. It is the only voiceless fricative without a voiced counterpart. Another way to understand the sound is as a kind of voiceless vowel, which is homorganic with the following vowel (in fact, /h/ occurs only syllable initially before a vowel in English). That is, you put your mouth in position to say the following vowel; then you constrict

---

10.   In Old English this sound was written *hw* rather than *wh*; the Old English spelling fairly closely approximates what you are doing in articulation.

11.   In the IPA, the symbol /r/ represents the "alveolar trilled r" one finds in many languages such as Spanish.

the air momentarily before setting the vocal cords in motion to produce the voiced vowel. Note the position of your tongue and lips when you say /h/ in each of the following words, each with a different vowel:[12]

/h/ + front vowel	/h/ + central vowel	/h/ + back vowel
heed		*hoop*
hid		*hood*
hate	*hut*	*home*
head		*horse*
hat		*hot*

This completes the inventory of consonants in English. In our discussion, we have also mentioned various phonological processes which alter the basic sound of consonants; we have also discussed the diacritics used in addition to the consonant symbols to denote these processes:

[ˌ]	devoiced
[ʰ]	aspirated
[~]	velarized
[ˌ]	dentalized
[˺]	unreleased

In the following chapter, we will discuss in more detail when and why these phonological changes occur.

Self-Testing Exercise: Do Exercise 2.2.

4. Vowel sounds

Turning now to vowels, we will again consider vowels in the abstract before examining the specific vowels found in English. To adequately define a **vowel**, we need to look at it in articulatory, acoustic, and functional terms:

–   In articulatory terms, vowels are sounds articulated with no obstruction of the air stream, that is, with open articulation. There is lack of central closure of the air stream, though the tongue may come into contact with the teeth on the sides.

---

12.   For this reason, /h/ can also be considered a voiceless glottal approximant (it would be the only voiceless approximant), and could be written with the appropriate vowel symbol with a devoicing diacritic [ˌ].

–   In acoustic terms, vowels are sounds that vary in pitch, which is determined by the quality of the sound wave. Pitch is modified by changing the shape of the resonating chamber (the oral and, sometimes, the nasal tracts) by changing the position and shape of tongue and lips and by lowering or raising the velum.

–   In functional terms, vowels constitute the nucleus, or necessary, part of the syllable.

4.1   Classification of vowels

Although there are fewer vowels than consonants, their classification is more difficult for the following reasons.

–   Vowels are articulated not by putting the articulators into discrete configurations, but by shaping the tongue in the mouth. Hence, there are theoretically infinite different vowel sounds, forming a continuum with no distinct boundaries.

–   There is significant regional and individual variation in the inventory of vowel sounds; in fact, phonologically, different dialects of English are distinguished primarily by their inventory of vowels, while the inventory of consonants is quite consistent across dialects.[13]

–   Authorities differ in their analyses of vowel sounds and in their methods of transcribing vowels; several (not entirely compatible) systems of vowel transcription are currently in use.

–   We can produce acceptable vowel sounds without the full complement of articulatory gestures, for example, with our teeth clenched or without the required lip rounding.

–   Differences in length combine with differences in quality in distinguishing vowels, but it is not always easy to separate these differences.

–   It is quite difficult to pinpoint exactly where the tongue is when a vowel is produced; this is especially true for back vowels. Thus the classification system in Table 2.2 below designates the general position of the tongue for each vowel. An exact auditory measurement of any given vowel might place its production in a slightly different area.

In some respects, however, vowels are easier to classify than consonants. For consonants, we must consider four criteria: voicing, orality/nasality, place, and manner of articulation. For vowels, we need to consider only one criterion: place of articulation. This is

---

13.   This book does not include any detailed description of the dialects of English. A comprehensive, 3-volume treatment of the dialects of the English-speaking world is found in Wells (1982). For specific information on British and North American dialects see Hughes, Trudgill, and Watt (2005) and Wolfram and Schilling-Estes (2005), respectively. Finally, for a discussion of issues of "dialect", "idiolect", "standard/nonstandard" and the teaching of English, see Chapter 12.

due to the fact that all vowels are voiced and oral. English does not regularly use voiceless or nasalized vowels.[14] Also, in terms of their manner of articulation, all vowels are produced with open approximation.

The place of articulation of vowels is understood rather differently than it is for consonants. Instead of determining which articulators are used and where stricture occurs, we determine where the highest point of the tongue is during the production of the vowel sound. In articulating vowels, the tongue is primary, though other articulators may change the size and shape of the resonating chamber: the larynx can move up and down slightly, the velum can be raised or lowered (giving one or two resonating chambers), the lower jaw is also raised or lowered in conjunction with the tongue position (moving through the close, half-close, half-open, and open positions as the tongue is lowered). The lips, also in conjunction with the tongue position, can be open and closed, as well as **rounded** (pursed) or **unrounded** (spread). The rounding of the lips has the double effect of changing the shape of the opening and lengthening the resonating chamber.

In classifying vowels, however, it is generally sufficient to talk about the position of tongue. The tongue is convex, with the front and back humped and the tip hanging down. The high point is measured on two axes: a horizontal, or front-back axis, and a vertical, or high-low axis. The vowel chart in Table 2.2 below, which is a schematic representation of a side-view of the mouth (viewed from the left), shows these two axes. The front-back axis is divided into three positions, **front, central**, and **back**, which range from the center of the palate to the back of the velum. The high-low axis is divided into from four to six positions, either the four positions of the jaw noted above or two positions in each of three sections, **high, mid**, and **low**. We will use the latter classification. There are thus 36 possible vowel positions, including the choice between rounded and unrounded vowels in each position.

There are two kinds of vowels:

1. A **monophthong** is a single or simple vowel sound constituting the nucleus of a syllable. The position of the tongue is more or less static, and there is a relatively constant acoustic property, or pitch, to the sound.
2. A **diphthong** consists of the tongue gliding from one vowel position to another within a single syllable; it is produced as one continuous sound, not as a succession of sounds. By definition, a diphthong involves a change in the position of the tongue, and it may involve a change in the shape of the lips as well.

In articulating diphthongs, we may make use of vowel positions not used in articulating monophthongs. There is quite a large range of beginning and ending points for diphthongs.

---

14. The only exceptions are vowels that co-occur with voiceless stops (and as a result may be partially devoiced) and vowels that precede nasal consonants (and hence are nasalized). These will be discussed in Chapter 3.

Because of the movement of the tongue, the articulation of a diphthong, unlike that of a monophthong, cannot be maintained; a diphthong is not necessarily longer (does not take more time to articulate) than a monophthong, though diphthongs are frequently, and erroneously, called "long vowels" in school.

Diphthongs always make use of one of the two semivowels, /j/ and /w/, hence their name of "glide"; we will, however, transcribe the semivowels in diphthongs using the symbols for their vowel equivalents /ɪ/ and /ʊ/, respectively. The glide component of a diphthong is shorter and less sonorous (hence "lower"); the vowel component is longer and more sonorous (hence "higher"). There are two types of diphthongs. A falling diphthong consists of a vowel portion followed by a glide portion. Because the glide is acoustically less prominent than the vowel, the diphthong is considered to be "falling"; the term has nothing to do with tongue position, which in fact usually rises. It refers to the fall or decrease in resonance. A "rising" diphthong consists of a glide portion followed by a vowel portion, thus consisting of a rise or increase in resonance.

4.2   Vowels of English and their phonetic notation

We will now consider which of the possible vowel positions are used in English by surveying the vowel inventory of English and learning the phonetic alphabet symbol used to transcribe each vowel. Combined with your consonant transcription skills acquired in the previous section, you will by the end of this section be able to transcribe entire words and sentences as well as read broad phonetic transcriptions.

As you read the following section, you should consult the vowel chart in Table 2.2. For ease in learning the sound represented by each symbol, a sample word containing that sound is given on the chart.

> **HINT:** You might find it useful to memorize the words associated with each symbol in Table 2.2, so that when faced with an unknown vowel sound you can check whether it rhymes with your sample word.

If no word appears next to a symbol in the chart, this means that the sound does not generally occur as a monophthong in English, but only as the nucleus in diphthongs, which are listed below the vowel chart. In giving a technical description of English vowels, it is traditional to begin with the high-low position, then give the front-back position, and finally list features of tenseness and rounding.

> **HINT:** Be sure to pronounce all of the sample words carefully. Because of the dialectal and individual diversity noted above for vowel sounds, you might find you do not pronounce all of the words the same way as indicated. Strike out any examples which are not appropriate for you. The vowels given are typical of many dialects of North American English.

Table 2.2. The Vowels of North American English

Monophthongs		Front	Central	Back	
High (close)					
	tense	i *seat*	ɨ *just* (Adv)	u *boot*	
	lax	ɪ *sit*		ʊ *put*	
Mid					
	upper	(e)	ə *sofa, about*	(o)	
	lower	ɛ *set*	ɝ *bird*	ɔ *port*	
			ʌ *putt*		
Low (open)					
		æ *sat*	(a)	ɒ *pot*	ɑ *father*
Diphthongs					
		eɪ *late*	aɪ *file*	oʊ *loan*	
		ɪu *cute*	aʊ *fowl*	ɔɪ *foil*	

Note: Vowels in parentheses represent the "pure" vowels, which do not typically exist in English. For this reason, no example words are given.

We will begin with the monophthongs, moving from front to back. The front vowels are produced with the high point of the tongue in the palatal region. The front vowels of Modern English are all unrounded. In the high front area, there are two vowels:

1. the high front tense vowel, represented with a Roman alphabet lower case *i* /i/; this is the "long e" sound of words such as *heed, he, bead, heat, keyed*.[15]
2. the high front lax vowel, represented with a Roman alphabet small capital *i* /ɪ/; this is the vowel in words such as *hid, bid, hit, kid*.

Try saying the two sounds in succession and note the position of your tongue.

In the mid front area, there are two possible vowels, only one of which is found as a monophthong in English:

1. the upper-mid front vowel, represented with a Roman alphabet lower case *e* /e/; this is the sound in German *leben* 'to live', French *été* 'summer', or Spanish *leche* 'milk'. If we compare the French and Spanish words with English *ate* or *lay*, we find that the English sound is really a diphthong; the tongue is not in a constant position, but moves to a glide at the end of the sound. Most dialects of English have no "pure e".
2. the lower-mid front vowel, represented with Greek epsilon /ɛ/; this is the sound in *head, bed, neck, bet, hair, care*. It is a very common vowel in English.

---

15. This sound is sometimes transcribed as /iy/ and may be analyzed as a diphthong; however, we will consider it a monophthong.

In the low front area, there is one vowel in English: the low front vowel represented by the Old English symbol called "æsc" or "ash" /æ/; it is the sound in words such as *lamb*, *hat*, *rap*, *fast*, *tram*.

> **HINT:** Ash is a ligature, that is, a single letter formed by linking two letters, in this case *a* and *e*; you should practice writing ash with a single stroke starting in the upper left-hand corner.

This sound is very susceptible to regional variation, especially between British and North American English.

> **HINT:** The front vowels are fairly evenly spaced. Say each of the front vowels in succession from the top. As you do so, notice that your lower jaw drops as your tongue is lowered, so that by the time you reach /æ/, your mouth is open quite wide. You may also notice your tongue moving back a little, as the lower front vowels are articulated a bit further back in the oral cavity than the upper ones.

The tongue is in the palatal-velar region when articulating the central vowels, all of which are lax and unrounded. In the mid central area, there are four sounds. All of these are "uh" sounds:

1. the upper-mid central vowel, represented by the Hebrew "schwa" /ə/.[16] This sound is found in unstressed syllables only, as in *sofa*, *about*, *subtract*, and *offend*, and therefore is classified as an **unstressed vowel**. Note that in the following words, the underlined vowels in the unstressed syllables tend to reduce to /ə/(stress is indicated by the acute accent mark ´):

catástrophe /æ/	catastróphic /ə/
depréciate /i/	déprecate /ə/
locátion /eɪ/	lócative /ə/
propóse /oʊ/	próposition /ə/
oblíge /aɪ/	óbligation /ə/
allége /ɛ/	allegátion /ə/
absólve /ɑ/	absolútion /ə/

As we discuss further in Chapter 3, this vowel also occurs in unstressed words in the stream of speech, as indicated by the underlined elements in the following sentences:

> He *and* I *are* ready.
> It's ten *to* two.
> Jake's strong *as* *an* ox.

---

16. In some transcription systems, the additional unstressed vowel symbol /ɚ/ is introduced to represent the unstressed "r-colored" /ə/ in words such as *butter*, *bitter*, *persist*, and *curtail*. We have opted not to introduce this additional symbol.

2. a variant of schwa, the high central vowel, represented by "barred i" /ɨ/. This is the reduced vowel found in very casual speech, as when you say the adverb *just* (as opposed to the adjective *just)*: compare *He just arrived* (Adv) and *He is a just person* (A). You should note that the /ɨ/ vowel in the adverb is somewhat higher. You might also have /ɨ/ in the second syllable in the following words: *chicken, women, roses, college, comic,* and *spinach.*[17]

3. the mid central vowel, represented by a "reversed open e with hook" /ɝ/. This sound occurs only in stressed syllables when followed by an "r" sound, as in *herd, her, bird, hurt, pert*. When transcribing this sound, the /r/ is not added, for example *third* /θɝd/.

4. the lower-mid central vowel, represented by an "inverted v" /ʌ/. This sound occurs only in stressed syllables, as in *cut, bud, hut, putt, mud*. This sound is lower and somewhat further back than schwa; in fact, it is sometimes analyzed as a lower-mid back vowel.

In the low central area, there is one sound, represented with a Roman alphabet lower case *a* /a/, but it does not generally occur as a monophthong in North American English; it is used as a starting point for diphthongs, as we will see later. It is the sound you might find in German *machen*. Because it is somewhat further forward than the mid central vowels, it is sometimes analyzed as a front vowel in other systems of transcription.

The back vowels are all articulated with the back of the tongue in the velar region. In English, the back vowels are all rounded, except one. There are two high back vowels:

1. the high back tense vowel represented by a Roman alphabet lower case *u* /u/. It is the vowel sound in words such as *who, booed, boot, hoot, cooed, do*. Note the strong rounding of your lips when you pronounce this vowel.[18]

2. the high back lax vowel, represented by Greek upsilon /ʊ/. It is the sound in *hood, put, good, look, could*.

> **HINT:** If you say the high back tense vowel /u/ and then the high back lax vowel /ʊ/, you should notice both that your tongue is lower in the second vowel and that your lips are somewhat less rounded.

Historically, /ʊ/ has become /ʌ/ in many words, so that words which appear from the spelling to contain "short u" do not, such as *fun, run, luck, spun, gun, cuff, gull, dull*; exceptions are *u*'s between labials and /l/, /ʃ/ or /tʃ/, which remain /ʊ/, such as *full, pull, mull, wool, bull, push, bush,* or *butcher*.

---

17. Note that there is a great deal of individual variation as to which unstressed vowel is used. Thus a speaker may pronounce the final unstressed vowel in all these words as either /ə/ or /ɨ/.

18. In some systems of transcription this vowel is analyzed as a diphthong with a following glide /uw/, but we will consider it a monophthong.

When we reach the mid and lower back areas, the vowel situation becomes considerably more murky: there is great dialectal differences as to which vowels are found as well as
differences of opinion concerning their transcription. In the mid back area, there are two
possible vowels:

1. the upper-mid back vowel, represented by a Roman alphabet lower case /o/; it is the
    sound in German *Boot* 'boat' or French *eau* 'water', *chaud* 'hot'. But it does not exist as a
    monophthong in most dialects of English, only as the beginning point of a diphthong,
    the sound found in, for example, *boat*.

    > HINT: As you say *boat*, you should notice that your tongue is not in a constant position,
    > but rises at the close; your lips will also round more at the end.

2. the lower-mid back vowel, represented by a backwards *c*, called an "open o", /ɔ/. While
    this vowel is common in many dialects of English, in some dialects, it occurs only before
    /r/, as in *fort, torte, more*.[19]

In the low back area, there are again two possible vowels:

1. the low back unrounded vowel, represented by a lower case script *a* /ɑ/. This is the
    vowel found in *father* and, for many speakers, also in *hot, cod, body, bomb, hard, bard,
    heart, card*. Note that this is the only back vowel which is not rounded. Compare the
    unrounded /ɑ/ in *moss, pot*, and *gosling* to the rounded /ɔ/ in *Morse, port, gorse*.
2. the low back rounded vowel, represented by an upside down script *a* /ɒ/. Speakers of
    British and Canadian English may have this sound in the words given immediately
    above, except *father*.

    > HINT: Say the above words and try to determine whether your vowel is the rounded
    > version /ɒ/ or the unrounded version /ɑ/. If you have /ɒ/, then it is likely that /ɑ/ is
    > restricted to the position before /r/, as in *part*, and to the word *father*.

British English and some dialects of North American English distinguish the vowels in the
following sets of words, using /ɔ/ in Column 1 and /ɑ/ or /ɒ/ in Column 2:

Column 1	Column 2
cawed	*cod*
caught	*cot*
auto	*Otto*
awed	*odd*
taught	*tot*
naught	*not*

---

19. In some transcription systems, /ɔ/ is considered a low back vowel.

However, Canadian English and some dialects of US English do not distinguish the vowels.

> **HINT:** Say the words in Columns 1 and 2 above and determine whether they are homophones for you. Then try to say all the back vowels in order from the top of the chart to the bottom: /u – ʊ – o – ɔ – ɑ/. Notice how your tongue drops, your jaw lowers, and your lips gradually unround.

This completes the inventory of monophthongs of English. We turn now to the diphthongs. English has six diphthongs, five of which are falling diphthongs, and one of which is a rising diphthong. As you read the following explanations, look at Figure 2.4, which shows the approximate starting and ending points of these diphthongs.

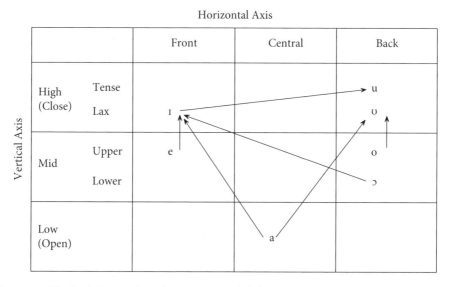

Figure 2.4. The Diphthongs of North American English (Approximate Starting and Ending Points)

1. The low central to high front (lax) diphthong /aɪ/ is the sound found in h*i*de, h*i*gh, b*i*de, h*ei*ght, *eye*, s*i*gh, t*i*red, h*i*re. This sound was probably called "long i" in school, but it is really a falling diphthong ending with a /j/ glide.
2. The low central to high back (lax) diphthong /aʊ/ is the sound in h*ow*, f*ou*nd, c*ow*ed, *out*, d*own*. Note that your lips round at the end with a /w/ glide.

There is a phenomenon affecting these two diphthongs which characterizes Canadian English; for this reason, it is often called "Canadian raising", though it is also found in American dialects, such as those of tidewater Virginia and Cape Cod. In Canadian raising, the beginning point of these two diphthongs is somewhat higher, closer to the mid central region, so that the resulting diphthongs are /ʌʊ/ and /ʌɪ/, as in the typical Canadian pro-nunciations of the following:

/aʊ/ > /ʌʊ/   _out, south, mouse, couch_
/aɪ/ > /ʌɪ/   _rice, type, tight, wife_

However, this raising occurs only before voiceless consonants, so that speakers have a contrast between a raised diphthong for the words in Columns 1 and 3 below and an unraised diphthong for the words in Columns 2 and 4, where the consonant following is voiced:

Column 1	Column 2	Column 3	Column 4
/ʌʊ/ ~	/aʊ/	/ʌɪ/ ~	/aɪ/
house	houses, (to) house	knife	knives
mouth	mouths, (to) mouth	advice	(to) advise
spouse	(to) espouse	tripe	tribe
lout	loud	ice	eyes
bout	bowed	write	ride

3. The (upper-)mid front to high front (lax) diphthong /eɪ/ is the sound in _hay, hate, bayed, mate, gate, late_. This sound has traditionally been called "long a", but it is, in fact, a falling diphthong. This diphthong substitutes for the "pure e" vowel of other languages such as Spanish and French.
4. The (upper-)mid back to high back (lax) diphthong /oʊ/ is the sound in _bode, hoe, boat, coat, no_. Known traditionally as "long o", it is a falling diphthong ending in a /w/ glide; note that your lips round with the glide.
5. The (lower-)mid back to high front (lax) diphthong /ɔɪ/ is the sound in _ahoy, Boyd, boy, ploy_. It too is a falling diphthong.
6. The high front (lax) to high back (tense) diphthong /ɪu/ is the sound in _hued, cute, cued, few, pure, fury_. It is the only rising diphthong of English: it begins with a /j/ glide and concludes with a /u/ vowel.[20]

Quite a common phenomenon for many speakers is the loss of the /j/ glide (or "yod-dropping"), that is, a shift from /ɪu/ to /u/, what can be called "monophthongization", after alveolar consonants, as in _Sue, suit, new, stew_. Note that if monophthongization occurs, the words in Columns 1 and 2 are homophones:

Column 1	Column 2
Tue(sday)	two, to
due, dew	do
lieu	loo
sue	Sue

---

20. In some transcription systems this diphthong is represented as /ju/.

In other environments, the diphthong is maintained, as in the words below, where /ɪu/ in Column 1 contrasts with /u/ in Column 2:

Column 1	Column 2
pew	*poo*
cute	*coot*
view	*voo(doo)*
beaut(y)	*boot*
few	*phoo(ey)*
music	*mood*

Self-Testing Exercises: Do Exercises 2.3, 2.4, and 2.5.

Two additional features of vowels still need to be discussed. The first is the feature of vowel "tenseness". Tenseness is a rather controversial concept, but it is generally thought to refer to the degree of tension in the muscles of tongue, which affects the total volume of the tongue, and is responsible for small variations in vowel quality. **Tense vowels** are longer, higher, and more marginal, while **lax vowels** are shorter, lower, and slightly more centralized. More importantly, tense and lax vowels can be distinguished by their occurrence in certain types of syllable. An open syllable is one which does <u>not</u> end in a consonant, though it may optionally begin with one or more consonants. A closed syllable is one which ends in one or more consonants; again it may or may not begin with consonants. While both tense and lax vowels can occur in unstressed syllables of any kind and in stressed closed syllables, only tense vowels can occur in stressed open syllables; lax vowels cannot occur in stressed open syllables. Table 2.3 classifies the vowels of English into the categories tense versus lax and illustrates their distribution in open versus closed syllables. Note that the asterisks mark impossible sequences (here, a lax vowel in an stressed open syllable).

The second remaining feature is that of **vowel length**, the time spent in articulating a vowel. Unlike many languages, English does not distinguish between long and short vowel pairs. It has been found that syllables in English are always the same length. In other words, they always take the same amount of time to articulate. However, we have already seen above that voiced and voiceless obstruents at the ends of words differ in length, the voiceless obstruents being longer than the voiced. In such cases, in order to compensate for the length of the consonants, the vowel length differs, thus keeping the length of the syllable constant. In Column 1 below, the vowel is followed by a voiceless obstruent, causing the vowel to be shorter and the obstruent longer. In Column 2, the opposite is true: the vowel is followed by a voiced consonant, causing the vowel to be longer and the obstruent to be shorter.

Table 2.3. The Tense and Lax Vowels of English

Tense	Lax	Open Syllable		Closed Syllable	
		Tense	Lax	Tense	Lax
i	ɪ	ki	*kɪ	kin	kɪt
eɪ	ɛ	keɪ	*kɛ	keɪk	kɛtʃ
	æ		*kæ		kæt
	ʌ[21]		*kʌ		kʌt
u	ʊ	ku	*kʊ	kut	kʊk
oʊ		moʊ		koʊt	
ɔ, ɑ[22]		pɔ, pɑ/ɒ		kɔt, kɑt/kɒt	
aɪ		laɪ		kaɪt	
aʊ		kaʊ		kraʊd	
ɔɪ		kɔɪ		kɔɪl	
ɪu		kɪu		kɪut	

Column 1	Column 2
[Vo C$_{vl}$ vowel shorter C obstruent longer]	[Vo C$_{vd}$ vowel longer C obstruent shorter]
seat	seed
safe	save
lace	laze

Note: Vo = vowel, C = consonant, vd = voiced, vl = voiceless

Final sequences of consonants also take longer to articulate than single consonants, as you would expect (initial consonants seem to have no effect). Moreover, vowels in open syllables will be longer than those in closed syllables. These facts combined give us the following, entirely predictable, sequence of vowel length:

Long	Half-long	Short	Shortest
CVo	CVoC$_{vd}$	CVoC$_{vl}$	CVoCC
see	seed	seat	ceased
lay	laid	late	laced
mow	mowed	moat	most
fee	feed	feat	feast

Note: Vo = vowel, C = consonant, vd = voiced, vl = voiceless

---

21. Note that /ʌ/ is the only mid central vowel given in this chart: /ɨ/ and /ə/ are not included since they occur only in unstressed syllables; /ɝ/ occurs only in conjunction with the "r" sound and thus can be analyzed as occurring always in a closed syllable (hence lax by definition).

22. For speakers who have /ɔ/ only before /r/, /ɔ/ will be lax by definition.

Vowel length may be indicated by diacritics: [ː] for long, [ˑ] for half-long, and nothing or [ˇ] for short. Alternatively, a macron [ˉ] may indicate a long vowel.

5.   The function of vowels and consonants

Speech sounds can be viewed in two ways, either with respect to their form or with respect to their function. Thus far we have discussed the form of vowels and consonants, noting that vowels are articulated with no restriction of the air stream (or with open approximation) while consonants are generally articulated with some restriction of the air stream.

In order to understand the difference between these two classes of speech sounds we should also consider their function. Vowels have a function that can be described as **syllabic**: that is, they constitute the obligatory nucleus of a syllable, which consists minimally of one vowel, as in the personal pronoun *I* /aɪ/. Vowels are also louder, longer, more sonorous, and acoustically more prominent than consonants. Consonants, on the other hand, generally have a "nonsyllabic" function. Though they can begin and/or end syllables, they are optional. They are also shorter and acoustically less prominent.

However, we have already seen that the distinction between consonant and vowel is not entirely absolute: glides are articulated as vowels but function as consonants. Further difficulty results from the fact that certain consonants have a "syllabic" function; that is, they are like a vowel in being able to stand alone in a syllable (without any other vowel). These consonants include the liquids and the nasals. They are commonly syllabic following a consonant at the end of a polysyllabic word. We indicate the syllabic function of consonants by a subscript bar [ˌ]. Read the following examples; you should notice that the underlined element may contain the vowel /ə/ or, alternatively, no vowel at all. In the latter instance, the consonant is syllabic, and serves the function of a vowel:

Syllabic Consonant	Examples
[r̩]	*ladder, butter, runner*
[l̩]	*fizzle, muddle, muscle, kettle*
[n̩]	*reason, beaten, sudden, and* (said rapidly)[23]
[ŋ̍]	*Jack and Kate* (said rapidly), *lookin' good*
[m̩]	*solemn, rhythm, prism, chasm*[24]

In sum, it is important when distinguishing consonants and vowels to consider both differences in form (i.e. articulated with or without closure in the vocal tract) and function (syllabic versus nonsyllabic). As we have seen, neither vowels nor consonants are entirely

---

23.   Note that nasal release and lateral release may yield syllabic consonants. Syllabic [l̩] and [n̩] occur following alveolars, but generally not following labials and velars.

24.   Syllabic [ŋ̍] and [m̩] are rare.

distinguished by either form or function since some consonants (namely, the approximants) are articulated as vowels with open approximation and some consonants (the syllabic consonants) function as vowels in certain environments.[25]

Self-Testing Exercise: Do Exercise 2.6. For more advanced work in phonological analysis, read the discussion of "distinctive features" on the website and do the problems in Exercise 2.7.

Chapter summary

Now that you have completed this chapter, you should be able to:

1.   list the differences between the written and oral media of communication;
2.   describe the human speech apparatus and production of speech sounds;
3.   give a technical description of English consonants and vowels and provide the phonetic symbol for each;
4.   transcribe English words in broad transcription; and
5.   discuss the classification of consonants and vowels using both formal and functional criteria.

Recommended additional reading

A very clear discussion of articulatory phonetics is found in Bickford and Floyd (2006) as well as in Catford (2002) and Ladefoged (2006).

More detailed discussions of English consonants and vowels include McMahon (2002, Chapters 3 and 5), Kreidler (2004, Chapters 3–4), Ladefoged (2006, Chapters 1–4), Yavaş (2006, Chapters 1, 3–4), and Celce-Murcia, Brinton, and Goodwin (with Griner) (2010). A definitive work on the vowels and consonants of the world is Ladefoged (2005).

---

25.   Because the traditional classification of sounds rests on both formal and functional criteria, it has proved useful in phonological work to break sounds down into smaller components. These are known as "phonological", or "distinctive, features". This alternative way of describing sounds originated in the "Prague School" of structural linguistics which flourished between World War I and World War II. It was promoted in America by the linguist Roman Jakobson and later incorporated into the approach know as "generative phonology" by Noam Chomsky and Morris Halle in their influential book, *The Sound Pattern of English* (1968). While this approach is considered somewhat too advanced for this text, you may find out more about it in Exercise 2.7 and in the sources listed in the "Recommended Additional Reading" section.

Textbooks which you might like to consult include Jeffries (2006, Chapter 1), Fromkin, Rodman, and Hyams (2007, Chapter 6), Finegan (2008, Chapter 3), Curzan and Adams (2009, Chapter 3), and O'Grady and Archibald (2009, Chapter 2). Murray (1995, Chapter 1) includes exercises with answers.

A dictionary of English words in phonetic transcription is Jones (2006).

For definitions of any of the terms used in this chapter, see Crystal (2008) and for a clear and concise explanation of all of the phonetic symbols used here, see Pullum and Ladusaw (1996).

On the difference between speech and writing, see Biber (1992, especially Chapters 2 and 3) and Delahunty and Garvey (1994, Chapter 12).

Chapter 3

Phonology, phonotactics, and suprasegmentals

1. Phonemes
2. Phonemic rules
3. Phonological processes
4. Phonotactics
5. Suprasegmental features
6. Syllable structure

Chapter preview

This chapter begins with a discussion of phonemes (the distinctive sounds of a language) and allophones (the predictable variants of these sounds). A number of phonemic rules for specific English phonemes and their allophones are stated. The chapter then treats the topic of phonological rules, which account generally for allophonic variation in English. This is followed by a description of the constraints on possible positions for sounds and possible sound combinations in English. The chapter then turns to the features of stress and intonation in English, features which extend over more than one sound. The characteristics of stress are defined, the rules of stress placement in English are explained briefly, and the functions of stress in different domains – morphology, syntax, and discourse – are described. The pitch patterns of different sentence types are exemplified, and intonation is related to the presentation of information in an English sentence. The chapter ends with a discussion of English syllable structure – a level of structure intermediate between the sound and the word.

Commentary

1. Phonemes

You will recall that we defined phonology as the study of the distinctive sounds in a language, and although we have mentioned in passing the difference between certain distinctive and nondistinctive variants (for example, between [tʰ] and [t]), we have not discussed this subject in any detail. The concept of distinctiveness is captured by the notion of a **phoneme**. A phoneme is a distinctive or contrastive sound in a language. What "distinctive" means in this context is that the sound makes a difference in meaning and has communicative value. Different phonemes make contrasts in words. For example, /n/, /l/ and /t/ are all phonemes because they serve to make contrasts in words, as in *nab, lab, tab*. Here we see how the phonemes of a language are determined, by means of what are called **minimal pairs**. A minimal pair is a set of different words consisting of all the same sounds except for one. The one sound which contrasts is then determined to be a phoneme since it makes a difference in meaning (it differentiates one word from another). For example, we could set up a *phonetic environment*, or a sequence of sounds, such as an environment containing the sound sequence /æt/. If we then establish a blank slot preceding this sequence, /_æt/, and substitute different consonants in this slot, we can see if we get different words. If we do, then each of these consonants is a phoneme. Examine the following:

/_æt/: p̲at, b̲at, s̲at, m̲at, g̲nat, f̲at, t̲hat, v̲at, c̲at …

We can conclude that /p/, /b/, /s/, /m/, /n/, /f/, /ð/, /v/, and /k/ are all phonemes. Thus, *bat* and *cat*, for example, form a minimal pair, as do *gnat* and *vat*.

This same concept of a minimal pair holds true for vowels as well. Consider, for example, a phonetic environment such as /p_t/. Substituting different vowels in the empty slot, we can generate numerous minimal pairs:

/p_t/: p̲it, p̲e̲at, p̲a̲te, p̲ot, p̲o̲ut, p̲ut, p̲utt, p̲at, p̲et …

We can conclude that /ɪ/, /i/, /eɪ/, /ɒ/, /aʊ/, /ʊ/, /ʌ/, /æ/, and /ɛ/ are all distinct phonemes.

Phonemes are said to be unpredictable, since their occurrence depends on what word you want to say rather than by any phonological rule. That is, whether /b/ or /k/ occurs in the environment /_æt/ depends on whether you wish to refer to the nocturnal flying mammal *bat* or to the family feline *cat*, not on whether the sound occurs in the context of /æ/ or word initially or any other factor which is solely phonetically determined. Phonemes are also said to be in **parallel distribution** since they occur in the same (or 'parallel') phonetic environments. Note that an ideal writing system would be phonemic, where each alphabetic symbol stands for one and only one phoneme.

There is some debate about the nature of the phoneme. One view is that it has some psychological validity; it is a concept in the mind. Another view is that it is an abstraction, or an ideal sound. A third view is that it refers to a class of sounds which are phonetically similar (but not identical) and have the same phonological function. The last two views are probably the easiest to comprehend, and they have the further advantage of incorporating the notion of the allophone.

An **allophone** (from *allos* 'other' *phōnē* 'sound') is a predictable variant of a phoneme. Allophones are the individual members of a class of sounds (a phoneme), or the pronounceable or concrete realizations of an abstraction (a phoneme). We speak of the phonetically similar variants of a sound as the "allophones of a (particular) phoneme". To take a real example from English, consider the aspirated [tʰ] and the nonaspirated [t] discussed in the previous chapter. They are phonetically very similar, but not identical. Allophones are nondistinctive (noncontrastive) variants of a phoneme, since substituting one allophone for another allophone of the same phoneme will not lead to a different word. Replacing [tʰ] with [t] in *top*, or [t] with [tʰ] in *stop*, will not lead to different words, just slightly odd-sounding ones.

Allophones of a phoneme are predictable: they are conditioned by the phonetic environment, which determines the appearance of one or another allophone. Thus, we can say that the aspirated version of /t/ is predicted by its position word (or syllable) initially before a stressed vowel; the nonaspirated version is predicted by all other phonetic environments. We can say that allophones are positional variants, which are in **complementary distribution**, meaning that where one occurs the other does not. They never occur in the same environment, always in different environments. They never overlap in distribution; rather, their distributions "complement" (or 'complete') one another. Our examples [tʰ] and [t] never occur in the same position: [tʰ] occurs syllable initial, and [t] occurs in all other environments. Thus, we can conclude that [tʰ] and [t] are allophones of the phoneme /t/. We enclose the phoneme in slashes to indicate that it represents a class of sounds, or an abstraction, and thus cannot be pronounced.

Note that *environment* in the context of phonemes and allophones is limited strictly to phonetic features, though it can refer to a number of such features; for example, it can refer to the position of the sound in the word or syllable (e.g. syllable initial or word final), the nature of the surrounding sounds (e.g. between vowels, following a voiceless stop, before an approximant), or even the placement of stress.

Occasionally, allophones are in "free variation". For example, stops may or may not be released word finally. A speaker will release or not release them arbitrarily, and whether or not they are released makes no difference in meaning.

Phonemes and allophones are always language- (or dialect-)specific. For example, in Greek [ɪ] and [i] are allophones of the same phoneme, while in English they are distinct phonemes. In Japanese [l] and [r] are allophones of the same phoneme, hence the difficulty many native Japanese speakers have with these two distinct sounds in English. In some dialects of North American English, specifically those which do not distinguish *pin* and *pen*, the phonemes /ɪ/ and /ɛ/ are allophones of the same phoneme.

Finally, while the phonemes of a language constitute its inventory of distinctive sounds, languages might also have a few marginal phonemes. These are sounds which occur in only a limited number of words. For example, one might consider the voiceless velar fricative /x/ occurring in words such as *Bach* (the German composer) or *loch* (a Scottish lake) as a marginal phoneme for some speakers of English.

2. Phonemic rules

The allophones of phoneme are predictable and hence can be stated in terms of a **phonemic rule**. Phonemic rules stipulate the different environments in which the allophones of a given phoneme are found.

In the previous chapter we introduced several diacritic marks that designate phonological processes such as devoicing, aspiration, and dentalization. In order to discuss phonemic rules, we must now expand this list as follows:

devoicing	[̥]	syllabic	[̩]	fronting	[̟]
aspiration	[ʰ]	nasal release	[ⁿ]	retracting	[̠]
unreleased	[̚]	lateral release	[ˡ]	nasalization	[̃]
dentalization	[̪]	length	[ː], [ˑ]	velarization	[~]
				labialization	[ʷ]

We also introduced the symbol for the flap allophone [ɾ] but here need to introduce one additional symbol, the symbol [ɱ] representing the labiodental nasal allophone of /n/.

The phonemic rules for allophonic variation can be formalized as follows:

/x/ →   [y]/
       [z]/ elsewhere

The symbol between the slashes /x/ represents the phoneme, while the symbols in square brackets represent the allophones [y] and [z]. The arrow → means 'is realized as' or 'has the allophones'. Thus, this rule reads "the phoneme x has the allophones y and z." Furthermore, the slash / means 'in the environment'. Following the slash, the phonetic environment in which the allophone is found is stated. The environment of the last allophone is always stated as "elsewhere", meaning all other environments. The "elsewhere allophone" is the one with the widest distribution, the one found in the greatest variety of environments. Note that "elsewhere" includes all environments excluding the environments already listed above in the rule; thus you always read the rule from top to bottom.

Environments are quite varied, and they are generally abbreviated in some way, e.g.:

Abbreviation	Meaning
#	word or syllable boundary
—	position of the allophone
#—	word or syllable initial
—#	word or syllable final
Vo—Vo	between vowels

#—Vó   word or syllable initial before a stressed vowel
C—   following a consonant

Let's look at some actual examples of phonemic rules in English, reviewing details that were presented in the previous chapter:

1. Since /h/ may be analyzed as a voiceless approximant that is homorganic with the following vowel, we could write a rule for the predictable variants of this phoneme as follows:

    /h/ → [i̥]/—i   _hee_d
        [ɪ̥]/—ɪ   _hi_d
        [æ̥]/—æ   _ha_t
        [u̥]/—u   w_ho_
        [ʊ̥]/—ʊ   _hoo_d
        etc.

    This rule says that /h/ is articulated as a voiceless approximant that takes on characteristics of the vowel it precedes. Thus before /i/ /h/ becomes [i̥], before /ɪ/ it becomes [ɪ̥], and so forth.

2. The voiceless stop /p/ has a number of variants:

    /p/ → [pʰ]/ #—Vó   _p_ort, _p_arty, com_p_uter, a_p_art
        [p˺]/ —C_stop_, —#   ca_pp_ed, o_p_t, sce_p_ter, ca_p_, ro_p_e,
        [p]/ elsewhere   s_p_ort, s_p_ring, a_p_ron, _p_roclaim, ti_p_sy

    This rule says that: (1) the phoneme /p/ is realized as aspirated [pʰ] syllable initially before a stressed vowel; (2) it is unreleased [p˺] before another stop consonant or word finally; and (3) it is [p] in all other environments.

3. The voiceless stop /t/ has more variants than /p/:

    /t/ → [tʰ]/ #—Vó   _t_ongue, re_t_urn, at_t_end
        [tⁿ]/ —[n, n̩]   fi_t_ness, mi_tt_en
        [tˡ]/—[l]   a_t_las, bu_t_ler
        [ɾ]/ Vó—Vo, Vó— [ɾ], Vó— [l̩]   ci_t_y, ma_tt_er, bo_tt_le
        [t̪]/ —[ð, θ]   a_t_ that, eigh_th_
        [t˺]/ —C_stop_, —#   foo_t_print, ha_t_pin, ra_t_, roo_t_
        [t]/ elsewhere   s_t_op, _t_ry, _t_win, a_tt_ract, ma_t_ron

    This rule reads that the phoneme /t/ has as its allophones: (1) an aspirated [tʰ] syllable initially before a stressed vowel; (2) a nasal-released [tⁿ] before [n] or syllabic [n̩]; (3) a lateral-released [tˡ] before [l] (and for some speakers before [l̩]); (4) a flap [ɾ] between a stressed vowel and a vowel or syllabic liquid; (5) a dentalized [t̪] before dental consonants; (6) an unreleased [t˺] before a stop consonant or syllable or word finally; and (7) [t] in all other contexts.

    Concerning the flap allophone [ɾ], note that a stressed vowel must precede a flap. Therefore in the following sets of words, there is flapping in Column 1 but not in

Column 2, where the stressed vowel follows rather than precedes the "t". In Column 2 the aspirated [tʰ] allophone occurs since it is found syllable initially preceding a stressed vowel:[1]

Column 1	Column 2
[ɾ]	[tʰ]
phótograph	*photógrapher*
fráternize	*fratérnal*
átom	*atómic*

4. The phoneme /n/ also has a number of predictable variants:

/n/ → [ɱ]/—C$_{labiodental}$ *infamous, information, confirm environment*
　　 [n̪]/—C$_{dental}$　　　 *month, ninth, in the*
　　 [ŋ]/—C$_{velar}$　　　 *incongruous, increase, ingrown*
　　 [n̩]/ C$_{obstruent}$—#　 *leaden, madden, kitten, listen*
　　 [n]/ elsewhere　　　 *noise, pound, tons, funny, pin*

This rule states that: (1) the phoneme /n/ is realized as the labiodental nasal [ɱ] before labiodental consonants; (2) as dentalized [n̪] before the dental consonants /θ/ and /ð/; (3) as velar [ŋ] before velar consonants; (4) as syllabic [n̩] word finally following obstruents; and (5) as [n] in all other environments.

> HINT: The symbol [ɱ] represents a labiodental nasal. Concentrate on the position of your upper lip and lower teeth when you articulate the above words. Also try to think up other examples of words in which labiodental nasals occur.

5. The rule for vowel length can be stated as follows:

/Vo/ → [Voː]/ —#　　　　 *fey*　　　 *grow*　　　 *eh*
　　 [Vo·]/ —C$_{vd}$　　　 *fade*　　　 *brogue*　　 *Abe*
　　 [Vo]/ elsewhere[2]　 *face, taste*　*broke, toast*　*ape, aced*

This rule states that: (1) vowels are longest at the end of an open syllable; (2) slightly shorter when followed by a voiced consonant; and (3) shortest in all other environments (i.e. when followed by a voiceless consonant or by a consonant cluster).

---

1. In casual speech a flap may also occur between two unstressed vowels as in *cávity, chárity, próperty, vísiting* (cf. *visitátion*).

2. "Elsewhere" could also be stated in terms of the two environments where short vowels occur: —C$_{vl}$ (before a voiceless consonant) and —CC(C)(C) (before a consonant cluster).

3.　Phonological processes

There are numerous general processes of phonological change involved in allophonic variation which apply to classes of sounds that share one or more features. Some examples of these classes, as we see below, are alveolar consonants, voiceless stops, front vowels, and lax vowels. These general processes may be stated in terms of **phonological rules** and are similar in formalism to phonemic rules.

Below are some examples of phonological rules. They are stated first in prose, then in abbreviated form using the formalism of rules, and finally illustrated with examples.

1.　All consonants are labialized before rounded vowels:

Phonological rule:　$/C/ \rightarrow [C^w]/ -Vo_{rounded}$

Note: "C" includes stops (_pool, boot, tool, dote, coke, good_), fricatives (_thorough, food, voice, sew, zoo, shone_), affricates (_chose, jury_), nasals (_note, moan_), and liquids (_lute, rude_).[3] $Vo_{rounded}$ includes /u, ʊ, oʊ, ɔ, ɔɪ, ʊ/.

2.　Liquids and nasals have a syllabic function following a consonant word finally:

Phonological rule:　$/l, r, m, n/ \rightarrow [ḷ, ɹ̩, m̩, n̩]/ C_{obstruent}-\#, C_{nasal}-\#$

Note: We saw this rule operating above in the case of the allophones of /n/. Examples of this rule are [m̩] in _chasm_, [n̩] in _button, omen_, [ḷ] in _paddle, camel, tunnel_ and [ɹ̩] in _latter, hammer, runner_.[4] We must specify obstruents and nasals in the phonetic environment of the rule above rather than consonants in general in order not to generate syllabic forms following liquids, as in _curl, turn, kiln, firm_, and _film_ (though some speakers say [fɪlm̩]).

3.　Alveolar sounds are dentalized before a dental:

Phonological rule:　$/s, t, d, n, l/ \rightarrow [s̪, t̪, d̪, n̪, l̪]/-[ð, θ]$

Examples of this rule are [s̪] in _sixth_, [t̪] in _eighth_, [n̪] in _tenth_, [l̪] in _wealth_, and [d̪] in _width_.

4.　Approximants and nasals, which along with vowels and glides comprise the natural class of **sonorants** (sounds involving a certain degree of resonance), are devoiced following a voiceless consonant:

Phonological rule:　$/j, w, r, l, m, n/ \rightarrow [j̊, w̥, ɹ̥, l̥, m̥, n̥]/ C_{vl}-$

3.　Note that /r/ is by nature labialized.

4.　/ŋ/ is syllabic only in connected speech as in _cookies and cake_.

Examples of this rule are [j] in _few_, _cute_, [w̥] in _twin_, _twelve_, [r̥] in _try_, _pry_, [l̥] in _play_, _claim_, [m̥] in _smart_, and [n̥] in _snore_.

5. Velars are fronted (to the palatal region) in the environment of a front vowel:

   Phonological rule: /k, g, ŋ/ → [k̟, g̟, ŋ̟]/ —Vo$_{front}$, Vo$_{front}$—

   Examples of this rule are [k̟] in _key_, _kit_, _kept_, _cape_, _cat_, _pick_, _peek_, [g̟] in _geese_, _give_, _get_, _gate_, _gad_, _fig_, _rag_, and [ŋ̟] in _ring_, _rang_.

6. Vowels are nasalized before a nasal:

   Phonological rule: Vo → Ṽ/ —[n, m, ŋ]

   Examples of this rule are [ʌ̃] in _sun_, [ĩ] in _sin_, [æ̃] in _Sam_, and [ũ] in _soon_.

7. /l/ becomes "dark" or velarized [ɫ] after a vowel or other approximant:

   Phonological rule: /l/ → [ɫ]/ Vo—, [r]—

Examples of this rule are _ball_, _wool_, _girl_, and _curl_.

> **HINT:** Both nasalization and velarization are indicated with a "tilde" diacritic, except that in the first case, the tilde is placed above the phonetic letter and in the second case it is superimposed over the letter.

8. Front vowels are **retracted** (articulated further back) before [ɫ]:

   Phonological rule: Vo → Vo̱/ —[ɫ]

Examples of this rule are [i̱] in _seal_, [ɪ̱] in _sill_, [ɛ̱] in _sell_, and [æ̱] in _Sally_.

> **HINT:** To feel the retraction, compare the vowels in the examples above to the words _seat, sit, same, set,_ and _Sam,_ where the same vowels are _not_ retracted.

9. Voiceless stops are aspirated word or syllable initially before a stressed vowel:

   Phonological rule: /p, t, k/ → [pʰ, tʰ, kʰ]/#—Vó

Examples of this rule are _peace_, _time_, _kind_, _apart_, _until_, and _across_.

10. Alveolar obstruents become alveolopalatal obstruents before /j/ in the following syllable:

   Phonological rule: /t, d, s, z/ → /tʃ, dʒ, ʃ, ʒ/—#/j/

This process, commonly referred to as **palatalization**, is quite common word internally. Examples of this rule include:

/t/ > /tʃ/	_posture, digestion, Christian_
/d/ > /dʒ/	_individual, residual, educate, soldier_
/s/ > /ʃ/	_passion, tissue, anxious, mission_
/z/ > /ʒ/	_occasion, leisure, vision, fusion_

Note: Palatalization may also occur between words in rapid speech: /tʃ/ *don't you, can't you*; /dʒ/ *would you, should you*; /ʃ/ *miss you, bless you*, /ʒ/ *as yet, as usual.* Sometimes palatalization occurs even when there is no syllable break, as in the pronunciation of *Tuesday* as /tʃuzdɪ/.[5]

11. Lax vowels /ɪ, ɛ, æ, ʌ, ʊ/ when unstressed are reduced to /ə/:

Phonological rule: $V_{lax} \rightarrow$ [ə]/ when unstressed

Examples of vowel reduction can be seen in the underlined vowels in the following pairs of related words:

átom	atómic	mélody	melódic	melódius	phótograph	photógrapher
/æ/ /ə/	/ə/ /a/	/ɛ/ /ə/	/ə/ /a/	/ə/ /oʊ/	/oʊ/ /ə/	/ə/ /a/
Cánada	Canádian	órigin	oríginal		cómedy	comédian
/æ/ /ə/	/ə/ /eɪ/	/ɔ/ /ə/	/ə/ /ɪ/		/a/ /ə/	/ə/ /i/

> HINT: Contrast the lax vowels given in the examples above with the unstressed vowels in the following words: *geography, psychology, calico, vacation.* Since the underlined vowels here are tense, they are not reduced.

12. The unstressed central vowel /ə/ may be deleted when followed by a liquid or nasal at the beginning of the next syllable:

Phonological rule: /ə/ → Ø/ —#[l, r, n, m]

Examples of this rule are the underlined vowels in *police, parade, suppose, gorilla, every, evening, generally, botany,* and *family.*

Note: The syllable following the deleted vowel generally carries some degree of stress. Unlike the preceding rules, which are obligatory, this rule is optional.

> HINT: It is also possible to state the above rules in terms of the distinctive features; see Exercise 3.2. Often the use of distinctive features makes clear how assimilation is working.

The motivation behind many, though not all, of the above phonological rules is ease of articulation, which allows the speaker to minimize his or her articulatory effort. This results in **assimilation**, where two neighboring (usually adjacent) sounds become more like one another in respect to one or more phonetic feature.

If we consider the rules above, we see that there is assimilation in voicing, as in rule (4) above, assimilation in place of articulation, as in rules (3, 5, 7, 8, and 10), and assimilation

---

5. Note that palatalization includes the rule of "yod-dropping" which deletes the /j/ of the following syllable; we have already encountered this rule in the monophthongization of /ɪu/ to /u/ (see Chapter 2).

in manner of articulation, as in rule (1 and 6). The deletion of a segment (12) or reduction of vowels (11) is probably also motivated by ease of articulation. Not all rules are clear cases of assimilation, however, as in rule (9), in which a segment (aspiration) is added, or rule (2).

Self-Testing Exercises: Do Exercises 3.1 and 3.2.

Below is a summary of the diacritics used in this chapter:

devoicing	[̥]	labialization	[ʷ]
aspiration	[ʰ]	fronting	[̟]
unreleased	[˺]	nasalization	[˜]
dentalization	[̪]	retracting	[̠]
syllabic	[̩]	velarization	[~]
nasal release	[ⁿ]	length	[ː], [·]
lateral release	[ˡ]		

4. Phonotactics

Phonotactics are the constraints on positions and sequences of sounds in a language. Phonotactics are always language-specific; that is, combinations of certain sounds may be permitted in another language which are not permitted in English, such as /pn/ beginning a word.

When discussing the possible positions of sounds in a language, we need to refer to word initial, medial, and final positions, as well as other positions, such as syllable initial, or other factors, perhaps the occurrence of a sound in monosyllabic or polysyllabic words. In the previous chapter, we considered in passing some of the constraints on the positions of sounds in English. Let's review those constraints:

– /ŋ/ is never word initial; it is word medial only after a stressed vowel as in *anger*;[6]
– /ʒ/ is very restricted word initially (occurring only in French words such as *gendarme*). It is common word medially (as in *pleasure*) and fairly rare word finally (again in French words such as *rouge*);[7]
– /h/, /j/, and /w/ are always syllable initial before a stressed vowel, as in *hit*, *yes*, and *wet*. /j/ and /w/ occur syllable finally only as part of a diphthong;
– /ð/ is word initial only in pronouns, adverbs, prepositions, demonstratives, and the definite article, never in nouns, verbs, and adjectives. Otherwise, it occurs freely word medially and word finally;

---

6. Historically, [ŋ] was an allophone of [n] occurring before [k] and [g]; as a cluster it could not occur word initially.

7. Unlike its voiced counterpart /ʒ/, /ʃ/ is quite common word initially, as in *sure*, *sugar*, *shirt*.

- the syllabic nasals [m̩] and [n̩] and the syllabic liquids [l̩] and [r̩] are never word initial; and
- unreleased stops only occur word finally, as in *tap* [p˺], or before another stop, as in *apt* [p˺t].

The above is not an exhaustive list of the positional constraints; however, it covers the most important ones.

When discussing the possible sequences or combinations of sounds in a language, we are primarily concerned with the combinations of consonants, called **consonant clusters**, which may begin or end a syllable. Unlike many other languages of the world, English rather freely allows for consonant clustering. In fact, it allows up to three consonants in an initial cluster and up to four consonants in a final cluster configuration:

initial consonant clusters	*glow*, *spruce*
final consonant clusters	*bird*, *ends*, *worlds*

In English we find that initial consonant clusters are much more restricted than final consonant clusters. In initial position, the phonotactics of English do not allow the following sequences:

stop + stop, such as /pt/[8]
stop + nasal, such as /pn/
nasal + stop, such as /np/
stop + fricative, such as /ts/
fricative + stop, such as /ft/[9]

The only permitted syllable initial sequences are the following:

voiced or voiceless stop + approximant	*play*, *price*, *bleed*, *break*, *clean*, *creek*
voiceless fricative + approximant	*fly*, *sled*, *three*, *shrew*
/s/ + voiceless stop	*spend*, *sting*, *scare*
/s/ + nasal[10]	*snail*, *sneak*, *small*, *smile*

There is only one possible combination of three consonants occurring initially:

/s/ + voiceless stop + approximant	*strong*, *split*, *scrape*, *spry*, *sclerosis*[11]

---

8.   The spelling "pt" can be found at the beginnings of some borrowed words such as *ptarmigan*, *Ptolemy*, *ptomaine*. However, this combination of letters is pronounced /t/ and is not articulated as a cluster.

9.   As we discuss shortly, the exception is where the fricative is /s/. Other exceptions include obviously foreign words such as *shtick*.

10.   Note that since /ŋ/ does not occur syllable initially in English, it cannot occur in an initial consonant cluster.

11.   The cluster /skl/ occurs quite infrequently.

The results of these restrictions are summarized in Table 3.1.

Table 3.1. Initial Consonant Clusters in English

stop +	/pl/	please	/bl/	black	*/tl/		*/dl/		/kl/	class	/gl/	glue
approximant	/pr/	prank	/br/	brown	/tr/	trace	/dr/	dry	/kr/	crew	/gr/	grow
	*/pw/		*/bw/		/tw/	twin	/dw/	dwell	/kw/	queen	/gw/	Gwyn
voiceless fricative + approximant	/fl/	flow	*/θl/		/sl/	slow	*/ʃl/		*/hl/			
	/fr/	free	/θr/	throw	*sr		/ʃr/	shrimp	*/hr/			
	*/fw/		/θw/	thwart	sw	swear	*/ʃw/		/hw/	where[12]		
/s/ + voiceless stop	/sp/	spy			/st/	stove			/sk/	sky		
/s/ + nasal	/sm/	smart			/sn/	snore			*/sŋ/			
/s/ + voiceless stop + approximant	/spl/	splash			*/stl/				/skl/	sclerosis		
	/spr/	spring			/str/	string			/skr/	scream		
	*/spw/				*/stw/				/skw/	square		

Note: An asterisk (*) before the consonant cluster sequence indicates that this cluster does not exist in English.

The gaps in Table 3.1 can be seen as either *systematic* or *accidental*:

–   Systematic gaps are those that can be explained by phonotactics, such as the restriction against two labials occurring together. This rules out the consonant clusters */pw/, */bw/, and */spw/, since all these consonants are classified as labials. Similarly, the restriction against two alveolars/dentals occurring together rules out the clusters */tl/, */dl/, */θl/, and */stl/.

–   Accidental gaps, on the other hand, include those sequences which do not violate any general principle but which simply do not occur in contemporary English, such as /stw/, /hl/, or /hr/.[13]

–   A general restriction against /ʃ/ + approximant rules out the clusters */ʃl/ and */ʃw/. However, the cluster /ʃr/ occurs since it represents the labialization of /s/ > /ʃ/ before /r/. Note that /sr/ in *Sri Lanka* is not a native pronunciation. Also in a few other foreign words, such as *schlepp*, *schlemiel*, containing /ʃl/, or *schwa*, containing /ʃw/, we find /ʃ/ plus approximant, but these are not English consonant clusters.

---

12.   Speakers of some dialects – those who do not distinguish between *whale* and *wail* or *which* and *witch* – have simplified /hw/ > /w/ and thus do not have this cluster in their speech.

13.   Interestingly, the latter two sequences did occur in an earlier period of English, as in Old English *hlūd* 'loud' and *hnutu* 'nut', but were subsequently lost.

–   As can be seen in Table 3.1, the only consonant preceding nasals in English is /s/. However, in a few non-native words we find /ʃm/ (as in *schmooze, schmuck*) or /ʃn/ (as in *schnapps, schnauzer*).

> **HINT:** See if you can think of other examples of the allowable consonant clusters in Table 3.1. Then, for the non-occurring clusters marked by the asterisk, see if you can determine whether they are systematic or accidental gaps. For example can you explain why [sŋ] does not occur? Is this a systematic or an accidental gap?

You might have noticed that the approximant /j/ has been omitted from the discussion. The reason for this is that it occurs following a consonant only in combination with the vowel /u/ and is therefore not considered to participate in consonant clusters. In fact, it may occur following a wide variety of consonants, voiced or voiceless. The following permissible sequences of consonant + /j/ are not considered consonant clusters:

pj	*pew*			tj	*tune*	kj	*cute*
bj	*beauty*			dj	*duty*	gj[14]	*gules*
mj	*music*			nj	*news*	*nj
fj	*few*	θj[15]	*thew*	sj	*sue*	*ʃj
vj	*view*	*ðj		*zj		*ʒj

There are some dialectal restrictions regarding the above consonant + /j/ sequences. For example, in some dialects /j/ is lost following alveolars. Thus in many if not most dialects of North American English the word *news* is pronounced /nuz/ rather than /njuz/. The same is true for the pronunciations of *tune, duty,* and *sue* in North American English, causing these words to be pronounced differently than in British English. Also, only certain dialects have /j/ following /tʃ/ and /dʒ/ and for this reason these consonant combinations have not been included in the list above. By the way, do you know the meaning of *gules* or *thew*?

Final consonant clusters are freer and more complex than initial clusters, containing up to four consonants. Space does not permit an exhaustive listing, but some possible combinations of two final consonants are the following:

liquid + consonant	*harp, harm, horse, hurl, help, helm, else*[16]
nasal + obstruent	*bend, bent, pins, tenth, lamp, rink*
obstruent + obstruent, e.g.	
fricative + stop	*lift, paved, disk, roast, bathed*
stop + fricative	*mats, lapse, grabs, cheeks*
fricative + fricative	*leaves, reefs, sheaths,*
stop + stop	*apt, ached, bobbed*

---

14.   The sequence /gj/ is extremley rare.

15.   The sequence /θj/ is also extremely rare.

16.   The cluster /lr/ does not occur since /r/ must precede /l/.

Not all possible combinations of these sounds occur, however. For example, /m/ precedes /p, f/ only and /ŋ/ precedes /k, g/ only, while in all other instances the nasal preceding the obstruent is /n/. Also, certain of these clusters are indicative of a particular grammatical context. Thus, the cluster of fricative + fricative or voiced consonant + /z/ always indicates a noun plural or possessive or third person singular of the verb; similarly, the voiced consonant + /d/ always indicates the past tense or past participle of a verb.

Sequences of three consonants include:

three obstruents (stop + fricative + stop)	/dst/ in *mid̲s̲t̲*; /kst/ in *bo̲x̲e̲d̲*
nasal + two obstruents, e.g.	
nasal + fricative + stop	/nst/ in *rin̲s̲e̲d̲*; /mft/ in *triu̲m̲p̲h̲e̲d̲*
nasal + stop + fricative	/mps/ in *gli̲m̲p̲s̲e̲*; /nts/ in *de̲n̲t̲s̲*
nasal + stop + stop	/mpt/ in *pro̲m̲p̲t̲*; /mbd/ in *thu̲m̲b̲e̲d̲*
liquid + two obstruents, e.g.	
liquid + stop + fricative	/rps/ in *co̲r̲p̲s̲e̲*; /lps/ in *gu̲l̲p̲s̲*
liquid + stop + stop	/lpt/ in *he̲l̲p̲e̲d̲*; /rpt/ in *wa̲r̲p̲e̲d̲*
liquid + fricative + fricative	/lvz/ in *she̲l̲v̲e̲s̲*; /rfs/ in *dwa̲r̲f̲s̲*
liquid + fricative + stop	/rst/ in *fi̲r̲s̲t̲*; /rvd/ in *sta̲r̲v̲e̲d̲*
liquid + nasal + fricative	/lnz/ in *ki̲l̲n̲s̲*; /rmz/ in *te̲r̲m̲s̲*

Sequences of four consonants occur, although more rarely:

/mpst/	*gli̲m̲p̲s̲e̲d̲*	/ndθs/	*thousa̲n̲d̲t̲h̲s̲*
/ksθs/	*si̲x̲t̲h̲s̲*	/ksts/	*te̲x̲t̲s̲*
/rlds/	*wo̲r̲l̲d̲s̲*	/mpts/	*te̲m̲p̲t̲s̲*
/lfθs/	*twe̲l̲f̲t̲h̲s̲*	/ŋkst/	*ji̲n̲x̲e̲d̲*

As you can see, in these cases, the fourth consonant is always an inflectional ending added to a word ending in three consonants. Words ending in four consonants without an inflectional ending are rare, if not impossible. In cases where the medial consonant in a cluster is a voiceless stop or /θ/, native speakers tend to simplify the cluster by omitting this consonant, saying [glimst] instead of /glimpst/, [twɛlfs] instead of /twɛlfθs/, etc. Importantly, the inflectional ending cannot be omitted in the process of consonant cluster simplification because of the grammatical information it carries.

Native speakers of a language intuitively know the permissible and nonpermissible sequences (it is part of their linguistic competence); newly-created words will always follow the phonotactic principles of the language: thus, while *pnark* could never be created in English, *plark* could be. Borrowed words which have not been fully assimilated into English may have nonEnglish sequences, such as /kn/ in *Knorr*. It is usual, however, to make the borrowed word conform to the phonotactics of English by eliminating nonEnglish clusters, such as /ps/ in *psychology*, which becomes /s/, and /ts/ in *Zeppelin*, which becomes /z/. Remember also that while certain sequences of sounds are not possible in English, they are humanly possible and may be found in other languages, for example, initial /ts/, /kn/, /gn/, /ps/, and /pf/ in German.

5. Suprasegmental features

Suprasegmental features are those articulatory features which are superimposed over more than one segment (i.e. vowel or consonant); they include stress and intonation.

5.1   Stress

Every word spoken in isolation has at least one stressed syllable. In articulatory terms, **stress** involves a rise in air pressure; an increase in the activity of the respiratory muscles forces more air out of the lungs during the articulation of a particular syllable. There may also be an increase in the activity of the larynx, resulting in higher pitch. In acoustic terms, the stressed syllable is perceived as longer, louder, and of higher pitch. The term *stress* is sometimes used interchangeably with *accent*, but "accent" should not be confused here with the other use of the term to refer to dialect features (as in "a British accent").

Certain languages in the world have an accentual system based on pitch differences, not stress differences. That is, syllables carry varying levels of pitch, and pitch differences alone can distinguish words. These "tonal" languages include Chinese, Thai, West African languages, and Amerindian languages. English, on the other hand, belongs to the group of languages which have stress accent.

Stress is a meaningful feature of speech in respect to both words and phrases in English. It has functions in the province of morphology, syntax, and discourse.

Traditionally, different degrees, or levels, of stress are differentiated at the word level:

> primary (level 1)   marked by an acute accent (´)
> secondary (level 2)   marked by a grave accent (`)
> unstressed (level 3)   unmarked or marked by a breve (˘)

For example, if you say *computation* in isolation or at the end of a sentence, the *ta* syllable will carry the strong stress, but the *com* syllable will also carry a seemingly weaker stress. What is actually happening here is superimposition of an intonational pattern (discussed in the next section) called a *tonic accent* onto the last stressed syllable. So we say that *ta* carries **primary stress** and *com* carries **secondary stress**, thus *còmputátion*. Secondary stress is sometimes difficult to hear, but generally it will be separated by at least one syllable – either before or after – from the syllable carrying primary stress, as follows:

> *intérrogàte*   *àccidéntal*   *ínventòry*
> *còncentrátion*   *épilèpsy*   *hallùcinátion*

That is, secondary stress will occur in words where the stressed syllable is followed by two or more syllables or where the stressed syllable is preceded by two or more syllables.

> **HINT:** To find the stressed syllable in English, say a polysyllabic word and tap your finger at the same time. You will naturally tap on the stressed syllable. The reason for this is that it is easier to produce one increase in muscular activity in conjunction with another, so you use your respiratory muscles and your hand muscles simultaneously. If you try to tap on an unstressed syllable, you will get a distortion in the pronunciation of the word. Try saying the following words while tapping your finger (the stressed syllable is marked):
> abóminable pátriarchy exécutive confidéntial interpretátion

In transcription, the IPA system of marking stress is the use of a superscript tick before the primary stressed syllable and a subscript tick before the secondary stressed syllable, e.g. *eligibility* /ˌɛlɪdʒəˈbɪləti/.[17] Alternatively, only primary stress is indicated. Unstressed syllables are not marked.

The rule for stress in Germanic words is very simple: words are always stressed on the first syllable (as in *ápple, fáther, húnger*), except prefixed verbs, which are stressed on the root syllable (as in *forgét, belíeve, withdráw*). However, English has borrowed many words from the Romance languages. These words have a different stress principle: stress falls on the penultimate syllable, as in *admónish*, unless there are two consonants or a tense vowel at the end, as in *adápt, exíst*. The result is that the stress system of Modern English is now very complex, and accent is not entirely predictable.

Some useful generalizations about stress at the word level include the following:

1. Stress can distinguish different parts of speech, as in the corresponding sets of nouns (with initial stress) and verbs (with final stress) below:[18]

noun	verb
próduce	*prodúce*
áddress	*addréss*
ímport	*impórt*
ínsult	*insúlt*
súrvey	*survéy*
íncline	*inclíne*
éxport	*expórt*

    There are also derivationally-related pairs that show the same stress pattern: *concéive* (V) and *cóncept* (N), *procéed* (V) and *prócess* (N), or *preténd* (V) and *prétense* (N). But note that there are many exceptions: *respéct* and *rewárd* are both a noun and a verb;

---

17. Alternatively, only primary stress is indicated.

18. According to Minkova and Stockwell (2009), this is a finite class of words consisting of approximately 130 word pairs.

cómment is both a noun and a verb; and *díffer* and *defér* are different verbs; compare also *belíeve* (V) and *belíef* (N).

2. Stress can distinguish a word from a phrase. A word, as we shall see in the next chapter, has only <u>one</u> primary stress (as in the case of *wálkout*, given below), though it may have both primary and secondary stress (as in the case of *hótdòg*). A phrase, on the other hand, has more than one stress (as in the case of *to wálk óut*). We can see this difference in stress patterns in the following word-phrase pairs:

a. where a noun or a verb combines with an adverbial particle such as *in* or *out*:

Word	Phrase
wálkout	*to wálk óut*
púshover	*to púsh óver*
rípoff	*to ríp óff*
cáve-in	*to cáve ín*

b. where an adjective combines with a noun to form either a single noun or a noun phrase:

Word	Phrase
hótdòg	*hót dóg*
bláckbòard	*bláck bóard*
híghchàir	*hígh cháir*

c. where two nouns combine to form either a single verb or a noun phrase:

Word	Phrase
to stónewall	*stóne wáll*
to bláckball	*bláck báll*
to máinstream	*máin stréam*

3. Stress patterns in derivationally related words distinguish parts of speech:

Noun (concrete)	Noun (abstract)	Adjective
díplomat	*diplómacy*	*diplomátic*
phótograph	*photógraphy*	*photográphic*
mónotone	*monótony*	*monotónic*
télegraph	*telégraphy*	*telegráphic*

Noun	Adjective
pícture	*picturésque*
jóurnal	*journalése*

That is, the affix affects the placement of stress.

4. There may be differences in the placement of stress in individual words. For example, the following words typically receive different stress placement in British and

North American English, as indicated in the designation of primary stress in the list below. However, there is a great deal of regional variation. Decide which syllable is stressed for you:

North American English	British English
ánchovy	anchóvy
préparatory	prepáratory
garáge	gárage
laméntable	lámentable
ápplicable	applícable
mústache	mustáche
mágazine	magazíne
advertísement	advértisement

There is a fairly general rule in British English that secondary stress is omitted on *-ery/-ory/-ary*. Compare the North American and British pronunciations of *batt<u>ery</u>* /bǽtəri/ vs. /bǽtri/, respectively. As a consequence, the penultimate syllable is lost in the British pronunciation of words ending in /-(ə)ri/, as in *secretⱥry, laboratⱥry, obligatⱥry, militⱥry,* and *dictionⱥry.*

5. In general, stressed vowels within a word are generally full, while unstressed vowels may or may not be reduced to /ə/ or another unstressed vowel:

    expl<u>ái</u>n /eɪ/   expl<u>a</u>nátion /ə/
    emph<u>á</u>tic /æ/   émph<u>a</u>sis /ə/

    > **HINT:** Remember that the reduction of vowel sounds is not due to "sloppiness" or "laziness", but is completely natural. You may have observed that when nonnative speakers do not reduce vowels as we would expect, their speech indeed sounds "foreign" and nonEnglish.

6. The vowel in the second half of a compound noun is reduced:

/mæn/ > /-mən/	*foreman, policeman, draftsman*
/lænd/ > /-lənd/	*Finland, England, highland*
/fʊl/ > /-fəl/	*helpful, thoughtful, rightful*
/badi/ > /-bədi/	*somebody, anybody, nobody*

    However, conscious factors, such as the newness of a word, may prevent an expected reduction, as in *superman* or *Disneyland*, which usually contain full vowels and carry secondary stress.[19]

---

19.   Note though that some words may be variably stressed (e.g. such as *madman*) while others may be subject to dialectal variation (e.g. Canadians invariably pronounce *Newfoundland* with a full vowel in *land*).

7. Reductions of other forms may likewise be predictable, as in the cases of *a, the, to,* which are reduced when they occur before a word beginning with a consonant:

a	/ə/	*a cup*	vs.	/æn/	*an apple*
the	/ðə/	*the man*	vs.	/ði/	*the apple*
to	/tə/	*to jail*	vs.	/tu/	*to university*

8. Sometimes we have full and reduced versions (**strong** and **weak forms**) of the same words. When spoken in isolation or used contrastively, function words are pronounced with full vowels, but when they occur in a sentence, they are generally unstressed (see Table 3.2):

Table 3.2. Strong and Weak Forms

Word	Strong	Weak	Example of Weak Form
and	/ænd/	/ənd, ən/, [n̩]	*I've got to make dinner and clean up.*
too, to	/tu/	/tə/	*She went to New York.*
can	/kæn/	/kən/	*I can help you.*
at	/æt/	/ət/	*Betsy's staying at home today.*
as	/æz/	/əz/	*He's as happy as possible.*
could	/kʊd/	/kəd/	*I could be there in ten minutes.*
than	/ðæn/	/ðən/	*She is richer than I am.*
you	/ju/	/jə/	*Can you give me a hand?*
had	/hæd/	/(h)əd/	*I had better leave now.*
would	/wʊd/	/(w)əd/	*Jack would know the answer.*
are	/ar/	/ər/, [r̩]	*We are going to Florida next week.*
them	/ðɛm/	/(ð)əm/	*Tell them to stop making so much noise.*

Self-Testing Exercise: Do Exercise 3.3.

At the phrasal level, stress also plays a role. In English, when we utter entire phrases, we do not, in fact, stress every word. Instead, we stress only certain words, and unstress others. Generally, we place stress on the major parts of speech, or content words (the nouns, verbs, adjectives, and adverbs); we do not place stress on the minor parts of speech, or function words (the prepositions, conjunctions, pronouns, articles, and so on). Consider the following sentence:

In autumn, the dry, yellow leaves fall from the trees.

Based on the above, we would expect the content words *autumn, dry, yellow, leaves, fall,* and *trees* to carry stress, and the function words *in, the,* and *from* not to.

Moreover, in English these stresses fall as much as possible at regular intervals, making English a "stress-timed" language. The amount of time necessary for an utterance depends upon the number of stressed syllables, with unstressed syllables occupying much less time than stressed ones.

> **HINT:** Say the following sentences and note where the stresses fall. Observe that certain content words which one might expect to carry stress do not do so:
>
> > A fúnny thing háppened on the wáy to the fórum.
> > Fíve pretty gírls kissed fífteen handsome bóys.
> > Thís is the hóuse that Jáck búilt.
>
> You can also try tapping out the rhythm. As you do so, note the regularity of the intervals between stresses. Finally, try stressing all the words equally to see how unnatural these sentences sound when the function words are stressed.

1. There are strong and weak forms of phrases:

Strong > Weak Form	Example
I am > I'm	[aɪæm > aɪəm > aɪm]
you are > you're	[juar > juwər > jɾ̩]
she is > she's	[ʃiɪz > ʃiːz > ʃiz]
it is > it's	[ɪtɪz > ɪɾiz > ɪts]

2. Variations in the placement of stress within an individual polysyllabic word may result from the position of the word in a sentence. Note the difference in stress for the following adjectives if they occur before the noun (in attributive position) or if they occur following the verb (in a predicative position), in the slot indicated:

Attributive Position	Predicative Position
Alex is an _____ person.	*Alex is very _____.*
ártificial	artifícial
ábsent-minded	absent-mínded
arístocratic	aristocrátic

    Because the placement of stress in a sentence is a matter of spacing out the stresses as evenly as possible and because it is usual to place stress near to the end of the sentence in English, on the last major part of speech, *pérson* carries stress; as a consequence, stress on the preceding adjective is placed as far from it as possible, on the first or second syllable. In contrast, since *véry* carries emphatic stress, the stress on the following adjective is placed as late as possible, on the penultimate syllable.

3. Stress is used for contrastive emphasis within phrase units. This is often indicated in writing by italics or underlining:

    > *I want the <u>réd</u> one, not the <u>blúe</u> one.*
    > *He <u>cán</u>, but he <u>wón't</u> finish his work.*

4.   Stress may be used in a discourse to signal new as opposed to old (given) information. For example, in a discussion of what food is wanted by the addressee for dinner, the speaker might use any of the questions below:

    a.   *Do yóu want pizza for dinner?*
    b.   *Do you want pízza for dinner?*
    c.   *Do you want pizza for dínner?*

In sentence (a), pizza is considered given information. By placing the stress on *you*, the speaker is questioning specifically whether it is the addressee who wants pizza (as opposed to another person in the group). In sentence (b), the speaker is questioning the addressee's wants for dinner ("pizza" as opposed to "spaghetti"). Finally, in sentence (c), the speaker is questioning which meal pizza should be served at ("dinner" rather than "lunch"). The third sentence – in which the last noun in the clause receives the greatest prominence – is also the most neutral version of this question, where no particular item is being unduly stressed (as we shall see in the next section). We will consider this aspect of stress in more detail in Chapter 11.

5.2   Intonation

Like stress, intonation is a meaningful suprasegmental feature of speech. Intonation refers to patterns of pitch variation in a sentence. It does not refer to the discrete pitches of different vowels, to pitch accent, or to physiologically determined variations in pitch due to the size and shape of a person's vocal apparatus (e.g. the difference in pitch between men's and women's voices). The pitch patterns of intonation are similar to tunes distributed over sentences in an organized and systematic way. They affect the meaning of the sentence as a whole by indicating different sentence types, such as statements or questions.

Intonation is represented in a gross fashion in writing by punctuation marks: ? , . ! ; –. Intonation patterns may also indicate the attitude or relation of the speaker to the hearer as well as various contextual features. Therefore, though intonation is a phonological feature, its meaning lies within the province of syntax and pragmatics. Intonation patterns differ quite substantially among different dialects of English, for example between British and American or American and Canadian English. Note that you cannot usually determine the national dialect of a singer because the tunes of the music supersede the distinctive intonational patterns of English sentences.

In describing intonation, we generally identify four different levels of pitch, which we can refer to as "extra high", "high", "middle", and "low". Within an utterance, the pitch tends to alternate between low and high. The extra high level is reserved for expressing a strong emotion such as surprise, enthusiasm, or disbelief; it is also the pitch level that signals contrastive or emphatic stress.

It has been the practice to recognize two basic intonation contours, **falling intonation** (where the end of the utterance is marked by low pitch) and **rising intonation** (where the end is marked by high pitch). In general, a fall signals certainty or finality while a rise signals uncertainty. Within these two basic contours, we can identify several different pitch patterns, which convey different meanings:

Pitch Pattern	Meaning
long falling	expresses finality, conclusion, affirmation, agreement
short falling	expresses an attenuated or qualified conclusion
long rising	expresses questioning and a lack of finality
short rising	expresses some degree of reservation or functions as a signal of attentiveness (continuation marker)
rising-falling	expresses finality with added emotion (e.g. emphasis. enthusiasm, certainty, annoyance)
falling-rising	expresses querulousness, skepticism, reservation

In essence, the difference between the "long" and "short" falling and rising patterns has to do with the time it takes for the speaker to change pitch within the utterance. In "long" patterns, the change in pitch (whether up or down) is more gradual; in "short" patterns it tends to be rather abrupt (typically over one or two words).

The listener uses the cues provided by pitch change to interpret the speaker's intent. We can see the meaning of these pitch patterns even in the different ways that the one-word utterance "Yes" can be produced:

Pitch Pattern	Utterance	Meaning
long falling	"Yes."	The answer is "'yes.'"
short falling	"Yes."	The answer is "yes", but I am impatient with your question or find it unimportant.
long rising	"Yes."	Did you say "yes"?
short rising	"Yes."	Perhaps. *or* Please go on – I'm listening.
rising-falling	"Yes."	I'm certain.
falling-rising	"Yes."	I'm doubtful.

Of course, we normally speak in sequences longer than an individual word. In analyzing intonation patterns, we need to divide longer sequences of discourse into **tone groups**. Tone groups are not necessarily syntactic, but correspond to units of information. A single tone pattern continues over a particular tone group. There may be more than one tone group per sentence. The number of tone groups may vary depending on style: in more formal, deliberate, or pompous style, there are a greater number of tone groups than in more colloquial styles. Consider the following sentence:

She sat by the window in the late afternoon, // reading a letter.

Here there are two tone groups, corresponding to syntactic units, both with falling intonation. A more formal style might consist of three tone groups:

> *She sat by the window // in the late afternoon, // reading a letter.*

Each tone group contains a **tonic syllable**, which carries the major shift in intonation. Usually, the tonic syllable is the last stressed syllable in the tone group. It expresses the information which the speaker considers new (unknown) and most important, as in the following sentences where the tonic syllable is underlined:

> *Did you get the job?*   vs.   *Did you lose your job?*
> *I visited my mother.*   vs.   *I visited your mother.*

Let's now examine pitch patterns in different sentence types.[20] In each example the tonic syllable is underlined.

1. A statement has a long falling intonation pattern.

    a. *A whale is a mammal.* (Here the topic of the conversation is whales. What the speaker is adding to the conversation is that these animals are mammals – as opposed to fish – so "mammal" is new information.)
    b. *A whale is a mammal.* (Here "mammal" is the topic, and "whale" is new information.)

2. A command also has long falling intonation when compliance is expected:

    a. *Close the window!*
    b. *Take your seats!*

3. A *yes/no* question has a long rising intonation pattern, since it expects an answer.

    a. *Do you want some coffee?*
    b. *Do you want cream in your coffee?*
    c. *Do you want coffee or tea?*
    d. *Do you want coffee, // or tea?* (This actually represents two *yes/no* questions, the second being a kind of afterthought to the first; the first has long rising intonation and the second has short rising intonation)[21]

---

20.   It is important to note that there is no complete correspondence between intonation patterns and grammatical structures. Thus, any generalizations about statements having falling intonation or questions having rising intonation are tempered by the discourse contexts in which these grammatical patterns are found and also by the speaker's intent.

21.   This pattern is not to be confused with the pattern used for alternative questions (see 7 below).

e.   *You are giving up coffee?* (Note that this is not syntactically a question, but the intonation shows that it is functioning as one.)

4.   An echo question, which asks for the repetition of what has been said before, also has rising or falling-rising intonation.

a.   *He said what?*
b.   *You did what?*

5.   A *wh*-question has a long falling intonation pattern (like a statement) since this type of sentence does not ask for but rather presupposes an answer.

a.   *Where did you put the paper?* (This is the neutral emphasis.)
b.   *Where did you put the paper?* (This focuses on "you" as new information.)

6.   A tag question has two tone groups; the first half is syntactically a statement, while the second half is syntactically a question.[22]

a.   *You will help, // won't you?* (This follows the expected pattern where the first tone group has falling intonation because it is a statement and the second tone group has short rising intonation because it is a *yes/no* question.)
b.   *He likes chocolate, // doesn't he?* (This is not a real question, but merely asks for confirmation, so unlike (a), the second tone group has short falling intonation.)

7.   An alternative question consists of two or more tone groups, the first one or more having question intonation and the final having statement intonation:

a.   *Did you buy a paper, // or not?* (The first pattern is long rising, and the second short falling.)
b.   *Did you eat a doughnut, // or a muffin?*
c.   *Do you want an apple, // an orange, // or a peach?*

8.   A list has a number of tone groups with short rising intonation patterns indicating that the discourse continues:

a.   *I bought some apples, // oranges, // and peaches.* (The last tone group is falling because this is a statement.)[23]
b.   *I ordered an endive salad, // pasta with sun dried tomatoes, // and tiramisu.*

---

22.   We look at the construction of questions in Chapters 8 and 9.

23.   Long falling intonation on the first two tone groups yields a very slow, deliberate, solemn style, while long rising intonation of these tone groups yields a highly dramatized style, often used when addressing children.

9. Complex sentences have a similar pattern – short rising followed by the appropriate end intonation – whether the subordinate clause precedes or follows the main clause:

    a.   *When she arrived <u>home</u> // she opened the <u>mail</u>.*
    b.   *She turned off the <u>radio</u> // when he <u>called</u>.*

10. A question expressing great doubt or surprise has a falling-rising intonation pattern.

    a.   *Are you <u>sure</u>?* (The vowel of the tonic syllable may be elongated.)
    b.   *It's <u>raining</u>?*

11. A statement expressing great certainty has a rising-falling intonation pattern.

    a.   (I've told you several times) *I don't <u>know</u>.*
    b.   (You have to wear your jacket) *It's <u>raining</u>.*

12. The intonation patterns of parenthetical expressions such as direct address (e.g. *Mr. Smith, James*), adverbials (e.g. *unfortunately, realistically*), expressions of opinion (e.g. *I believe, you know*), and expletives (e.g. *damn*) differ depending on where the parenthetical expressions appears within the utterance.

    a.   *Your <u>taxi</u>, // Ms. <u>Jones</u>, // is waiting <u>downstairs</u>.* Sentence initial and sentence medial expressions tend to have short rising intonation signaling that the speaker has not completed the utterance.
    b.   *We're in for some hard <u>times</u>, // I <u>think</u>.* Sentence final parenthetical expressions generally have short falling intonation. In some cases, there may also be short rising intonation on the parenthetical to lighten up the utterance.[24]

Self-Testing Exercise: Do Exercise 3.4.

6.   Syllable structure

We will end this chapter by examining the level intermediate between sounds (meaningless segments) and affixes/words (meaningful segments), namely the **syllable (Sy)**. The syllable represents a level of structure intuitively recognized by speakers of the language; it figures importantly in the rhythm and prosody of the language. As noted earlier, a syllable consists obligatorily of a vowel (or syllabic consonant); this is the acoustic peak, or **nucleus (Nu)**,

---

24.   Note that if the final parenthetical element is short, the speaker may not separate the utterance into two tone groups. In this case the parenthetical element is subsumed into the first tone group and the intonation contour of the first tone group extends over the entire utterance.

of the syllable and potentially carries stress. As discussed above, a syllable may optionally begin with one to three consonants – the **onset (On)** of the syllable – and may close with one to four consonants – the **coda (Co)** of the syllable:

(C) (C) (C) Vo (C) (C) (C) (C)

The nucleus and coda together form the rhyme (Rh). Syllable structure can be represented in the form of trees, as in the diagrams below for *spring* and *quartz* (using conventional orthography rather than transcription):

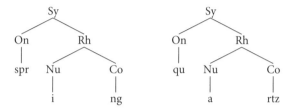

With polysyllabic words, the question of syllable division arises. If there is no medial consonant, the syllable division falls between the vowels, as in *po.et*, *ne.on*, or *gi.ant*:

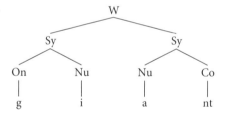

(W = word. For simplicity, we will ignore the intermediate level of the rhyme.)[25] If there is one medial consonant, and stress follows the consonant, the medial consonant forms the onset of the second syllable, as in *ba.ton*, *re.gard*, or *a.bout*:

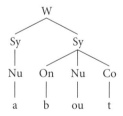

---

25. While is it conventional to use the symbol σ for "syllable" and Σ for "word", for the purposes of this introductory text, we are using the more intuitively more obvious "Sy" and "W."

However, if stress falls on the initial syllable, speakers syllabify sometimes with the consonant as coda of the first syllable, sometimes as onset of the second, as in *read.y/rea. dy, op.en/o.pen,* or *rig.id/ri.gid.* The consonant is said to be **ambisyllabic** (*ambi-* Greek for 'both'), belonging to both syllables:

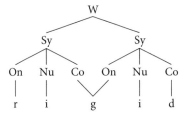

Ambisyllabicity may occur as well when the syllable preceding and following the consonant are both unstressed, as in *man.i.fest/man.if.est,* or *or.i.gin/or.ig.in.* Of course, the first consonant is also ambisyllabic (hence also *ma.ni.fest* and *ma.nif.est* or *o.ri.gin* and *o.rig.in*):

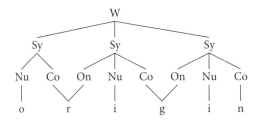

When a consonant cluster occurs word medially and stress falls on the vowel following, the consonants form the onset of the second syllable (compare *about* above), as in *su.blime* or *re.strain* (not *rest.rain, res.train* or *sub.lime;*[26] **subl.ime* would not be possible since **bl* is not a possible final cluster):

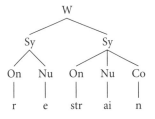

---

26.   Syllabification practices used in dictionaries are conventional and not entirely phonologically based. Often, morphological boundaries are also used in establishing syllables. This would be the case for *sublime,* where the prefix *sub-* would be recognized for the purposes of syllabification.

When stress falls on the vowel preceding the consonant cluster, the cluster forms the onset of the second syllable with the initial consonant being ambisyllabic (compare *rigid* above), as in *mi.stress/mis.tress* or *na.sty/nas.ty* (but not *nast.y* or *mist.ress*):

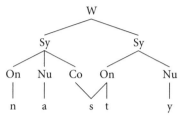

However, if the consonant cluster is not a possible initial cluster in English, the consonants are split between the two syllables, as in *at.las* (not **a.tlas*) or *on.set* (not **o.nset*), with the longest possible sequence (according to phonotactic constraints) forming the onset of the second syllable, as in *em.blem* (not *emb.lem* or **e.mblem*).

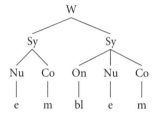

Self-Testing Exercise: Do Exercise 3.5.

A phenomenon similar to ambisyllabicity arises not at syllable boundaries, but at word boundaries, in cases of apparent ambiguity, as in these well-known examples:

my train/might rain	*this kid/the skid*
mice fear/my sphere	*syntax/sin tax*
that scum/that's come	*not at all man/not a tall man*
night rate/nitrate	*an aim/a name*
Grade A/gray day	*we dressed/we'd rest*
lighthouse keeper/light housekeeper	*that's tough/that stuff*

For example, the sequence of sounds /aɪskrim/ could be divided as follows:

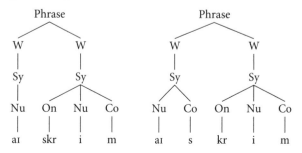

That is, /s/ could form the coda of the first word or the onset of the second word, just as in ambisyllabicity, a consonant can form the coda of the first syllable or the onset of the second. Nonetheless, various phonetic features seem to permit disambiguation of these sequences.[27] For example, the /k/ in *ice cream* would be aspirated, whereas that in *I scream* would not be. Vowel length would distinguish *my train* (with [aɪː]) from *might rain* (with /aɪ/); nasalization and vowel quality would distinguish *an aim* (with [æ̃n]) from *a name* (with /ə/); and stress would distinguish *líghthòuse kéeper* from *líght hóusekèeper*.

Chapter summary

Now that you have completed this chapter, you should be able to:

1. write rules for phonemes of English, given appropriate data;
2. identify a number of phonological processes at work in English;
3. state the restrictions on positions of sounds and combinations of sounds in English;
4. determine the placement of primary and secondary stress in English words;
5. describe the different functions of stress in English;
6. identify the tonic syllable and pitch pattern within a tone group; and
7. determine the syllable structure of English words.

Recommended additional reading

More detailed discussions of English phonology can be found in Giegerich (1992, Chapters 6–10), McMahon (2002, Chapters 2, 4, 5, 7, and 9), Kreidler (2004, Chapters 5–7, 9–10, 13–14), Ladefoged (2006, Chapter 3, pp. 71–76 and Chapter 4, pp. 98–100), and Clark, Yallop, and Fletcher (2007).

Textbook discussions of the topics covered by this chapter include Jeffries (2006, Chapter 2), Fromkin, Rodman, and Hyams (2007, Chapter 7), Finegan (2008, Chapter 4), and Curzan and Adams (2009, Chapter 3). Murray (1995, Chapter 2) is an elementary discussion, complete with exercises and answers.

A generative approach to English phonology is Carr (1999), see also Clark, Yallop, and Fletcher (2007, Chapter 6). General linguistics treatments of phonology include Katamba (1989) and Odden (2005).

For a more detailed discussion of English intonation, see Wells (2005), and, for a more individualistic account, Bolinger (1986).

---

27. Such phenomena used to be explained by postulating a suprasegmental feature called "juncture", a kind of pause which demarcated the boundary between words and which differed from the pauses between sounds within words ("open" versus "close" juncture).

Chapter 4

The internal structure of words and processes of word formation

1. Defining the word
2. Morphemes
3. Processes of word formation
4. Idioms

Chapter preview

This chapter first introduces the criteria used for distinguishing a word from a phrase. It then considers the internal structure of words, making use of the abstract notion of a morpheme (meaningful unit) and the concrete notion of a morph. The different types of morphemes and morphs are described. It is shown that there is not always a correspondence between the morphemes and morphs of a word and that morphemes may be realized in different ways as morphs. The chapter then introduces allomorphs (predictable variants) of morphemes, and the writing of morphemic rules is explained. Both stem and root allomorphy is treated. The next section of the chapter explores the different processes of word formation in English, focusing on the complexities of derivation and compounding; minor processes of word formation – reduplication, conversion, blending, shortening, and root creations – are treated in less detail. The chapter ends with a brief discussion of idioms.

Commentary

1. Defining the word

We move now from an examination of the smallest segments of language (sounds) to the larger units: words. However, since speech is a phonetic continuum, without pauses between words (we generally pause between larger syntactic units such as phrases or clauses), we need some means of determining the boundaries of words. We all have an intuitive feel for the words of the language and we think immediately of the written word, but even nonliterate speakers can divide the speech chain into words. Thus, there must be some formal criteria for wordhood which all speakers use. These might be of various kinds:

1. Orthographic: a word is what occurs between spaces in writing.
2. Semantic: a word has semantic coherence; it expresses a unified semantic concept.
3. Phonological:
    a. potential pause: a word occurs between potential pauses in speaking. Though in normal speech, we generally do not pause, we may potentially pause between words, but not in the middle of words.
    b. stress: a word spoken in isolation has one and only one primary stress.
4. Morphological: a word has an internal cohesion and is indivisible by other units; a word may be modified only externally by the addition of suffixes and prefixes.
5. Grammatical: words fall into particular classes.
6. Syntactic: a word has external distribution or mobility; it is moved as a unit, not in parts.

We can see the usefulness of these criteria if we look at some problematical examples of word delimitation:

supermarket	*jack-of-all-trades*
travel agency	*noteworthy*
runner-up	*try out*
forget-me-not	*pins and needles*

By the criterion of orthography, *supermarket* and *noteworthy* would be considered a single word, as would hyphenated forms such as *jack-of-all-trades, forget-me-not,* or *runner-up,* while phrases such as *travel agency, take out,* or *pins and needles* must be considered as multiple words, or phrases. Yet by the second criterion, semantic unity, the words and the phrases all appear to be equally unified conceptually. The discrepancy is especially apparent if you compare *supermarket* with related concepts such as *toy store* or *grocery store.* In fact, the conventions of spacing between words, as well as hyphenation practices, are often quite arbitrary in English. As well as being hyphenated, *forget-me-not, jack-of-all-trades,* and *runner-up* meet the syntactic criterion of wordhood: they are moved as a single unit. However, they differ in respect to the morphological criterion; while *forget-me-not* always behaves as a single word, with external modification (*two forget-me-nots, forget-me-not's*), *runner-up* is inconsistent, behaving as a single word when made possessive (*runner-up's*), but as a phrase, that is, with internal modification, when pluralized (*runners-up*); *jack-of-all-trades* is similarly inconsistent. The third criterion, a single primary stress, would seem to be the most reliable, but even here compound adjectives such as *noteworthy* pose a problem: they have two primary stresses and are phonologically phrases but are treated orthographically, morphologically, and syntactically as single words. "Phrasal verbs" such as *try out* also present an interesting case.[1] Though having many of the qualities of a phrase – internal modification occurs (*tried out*), material may intercede between the parts (*try out the car*, but also *try the car out*), and both *try* and *out* receive primary stress – phrasal verbs seem to express a unified semantic notion, the same as expressed in this case by the single word *test*. As this chapter progresses, we examine these problems in more detail.

Another difficulty when treating words is the term *word* itself, which may be used in a number of different ways:

1. It may refer to the word form, the physical unit or concrete realization, either the orthographical word (the written form) or the phonological word (the uttered or transcribed form).
2. It may refer to the **lexeme**, which is rather like a dictionary entry. A lexeme includes all inflected forms of a word. It is thus a kind of abstraction or class of forms and is indicated by small capitals, as in the following examples:

    > WALK – *walk, walks, walked, walking*
    > RUN – *run, runs, ran, running*
    > SING – *sing, sings, sang, sung, singing*

    Note that since the lexeme is an abstraction, it is conventional to choose one of the inflected forms to represent it, such as the infinitive of the verb or the singular of the noun. The same word form may in fact represent different lexemes:

    a. A homonym is a single orthographic and phonological word standing for two lexemes, as *bear* is either the verb or the noun.
    b. A homograph is a single orthographic word (but separate phonological words) standing for two lexemes, as *lead* is either the noun /lɛd/ or the verb /lid/.
    c. A homophone is a single phonological word (but separate orthographical words) standing for two lexemes, as /mit/ is either the noun *meat* or the verb *meet*.

    The same lexeme might also have quite distinct word forms, as in the case of the definite article *the*, represented by /ði/ or /ðə/, or the indefinite article *a/an*, represented by /eɪ/, /ə/, /ən/, or /æn/.
3. Finally, *word* may also refer to a morphosyntactic word (or grammatical word). A morphosyntactic word consists of a lexeme and associated grammatical meaning. For example, in:

    > *I take the garbage out every week.* (TAKE + present)
    > *I took the garbage out yesterday.* (TAKE + past)
    > *I have taken the garbage out already.* (TAKE + past participle)

---

1. Phrasal verbs consist of a verb plus a following particle such as *up* or *out* (e.g. *fill up, fill out*); they will be discussed in more detail below and in Chapter 8.

the different morphosyntactic words are represented by different word forms (*take, took, taken*). But in

> *I put the garbage out every week.* (PUT + present)
> *I put the garbage out yesterday.* (PUT + past)
> *I have put the garbage out already.* (PUT + past participle)

the different morphosyntactic words are represented by the same word form (*put*).

2. Morphemes

We begin the study of morphology by taking words as given and examining their internal structure.

2.1 Morpheme versus morph

We must start by identifying the **morpheme**, the smallest meaningful unit in a language; the morpheme is not necessarily equivalent to a word, but may be a smaller unit. For example, the word *headphones* consists of the three morphemes *head, phone,* and *-s*; the word *ringleader* consists of three morphemes, *ring, lead,* and *-er.* Some of these morphemes may stand alone as independent words (*head, phone, ring, lead*), others must always be attached to some other morpheme (*-er, -s*).

Like the phoneme, the morpheme refers to either a class of forms or an abstraction from the concrete forms of language. A morpheme has the following characteristics:

- it is internally indivisible; it cannot be further subdivided or analyzed into smaller meaningful units.
- it has internal stability since nothing can be interposed in a morpheme.
- it is externally transportable;
- it has positional mobility or free distribution, occurring in various contexts.

Morphemes are represented within curly braces { }.

> HINT: Like the phoneme, the morpheme refers to either a class of forms or an abstraction from the concrete forms of language. For example, the feminine morpheme is an abstraction which can be realized in a number of different ways, by *-ess*, as in *actress*, or by a personal pronoun such as *she*. Because morphemes are abstractions we place them within curly braces { } using capital letters for lexemes and descriptive designations for other types of morphemes. For *actress*, the morphemes are {ACTOR} and {f} (for {feminine]).

Based on meaning, there are a number of types of morphemes, as shown in Figure 4.1.

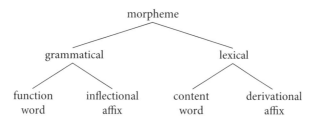

Figure 4.1. Types of Morphemes

Lexical morphemes express lexical, or dictionary, meaning. They can be categorized into the major lexical categories, or word classes: noun, verb, adjective, or adverb; these are frequently called "content words". They constitute open categories, to which new members can be added. Lexical morphemes are generally independent words (free roots) or parts of words (derivational affixes and bound roots). **Grammatical morphemes** express a limited number of very common meanings or express relations within the sentence. They do not constitute open categories; they can be exhaustively listed. Their occurrence is (entirely) predictable by the grammar of the sentence because certain grammatical meanings are associated with certain lexical categories, for example, tense and voice with the verb, and number and gender with the noun. Grammatical morphemes may be parts of words (inflectional affixes) or small but independent "function words" belonging to the minor word classes: preposition, article, demonstrative, conjunction, auxiliary, and so on, e.g. *of, the, that, and, may.*

In the case of the morpheme – which is an abstraction – we must also recognize the level of the **morph**, the concrete realization of a morpheme, or the actual segment of a word as it is spoken or pronounced. Morphs are represented by phonetic forms. We must introduce the concept of the morph distinct from the morpheme because sometimes although we know that a morpheme exists, it has <u>no</u> concrete realization (i.e, it is silent and has no spoken or written form). In such cases, we speak of a **zero morph**, one which has no phonetic or overt realization. There is no equivalent on the level of the phoneme. For example, plural *fish* consists of the morphemes {fish} + {pl}, but the plural morpheme has no concrete realization (i.e. the singular and plural forms of *fish* are both pronounced /fɪʃ/). Another example of a zero morph is the past tense of *let*; although the past consists of the morpheme {let} plus the morpheme {past}, the past tense morpheme has no concrete expression (i.e. the present and past forms of *let* are both pronounced /lɛt/).

We say that a morpheme is "realized" as a morph.

Based on form and distribution, there are different types of morphs (see Figure 4.2).

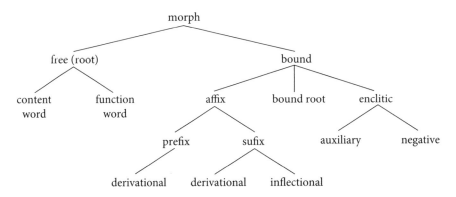

Figure 4.2. Types of Morphs

A **free morph** may stand alone as a word, while a **bound morph** may not; it must always be attached to another morph. A free morph is always a **root**.[2] That is, it carries the principal lexical or grammatical meaning. It occupies the position where there is greatest potential for substitution; it may attach to other free or bound morphemes. Examples of roots are underlined in the following words:

> un*avoid*ably   over*grown*   al*tru*istic   *decor*ation   pro*voc*ative
> dis*heart*ened   re*class*ify   hetero*sex*uality   up*bring*ing   *real*ization

Roots are also occasionally bound morphs. These are called **bound roots**. Bound roots are often foreign borrowings that were free in the source language, but not free in English. For example, in the following sets of words, we would all intuitively identify the root *-vert*, *-mit*, *-ceive*, or *-fer* (in part because it occurs in a number of words, as do the prefixes):

> -vert   con*vert*, re*vert*, sub*vert*, intro*vert*, per*vert*
> -mit   trans*mit*, com*mit*, re*mit*, ad*mit*, o*mit*, sub*mit*
> -ceive   con*ceive*, per*ceive*, re*ceive*, de*ceive*
> -fer   trans*fer*, re*fer*, pre*fer*, de*fer*, con*fer*

However *-vert*, *-mit*, *-ceive*, and *-fer* cannot stand alone as independent words, and we would also find it very difficult to state the meaning of any of these roots, unless we know

---

2.   A root is often distinguished both from a "base" (a root plus associated derivational affixes, to which derivational affixes are added) and from a "stem" (a root plus associated derivational affixes, to which inflectional affixes are added). Thus, in the word *engagement, gage* is the root, *engage* is the base, and *engagement* is the stem.

Latin, from which these words derive: -*vert* is from Latin *vertere* meaning 'to turn', -*mit* is from Latin *mittere* meaning 'to send', -*ceive* is from Latin *capere* meaning 'to seize', and -*fer* is from Latin *ferre* meaning 'to bring'. Other examples of bound roots borrowed from the Romance languages include *disgruntled*, *nonchalant*, and *incognito*. Bound roots may also be native English, as with -*kempt* (< *unkempt*) and -*couth* (< *uncouth*), where the positive form no longer exists. You could say that the bound roots have a meaning only if you know their history, or etymology.[3]

Unlike a root, an **affix** does not carry the core meaning. It is always bound to a root. It occupies a position where there is limited potential for substitution; that is, a particular affix will attach to only certain roots. English has two kinds of affixes, **prefixes**, which attach to the beginnings of roots, and **suffixes**, which attach to the end of roots. Some languages regularly use "infixes", which are inserted in the middle of words. In Modern English, infixes are used only for humorous purposes, as in *im-bloody-possible* or *abso-blooming-lutely*. While it might initially be tempting to analyze the vowel alternation indicating plural (as in *man*, *men*) or past tense (as in *sing*, *sang*) in Modern English as a kind of infix, the vowels are not added or inserted but actually replace the existing vowels.

Self-Testing Exercise: To practice identifying roots, prefixes, and suffixes, do Exercise 4.1.

Affixes may be of two types, derivational or inflectional, which have very different characteristics. A **derivational affix** in English is either a prefix or a suffix. There may be more than one derivational affix per word. A particular derivational affix may attach to only a limited number of roots; which roots it attaches to is not predictable by rule, but highly idiosyncratic and must be learned. A derivational affix has one of two functions: to convert one part of speech to another (in which case, it is class changing) and/or to change the meaning of the root (in which case, it is class maintaining). Such affixes function, then, in word formation and are important in the creation of new lexemes in the language. They always precede an inflectional affix. An **inflectional affix** in English is always a suffix. A particular inflectional affix attaches to all (or most) members of a certain word class. The function of inflectional affixes is to indicate grammatical meaning, such as tense or number. Because grammatical meaning is relevant outside the word, to the grammar of the entire sentence, inflectional affixes always occur last, following the root and any derivational affixes, which are central to the meaning or class of the root. The differences between derivational and inflectional affixes are summarized in Table 4.1.

---

3.   For this reason, they have been termed "etymemes".

Table 4.1. Derivational vs. Inflectional Affixes in English

Derivational affixes	Inflectional affixes
either prefixes or suffixes	only suffixes
optionally more than one per word	only one per word[4]
attach idiosyncratically to only a limited number of roots	attach to all (or most) members of a word class
have two functions	have one function
1. to convert one part of speech to another	1. to indicate grammatical meaning
2. to change the meaning of the root	
precede the inflectional suffix	follow derivational suffix(es)

A distinction can be made between productive inflections, which would attach to any new word entering the language to express a particular grammatical category, and nonproductive, or remnant, inflections, which are found on select members of a class, but would never be added to a new word. There are only eight productive inflections in Modern English, as shown in Table 4.2. Some examples of nonproductive inflections are the plural vowel alternation *tooth-teeth*; the *-most* superlative of *foremost*; the *-en* past participle of *write-written*; or the past tense vowel alternation of *ring-rang*.

Table 4.2. The Productive Inflections of Modern English

plural number	*-s*	
possessive case	*-s*	Noun
present (nonpast) tense, 3rd p sg	*-s*	
past tense	*-ed*	
past participle	*-ed*	Verb
present participle	*-ing*	
comparative degree	*-er*	
superlative degree	*-est*	Adjective

> HINT: As you can see in Table 4.2, the *-ed* ending has two distinct functions, as a past tense marker and as past participle marker. These two functions are distinguished as follow: past tense forms serve as the sole verb in a sentence (e.g. He _walked_ along the shore, The teacher _helped_ the student with the problem), while past participles must occur with a preceding auxiliary BE or HAVE (e.g. He _has walked_ along the shore for an hour; The student _was helped_ with the problem (by the teacher)). Depending on the verb, the past tense and past participle may be either the same (e.g. walked~walked) or different

---

4.   A form such as *men's* has two inflectional morphemes (plural and possessive), though only one inflectional suffix (*-s*).

(e.g. *drove~driven*). Note also that the *-s* ending has different functions for nouns and verbs. This does not usually pose a problem unless the same word functions as either a noun or a verb (e.g. *His <u>hopes</u> to win the lottery were dashed* [-s plural on the noun] vs. *He <u>hopes</u> to win the lottery* [-s 3rd person present indicative on the verb]).

Self-Testing Exercises: To learn to identify inflectional suffixes, do Exercise 4.2. Then to better understand the difference between inflection and derivation, do Exercise 4.3.

An **enclitic** is a kind of contraction, a bound form which derives from an independent word and must be attached to the preceding word.[5] In English, we have two kinds of enclitics: contracted auxiliaries, which are attached to the preceding subject, and the negative contraction *-n't*, which is attached to the preceding auxiliary. Certain auxiliaries (e.g. *may, can, must, should, might, was*) cannot be contracted, while the contraction of *not* produces marginally acceptable forms in some cases (e.g. *ʔmayn't, ʔmightn't*) or unacceptable forms in other cases (e.g. **am't*).

Contracted auxiliaries	Contracted negatives -n't
will, shall > 'll	*won't, ʔshalln't*
would, had > 'd	*wouldn't, hadn't*
is, has > 's	*isn't, hasn't*
have > 've	*haven't*
am > 'm	**am't (ain't)*
are > 're	*aren't*
was > *'s	*wasn't*

Words are analyzed morphologically with the same terminology used to describe different sentence types:

- a "simple" word has one free root, e.g. *hand*;
- a "complex" word has a free root and one or more bound morphs e.g. *unhand, handy, handful*, or it has two or more bound morphs, e.g. *transference, reception, conversion*
- a "compound" word has two free roots, e.g. *handbook, handrail, handgun*; and
- a "compound-complex" word has two free roots and associated bound morphs, e.g. *handwriting, handicraft*.

2.2   The analysis of words into morphs and morphemes

The importance of the distinction between morph and morpheme is that there is not always a one-to-one correspondence between morph and morpheme, and morphemes can

---

5.   Some languages have "proclitics", originally free words which must be attached to the word that follows; the articles in French are proclitics, e.g. *la auto > l'auto*. Also, the archaic forms in English *'twas* (< *it was*) or *'tis* (< *it is*) contain proclitics.

combine or be realized in a number of different ways. We can thus analyze words in two different ways:

1.   into morphs following formal or structural divisions, or
2.   into morphemes, recognizing the abstract units of meaning present.

If we start first with nouns, we would arrive at the two analyses of each of the following words:

	Morphs	**Morphemes**
writers	3 morphs *writ/er/s*	3 morphemes {WRITE} + {-er} + {pl}
authors	2 morphs *author/s*	2 morphemes {AUTHOR} + {pl}
mice	1 morph *mice*	2 morphemes {MOUSE} + {pl}
fish	1 morph *fish*	2 morphemes {FISH} + {pl}
children	2 morphs *child/ren*	2 morphemes {CHILD} + {pl}
teeth	1 morph *teeth*	2 morphemes {TOOTH} + {pl}
man's	2 morphs *man/s*	2 morphemes {MAN} + {poss}
men's	2 morphs *men/s*	3 morphemes {MAN} + {pl} + {poss}

> **HINT:** Inflectional morphemes can often be realized by a number of different forms, or the same form may denote a number of different inflectional morphemes. Therefore, it is usual to use descriptive designations for inflectional morphemes, such as {pl} (rather than {-s} or {-es}) for the plural marker and {poss} (rather than {-s}) for the possessive marker. The descriptive designations that we will use should be self-evident in the following discussion (also see the list of abbreviations in Appendix I).

A noun such as *sheep* raises a difficulty for morphemic analysis, since it is either singular or plural. Should we postulate two morphemic analyses?

{SHEEP} + {pl}
{SHEEP} + {sg}

This seems a good idea. If we postulate a morpheme for singular, even though it is never realized, we can account for number systematically. Thus, we will analyze all singular nouns as containing an abstract {sg} morpheme, so that *man's* above would have the analysis {MAN} + {sg} + {poss}, *writer* the analysis {WRITE} + {-er} + {sg}, and *author* the analysis {AUTHOR} + {sg}.

Let us look at how morphological and morphemic analysis works in adjectives:

	Morphs	**Morphemes**
smaller	2 morphs *small/er*	2 morphemes {SMALL} + {compr}
smallest	2 morphs *small/est*	2 morphemes {SMALL} + {supl}
better	1 morph *better*	2 morphemes {GOOD} + {compr}
best	1 morph *best*	2 morphemes {GOOD} + {supl}

(Here, compr = comparative degree and supl = superlative degree, as will be discussed in the next chapter.) Again, we need to postulate a morpheme positive degree {pos}, even though it is never realized, to account systematically for the inflected forms of adjectives:

> *good*   1 morph *good*   2 morphemes {GOOD} + {pos}

For verbs, the two analyses work as follows:

	Morphs	Morphemes
worked	2 morphs *work/ed*	2 morphemes {WORK} + {past}
		2 morphemes {work} + {pstprt}
wrote	1 morph *wrote*	2 morphemes {WRITE} + {past}
written	1 morph *written*	2 morphemes {WRITE} + {pstprt}
working	2 morphs *work/ing*	2 morphemes {WORK} + {prsprt}
		3 morphemes {WORK} + {gerund}+ {sg}
put	1 morph *put*	2 morphemes {PUT} + {past}
		2 morphemes {PUT} + {pstprt}

(Here, pstprt = past participle, prsprt = present participle; see further Chapter 9.) Note that we have to analyze *-ing* verbal forms not only as present participles, but also as "gerunds".[6] Since gerunds are functioning as nouns, they may sometimes be pluralized, e.g.:

> *readings*   3 morphs *read/ing/s*   3 morphemes {READ} + {gerund} + {pl}

We need to postulate a morpheme {pres}, which is never realized, to account coherently for the distinction past versus present:[7]

> *work*   1 morph *work*   2 morphemes {WORK} + {pres}
> *write*   1 morph *write*   2 morphemes {WRITE} + {pres}

---

6.   Gerunds are word forms that are derived from verbs – by the addition of the suffix *-ing* – but function grammatically as nouns; they are "verbal nouns". Thus, in *Swimming is good exercise, swimming* is derived from the verb *swim*, but since it serves as the subject of the sentence, it functions as a noun; in *I enjoy singing in the shower, singing* is derived from the verb *sing*, and the entire phrase *singing in the shower* functions as a noun phrase direct object. As shown above, (some) gerunds can be pluralized and function as sentential subjects or objects: e.g. *Readings by local authors are given at the local book store; I detest poetry readings.* (Gerunds will be discussed in more detail in Chapter 9.)

7.   The 3rd person singular form *works* or *writes* causes some difficulty for our analysis. Would we need to propose the following analysis for *works*: {WORK} + {pres} + {sg}? If we do this, we would also have to postulate a {pl} morpheme, which is never realized. However, we won't do this, but will assume that *-s* is added by a rule of grammar, that of concord, which copies the feature of number from the noun subject to the verb.

The morphemic analysis of pronouns is somewhat more complicated:

	Morphs	Morphemes
we	1 morph *we*	3 morphemes {1st p} + {pl} + {nomn}
him	1 morph *him*	4 morphemes {3rd p} + {sg} + {m} + {obj}
its	2 morphs *it/s*	4 morphemes {3rd p} + {sg} + {n} + {poss}

(Here, nomn = nominative case and obj = objective case; see the following chapter.)

Morphemes combine and are realized by one of four **morphological realization rules**:

1. agglutinative rule: two morphemes are realized by morphs which remain distinct and are simply "glued" together, e.g. {WRITER} + {pl} > *writers*
2. fusional rule: two morphemes are realized by morphs which do not remain distinct but are fused together, e.g. {TOOTH} + {pl} > *teeth*
3. null realization rule: a morpheme is never realized as a morph in any word of the relevant class, e.g. {sg} on nouns, which never has concrete realization in English.
4. zero rule: a morpheme is realized as a zero morph in particular members of a word class, e.g. {SHEEP} + {pl} > *sheep*. Note that in most other members of the class noun, {pl} has concrete realization as *-s*.

Examples of the four different morphological realization rules, or combinations of these rules, are the following:

agglutinative	{WORK} + {past} > *worked*
fusional	{WRITE} + {past} > *wrote*
null	{WORK} + {pres} > *work*
zero	{PUT} + {past} > *put*, {PUT} + {pstprt} > *put*
fusional and agglutinative	{MAN} + {pl} + {poss} > *men's*

> **HINT:** Distinguishing between the concept of a null rule and a zero rule can be difficult. Remember that in the case of a null rule, the morpheme is never concretely realized. For example, {pres} on verbs is always unmarked. No verb has an overt marker of the present. In contrast, when a morpheme is usually concretely realized, but is not realized on certain words, then we have a zero rule. For example {pl} on nouns is typically expressed by *-s*, but on a noun such as *deer*, it is not marked and hence a zero rule.

Self-Testing Exercise: Do Exercise 4.4.

2.3 Allomorphs and morphemic rules

Just as phonemes have predictable variants, called allophones, morphemes have predictable variants called **allomorphs**. Allomorphs are the members of the class, morpheme, or the phonetic realizations of the abstraction, morpheme. Allomorphs are semantically similar and in complementary distribution. They needn't be phonologically similar, however. Allomorphs are predicted, or "conditioned", in one of three ways:

1. the appearance of a particular allomorph is predictable from the phonetic environment, hence phonologically conditioned;
2. the appearance is unpredictable phonologically but is determined by the grammar of the language, hence grammatically conditioned; or
3. the allomorphs are used interchangeably in all environments, hence in free variation.

Let's consider the following example involving regular plural formation in nouns in English, as shown in Table 4.3.

Table 4.3. Regular Plural Formation in Nouns

A	B	C	
bushes /ʃ/	maps /p/	knobs /b/	rays /eɪ/
buses /s/	cats /t/	rods /d/	sofas /ə/
mazes /z/	racks /k/	logs /g/	toys /ɔɪ/
judges /dʒ/	ropes /p/	seals /l/	keys /i/
matches /tʃ/	laughs /f/	mirrors /r/	news /ɪu/
boxes /s/	paths /θ/	pans /n/	lathes /ð/
garages /ʒ/		tombs /m/	coves /v/
rouges /ʒ/		rings /ŋ/	

Although the orthographic form of the plural is *s* or *es* in all cases, you will notice that the phonological form of the plural morpheme in column A is /əz/, in column B /s/, and in column C /z/. Thus, there are three allomorphs of the plural morpheme. These allomorphs are phonetically similar, as well as semantically similar, all expressing the concept 'more than one'. A speaker of English knows which of these three forms to choose in any particular case. For the made-up noun, *prat*, the speaker would know to add the /s/ plural, whereas with the made-up noun *stad*, the speaker would add /z/. Thus, the particular endings, or allomorphs, are predictable – but how? If they are phonologically conditioned, there must be something about the phonetic environment of the noun which determines the choice of allomorph. In fact, it is the final sound of the root of the noun which is the determining factor. Note that in column A, all of the nouns end with a fricative or an affricate, in column B, with a voiceless consonant, and in column C, with a voiced consonant or vowel. We can refine this information and state it in terms of a **morphemic rule** similar in form to a phonemic rule (as in Chapter 3) We must first recognize that the sounds found in column A /s, z, ʃ, ʒ, tʃ, dʒ/ constitute a natural class called sibilants. It would be inaccurate to say that /əz/ occurs after fricatives, since certain fricatives such as /f/ take the /s/ allomorph while others such as /v/ take the /z/ allomorph. Once we recognize the class of sibilants, we can state the rule as follows: [8]

$$
\{pl\} \rightarrow \quad
\begin{array}{l}
\text{[əz]/ sibilants —} \\
\text{[s]/ voiceless consonants —} \\
\text{[z]/ elsewhere}
\end{array}
$$

Remember that the rule is read downward, so that "voiceless consonants" in the second line would exclude any voiceless consonants already included in the first line among sibilants.

As with phonemic rules, we specify one allomorph as "elsewhere". This is the form with widest distribution or the one found in the most diverse phonetic environments, in this case, after voiced consonants and vowels. It should also be the form from which the other forms can be derived with the simplest set of phonological rules. For example, if we take /z/ as the underlying form,[9] then we can derive the other forms:

- by inserting schwa between two sibilants (giving the [əz] allomorph); and
- by devoicing [z] when it immediately follows a voiceless consonant (giving the [s] allomorph).

Note that we must make these changes in this order. Although we could assume [s] or [əz] as the underlying form, the phonological changes that would need to occur are less natural than the ones suggested above.

Table 4.3 above gives the forms of noun plural in English that are phonologically conditioned, but certain noun plurals are grammatically conditioned:

Ø	*fish, sheep, deer*
vowel alternation	*mice, lice, geese*
-en	*children, brethren, oxen*
foreign plurals	
-a	*phenomena, data, criteria*
-i	*stimuli, foci*
-ae	*alumnae, formulae*
-ices	*indices, appendices*
-es	*bases, axes*
-im	*kibbutzim, cherubim*

These endings are not productive: they are either linguistic fossils (remnant forms from an earlier stage of English) or foreign borrowings. Note that if a noun such as *mouse* took a productive ending, it would be the [əz] allomorph, *child* would take /z/, and *tooth* would take /s/.

---

8. This rule will also account for the allomorphs of the possessive morpheme (as well as of the 3rd p sg pres morpheme on verbs and contractions of 3rd p sg pres of HAVE and BE).

9. The underlying form need not correspond to the actual historical form.

Let's look at one set of forms that does not seem to follow the morphemic rule for plural allomorphs given above. We would expect the plural allomorph of words ending in /f/ (a voiceless non-sibilant consonant) to be /s/, as in the following words:

belief – beliefs   chief – chiefs
proof – proofs   safe – safes

However, what we find in the following set of forms is not /s/, but instead the plural allomorph /z/, with a simultaneous voicing of the final root consonant:

wolf – wolves   leaf – leaves
knife – knives   loaf – loaves
sheaf – sheaves   wife – wives
elf – elves   life – lives
shelf – shelves   calf – calves
thief – thieves   self – selves

In some cases, we also find variation between the phonologically expected and unexpected forms:

wharf – wharfs/wharves   dwarf – dwarfs/dwarves
hoof – hoofs/hooves   scarf – scarfs/scarves

A similar irregularity appears in the following words ending in /s/; the expected /əz/ allomorph is found, but there is also voicing of the final root /s/:[10]

house – houses   blouse – blouses

How do we account for these irregularities in the plural forms? We could have a morphological realization rule which changes final voiceless fricatives to voiced fricatives when {pl} is added. However, such a rule would have to apply generally to all roots ending in voiceless fricatives, and it does not. Instead, we say that there are two predictable variants of the root, what is called **root allomorphy**. The two allomorphs of the root are grammatically conditioned, by the presence of either a following {sg} and {pl} morpheme. The rule for *leaf/leaves* is as follows:

{lif} → [liv]/ -{pl}
          [lif]/ elsewhere

Note that "elsewhere" would include the environment before both {sg} and {poss}. Hence, this form has the widest distribution. Actually, the -{pl} environment is too restricted since

---

10. It is interesting to note that in these cases, the possessive morpheme *-s* is altogether regular: *wolf's, knife's, life's, thief's, elf's*, and so on.

we also have voicing when a verb is formed from the noun (for example, *to shelve, to calve, to halve*).[11]

A similar kind of root allomorphy is thus seen in cases of shifts from noun to verb where (a) the nominal forms have /s/ and the verbal forms have /z/ (Table 4.4a), or (b) the nominal forms have /θ/ while the verbal forms have /ð/ (Table 4.4b).

Table 4.4. Root Allomorphy

a. N: /s/	V: /z/	b. N: /θ/	V: /ð/
house	to house	bath	to bathe
blouse	to blouse	cloth	to clothe
use	to use	breath	to breathe
excuse	to excuse	mouth	to mouthe
advice	to advise	teeth	to teethe
abuse	to abuse	wreath	to wreathe

Finally, it is interesting to note that bound roots may show root allomorphy; for example, *-cept* is a predictable variant of *-ceive* before *-ion*, as in *conception, perception, reception,* and *deception*.

Generally, English is not rich in allomorphy, though we have inherited quite a lot of it with the Latinate vocabulary that we borrowed, as you will see in Exercise 4.5. However, two other examples of native allomorphy are the [ðə]/[ði] variants of the definite article {THE} – can you determine how these are conditioned? A further example of root allomorphy is *staves/staffs* (< *staff*), where the root-allomorphic plural and the regular plural have become semantically distinguished, the former being restricted to music.

Self-Testing Exercise: To practice writing morphemic rules, do Exercise 4.5.

3.   Processes of word formation

English has a number of means by which morphs combine or are altered to form new words. However, only two of these processes of word creation, derivation and compounding, are responsible for significant numbers of new words.

3.1   Derivation

The addition of a word-forming affix is called **derivation**. We have already looked at the features of derivational affixes (in contrast to inflectional suffixes) (see Table 4.1). The addition

---

11.   Voicing even occurs in some cases where there is no voicing in the noun plural (as in *to believe, to prove, to grieve*).

of a derivational affix to a root produces a new word with one or more of the following changes:

–   a phonological change (including stress change): *reduce > reduction, clear > clarity, fuse > fusion, include > inclusive, drama > dramatize, relate > relation, permit > permissive, impress > impression, eléctric > electrícity, phótograph > photógraphy*;
–   an orthographic change to the root: *pity > pitiful, deny > denial, happy > happiness*;
–   a semantic change, which may be fairly complex: *husband > husbandry, event > eventual, post > postage, recite > recital, emerge >emergency*; and/or
–   a change in word class: *eat* (V) *> eatable* (A), *impress* (V) *> impression* (N) (see further below).

In English, derivational affixes are either prefixes or suffixes. They may be native (deriving from Old English) or foreign (borrowed along with a word from a foreign language, especially French). Their productivity may range from very limited to quite extensive, depending upon whether they are preserved in just a few words and no longer used to create new words or whether they are found in many words and still used to create new words. An example of an unproductive suffix is the *-th* in *warmth, width, depth*, or *wealth*, whereas an example of a productive suffix is the *-able* in *available, unthinkable, admirable*, or *honorable*. But which affix attaches to which root is always quite arbitrary and unpredictable; it is not a matter of rule but must be stated separately for each root (as, for example, in a dictionary). That is, derivation is part of the lexicon, not part of the grammar of a language.

   Only three prefixes, which are no longer productive in English, systematically change the part of speech of the root:

a-	N/V > A	*ablaze, asleep, astir, astride, abed, abroad*
be-	N > V	*betoken, befriend, bedeck, becalm, besmirch*
en-	A/N > V	*enlarge, ensure, encircle, encase, entrap*

Other prefixes change only the meaning of the root, not its class. Prefixes fall into a number of semantic classes in English, depending upon the meaning that they contribute to the root, as shown in Table 4.5. Note the difference between privation and negation: a privative prefix expresses the reverse of an action (as in *undo*) or the absence of a quality (as in *amoral* 'without morals'), whereas the negative prefix expresses 'not' (as in *immoral* 'not moral'). The list given in Table 4.5 is not an exhaustive one; other semantic categories would be needed to classify all the prefixes of English, such as "completeness" (e.g. *fulfill*), "reversal" (e.g. *counterattack*), or "subordination" (e.g. *vicechair*). Furthermore, some prefixes may fit into more than one category; e.g. *under-*, expresses both degree (in *underpayment*) and place (in *underwater*). Prefixes may often attach to more than one part of speech, e.g. *mislead* (V) and *misfortune* (N).

Table 4.5. Semantic Classes of Prefixes in English

a.	Time	
	pre-	prearrange, presuppose, preheat
	after-	aftershock, afterthought, afterglow
b.	Number	
	tri-	tricycle, triannual, triconsonantal
	multi-	multinational, multilingual, multimillionaire
c.	Place	
	in-	infield, in-patient, ingrown
	inter-	interconnect, interbreed, interlace
d.	Degree	
	super-	supersensitive, supersaturated, superheat
	over-	overanxious, overconfident, overdue
e.	Privation	
	a-	amoral, apolitical, asymmetric
	un-	unlock, untie, unfold
f.	Negation	
	un-	unafraid, unsafe, unwise
	anti-	antisocial, antitrust, antiwar
g.	Size	
	micro-	microcosm, microchip, microfilm
	mini-	miniskirt, minivan, minimall

Of the prefixes given in Table 4.5, *after-*, *in-*, *over-*, and *un-* are native English, while *pre-*, *inter-*, *super-*, and *mini-* are Latin and *tri-*, *a-*, *micro-*, and *anti-* are Greek. Note that many of the native prefixes, such as *over-*, *under-*, *out-*, or *in-* (as in *over-skilled*, *underpayment*, *outcast*, *infield*), also exist as independent prepositions and adverbs.

Suffixes have two functions: to change the meaning of the root and to change the part of speech of the root. Many suffixes attached to nouns change their meaning but not their class:

- the diminutive suffixes *-ling, -let, -y, -ie* (as in *princeling, piglet, daddy, hoodie*),[12]
- the feminine suffixes *-ess, -ette, -rix, -ine* (as in *actress, usherette, aviatrix, heroine*) – which, for social and cultural reasons, are now falling out of use,
- the abstract suffixes *-ship, -hood, -ism*, making abstract nouns out of concrete nouns (as in *friendship, neighborhood, hoodlumism*), or
- suffixes denoting people such as *-(i)an, -ist, -er* (in *librarian, Texan, Canadian, Marxist, Londoner*).

Some suffixes attached to adjectives likewise change only their meaning

- *-ish* means 'nearly, not exactly' in *greenish, fortyish, coldish*
- *-ly* express 'resemblance' in *goodly, sickly, lonely*

---

12.   Diminution (e.g. *doggy*) is not the only use for the diminutive suffix; it may also express degradation (e.g. *dummy*), amelioration (e.g. *hubby*), and intimacy (e.g. *Jenny < Jennifer*).

More often, however, suffixes change the word class of the root. As shown in Table 4.6a and b, the suffix may produce a noun from a verb or an adjective. Any suffix which produces a noun is called a **nominalizer**. This constitutes the largest set of class-changing suffixes. A highly productive nominalizer is the agentive suffix *-er*, which may be added to many verbs to produce agent nouns. A suffix which produces a verb from a noun or an adjective is called a **verbalizer**, as exemplified in Table 4.6c, while one which produces an adjective from a noun, a verb, or another adjective is called an **adjectivalizer** and is exemplified in Table 4.6d and e. The smallest set of class-changing suffixes is the **adverbializer**, as shown in Table 4.6f.

Table 4.6. Derivational Suffixes in English

Nominalizer	a. V > N	-ment	arrangement, judgment, advancement
		-er	worker, helper, leader
		-(c)ation	legalization, simplification, taxation
		-al	disposal, refusal, arrival, trial
		-ance/-ence	ignorance, performance, reference
	b. A > N	-dom	freedom, officialdom, Christendom
		-ness	happiness, cleverness, bitterness
		-ity	legality, purity, equality
Verbalizer	c. A/N > V	-ify	pacify, simplify, purify
		-ize	prioritize, publicize, centralize
		-ate	hyphenate, orchestrate, chlorinate
		-en	lighten, soften, tighten, moisten
Adjectivalizer	d. N > A	-y	flowery, thirsty, bloody
		-ous	poisonous, famous, glamorous
		-ful	delightful, sinful, pitiful
	e. V > A	-ive	supportive, generative, assertive
		-able	acceptable, livable, changeable
		-ful	hopeful, thankful, useful
		-ent/-ant	absorbent, flippant, repellent
Adverbializer	f. A/N > Adv	-ward	homeward, eastward, downward
		-ly	quickly, terribly, gradually
		-way(s)	sideway(s), anyway(s), someway

The formation of complex words is not always entirely predictable or regular. For example, *-ist* is typically added to common nouns (e.g. *cyclist*) and occasionally to proper nouns (e.g. *Platonist*). The addition of *-ist* results in a phonetic change /-ɪst/ and a semantic change 'one connected with X'. However, some words have an additional phonetic change, as in *Platonist* above or in *publicist, historicist* (< *public, historic*), where the final /k/ consonant changes to /s/. The semantics of *-ist* words is also more complex than first suggested since such words may denote persons adhering to a theory (e.g. *anarchist, realist,* *hedonist*), persons exercising a scientific profession (e.g. *linguist, dentist, psychiatrist, botanist*), or persons addicted to an ideology (e.g. *perfectionist, extremist, nationalist, fascist*). In the last category would fall *racist, sexist, lookist,* or *ageist,* which denote not just people addicted to race, sex, looks, or age, but those who make discriminations or hold prejudices based on these qualities. Note too that many such words have acquired negative connotations (as has, in fact, the notion of 'addiction'). The morphology of *-ist* words is also not entirely regular; some *-ist* words are related to abstract nouns ending in *-y* (e.g. *botany, psychiatry*) and some to ones in *-ism* (e.g. *realism, fascism*), while some *-ist* words take an *-ic* adjectivalizer and others do not (e.g. *hedonistic,* *dentistic). And the combination of *-ist* with a particular root is not predictable: while *balloonist* and *cyclist* are possible, for example, *boatist and *skatist are not. The suffix *-ist* is often in competition with either *(i)an* (e.g. *pedestrian, grammarian, barbarian*) and *-ite* (e.g. *suburbanite, socialite, Troskyite*). In the case of a follower of Darwin, all three forms – *Darwinian, Darwinist,* and *Darwinite* – exist.

Finally, the false morphological division of words may result in more or less productive suffixes, which one scholar calls "splinters", as in the following:

ham/<u>burger</u>	>	*cheeseburger*
		fishburger
		mushroomburger
		vegieburger
alc/<u>oholic</u>	>	*workaholic*
		chocaholic
		rageaholic
mar/<u>athon</u>	>	*workathon*
		telethon
		swimathon
		walkathon
pano/<u>rama</u>	>	*autorama*
		motorama
caval/<u>cade</u>	>	*aquacade*
		motorcade
<u>heli</u>/copter	>	*heliport*
		helidrome
		helistop

For instance, in *alcohol,* a word derived from Arabic, *al* is a definite article and the root is *-cohol-* (related to the word *kohl* 'powder used to darken eyelids'); therefore, dividing the word between *alco-* and *-holic* (or *alc-* and *-oholic*) is a mistake. *Helicopter* is derived from Greek roots meaning 'spiral' (cf. *helix*) + 'wing' and should correctly be divided between *helic-* and *-opter* (or *helico-* and *-pter*); that is, the *-c-* belongs with the root.[13]

---

13.   These forms might also be analyzed as blends; see below.

Derivation can be stated in terms of lexical rules:

mis- + align (V) + -ment   >   *misalignment* (N)
image (N) + -ine + -ary   >   *imaginary* (A)
false (A) + -ify   >   *falsify* (V)

Or they can be expressed by tree diagrams, which have the advantage that they indicate the hierarchical arrangement and order of derivation of complex words. Possible representations of the derived form *nonsmoker* are the following:

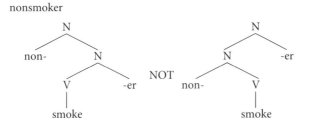

The reason that the second derivation is impossible is that one must be able to stop at any point in the derivation and still have a word of English. The second derivation produces the nonword **nonsmoke*. The form *unimpressionable* has two possible derivations:

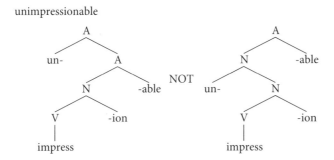

(Here we are not analyzing *impress* into its bound root -*press* and prefix *im*-.) Again, the second derivation produces the nonword **unimpression*. Look at the two possible trees for *informality*:

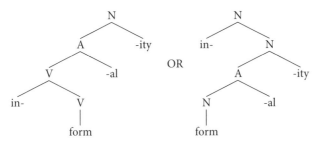

While neither derivation produces a nonword, the reason for preferring the second derivation in this case is semantic. *Informality* means 'not having the quality of form' and is related to the noun *form*. The prefix is negative. It is not related to the verb *inform*, which does not contain a negative prefix. Compare the following derivations of *information*:

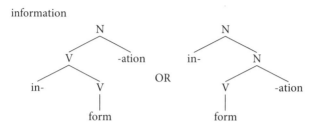

information

Again, there are semantic reasons for preferring the first derivation here, since *information* is related to the action of informing, not to a formation.

> **HINT:** In writing or reading these tree diagrams, you should work from the bottom up; that is, you should begin with the root and then add the prefixes and/or suffixes. They should yield the word when read from left to right.

Self-Testing Exercises: Do Exercises 4.6 and 4.7 on derivation.

3.2   Reduplication

Reduplication is a process similar to derivation, in which the initial syllable or the entire word is doubled, exactly or with a slight phonological change. Reduplication is not a common or regular process of word formation in English, though it may be in other languages. In English it is often used in children's language (e.g. *boo-boo, putt-putt, choo-choo*) or for humorous or ironic effect (e.g. *goody-goody, rah-rah, pooh-pooh*). Three different kinds of reduplication can be identified:

1. exact reduplication: *papa, mama, goody-goody, so-so, hush-hush, never-never, tutu, fifty-fifty, hush-hush*;
2. ablaut reduplication in which the vowel alternates while the consonants are identical: *criss-cross, zig-zag, flip-flop, mish-mash, wishy-washy, clip-clop, riff-raff, achy-breaky*, and
3. rhyme reduplication in which the consonants change while the vowel remains the same: *hodge-podge, fuddy-duddy, razzle-dazzle, boogie-woogie, nitty-gritty, roly-poly, hob-nob, hocus-pocus*.

Reduplications can be formed with two meaningful parts, for example, *flower-power, brain drain, culture vulture, boy toy,* or *heart smart*.

Reduplication has many different functions: it can express disparagement (*namby-pamby*), intensification (*super-duper*), diminution (*teeny-weeny*), onomatopoeia (*tick-tock*), or alternation (*ping-pong*), among other uses.

3.3   Conversion or functional shift

A **functional shift** involves the **conversion** of one part of speech to another without the addition of a suffix, as in *a phone* (N) > *to phone* (V). It is sometimes said that a zero (Ø) derivational suffix is added (since it is usual for derivational suffixes to change the part of speech, as discussed above). The only concrete change that may occur in a functional shift is a change in stress.

The following kinds of functional shifts are most common in English:

V > N	*(a) run, drive, walk, bruise, cut, look, call, dump, spy, bite, sneeze*
N > V	*(to) man, head, shoulder, telephone, lust, contact, ship, sign, skin, mail*
A > V	*(to) weary, better, empty, idle, dirty, bare, quiet, tame, lower*
A > N	*(a) daily, double, private, commercial, formal, red, elder, roast*
Prt > V	*(to) down, up, off, thwart, out*

("Prt" denotes "particle", a super-class of words including prepositions, adverbs, and some conjunctions, as will be discussed in Chapter 5.) Less common kinds of conversions are a preposition to a noun (*ins and outs, ups and downs*), an adverb to a noun (*whys and where-fores, the hereafter*), or even a prefix to a noun (*pros and cons*). Once a word has been converted, it can normally take the inflections of the new class, for example, *two runs, telephoned/telephoning, dirtied*.

What happens semantically when a word is converted may be quite varied. For example, in the V > N shift, an action is treated as:

- an object or thing, though the emphasis may be on the action (e.g. *an attack, a fight, a kiss, a kick, a groan*),
- the result of the action (e.g. *an award, a find, a bruise, a crease*),
- the person performing the action (e.g. *a spy, a cook*),
- the time of the action (e.g. *the spring, the fall*),
- the place of the action (e.g. *a sink, a drain, a speak-easy*), or
- the range of the action (e.g. *an overlap*).

Note that with such shifts, actions become easily countable (e.g. *two kisses, several fights*).

With the N > V shift, the noun used as a verb denotes:

- the thing moved to a location (e.g. *to paint, to water*) or from a location (e.g. *to milk, to skin*),
- the location to which something is moved (e.g. *to bottle, to box*) or from which it is moved (e.g. *to mine*), or
- the instrument used to perform an action (e.g. *to lock, to mail, to whistle, to rattle*).

A > V gives the inchoative ('to become X') or the causative ('to cause to become X') meaning (see Chapter 10). The shift A > N treats a quality as an entity (and hence quantifiable).

It is often difficult to know in conversions which is the original (or basic) form and which the converted form. Sometimes semantics or morphological modification will offer a clue. When the noun is primary, the verb necessarily includes the meaning of the noun. Thus, *to butter toast with margarine* sounds odd because the converted verb *butter* includes the meaning of the noun. Similarly, *to garage the car in the shed* is not entirely natural. However, *to anchor the ship with a rock* or *to comb one's hair with one's fingers* is acceptable because the verb is original and the noun derived by conversion. What do you think in the case of *to hammer the stake with a rock*? Is the noun or the verb original? Another distinguishing feature is the regularity of inflection. Converted forms will always take the regular, productive inflection, never a remnant or irregular inflection. For example, *grandstand*, *highlight*, or *highstick* may originally be either nouns or verbs. Since the past tense forms are *grandstanded*, *highlighted*, and *highsticked*, we conclude that the verb must be derived from the noun; otherwise, the past tense would be *grandstood*, *highlit*, or *highstuck*. Similarly, the past tense of *ring (the city)* is *ringed*, not *rang (the city)*, showing that *ring* in this case is a verb converted from a noun rather than an original verb. In contrast, the past tense of *deepfreeze* is *deepfroze*, not **deepfreezed*, and thus the noun (*a deepfreeze*) must derive from the verb.

Stress changes accompany the conversion of phrasal verbs to nouns. The primary stress on the particle is lost in each case, as was discussed in Chapter 3:

V + Prt > N   *cómeback, rúnoff, tákeover, mákeup, rúndown, stándby, shówoff, wríteoff, lóckout, pútdown, chéckup*

Another fairly large set of converted forms shows a difference in stress, with stress on the first syllable (prefix) of the noun and the second syllable (root) of the verb (see Chapter 3):

Verb	Noun
condúct	*cónduct*
rebél	*rébel*
permít	*pérmit*
recórd	*récord*
objéct	*óbject*

Note that unstressing of the syllable may also lead to reduction of the vowel, e.g. *rebél* (V) /rəbɛl/ (stress on second syllable, hence full vowel) vs. *rébel* (V) /rɛbəl/ (stress on first syllable, hence reduced vowel in second syllable).

A special kind of functional shift is what we may call **commonization**, in which a proper noun is converted into a common word. A proper noun, naming a real or fictional person or place, tribe, or group, may undergo commonization to a noun, verb, or adjective, often with no phonological change:

N: *cashmere, china, sandwich, odyssey, valentine, bourbon, Braille, madras, spa, Chablis, dunce, canary*

V: *lynch, pander, canter, welsh, boycott, meander, hector*

A: *maudlin, zany, frank, bantam*

In other cases, however, a derivational suffix is added to convert the noun into the appropriate part of speech:

N: *sadism, chauvinism, marionette, tangerine, bayonet, bobby* ('policeman'), *panic*
V: *tantalize, pasteurize, mesmerize*
A: *quixotic, platonic, spartan, machiavellian, jovial*

3.4   Compounds

A **compound** is the combination of two or more free roots (plus associated affixes). It can sometimes be difficult to distinguish a compound – which is considered a single word – from a syntactic phrase consisting of a number of distinct words. As we saw at the beginning of the chapter, English orthography is often unhelpful: compounds may be written as a single word or as two words, hyphenated or not, e.g. *icecream, ice cream, ice-cream.* Phrases may likewise be written as separate words or hyphenated. Both compounds and phrases may express semantically cohesive notions. Compare *shipyard* and *automobile assembly plant*; the meanings of the compound and the phrase might be considered equally unified. It is sometimes pointed out that the order of elements in a compound tends to be nonliteral, while in a phrase it is literal, as in the difference between *forthcoming* and *come forth*, or *offputting* and *put off*, but this rule cannot be extended very far.

A better means of differentiation is internal coherence, since compounds are externally modified (at the single word boundary), whereas phrases may be internally modified (at any of the word boundaries). For example, the plural of the compound *manhole* is *manholes* not **menhole*, with the plural marker at the end, whereas the plural of the phrase *man-of-war* is *men-of-war* not **man-of-wars*, with the plural marker internal to the phrase. Another good means of distinguishing compounds is their external mobility; that is, they move in a sentence as a whole, not in parts. For example, the compound *cross-examination* moves as a unit (*The lawyer conducted the cross-examination, The cross-examination was conducted by the lawyer*), while part of the phrase *check out* may be moved (*He checked out the witness, He checked the witness out*). However, stress seems to offer the most reliable means of distinguishing a compound from a phrase. As a single word, a compound will carry only one primary stress, whereas a phrase, as a group of words, will carry more than one primary stress. The second half of the compound carries secondary stress and the vowel may be reduced (see Chapter 3). Compare the stress patterns in the following sets:

Compound	Phrase
stónewall	*stóne wáll*
sáfeguard	*sáfe guárd*
bréakdown	*bréak dówn*

This principle holds for compound nouns and some compound verbs. Compound adjectives, however, may carry more than one primary stress, as *dúty-frée* or *chíld-próof.*

Both the semantics and the syntax of compound are complex. Often the semantics of compounds are not simply a sum of the meaning of the parts; that is, if we know the meaning of the two roots, we cannot necessarily predict the meaning of the compound, as in *firearm*, *highball*, *makeup*, or *handout*. Note the various ways in which the meanings of the roots of these compounds interact with *home*:

homeland	'land which is one's home'
homemade	'something which is made at home'
homebody	'someone who stays at home'
homestead	'a place which is a home'
homework	'work which is done at home'
homerun	'a run to home'
homemaker	'a person who makes (cares for) the home'

The syntax of compounds is even more complex. Any combination of parts of speech seems possible, with almost any part of speech resulting. One principle which holds is that the word class of the compound is determined by the head of the compound, or its rightmost member, whereas the leftmost member carries the primary stress. The only exception to this rule is a converted compound or one containing a class changing suffix. Look at the syntactic patterns of compounding shown in Table 4.7.

Note that in addition to combining two roots, compounds may contain derivational or inflectional affixes; when the present or past participle inflectional suffix (represented by *-ing* and *-en* in Table 4.7) is added to a verb, the resulting unit functions as an adjective. Compounds may also involve conversions and back formations (discussed later in this chapter).

Self-Testing Exercise: Do Exercise 4.8 on compounding.

A problem for the differentiation of compounds and phrases is the **phrasal verb**. Older English preferred prefixed verbs, such as *forget*, *understand*, *withdraw*, *befriend*, *overrun*, *outdo*, *offset*, and *uproot* (note the position of stress on the root morpheme rather than on the prefix), but prefixing of verbs is not productive in Modern English, except for those with *out-* and *over-*. Modern English favors verbs followed by postverbal particles, such as *run over*, *lead on*, *use up*, *stretch out*, and *put down*. Like compounds, phrasal verbs have semantic coherence, evidenced by the fact that they are sometimes replaceable by single Latinate verbs, as in the following:

break out – erupt, escape	*think up – imagine*
count out – exclude	*put off – delay*
take off – depart, remove	*egg on – incite*
work out – solve	*put out – extinguish*
bring up – raise	*put away – store*
go on – continue	*take up – adopt*

Table 4.7. Syntactic Patterns in English Compounds

Compound Nouns	
N + N > N	airplane, lipstick, gold-mine, deathblow, figurehead, peppercorn
V + N > N	cut-throat, pickpocket, spoil-sport, leapfrog, drawbridge, crybaby
A + N > N	madman, blackbird, fast-food, software, hotbed, mainland, busybody
Prt + N > N	background, in-crowd, off-Broadway, afternoon
Prt + V > N	outcast, downpour, outbreak, offspring (converted prefixed or compound V)
V + Prt > N	put-down, drop-out, lockout, sit-in, fallout, runaway, drawback (converted phrasal V)
N + V > N	bloodshed, fleabite, bus-stand, sunrise, handshake, nosebleed, earthquake (converted V)
N + -'s + N > N	bachelor's degree, bull's eye, cow's milk, housemaid's knee
V + -ing + N > N	mocking bird, spending money, closing time, freezing point
N + V + ing > N	handwriting, housekeeping, foxhunting (gerund)
N + V + -er > N	hairdresser, nutcracker, landowner, peacemaker

Compound Verbs	
N + V > V	babysit, carbon-date, head-hunt, skydive, housekeep, proofread (backformations)
A + V > V	free-associate, double-book, fine-tune, whitewash, ill-treat (back-formations)
Prt + V > V	outdo, overcook, underrate, overeducate
V + V > V	blow-dry, play-act, sleep-walk, tap-dance, force-feed
A + N > V	strong-arm, blacklist, brownbag, mainstream (converted N)

Compound Adjectives	
N + A > A	headstrong, colorblind, childproof, duty-free, lifelong, carsick
A + A > A	bittersweet, icy-cold, red-hot, blue-green
N + N > A	seaside, coffee-table, back-street (converted N)[14]
A + N > A	redneck, blue-collar, solid-state (converted N)
V + Prt > A	tow-away, see-through, wrap-around (converted phrasal V)
N + V + -ing > A	man-eating, seed-bearing, heart-breaking, card-carrying, life-giving
A + V + -ing > A	easygoing, hard-hitting, good-looking, quick-cooking, high-flying
N + V + -en > A	manmade, hand-woven, housebroken, crest-fallen
A + V + -en > A	high-born, widespread, far-fetched, new-found
A + N + -ed > A	cold-blooded, thick-skinned, double-barreled, old-fashioned, public-spirited, heavy-handed

position dictates parts of speech

Furthermore, the meaning of the combination of verb and particle in the phrasal verb may be opaque, that is, not predictable from the meaning of the parts. Often, the difference in

---

14. Bauer (1983, p. 210) observes of forms like these that it might be "misleading to term them adjectives at all". They function in only very limited ways as adjectives. At the end of Chapter 5 we will look at a different way to analyze these forms.

meaning between the simple and the phrasal verb is 'completive'; the phrasal verb expresses termination or completion of the action:

burn vs. *burn down, up, on, out*	*work* vs. *work out, up*
eat vs. *eat up, through*	*wash* vs. *wash up, down, out*
pay vs. *pay up, off*	*read* vs. *read through*

Unlike compounds, however, phrasal verbs exhibit internal modification (*burn down/ burned down, burning down*), carry two primary stresses (*wórk óut*), and behave syntactically like phrases since the particle may move after the object, or an adverb may intercede between the verb and the particle:

> *He burned down the house.*
> *He burned the house down.*
> *He burned the house right down.*
> cf. **He burned right down the house. *He burned right the house down.*

For these reasons, we must conclude that phrasal verbs are phrases, not compounds.

A further problem in the analysis of compounds is **phrase compounds**, formed from entire phrases, such as *lady-in-waiting, dog-in-the-manger, forget-me-not, has-been, run-of-the-mill, break-and-enter, nuts-and-bolts, whiskey-and-soda, bubble-and-squeak,* or *son-in-law*, which are generally written as compounds (hyphenated) and have semantic unity. Many of these behave normally as compounds by being externally modified, such as *all has-beens, five whiskey-and-sodas* (rather than *whiskies-and-soda*). But some are internally modified like a phrase, as in the *all her ladies-in-waiting* or *our two sons-in-law*.[15] When they are inflected for the possessive, however, they show external modification like a compound, as in *son-in-law's (new car)*.[16] What precedes the possessive ending need not be a single-word compound but can be a phrase, as in *my neighbor next door's dog*, or even a clause, as in *a woman I know's niece*. By no criteria would *my neighbor next door* be considered a compound. Thus, phrase compounds seem to be phrasal in nature.

Another problem for analysis is **amalgamated compounds**. These are words which in origin are compounds, but which in the course of time have become fused and no longer separable into two distinct parts. Some examples are the following:

> *barn* < bere 'barley' + ærn 'place'
> *halibut* < hālig 'holy' + butte 'flatfish'
> *garlic* < gar 'spear' + lēac 'leek'
> *neighbor* < neah 'near' + gebur 'dweller'
> *cobweb* < coppe 'kind of spider' + web

---

15. These forms are increasingly taking external modification, e.g. *our two son-in-laws*.

16. Historically, this has not always been so: prior to the sixteenth century, such phrases had internal modification in the possessive, as in *kings crown of England* (= 'king of England's crown'), which has the possessive ending *-s* on *king*. Then it became possible to add the possessive ending to an entire phrase, a construction called the "group genitive".

midrif < mid + hrif 'belly'
earwig < ear + wicga 'one that moves'
mildew < mele 'honey' + dew

Since these words are no longer recognizable as compounds, all are considered single, unanalyzable morphemes.[17]

3.5   Blends

A **blend** involves two processes of word formation, compounding and "clipping" (see below). Two free words are combined and blended, usually by clipping off the end of the first word and the beginning of the second word, although sometimes one or the other morpheme is left intact. Blends are sometimes called "portmanteau" words. Examples of blends are the following:

sm(oke) + (f)og	>	*smog*
mo(tor) + (ho)tel	>	*motel*
info(rmation) + (com)mercial	>	*infomercial*
simul(taneous) + (broad)cast	>	*simulcast*
trans(fer) + (re)sistor	>	*transistor*
sky + (hi)jacker	>	*skyjacker*
motor + (caval)cade	>	*motorcade*
perma(nent) + frost	>	*permafrost*
docu(mentary) + drama	>	*docudrama*
para(chutist) + trooper	>	*paratrooper*
film + (bi)ography	>	*filmography*

In the last six examples, where one half remains intact, it might also be possible to analyze *-jacker, -cade, perma-, docu-, para-*, and *-ography* as new (and perhaps productive) derivational affixes attached to free roots (think of *paramilitary/paralegal/paramedic, discography*).

A rather interesting blend is *blog* < *web* + *log*, where only the final sound of the first word is part of the blended word.

3.6   Back formations

In **back formation**, speakers derive a morphologically simple word from a form which they analyze, on the basis of derivational and inflectional patterns existing in English, as a morphologically complex word. For example, by analogy with the very common derivational pattern in English in which the agentive suffix *-er* is added to a verb to produce a noun (*sing* + *-er* > *singer, work* + *-er* > *worker, buy* + *-er* > *buyer*), verbs have been formed from the following nouns by the removal of an agentive suffix, as in *sightseer – -er* > *sightsee*,

---

17.   In the last four examples only half of the compound is opaque (*cob-, -rif, -wig, mil-*); the other half is identifiable.

babysitter – -er > baby-sit, or *typewriter – -er > typewrite*. Since the nouns predate the verbs in these cases, we say that the verbs are "back-formed". Back formation is thus the opposite of derivation: C – B > A as opposed to A + B > C. Without knowledge of the history of an individual word, it is usually impossible to know whether related forms result from derivation or back formation. In many cases of back formation a presumed affix is removed which is in fact not truly an affix, as in the following words where the *-or*, *-ar*, and *-er* are not the agentive suffix, but part of the root:

orator – -er > orate	*lecher – -er > lech*	*peddler – -er > peddle*
escalator – -er > escalate	*editor – -er > edit*	*swindler – -er > swindle*
sculptor – -er > sculpt	*hawker – -er > hawk*	*burglar – -er > burgle*
housekeeper – -er > housekeep	*babysitter – -er > babysit*	*panhandler – -er > panhandle*

These new words are called back formations. Note that some of them are colloquial or marginal, while others are fully accepted.

Other examples of back formations are the following, where a presumed derivational suffix has been removed:

-ion	*intuition > intuit*	-ive	*sedative > sedate*
	resurrection > resurrect	-al	*paramedical > paramedic*
	emotion > emote	-asm	*enthusiasm > enthuse*
	transcription > transcript	-y	*sleazy > sleaze*
	orientation > orientate		*lazy > laze*

In the case of *joyride < joyriding* or *henpeck < henpecked*, inflectional affixes (*-ing* and *-ed*) have been removed.

3.7   Shortening

The three types of shortening – acronyms, initialisms, and clipped forms – have in common the deletion of sound segments without respect to morphological boundaries. That is, parts of words, but not usually entire morphemes, are deleted.

Clipping.   A **clipping** is the result of deliberately dropping part of a word, usually either the end or the beginning, or less often both, while retaining the same meaning and same word class, as in the following examples:

end

ad/advert < advertisement	*hack < hackney*
mike < microphone	*porn < pornography*
tarp < tarpolin	*condo < condominium*
rehab < rehabilitation	*fax < facsimile*
fan < fanatic	*mitt < mitten*

beginning

burger < hamburger	*venture < adventure*
spite < despite	*gin (cotton gin) < engine*
cello < violoncello	*phone < telephone*

beginning and end

fridge < refrigerator
flu < influenza
shrink < head-shrinker

The word *taxicab* has provided two clipped forms, *taxi* and *cab*, depending on whether the beginning or the end was clipped. Sometimes a word or part of a word in a phrase is clipped:

women's lib < women's liberation	*soap < soap opera*
high tech < high technology	*movie < moving picture*
narc < narcotics agent	*chauvinist < male chauvinist*

A diminutive affix may be attached to the clipped form, as in *movie, jammies, hankie*, and *nightie*. A clipping may leave behind a prefix or suffix rather than (part of) the root:

ex < ex-husband
bi < bi-sexual
bus < omnibus[18]

Clipping is generally not sensitive to morphological boundaries, though it does usually reflect phonological processes, selecting the longest possible syllable, what is called a maximal syllable, such as *narc* rather than *nar*.

Clippings often begin life as colloquial forms, such as the clipped forms *prof* (< *professor*), *gym* (< *gymnasium*), *chem* (< *chemistry*), *psych* (< *psychology*), or *lab* (< *laboratory*) one hears at university, but many have become fully accepted in the standard language and are no longer recognized as clipped forms.

Acronyms and initialisms.   An extreme form of clipping results in acronyms and initialisms. In an **acronym**, the initial letters of words in a phrase are pronounced as a word, as in the following examples:

WASP	<	W(hite) A(nglo)-S(axon) P(rotestant)
SALT	<	S(trategic) A(rms) L(imitation) T(alks)
NATO	<	N(orth) A(tlantic) T(reaty) O(rganization)
AIDS	<	a(cquired) i(mmune) d(eficiency) s(yndrome)
radar	<	ra(dio) d(etecting) a(nd) r(anging)
laser	<	l(ight) a(mplification) (by) s(timulated) e(mission) (of) r(adiation)
sonar	<	so(und) na(vigation) r(anging)

---

18.   In the last example, *bus* is actually part of the dative plural inflectional ending *-ibus* of the Latin word *omnis*, meaning 'all'.

Note that acronyms are not formed in an entirely systematic way; a word or words may be skipped, or the first two letters of a word may be chosen, always in order to produce a word which conforms to English phonotactics. Acronyms are written with capital letters when formed from a proper noun. In an **initialism**, the initial letters of words in a phrase are pronounced as letters, as in *r.s.v.p., a.m., p.m.,* B.C., A.D., *v.d., b.m.* (What are the sources of these initialisms? Check a dictionary if you are uncertain.) Sometimes an initialism may involve only a single word, as in *i.d.* or *t.v.* Spelling and punctuation conventions are somewhat inconsistent: periods are normally used between the letters with proper nouns indicated with capitals. In a few cases such as *okay/o.k., emcee/m.c.,* or *jeep* (for *G. P. = General Purpose*), the form is treated variously as an acronym or an initialism.

3.8   Root creations

The rarest form of word formation is **root creation**, the invention of an entirely new root morpheme. Brand names are the most likely examples of root creations (e.g. *Xerox(graphy), Oreo*), but when examined closely, they often prove to be based on existing words or names (e.g. *Levis,* named for the inventor Levi Strauss; *McDonald's,* named for the original owners Maurice and Richard McDonald; *Perrier,* named for the spring in France, itself named for Dr. Perrier; *Spandex* based on *expand; Thermos,* from the Greek word for 'warm'), or to follow patterns of word formation such as shortening or blending (e.g. *IBM,* an initialism for *International Business Machines; Q-tip,* an initialism for *quality tip; coke,* a clipped form of *Coca-cola; Jello,* a modified form of *jelly; Alka-Seltzer,* a blend of *alkali + seltzer; Amtrak,* a blend of *American + track; Botox,* a blend of *botulinum toxin; Cineplex,* a blend of *cinema + complex; Spam,* a blend of *spiced + ham*). A few recent root creations are *granola, quark,* and *googol* 'ten raised to the hundredth power'.[19] Onomatopoeic words, which in their pronunciation are imitative of animal sounds (e.g. *bow-wow, baa, cuckoo, moo, meow*) or other natural sounds (e.g. *twitter, gulp, hiss, sizzle, squeak, boom, blab*), can presumably be created at will as the need arises, though they are highly conventionalized and language-specific. Some new words are considered **literary coinages**, such as Shakespeare's *dwindle,* Milton's *sensuous,* and Spenser's *blatant* or *askance.* However, it is often difficult to know whether an author actually invented the word or whether he or she was simply the first to record it in writing.

Self-Testing Exercise: Using a dictionary, when necessary, identify the processes of word formation in Exercise 4.9.

---

19.   This word is thought to be the basis for the internet search engine, *Google,* because of the large amount of information available on the internet.

4. Idioms

A final consideration in regard to words is the existence of special kinds of phrases called idioms. An **idiom** is a sequence of words which functions as a single unit; it is syntactically fixed and semantically conventionalized. Examples include the following:

spill the beans	*saw logs*	*shoot the breeze*
keep tabs on	*add fuel to the fire*	*lose one's cool*
steal the show	*bite the dust*	*rock the boat*
take stock of	*flog a dead horse*	*hold your horses*
search high and low for	*find fault with*	*take heart*
take fright	*hit the road*	*run the gamut*
be under the weather	*let the cat out of the bag*	*be dead to the world*

Idioms have the following characteristics:

– No, or little, variation is allowed in the words that constitute the phrase, so that you can't say, for example, **hold your stallions, *bite the dirt, *shoot the wind*, or **spill the rice*. (Note that when the wording of an idiom is changed, as in *spill the rice* above, the phrase can be interpreted only literally.)

– The semantics of the idiom are usually not predictable from the meaning of the individual words; this is what linguists call "noncompositionality". For example, you can't calculate the meaning of 'being sick' or 'feeling ill' from the meanings of *under* and *weather*.

– The meaning of idioms is often thought to be metaphorical or proverbial; they are emotionally-charged rather than neutral in meaning.

– Idioms are frequently quite colloquial.

Note that some idioms, such as *sit tight* or *easy does it*, are syntactically ill-formed.

Since idioms are not like free syntactic phrases – which can be accounted for the syntactic and semantic rules of the grammar – but are rather more like single words, the question arises as to whether they should be treated in the morphological component of the grammar, that is, whether they should be treated as unanalyzable wholes. The difficulty with doing so is that there appear to be degrees of idiomaticity, with some idioms permitting syntactic changes and some being more literal in meaning than others. *Pull some strings*, for example, seems to be much less idiomatic than *shoot the breeze* in respect to its flexibility:

> internal modification:
>> *She pulled some important strings for him.*
>> *?They shot a little breeze today.*
> fronting on object:
>> *Those strings, he won't pull for you.*
>> **The breeze, we shot yesterday.*

passive:
> *Some strings were pulled for him.*
> **The breeze was shot yesterday by us.*

Like *pull some strings* are *keep tabs on, lay eyes on, break the ice*, whereas like *shoot the breeze* are *saw logs, be under the weather, kick the bucket*. We don't intend to propose an answer to the question of the analysis of idioms here, but to leave it for you to ponder. Some scholars distinguish between "collocations", fixed groups of words, and true idioms. How do you think we should account for them in our grammar?

Chapter summary

Now that you have completed this chapter, you should be able to:

1. give the criteria used to distinguish a word from a phrase;
2. define the different types of morphemes and morphs;
3. analyze a word into its constituent morphs and morphemes and specify how the morphemes are concretely realized as morphs;
4. differentiate a morpheme from an allomorph;
5. write a morphemic rule for the allomorphs of a morpheme in English;
6. explain and identify the most common processes of word formation in English; and
7. analyze derived and compound words into their constituent morphs.

Recommended additional reading

Still the most complete treatment of English morphology is Marchand (1969). Bauer (1983, see especially Chapter 7) remains a useful treatment of the topic. More up-to-date treatments include Minkova and Stockwell (2009), Carstairs-McCarthy (2002), and Harley (2006). A classic discussion of morphology in the structuralist tradition may be found in Bloomfield (1933, Chapters 13 and 14) with many interesting examples. General linguistic accounts of morphology are Matthews (1991) and Bauer (2003), and an advanced treatment in a generative framework is Spencer (1991).

Textbooks which you might want to consult for a somewhat different perspective are Plag, Braun, Lappe, and Schraum (2009, Chapter 3), Jeffries (2006, Chapter 3), Fromkin, Rodman, and Hyams (2007, Chapter 3), Klammer, Schulz, and Della Volpe (2010, Chapter 3), Finegan (2008, Chapter 2), Curzan and Adams (2009, Chapter 4), or O'Grady and Archibald (2009, Chapter 4). A workbook, with exercises and answers, is Coates (1999).

Chapter 5

Grammatical categories and word classes

1. Grammatical categories
2. Determining word classes

Chapter preview

The first half of the chapter defines the grammatical categories (number, person, gender, case, degree, definiteness, tense, aspect, mood, and voice) and the distinctions within each category, explaining how each of these categories is expressed in the different parts of speech in English. The second half of the chapter considers the classification of words using formal (inflectional and distributional) tests. Tests for the categories of noun, adjective, verb, auxiliary, and particle are examined.

Commentary

1. Grammatical categories

In the previous chapter, we introduced the distinction between lexical and grammatical morphemes, but apart from listing the inflectional affixes of English, we were – in our discussion of the processes of word formation – primarily concerned with lexical morphemes. We return now to grammatical morphemes, focusing on the diversity of their meanings and forms in English. You will recall that grammatical morphemes may be either free roots (function words) or bound affixes (inflectional suffixes). Semantically, grammatical morphemes express grammatical notions such as number or tense, what are called the **grammatical categories**. In this section, we will look in more detail at the different grammatical categories, the terms of each category (the distinctions made within each category), and the means by which they are expressed in English. In synthetic languages, such as Classical

Latin or Greek, the grammatical categories are expressed almost exclusively by inflectional endings, whereas in analytic languages, such as Present-day English or French, the grammatical categories are expressed primarily by word order (the position of a word in a sentence) and by function words, as well as by a few inflections.[1] A phrase containing a function word which is functionally equivalent to an inflection is called a **periphrasis**, or **periphrastic form**. For example, in English, we can express the possessive either by an inflection -'s (as in *Alicia's cat*) or by a periphrasis with *of* (as in *the leg of the table*).

Let us look first at the concept of a grammatical category, which is rather difficult to define. It is important to keep in mind that a grammatical category is a linguistic, not a real-world category, and that there is not always a one-to-one correspondence between the two, though they are usually closely related. For example "tense" is a linguistic category, while "time" is a category of the world. If we consider the following two past-tense forms underlined below:

> a.   I <u>saw</u> a movie last night.
> b.   I wish you <u>would</u> go.

we see that the past tense expresses past time in (a), as is usual, but that it expresses future time in (b). And if we consider the following two present-tense forms underlined below:

> a.   I <u>bite</u> my nails.
> b.   I <u>leave</u> tomorrow.

we see that the present tense expresses a timeless habit in (a) and a future time in (b), neither expressing an action occurring at the present moment. Grammatical categories can thus be identified either by formal or notional means. In the first case, we look at the formal distinctions made in a language solely by means of inflection. By these criteria, English has only two tense distinctions, past and present (as in *work/worked*). In the second case, however, there is assumed to be a universal set of grammatical categories and terms, which for tense are past, present, and future. These are expressed in English by means of inflection and, in the case of the future, by periphrasis (as in *will work*). Languages will express different subsets of these universal distinctions and will do so in different ways. We can also differentiate between overt and covert categories. Overt categories have explicit or formal realization on the relevant part of speech, such as past tense in English (the -*ed* inflection on the verb), while covert categories are expressed only implicitly by the cooccurrence of particular function words, such as the future tense in English (the *will* auxiliary occurring with the verb). Finally, we must decide whether a distinction is expressed systematically

---

1.   Languages are situated on a cline between these language types. A language such as Modern German, for example, is more synthetic than Present-day English but more analytical than classical Latin. Modern French is probably somewhat more synthetic than Present-day English.

and regularly in a language, by a regular grammatical marker, or whether it is expressed idiosyncratically and lexically, by the meaning of content words. For example, the distinction "dual" (the concept of 'two') is expressed grammatically in Old English by special forms of the personal pronouns, that is, by *wit* 'we two' and *git* 'you two'. In Present-day English dual is expressed lexically only with the words *both* or *two*, not grammatically by an inflection or function word.

The following inventory of grammatical categories proceeds through the nominal categories (number, gender, person, case, degree, definiteness) and then the verbal categories (tense, aspect, mood, and voice).

1.1 Number

The first category, **number,** is relatively simple. There are two terms of this category in English: singular (the concept of 'one') and plural (the concept of 'more than one'). Number is expressed by inflection in:

–   count nouns, generally by -s (*dog/dogs*)
–   demonstratives (*this/these, that/those*)
–   the 1st and 3rd p (but not in the 2nd p) of pronouns
    personal pronouns (*I/we*)
    possessive determiners (*my/our*)
    possessive pronouns (*mine/ours*)
    reflexive pronouns (*myself/ourselves*)

> **HINT:** For historical reasons the idiosyncratic forms of the personal pronouns are considered "inflected forms", though they do not always contain separable inflectional endings.

Number is also expressed by distinct forms of certain pronouns and adjectives:

–   singular: *every, each, someone, anybody, a/an*
–   plural: *all, many, few, several, most*

It is also indicated in a limited way in verbs, by the singular -s of the 3rd p which occurs in the present but not in the past tense (*he writes* versus *they write, he wrote*). Number is expressed more fully in the inflected forms of the verb BE (singular *am, is, was*, plural *are, were*), which because of its high frequency, tends to preserve inflections more fully than do other verbs.[2]

---

2.   The history of the English language has involved a gradual loss of inflections in all parts of speech.

The concept of **generic number**, which incorporates both singular and plural and is used when one doesn't want to specify number, is expressed in English in three ways:

1. the definite article + singular noun (*The tiger may be dangerous*),
2. the indefinite article + singular noun (*A tiger may be dangerous*), and
3. Ø article + plural of count nouns or singular of mass nouns (*Tigers may be dangerous* or *Gold is valuable*).

Finally, an "odd" use of number is use of the plural when singular is denoted, in the so-called "royal *we*" or "editorial *we*".

1.2   Gender

English has a rather straightforward system of gender called **natural gender**, in which gender distinctions made in language depend upon the sex of the object in the real world. English distinguishes masculine, feminine, **common gender** (m or f), and neuter (sexless) genders.

> **HINT:** A system of gender found in many languages, such as German, French, or Italian, as well as in an earlier stage of English, is called **grammatical gender**. Grammatical gender appears to be arbitrary, not related to the sex of the object denoted, as in German *das Mädchen* 'the girl' (neuter gender) or French *le jour* 'the day' (masculine gender) or Italian *la vita* 'the life' (feminine gender). Historically, there is probably motivation for grammatical gender since it serves as a means of subcategorizing nouns, but for the contemporary speaker, the motivation is generally not obvious.

In English, gender is expressed by inflection only in personal pronouns, and only in the 3rd person, singular *he*, *she*, *it*; the 1st and 2nd person forms *I*, *we*, and *you* are common gender, while the 3rd person plural form *they* is either common gender or neuter (*the people … they, the boats … they*). Relative and interrogative pronouns and some other pronouns inflectionally express a related category of "animacy" (animate/inanimate): *somebody/one* vs. *something, anybody/one* vs. *anything, who, whom* vs. *what, which*. Distinctions of animacy are variable, but commonly speakers distinguish between human beings and higher animals (*the {woman, dog} who …*) and lower animals and inanimate things (*the {ant, stone} which …*).

There is nothing about the morphological form of nouns such as *boy* and *girl* which would indicate that they are masculine or feminine gender. Instead, gender is shown by the cooccurrence of relevant pronouns, *he* and *she*, which refer back to the noun: *the boy … he, the girl … she*. Thus, we say that gender is a covert category of the noun.[3] However, gender may also be expressed overtly on the English noun in a number of limited ways:

---

3. It is also generally the case in languages with grammatical gender that the accompanying article or demonstrative, not the shape of the noun, reveals its gender.

1. by derivational suffixes, such as the feminine suffixes *-ine* (*hero/heroine*), *-ess* (*god/god-dess*), *-rix* (*aviator/aviatrix*), and *-ette* (*suffragist/suffragette*) or the common gender suffixes *-er* (*baker*), *-ist* (*artist*), *-ian* (*librarian*), *-ster* (*prankster*), and *-ard* (*drunkard*);
2. by compounds, such as *lady-, woman-, girl-, female-, -woman* (*lady friend, woman doctor, girl friend, female fire fighter, chairwoman*) or *boy-, male-, gentleman-, -man* (*boy friend, male nurse, gentleman caller, chairman*);
3. by separate forms for masculine, feminine, and common genders, such as *boy/girl/child* or *rooster/hen/chicken*; and
4. by separate forms for masculine and feminine genders, such as *uncle/aunt, stallion/mare, bachelor/spinster* and proper names such as *Joseph/Josephine, Henry/Henrietta*.

You can see that none of these means is systematic. It is significant that the feminine is always derived from the masculine, except in the case of *widow/widower*,[4] presumably because women outlive men. Also, it is typical for the masculine form to double as the common gender form, as with *dog* (cf. the feminine form *bitch*), though in the case of *cow/bull, goose/gander* or *drake/duck*, the feminine form is the common gender form, presumably because the female is more important in the barnyard economy.

The marked use of the feminine gender with ships, cars, countries, fortune, art, music, and nature in Present-day English is sometimes considered a remnant of grammatical gender, as in:

> *Isn't she a beauty?* (referring to a car or a ship)
> *Every country must defend her sovereignty.*
> *Fate has exacted her revenge.*
> *Mother Nature can be cruel.*

But it is better seen either as a kind of personification or what George Curme calls "gender of animation", by which the object is animated and an emotional attachment is expressed. The use of neuter gender with babies (*What a cute baby. What's its name?*) or callers (*A person is calling for you. Who is it?*) is an expediency used when the gender is unknown.

The lack of a common gender for the 3rd person singular, especially for use following a singular indefinite pronoun such as *each* or *every*, has long been a source of difficulty in English. Traditionally, the masculine form has been used for the generic (e.g. *Every child should put on his coat*), but this expediency is now out-of-favor. In fact, the use of the plural *their*, which is gender-neutral but which violates number agreement (e.g. *Every child should put on their coat*), has a long history and is very common in Present-day English. Forms such as *his or her, his/her, s/he* (e.g. *Every child should put on his or her coat*) are newer attempts to correct this deficiency.

---

4. Also perhaps in the case of *ballerina/ballet dancer,* though the musculine is a compound, not a simple form.

1.3   Person

The category of **person** has three terms:

> 1st person: the speaker, person speaking;
> 2nd person: the addressee/hearer, person spoken to; and
> 3rd person: the person or thing spoken about.

Person distinctions are expressed by the inflected forms of the pronouns, for example:

personal pronouns:	*I*	*you*	*he, they*
personal possessive determiners:	*my*	*your*	*his, their*
personal possessive pronouns	*mine*	*yours*	*his, theirs*
personal reflexive pronouns	*myself*	*yourself*	*himself, themselves*

As *I* denotes the person speaking, the referent of *I* changes depending on who is speaking; the referent of *I* is always related to the specific speech situation. This means that the personal pronouns are what linguists call "deictic",[5] that is, an expression whose meaning depends upon the time and place of speaking (the speaker's here and now).

Nouns are all 3rd person, but this is shown only covertly by the cooccurrence of pronouns: *the house … it (*I, *you), the houses … they (*we, *you).*

Person is also expressed inflectionally in the singular, present tense, indicative of verbs by the *-s* inflection on the 3rd person (but on no other persons or numbers): *she/he/it writes* vs. *I/you/we/they write.*

> **HINT:** Both number and person are expressed more fully in the verb BE, which because of its high frequency tends to preserve inflections more fully than do other verbs. Hence, we have
> singular *am, is, was* vs. plural *are, were*
> 1st person *I am/was, we are/were* vs. 2nd person *you are/were* vs.
> 3rd person *he/she/it is/was, they are/were*

The form *one* expresses **generic person** (all persons) in English, but since it is often considered rather formal, it coexists with other forms that also express generic:

1st p pl	we	*We're often misinformed by the media.*
2nd p	you	*You never can tell.*
3rd p sg	one	*One doesn't do that in polite company.*
3rd p pl	they	*They'll find a cure for cancer soon.*

---

5.   The term *deictic* is from the Greek word meaning 'to point'.

The generic *you* is the most common in informal usage. Finally, a few apparently deviant uses of person are the following:

3rd p for 2nd p	*your excellency, your honor*
3rd p for 1st p	*present company, the writer, your teacher,*
	Caesar (spoken by Caesar himself)
1st p for 2nd p	*we won't do that anymore, will we* (spoken by a parent to a child)

Finally, an interesting use of the personal pronouns is for social purposes, to mark a person who is socially close to or remote from the speaker, such as the use of *tu/vous* in French or *du/Sie* in German. For example, when asking in German *Have you eaten everything?*, one can say *Hast du* [familiar form] *alles gegessen?* when addressing an intimate or child in an informal context, or *Haben Sie* [formal form] *alles gegessen?* when addressing a more distant acquaintance or stranger in a formal context.

1.4 Case

Case may be defined rather simply as an indication of the function of a noun phrase, or the relationship of a noun phrase to a verb or to other noun phrases in the sentence. Case is most fully expressed in the personal and interrogative/relative pronouns, which distinguish **nominative case** (the function of subject), **genitive case** (the function of possessor), and **objective case** (the function of object) by different inflected forms:

nominative:	*I, we, you, he, she, it, they, who;*
genitive:	*my/mine, our/ours, his, her/hers, its, their/theirs, whose;* and
objective:	*me, us, you, him, her, it, them, whom.*

There is no distinction between the nominative and objective form of *it*, nor of *you* (though historically the nominative form was *ye*, as in the archaic expression *Hear ye, hear ye*). The genitive includes forms which function as determiners, such as *my* and *our*, as well as forms which function as pronouns, such as *mine* or *ours*.

Nouns differentiate inflectionally between the nongenitive, or **common**, **case** and the genitive:

common case	genitive case
cat, cats	*cat's, cats'*
man, men	*man's, men's*

While orthographically there appear to be four distinct forms of nouns when singular and plural, common and genitive case are considered, you should keep in mind that the apostrophe is merely orthographic so that the forms *cats*, *cat's*, and *cats'* are phonologically indistinguishable. Only irregular plurals such as the noun *man* actually distinguish four forms both orthographically and phonologically.

Beyond this, nouns can be said to distinguish nominative and objective case only by word order, by the placement of the noun before or after the verb, respectively, in the usual positions for subject and object in a Subject-Verb-Object language such as English. Hence, in the sentence *The ship struck the dock*, "the ship" could be called nominative case and "the dock" objective case, though morphologically both are common case. This ordering principle is so strong that it may even override grammatical principles. The sentence *Who did you see?* is more natural than the grammatically correct *Whom did you see?* because in this structure the object (*who*) precedes rather than follows the verb, so the nominative form *who* is preferred. Another case distinction which can be made is **dative case** (the function of indirect object); this is really a subcategory of the objective case. It is shown by periphrasis with *to* or *for* or by word order (V iO dO): *He gave the book to Jane, He gave Jane the book*.

What we have just presented is a simplified picture of case usage:

- There are other traditional cases (such as the "instrumental" case) which are expressed only periphrastically in Present-day English, for example, with the prepositions *with* or *from* (*I broke the glass with a rock*).
- There are many conventional uses of cases, such as use of the nominative case after the verb BE (e.g. *It is I*)
- The same function can be expressed by different cases, as in instances where the concept of possession is expressed by either the genitive or dative case (e.g. *The book is <u>mine</u>, The book belongs <u>to me</u>*).
- One case can express several different functions or meanings.

The genitive case is an excellent example of this latter situation. It does not simply express the notion of possessor, but it indicates a variety of other notions. The following types of genitives have been identified, based on the meaning relationship between the noun in the genitive and the head noun:

possessive genitive:	*Felix's car, Maureen's inheritance*
subjective genitive:	*the movie star's entrance, the hero's actions*
objective genitive:	*the city's reconstruction, the play's conclusion*
genitive of origin:	*Shakespeare's plays, the baker's cakes*
descriptive genitive:	*person of integrity, a woman of courage*
genitive of measure:	*an hour's time, a stone's throw*
partitive genitive:	*a member of the crowd, a spoke of the wheel*
appositive genitive:	*the city of Vancouver, the state of California*

Only the first, the possessive genitive, expresses the prototypical meaning of the genitive: *Felix owns his car*. In contrast, the "subjective genitive" expresses the same relation as a subject does to a verb (*the movie star enters*), while the "objective genitive" expresses the same relation as a direct object does to a verb (*X reconstructs the city*); it is certainly not the case that the movie star owns her entrance or that the city owns its destruction. The "genitive of origin" expresses the source, person, or place from which something originates. The "descriptive genitive" is usually expressed periphrastically; the genitive noun is often equivalent to a descriptive adjective, as in *man of wisdom* = 'wise man'. The "genitive of measure" expresses an extent of time or space, the "partitive genitive" the whole in relation to a part. Finally, the genitive noun of the "appositive genitive" renames the head noun.

> **HINT:** Although the genitive can be expressed inflectionally with *'s* or periphrastically with *of NP*, it is not always possible to substitute one means of expression for the other. For example, while *the Queen's arrival* is interchangeable with *the arrival of the Queen*, *a person of integrity* is not interchangeable with **an integrity's person* nor is *a stone's throw* interchangeable with **a throw of a stone*. Certain types of genitives, such as the partitive, descriptive, or appositive, are typically expressed only periphrastically.

The phrase *the shooting of the hunters* is ambiguous between subjective and objective genitive readings because it can mean either 'the hunters shoot X' or 'X shoots the hunters'. *The child's picture* is likewise ambiguous – has the child drawn the picture or has someone taken the picture of the child? And *the woman's book* could be ambiguous between the possessive genitive and the genitive of origin – does the woman own the book or has she written the book?

Another complex aspect of the genitive is the **double genitive**, in which periphrastic and inflectional forms cooccur: *a friend of Rosa's, no fault of his*. The double genitive is necessarily indefinite (**the friend of Rosa's*) and a human inflected genitive (**a leg of the table's*). It normally has a partitive sense (= 'one friend among all of Rosa's friends), though it is also possible to use it when Rosa has only one friend. Contrast *a portrait of the king's* (= 'one among all the portraits (of others) that the king owns') and *a portrait of the king* (= 'a portrait which depicts the king').

1.5 Degree

Degree, unlike the nominal categories that we have been discussing, is a category that relates to adjectives and adverbs. It has three terms, **positive, comparative,** and **superlative degree.** While positive degree expresses a quality, comparative degree expresses a greater degree or intensity of the quality in one of two items, and superlative degree expresses the greatest degree or intensity of the quality in one of three or more items. The positive degree is expressed by the root of the adjective (e.g. *big, beautiful*) or adverb (e.g. *fast, quickly*) – that is, it is null-realized – while the comparative and superlative degrees are expressed either by inflection (by means of *-er, -est*) or by periphrasis (using *more, most*):

positive	Ø	*big*	*fast*	*beautiful*	*quickly*
comparative	-er, more	*bigger*	*faster*	*more beautiful*	*more quickly*
superlative	-est, most	*biggest*	*fastest*	*most beautiful*	*most quickly*

Whether the inflection or the periphrasis is used depends upon the phonological shape of the root. The inflection is used with:

monosyllabic forms   *neater, thinner, wider*
certain disyllabic forms
      -y   *holier*   *-le*   *littler*
      -er   *bitterer*   *-ow* *narrower*
    -some *handsomer*

All other forms occur in the periphrasis, including adverbs ending in *-ly* (e.g. **quicklier*). Lesser degree can be expressed periphrastically with *less* and *least*, as in *less big, least beautiful*. Sometimes, the three degrees of a particular word are expressed by different roots, as in *bad/worse/worst* or *good/better/best*. This is called **suppletion**. The paradigm of the adjective *old* (*older/elder, oldest/eldest*) shows irregularities but is not suppletive; the irregular forms *elder/eldest* are specialized semantically to refer to familial relations, while the regular forms *older/oldest* are used in all other functions. An interesting set of inflected forms is *nigh, near, next*; the positive form has been lost, the old comparative has become the positive, new comparative and superlative have developed (*near/nearer/nearest*), and the superlative form no longer exhibits degree.

> **HINT:** For semantic reasons, not all adjectives can be inflected for degree, such as *perfect, unique, round, full, empty, married*, and *dead*. These adjectives are incomparable because they express absolute qualities. Something is either 'dead' or not; it cannot be more or less dead. Superlatives such as *most unique* are thus logically impossible, though one frequently hears such forms, where either *most* can only be understood as an emphatic or *unique* can be understood as meaning 'unusual'.

A form such as *best time, rudest remark*, or *closest of friends* often expresses a high degree rather than a true comparison, with the superlative equivalent to 'very'. Finally, it is also common to hear the superlative used in the comparison of two items, as in *put your best foot forward, the most advantageous of two alternatives*.

1.6   Definiteness

The concepts of definiteness and indefiniteness are intuitively quite simple: definite denotes a referent (a thing in the real world denoted by a noun) which is known, familiar, or identified to the speaker and hearer, while indefinite denotes a referent which is novel, unfamiliar, or not known. If we consider nouns on their own, definiteness is a covert category, obvious only in the cooccurrence of an article with a noun, either the **definite article** *the* or the **indefinite article** *a/an*, though all proper nouns and most pronouns are intrinsically definite. In actual practice, definiteness can be quite confusing. First, it intersects with the category of specificity.[6] Second, article usage in English is complex and in many instances arbitrary. There are several different uses for each article, articles are often omitted, and there are dialectal differences in the use of articles. Thus, article usage can be an area of grammar which is very difficult for nonnative speakers to master.

In broad outline, the major uses of *the* are the following:

1.   for something previously mentioned: *yesterday I read a book … the book was about space travel* (This is the **anaphoric**, or 'pointing back', function of the definite article);
2.   for a unique or fixed referent: *the Prime Minister, the Lord, the <u>Times</u>, the Suez Canal*;
3.   for a generic referent: *(I love) the piano, (We are concerned about) the unemployed*;
4.   for something which is part of the immediate socio-physical context or generally known: *the doorbell, the kettle, the sun, the weather*;
5.   for something identified by a modifying expression either preceding or following the noun: *the gray horse, the house at the end of the block*; and
6.   for converting a proper noun to a common noun: *the England he knew, the Shakespeare of our times, the Hell I suffered*.

> **HINT:** Article usage with proper nouns often depends on the category of proper nouns (e.g. *Lake Superior* vs. *The Red Sea*; *The Mississippi River* vs. *Cache Creek*) or even on the specific example within a category (e.g. *The Sudan* vs. *Ethiopia*; *Sears Tower* vs. *The Eiffel Tower*; *Washington Monument* vs. *The Lincoln Memorial*). One useful rule of thumb is that proper nouns with *-s* (in the plural form) generally take the definite article: *The Everglades, The Great Plains, The Rocky Mountains, The Seychelles*.

Many times in actual usage the definite article is omitted when it would be expected:

–   with institutions (e.g. *at school*)
–   with means of transportation (e.g. *by car*)
–   with times of day (e.g. *at noon*)
–   with meals (e.g. *at breakfast*), and
–   with illnesses (e.g. *have malaria*).

These omissions are not always possible to predict and may depend on dialect.

The major uses of *a/an* are the following:

1.   for something mentioned for the first time (see above);
2.   for something which cannot or need not be identified: *(I want) a friend*;
3.   for a generic referent: *(He is) a teacher*;

---

6.   This topic is taken up in Chapter 11.

4.   equivalent to 'any' : *a (any) good book*;[7]
5.   equivalent to 'one' : *a week or two*; and
6.   for converting a proper noun to a common noun: *a virtual Mozart, a real Einstein*.

Self-Testing Exercise: Do Exercise 5.1 on nominal categories.

1.7   Tense

We turn now to categories that relate to the verb. The first such category is **tense**, which, in simple terms, is the linguistic indication of the time of an action. In fact, tense establishes a relation: it indicates the time of an event in respect to the moment of speaking (or some other reference point). If we consider the time line below, for example, we see that a past-time statement, such as *It rained*, or a future-time statement, such as *It will rain*, denotes a situation that did hold before the present moment or will hold after the present moment, respectively:

Past   Present   Future

This relational aspect of tense makes it a "deictic" category, since whether a situation is past, present, or future depends upon the moment of speaking and changes as that moment changes.

HINT: You should remember that adverbs are also a common means of expressing time in language. Temporal adverbs may be either deictic, expressing time in relation to the speaker and moment of speaking, such as *then/now/then, yesterday/today/tomorrow* (i.e. past, present, future), or nondeictic, expressing absolute time, either calendric, such as *Tuesday*, or clock, such as *at 4:00*. Tense, on the other hand, is always deictic.

The only tense distinction expressed inflectionally in English is that between present and past, as in *walk/walked* or *sing/sung*, even though it is conventional to talk about a three-way distinction between past, present, and future tense. However, the future is expressed periphrastically and thus is not formally parallel to the past and present.

Beginning with an examination of the uses of the **present tense** form in English, we find that it is not, in fact, used to denote actions which are actually going on at the present time. For this, the present progressive is used, as in *I am reading at this moment*, not **I read at this moment*. Instead, the present is used for the expression of a number of other types

---

7.   "Generic" makes reference to a (characteristic) member of the class (e.g. *A book makes a good travel companion*); 'any' is indifferent in its reference to a particular member of the class (e.g. *I need a book to read on my trip*).

of temporal as well as nontemporal situations; for this reason, the term *nonpast* is preferred to *present*:

1. habits: *I walk to work everyday. She smokes. We eat dinner at 6:00.*
2. states: *She lives at home. I like chocolate. I believe you. I have lots of work to do. The dog sees well. I feel sick.*
3. generic statements: *Beavers build dams. Tigers are ferocious.*
4. timeless statements: *The sun sets in the west. Summer begins on June 21st. Two plus two is four.*
5. gnomic (proverbial) statements: *A stitch in time saves nine. Haste makes waste.*
6. future statements: *We leave tomorrow. I see the doctor this afternoon.*
7. instantaneous commentary: *He shoots; he scores. Now I beat in two eggs. He pulls a rabbit out of the hat.*
8. plot summary: *Hamlet dies at the end of the play. Emma marries Mr. Knightley.*
9. narration in the present (the "historical present"): *Then he says …*
10. information present: *I hear/see that Manfred has been promoted.*

A habit indicates a series of events that are characteristic of a period. These events constitute a whole. For habits to exist, the event (of walking to work, smoking, etc.) need not actually be going on at the present moment. States include nondynamic situations such as:

– emotional states (*love*),
– cognitive states (*understand*),
– perceptual states (*feel*),
– bodily sensations (*ache*), and
– expressions of having and being (*own, resemble*)

A generic statement says something ('being ferocious') about a class of things ('tigers'). Note that the difference between a state such as *I am happy* and a generic statement such as *Tigers are ferocious*, in addition to the nongeneric (*I*) vs. generic (*tigers*) subject, is that the state refers to a specific situation and can occur with adverbs such as *still, already, not yet* (e.g. *I am still happy/*Tigers are still ferocious*). Timeless statements express eternal truths and laws of nature. Gnomic statements express proverbs, which though similar to eternal truths, aren't necessarily timeless. Futures expressed with the simple present generally refer to situations that are predetermined and fixed. Instantaneous commentary occurs in sports reporting, cooking demonstrations, and magic shows, though the progressive is also possible in these contexts. This is the only use of the nonpast form for actions actually going on at the current moment. The present is used in summarizing works of literature and in talking about artists as artistic figures, though not as actual persons (*Shakespeare is the greatest writer in English* vs. *Shakespeare was born in Stratford on Avon*). The historical present is the use of present tense for narrating informal stories and jokes, though it is being used increasingly frequently in serious literature. Finally, the information present is the use of present tense with verbs of hearing or seeing where one might expect the past tense.

The uses of the **past tense** are more unified; generally it denotes a past time divorced from, or distinct from, the present moment:

1. an event or a state in past time: *Haydn composed the symphony in 1758* or *Handel lived in England for a number of years;*
2. narration: *Two days after the war ended, my sister Laura drove a car off a bridge* (Atwood, 2000, p. 1)
3. past habit: *I drove to work last year.*

The past tense is the usual tense of narration (even for narratives set in the future!). If the simple past denotes a past habit, an appropriate time adverbial is required; however, there is also a special past habitual form, *used to*, as in *I used to drive to work*, which does not normally require a time adverbial. The past tense may also be used nontemporally for purposes of the politeness or to denote the unreal:

4. politeness: *I was hoping you would help.* (present hope; future help)
5. hypothetical: *If you studied more, you would do better.*

These are "modal" uses of the past, as we will discuss more fully below.

As noted above, the **future tense** is expressed by a variety of periphrases as well as by the inflected simple tense:

1. *will/shall* + infinitive: *I will help you tomorrow.*
2. the simple present: *The party begins at 4:00.*
3. the present progressive: *We're having guests for dinner.*
4. *be going to, be about to* + infinitive: *The child is going to be sick. The boat is about to leave.*
5. *shall/will* + the progressive: *I will be moving next week.*

All of the forms of the future are subtly different in meaning. For example, *It's going to rain today* or *It's about to rain* might be uttered while looking up at a threatening rain cloud, while *It will rain today* could only be the prediction of the meteorologist or a report of this person's prediction, but *It rains today* is distinctly odd because it denotes the future as fact, or predetermined, and as punctual; the progressive *It's raining today* could not function as a future in this instance either. *It will be raining today (when you want to mow the lawn)* is possible if it denotes a situation surrounding another event. Note that commands (e.g. *Wash the dishes!*) always carry a future meaning as well since you cannot command someone to do something in the past nor to be doing something at the present moment. Despite the designation of future as a tense, however, it bears a closer relation to modality than to tense since it expresses what is not (yet) fact (see below).

1.8   Aspect

The so-called "compound tenses" – the perfect and the progressive – are better treated as expressions of the category of **aspect**, which can be defined as the view taken of an event, or the "aspect" under which it is considered, basically whether it is seen as complete and whole (**perfective aspect**) or as incomplete and ongoing (**imperfective aspect**). The simple past tense in English is perfective in aspect since it views events as complete and whole, e.g. *Yesterday, I drove to town, ran some errands, and visited with my friends.* The **progressive** periphrasis, consisting of BE + the present participle, presents actions as in progress, ongoing, and incomplete (not yet ended). It thus expresses imperfective aspect. It is the usual way to express a situation happening at the very moment of speaking, which by definition is incomplete. However, depending upon the temporal nature of the situation expressed by the verb – whether it is punctual (e.g. *flash, solve*) or durative (e.g. *swim, clean*)[8] – the progressive may denote somewhat different situations:

– a continuous activity: *She is swimming. They were cleaning the house when I called.*
– a repeated activity ("iterative aspect"): *He is bouncing the ball. The light was flashing when I entered the house. He is washing dishes (*a dish). People (*a person) will be leaving early.*
– a process leading up to an endpoint: *The child is finishing the puzzle. She was solving the problem when she was interrupted.*

Note that in all cases, the activity in question is ongoing and hence not complete, either at the present moment or in reference to some time in the past (expressed in the *when*-clause).

> HINT: The progressive is generally incompatible with static situations since they are nondynamic and hence cannot been seen as ongoing or in progress, e.g. **I am liking chocolate, *I am having lots of work to do.*[9]

Both the meaning and categorization of the other periphrasis in English, the **perfect**, consisting of HAVE + the past participle, pose difficulties for scholars. However, it is widely agreed that the perfect is an aspect category (rather than a tense category) and that it presents the "current relevance" of a past event. The past event is relevant either by its continuation into the present or by its results in the present. When a state or event that has duration, that is, that extends over a period of time, is expressed in the perfect, it denotes a situation

---

8.   The topic is treated in more detail in the next chapter.

9.   There are a number of "marked" uses of the progressive with state verbs, such as to change a state verb into a dynamic one (e.g. *Fred is being very silly* = 'behaving in a silly way'), to indicate a temporary state (e.g. *She is living with her parents this summer*), to denote a waxing or waning state (e.g. *Gasoline is costing a lot these days, I'm understanding economics better now*), or for purposes of politeness (e.g. *I'm not recalling your name*).

that began in the past but continues to the present and possibly beyond (e.g. *she has stayed for a week*). This is called a "continuative perfect". When an event that is punctual or has a necessary endpoint is expressed in the perfect, it denotes a situation that is completed but has results in the present (e.g. *she has opened the door*). This is called the "resultative perfect".

continuative:	
state	*I have lived here since childhood.*
habit	*She has sung in the choir for ten years.*
activity (continuous)	*The preacher has talked for the last hour.*
activity (iterative)	*The child has coughed all night.*
resultative:	
activity with a necessary endpoint	*She has recovered from the flu.*
	I have read the novel.
punctual event	*I have lost my keys.*
	I have just seen a movie star.

The perfect differs from the simple past in the following way. While *I have eaten breakfast (today/*yesterday)* would imply that one is still full (and could be said only in the morning), *I ate breakfast (today/yesterday)* would have no such implication (and could be said at any time of the day or subsequent days). Similarly, *I have lost my keys* could not be uttered if one had subsequently found one's keys, though *I lost my keys* could be. Expressions such as *I have read that novel* belong to the subcategory of "perfect of experience". Here the event ('reading that novel') occurred at least once in the past; the present results that it has may not be tangible results, as in the case of finding one's keys, but the results may be in the memory of the subject *I* (the subject's recollection of the novel). The last example of the resultative perfect given above (*I have just seen a movie star*) belongs to the subcategory of the perfect which one linguist calls "hot news perfect"; here, the simple past would be equally possible (and would be more common in North American English: *I just saw a movie star*).

The aspectual periphrases combine with tense forms – tense is expressed on the auxiliary verb BE or HAVE– to give the following forms:

present progressive:	*she is singing*	action ongoing at the present moment
past progressive:	*she was singing*	action ongoing at some moment in the past
future progressive:	*she will be singing*	action ongoing at some moment in the future
present perfect:	*she has sung*	past action with results in the present
past perfect:	*she had sung*	past action with results at some past moment or completed prior to some past moment
future perfect:	*she will have sung*	future action with results at some future moment or completed prior to some future moment

> **HINT:** The two aspectual periphrases may also combine in the order perfect + progressive, as in *I have been reading the novel for the last hour*, to express an action which has been ongoing from some moment in the past to the present (and possibly beyond). What would the past + perfect + progressive (e.g. *I had been reading the novel for the last hour*) and future + perfect + progressive (e.g. *I will have been reading the novel for the last hour*) mean?

A number of other aspectual periphrases in English distinguish the beginning of situations, the continuation of situations, and the end or termination of situations, e.g. *It started/continued/stopped raining*.[10] In contrast to the perfect aspect, we can recognize a "prospective aspect" consisting of BE + infinitive, e.g. *she is to see her doctor tomorrow*. The "habitual aspect", which views a situation as repeated on different occasions, has been treated in the discussion of the nonpast and past tenses above.

1.9   Mood

Simply defined, mood is an indication of the speaker's attitude towards what he or she is talking about, whether the event is considered fact or nonfact. The **indicative** is the mood of fact; it is expressed by the simple and compound tenses of the verb. Nonfact encompasses a number of different degrees of reality, including wishes, desires, requests, warnings, prohibitions, commands, predictions, possibilities, and contrary-to-fact occurrences. It has two primary subcategories, the imperative and the subjunctive.

The **imperative** is a one of the two nonfact moods. It is used to expresses direct commands. In English the imperative has a special syntactic form: it is a subjectless sentence containing a bare form of the verb, as in *Go!, Be quiet!, Don't disturb me!*. The imperative is addressed to a second person *you*. There are also an imperative with *let's* addressed to the 1st person plural, to oneself and to others present, as a kind of suggestion (e.g. *Let's see a movie tonight*) and an imperative with *let* addressed to the 3rd person (e.g. *Let him see to that*).[11]

The **subjunctive** is the other non-fact mood. In Present-day English, the subjunctive is expressed by the modal auxiliaries or their phrasal equivalents, as in:

He *may* leave.	You *shouldn't* wait.
I *can't* find my keys.	*Would* you pass the salt?
It *might* rain.	You *ought to* try harder.
I *have to* run an errand.	We *have got to* be more careful.

---

10.   These aspects will be treated further in Chapter 10.

11.   The 1st person imperative with *let's* must be distinguished from a true 2nd p command *Let us stay up late tonight*, spoken, for example, by children to their parents (= 'allow us to stay up late tonight').

Modal adverbs such as *maybe, possibly*, or *perhaps* are also used, as are modal adjectives such as *possible, probable*, or *necessary*. A more colloquial, but very common, means of expressing the subjunctive is by the use of first-person parentheticals, or what have been called comment clauses: *He would be happy to help, I think* or *You're right, I guess.*

In earlier stages of English, the subjunctive was expressed by special inflected forms of the verb, as it still is in many of the European languages such as French, German, and Spanish. In Present-day English, most inflected subjunctives have disappeared (and been replaced by modal auxiliaries). However, a few remnant forms of the inflected subjunctive remain in Present-day English; they are identifiable by the lack of *-s* in the 3rd p sg pres and by use of *be* for all persons and numbers of the present tense and of *were* for the past tense. In main clauses, these remnants tend to be highly formulaic, such as *Long live the Queen, Have mercy on us, Heaven preserve us, Be that as it may, Suffice it to say*, or *Far be it from me*.[12] In dependent clauses, they are restricted to a few contexts:

- *that*-clauses following verbs such as *insist, suggest, recommend, move, beg, ask, be required* (*I recommend that he leave*);[13] adjectives such as *advisable, imperative, desirable* (*It is advisable that he leave*); and nouns such as *decision, requirement, resolution* (*It is a requirement that that he leave*). (The use of the subjunctive here is more common in North American than in British English.)
- *if*-clauses: *If she had the time* … , *If we were rich* … , … *as if he liked it, if only he were smarter* … [14]
- clauses following verbs of wishing: *I wish I were rich.*

In the latter two cases, the indicative is rapidly replacing the subjunctive, that is, *If I was rich* rather than *If I were rich*. Note that these cases resemble the "polite" use of the past tense discussed above. Finally, another means of expressing the subjunctive is by means of inversion: *Had I the time …, Were I in control …* .

1.10   Voice

The category of voice, though usually considered a category of the verb, is actually relevant to the entire sentence. Voice is an indication of whether the subject is performing the action of the verb or being something (**active voice**) or whether the subject is being

---

12.   While a form such as *God save the Queen* might resemble a command to God to save the Queen, it differs from a command in having an explicit 3rd p subject; furthermore, it would be quite presumptuous to command God to do anything.

13.   Note that the indicative would be *I recommend that he leaves*; it is only in the 3rd p sing that the difference between indicative and subjunctive is obvious since the other persons and numbers have no *-s* ending on the verb.

14.   Subjunctives in *whether-, though-,* or *lest-*clauses (e.g. *I wonder whether that be true or not*) are now obsolete.

affected by the action or being acted upon (**passive voice**). While the active is expressed by the simple forms of the verb, the passive is expressed periphrastically:

- by BE + the past participle, as in *The report was written (by the committee)*; or
- by GET + the past participle, as in *The criminal got caught (by the police)*.

The difference between the *be*-passive and the *get*-passive is that the former focuses on the resultant state ('the report is in a written state') while the latter focuses on the action bringing about the state.

> HINT: In the passive, the logical subject – the agent – moves out of the position of grammatical subject and is relegated to a *by*-phrase. However, it is common to delete the *by*-phrase in the passive, to omit mention altogether of the agent who performed the action. This is a manifestation of one of the rhetorical functions of the passive (see Chapter 11).

Another distinction of voice is the "middle" voice, in which the action of the verb reflects back upon the subject; in English, the middle is generally expressed with a reflexive pronoun (a form in -*self*), which indicates the sameness of the subject and the object, as in *Henry shaved (himself)*, *Terry bathed (herself)*, *Felicia cut herself*. A form which resembles the middle is what Otto Jespersen calls a **notional passive**; this is a sentence which is active in form but passive in meaning, for example:

The shirt washes easily.	= 'the shirt is easily washed'
These oranges peel easily.	= 'these oranges are easily peeled'
The cake should cook slowly.	= 'the cake should be slowly cooked'

Note that nearly all notional passives contain a manner adverb. They differ from regular passives in that, not only do they occur without explicit agents, there is never even an implicit agent (**these oranges peel easily by you*). Some infinitives may also be active in form but passive in meaning, such as the following:[15]

These apples are ready to eat.	= 'these apples are ready to be eaten'
There are the dishes to do.	= 'there are the dishes to be done'

In conclusion, we can approach the categories from a different perspective by noting which different word classes each of the grammatical categories is relevant to:

- nouns: number, gender, case, (person), and definiteness;
- pronouns: number, gender, case, and person;
- adjectives and some adverbs: degree; and
- verbs: number, person, tense, aspect, mood, and voice.

---

15. Constructions such as *that movie is filming in Vancouver*, which is also active in form but passive in meaning (= 'that movie is being filmed in Vancouver'), or *your order is shipping* (= 'your order is being shipped') are remnants or an earlier period when it was not possible to combine the progressive and the passive.

No grammatical categories are relevant to prepositions and conjunctions, which are invariable.

Self-Testing Exercises: Do Exercise 5.2 on verbal categories and Exercise 5.3 as a review.

2.   Determining word classes

We have completed our examination of the internal structure of words, but there remains one aspect of morphology that we have yet to examine: the classification of words into what are known variously as **word classes**, lexical categories, or parts of speech. Traditionally, eight word classes are recognized: noun, verb, adjective, adverb, pronoun, preposition, conjunction, and interjection (or article). The reason for eight word classes is that the first Greek grammarian recognized that number of word classes in Classical Greek. Changes in the inventory of word classes have subsequently been required to account for other languages, but the number eight has remained constant.

The traditional word classes are identified by a mixed combination of criteria, both notional (according to the meaning of words) and formal (according to the form, function, or distribution of words). The notional criteria are particularly problematical. For example, nouns are traditionally said to name people, places, and things, but they also denote abstractions (e.g. *truth*, *existence*), nonentities (e.g. *void*, *vacuum*), and events (e.g. *picnic*, *race*, *thunderstorm*). In fact, word classes are purely a matter of language, not of the external world; they do not correspond in a one-to-one way with things in the real world. We tend to equate nouns with things and verbs with events, but there are other languages which make different correspondences.[16] Furthermore, the inventory of word classes does not appear to be universal, but differs from language to language (Vietnamese has 12, Nootka has 2 word classes).

The student of language should not bring preconceptions about word classes to bear on a particular language. Approaching English as if it were an unknown language, the linguist C.C. Fries determined that there were 19 word classes in English (see Table 5.1). He did so using the formal tests that we will examine below (we have supplied the names for the categories).

---

16.   For example, it might be possible to put in one class words denoting things of long duration, such as *house* and *live* (N and V, respectively, in English) and in another class words denoting things of short duration, such as *kick* and *fist* (V and N, respectively, in English).

Table 5.1. The Nineteen Word Classes of English (C.C. Fries, 1952)

Class 1: (noun)
Class 2: (verb)
Class 3: (adjective)
Class 4: (adverb)
Class A: *the, this, a/an, both our, every, two, each*, etc. (determiners)
Class B: *may, might, can, will*, etc. (modals)
Class C: *not*
Class D: *very, rather, pretty, quite*, etc. (degree adverbs)
Class E: *and, or, but, rather*, etc. (coordinating conjunctions)
Class F: *at, by, for, from*, etc. (prepositions)
Class G: *do*
Class H: *there* (existential *there*)
Class I: *when, why, where*, etc. (*wh*-words)
Class J: *after, when, although*, etc. (subordinating conjunctions)
Class K: *oh, well, now, why* (discourse markers)
Class L: *yes, no*
Class M: *look, say, listen*
Class N: *please*
Class O: *let's*

Finally, the traditional analysis of parts of speech seems to suggest that all parts of speech are of the same semantic and functional importance. However, as we saw when we examined morphemes, words fall into one of two quite different categories: content words (lexical morphemes) or function words (grammatical morphemes).

Content words:

-   carry the primary communicative force of an utterance
-   are open or productive classes
-   are variable in form (inflected)
-   fall into the major parts of speech, including nouns, verbs, adjectives, adverbs, and some pronouns

Their distribution is not definable by the grammar.
In contrast, **function words**, whose distribution is definable by the grammar:

-   carry less of the communicative force of an utterance
-   express grammatical meaning (by relating sentence parts)
-   express the terms of grammatical categories (the meanings often expressed by inflections)
-   are closed or unproductive classes
-   are generally invariable in form (except demonstratives, modals, and some pronouns)
-   fall into the minor parts of speech, including prepositions, conjunctions, interjections, particles, auxiliaries, articles, demonstratives, and some adverbs and pronouns.

2.1   Inflectional and distributional tests

Because of the problems associated with notional definitions of the parts of speech, we
need some formal means for determining the word classes of a language. Two types of
tests have been developed in structural linguistics as an objective (formal), not subjective
(notional), means of determining the parts of speech.

In a **distributional test**, words that fill the same syntactic slot, that is, fit into the same
syntactic position and function, are considered to belong to the same class of words. In
such a test, semantics is ignored as much as possible. For example, the words *large, green,
exciting,* and *damaged* belong to the same class because they all fill the following test frame,
while the other words do not:

> The _____ book is on the shelf.
> | | | |
> |---|---|---|
> | large | *read | *man |
> | green | *while | *up |
> | exciting | *very | *oh |
> | damaged | *that | *him |

Note that this test is very similar to the test frame used to identify phonemes that we discussed in Chapter 3.

In an **inflectional test**, all words that take a particular inflectional suffix are considered
to belong to the same class of words. This test depends, of course, on the prior identification of the inflectional suffixes of a language. Thus, for example, *big* takes the inflection *-er,*
but *hand, arrive, and,* and *him* do not:

> The _____ {-er, -est} book
> | | | |
> |---|---|---|
> | bigger | *hander | *ander |
> | biggest | *arrivest | *himest |

Derivational morphology is generally not very helpful in such a test because it is highly
idiosyncratic and individual in its combinatory possibilities.[17] In general, inflectional tests
have fairly limited applicability in a language such as English, which has very few inflections. They are also suitable only for the major parts of speech since the minor parts of
speech are invariable.

Distributional and inflectional tests must be used in combination, because words
belonging to the same class may not meet all of the tests. When words meet *most* tests for a
particular class, but fail to meet some, then we have evidence for the subcategorization, or
subclassification, of a particular word class.

---

17.   Extremely productive derivational affixes such as the agentive *-er* on Vs and the adverbial *-ly*
on As may be of some use, however.

2.2   Tests applied to various word classes

Noun.   Inflectional tests for the category **noun** (N) include the plural -*s* inflection and the genitive -*'s* inflection. The plural inflection attaches to certain types of nouns, but not to others:

count noun:	*pencils, dogs, hats, pies, accountants*
mass (noncount) noun:	**honeys, *rices, *golds, *muds*
abstract noun:	**existences, *friendships, *happinesses*
collective noun:	*committees, herds, *furnitures, *cutleries*

Proper nouns are distinguished from **common** nouns in that they denote a unique referent. Most proper nouns occur in the singular and are not pluralizable (e.g. **Susans, *Jims, *Seattles, *Gandhis*). However, some proper nouns invariably occur in the plural form (e.g. *The Everglades, The Great Plains, The Rocky Mountains, The Seychelles*) and are never singular in form. **Count** nouns denote items that are individuated and can be pluralized and counted, while **noncount** (**mass**) nouns denote substances that exist in bulk or unspecified quantities. While they may be divided into portions (*a spoon of honey, a cup of rice, an ounce of gold*), in their bulk form, they cannot be counted. Note that some mass nouns name continuous substances (e.g. *honey, gold*), whereas other names substances whose parts are generally too small or insignificant to be counted (e.g. *rice, sand*). **Abstract** nouns are distinguished from **concrete** nouns in that they denote things which are not tangible and cannot be known through the senses; they are often mass as well. **Collective** nouns name groups of individuals which together form a unit. Collectives are generally countable, though some are not. Thus, we see that the plural inflectional test serves as an important means of subcategorizing nouns.[18] The genitive inflection can be added to all kinds of nouns, though it is sometimes a bit odd with inanimates (e.g. *?the cupboard's back* vs. *the back of the cupboard*).

---

18.   Apart from instances of recategorization, which are discussed below, the mass/count distinction involves quite a number of complexities of number, which cannot be treated in detail here (but see any standard reference grammar of English). For example, some mass nouns are plural in form and take a plural verb (e.g. *brains, savings, wages, ashes*), some singular nouns end in -*s* and take a singular verb (e.g. *news, politics, mumps, dominoes*), nouns denoting singular bipartite items end in -*s* and take a plural verb (e.g. *scissors, binoculars, pajamas, pants*), and some singular nouns may follow plural numerals (e.g. *five staff, six offspring, two bear*). Collective nouns may be count (e.g. *family, team*), mass and singular in form (e.g. *shrubbery, gentry*), or mass and plural in form (e.g. *groceries, leftovers*); moreover, collective nouns take a singular verb or a plural verb depending on whether the collective is seen as a unit or an abstraction (e.g. *The family is a dying institution*) or whether the individual members of the collectives are emphasized (e.g. *The family are all coming home for Christmas*), though there are some dialectal differences here as well.

We can consider three distributional tests for the category noun:

1.   Det _____

That is, nouns can follow a subclass of words called **determiners (Det)**, which include articles (such as *a, the*), demonstratives (such as *this, that*), possessives (such as *my, her*), *wh*-words (such as *which, whose*), and quantifiers (such as *many, several*). The occurrence of nouns with determiners depends on their subclass and number:

–   proper nouns, when singular in form, seldom follow a determiner (**the Seattle*), but when plural in form invariably take the definite article (*The Times*)[19]
–   single count nouns always follow a determiner (*the dog, *dog*)
–   plural count nouns may or may not follow a determiner (*dogs, the dogs*)
–   mass nouns may or may not follow a determiner (*the honey, honey*), though they never follow the indefinite article (**a honey*)
–   collectives behave either like count nouns (**herd, herds, the herd, the herds*) or like mass nouns (*furniture, the furniture, *a furniture*)

Quantifiers are rather complex since some (such as *much, a little, a large amount of, less*) are restricted to mass nouns: *much violence, a large amount of money, less homework*. Others (e.g. *many, a few, several, a large number of, fewer*) are restricted to count nouns: *many protesters, several reporters, fewer regulations*. Finally, yet other quantifiers (e.g. *more, most, a lot of*) may occur with both: *more time/reasons, most people/parents, a lot of trouble/magazines*.[20]

2.   A _____

Plural count nouns and mass nouns may follow an adjective (*fierce dogs, sticky honey*), but single count nouns and proper nouns cannot (**big dog, *beautiful Seattle*).

3.   Det A _____

All nouns except proper nouns can follow the sequence of determiner and adjective (*the big dog, two fierce dogs, the sticky honey, *the beautiful Seattle*). There are a number of other elements which can occur in the noun phrase (NP), but these three distributional tests are sufficient for our purposes here. (We will consider the structure of the NP in Chapter 7.)

---

19.   A limited number of proper nouns in the singular form include the definite article, such as *The Hague, The Empire State Building, The White House, The Metropolitan*.

20.   It is amusing to observe that the usage of all supermarkets – in their signs for express lanes which declare "nine items or less" – ignores the distinction between mass and count. These signs should, of course, read "nine items or fewer". Rather than seeing this usage as an "error", we should probably consider it a "change in progress".

Adjective.   Inflectional tests for the category **adjective (A)** include the comparative *-er* and the superlative *-est* degree endings, as in *larger/largest* or *prettier/prettiest*. As discussed earlier in the chapter, some adjectives cannot take these inflections for phonological reasons, while other are excluded for semantic reasons. Another difficulty with this inflectional test is that it admits certain adverbs, such as *late/latest, sooner/soonest*, though not others *quicklier/quickliest*. As we discussed in the previous chapter, *-ly,* though a common derivational suffix added to adjectives, does not function as an inflectional test.

Distributional tests for the category of adjective include the following:

1.   Det _____ N

This is called the "attributive" position of adjectives, the position preceding the noun (as in *the fierce dog*). A few adjectives, such as *afraid, asleep*, or *afire*, cannot appear in this position. Another position in which adjectives are found is the following:

2. V_{cop} _____

This is called the "predicative" position of adjectives, following a copula verb (see below) in the predicate of a sentence (as in *the dog is fierce*). A few adjectives cannot appear in this position, such as *principal, utter, mere, outright, entire*, or *same*. Also note that certain adjectives have quite different meanings in attributive and predicative positions, e.g. *That poor heiress has no friends* (here *poor* expresses the speaker's sympathy for the heiress; the heiress is likely quite rich) vs. *That girl is very poor* (here *poor* means 'impecunious, without wealth'). Adjectives may also follow a subclass of words called **degree words (Deg)**, or intensifiers:

3.   Deg _____

Degree adverbs include *so, too, very, somewhat, rather, quite, slightly, highly, moderately, completely, awfully, incredibly*, or *unbelievably* (as in *very fierce dog*). Also included among the degree adverbs are the periphrastic forms for degree, *more* and *most*. The degree word and the adjective together form the adjective phrase (AP). A problem with this test is that it will also include most adverbs, as in *very quickly, quite soon*, or *most helpfully*.

Verb.   The category of **verb (V)** has the greatest number of inflectional tests of all the word classes:

1.   the present participle *-ing*, which attaches to all verbs;
2.   the 3rd p sg pres *-s*, which also attaches to all verbs;
3.   the past tense *-ed*, which attaches to "weak" verbs, but not to "strong" verbs (which form their past tense by vowel alternation) or to other irregular verbs; and
4.   the past participle *-ed*, which likewise attaches to weak, but not to strong verbs (which may take the nonproductive ending *-en* or some other ending).

The agentive suffix *-er*, though a common ending to verbs (*singer, worker, writer, helper*), is not inflectional; in fact, there are many members of the class which cannot take it, e.g. **knower, *hurter, *realizer*, or **beer* (< *be* + *-er*).

There are several distributional tests for the category verb; these serve to subclassify verbs. Certain verbs, known as transitive verbs, such as *buy, help, learn, give*, or *hit*, may precede noun phrases (e.g. *buy stocks, help people, learn French, give advice, hit the ball*):

1.   _____ NP

Other verbs, known as intransitive verbs, such as *appear, rise, arrive*, or *fall*, cannot precede noun phrases:

2.   _____ #

(The pound sign # indicates a clause boundary; in other words, no word needs to follow an intransitive verb, though an adverb often does.)
A third subclass of verbs, known as copula verbs (or "linking verbs"), such as *seem, feel, become, appear*, or *happen*, precede adjective phrases. The copula *be* may also precede a noun phrase.

3.   _____ AP/NP

Two distributional tests apply to all verbs. First, verbs may follow an auxiliary verb and *not*:

4.   Aux (*not*) _____

Second, they may follow the periphrastic marker of the infinitive *to* (which replaces the infinitival inflectional ending *-an* in older English):

5.   to _____

(We have treated the different types of verbs cursorily, since they will be treated in some detail in Chapter 7.)

Self-Testing Exercise: In order to explore the tests for verbs more fully, do Exercise 5.4.

Adverb.   The category of **adverb (Adv)** is rather difficult to differentiate. A small number of what are traditionally recognized as adverbs take the comparative inflectional endings *-er* and *-est*, but most are uninflected. In respect to distribution, adverbs are very free:

> *Maria worked quickly.*
> *Maria completed the work quickly.*
> *Maria quickly completed the work.*
> *Quickly Maria completed the work.*

It is traditional to say that an adverb modifies verbs, adjectives, and other adverbs. However, the possible distributional tests for adverb as modifier are inadequate: _____ A would include adjectives as well (as in *large, fierce dog*); _____ Adv would isolate the subclass of degree words only; and _____V would draw in nouns, auxiliary verbs and *not*. Adverbs also "modify" entire sentences; such sentence adverbs may occur in initial and final position in the sentence (hence _____S or S_____) as well as medially:

> *Surprisingly, Maria (surprisingly) completed the work (surprisingly).*

In fact, there is considerable overlap in word forms among adverbs and other parts of speech. For example, *since* and *before* may have the following functions:

> adverb: *He hasn't been here <u>since</u>. I've never seen it <u>before.</u>*
> preposition: *I haven't seen him <u>since</u> lunch. I saw him <u>before</u> his exam.*
> conjunction: *He's been asleep <u>since</u> I arrived. I spoke to her <u>before</u> she left.*

Because of this overlap and because of the difficulty of isolating adverbs from other parts of speech, some scholars have proposed a larger category of **particle (Prt)**, or adposition, which would include **prepositions (P)**, some adverbs, some conjunctions, and the particles of phrasal verbs. There would be no inflectional tests for this category, because these words are generally invariable, but there are several distributional tests:

1. *right* _____
   look it right <u>up</u> (particle of phrasal verb)
   go right <u>home</u> (adverb)
   land right <u>on</u> top (preposition)
   he left right <u>after</u> the music started (conjunction)
2. measure phrases _____
   three feet <u>behind</u> me (preposition)
   twice <u>before</u> (adverb)
   he was here two hours <u>before</u> I was (conjunction)
3. _____ NP
   <u>in</u> the garden (preposition)
   <u>after</u> the man leaves (conjunction)
   blow <u>out</u> the candle (particle of phrasal verb)
   (Note that this test does not distinguish particle from verb.)
4. _____ P
   out of   up from
   away with   up from under

The last test works for prepositions, but not for the other members of the category of particle.

Self-Testing Exercise: Do Exercise 5.5.

2.3   Recategorization

A major difficulty for word classification is that the same word can often belong to different parts of speech. The word *round*, for example, can function as a noun, an adjective, a verb, a preposition, and perhaps even an adverb:

N	a *round* of parties
A	a *round* table
V	*round* off the figures
Prep	come *round* the corner
Adv	come *round* with some fresh air

We can account for some of these forms by functional shift, or conversion, but we might also have to say that there are a number of homophones here.

A related problem is how to deal with an expression such as *the good, the bad, and the ugly*. The forms *good, bad*, and *ugly* seem to be functioning as nouns because they follow a determiner, but they are unlike nouns in the following respects:

–   they do not pluralize (**the bads)
–   the possessive is odd (*?the bad's horse*)
–   they do not follow an adjective (**the remarkable good*)[21]

In some respects, they behave like adjectives in that they can follow a degree adverb (*the remarkably/truly good*) and perhaps be inflected for degree (*?the best, the worst, the ugliest*). There would appear to be four possible ways to analyze these forms:

1.   There are two distinct lexemes in each case, a noun and an adjective, which are homophones.
2.   The forms are adjectives with an understood, or elliptical, noun such as *ones*.
3.   The adjectives have been recategorized as nouns.
4.   The forms belong to the class of adjective, but syntactically function as nouns.

While the first analysis works, it is a cumbersome solution and it does not serve to show how the adjective and the noun forms might be related (which intuitively we feel they are).

---

21.   A possible counter example is *the working poor*, with a present participle functioning as an adjective.

The second analysis looks appealing, but it has problems since sometimes you would have to understand a singular noun *one* rather than *ones* (e.g. *the {deceased, Almighty, accused, departed} one*), while at other times, the adjective refers to an abstraction and hence *one* seems inappropriate (*the known *one*). Between the third and fourth analyses, the fourth seems preferable; if recategorization had occurred, one would expect the recategorized word to have all of the behavioral characteristics of its new class, including its inflectional forms. Since it doesn't, it seems that these forms are still lexical adjectives, but are functioning as nouns in this instance.

Recategorization can occur both within a class (from one subcategory to another) or between classes. For example, the subcategories of a noun can be shifted in the following ways:

from abstract to concrete:	*a beauty* (= 'a horse'), *a youth* (= 'a boy'), *a personality* (= 'a well-known person'), *a terror, a help*
from mass to count:	*wines, milks, difficulties, hairs, teas, cakes*
from count to mass:	*(a taste of) garlic, (the smell of) lilac*
from proper to common:	*the Susans I know* (= 'the women named Susan whom I know'), *an Einstein* (= 'a genius'), *a Benedict Arnold* (= 'a traitor')

Again, to account for the shift – e.g from mass to count noun – there are four possibilities:

1. A word such as *difficulty* would be entered in the dictionary as two separate lexemes, one mass and one count.
2. The count noun is understood as having an elliptical quantifying expression, e.g. *(pieces of) cake = cakes*.
3. The mass noun has been recategorized as count.
4. The mass noun is functioning syntactically as a count noun.

The first analysis is again ungainly and doesn't show the relation between the two uses of the nouns. The second analysis runs into difficulties because it would be necessary to postulate a different quantifying expression for each shifted noun, as in <u>bottles</u> of wine, <u>glasses</u> of milk, or <u>strands</u> of hair, while in some cases, there does not appear to be any quantifying expression, as with *difficulties*. Furthermore, the plural forms occasionally refer to types not quantities, as in *the wines of France* or *the teas of China*. One would also have to shift the plural inflection from the quantifier to the noun (e.g. from *pieces* to *cakes*) by some yet unknown syntactic process. However, in contrast to the case of *the good*, it seems plausible to explain the shift in this case as a true instance of recategorization since the words behave both inflectionally and distributionally like count nouns.

Self-Testing Exercise: Do Exercise 5.6 on recategorization.

In conclusion, there appear to be a number of general problems with the inflectional and distributional tests that we have been discussing. First, there is an inherent circularity to the tests: the first test frame usually contains some word class, such as "determiner" in the test for noun; we are then assuming what we are trying to prove. Or the first test frame contains some lexical item; in this case, meaning (which we were trying to exclude) necessarily enters in. We must also ignore certain violations (which subcategorize words) and take certain tests as the basic one for a category. But there are no reasons, on inflectional and distributional grounds, why one test should be more important than any other. Finally, it is not clear how far subcategorization should be taken: we could conceivably continue until each word is a separate subclass, though doing so would not be very useful. Despite these difficulties, the inflectional and distributional tests discussed here represent a more precise means of categorization than does the traditional approach which is based on a combination of meaning and form.

Chapter summary

Now that you have completed this chapter, you should be able to:

1. define the grammatical categories and their terms;
2. say how the terms of each grammatical category are expressed in English (by means of inflection, periphrasis, word order, and so on) and in which parts of speech; and
3. apply the inflectional and distributional tests for the categories noun, adjective, verb, auxiliary, and adverb in English.

Recommended additional reading

Both of the topics treated in this chapter are generally covered in traditional grammars of English (see the references in Chapter 1). A very clear account of tense, aspect, and modality in English is Leech (2004). The classic structuralist treatment of parts of speech is Fries (1952, pp. 65–141).

Leech, Deucher, and Hoogenraad (2006, Chapter 4) and Klammer, Schulz, and Della Volpe (2010, Chapters 4, 5, and 6) discuss the distinction between content and function words. Carstairs-McCarthy (2002, Chapter 4), Miller (2009, Chapter 12 and 13), and Finegan (2008, Chapter 2, pp. 35–41, pp. 54–59, and Chapter 6, pp. 191–197) include discussions of the grammatical categories; Hurford (1994) defines the grammatical categories in English.

Chapter 6

Lexical semantics

Chapter preview

This chapter first considers some common assumptions about word meaning. The technical terms that linguists use in naming various relationships between words and sentences are introduced. The chapter then examines one way of approaching the problem of lexical meaning called *structural semantics*. The inherent meaning of nouns, verbs, and modal auxiliaries is next analyzed, using the concept of semantic features. Brief consideration is then given to an alternative approach to semantic features based on the concept of prototypes. Semantic restrictions on the combinations of words and the concept of semantic anomaly are then discussed. The chapter enumerates the different types of figurative language, focusing on how metaphors are recognized and interpreted. The chapter ends with a brief section on cognitive semantics.

Commentary

Semantics is the study of linguistic meaning. We can study meaning on a number of different levels: **lexical semantics** is the study of the meaning properties of individual words (lexical items) in isolation; **sentence semantics** is the study of the meaning properties of a sentence, of the semantic relationships among the parts of sentence; and **discourse** (utterance) **semantics** is the study of the meaning of extended discourse (spoken or written), of the semantic relationship among utterances used in context. In this chapter, we will be concerned with the semantics of words, focusing on lexical rather than grammatical meaning (the latter was treated in Chapter 5). However, because of the complexity of semantics, we can only sample a number of different approaches towards lexical semantics, such as structural semantics, semantic features or components, prototypes, and cognitive semantics. Once we have treated the syntax of the sentence, we will consider sentence semantics (Chapter 10), and after that, we will turn to some aspects of discourse semantics (Chapter 11).

1. Traditional semantics

We begin by looking at some of our preconceptions about meaning. This approach to meaning, which can be termed "traditional semantics", like traditional grammar, tends to be prescriptive and is often embodied in our attitudes towards dictionaries.

The first preconception of traditional semantics is that the meaning of a phrase or a sentence consists of a sum of the meaning of its parts; therefore, if we don't know what a sequence of words means, we assume that we simply have to look the words up in a dictionary. In popular thinking about language, there is one correct and accepted meaning for each word in the language; people generally rely upon dictionaries to provide this "correct" meaning and to act as arbiters of meaning. However, the assumption that there is one "true" meaning for a word is mistaken. Even if such unequivocal meanings existed, dictionary makers would have no direct access to them; they can only consult usage (often aided now by the use of computerized collections of the language) to discover the meanings of a word in the different contexts in which it is used. Word meanings are a matter of both social agreement (see Chapter 1) and use, and are thus imprecise and fluid. Native speakers do not always agree on the meanings of words, even common words, and dictionaries cannot be expected to record individual variation in word meanings. For example, for different speakers, *brother-in-law* may refer to

> your sister's husband
> your husband's brother,
> your wife's brother, or
> any combination of these meanings.

Meanings may change more rapidly than can be recorded in dictionaries, despite the best efforts of lexicographers; for example, if asked the meaning of the word *desultory*, most people would respond with the meaning 'aimless, slow, casual', as in:

> *Dwayne, who'd been lounging in a deck chair, was now making <u>desultory</u> calls on his cell phone.* (COCA: FIC)

Yet many dictionaries, including the *American Heritage Dictionary*, list its meaning as 'moving or jumping from one thing to another' based on its origin in Latin *dēsultōrius* 'leaping'. While this may have been the word's meaning at an earlier period of the language, it is not, at least judging from contemporary quotations, its current sense.[1] Finally, the traditional view of semantics also ignores many aspects of meaning apart from the meanings of words, such as the function of meaningful phonological features (i.e. stress and intonation), the meaning of the grammatical structure of the utterance, and the significance of the communicative context (pragmatics).

A second assumption of traditional semantics is that the correspondence between a word and a thing is simple and direct. In fact, the relation between a word and the world may be quite complex. For example,

- *disappointment* names an emotional state, but to understand the word we must know that this is the state which results from one's hopes or expectations of something pleasant not being satisfied. Under normal circumstances, you wouldn't be 'disappointed' that you didn't get hurt in an accident, but you might be disappointed that you did not get the raise you expected.
- The word *widow* denotes a type of woman, but again we must know something about the history of that woman, that she was married and that her husband has died.
- To understand meanings of the word *stingy* or *lazy*, as well as their negative associations, we must know something about the cultural values of the English-speaking linguistic community.
- Even the meaning of the expression *apple core* – or the image we associate with this meaning – depends upon our knowledge of the way in which apples are typically eaten in our society!

A third assumption of traditional semantics – and perhaps the most problematical one – is that words name things or objects in the real world, that meaning is always in reference to phenomena outside language. In fact, many words do not name things at all, such as words denoting abstractions or nonentities, or function words. Linguists believe that a clear distinction must be made between:

---

1. Another example is the expression *hoi polloi*, from Greek meaning 'the (ordinary) people'. Again, current usage differs, with the directly opposite meaning of 'the upper classes' predominating. Dictionaries tend to list the etymological meaning, while perhaps noting that the expression is used "improperly" with the meaning 'people of distinction'. One dictionary simply lists both meanings without comment. Imagine the difficulties for a learner of the language when faced with such a contradictory definition! These examples were discussed by Justice (1987, December).

- the **extension** of a word, the set of entities that a word denotes in the world (its referents) – if it denotes any entity at all – and
- the **intension** of a word, the set of properties shared by all the referents of a word, their defining characteristics.

This distinction is important because the extension may be the same while the intension differs: e.g. the same man may be denoted by *Mr. Jones, my neighbor, that man mowing the lawn*, or *an accountant*. In contrast, the intension may be the same while the extension differs: e.g. *I* always names the property of being the speaker, but the extension differs as the speaker shifts or *the Prime Minister of England* always names the same position within the government of England, but over time, the extension differs.

A final assumption of traditional semantics is that it is possible to treat the meanings of individual words separately. However, words refer to things in the real world not directly, but by means of concepts existing in the mind, or meanings internal to language (linguistic meaning) – what is known as the **sense** of a word – and words enter into various sense relationships with other words in the language. For example, words expressing movement towards and away from the speaker form a network based on directionality and transitivity:

	towards speaker	away from speaker
intransitive	*come*	*go*
transitive	*bring*	*take*
	–	*send*

Likewise, words expressing vision form a network based on the distinction between chance happening and willful act as well as duration:

	happening	act
longer duration	*see*	*look (stare, gawk)*
shorter duration	*glimpse*	*glance*

In these networks, the meanings of the words are interdependent; it is impossible to know the meaning of *look*, for example, without also knowing the meaning of the word *see*.

Self-Testing Exercise: Do Exercise 6.1.

2.   Basic semantic relationships

As speakers of the language, we all have an implicit understanding of a number of semantic relationships that hold between either words or sentences in the language. Let's examine briefly the technical terms that linguists use to describe the different types of relationships.

1. **Paraphrase**: an utterance is a paraphrase of another when it has the same meaning as another, as *Philip purchased an automobile* is a paraphrase of *Philip bought a car* (we will look at synonymy – sameness of meaning between words – below).

2. **Entailment**, or implication: one utterance entails another when the second is a logically necessary consequence of the first, as *Alan lives in Toronto* entails *Alan lives in Canada*. Note that the relationship of entailment, unlike that of paraphrase, is one-way: it is not the case that *Alan lives in Canada* entails *Alan lives in Toronto*.

3. **Inclusion**: one utterance encompasses another, as *I like fruit* includes *I like apples*. Again, this relationship is unidirectional: *I like apples* does not include *I like (all) fruit*.

> **HINT:** The following example may help you distinguish entailment from inclusion. To say *I am allergic to dairy* INCLUDES *I am allergic to yoghurt, milk, cottage cheese, ice cream, etc.* To say the same thing ENTAILS *I get sick when I eat dairy.*

4. **Contradiction**: a statement or sequence of utterances is logically contradictory; that is, if one is true, the other must be false: *He is an orphan* contradicts *His parents are living* or *I was fatally ill last year* is internally contradictory.

5. **Anomaly**: an utterance has no meaning in the everyday world; it violates semantic rules, for example, *He swallowed a dream* or *The rock giggled.* (We will examine anomaly below, as some apparent anomaly is actually figurative language.)

6. **Lexical ambiguity**: a word or phrase allows more than one meaning in context, as in *an old friend*, which may denote a friend who is aged or a friend whom one has known for a long time (two different meanings of *old*), or *a large bill*, which may denote a large beak of a bird or a large check at a restaurant (two different words *bill*), or *he lost his head*, which may mean that he became discomposed (a metaphorical interpretation) or that he was decapitated (the literal interpretation).[2]

7. **Denotation/connotation**: words have literal or referential meanings (denotation) but also evoke feelings, attitudes, or opinions (connotations). The following words, whose denotations are similar if not identical, carry differing connotations, either good or bad:

soldier – warrior	*relax – loaf*
insect – bug	*hound – dog*
illness – disease – ailment – condition	*generous – extravagant – wasteful*
fat – obese – plump – portly – stout – substantial	*plan – trick – ruse -stratagem*

---

2. Lexical ambiguity differs from structural ambiguity, where no single word in a sentence is ambiguous, but the structure permits more than one interpretation, as in *He found her home* (which may mean either that he found her at home or that he found the home belonging to her). See Chapter 8.

For example, some air blowing through a window is called a *draft* when it is cold and undesired, but a *breeze* when it is cool and desired; a *plan* points to careful foresight, while a *scheme* suggests deviousness or manipulation.

> **HINT:** Sometimes the connotations of synonymous words are associated with their language of origin, as in:
>
> | English | French | Latin |
> |---------|----------|--------------|
> | fire | flame | conflagration |
> | fear | terror | trepidation |
> | rise | mount | ascend |
> | ask | question | interrogate |
>
> These words differ in their register, or level of formality. The English words are most colloquial or informal, the French words are more literary, and the Latin words are most technical or formal.

In any but the most mundane uses of language, connotations are an important aspect of meaning. Words may also carry social meaning, indicators of the identity of the speaker (age, sex, social class, race) or the formality of the context. These are also significant to the meaning of a discourse.

8. **Polysemy**: a word has more than one meaning out of context; the meanings are related to one another, e.g.:

court:	'enclosed area', 'retinue of a sovereign', 'judicial tribunal';
mouth:	'opening through which an animate being takes food', 'the part of a river which empties into a lake or sea';
bug:	'insect', 'enthusiast', 'electronic device for eavesdropping', 'design defect in a computer';
fire:	'to burn or ignite', 'to shoot a gun', 'to discharge from one's employment'

9. **Homonymy**: two words sound and are written the same but are different in meaning, e.g.:

$bark_1$	'outer covering of wood'	$bark_2$	'harsh sound, uttered by a dog'
$sound_1$	'noise'	$sound_2$	'body of water'
		$sound_3$	'free from defect'
$band_1$	'group of people'	$band_2$	'thin strip for encircling an object'
$swallow_1$	'to ingest'	$swallow_2$	'a type of bird'

Homonyms represent different entries in a dictionary, while the different meanings of a polysemous word are listed under a single entry. However, without consulting a dictionary, it is often difficult to distinguish between polysemy and homonymy, that is, when one is dealing with two meanings for a single word or two different words.

> **HINT:** If the two forms belong to different parts of speech, one can usually conclude that they are homonyms, as in the case of *grave* (A – 'serious, weighty') and *grave* (N – 'hole for burying a person')

In the case of polysemy, the meanings are related (either literally or figuratively), though the connection between different meanings may sometimes be difficult to perceive (as in the meanings 'a series of connected mountains' or 'a unit for cooking' for *range*). In some cases, the meanings may have become so far apart from one another over time that an originally single word is divided into two dictionary entries (as in *pupil* 'a student' and *pupil* 'the opening in the center of the iris of the eye').

10. **Meronymy**: a word denotes part of a whole, as *fender* is to *car*, *week* is to *month*, *head* is to *body*, *branch* is to *tree*, *binding* is to *book*.

11. **Presupposition**: what is assumed beforehand by an utterance, or what is taken for granted, is said to be presupposed. Minimally, the existence of the thing or person talked about (the topic) is presupposed, as in *My teacher gave a boring lecture*, where the existence of teacher is presupposed.

> **HINT:** The test for presupposition is that when an utterance is negated, what is presupposed remains true; what is presupposed "holds up under negation". When the sentence above is negated – *My teacher didn't give a boring lecture* – the teacher is still assumed to exist, though a lecture may or may not have been given (she may have given an exciting lecture or she may have led a discussion).

Individual words may carry or "trigger" presuppositions:

"Trigger"	Presupposition
Have <u>another</u> cup of coffee	addressee has already had a cup of coffee
You should hit him <u>back</u>	he has hit the addressee
I <u>responded</u> to him	he has asked the speaker something
I read the article <u>again</u>	the speaker has already read the article at least once
I {<u>continued, stopped, finished</u>} drawing	the speaker was drawing in the time immediately preceding the moment of speaking
I <u>resumed</u> drawing	the speaker was drawing in some time not immediately preceding the moment of speaking
I {<u>began, started</u>} drawing	the speaker was not drawing in the time immediately preceding the moment of speaking
They have a bigger house <u>than</u> we do	both their house and our house exist

If what is presupposed does not hold, then presupposition failure occurs, and the communication is pragmatically odd. In a *wh*-question, everything is presupposed except the information requested:

> *Where did you put the paper?* (presupposes that the addressee put the paper somewhere).

Indirect questions have the same presupposition: *I asked where she put the paper.* Compare a *yes/no* question such as *Is Karen attending the conference?*, where only the existence of Karen is presupposed.

Entire propositions may also be presupposed when they are expressed in the complement clauses of what have been termed **factive** expressions:

> It is {tragic, exciting, amusing, terrible, odd, significant, relevant, a bother} that it is raining.
> I {regret, am happy, remember, concede, understand, hear, notice, resent, accept, appreciate, deplore, tolerate} that it is raining.

Notice that it is impossible to add **but it isn't raining* to the above statements since they presuppose that it is raining. An entire proposition may also be presupposed if it is nominalized (*His refusal to help annoyed me, What annoyed me was his refusal to help*). If the proposition of the complement clause is not presupposed, the expression is **nonfactive**:

> I {believe, guess, think, agree, doubt, fear, imagine, assert, am dreaming} that it is raining.
> It {appears, seems, is likely, is possible, is certain, is true/false, is probable} that it is raining.

Both factive and nonfactive contrast with counterfactive, which denotes an event that has not occurred and probably will not occur, as in *She pretended to be listening, He wishes that he were rich.*

> **HINT:** It is important to distinguish presupposition from entailment. The clearest distinguishing test is that entailment does not hold up under negation. Thus, *Alan does not live in Toronto* does not entail that *Alan lives in Canada* (in fact, he may live anywhere).

Self-Testing Exercise: Do Exercise 6.2.

3. Structural semantics

One description of the meaning relationships of words in a language is that of the British linguist John Lyons and is called "structural semantics". Lyons recognizes three major types of relationship: synonymy, hyponymy, and oppositeness.

The concept of **synonymy** is, of course, well-known and intuitively obvious; it denotes sameness in meaning, or sense, as with the words:

unhappy/sad	*huge/enormous*
correct/right	*casual/informal*
prisoner/convict	*present/gift*
flourish/thrive	*donate/contribute*

Synonymy is context-dependent: *pedigree* refers only to animals, while *ancestry, genealogy,* and *lineage* refer only to human beings, and *descent* may refer to either; *carcass* refers only to animals, *corpse* only to human beings. Two words may have the same meaning in a particular context, but not necessarily in all contexts, as in the case of *pale/light* or *peel/skin*:

Synonymous   *The shirt is {pale/light} in color.*   *The {peel, skin} of the orange is thick.*
Not synonymous *The book is {light, *pale} in weight. The girl's {skin, *peel} is sunburned.*

Synonymy ignores the connotations of words and recognizes only their denotations. In fact, many synonyms differ only in respect to their connotations, as in *horse/steed/nag*. Synonyms may also differ in degree or intensity, as in *rain/showers/sprinkles/downpour*. Synonymy also ignores stylistic aspects – the colloquial, familiar, or formal "register" of the word – or its social or geographic dialect distribution. Consider the following sets of synonyms and note the differences in formality among the terms as well as their distribution in Canadian, US, or British English:[3]

> *sofa, couch, chesterfield, davenport*
> *privy, loo, w.c., bathroom, restroom, washroom, toilet*
> *dear, expensive, costly*

Hyponymy is a relation of inclusion or entailment. For example, for the set of terms *red, scarlet, crimson, vermilion, pink, maroon,* and so on, *red* is what Lyons calls a **superordinate term**, and *scarlet,* etc. are what he calls **cohyponyms** (or hyponyms).[4] The meaning of the hyponym includes the meaning of the superordinate term (*red* includes *scarlet, crimson,* etc.). The meaning of the hyponym entails the meaning of the superordinate term (*scarlet* entails *red*). However, this relationship works in only one direction: if *roses* is a hyponym of the superordinate term *flowers*, then *I bought some roses* entails *I bought some flowers*, but *I bought some flowers* does not entail *I bought some roses*.

> **HINT:** Another way to understand the concept of a superordinate term is as the name of a class of entities, as *musical instrument* is a class term including *piano, violin, flute, guitar, drum, cello, marimbas, accordion*, and so on.

There may be different levels of hyponyms, a hierarchy, as shown in Figure 6.1. The lower one moves in this hierarchy, the more specialized, or "marked", the terms become.

---

3.   *Sofa* is the usual term in US English and *davenport* may still be found; *chesterfield* is uniquely Canadian, but is falling out of use. US English favors *bathroom* or *restroom*, while Canadian English prefers *washroom*; the standard term in British English is *toilet*, while *loo* is a slang term.

4.   The prefix *hypo-* is Greek for 'below'. Logically the superordinate term should be called a "hypernym" (from the Greek prefix *hyper-* meaning 'above'), though to avoid confusion Lyons uses the corresponding Latin prefix *super-*.

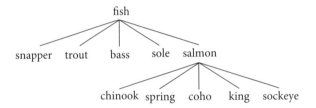

Figure 6.1. A Hierarchy of Fish Hyponyms

A number of complexities may arise in the identification of superordinate terms and hyponyms:

- The hyponyms *brother* and *sister* have only the technical superordinate *sibling*, while the hyponyms *uncle* and *aunt* have none.
- The only possible superordinate term for the hyponyms *cow* and *bull* is *cow*, which is identical with one of the hyponyms; the term *cattle* is a collective term, while *bovine* is only technical.
- For the cohyponyms *chair, table, desk*, there likewise exists no simple superordinate term, but merely the phrase *a piece of furniture*.
- Color terms, such as *red, green*, and *pink*, also have no obvious superordinate since the term *colored* sometimes means 'not white' and sometimes 'not transparent'.
- The superordinate term *animal* (which contrasts with *vegetable* and *mineral*) is a hyponym of itself, where it contrasts with *human being*.

Lyons recognizes three different relationships of oppositeness.

1. **Complementarity** is a relation of contradiction, in which the denial of one term is the assertion of its complementary term. X is not Y and Y is not X (e.g. *right is not wrong* and *wrong is not right*). Other examples include the following:

single – married	*male – female*
dead – alive	*pregnant – not pregnant*
legal – illegal	*on – off*
asleep – awake	*pass – fail*
true – false/untrue	*raw – cooked*

Sometimes there are separate lexical items to express the complementary terms, while at other times negative prefixes such as *un-* or *in-* occur or the negative particle *not* is used. Although it may be possible to think of intermediate cases where the denial of one is not, strictly speaking, the assertion of the other, as in the case of *mermaid* or *satyr* (which is not strictly either *human* nor *nonhuman*), *retired* (which is not strictly either *unemployed* nor *employed*), *ambidextrous* (which is not strictly either *left-handed* or *right-handed*) and *divorced* (which is not strictly either *single* nor *married*), these are not usual. Because complementary terms denote incompatible extremes, it is abnormal to compare or qualify them with *more* or *less*: **more false, *less failing, *somewhat dead*. However, we may do so for humorous purposes when referring not to the quality itself, but to physical, emotional, or behavioral characteristics associated with a quality, as in *more (very) pregnant* (referring, perhaps, to appearance) or *more (very) married* (referring, perhaps, to behavior).

2.   **Antonymy** (a term Lyons uses in a restricted sense) refers to gradable concepts, which may be explicitly or implicitly compared, such as:

big – small/little	*old – young/new*
high – low	*wide/broad – narrow*
proper – improper	*thick – thin/narrow*
fat – thin	*good – bad*
small – large	*many – few*
hot – cold	*rich – poor*
warm – cool	*sweet – sour/bitter*
smart – dumb	*noisy – quiet*
wet – dry	*intelligent – unintelligent*

(Note that the prefixes *un-* and *in-* may denote antonymy as well as complementarity.) Such sets of adjectives are called **scalar adjectives**. In the use of these adjectives, there is always an implicit comparison to a norm. The norm varies from context to context, e.g.:

> *A small elephant is a large animal.*
> *A large mouse is a small animal.*
> *A large child is a small adult.*
> *A quiet concert is a noisy library.*

A warm beer and a cold coffee may be the same temperature since the temperature norms for beer and coffee differ. Depending upon the context, the form that a scalar adjective is paired with may differ. For example, with animate beings, *young* is used, while for inanimate things, *new* is used, but *old* is used for both; beer is *bitter* or *sweet* whereas fruit is *sour* or *sweet*; a building is *tall* or *low* while a person is *tall* or *short*. In other instances, terms seem to be interchangeable; a river is *broad* or *wide*, or an animal may be *small* or *little*. Unlike complementary pairs, antonymous pairs, since they mark points on a scale, typically permit intermediate stages; thus, between *often* and *seldom*, we find *occasionally* and *sometimes*, between *love* and *hate*, we find *like* and *dislike*, and between *hot* and *cold*, we find *warm* and *cool*.

With scalar pairs, one is "unmarked" (positive, unbiased) and one is "marked" (negative, biased). The unmarked member will fit more naturally into the following slots than will the marked member:

> How _____is it?
> Twice as _____
> Half as _____

Again, the markedness can be context-dependent; for example, in summer one might ask *how hot is it?*, while in winter one might ask *how cold is it?*. Scalar adjectives differ as to whether they are uni- or multidimensional:

unidimensional	e.g. *hot – cold, tall – short, wet – dry*
multidimensional	e.g. *attractive – unattractive, big – small, rich – poor*

We can also distinguish between the normal scalar adjective and the end-of-scale scalar adjective by using the following slots:

normal	*very* _____	e.g. *big, tasty, interesting, beautiful, old, cold, hot*
end-of-scale	*absolutely* _____	e.g. *enormous/huge, delicious/scrumptious, fascinating, gorgeous/stunning, aged/ancient, freezing/frigid, boiling/scorching/stifling*

The end-of-scale adjective is much more varied and connotationally rich than the normal adjective.

3. **Converseness** denotes a kind of reversal, expressed by:

verbs expressing reciprocal actions	*buy/sell, rent/rent (lease), lend/borrow, give/receive*
verbs expressing reverse actions[5]	*zip/unzip, tie/untie, wrap/unwrap, connect/disconnect, appear/disappear, exhale/inhale, progress/regress, inflate/deflate*
expressions of time and space	*in front of/behind, in back of, north of/south of, outside/inside*
kinship terms	*husband/wife, brother/sister*
professional relationships	*teacher/student, employer/employee, host/guest, master/servant, lawyer/client*

All converse terms permit reversal; for example, *Andy bought the car from Christy* entails and is entailed by *Christy sold the car to Andy* or *Bill is Trudy's son* entails and is entailed by *Trudy is Bill's mother*. Logically *The bike is in front of the garage* entails *The garage is behind the bike*; however, the second sentence is perspectively odd since we tend to place the figure in respect to the ground rather than the ground in respect to the figure.

Syntactically, active sentences and their corresponding passives denote converseness, though, again, the correspondences may sound odd because of the tendency for the topic of the discourse to be expressed in the subject position (e.g. *Sandy ate the strawberries* entails *The strawberries were eaten by Sandy*). Comparative expressions, though they usu-

---

5. These have been seen as a special case of converseness called "reversive" (Cruse, 1986). Privative verbs such as *zip/unzip* or *tie/untie* are discussed in Chapter 4.

ally contain scalar adjectives, are themselves converse (e.g. *The castle is larger than the fort* implies *The fort is smaller than the castle*). We must be careful to distinguish true cases of converseness from apparent ones:

ask/answer	an answer is only expected, not necessary
command/obey	a command is not always obeyed
seek/find	seeking does not necessarily result in finding
try/succeed	trying does not necessarily result in succeeding

Teach/learn may also be a case of apparent converseness if one assumes that teaching does not necessarily imply learning.

A special kind of converseness is called **symmetry**. An example is *married*; while it is possible to say *Helen is married to David* and *David is married to Helen*, it is also possible to say *Helen and David are married*. Other examples of symmetry are *be {synonymous with, identical to, different from, adjacent to, related to, neighbors with, the same size as}*. The term *sister* can be symmetrical when the sex of both referents is female (*Dora is the sister of Sally, Sally is the sister of Dora*, and *Sally and Doris are sisters*), but when the sex differs, the symmetrical term *sibling* must be used (e.g. *Lois is the sibling of Don, Don is the sibling of Lois, and Don and Lois are siblings*).[6]

> *Self-Testing Exercise:* Do Exercise 6.3. A concept related to that of hyponymy is that of the semantic field. Read about this in Exercise 6.4.

4.   Semantic features

Componential analysis is an attempt to give a semantic analysis of words in terms of **semantic features** or **components** (Katz & Fodor, 1963). It consists in determining the basic components constituting the semantic content, or sense, of a word. These components, sometimes called *semantic primitives*, are assumed to be the most basic notions expressed by linguistic meaning, the "givens" of the semantic system which cannot be broken down further by semantic analysis. Furthermore, they are thought to be universal, not language specific, part of the cognitive and perceptual system of the human mind. According to the linguist Manfred Bierwisch, "all semantic structure might finally be reduced to components representing the basic dispositions of the cognitive and perceptual structure of the human organism". These components combine in different ways to form the meaning of

---

6.   A verb such as *agree with* would appear to be symmetrical (e.g. *Tom agreed with Paul, Paul agreed with Tom*, and *Tom and Paul agreed*), but note that the relation may be unidirectional (when Tom and Paul agree, it may be that Tom agrees with Paul, but that Paul does not necessarily do anything). This type of unidirectional relationship is called "reciprocity"; other examples include *collide with, concur with, cooperate with, fight with*.

individual words; thus, features are the shared semantic characteristics of words. Every word in the language consists of a unique bundle of semantic features. Semantic features combine in different ways in different languages; that is, they are lexicalized differently, resulting in the varied vocabularies of different languages.

Semantic features are usually presented as a matter of opposition, paired positive and negative features, denoting the presence or absence of the particular feature in the meaning of the word.

> **NOTE ON NOTATION:** Semantic features are theoretical elements, not part of the vocabulary of the language. But since we have no metalanguage (special language for talking about language), we must use the words of English to represent features. To indicate that we are referring to a feature rather than a word of the language, we capitalize the feature and place it in square brackets. Thus, the feature of 'humanness' is represented as [±HUMAN]. The feature label that we use can be understood as only accidentally resembling a word of English.

The determination of semantic features is a kind of "factoring out" of semantic components. This process can be seen most clearly in a semantic feature analysis of a livestock paradigm (see Table 6.1).[7]

Table 6.1. Componential Analysis of a Livestock Paradigm

man	boar	bull	cock	dog	stallion	ram	[+MALE] [+ADULT]
woman	sow	cow	hen	bitch	mare	ewe	[–MALE] [+ADULT]
child	piglet	calf	chick	puppy	foal	lamb	[±MALE] [–ADULT]
boy	shoat	bullock	chick	dog puppy	colt	ram lamb	[+MALE] [–ADULT]
girl	gilt	heifer	chick	bitch puppy	filly	ewe lamb	[–MALE] [–ADULT]
crowd	drove	herd	flock	pack	herd	flock	[+COLLECTIVE]
[+HUMAN]	[+SWINE]	[+BOVINE]	[+CHICKEN]	[+CANINE]	[+EQUINE]	[+SHEEP]	
	[–HUMAN]	[–HUMAN]	[–HUMAN]	[–HUMAN]	[–HUMAN]	[–HUMAN]	

The table is read as follows: all of the words in the second row, for example, share the features [–MALE] and [+ADULT], while all of the words in the third column share the feature [+BOVINE], and so on. While the words in the first column share the feature [+HUMAN], those in the other columns share the feature [–HUMAN]. However, for each word to be distinguished from every other word by at least one feature, [–HUMAN] is much too broad a category, suggesting that we need the further distinctions [+SWINE], [+BOVINE], and so on. But if we add one of these positive features to a column, we must, for completeness, also add all the others as negative features to that column, leading to a very cumbersome feature analysis. A second difficulty is deciding which is the positive and which is the negative member. Sometimes the choice is arbitrary, but often the positive term is more

---

7.   Some of the words in this table are not part of everyday speech but are part of the specialized vocabulary of people in animal husbandry. We give them here for illustrative purposes only.

inclusive or more generalized than the negative term. For example, *dog*, which we analyze as [+ADULT], [+MALE] is often used to refer to both male and female canines (thus [±MALE]) and young and old canines (thus [±ADULT]). Likewise, the term *man* may be [±MALE] in the sense of "mankind" and [±ADULT] in its use, for example, on the door of a washroom. The positive feature often has more extended and metaphorical meanings than the negative feature, as can be seen with *stallion*, *cock*, or *bull* (*bitch* and *cow* are perhaps exceptions to this generalization).

Other sets of words can likewise be differentiated by the use of semantic features. For example, we could distinguish types of clothing as in Table 6.2a or bodies of water (6.2b). Departing from the livestock paradigm, it becomes clear how arbitrary the choice of supposedly universal features becomes, since the clothing terms given in (6.2a) could certainly be analyzed with quite a different set of features, for example, with a feature such as [±SLEEVE] rather than one such as [±UPPER BODY]. Once more specialized garments such as *vest*, *nightgown*, or *turtleneck* are included, it would become necessary to add many more specific semantic features. Another weakness evident in the examples in (6.2b) is that, although the eight terms are all distinguished by at least one feature, there is not a sense that the features used satisfactorily capture the meaning of the terms since, for example, *bay* and *inlet* contain some feature of [+INDENTATION].

There are two conclusions to be drawn from this discussion:

- in theory, every word can be accounted for by a unique set of features
- features (or feature matrices) can be used to compare words and talk systematically about sense relations.

For example, we can define more precisely certain relationships that we have already discussed. Two synonymous words – W_1 (W = word) and W_2 – are analyzable in terms of the same semantic components. Polysemy and ambiguity both involve a word's having more than one complex of components assigned to it, either out of or in context. Antonymy (in the broad sense, not Lyons' restricted sense) is a case where W_1 and W_2 share the same features except that for W_1 the feature is [+] and for W_2 the same feature is [−]. Hyponymy may be defined as follows: W_1 is a hyponym of the superordinate term W_2 if all features of W_1 are features of W_2 but not vice versa. For example, in the case of *woman*, the superordinate term *adult* contains all of the features of the hyponym *woman*, but *woman* does not contain all features of *adult* (i.e. [+MALE])

Woman W_1	Adult W_2
[+HUMAN]	[+HUMAN]
[+GROWN]	[+GROWN]
[−MALE]	[±MALE]

That is, all features of W_1 are features of W_2 but not vice versa.

Table 6.2. Componential Analysis of (a) Types of Garments and (b) Bodies of Water

a. garments

coat	jacket	shirt	blouse	skirt	pants	shorts
[+UPPER BODY]	[+UPPER BODY]	[+UPPER BODY]	[+UPPER BODY]	[−UPPER BODY]	[−UPPER BODY]	[−UPPER BODY]
[±FULL LENGTH]	[−FULL LENGTH]	[−FULL LENGTH]	[−FULL LENGTH]	[±FULL LENGTH]	[+FULL LENGTH]	[−FULL LENGTH]
[±MALE]	[±MALE]	[±MALE]	[−MALE]	[−MALE]	[±MALE]	[±MALE]
[+OVER GARM.]	[+OVER GARM.]	[−OVER GARM.]	[−OVER GARM.]	[−OVER GARM.]	[−OVER GARM.]	[−OVER GARM.]

b. bodies of water

lake	sea	ocean	river	brook	pond	bay	cove
[−FLOWING]	[−FLOWING]	[−FLOWING]	[+FLOWING]	[+FLOWING]	[−FLOWING]	[−FLOWING]	[−FLOWING]
[−SALINE]	[+SALINE]	[+SALINE]	[−SALINE]	[−SALINE]	[−SALINE]	[±SALINE]	[±SALINE]
[±LARGE]	[±LARGE]	[+LARGE]	[±LARGE]	[−LARGE]	[−LARGE]	[±LARGE]	[−LARGE]

4.1 Feature analysis of nouns

In Chapter 5, various subclasses of nouns were introduced, including count, concrete, and collective nouns. However, these are not mutually exclusive categories. Nouns can be count/concrete/collective (e.g. *team*), noncount/abstract/noncollective (e.g. *truth*), count, concrete/noncollective (e.g. *pear*), noncount/concrete/collective (e.g. *police*), and so on. The use of a set of semantic features thus provides for a better means for analyzing nouns into subclasses as it allows for cross-categorizations of this type. We will analyze nouns with the following set of semantic features:

[±COMMON]   [±ANIMATE]   [±COLLECTIVE]
[±COUNT]   [±HUMAN]
[±CONCRETE] [±MALE]
[±COLLECTIVE]

The features [±COMMON], [±COUNT], [±CONCRETE], and [±COLLECTIVE] were defined in Chapter 5. The meaning of the features [±HUMAN] and [±MALE] is self-evident. [±ANIMATE] usually refers to animal rather than vegetable life, with a secondary meaning of 'living'. Thus, *tree* and *beef* should be analyzed as [−ANIMATE], the first not being animal life and the second not being living. In Table 6.3 are some examples of the componential analysis of different sample nouns. Note that there is a hierarchy of features: if something is [−ANIMATE], then [HUMAN] and [MALE] are irrelevant; if [−CONCRETE], then [ANIMATE] is irrelevant. For some terms, the semantic analysis depends on our conception of the object: a university, for example, may be thought of in terms of the concept (*university₁*), the collective body of people constituting the university (*university₂*), or the physical structure (*university₃*).

Using these semantic features, however, we could not distinguish between the terms *father* and *man*. Certain classes of nouns, such as kinship terms, require a different kind of feature, namely relational features. The term *father* could be analyzed in the following way:

X [+PARENT OF] Y
    X [+ANIMATE] [±HUMAN], [+ADULT], [+MALE]
    Y [+ANIMATE], [±HUMAN], [±ADULT], [±MALE]

The term *daughter* would be analyzed as follows:

X [+OFFSPRING OF] Y
    X [+ANIMATE], [±HUMAN], [±ADULT], [−MALE]
    Y [+ANIMATE], [±HUMAN], [+ADULT], [±MALE]

Scalar adjectives, which are always understood in respect to a norm, also lend themselves to an analysis using relational features:

high: Y [+GREATER THAN] Norm
        Y [+DIMENSION OF] X
        Y [+VERTICAL]

Table 6.3. Feature Analyses of Sample Nouns

butter	*cabbage*	*commitment*
[+COMMON]	[+COMMON]	[+COMMON]
[–COUNT]	[+COUNT]	[–COUNT]
[+CONCRETE]	[+CONCRETE]	[–CONCRETE]
[–ANIMATE]	[–ANIMATE]	[–ANIMATE]
weather	*sunrise*	*experience*
[+COMMON]	+COMMON]	[+COMMON]
[–COUNT]	[+COUNT]	[+COUNT]
[+CONCRETE]	[+CONCRETE]	[–CONCRETE]
[–ANIMATE]	[–ANIMATE]	[–ANIMATE]
The Rockies	*aid*	*leftovers*
[–COMMON]	[+COMMON]	[+COMMON]
[–COUNT]	[+COUNT]	[–COUNT]
[+CONCRETE]	[±CONCRETE]	[+CONCRETE]
[–ANIMATE]	[–ANIMATE]	[–ANIMATE]
[+COLLECTIVE]		[+COLLECTIVE]
cook	*aide*	*measles*
[+COMMON]	[+COMMON]	[+COMMON]
[+COUNT]	[+COUNT]	[–COUNT]
[+CONCRETE]	[+CONCRETE]	[–CONCRETE]
[+ANIMATE]	[+ANIMATE]	[–ANIMATE]
[+HUMAN]	[±HUMAN]	
[±MALE]	[±MALE]	
whale	*lioness*	*clergy*
[+COMMON]	[+COMMON]	[+COMMON]
[+COUNT]	[+COUNT]	[–COUNT]
[+CONCRETE]	[+CONCRETE]	[+CONCRETE]
[+ANIMATE]	[+ANIMATE]	[+ANIMATE]
[–HUMAN]	[–HUMAN]	[+HUMAN]
[±MALE]	[–MALE]	[±MALE]
		[+COLLECTIVE]
university₁	*university₂*	*university₃*
[+COMMON]	[+COMMON] or	[+COMMON]
[+COUNT]	[+COUNT]	[+COUNT]
[–CONCRETE]	[+CONCRETE]	[+CONCRETE]
	[+ANIMATE]	[–ANIMATE]
	[+HUMAN]	
	[±MALE]	
	[+COLLECTIVE]	

Verbs could also be analyzed using relational features; we will turn to this type of verbal analysis in Chapter 10.

Self-Testing Exercise: Do Exercise 6.5.

4.2 Feature analysis of verbal predicates

It is possible to characterize the inherent temporal nature of the situation named by the verb[8] by using a number of semantic features. This temporal nature is referred to as "inherent aspect" or "situation aspect".[9] As the use of the term "aspect" suggests, inherent aspect interacts with verbal aspect (perfective/imperfective aspect), which was discussed in Chapter 5. There are a number of ways in which inherent aspect can be defined, but it is sufficient for our purposes to identify four semantic features for verbal predicates:

1. [±STATIVE]: this feature recognizes whether the situation denoted by the verb involves change [–STATIVE] or not [+STATIVE]; it is said that a [–STATIVE] (or dynamic) situation requires the input of energy, whereas a [+STATIVE] situation does not;
2. [±DURATIVE]: this feature recognizes whether the situation goes on in time [+DURA-TIVE] or occurs at a moment in time (punctual/instantaneous) [–DURATIVE];
3. [±TELIC]: this feature recognizes whether the situation has an endpoint or goal which is necessary for the situation to be what it is [+TELIC] or has no necessary conclusion [–TELIC]; and
4. [±VOLUNTARY]: this feature recognizes whether the situation is a matter of an agent's voluntary or willful action [+VOLUNTARY] (intentional) or not [–VOLUNTARY].[10]

On the basis of these features, different situation types are identifiable. The best-known typology is that of Zeno Vendler (1967), which distinguishes four situation types: states, activities, accomplishments, and achievements. Each situation can be analyzed by a unique combination of semantic features, as shown in Table 6.4.

---

8. Terminology in this area is quite confusing, so in recent years the term "situation" has come to be used as a neutral term to denote any state, event, process, act, or activity named by a verb.

9. The German word "Aktionsart" 'type of action' is also commonly used.

10. This feature is, strictly speaking, not a matter of the temporal qualities of a situation, but it has traditionally been treated with inherent aspect.

Table 6.4. Features of Situation Types

state e.g. *love, resemble*	activity e.g. *push, run*
[+STATIVE]	[–STATIVE]
[+DURATIVE]	[+DURATIVE]
[–TELIC]	[–TELIC]
[–VOLUNTARY]	[±VOLUNTARY]
accomplishment e.g. *dress, use up*	achievement e.g. *kick, blink*
[–STATIVE]	[–STATIVE]
[+DURATIVE]	[–DURATIVE]
[+TELIC]	([+TELIC])
[±VOLUNTARY]	[±VOLUNTARY]

States denote unchanging situations such as emotional, cognitive, and physical states, conditions, or qualities. States are continuous over the entire time period in which they exist. Examples of states are the predicates in *Philip {loves, suspects, resembles, expects, doubts} Brigit*. Stative expressions can be identified by a number of formal properties:

- A state is generally expressed in the simple, not the progressive form, because the progressive indicates a situation which is ongoing and changing: **Philip is loving Brigit*.
- A state lasts in time indefinitely, for a given period of time, with no necessary end; it answers the question "for how long?".
- A person cannot be commanded, forced, or persuaded to be in a state because a state is not a matter of volition or will: **Love Brigit! *His mother forced him to love Brigit*.
- For the same reason, no manner adverbs can accompany a stative expression: **Philip loved Brigit {deliberately, studiously, attentively, carefully}*.
- A state cannot occur in a pseudocleft sentence since a state is not "done": ** What Philip did was love Brigit*.
- A states starts and stops, but it cannot be finished: *Philip {started, stopped, *finished} loving Brigit*.

Other examples of states (taken from Vendler) are the following:

know	*believe*	*be X*
be married	*dominate*	*think that*
like/dislike	*see*	*know that/how*
have	*possess*	*believe that/in*
desire	*want*	*understand*
hate	*rule*	*see*

Activities are dynamic situations which go on in time (potentially indefinitely). Examples of activities are the predicates in *Jesse is {reading, pushing the cart, daydreaming, talking with Janice, staring at the picture, sitting on the bed}*.

–   An activity lasts for a period of time and answers the question "for how long?".
–   An activity does not take any definite time nor have any definite end and hence cannot
    be "finished", though like states, activities can begin and end.
–   An activity goes on in a homogeneous way; it is constant over the period of time in
    which it happens.
–   With an activity, one can "spend a certain amount of time V-*ing*".
–   An activity may be either continuing (e.g. *argue, talk, walk*) or changing (e.g. *grow,
    improve, decline*).
–   A test for activities is that if *one stops* V-ing, then *one has* V-ed (if *Jesse stops pushing the
    cart*, then *he has pushed the cart*).

Other examples of activities from Vendler are the following:

run	*swim*	*think about*
walk	*watch*	*housekeep*
look	*observe*	*keep in sight*
pull	*gaze upon*	*follow with one's eyes*
pay attention to	*scrutinize*	*focus one's eyes on*

Although activities are frequently [+VOLUNTARY], they may also be [–VOLUNTARY], as is
the case with, e.g. *The water is flowing, Her arm is bleeding, The child is growing*. Such activities cannot be commanded.

   Accomplishments are dynamic situations with a terminal point or "climax" which is
logically necessary for them to be what they are, as in the examples *Sybil {wrote a letter,
went to the store, cooked dinner}*.

–   In an accomplishment, it is necessary for the endpoint to be reached (i.e. the letter to
    be produced, the store to be reached, and the dinner to be completed) for the accom-
    plishment to occur.
–   A test for accomplishments is that if *one stops* V-ing, then *one has not* V-ed: if *Sybil stops
    writing the letter*, then she has not written a letter; she has simply worked on a letter.
–   An accomplishment, unlike a state and an activity, can be "finished": if *Sybil finishes
    writing the letter*, then she has written a letter).
–   Because of its necessary endpoint, an accomplishment takes a certain amount of time
    and answers the question "how long did it take?".
–   With an accomplishment, one Vs "in a certain amount of time", not "for a certain
    amount of time".
–   An accomplishment does not go on in a homogeneous way, but consists of an activity
    phase and a terminal point, which are different in nature.
–   An accomplishment is ambiguous with *almost*; if *Sybil almost wrote a letter*, then
    she may have written a partial letter or she may not have even begun the letter (just
    thought about it).

Other examples of accomplishments drawn from Vendler are the following:

run a mile	draw a circle	recover from an illness
write a letter	get exhausted	get ready
paint a picture	make a chair	see Carmen
build a house	write/read a novel	play a game of chess
deliver a sermon	give/attend a class	grow up
watch (the passage		
of Venus across the sun)		

Accomplishments can be [+VOLUNTARY], e.g. *run a mile, get ready*, or [−VOLUNTARY], e.g. *get exhausted, grow up.*

Achievements are dynamic situations that are conceived of as occurring instantaneously, as in *Roger {reached the top of the mountain, flicked the switch on, solved the problem}*. They are punctual acts or changes of state. [TELIC] is not really a relevant category here because achievements, since they are punctual, end as soon as they begin (though they are often described as [+TELIC]).

–   An achievement occurs at a single moment in time and answer the question "at what time?".
–   The progressive is either incompatible with an achievement (*She is recognizing a friend*) or denotes the repetition of the achievement either by a singular subject (*He is kicking the ball*) or multiple subjects (*The guests were arriving gradually*).
–   An achievement is incompatible with *start* and *stop* (*She stopped recognizing a friend*); stopping and starting are themselves achievements.

Some achievements can also answer the question "how long did it take?", as in the case of *solve the problem*:

> How long did it take for Roger to solve the problem?
> It took Roger an hour to solve the problem.

This does not imply that at every point during that hour he was necessarily working on the problem.[11] This behavior of achievements seems to suggest that they fall into two subclasses: those that are truly instantaneous (such as *kick, flick, tap*) and those that involve a preliminary process such as *find* (generally preceded by looking for) or *reach the top* (generally preceded by working one's way towards the top). When the process leading up to the endpoint and the endpoint are named by the same verb, the progressive is possible: *He*

---

11.   The meaning of an accomplishment with an expression of duration is quite different. For example, *It took Sybil an hour to write a letter* implies that at every point during that hour she was working on the letter.

died at 5:00/He is dying, The plane arrived at 5:00/The plane is arriving. Other examples of achievements from Vendler are the following:

die	*topple the tree*	*understand*
win the race	*spot (something)*	*get married*
recognize	*find*	*know*
start V-ing	*stop V-ing*	*notice*
realize	*lose*	*see*
cross the border	*resume V-ing*	*catch a dog*
be born	*?think of*	

Achievements are often [–VOLUNTARY] (e.g. *find, spot, catch a dog*), though they can be [+VOLUNTARY] as well (e.g. *cross the border, kick the ball, tap the window*).

> HINT: In Vendler's lists given above, the verbs *understand, see*, and *know* occur in both the categories of states and of achievements. As states, these verbs denote an unchanging condition (e.g. *I understand German, I see poorly, I know how to tune a car*), while as achievements, they denote the dynamic event of coming into a state (e.g. *Now I understand what you mean, I see a parking spot over there, Now I know what to do*). This exemplifies the "multivalency" of verbs in English, that fact that they are often able to name more than one situation type.

You may have noticed that it is often not just the verb alone, but also other parts of the predicate that figure in the determination of situation type. First, the addition of a nominal object may contribute the notion of goal and thus change an activity into an accomplishment:

> *She sang.* (activity) > *She sang a song.* (accomplishment)
> *I worked.* (activity) > *I worked the crossword puzzle.* (accomplishment)

Moreover, the count qualities of the object are significant; with mass and indefinite plural objects, the activity status is unchanged, while with definite plural objects, the activity is converted into an accomplishment:

Activity
Mass noun   *She sang folk music.*
Indefinite plural   *She sang songs.*
Accomplishment
Definite plural   *She sang two songs.*

Prepositional phrases which denote either a spatial goal or temporal limit may also convert an activity into an accomplishment:

> *He walked.* (activity)   >   *He walked {to the store, from dawn to dusk}.*
> (accomplishment)

Particles such as *up, down, out, off,* and *through* may have the same effect:

> *She used the paper.* (activity)   >   *She used up the paper.* (accomplishment)

However, not all prepositional phrases and particles change an activity into an accomplishment:

> *He walked in the woods. I worked at/on the crossword puzzle.*
> *He walked along/on.*
> *I worked on the machine.*

The count qualities of the subject may affect the situation type as well:

achievement	*The runner crossed the line.*
accomplishment	*Two runners crossed the line.*
activity	*Runners crossed the line.*

For these reasons, we speak of *situation type* rather than *verb type*.

Table 6.5. Feature Analyses of Sample Situations

push the buzzer	*take a nap*	*play the piano*
[–STATIVE]	[–STATIVE]	[–STATIVE]
[–DURATIVE]	[+DURATIVE]	[+DURATIVE]
[+TELIC]	[+TELIC]	[–TELIC]
[+VOLUNTARY]	[+VOLUNTARY]	[+VOLUNTARY]
lie down	*hope for*	*set the table*
[–STATIVE]	[+STATIVE]	[–STATIVE]
[–DURATIVE]	[+DURATIVE]	[+DURATIVE]
([+TELIC])	[–TELIC]	[+TELIC]
[+VOLUNTARY]	[–VOLUNTARY]	[+VOLUNTARY]
hurt[12]	*doodle*	*unwrap the package*
[+STATIVE]	[–STATIVE]	[–STATIVE]
[+DURATIVE]	[+DURATIVE]	[+DURATIVE]
[–TELIC]	[–TELIC]	[+TELIC]
[–VOLUNTARY]	[+VOLUNTARY]	[+VOLUNTARY]
do homework	*crack eggs*	*sleep*
[–STATIVE]	[–STATIVE]	[–STATIVE]
[+DURATIVE]	[+DURATIVE]	[+DURATIVE]
[+TELIC]	[–TELIC]	[–TELIC]
[+VOLUNTARY]	[±VOLUNTARY]	[–VOLUNTARY]
trip on the step	*go bald*	*write poetry*
[–STATIVE]	[–STATIVE]	[–STATIVE]
[–DURATIVE]	[+DURATIVE]	[+DURATIVE]
([+TELIC])	[+TELIC]	[–TELIC]
[±VOLUNTARY]	[–VOLUNTARY]	[+VOLUNTARY]

---

12.   This is in the sense 'My hand hurts', not 'He hurt me'.

Table 6.5 presents feature analyses of different situations: *hurt* and *hope for* are states; *doodle, crack eggs, write poetry, play the piano,* and *sleep* are activities; *push the buzzer, lie down, trip on the step* are achievements; and *take a nap, set the table, unwrap the package, do homework,* and *go bald* are accomplishments. Note that for the achievements the feature [TELIC] is put in parentheses as it is not entirely relevant.

The situation type interacts in complex ways with verb aspect, as suggested in the previous chapter. Here it is sufficient to emphasize that changing the aspect of an expression does not alter its situation type. Thus, *she was singing* and *she sang* are both activities, although the first is viewed imperfectively (as ongoing) while the second is viewed perfectively (as a whole or "bounded"). In contrast, *she sings* is an activity which is viewed habitually, that is, is seen as happening in bound segments on different occasions; this constitutes the situation type of habit.[13] Any situation type can be seen as occurring on different occasions over time (as a habit), e.g. *He writes poems* (accomplishment), *He crosses the border everyday* (achievement), *She runs* (activity), *He enjoys every movie he sees* (state).

Self-Testing Exercise: Do Exercise 6.6.

4.3 Feature analysis of modals

Another application of semantic features is in the analysis of the modal meaning, which is most often expressed by the modal auxiliaries and their phrasal equivalents:

will (*would*)	*have to,* often pronounced /hæftə/
can (*could*)	*have got to,* often pronounced /hævgɑtə/
shall (*should*)	*ought to,* often pronounced /atə/
may (*might*)	*need to*
must	*be supposed to,* often pronounced /spoustə/
	be able to

Modal meaning refers to matters of possibility and necessity and can be analyzed using two features:

1. [+**EPISTEMIC**]: epistemic meaning which is a matter of belief (inference, deduction), such as potentiality, possibility, probability, prediction, or certainty; or
2. [+**DEONTIC**]: deontic meaning is a matter of action, such as permission, duty, responsibility, obligation (weak or strong), or command.

Epistemic meanings answer the question "How do you know?", while deontic meanings answer the question "What should I do?". Epistemic modality relates to the entire proposition: *It may rain* = 'it is possible that it will rain'. Deontic modality is subject-oriented: *You*

---

13. Some scholars consider habits to be states, but because they are volitional and consisting of multiple events, they are better understood as a separate situation type.

may leave the table = 'you are permitted to leave the table'. Sentences with modal auxiliaries or their phrasal equivalents are either epistemic or deontic in meaning, or ambiguous between the two readings. Each of the modals may denote both types of meaning, as shown in Table 6.6.

Table 6.6. Epistemic and Deontic Meanings of the Modal Auxiliaries

[+EPISTEMIC]	[+DEONTIC]
may	
He may commit suicide.	You may go to the movies.
Sally may have left.	May I be excused from the table?
must	
I must be dreaming.	I must convince him to reform.
The wet weather must be the result of La Niña.	You must not do that.
will	
John will know the answer.	I will certainly be there.
She will be home soon.	I will marry you.
shall	
I shall be in my office today.	Lesley shall see to it.
We shall finish it by tomorrow.	He shall be there.
can	
Oil can float on water.	You can come in now.
Winters can be very cold here.[14]	Can I be excused from the table?
She can sing beautifully.	
should	
We should be home soon, children.	You should see that movie.
You should know our decision soon.	I should go.
would	
He would know, if anyone does.	Would you please be more attentive.
Would it be safe to travel there?	Would you open the door for me?
could	
She could have known.	She could help you more often.
She could die.	As a child I could climb trees.
might	
That might be the correct answer.	You might check into it.
You might have killed yourself.	You might have been more helpful.
ought to	
According to the information on the board, the plane ought to be here.	The children ought to go to bed now.

(Continued)

---

14.   Positive *can* is somewhat rare in the epistemic sense, though negative *can* is frequently epistemic, as in *It can't be five o'clock already*.

Table 6.6. (Continued)

have to	
This has to be the right house.	I have to finish my paper today.
This has to be the tallest building in the world.	I had to return the library book.
have got to	
This has got to be the one he was referring to.	I have got to be more efficient with my time.
be supposed to	
It is supposed to rain today.	I am supposed to be there now.
be able to	
This car is able to go very fast.	He is able to wiggle his ears.

The different modals are distinguished by the intensity or strength of epistemic or deontic meaning they express. Note that the past-tense forms *would, could, should,* and *might* do not express past-time meaning (except in indirect speech), but rather different degrees of epistemic or deontic meaning.

While the distinction between epistemic and deontic is often quite obvious:

I must leave now	=	'I am obliged to leave now' ([+DEONTIC])
I must be dreaming	=	'it is possible that I am dreaming, I think I am' ([+EPISTEMIC])
		NOT 'I am under an obligation to be dreaming' ([+DEONTIC])

it may also be more subtle:

She will be home soon	=	'I predict that her arrival is imminent, I think it is' ([+EPISTEMIC])
I will marry you	=	'I intend to marry you, this is my intended course of action' ([+DEONTIC])
		NOT 'I predict I will marry you in the future' ([+EPISTEMIC])

Note that permissive *may* is often replaced by *can* for many speakers. The 'ability' sense of *can* (as in *She can sing beautifully*), which cannot be expressed by *may*, is sometimes put in a separate category of "dynamic modality"[15] but for our purposes will be interpreted as epistemic. For most North American speakers, the modal auxiliary *shall* is now quite rare, having been replaced by *will*, so the examples given above may not be very meaningful;[16]

---

15. Unlike deontic modality, which expresses social constraints, and epistemic modality, which expresses inferential constraints, 'ability' refers to constraints within the individual (person or thing) denoted by the subject.

16. The use of *shall* and *will* in dialects which contain both modals is controlled by a complicated set of rules known as the "Wallis Rules" (originally formulated by John Wallis, who wrote a

however, we can still see the contrast between *will* and *shall* in the questions *Will we eat before we leave?*, which asks for a prediction, and *Shall we eat before we leave?*, which asks for a recommendation. Finally, *had to* is the only way to express obligation in the past (because *must* is unpaired).

Sentences may also be ambiguous between epistemic and deontic readings. For example:

- *They must (have to) be married* may mean either that the speaker surmises, perhaps from appearances, that the couple is married ([+EPISTEMIC]) or that the couple is obliged to be married, perhaps in order to do something ([+DEONTIC]). In contrast, *They have to get married* can be only deontic in meaning.
- The sentence *You might have said something* can mean that the speaker believes either that the hearer did probably say something ([+EPISTEMIC]) or that the hearer should have said something ([+DEONTIC]).
- A sentence appearing in a departmental memorandum read *A student whose file of essays is incomplete may not be considered for appeal*; this can interpreted epistemically as a statement of a possible outcome or deontically as a statement of an impermissible course of action.
- *Bill won't go* is either the speaker's prediction about Bill's not going ([+EPISTEMIC]), 'I don't believe he will go', or the speaker's report of Bill's statement about his volition ([+DEONTIC]), 'Bill says that he is unwilling to go'.

Below are some further examples of ambiguous modals. Try to paraphrase the two readings in each case:

> *You must help your mother.*
> *Frank may go out to buy a newspaper.*
> *She must not care.*
> *You may see him.*

> **HINT:** if you put the sentence in the perfect, only the epistemic reading is possible; thus *You must have helped your mother* can only be a surmise about what happened (hence epistemic), not a suggestion about what would be appropriate for you to do (hence deontic).

---

grammar of English – in Latin – in the seventeenth century). In declarative sentences, in the 1st person *shall* makes a prediction (e.g. *I shall be there in an hour*), while *will* expresses the speaker's intention (e.g. *I will marry you*). In the 2nd and 3rd persons, the situation is reversed so that *shall* expresses obligation, while *will* expresses a prediction (e.g. *you shall help your mother* vs. *he will be there in an hour*). In interrogative sentences, the modals operate differently: in the 1st and 3rd persons, *shall* is deontic and *will* is epistemic, while in the 2nd person *shall* is epistemic and *will* is deontic.

Epistemic and deontic meaning can be expressed by parts of speech other than the modal auxiliaries, as exemplified below:

1. modal verbs:

    I assume that he's left.   ([+EPISTEMIC])
    I suggest that he learn the answer.   ([+DEONTIC])
    I suggest that he knows the answer.   ([+EPISTEMIC])
    I insist that he do it.   ([+DEONTIC])
    I insist that he did it.   ([+EPISTEMIC])
    I {guess, think} that you're right.   ([+EPISTEMIC])
    We recommend that he step down.   ([+DEONTIC])

I expect him to go is ambiguous: either 'it is possible that he will go' ([+EPISTEMIC]) or 'I place him under some obligation to go' ([+DEONTIC]).

2. modal adjectives:

    It is obligatory to understand modals.   ([+DEONTIC])
    It isn't necessary to read that chapter.   ([+DEONTIC])
    It is possible to understand modals.   ([+EPISTEMIC])
    It is probable that the results are known. ([+EPISTEMIC])

3. modal adverbs: *probably, possibly, certainly*

4. modal nouns:

    It is your {duty, obligation} to look after your parents.   ([+DEONTIC])
    There is a {likelihood, probability, possibility} of rain today. ([+EPISTEMIC])

5. epistemic parentheticals:

    You are right, I {guess, think, suspect, believe, reckon, feel, assume}.
    Your cat will come back, I'm {certain, sure, confident}.

Self-Testing Exercise: Do Exercise 6.7.

4.4 Postscript on semantic features

The goal of analyzing all words of a language in terms of combinations of semantic features has never been met. Once one departs from the clear-cut cases of livestock terms or even concrete nouns and verbs, it becomes quite difficult to decide what the primitive components of meaning are, which concepts cannot be further analyzed, when one should stop making distinctions, and so on. No one has yet determined all the possible semantic components of a one language (let alone a universal list). To do so, it would probably be necessary to postulate many semantic components that occur in only one word. But components are supposed to be recurrent, so such unique features undercut the purpose of semantic feature analysis. Moreover, many aspects of meaning are not binary and are not susceptible to analysis into binary features. We also saw that for different parts of speech, we had to postulate very different kinds of semantic features. Furthermore, in any particular use of a word, only some or perhaps none of the postulated semantic features may be relevant. As we will see below, in cases of metaphorical language, it appears that only certain features of a word may be important: in a sentence such as *He's a pig* (meaning 'he has terrible table manners'), the intrinsic feature of [+ANIMATE], [–HUMAN], [+SWINE] are not relevant to the intended meaning; rather, the emphasis is on certain behavioral characteristics. We seem to use different features for different purposes, such as to identify something, to give synonyms or definitions, or to make inferences. It is uncertain how clearly features are marked, especially in our passive vocabulary. In fact, there is little evidence that semantic features have any psychological reality, that when we use words, we "think" of any of the constituent components, or even that the features are relevant in our understanding of the meaning of the word.

5.   Prototypes

An alternative to feature analysis, which is intended to have psychological validity is called **prototype** theory (proposed by psychologist Eleanor Rosch, 1973). It argues that we understand the meaning of a word because we have a prototypical concept of the category to which the thing belongs. A prototype is a good, clear exemplar of a category.[17] All members of the category are judged in relation to this prototype. That is, it is not a case of ascertaining whether an entity possess the attributes characterizing a category or not, but how closely it approximates an optimal instance of the category. The result is graded membership in a category: things are more or less good exemplars of a category. When members can be ranked in this way, the set is said to be "fuzzy". Thus, for example, we have a prototypical concept of a sport (perhaps soccer) and we understand all other sports in relation to this prototype. **Core members** would be those sports most closely resembling the prototype, such as rugby, football, basketball, hockey, baseball, and volleyball, whereas more **peripheral members** would include those which are not as easily, or quickly, identified as a sport, including golf, table tennis, curling, and badminton. The defining characteristics of a sport would seem to have something to do with physical activity regulated by a set of rules, involving competition between individuals or teams. Less "sport-like" and hence more peripheral would be shuffleboard, archery, arm wrestling, kite flying, square dancing, apple bobbing, skeet shooting, etc., which may not have all of the essential attributes. The core members elicit more shared attributes than the more peripheral members.

---

17.   A prototype has also been understood both as a subcategory (exhibiting a certain set of attributes) and as an abstraction of a category.

Another example might be the category of birds. Core members would be birds such as robins, sparrow, starlings, jays, and eagles, whereas more peripheral members would be emus, ostriches, penguins, and chickens.

If we consider what makes a cup a cup and not a bowl, we would focus on physical characteristics (handle or not), function (for drinking or eating out of), and possible contents (tea vs. noodles). Or if we consider the concept of jewelry, we would certainly judge necklaces, pins, and rings to be core members; there might be some disagreement about items such as wristwatches, tie-clasps, and cufflinks, while many would probably reject altogether items such as eyeglasses, medic-alert bracelets, and belt buckles. Thus, our prototype of jewelry seems to have the notion of 'purely ornamental, nonfunctional' as central. In an experiment, subjects were asked to rank things as good or bad members of a particular category (e.g. fruit, sport, vegetable, vehicle, even numbers, odd numbers, female, plane geometry) and their responses were timed: they were faster with familiar, typical things, thus suggesting the validity of prototypes (Armstong, Gleitman, & Gleitman, 1983).[18]

The concept of prototype is related to what is called the **basic level term.** This is the level at which people normally conceptualize and name things. Thus, "chair" is a basic level term and occurs most frequently, while "kitchen chair" occurs on a lower level and "furniture" on a higher level. Basic level terms tend to be structurally simple, while those on a lower level are frequently compounds and those at a higher levels may be morphologically deviant, denoting conceptually vague and undifferentiated entities. A basic level term maximizes the number of attributes shared by members of each category and minimizes the number of attributes shared by different categories. It is often easier to specify the attributes of a basic level category than of the higher-level (superordinate) category. The features of the superordinate term that emerge are so general that they often do not define the category. A basic level term has to do with "what things are called"; in contrast, a prototype has to do with "what words refer to" (Taylor 2003, p. 53). In respect to what I am reading, I would refer to it with the basic level term "book" (regardless of whether it is a novel, a textbook, a book of poetry, a non-fiction book, etc.) because this is the level in a categorization hierarchy at which a book is normally named. In respect to "reading matter", I would apply it to prototypical instances such as books and magazines rather than cereal cartons or packing lists.

Let's look at one extended example of prototypes. If we consider the concept of "vehicles", we might first divide the concept into three divisions – land, air, and water vehicles – and then list the core and peripheral members as a means of arriving at the defining characteristics of the category (see Table 6.7). It is obvious that there would be a fair amount of disagreement among speakers concerning both the members of this category and the division into core and peripheral. The general definition of 'a conveyance for the transport

---

18.   Oddly, while the range of acceptability for categories like fruit was quite large, there was also a range for even and odd numbers, which should not logically be rankable.

of people or cargo' would undoubtedly be unproblematic (but very vague and abstract). However, for some speakers, the prototype of a vehicle includes the concept of movement over land, so neither air nor water conveyances are considered "vehicles". Many speakers might include in their prototype a notion of running on wheels or tires and thus exclude water conveyances and perhaps trains as well. Most speakers view a vehicle as motorized or capable of moving independently, thus excluding conveyances propelled through human or animal power, such as wagons or rickshaws; conveyances such as wheelchairs or go-carts, which may or may not be motorized, also create a problem. Students asked to perform this exercise with the concept of vehicle have actually come up with a wide variety of defining characteristics for vehicles – such as that a vehicle must be enclosed or that it must be something one sits in – suggesting that individual speakers may have quite divergent prototypes of categories.

Table 6.7. Core and Peripheral Members of the Category "Vehicle"

Type	Core Members	Peripheral Members		
Land	*car*	*truck*	*bicycle*	*tricycle*
	motorcycle	*scooter*	*skateboard*	*wagon*
	limousine	*van*	*baby carriage*	*shopping cart*
	bus	*ambulance*	*wheel barrow*	*sled*
	hearse	*taxi*	*toboggan*	*rickshaw*
	tractor	*go-cart*	*wheelchair*	*cart*
	combine	*train*	*buggy*	*carriage*
Air	*airplane*	*helicopter*	*hot air balloon*	*glider*
	spaceship	*satellite*	*jet*	*parachute*
Water	*ferry*	*yacht*	*canoe*	*kayak*
	tanker	*motorboat*	*sailboat*	*(life)raft*
	ship	*tugboat*	*rowboat*	*catamaran*
	hovercraft	*steamboat*	*dinghy*	
	hydrofoil	*tugboat*	*barge*	

Self-Testing Exercise: Do Exercise 6.8.

6. Semantic anomaly

One of the basic semantic concepts mentioned at the beginning of the chapter was semantic anomaly. How is it that speakers of the language are all able to recognize that certain expressions, say, *the birth of a peanut* or *the birth of a lamp*, are meaningless? At the same time, how is it also possible that we can provide an interpretation – a figurative interpretation – for other expressions, say, *the birth of the morning, the birth of a nation*, or *the birth of linguistics*, which on the surface are equally anomalous, since only animate beings are born?

6.1   Selectional restrictions

Semantic anomaly follows from restrictions on the compatibility or combinability of words. Not only does a word contain certain semantic features, but it may also require that words with which it cooccurs contain certain features. These are called its **selectional restrictions**. Frequently a verb selects features in its noun arguments (subject or object) and an adjective selects a noun. In Table 6.8, we see examples of selectional restrictions for certain words. Even keeping in mind that we are considering only absolutely literal uses of

Table 6.8. Examples of Selectional Restrictions

---

trot – requires [+QUADRUPED] subject

> *{The horse, *the money, *the spider} trotted home.*

fly – requires [+WINGED] subject

> *{The airplane, the bird, *the goat} flew north.*

sing – requires [+HUMAN] or [+AVIAN] subject

> *{The woman, the bird, *the motor} sang sweetly.*
> cf. *The motor hummed softly.*

talk, think, dream – require [+HUMAN] subject (or possibly [+ANIMATE])

> *{The man, *the rock} is talking/thinking/dreaming.*
> *My dog is talking to me/thinking about his dinner/dreaming about cats.*

admire – requires [+HUMAN] subject

> *{Judy, *the goldfish} admires Mozart.*

pray – requires [+HUMAN] [±COLLECTIVE] subject

> *{The man, the nation, *the treaty} is praying for peace.*

pregnant – requires [+ANIMATE] and [–MALE] subject

> *{Mary, the mare, *the bull} is pregnant.*

marry – requires [+HUMAN] subject and object

> *Carl married Susan. *The goose married the gander.*

terrify – requires [+ANIMATE] object

> *The thunder terrified {the dog, the child, *the house}.*

anger – requires [+ANIMATE] object

> *Intruders anger {dogs, homeowners, *houses}.*

drink – requires [+ANIMATE] subject and [+LIQUID] object

> *{The child, *the glass} drank {the milk, *the candy}.*

melt – requires [+SOLID] object or subject

> *The sun melted {the candy, *the smoke, *the water}. The candy melted.*

fall – requires [+CONCRETE] subject

> *{The book, *the truth} fell to the floor.*

shatter – requires [+SOLID] subject or object

> *The hammer shattered {the rock, *the pudding}. The rock shattered.*

tall – requires [+VERTICAL] object

> *{The building, the person, *the road} is tall.*

long – requires [+HORIZONTAL] object

> *{The ribbon, *the tree} is long.*

---

language, we can see that there are certain limitations with selectional restrictions. For example, although *fly* typically requires a [+WINGED] subject, we can also say (non-literally) *The paper flew out the window, Dust flew into my face*, where the subject does not have the requisite feature. We can either change the selectional restriction to something broader (e.g. [+CAPABLE OF BEING LIFTED BY WIND] or simply say that prototypically the verb *fly* requires a [+WINGED] subject.

When selectional restrictions are violated, when there is an incompatibility in the selectional restrictions of a word and the inherent features of a word in combination with it, we have semantic anomaly. There is generally an implied rather than an explicit contradiction, as in **The rooster laid an egg*: *lay an egg* requires a [–MALE] subject, while *rooster* is [+MALE]. (Compare the explicit contradiction of **The rooster is a hen*, where *rooster* is [+MALE] and *hen* is [–MALE].)

6.2   Figurative language

To this point, we have been concerned with literal or "normal" uses of language, because figurative uses of language (personification, metaphor, etc.) routinely violate or break selectional restrictions. With figurative uses of language, as opposed to true anomaly, however, we can supply some interpretation. We do this, it seems, by allowing certain semantic features to override others in context. Compare the following three sentences:

Literal:	*An intruder attacked me.*
Metaphorical:	*Envy attacked me.*
Anomalous:	*The rock attacked me.*

Both the second and third sentences violate the selectional restriction that *attack* requires a [+ANIMATE] subject, but the second one permits interpretation, while the third one does not.

Types of figurative language.   Let's first consider some of the different ways in which selectional restrictions may be violated. When these violations are interpretable, we are dealing with types of figurative language:

1.   **Oxymoron (paradox)** refers to expressions which contain an explicit contradiction, such as *delicious torment, living death, sweet sorrow, silent scream, cold comfort, good grief, pleasing pain*, or the Shakespearean "I must be cruel only to be kind". Other more mundane and apparently paradoxical expressions include *soft rock, taped live, resident alien,* or *sanitary landfill*.

2.   **Tautology** refers to expressions which are "true by definition", offering no new information, such as *A gander is a male goose* or *An orphan is a parentless child*. Most

dictionary definitions are tautologies of sorts. Other examples of tautologies include the following:

exclusive prerogative	*Boys will be boys.*
new innovation	*Business is business.*
past history	*He is his father's son.*
end result	*What will be will be.*
main protagonist	*It ain't over till it's over.*
scrutinize carefully	*His moustache is on his upper lip.*

The purpose of a tautology such as *free gift* seems to be to emphasize or highlight the feature [+FREE] inherent in the word *gift* by expressing it in a separate word. However, in the case of an expression such as *boys will be boys* we appear not to have a true tautology, but an **apparent tautology**, since the second instance of *boy* is not understood in respect to its core inherent features [+HUMAN], [+MALE], [–ADULT], as is the first instance of *boy*, but in respect to certain behavioral characteristics of boys, for example, loudness, rowdiness, carelessness, and so on. (Which of the above are true tautology and which apparent tautology?)

3. **Synesthesia** refers to expressions which combine a word from one sensory domain with a word from another sensory domain, such as *cold response, sweet sound, cool reception, sharp rebuke, flat note, quiet color,* or *soothing color.* A common type of synesthesia is the use of a color terms (from the visual domain) in conjunction with an emotional states (*blue/black mood, green with envy, yellow with cowardice, red with anger*). Again, it appears that secondary features of a word are brought to the forefront so that, for example, the soothing or calming features of *quiet*, not its feature of low audition, are emphasized in *quiet color.*

4. **Synecdoche** refers to expressions which refer to a thing by naming part of it, such as *a new face* or *new blood* (= a new person). A typical kind of synecdoche is the naming of something by naming the material of which it is composed, such as *a cork, an iron, a glass,* and more recently *plastic* (= credit card).

5. **Metonymy** refers to expressions which denote a thing by naming something associated with it:

the bar (= the legal profession)	*the law* (= the police)
the church (= religion)	*runners* (= athletic shoes for running)
(man of) the cloth (= clergyman, priest)	*rush hour* (= commuting time before and after work)
the crown, the throne (= the king)	*the bench* (= the judiciary)
backbencher (= member of parliament without power)	*a suit* (= a businessman, and perhaps businesswoman)

6. **Personification** refers to expressions which attribute human qualities to nonhuman or inanimate objects, such as *The idea grabbed me, The vending machine ate my money.*

7. **Metaphor** refers to expressions which transfer a word from one conceptual domain to another, such as the following, which all violate the selectional restrictions given in Table 6.8 for the relevant words:

Stock prices are falling.	*The bell sang out when struck.*
There was a pregnant pause.	*He flew into a rage.*
The bad news shattered her.	*She was away a long time.*
That is certainly a tall order.	*He eagerly drank up the new ideas.*

A typical type of metaphor is the use of body parts to name the parts of other entities:

lip of a glass	*mouth of a river*
eye of a storm	*shoulder of a road*
heart of a problem	*ribs of a ship*
legs of a table	*head of a committee*
neck of a bottle	*guts of a machine*

The transference of terms from the physical domain to the mental domain, as in *grasp the point, get a joke*, or *wrestle with an idea*, is also very common; in fact, much of our Latinate vocabulary denoting cognitive processes, such as *translate, deduce, abstract, explain, compose, conceive*, and *affirm*, originally denotes physical processes. The use of animal terms to denote human beings held in low esteem is also typical: *a rat, wolf, snake (in the grass), pit bull, tiger*, and so on.

The interpretation of metaphors.   In metaphor, selectional restrictions may be violated in one of two ways, depending on whether the noun or the verb must be interpreted metaphorically:

–   The noun is interpreted metaphorically: *Ralph is married to a gem, Juliet is the sun, Billboards are warts on the landscape.*
    The verb BE selects subjects and objects with the same semantic features; thus, *gem, sun*, and *warts* are incompatible with the verb and are read figuratively.)
–   The verb is interpreted metaphorically: *My car drinks gasoline, Craig ate up the compliments, Kevin is married to his work, The moonlight sleeps upon the bank.* The selectional restrictions of the subjects or objects of these sentences are incompatible with the features of *drink, eat, be married*, and *sleep*, and thus the verbs are read figuratively.

Sometimes, however, there is no apparent violation of selectional restrictions in the immediate context, as in *They have swerved from the path* or *He bit off a larger bite than he could chew*. The larger context will undoubtedly reveal a violation of selectional restrictions.

While the interpretation of metaphors is a difficult matter, it seems that in general we interpret them by selecting only some, but not all of the features of a word, and often not the core but rather the peripheral features and transferring them to the other domain. Thus, for *the vending machine ate my money*, it is not the feature of 'consuming for nutriment' for *eat* which is evoked, but the features of 'consuming' without giving anything obvious in return. By substituting these features, we arrive at the literal meaning: *the vending machine used up my money*. However, such a reading overlooks the specifically figurative meaning – that of attributing human qualities to a machine – which motivates the use of the figurative expression. We transfer the features of eating (of intentional action) onto the inanimate subject to arrive at the metaphorical meaning, thus animating or personifying an inanimate object.

Looking specifically at the novel metaphors of literary works, linguist Tanya Reinhart (1980) has proposed a system for analyzing metaphors which takes into account this two-part process of literary and metaphorical reading. She uses as an example the following metaphor from T. S. Eliot's "The Love Song of J. Alfred Prufrock":

> *The yellow fog that rubs its back upon the window-panes …*

We first assign this metaphor a "focus interpretation",[19] which yields its "literal" meaning, what the metaphor is about. In this reading, the features of rubbing one's back which are relevant in context are transferred to the movement of fog. Thus, the fog is seen to be moving and touching up against the window panes. Literally, the fog is swirling up against the window panes. But there is also a "vehicle interpretation", in which the features of cats relevant in context – such as their fuzziness, yellowness, sensuousness, even stealth – are transferred to the fog. This evokes the intended image of the fog as a cat. Notice that the vehicle interpretation is much more open-ended than the focus interpretation.[20]

Reinhart discusses a second metaphor from the same poem:

> *I have seen the mermaids riding seawards on the waves …*

In the focus interpretation, the relevant features of riding – the rising and falling motion – are transferred to the mermaids' movement. Literally, the mermaids are advancing by sitting on the waves. In the vehicle interpretation, the relevant features of horses – their force, their nobility, their need to be tamed, and so on – are transferred to waves. This evokes the image of the waves as horses.

Self-Testing Exercise: Do Exercise 6.9, questions 1–4.

7.   Cognitive approaches to meaning

Another approach to the understanding of metaphors is provided by George Lakoff and Mark Johnson in their book *Metaphors We Live By* (1980). They argue that not only is language metaphorical, but the cognitive processes underlying language are themselves

---

19.   This has also been called the "tenor".

20.   Another way to see this distinction is to associate the tenor interpretation with the concept that is being described, the "target domain" (i.e. fog in this case) and the vehicle interpretation with the comparison or analogy that is being made, the "source domain" (i.e. cats in this case).

metaphorical. That is, "a metaphor is essentially a device that involves conceptualizing one domain of experience in terms of another" (Lee, 2001, p. 6). For example, consider metaphors such as the following:

> *I won the argument.*
> *He retreated from his initial position.*
> *She buttressed her position with several examples.*
> *He shot down all my arguments.*

Here, we conceptualize arguing (the target domain) in terms of warfare (the source domain). What is conceptualized in terms of what is not random. Source domains tend to relate to concrete and more immediate areas of human experience, whereas target domains are more abstract. Quite systematic mappings or correlations between conceptual domains underlie coherent sets of structural metaphors; metaphors come together in "a coherent system of metaphorical concepts and a corresponding coherent system of metaphorical expressions of those concepts (Lakoff & Johnson 1980, p. 9). Importantly, these coherent mappings permit us to interpret metaphors. For example, loss of consciousness is associated with being or going down (e.g. *fall into a coma, be under a spell, drop off to sleep*) while gaining consciousness is associated with being or going up (e.g. *come out of a coma, wake up*). That is, we conceptualize consciousness in terms of the spatial orientation. Other examples of metaphors based on unifying cognitive mappings are the following:

ideas are objects (to be sensed)
    building: *The argument is shaky.*
    food: *That notion is half-baked.*
    people: *He is the father of linguistics.*
    plants: *The seeds of the idea were planted.*
time is money

I've invested a lot of time.	*I haven't enough time.*
You're running out of time.	*You've wasted my time.*
He's living on borrowed time.	*Can you spare me a moment.*
Put aside some time this evening.	*That cost me a day's delay.*

love is a physical force
    There isn't any electricity between us.
    They gravitated towards each other.
love is a patient
    Their relationship is {sick, healthy}.
love is madness/illness

She drives me crazy.	*He is mad about her.*
Love is blind.	*She's consumed by jealousy.*

love is magic

She cast her spell.	*She charmed him.*

love is war

He made a conquest.	*He made an advance.*
She has to fend off suitors.	*She rebuffed his advances.*

time is a line

> *the days ahead/behind*   *Don't look back/ahead.*
> *the weeks to come*   *That is behind us.*
> *We set the meeting back/forward.*

In some cases (e.g. 'consciousness is up') these mappings are based on our bodily experience of the world. And there are other metaphors based on a systematicity of mapping between the 'up-down' domain and some other domain, such as moral goodness/badness (e.g. *he has high standards, he's sunk into depravity*) or physical health/illness (e.g. *she's in peak form, she fell ill*). We saw above the mapping between body parts and other domains (e.g. *head of a pin, shoulder of a road*) and between the physical and cognitive domains (e.g. *grasp the idea, get the joke*). Note that mapping works in one direction – from up-down to health but not the reverse. These types of mapping can license the creation of novel metaphors and indeed new vocabulary.

Lakoff and Johnson (1980) also argue that metonymy (see above) operates by very similar cognitive processes, but in this case involving connections within a single domain rather than across domains. Thus, for example, a pervasive kind of metonymy involves conceptualizing a person by means of the object or place associated with that person:

> <u>*The stroller*</u> *needs to get off at the next stop* (= 'the person with the stroller').
> <u>*The fish-and-chips*</u> *was a good tipper* (= 'the person who ordered fish-and-chips at the restaurant').
> <u>*The taxis*</u> *are on strike* (= 'cab drivers')
> *He is* <u>*a hired gun*</u> (= 'assassin')
> <u>*The green car*</u> *is driving too fast* (= 'person in the green car')
> *High level talks are taking place between* <u>*Washington and Beijing*</u> (= 'representatives of the governments of the US and China').

This view of metaphor and metonymy forms the germ of a more fully-developed theory of meaning called "cognitive semantics", which has been developed in recent years. According to this approach, "because of our physical experience of being and acting in the world … we form basic conceptual structures which we then use to organize thought across a range of more abstract domains" (Saaed, 2009, p. 366). These conceptual structures are called "image schema" and include such abstract concepts as up-down, front-back, part-whole, inside-outside (container-contained), force, path, balance, and containment. For example, the "Path schema", which is based on our experience of moving in the world and of witnessing the movement of other items, underlies the following metaphors:

> *at the end of his life*   *past his prime*
> *embark on a new life*   *get side-tracked in life*
> *get on (in life)*   *be in a dead-end job*
> *give him a good start in life*   *get off on the wrong foot*
> *at the mid-point in his life*   *at a good point in his life*

Paths generally involve directional movement, a beginning and an end, as well as places along the way.

The "Force schema" involves a force acting on an entity; the force may continue or it may encounter a blockage (a barrier), which then may be removed. It is possible to analyze the meaning of the deontic and epistemic senses of the modal auxiliaries (see above) using the Force schema. A force-dynamic view of deontic meaning – which relates to action – seems intuitively obvious: deontic meanings refer to internal and external sociophysical forces. For example, deontic (obligatory) *must* as in *You must leave now* involves a compelling force directing the subject towards an act; deontic (permissive) *may* as in *You may turn in your paper tomorrow* involves a potential but absent barrier, or the elimination of a barrier. However, a force-dynamic view of epistemic meaning – which relates to belief – is not as intuitively obvious. Sweetser (1990) argues that epistemic meaning involves a metaphorical extension from social and physical force to the world of reasoning. For example, epistemic *may* as in *Jane may visit today* involves a metaphorical extension of the potential but absent barrier meaning seen in deontic *may* (i.e. here it is the absence of the barrier preventing the conclusion being reached that Jane will visit); epistemic *must* as in *Barry must be home by now* involves a force compelling the speaker to reach the conclusion that Barry is home.

In conclusion, the overarching view of cognitive linguistics is that the meanings of words are a reflection of general conceptual organization (mappings between and within conceptual domains) and principles of linguistic categorization (prototypicality, core and peripheral meanings). Words act as a set of instructions to create meaning (often multiple meanings) in particular contexts, and thus no strict distinction can be made between semantics and pragmatics (which we will discuss in Chapter 11).

Self-Testing Exercise: Do Exercise 6.9, question 5–6.

Chapter summary

Now that you have completed this chapter, you should be able to:

1. identify semantic relationships such as entailment, inclusion, contradiction, anomaly, ambiguity, connotation/denotation, hyponomy, polysemy, meronymy, and presupposition;
2. recognize the structural relations of synonymy, hyponymy, antonymy, complementarity, and converseness between words;
3. analyze nouns using seven inherent features and verbal predicates using four inherent features;
4. determine whether modal forms are epistemic, deontic, or ambiguous, and give paraphrases of these readings;
5. recognize and name different kinds of figurative language – oxymoron, paradox, tautology, apparent tautology, metonymy, synecdoche, personification, and synesthesia;

6.   give a vehicle and focus interpretation of a novel metaphor; and

7.   identify image schema that underlie metaphors in the language.

Recommended additional reading

Overviews of many of the topics discussed in this chapter may be found in Jeffries (2006, Chapter 6), Fromkin, Rodman, and Hyams (2007, Chapter 5, pp. 186–197), Finegan (2008, Chapter 6, pp. 172–191), and Curzan and Adams (2009, Chapter 7). General discussions of lexical semantics include Palmer (1981), Cruse (1986), Lyons (1995), Kearns (2000), Saeed (2009), and Griffiths (2006). Hurford, Heasley, and Smith (2007) contains a series of practice exercises and answers which cover most of the topics in this chapter. An excellent discussion of English semantics is Kreidler (1998). A comprehensive treatment of semantics is Allan (1986).

More specialized treatments of the topics of this chapter include Kiparsky and Kiparsky (1971), Levinson (1983, Chapter 4), and Saeed (2009, Section 4.5) on presupposition; Lyons (1995, Chapter 4), Cruse (1986), and Saeed (2009, Section 3.5) on structural semantics; Katz and Fodor (1963) and Saeed (2009, Chapter 9) on componential analysis; Taylor (2003) and Ungerer and Schmid (2006, Chapters 1 and 2) on prototypes; Lakoff and Johnson (1980), Johnson (1987), Fauconnier (1994), Saeed (2009, Chapter 11), and Ungerer and Schmid (2006, Chapter 3) on cognitive semantics. Lee (2001) provides a good introduction to cognitive linguistics and Evans and Green (2006) a much more comprehensive treatment.

The modal auxiliaries in English have been treated extensively; for good discussions, see Palmer (1990), Frawley (1992, Chapter 9), and Leech (2004, Chapter 5). More advanced readings can be found in Facchinetti, Krug, and Palmer (Eds.) (2003).

Discussions of inherent aspect, or situation types, may be found in Vendler (1967, "Verbs and Times"), Frawley (1992, Chapter 4), Smith (1997, Chapters 2–3), Kearns (2000, Chapter 9), and Brinton (2009 [1988], Chapter 1).

A dictionary of terms in semantics is Cruse (2006).

Chapter 7

Phrasal structure and verb complementation

Chapter preview

This chapter treats the syntax of simple sentences in English. It begins with a brief description of generative grammar, defining the notion of a syntactic constituent and discussing the different relations of dependency between members of a constituent. The remainder of the chapter is concerned with the phrase structure grammar of English. Following an introduction to the formalisms of phrase structure rules, the distinction between subject and predicate is discussed. The internal structure of the noun phrase, the adjective phrase, the adverb phrase, and the prepositional phrase is then considered. Finally, the complement structures found in the verb phrase are treated, a number of grammatical functions are identified, and a categorization of verb types emerges.

Commentary

1. Introduction to generative grammar

We move now from the study of individual words to the study of the sequences of words which form the structure of sentences. This is the study of syntax. Although there are many ways to approach this study, we will take a primarily "generative" approach. This approach to syntax came into being over fifty years ago, and has been the dominant approach ever since.[1] This chapter makes use of some of the core notions of generative grammar which are most useful for empirical and pedagogical purposes without concerning itself with the now strongly theoretical and quite abstract aspects of this approach.

A fundamental tenet of generative grammar is that not only do words occur in a linear order (or "string") but they also enter into hierarchical relationships with one another within coherent units known as "constituents". Constituents are the proper subparts of sentences, as we will see below. Generative grammar inherited the notion of constituents from the approach to grammar which preceded it called "American Structural Linguistics". The form of sentence analysis used by the American structuralists was known as "immediate constituent analysis". (An even older form of sentence analysis which recognizes the existence of hierarchical structures in sentences is the "sentence diagramming" of traditional grammar; see Chapter 12.)

In a book entitled *Syntactic Structures* originally published in 1957, which inaugurated generative grammar, Noam Chomsky argued that immediate constituent analysis, though not wrong, was insufficient since it dealt only with the surface order (Chomsky, 2002). It could not account for the relation between an active and corresponding passive sentence (e.g. *Sam walked the dog* ~ *The dog was walked by Sam*) or a declarative and corresponding interrogative sentence (e.g. *Sam walked the dog. ~ Did Sam walk the dog?*), which have different linear orders (different strings of words) but are understood by speakers as related. It could also not account for the difference between sentences such as *Samantha is eager to please* and *Samantha is easy to please*, which on the surface seem to have the same structure but are in fact structurally very different (note that one can say *It is easy to please Samantha* but not **It is eager to please Samantha*). Nor did immediate constituent analysis provide a means of distinguishing between structural ambiguous sentences such as the following:

> *The missionary is ready to eat.*
> *Norah's writing occasioned him some surprise.*
> *Visiting relatives can be tiresome.*
> *Flying planes can be dangerous.*
> *The tourists objected to the guide that they couldn't hear.*
> *They took the animal to the small animal hospital.*

---

1. In that time, generative grammar (originally known as "Transformational-Generative (T-G) Grammar") has undergone many changes, including versions known as "Standard Theory", "Extended Standard Theory", "Government and Binding Theory", "Principles and Parameters", and "Minimalism" (see advanced textbooks in "Recommended Additional Reading" section). As is also to be expected, alternative approaches have also arisen, including "Lexical Functional Grammar (LFG)", "Systemic Grammar", "Optimality Theory", and so on.

For example, is it the relatives (who happen to be visiting) who are tiresome or is it the fact of a visit to relatives that can be tiresome? (Try to determine the ambiguity in each case.)

Chomsky argued for the need to distinguish between **deep** (or **underlying**) **structure** (**D-structure**) and **surface structure** (**S-structure**). D-structure is the abstract level in which all meaning resides, determining the structure of simple sentences, the lexical and phrasal categories to which words in the sentence belong, and the hierarchical relationships in which the words enter. S-structure is the actual linear order of words. It is important to distinguish between the two levels for two reasons:

1. different sequences on the surface – as in an active sentence and its passive counterpart such as *The dog uncovered the bone* and *The bone was uncovered by the dog* – may have (roughly) the same meaning and hence identical D-structures, but different S-structures.
2. similar or identical sequences on the surface – as in a case of structural ambiguity such as *Flying planes can be dangerous* – may have different meanings and hence different D-structure, though their S-structures are the same.

In the classical "standard" form of generative grammar, it was argued that syntax consisted of two types of rules, **phrase structure rules** and **transformations**.[2] Phrase structure rules account for the form of D-structures, which are simple (as opposed to complex), active (as opposed to passive), declarative (as opposed to interrogative or imperative), and positive (as opposed to negative) sentences. The phrase structure rules specify what is a constituent of what, or in other words, they reveal the hierarchical structures of sentences. Transformations perform various syntactic operations on the output of the phrase structure rules to produce surface structures. They may move, transpose, add, and delete elements, but they may not change meaning.

What gives generative grammar its name **generative**? It is the view that in order for a speaker to acquire a language, the rules of the grammar must be finite in number. No speaker could master an infinite number of rules. At the same time, this finite set of rules must be able to "generate", or produce, any possible sentence of English (and no impossible sentence of English). This finite set of rules must account for the infinite number of sentences that can be produced and comprehended by speakers of a language.

Finally, generative grammar is concerned exclusively with the form of sentences, distinguishing between "grammatical" (or "acceptable") and "meaningful". For example, the sentence (coined by Noam Chomsky) *Colorless green ideas sleep furiously* is grammatical, though not necessarily meaningful, while the sentence *Furiously sleep ideas green colorless* is ungrammatical (unacceptable) since it violates the rules of syntax. In other words, it is

---

2. Note that these rules are constitutive rules (determining grammatical structure) rather than regulatory rules (legislating the "good" forms to use, see Chapter 1).

believed that syntax and meaning are completely separate: grammar is autonomous and independent of meaning. (We will look at the semantics of sentences in Chapter 10.)

In this chapter and the next two chapters, we will study the phrase structure rules and syntactic operations needed to account for the syntax of English.

2. Constituents

As observed above, **constituents** are the proper subparts of sentences. The study of syntax is the analysis of the constituent parts of a sentence:

-   their form (the types of elements, the internal arrangement of elements, and the relation among elements within the constituent),
-   their (external) positioning in respect to other constituents, and
-   their function.

Constituents may themselves be complex, containing other constituents. The structure of a sentence is hence hierarchical.

Note that the same sequences of words may not always function as a constituent. It is the context which determines whether a particular sequence forms a constituent or not. In the following three sentences:

> *Suzie took in the winter scene.*
> *They won't survive in the winter.*
> *He is happy in the winter.*

"in the winter" is a constituent in the second and third sentences, but not in the first. In the first sentence "in" forms a constituent with "took". The sequence of words "beautiful flowers" is a constituent in *I received beautiful flowers for my birthday* but not in *Though they are beautiful, flowers cause me to sneeze*. The sequence "the house on the hill" is a constituent in one reading of the ambiguous sentence *I bought the house on the hill*, namely, in the sense 'I bought the house which is on the hill', but not in the sense 'I bought the house while standing on the hill'.

How can we determine what is a constituent in a particular sentence? Constituents can be identified by a number of different "constituency tests". Constituency tests are based on the principle that only entire constituents may be manipulated by syntactic operations. They can be replaced (by pronominal forms), they can be moved, they can be conjoined, or they can stand alone. For example, the constituent "beautiful flowers" in the first sentence above can be:

replaced by pro-forms   *I received <u>them</u> for my birthday.*
<u>What</u> did you receive for your birthday?

moved	*It was <u>beautiful flowers</u> that I received for my birthday.*
	What I received for my birthday was <u>beautiful flowers</u>.
	Did you receive <u>beautiful flowers</u> for your birthday?
conjoined	*I received <u>beautiful flowers</u> and chocolates for my birthday.*
interrogated	*(What did you receive for your birthday?) <u>Beautiful flowers</u>*

Self-Testing Exercise: For more practice in applying constituency tests, do Exercise 7.1 question 1.

There are two basic relationships possible between the members of a constituent:

1. one-way dependency, or **modifier-head**: one of the members of the constituent, the modifier (**Mod**), can be omitted, but the other, the head, cannot. The head is the essential center of the constituent and is obligatory; the modifier depends upon the head and cannot occur without it. The modifier expresses some quality or aspect of the head. The relation of adjective to noun is one example of modifier-head. In *blue eyes*, the modifier *blue* modifies the head *eyes*. In *deep blue eyes*, *deep* modifies *blue*, and *deep blue* modifies *eyes*. It is not the case that *blue* modifies *eyes* and *deep* modifies *blue eyes*, because this would suggest the incorrect reading "blue eyes which are deep" rather than the correct "eyes which are deep blue". In *the woman beside me*, *beside me* is the modifier of the head *woman*. The modifier also follows the head in *he swam quickly*, where *quickly* is the modifier of the head *swam*.

2. mutual dependency, or **governor-complement**: neither member of the constituent can be omitted and one cannot occur without the other; neither is more central. The first "governs" or controls the presence of the second, and the second "completes" the first. The relation between the subject and the predicate of sentence is a special case of mutual dependency (as in *The weather/is improving*). Other relations of governor to complement hold between:

    a. a preposition and its complement (as in *on/the shore*),
    b. an adjective and its complement (as in *dear/to me*),
    c. a verb and its complement (as in *be/a fool*), and
    d. a verb and its object (as in *swim/a race*).

Self-Testing Exercise: Do Exercise 7.1 questions 2 and 3.

3.   A phrase structure grammar of English

We will now attempt to construct a phrase structure grammar of English, a set of rules that will "generate" any possible (simple) sentence of English. In reality, our grammar will be incomplete, partial, possibly wrong, but it will be illustrative. We will not be overly concerned with syntactic argumentation – with the niceties of arguments or the merits of alternative accounts – but you will learn to analyze most of the basic structures and types of English sentences. When trying to write rules to generate all possible but no impossible structures in English, it is reassuring to remember that no one has yet written a complete and flawless generative grammar of English. The grammar we write will always be subject to revision and testing: the phrase structure rules can be changed if they aren't formulated correctly, or a particular structure might be accounted for in a different component of the grammar (by transformations rather than phrase structure rules or the reverse).

3.1   The form of phrase structure rules

Before we can begin actually constructing our grammar, we must learn the formalism used to represent phrase structure rules.

A phrase structure grammar consists of a set of ordered rules known as rewrite rules, which are applied stepwise. A rewrite rule has a single symbol on the left and one or more symbols on the right:

$$A \rightarrow B + C$$
$$C \rightarrow D$$

More than one symbol on the right constitutes a string. The arrow is read as 'is rewritten as', 'has as its constituents', 'consists of', or 'is expanded as'. The plus sign is read as 'followed by', but it is often omitted. The rule may also be depicted in the form of a **tree diagram**:

(1)

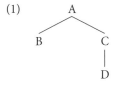

B and C are called labeled nodes; a node is a point on the tree diagram. Two metaphors are used here:

1. In the family tree metaphor, B and C are daughters of A and they are sisters of each other; less often, A is referred to as the "mother" or "parent" of B and C. (The view taken here is entirely matriarchal!) Also, in the tree metaphor, A is seen as a branching node, as opposed to C, which is a nonbranching node.
2. In the domination metaphor, a distinction is made between immediate domination and domination: a node dominates everything below it (hence, A dominates B, C, and D); a node immediately dominates those nodes for which there are no intervening nodes (hence, A immediately dominates B and C, but not D).

Finally, B and C form a constituent: a constituent is all and only the nodes dominated by a single node, in this case, A.

The phrase structure rules also allow for choices. The optional choices are indicated with parentheses:

$$A \rightarrow (B)\ C$$

This rule reads that A is expanded as optionally B and obligatorily C. In every rewrite rule, at least one element must be obligatory. There may also be mutually exclusive choices of elements in a string; these are indicated with curly braces:

$$A \rightarrow \{B,C\}\ or\ A \rightarrow \begin{Bmatrix} B \\ C \end{Bmatrix}$$

This rule states that if you choose B, you can't choose C, but you must choose one – either B or C, but not both. Whether the mutually exclusive items are written on one line separated by commas or on separate lines does not matter, as long as they occur within braces.

These two types of choices can be combined:

$$A \rightarrow (\{B, C\})\ D$$

This rule leads to the following possibilities:

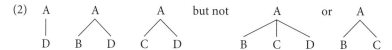

(2)   A   A   A   but not   A   or   A

In every phrase structure rule, there must be an initial symbol, a first left-hand symbol, such as A above. Thereafter, every symbol appearing on the left has already been introduced on the right-hand side. The symbols that occur on the right, but never on the left are the terminal symbols; another way of defining them is that they occur at the bottom of a tree diagram. In our brief grammar above, B, C, and D are terminal symbols. They immediately dominate lexical items, or words.

Phrase structure rules account for the linear order of elements in a sentence in D-structure, as well as for the hierarchical arrangement of sentence structure. They can also account for the infinite generating capacity of language. If a symbol introduces itself, it is known as a **recursive** symbol, as A in the following rule:

$$A \rightarrow B + C + (A)$$

Or if A introduces a symbol, and that symbol later introduces A, we also call A recursive, as in the following:

$$A \rightarrow B + C$$
$$B \rightarrow (A) + D$$

(Note that if we don't make the second occurrence of A optional, there would be no end to our expansion.) Recursiveness leads to the "nesting" property of language, the embedding of elements within other elements. Thus, recursiveness, along with the options provided by the parentheses and curly braces formalism and with the choices to be made among a large number of lexical items, accounts for the infinite nature of language.[3]

Self-Testing Exercise: If you are having trouble understanding this formalism, do Exercise 7.2.

3.2   Subject and predicate

In constructing our phrase structure grammar of English, we begin with the initial symbol S = **sentence**. We all have an intuitive idea of what counts as a sentence. It is a tenet of both traditional and generative grammar that S consists of two constituents: the **subject (Su)** and the **predicate (pred)**. The subject is variously defined as the topic, the actor, or that which is spoken about. The predicate is defined as the comment, the action, or that which is said about the subject; it says something true or false about the subject.

Note the different structures serving the function of subject in the following sentences:

The chocolate was later confiscated (read: inhaled) by his counselors. (COCA:MAG)

House plants add to humidity. (COCA:MAG)

The woman with the yellow hair clapped her hands together with joy. (COCA:FIC)

They hoped to make it before midnight. (COCA:FIC)

Girls and boys performed equally well in all types of classes. (COCA:MAG)

There are also gender gaps on issues. (COCA:MAG).

The book that changed my life professionally was Catch-22. (COCA:FIC)

It's snowing in summer! (COCA:FIC).

It is possible to overdo the jargon. (COCA:FIC)

Wrinkles disappeared. (COCA:FIC)

There are two tests for identifying subject:

1. subject–auxiliary inversion, or the "question test", e.g. *Was [the chocolate] later confiscated?*; and
2. the "tag question" test, in which the pronoun in the tag agrees with the subject in gender, number, and person, e.g. *[It] is possible to overdo jargon, isn't [it]?*

---

3. In addition to tree diagrams, there is the "notational variant" known as labeled bracketing. In this system, the terminal symbols are placed on the line and the nodes dominating them are subscripted. Square brackets indicate constituents. Our brief grammar immediately above would permit expansions such as the following with labeled bracketings: $_A[_B[D]C]$ or $_A[_B[_A [B C]D]C]$. Note that there must be as many left-facing as right-facing brackets.

The main element constituting the subject appears to be the noun with its accompanying modifiers; we will see below that this is the phrasal category of the noun phrase. Note that a noun may stand alone as subject (*wrinkles* above); a pronoun may also stand alone as subject since it replaces an entire noun phrase (*they* above). *It* and *there* are special kinds of "dummy" subjects called "expletives"; structurally they fill the position of subject but are lexically empty. There are two kinds of meaningless *it*, the impersonal *it* in *It's snowing in summer*, where there is no personal subject, and the anticipatory *it* in *It is possible …*, where the real subject *to overdo the jargon* occurs at the end of the sentence and *it* fills the normal subject position.

The predicate is generally what remains of a simple sentence after the subject is removed. As you can see in the sentences above, a verb stands alone in the predicate (*disappeared*) in one example and is the main element constituting the predicate in the other examples. The category of the predicate is thus the verb phrase. A test for predicate is to see whether the sequence may be replaced by *so do/do too*:

> *Wrinkles disappeared, and so did the brown spots.*

We can formalize our recognition of the subject and predicate as key elements in the sentence in the following phrase structure rule:

$$S \rightarrow NP + VP$$

This gives us a formal definition of subject and predicate: the subject is the NP immediately dominated by S and the predicate is the VP immediately dominated by S. The rule will account for declarative sentences, but not for imperatives, which have no subject (e.g. *Remove the pan from the fire!*) nor for interrogatives, which have a different word order (e.g. *Are you hungry?*). We account for these types of sentences later by means of syntactic operations (see Chapter 8). It is important to keep in mind that subject and predicate are **functions**, not categories; not all noun phrases serve the function of subject.

Self-Testing Exercise: Do Exercise 7.4, question 1.

Now that we have established that two phrasal categories – NP and VP – perform the major functions of the sentence, subject and predicate, we can look more closely at the internal structure of these categories. We will assume that there are **phrasal categories** corresponding to the major parts of speech, or **lexical categories**, namely noun, verb, adjective, adverb, as well as preposition (the parts of speech were treated in Chapter 5). The category of each phrasal category is determined by the lexical category of the head of a modifier-head construction or by the governor of a governor-complement construction; the head or governor is always obligatory. Phrases can be classified as belonging to the same phrasal category if they have the same internal structure and the same distribution in the sentence. We will see below that phrasal categories always occur on the left side of a phrase structure rule and are composed of other categories (lexical and phrasal).

> **NOTE ON TERMINOLOGY:** In traditional grammar, "phrases" are groups of words (without subject and predicate) forming a coherent group. In generative grammar, **phrases** are defined as sequences of words – or a single word – having syntactic significance: that is, they form a constituent. Since tree diagrams indicate the phrases functioning as constituents, they are also called phrase markers.[4]

3.3   Noun phrase

The **noun phrase** (NP) can be expanded in many different ways (see Table 7.1).[5]

Table 7.1. Expansions of NP

NP →	N	*dogs*
	Det N	*the dogs*
	Det A N	*the large dogs*
	Det AP N	*the loudly barking dogs*
	Det N PP	*the dog in the yard*
	Det A N PP	*the ferocious dog behind the fence*
	Det AP N PP	*the wildly yapping dog on the sofa*
	Pro	*He*
	PN	*Goldy*

The noun (N) is the only obligatory element in the first seven expansions of NP below and serves as head; the other elements are all optional. The adjective (A) or adjective phrase (AP) precedes the N and the prepositional phrase (PP) follows the N; both serve as modifiers of the noun (**modifier of N**), expressing a quality of the noun, answering the question "which dogs?".

"Det" here stands for determiners (introduced in Chapter 5), a set of grammatical words that are somewhat like modifiers, but actually serve the function of **specifier of N** (a one-way

---

4.   In current generative theory, phrases are called "projections" (because a phrase is a projection of its head), but we will use the older, more intuitively obvious terminology.

5.   For the present, we are simplifying the structure of the NP by not considering the presence of subordinate clauses in the NP, that is:

NP → Det N S   *the fact that I bought a dog, the dog which I bought*
         S   *that I own a dog*

Later in this chapter, we will be simplifying the structure of the AP and the PP in a similar way by ignoring the possibility of subordinate clauses as complements to A and as objects of P:

AP → A S   *worried that he might bite*
PP → P S   *about what it takes*

These phenomena will be treated in Chapter 9.

dependency), making more precise or definite the phrase that follows. Det includes quite a diverse set of grammatical words: demonstratives (Dem), articles (Art), *wh*-words (*Wh*-), possessives (Poss), and quantifiers (Q). We can write a rule for Det as follows:

Det → {Dem, Art, *Wh*-, Poss, Q}
Dem → {*this, that, these, those*}
Art → {*a, an, the*}
Wh- → {*which, what, whose*}
Poss → {*my, our, their, John's, the man's …*}
Q → {*some, any, every, each, neither, more …*}

The ellipses (…) indicate that these are not complete listings of the members of the sets Poss and Q. Note that Poss includes both possessive adjectives such as *my* and possessive nouns such as *John's* or *Sally's*. (It may even include an entire noun phrase, as in *that angry man's (dog)*, where the -*'s* inflection is being attached to the end of the noun phrase *that angry man*.) We can account for this phenomenon by the following rule:

$$\text{Poss} \rightarrow \left\{ \begin{array}{l} \text{NP -'s} \\ \textit{my, our, their …} \end{array} \right\}$$

In the last two cases in Table 7.1, the pronoun (Pro)[6] and the proper noun (PN) stand alone and cannot cooccur with the AP, the Det, or the PP:

    **The fierce he in the yard*
    **The fierce Goldy in the yard*

Our rule for NP, therefore, must indicate the optionality of Det, AP, and PP and the mutual exclusiveness of Pro and PN with the other elements.

    A preliminary structure for the NP *the large dogs* might be the following:

(3)

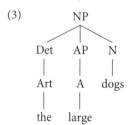

Here, Det is shown as sister of both AP and N. In fact, the determiner really relates to the rest of the noun phrase as a whole, not the AP and N separately. For this reason (and for reasons that will become clearer in Chapter 9), we will introduce the intermediate category of N-bar (N̄):

    N̄ → (AP) N (PP)

---

6. Certain pronouns are identical in form to determiners and take the place of the entire NP (e.g. <u>*That*</u> *is a fierce dog*); however, the determiner form sometimes differs slightly from the pronominal form, as in <u>*My*</u> *dog is gentle* vs. <u>*Mine*</u> *is a gentle dog.*

N-bar consists of N and it modifiers (but not its specifiers). Our rule for NP is then the following: [7]

$$NP \rightarrow \left\{ \begin{array}{l} (Det)\ \bar{N} \\ PN \\ Pro \end{array} \right\}$$

And our revised structure for *the large dogs* would be the following:

(4)

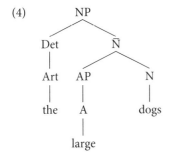

The validity of this "nested" structure is shown by the fact that the word *one*, which is a kind of substitute noun, can replace both *dogs* and *large dogs*:

I like large dogs rather than small ones. (ones = dogs)
The ones that I like best are Rottweilers. (ones = large dogs)

---

7. We are adopting here – in part – a formalism called "X-bar theory". In this theory, all phrasal categories are seen as having the same structure, namely:

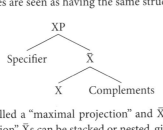

XP is called a "maximal projection" and $\bar{X}$ is called an "intermediate projection". By a process of "adjunction", $\bar{X}$s can be stacked or nested, giving us the structure we see in the NP:

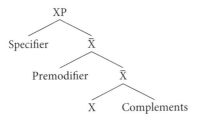

According to X-bar theory, the grammar has only binary branching nodes. You will notice that some of our nodes have three or more branches. In this way and others, we depart from the strict theory (see Footnotes 11 and 12, also Chapter 8, footnote 4 and Chapter 9, Footnote 2).

By our rule for NP, a more complex phrase, *that angry man's fierce dog*, would have the following phrase marker:

(5)

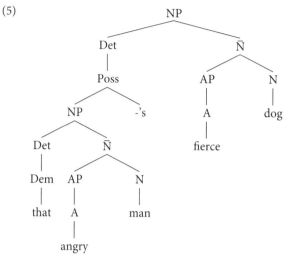

We are ignoring the presence in the NP of what are called predeterminers (*all, both, half*) and postdeterminers, such as some quantifiers (*many, few*), as in the following:[8]

[all] the [many] very happy people

Numerals, too, present a similar problem. In one respect, they would appear to be determiners (e.g. *two trees, two large trees*), but they also seem to fill the position predeterminers (e.g. *the two large trees*). We will not be accounting for numerals here.

To this point in our grammar, the only function for NP that we have examined is that of subject (S → NP VP); numerous other functions will be recognized later in this chapter.

3.4   Adjective phrase

The **adjective phrase (AP)** can be expanded in several different ways (see Table 7.2).[9]

Table 7.2. Expansions of AP

AP →		
	A	*happy*
	Deg A	*very happy*
	Adv A	*blissfully happy*
	Deg Adv A	*very blissfully happy*
	A PP	*dear to me, tired of him, glad about that*

---

8.   We are also not accounting for structures such as *all of (the dogs)* or *some of (the dogs)*.

9.   We are ignoring adjectives that can follow the noun, as in *the people responsible for the budget* or *the members present*, or even the pronoun, as in *someone responsible*.

The category of degree adverbs (Deg) (introduced in Chapter 5) includes words which are traditionally defined as adverbs, since they modify both adjectives and adverbs:

> Deg → {*more, most, less, least, very, quite, rather, least, exceedingly, awfully, absolutely, pretty* … }

However, they occupy a special syntactic position; unlike other adverbs – "general adverbs" – degree words cannot be modified by other adverbs. Degree words express a quality, intensity, or degree of the following adjective or adverb; in other words, they function, like determiners, as specifiers of the head.

> **HINT:** A test to distinguish between degree adverbs and general adverbs is to see if the adverb can be preceded by *very* or *quite*. If it can, then it is a general adverb (e.g. *very happy, very blue, quite rigid, quite patriotic*); if it cannot, then it is a degree adverb (e.g. **very rather, *quite awfully, *very absolutely*).
>
> There are two problems with this test. The first is that some adverbs can be both general adverbs and degree adverbs (but with different meanings). Thus, *pretty* is a degree adverb in the sense 'somewhat' and cannot be preceded by another degree word. If it is – i.e. *very pretty* – it becomes a general adverb and has the sense 'attractive'.
>
> The second problem is that although participles which occur before the noun are general adjectives, they often cannot be modified by Deg (**very smiling, *rather broken*), though they can be modified by AdvP (*very sweetly smiling, rather badly broken*). Note that one cannot say *very married* (except humorously), but one can say *very happily married*.[10]

We can see that in all cases above, A is the obligatory element and head of the phrase; all of the other elements are optional. The elements preceding the A are modifiers or specifiers, but the PP following bears a different relationship to the A; it serves as complement (**complement of A**). Although we will indicate it as optional in our rules, it is not optional if a complement-taking adverbial structure such as *aware of, afraid of, curious about, obvious to,* or *angry at* is selected. Note that the PP does <u>not</u> express a quality or degree of the A but rather "completes" it; the A serves as governor of the PP.

The initial tree structure for the NP *the very fiercely barking dog* might be the following:

(6)

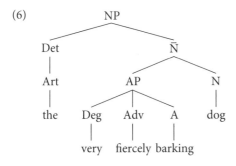

---

10.   Participles which occur after the noun (e.g. *the girl smiling sweetly* …) will be accounted for in Chapter 9.

However, this structure incorrectly shows *very, fiercely,* and *barking* as sisters, all modifying *dog,* that is, a 'very dog', a 'fiercely dog', and a 'barking dog'. Obviously, this is not what is being said, but rather "very fiercely" is modifying "barking", and "very" is modifying "fiercely". As we will see in the next section, the sequence [Deg Adv] constitutes an adverb phrase, so the correct structure is the following:

(7)

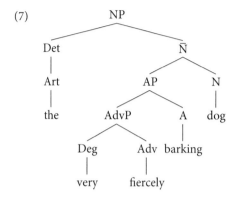

We must also recognize in our rule that Deg can modify A directly, as in *the very fierce dog*:

(8)

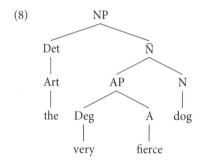

Thus, the following is our formulation of the rule for AP:[11]

$$AP \rightarrow \left(\left\{ \begin{array}{c} \text{Deg} \\ \text{AdvP} \end{array} \right\} \right) \text{A (PP)}$$

We have seen above that the AP is introduced in our phrase structure rules under N̄, functioning as modifier of the noun; we now have a structural definition for the "attributive" position of the adjective mentioned in Chapter 5: it is the adjective dominated by N̄. Later in this chapter we will also introduce AP under the verb phrase, functioning as complement of the verb; this is the "predicative" position. Note that if an adjective has a complement, it can only occur in predicative position in English (*the lake is near to me* but not **the near to me lake*) unless it is compounded (*twenty-year-old house*).

---

11.   Although a nested structure with an intermediate category Ā – dominating A and PP – is warranted here, we will not introduce it because it is not important for our purposes.

It is quite common for more than one adjective to occur as modifier of the N, as in *the long, blue, silken scarf*. Moreover, each of the adjectives can be modified by Deg or AdvP, as in *the very long, quite pale blue, silken scarf*. To account for this possibility, we must introduce a modification to our rule for NP which permits more than one AP in a single NP. One way to do so would simply be to allow for multiple APs in a "flat" structure as follows:

(9)

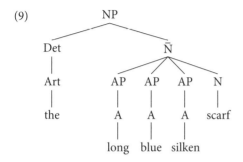

Apart from the fact that we don't actually have a mechanism in our rules for generating more than one AP, a hierarchical, or "nested", structure such as the following better captures the meaning of the phrase:

(10)

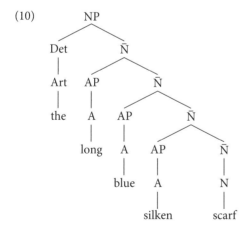

That is, rather than being a 'scarf which is silken and blue and long', it is a 'silken scarf which is blue' and a 'blue silken scarf which is long'. Note that changing the order of the adjectives produces unnatural phrases: ? *blue long silken scarf*, ? *silken blue long scarf*.

In order to account for this structure, our rule for N̄ must be rewritten as follows:

$$\bar{N} \rightarrow \begin{Bmatrix} (AP)\ \bar{N}\ (PP) \\ N \end{Bmatrix}$$

3.5 Adverb phrase

The **adverb phrase (AdvP)** can be expanded as in Table 7.3a. We note that Deg is an optional modifier and that the Adv is head; our rule for AdvP is thus formulated as follows:

AdvP → (Deg) Adv

Table 7.3. Expansions of (a) AdvP and (b) PP

(a)	AdvP →	Adv	*quickly*
		Deg Adv	*very quickly*
(b)	PP →	P NP	*on the beach*
		P P NP	*from behind the door*
		P P P NP	*out from under the table*

So far we have looked at the AdvP only as modifier of the adjective, but we will look at its other functions in the next chapter.

3.6 Prepositional phrase

The **prepositional phrase (PP)** may be expanded as in Table 7.3b. Again, we observe that the P is the head of the PP, but unlike the other categories we have examined, the P cannot stand alone in the PP. It must be followed by an NP, what is traditionally known as an **object of the preposition (OP)**.

It also appears that Ps can have specifiers as well as objects. Like determiners or degree adverbs, these forms specify or limit the prepositional phrase. They include the words *right*, *straight*, and *slap* (in some dialects) and phrases measuring time and space, such as *three seconds* or *one mile*:

> right after lunch   two feet behind me
> straight along this route   two minutes before my arrival

For lack of a simpler name, we will term these **specifiers of P (PSpec)**:

PSpec → {*right, straight, slap, one mile, three seconds* … }

Finally, we must also account for the sequences P P NP and P P P NP. Writing the rule as PP → P (P) (P) NP would incorrectly show the NP as object of all the Ps, when it is actually complement of only the last P. Thus, we write our rule as follows:[12]

$$PP \rightarrow (PSpec) \ P \left\{ \begin{matrix} NP \\ PP \end{matrix} \right\}$$

---

12. This rule is actually too powerful, since it would allow PSpecs to precede all Ps, whereas they appear to be possible only before the first P: cf. *right out from under the table* but not **out right*

So far, we have seen PPs functioning as modifier of the N and complement of the A; further functions will be identified later in this chapter and in the next chapter.

The rule for PP is a recursive rule since PP (on the left) introduces a PP (on the right). And since NP introduces PP which introduces NP, NP is also a recursive symbol. The latter recursion leads to structures such as the following:

(11)

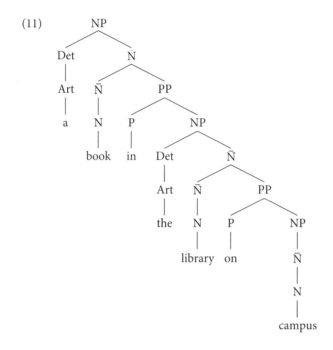

Here, "in the library" modifies "book" and "on campus" modifies "the library". Note that *a cat on the mat in the hallway* would have the structure given above, but the superficially similar *a cat on the mat with long whiskers* would not since "with long whiskers" modifies "the cat", not "the mat". A possible analysis of the phrase with a "flat" structure would give the following:

---

from under the table or *out from right under the table*. Again, a "nested" structure in which an intermediate category P̄ dominates P and its complements would solve this problem (but would unnecessarily complicate our tree structures):

$$PP \rightarrow (PSpec) \ \bar{P}$$
$$\bar{P} \rightarrow P \ \{NP, PP\}$$

(12)

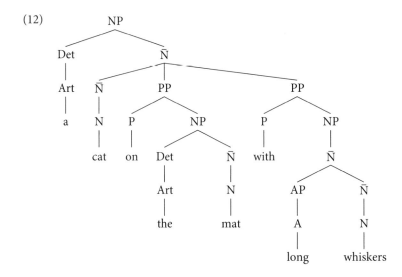

But the revision of our rule which permits more than one AP in the NP will also permit more that one PP, so the correct phrase marker for *the cat on the mat with long whiskers* is the following:

(13)

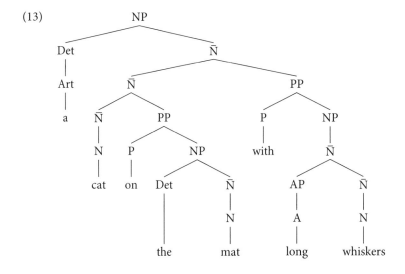

A further complication arises if there is a modifier both preceding and following the noun, as in *heavy rain in the night*. Should this be analyzed as a "flat" structure?

(14)

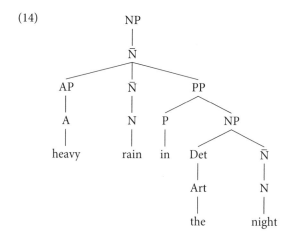

While this structure is probably not correct, it will suit our purposes, since there seems to be no reason to prefer one of the following hierarchical structures over the other:

(15)

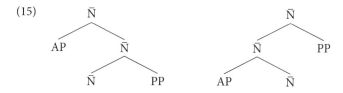

The phrase marker on the left would be 'night-rain which is heavy' and the phrase marker on the right would be 'heavy rain which is in the night'.

3.7   Conjunction

Our phrase structure rules do not yet account for the conjunction of elements (with *and*, *but*, *or*). It is possible to conjoin two or more <u>like</u> constituents, either phrasal or lexical categories (see Table 7.4).

Table 7.4. Conjunction

PP + PP	*on the table and under the chair*
P + P	*over or under*
NP + NP	*the tortoise and the hare*
N̄ + N̄	*cold coffee and warm beer*
N + N	*cats and dogs*
AP + AP	*very slow and quite tedious*
A + A	*long and boring*
AdvP + AdvP	*very cautiously but quite happily*
Adv + Adv	*quietly and smoothly*

The combined category will be the same as the individual categories conjoined. Thus, the supercategory of two conjoined Ps is P, while the supercategory of two conjoined APs is AP. The conjunction of lexical categories (Ps) [in and out] the window, is shown below:

(16)

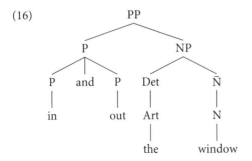

The conjunction of phrasal categories (APs) is found in a [rather expensive and ugly] car:

(17)

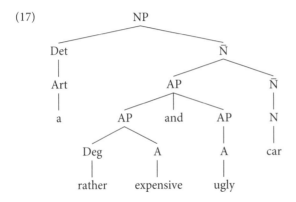

Note that we interpret *ugly* as AP rather that just A in order to have the conjunction of two like constituents. Generally, it is not possible to conjoin unlike categories, such as AP + NP, *very polite and the quick response*, unless the unlike categories are functioning the same way; in *The instructor will be away [on Tuesday] and [next week]*, for example, the PP *on Tuesday* and the NP *next week* are both functioning adverbially.

A phrase such as *a very rich and fattening dessert* is ambiguous; either *very* modifies *rich* only or it modifies both *rich* and *fattening*:

(18)

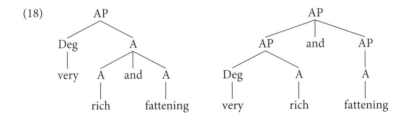

A phrase such as *soup or salad and french fries* is also ambiguous, as shown below:

(19)

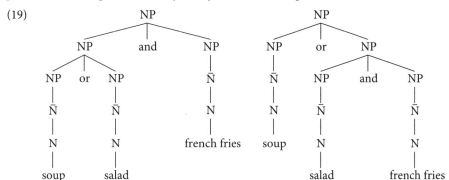

When APs are conjoined, and the As are of the same semantic type, it is common to omit the conjunction, as in *a happy and carefree child* > *a happy, carefree child* or *a delicious and bracing burgundy* > *a delicious, bracing burgundy*. Note that unlike the nested AP structures discussed above (i.e. *a long blue silken scarf*), it is entirely natural in these cases to change the order of the adjectives, i.e. *a carefree, happy child*, or *a bracing, delicious burgundy*.

Nominal compounding (which we treated in Chapter 4 as a matter of word formation), such as *french fries* and *ice cream* could also be represented in our syntactic trees as a kind of conjunction without an explicit conjunction, but we will not do so here:

(20)

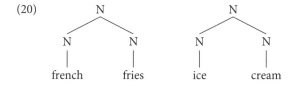

Self-Testing Exercise: Do Exercise 7.3.

3.8   Verb phrase

In order to study the structure of the VP, we will introduce the intermediate category of V_{gp} = **verb group** consisting of the lexical verb with or without a particle.[13] For the present we are not going to concern ourselves with the specifiers of the verb, including both tense and the auxiliary verbs; we will deal with these in Chapter 8. In this chapter, the V_{gp} may be thought of as the verb in its base form.

---

13.   A verb plus a post-verbal particle forms a "phrasal verb", as was introduced in Chapter 5 and will be discussed in more detail in Chapter 8.

Verb complementation. What we will consider now is the type(s) of complements that follow a verb. Verbs fall into different classes based on the type of complement structures that they require. This is called the **verb subcategorization** (as we noted briefly in Chapter 5). The particular structure or structures in which a verb can occur can be represented formally in a subcategorization frame:

    ____ NP   ____ AP   ____ PP

The verb occurs in the slot indicated by the line, with the possible complement(s) specified afterwards.

> **HINT:** Note that only obligatory complements (NPs, APs, and PPs) are relevant to the subcategorization of a verb, not the optional PPs which often follow a verb or verb phrase. Distinguishing obligatory from optional PPs can often be very difficult. Generally, it is the case that the obligatory complements cannot be omitted without affecting the grammaticality or meaning of the sentence: e.g. in *She identifies with her mother* or *She talked with her mother*, omitting *with her mother* produces an ungrammatical sentence in the first instance (**She identifies*) and one with a different meaning in the second (*She talked*). In contrast, optional PPs, which are functioning as adverbials, can be omitted or can be moved to the beginning of the sentence: e.g. *They ordered a pizza for dinner* cf. *They ordered a pizza, For dinner they ordered a pizza.* (This topic will be treated in detail in Chapter 8.)

Based on the type of complement a verb takes, a number of subcategories of verbs can be identified:

1. **Intransitive verb (intrans)**, e.g. *arrive, cry, laugh,* or *swim,* with the following subcategorization frame:

       ____ #   *By then aunts, uncles and cousins had arrived.* (COCA:SPOK)
            Some in the audience laughed. (COCA:NEWS)

   With an intransitive verb, no complement is required or allowed.

   > **HINT:** Intransitive verbs often sound more "natural" when followed by adverbials, especially if the verb is in the simple present or past tense: e.g. *The package arrived <u>on Tuesday</u>, The package arrived <u>yesterday</u>, The package arrived <u>after I got home</u>.* But adverbials, as we will see in more detail in Chapter 8, do not affect the subcategorization of the verb. It remains an intransitive verb.

2. **Transitive verb (trans)** (also known as "monotransitive"), e.g. *hit, eat, kill,* or *tie,* with the following subcategorization frame:

       ____ NP *I dug a giant hole.* (COCA:MAG)

   The complement of the verb here is a noun phrase functioning as a **direct object (dO)**. While traditionally a direct object is defined as the person or thing affected by the action of the verb, we are now able to give it a formal definition: it is the NP immediately dominated by the VP, or it is the NP which is sister of the V_{gp}. Note that the direct object follows the verb directly (i.e. it is not preceded by a preposition).[14]

3. **Ditransitive verb (ditrans)**, e.g. *give, send, tell, lend, buy, offer*, or *show*, with the following subcategorization frames:

    ____ $NP_1 \, NP_2$ *Maggie's niece sent her flowers.* (COCA:NEWS)   OR
    ____ $NP_2 \, _{PP}[to/for \, NP_1]$ *Huber sent flowers to teachers.* (COCA:NEWS)

We can write this subcategorization frame more economically as follows:

    ____ NP {NP, $_{PP}[to/for$ NP]}

> **HINT:** In our discussion of the structure of the NP above, we saw that a PP could serve as the optional modifier of the N, as in *the snow on the roof*. Here we see that the PP in a very different function as an obligatory complement of the verb.

NP_1 serves the function of **indirect object (iO)**, while NP_2 serves the function of direct object. An indirect object is the goal or benefactive of the action; it always denotes something which is animate or is conceived of as animate. It is important to distinguish the indirect object *to* marker (a) from the one meaning 'place to which' (b):

a. *Some friends sent flowers to Jon.* (COCA:FIC)
b. *Helen's husband had sent flowers to the party.* (COCA:SPOK)

and the indirect object *for* marker (c) from the one meaning 'in the stead of', 'in the place of' (d):

c. *When was the last time you cooked a meal for the family?* (COCA:FIC)
d. *so you do the dishes for them* (COCA:MAG)

The test to distinguish indirect objects from the other cases is known as the **indirect object movement** transformation: if the noun following *to* or *for* is an indirect object, it should be able to move to a position before the direct object (V NP_2 *to/for* NP_1 ⇒ V $NP_1 \, NP_2$):[15]

a. ⇒ *Some friends sent Jon flowers.*
b. ⇒ **Helen's husband had sent the party flowers.*

---

14. A direct object can also be a subordinate clause: *Vivian wrote <u>that she was unhappy</u>*. However, since we will be considering subordinate clauses in Chapter 9, they will be omitted from our current discussion.

15. We are assuming that the order V NP_2 *to/for* NP_1 is the order in D-structure and that V NP_1 NP_2 is the derived order (as S-structure), though this assumption can be debated.

c. ⇒ *When was the last time you cooked the family a meal?*
d. ⇒ **so you do them the dishes*

(⇒ means 'is transformed into'.) The test works no matter how lengthy either of the NPs is, that is, how many modifiers it has preceding or following it:

> *Iranian authorities gave [plastic keys to paradise to hang around their necks] to [young Iranians, some only twelve years old]* ⇒
> *Iranian authorities gave young Iranians, some only twelve years old, plastic keys to paradise to hang around their necks.* (COCA:ACAD)
> *the state sent [a letter to inform them about the survey] to [each school district]* ⇒
> *the state sent each school district a letter to inform them about the survey* (COCA:NEWS)

There are, however, certain restrictions with pronouns. If both the direct and indirect object are pronouns (a), or if the direct object alone is a pronoun (b), then indirect object movement cannot normally occur, but if the indirect object alone is a pronoun (c), then it can occur:

a. *My father gave it to her.* (COCA:FIC) ⇒ *?My father gave her it.*[16]
b. *Then I gave it to my nephew.* (COCA:FIC) ⇒ *?Then I gave my nephew it.*
c. *Besides, Hilda gave the money to you.* ⇒ *Besides, Hilda gave you the* (COCA:MAG) *money.*

(This restriction results from the weakly stressed nature of pronouns.)

4. **Copula(tive) verb (cop)**, e.g. *become, seem, appear, feel, be, grow,* or *look,* and with the following subcategorization frame:

> ____ NP *She is a computer software analyst.* (COCA:NEWS)
> ____ AP *She seems perfectly relaxed.* (COCA:MAG)
> ____ PP *He was in a good mood.* (COCA:SPOK)

Or, more concisely:

> ____ {NP, AP, PP}

The complement here serves the function of **subject complement (sC)**.[17] A subject complement characterizes the subject: it identifies, locates, or describes the subject, as in *Bill is the leader, Bill is in the living room,* and *Bill is irritable.* It expresses either a current state or a resulting state of the subject, as in *Bill is rich* vs. *Bill became rich.* Any copulative verb can usually be replaced by BE (*She seems perfectly relaxed* ⇒ *She is perfectly relaxed*).

---

16. British English allows *I gave it her,* and colloquially one might find both of the asterisked sentences in North American English.

17. You may know this function by one of its other names: *predicative nominative, subject(ive) predicative,* and so on.

> **HINT:** It is important to distinguish an NP serving as direct object from an NP serving as subject complement. A test distinguishing dO from sC is that the dO can become the subject of a passive sentence, while the sC cannot.
> Here *a lawyer* is sC:
>
> > *Martina became a lawyer.* ⇒ **A lawyer was become by Martina.*
>
> Here *a lawyer* is dO:
>
> > *Martina hired a lawyer.* ⇒ *A lawyer was hired by Martina.*

5. **Complex transitive verb (complex trans)**, with the following subcategorization frame:

_____	NP NP	*I consider him a real colleague.* (COCA:SPOK)
_____	NP AP	*She made him uneasy.* (COCA:FIC)
_____	NP PP	*You regard that as a problem?* (COCA:FIC)

Or more concisely:

   _____ NP {NP, AP, PP}

There are two subclasses of verbs in this category:

a. nonlocative: *find, consider, make, think, elect, call, hold, regard (as), take (for), devote (to)*; and
b. locative: *hang, put, place, lay, set, touch, shoot, pierce.*

The complex transitive verb combines the transitive and the copulative structures. The first NP is a direct object; the second element is an **object complement** (oC).[18] The object complement characterizes the object in the same way as the subject complement characterizes the subject: it identifies, describes, or locates the object (as in *We chose Bill as group leader, We consider him a fool, She laid the baby in the crib*), expressing either its current state or resulting state (as in *They found him in the kitchen* vs. *She made him angry*). It is not possible to delete the object complement without either radically changing the meaning of the sentence (e.g. *She called him an idiot* ⇒ *She called him*) or making the sentence ungrammatical (e.g. *He locked his keys in his office* ⇒ **He locked his keys*). Note that BE or some other copula verb can often be inserted between the direct object and the object complement (e.g. *I consider him to be a fool, We chose Bill to be group leader, They found him to be in the kitchen*).

---

18. This is also known as an *object(ive) predicative.* Object complement structures are sometimes analyzed as clauses with the infinitive of the verb BE understood: *They found the idea (to be) ridiculous.* However, in some object complements, the presence of BE is less natural, e.g. *We made him (to be) captain.*

HINT: Like the subject complement, the object complement cannot usually become the subject of a passive sentence:

> *Queen Elizabeth II made her a dame.*   ⇒ **A dame was made her by*
> *Queen Elizabeth II.*

But note that the direct object in the same sentence can become the subject of a passive sentence

> *Queen Elizabeth II made her a dame.*   ⇒ *She was made a dame by Queen*
> *Elizabeth II.* (COCA:NEWS)

6. **Prepositional verb (prep)**, with the following subcategorization frame:

> ____ PP   *Arvydas had insisted on the scorpion.* (COCA:FIC)
> *Colleen stood on her tiptoes.* (COCA:FIC)

Here the entire prepositional phrase serves as a complement of the verb. Thus *on the scorpion* is the complement of *insisted*. We call this PP a **prepositional complement (pC)**. There are two subclasses of verbs in this category:

a. locative: *stand, lie, lean, hang, sit, flow*; and
b. nonlocative (idiomatic): *agree (to), work (for), depend (on), look (into), refer (to), insist (on), respond (to)*.

In the case of nonlocative prepositional verbs, the verb and preposition seem to form a close syntactic and semantic unit, and the particular preposition occurring with a verb is idiosyncratic and must be learned (e.g. *to* is used rather than *on* with *refer*: *refer to, *refer on*). In the nonlocative cases, it is often possible to replace the prepositional verb with a simple verb (e.g. *She asked for a raise* ⇒ *She requested a raise*).

The locative cases often express a copulative relationship (e.g. *Colleen stood on her tiptoes* ⇒ *Colleen is on her tiptoes*).

HINT: It is easy to confuse pC "prepositional complement" and oP "object of the preposition", but they are different. oP refers to the NP which serves as the complement of the preposition (e.g. *my head* in *on my head*), whereas pC refers to the PP which serves as the complement of the verb (e.g. *on my head* in *The bird landed on my head*).

Earlier we also encountered prepositional complements of adjectives, as in *similar to my handwriting*, where *to my handwriting* is the complement of the A *similar*, as well as prepositional complements of prepositions, as in *up on the table*, where *on the table* is the complement of the P *up*.

7. **Diprepositional verb (diprep)**, e.g. *confer, talk,* or *consult*, with the following subcategorization frame:

> ____ PP PP   *I argued with the officers about little things.* (COCA:FIC)

This is a limited set of verbs that can often be prepositional, with only a slight difference in meaning:

a.   diprepositional: *We talked with our parents about buying a house.* (discussed a specific topic)
b.   prepositional: *We talked with our parents.* (conversed generally)

Thus, for the category VP, we have the possible expansions shown in Table 7.5.

Table 7.5. Expansions of VP

VP →	V NP	*open a package*
	V NP NP	*write a friend a letter*
	V NP PP	*give an excuse to the teacher*
	V AP	*feel lonely*
	V NP AP	*make the dog angry*
	V PP	*jump into the pool*
	V PP PP	*talk about the problem with a friend*

We need to write a single rule for the verb phrase. There are a number of ways to do so; we will do it in the following way:

$$(21) \quad VP \rightarrow V_{gp} \left\{ \begin{array}{l} \left[NP \left\{ \begin{array}{l} \left(\begin{array}{l} NP \\ \left\{ \begin{array}{l} PP \\ AP \end{array} \right\} \end{array} \right) \end{array} \right] \right] \\ AP \\ PP \quad (PP) \end{array} \right\}$$

We must make sure that our rule generates all possible structures and does not generate any impossible structures. You should see if it might be possible to write the rule differently.

Latent objects.   One of the difficulties for verb subcategorization in English is that it is sometimes possible to omit the direct object when it is understood from context, as in the case of *He ate* being understood as 'He ate dinner' in a certain context. In such cases, the object can be understood as being latent. How can you tell, then, when the verb is really transitive with a "latent" object (i.e. present but not overt at the level of S-structure), and when it is really intransitive? A few tests can be applied to the verbs in question. When the verb has a remarkably different meaning without an object than with an object, then we can assume that it is truly intransitive, not transitive with a latent object:

intransitive		transitive
From time to time the workers struck, of course. (COCA:ACAD)	vs.	*She struck the match.* (COCA:FIC)
I just played outside. (COCA:NEWS)	vs.	*As a girl in Manchester, Elizabeth played tennis.* (COCA:FIC)

If the object is irrelevant, then the verb is likewise intransitive since the object is not necessary at all:

> Jeff _smokes_ and is male. (COCΛ:SPOK)
> He was in bed and he _was reading_. (COCA:SPOK)
> Was there an argument after we _left_ yesterday? (COCA:FIC)

In the first sentence, it is not important what Jeff smokes; you are simply saying that 'Jeff is a smoker'. In the second sentence, what he was reading is immaterial, as is where we left from (home, town, country) in the third sentence.

If the object is completely predictable, however, then the object is latent because in those cases the object is "understood from context":

They elected a movie star president.	_They elected a movie star – Ronald Reagan_ (COCA:NEWS)
They played the game very well.	_They played very well._ (COCA:NEWS)
I bathed myself already.	_I bathed already._ (COCA:SPOK)

In the corpus examples, then, we would say that _elect_ is a complex transitive verb with the latent object complement _president_, _played_ is a transitive verb with the latent direct object _the game_, and _bathed_ is a transitive verb with the latent object _myself._

> _Self-Quiz:_ Try to determine whether the verb _write_ is intransitive, monotransitive, or ditransitive on the basis of the following sentences:[19]
>
> a.   _Margaret writes._
> b.   _Margaret wrote yesterday._
> c.   _Margaret wrote to George yesterday._
> d.   _Margaret wrote a letter yesterday._
> e.   _Margaret wrote a novel._

In the following case, while _start_ does not appear to have radically different meanings in the two uses, it is impossible to recover from the context who or what started the trouble in the second case:

---

19.   ANSWER: There is no missing object in (a) because an object is irrelevant; the sentence means 'Margaret is a writer'. The object in (b) and in (c) is latent because an object must be understood from context (e.g. _a poem, a letter, a memo_). In (d), the indirect object is latent because it must be understood from context (e.g. _to her mother, to Nadine_). Sentence (e), on the other hand, has no latent indirect object, because novels, unlike letters, are not written to anyone. Therefore, we need to assign _write_ to all three verb subcategories, intransitive (a), transitive (b, e), and ditransitive (c, d).

They started their first diet. (COCA:ACAD)
The trouble started again. (COCA:ACAD)

Thus, *start* is analyzed as both transitive and intransitive.

Self-Testing Exercise: Do Exercise 7.4.

4. Review of phrase structure rules

The following are the phrase structure rules for English which we have established so far:

S	→	NP VP
NP	→	{(Det) N̄, PN, Pro}
N̄	→	{(AP) N̄ (PP), N}
Det	→	{Art, Dem, Poss, Q, *Wh-*}
Dem	→	{*this, that, these, those*}
Art	→	{*a, an, the*}
Wh-	→	{*which, what, whose*}
Poss	→	{NP-'s, *my, our, their* ...}
Q	→	{*some, any, every, each, neither, more* ...}
AP	→	({Deg, AdvP}) A (PP)
AdvP	→	(Deg) Adv
PP	→	(PSpec) P {NP, PP}
VP	→	V$_{gp}$ ({NP ({NP, PP, AP}), AP, PP (PP)})

We have identified the following grammatical functions:

Subject (Su)	Object of the Preposition (OP)
Direct Object (dO)	Prepositional Complement (pC)
Indirect Object (iO)	Modifier of Noun (Mod of N)
Subject Complement (sC)	Specifier of Noun (Spec of N), Specifier of Preposition (Spec of P)
Object Complement (oC)	Complement of Adjective (Comp of A)

The phrasal categories we have studied can serve the following functions:

NP: Subject, Direct Object, Indirect Object, Subject Complement, Object Complement, Object of Preposition

AP: Modifier of Noun, Subject Complement, Object Complement

PP: Modifier of Noun, Subject Complement, Object Complement, Indirect Object, Prepositional Complement of Verb, of Preposition, or of Adjective

AdvP: Modifier of Adjective

We are now in the position to give D-structure trees for complete sentences. Here are a couple of examples:

The architect's plans for that renovation proved completely unworkable.

(22)

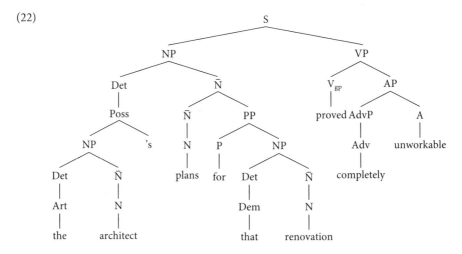

Mr. Richardson assigned her a very challenging new job on our newspaper.

(23)

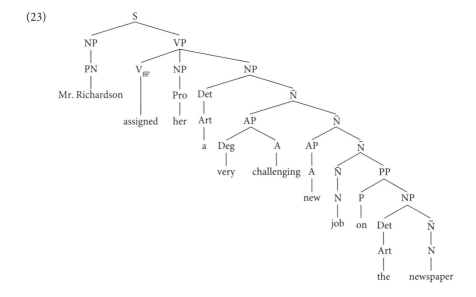

Self-Testing Exercises: Do Exercise 7.5 as a review of the material covered in this chapter

Chapter summary

Now that you have completed this chapter, you should be able to:

1. manipulate the formalisms of phrase structure rules;
2. determine the type of dependency relation (subject–predicate, modifier-head, governor-complement) between elements within a constituent;
3. analyze the structure of noun, adjective, adverb, and prepositional phrases in English using tree diagrams and identify their grammatical functions; and
4. determine the subcategory of verbs in English on the basis of their complement structures.

Recommended additional reading

> **NOTE:** You should be aware that in the works cited here, the order in which the material is presented may diverge quite markedly from the order followed in this textbook and that the formal system used may differ from the form of the grammatical rules introduced in this text.

Less detailed textbook treatments of syntax which take a similar approach to that taken in this chapter include Jeffries (2006, Chapters 4 and 5, pp. 124–143), Fromkin, Rodman, and Hyams (2007, Chapter 4), Plag, Braun, Lappe, and Schramm (2009, Chapter 4), Finegan (2008, Chapter 5), Curzan and Adams (2009, Chapter 6), and O'Grady and Archibald (2009, Chapter 5).

Treatments of English syntax which are similar in depth and level of formality to the treatment in this chapter include Brown and Miller (1991, Chapters 1–6 and 8), Kaplan (1995, Chapter 6, pp. 207–250, and Chapter 7), Burton-Roberts (1997, Chapters 1–4 and 7), Hopper (1999, Chapters 3–5 and 8–9), Miller (2009, Chapters 2–5 and 8), Morenberg (2002, Chapters 1–4), Disterheft (2004, Sections I and II), and Tallerman (2005, Chapters 4–6). Wardhaugh (1995, Chapters 2–4) and Klammer, Schultz, and Della Volpe (2010, Chapter 8) are clear, but less formal treatments.

More advanced textbook treatments of generative syntax (with a focus, but not an exclusive focus on English) include Haegeman and Guéron (1999), Ouhalla (1999), Carnie (2002), Radford (2004), and Haegeman (2006).

Chapter 8

Adverbials, auxiliaries, and sentence types

Chapter preview

This chapter continues discussion of the syntax of simple sentences in English. Three types of adverbial modification, which must be distinguished from verbal complements, are discussed first. The chapter then turns to the form of the verb specifiers – the auxiliary phrase – consisting of tense, mood, aspect, and voice. The structure of the passive sentence and the interaction of passive with verb subcategories are then treated. The chapter continues with a discussion of the structure of *yes/no* questions and negatives in English, followed by a consideration of tag questions and imperative sentences. A review of phrase structure rules, grammatical functions, and verb types ends the chapter.

Commentary

1. Adverbials

In the previous chapter, we discussed the obligatory complements within the verb phrase. We turn now to optional modifiers, both at the level of the verb phrase and at the level of the sentence. These are traditionally called *adverbs*. Three different types of adverbial functions are distinguished:

1. adjunct adverbial,
2. disjunct adverbial, and
3. conjunct adverbial.

We will see that the adverbial function may be filled by a number of different categories: AdvP, PP, NP, and S (the last will be treated in Chapter 9).

1.1 Adjunct adverbials

Adjunct adverbials (aA) generally answer one of the following questions:

How?	(manner)	e.g. *carefully, with enthusiasm*
When?	(time)	e.g. *yesterday, on Tuesday, after I left*
Where?	(place)	e.g. *there, in the kitchen, where I was*
Why?	(reason)	e.g. *for no reason, since I am poor*
How often?	(frequency)	e.g. *twice, monthly*
How long?	(duration)	e.g. *for two years*

The four most common types of adjunct adverbials are manner, time, place, and reason. The examples given above show AdvPs, PPs, and Ss functioning as adverbials. NP's can also occasionally function as adverbials; these fall into a number of different types:

> directional adverbs: *home, upstairs, outside*
> measure phrases: *ten miles, two hours*
> time expressions: *today, this morning, last year, Tuesday*

Adverbials are optional modifiers. Traditionally they are said to be modifying the verb, but they are better understood as modifying the verb together with its complements, which we can call **V-bar** ($\bar{V}$). Thus, we will introduce adverbials into our phrase structure grammar as optional sisters of the $\bar{V}$ in the following way (ignoring S for the present):

$$VP \rightarrow \bar{V} \left(\left\{ \begin{array}{l} PP \\ AdvP \\ NP \end{array} \right\} \right)$$

Our rule for $\bar{V}$ is then the following:

$$\bar{V} \rightarrow V_{gp} \left(\{NP \left(\{NP, AP, PP\} \right), AP, PP \text{ (PP)} \} \right)$$

It is common for more than one type of adverbial to appear in a sentence, as in

> *We came here today for a breather.* (COCA:NEWS)

where there is an adverbial of place (*here*), time (*today*), and reason (*for a breather*). If there is more than one adverbial present, there will have to be more that one $\bar{V}$ node; thus we need to revise our rule for $\bar{V}$ as follows:

$$\bar{V} \rightarrow \left\{ \begin{array}{l} V_{gp}\,(\{NP(\{NP,AP,PP\}),AP,PP(PP)\}) \\ \bar{V}\,(\{PP,AdvP,NP\}) \end{array} \right\}$$

The sentence above would have the following tree diagram. (Note that in this tree we are using a shorthand "triangle notation" where we do not indicate the internal structure of minor phrasal categories or those that are irrelevant for our purposes. We will call these "generalized" trees.)

(1)

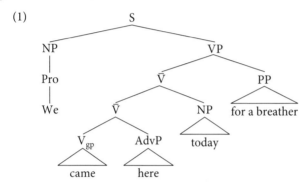

> **HINT:** In drawing your tree diagram, it is best in these cases to work backwards from the end of the sentence.

As many as four adverbials may occur, although the order does not seem to be entirely fixed, e.g. *He left [for town] [quickly] [a few minutes ago] [for help].*

Corpus examples show us that adverbials are very free in their placement, appearing in different positions in the sentence, not just sentence final:

sentence initial	*Yesterday I saw her blow a bubble.* (COCA: FIC)
sentence final	*Roads remained dangerous and slow in many parts of the region yesterday.* (COCA: NEWS)
preverbal	*You always see new faces at those stops.* (COCA: NEWS)
after the verb complement	*They sold their house quickly for a big profit.* (COCA: FIC)
within the auxiliary	*My mother and I have always been exceptionally close.* (COCA: MAG)

The various types of adverbials behave differently, however; while all can occur sentence finally, time adverbials are acceptable sentence initially and sometimes preverbally, place adverbials are clumsy sentence initially, and manner adverbials frequently occur preverbally but are less good sentence initially. One position which is impossible for adverbials is between the verb and the direct object (e.g. *They sold quickly their house for a big profit*). We will ignore the different positions of the adverbial. No matter what their position in surface structure, we will generate all adjunct adverbials in sentence-final position in D-structure and assume that they are moved in a later operation.

1.2   Disjunct adverbials

The second type of adverbial is the **disjunct adverbial (dA)**. Traditionally, these are known as *sentence adverbs*. They denote the speaker's attitude toward or judgment of the proposition, expressing, for example, the speaker's degree of truthfulness or his manner of speaking. As in the case of adjunct adverbials, AdvPs or PPs (or Ss) may serve as disjunct adverbials:

AdvP: *seriously, truthfully, frankly, certainly, hopefully, sadly, personally, confidentially, literally, foolishly, stupidly, oddly, surely, clearly*

PP: *in all frankness, to my surprise, in broad terms, to my regret, of course, on paper*

Unlike adjunct adverbials, disjunct adverbials modify the entire S, not just the VP, so they are generated by the phrase structure rules as the optional sister of S, as follows:

$$S \rightarrow S \quad \left(\left\{ \begin{matrix} AdvP \\ PP \\ NP \end{matrix} \right\} \right)$$

Note that disjunct adverbials appear most naturally at the beginning of the sentence; they are moved to this position on the surface.

Sometimes, the same lexical item can be both an adjunct and a disjunct:

aA: *I have <u>seriously</u> considered banning Christmas gifts this year.* (COCA:MAG)

dA: *<u>Seriously</u>, it's a pretty funny show.* (COCA:FIC)

In the first sentence, *seriously* means 'in a serious manner', while in the second it means 'I am being serious when I say'.

1.3   Conjunct adverbials

The third type of adverbial is the **conjunct adverbial (cA)**. Traditionally, these are known as *conjunctive adverbs*. They express textual relations, serving to link clauses; they have no function in their own clause. They may be AdvPs or PPs:

AdvP: *moreover, however, nonetheless, nevertheless, furthermore, next, finally, consequently, therefore, thus, instead, indeed, besides, hence*

PP: *in addition, in conclusion, on the contrary, on one/the other hand, in other words, for example, as a result, in the second place*

Conjunct adverbials denote a logical connection between the clause that follows and the clause or clauses that precede: for example, the second clause may express result (*hence*), contrast (*however*), addition (*moreover*), apposition (*namely*), summation (*overall*), listing (*next*), inference (*then*), and several other connections.

Like disjunct adverbials, conjunct adverbials are sisters of S; the rule given in the preceding section thus generates conjunct as well as disjunct adverbials.

Self-Testing Exercise: Do Exercise 8.1.

2. Functions of postverbal prepositional phrases

PPs which follow the verb – postverbal PPs – can serve a number of different purposes. The functions of postverbal PPs include prepositional complement, adjunct adverbial, and postmodifier of the noun, but these can often be difficult to distinguish.

The first difficulty arises with the sequence V PP, which can represent the following structures:

1. $\bar{v}[V_{cop} \; PP]$ *His wife was in her rabid matchmaking mode.*   (sC)
   (COCA:FIC)
2. $\bar{v}[V_{prep} \; PP]$ *His glower changed into a snarl.*   (pC)
   (COCA:FIC)
3. $_{VP}[\bar{v}[V_{intrans}] \; PP]$ *The face of poverty has changed*   (aA)
   in America. (COCA:SPOK)

In sentence 1, *in her rabid matchmaking mode* is a subject complement referring back to *his wife*. In sentence 2, *into a snarl* is a prepositional complement of *changed*, and in sentence 3, *in America* is an adjunct adverbial modifying *has changed*. The PP can be either an obligatory complement of the verb (as in sentences 1 and 2) or an optional modifier of the $\bar{V}$, an adjunct adverbial (as in the third case).

If the PP has at least some of the following qualities, then it is likely to be an adjunct adverbial:

- it is optional and hence can be omitted; the sentence is grammatical without it (*The face of poverty has changed*);
- it can usually (but not always) be moved to the beginning of the sentence (*In America, the face of poverty has changed*);
- it expresses time, place, manner, or reason, answering the questions "when?", "where?", "how?", or "why?", not "what?" or "whom?" (but note that many prepositional complements answer these questions as well) (*Where has the face of poverty changed?*);
- it can occur in a separate predication (*It happened in America*);

- it can occur in a *do so/too* structure, as in *The face of poverty changed in America and it did so in Europe as well* (here, *do so* substitutes for the VP);
- it may be replaced by a lexical adverb (*The face of poverty changed there*); and
- it does not figure in the subcategorization of the verb.

No PP will meet all of the tests for adjunct adverbials, but it will meet at least some of them.

Look at the following three sentences:

> *They agreed on the terms.*
> *They agreed in an instant.*
> *They agreed on the boat.*

The PP in the first sentence is a complement of a prepositional verb, while the PP in the second sentence is an adjunct adverbial. The third sentence is structurally ambiguous since the PP can serve either of these functions. The two meanings are that 'They decided while they were on the boat' (the aA reading) or 'They decided (to buy) the boat' (the pC reading). The following (generalized) tree diagrams represent the two structures:

(2)   (aA)   or   (pC)

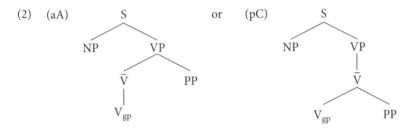

A second difficulty arises with the sequence V NP PP. This may represent a complex transitive verb structure, a transitive verb structure followed by an adjunct adverbial, or a transitive verb structure whose direct object is postmodified by a prepositional phrase, as in the following sentences:

1. $_{\bar{v}}[V_{gp}$ NP PP]   *Chadric exchanged a smile <u>with his wife.</u>*   (pC/oC)
                                             (COCA:FIC)

2. $_{VP}[_{\bar{v}}[V_{gp}$ NP] PP]   *My mother played piano <u>with skill.</u>*   (aA)
                                             (COCA:FIC)

3. $_{\bar{v}}[V_{gp\ NP}[\bar{N}$ PP]]   *She ... wore a dress <u>with a low-cut back.</u>*   (Mod of $\bar{N}$)
                                             (COCA:FIC)

Here *with his wife* is a prepositional complement of the transitive structure (*exchanged a smile*); *with skill* is an adjunct adverbial answering the question *how?* and expressing the manner in which the mother played the piano; *with a low-cut back* is an optional modifier of the direct object *a dress*.

Self-Quiz: Compare the following sentences:

    a. *Isaac played the violin with great skill.*
    b. *Isaac played the violin with the loose bridge.*
    c. *Isaac played the violin with a new bow.*

Analyze the function of the final PP in each case.[1]

These different possibilities may yield ambiguous sentences such as *I helped the man with a shovel*, meaning either that 'I helped the man using a shovel' (the pC reading) or 'I helped the man who had a shovel (the shovel-man)' (the modifier reading), represented by the following generalized trees:

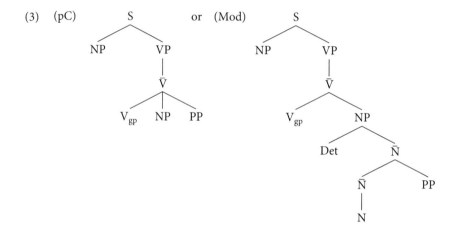

A third difficulty arises with the sequence V PP PP, where the second PP may be the second prepositional complement in a dipertositional verb structure, an adjunct adverbial, of the modifier of the preceding noun, , as in the following sentences:

1. $_{\bar{V}}[V_{gp}$ PP PP]   *She often argued with him <u>about their</u>*   (pC)
                                            <u>responsibility.</u> (COCA:FIC)

2. $_{VP}[_{\bar{V}}[V_{gp}$ PP] PP]   *The warden argued with them <u>for hours</u>.* (aA)
                                            (COCA:FIC)

3. $_{\bar{V}}[V_{gp\ pp}[P_{NP}[\bar{N}$ PP]]]   *Few advertisers argued with the success <u>of</u>* (Mod of N)
                                          <u>these commercials.</u> (COCA:SPOK)

Here, *with him* and *about their responsibility* are prepositional complements of *argued*; *for hours* is an optional adjunct adverbial modifying the prepositional verb and its complement

---

1. ANSWER: (a) aA; (b) Mod of N̄; (c) pC.

(*argued with them*); and *of these commercials* is a modifier of *the success*, with *argued with the success* being a prepositional verb and its complement.

> *Self-Quiz:* Compare the following sentences:
>
> > a. *Monica stepped on a bee on Tuesday.*
> > b. *Monica consulted with her doctor about the bee sting.*
> > c. *Monica stepped on a bee with a large stinger.*
>
> Analyze the function of the final PP in each case.[2]

Again, structural ambiguities arise, as in the case of the sentence *I ran into the girls with the flowers.* Here, "with the flowers" may be either a prepositional complement ('I ran into the girls with (using) the flowers') or a modifier of the noun "girls" ('I ran into the girls who had the flowers'), as shown below:

(4)   (pC)   S   or   (Mod)   S

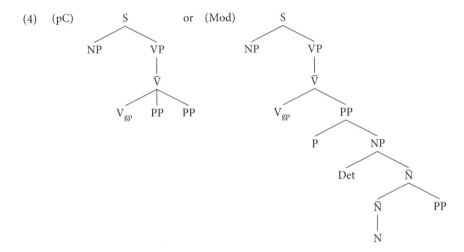

The last difficulty arises with phrasal verbs (introduced in Chapter 4), which must be distinguished from prepositional verbs. Transitive phrasal verbs consist of a verb, a direct object, and a particle, which is movable, occurring either before or after the object (unlike prepositions which can occur only before their objects). With prepositional verbs, the preposition is not moveable. Compare the following phrasal verbs with the corresponding prepositional verbs:

–   phrasal verb: *Psycho slipped on a black T-shirt.* (COCA:FIC)
                             Psycho slipped a black T-shirt on.
–   prepositional verb: *He slipped on a rock.* (COCA:NEWS)
                             *He slipped a rock on.

---

2.   ANSWER: (a) aA; (b) pC; (c) Mod of N̄.

– phrasal verb: *Insurgents blew up the last one.* (COCA:NEWS)
                          Insurgents blew the last one up.
– prepositional verb: *A cool wind blew up the canyon.* (COCA:FIC)
                          *A cool wind blew the canyon up.
– phrasal verb: *He ate up his dinner.* (COCA:FIC)
                          He ate his dinner up.
– prepositional verb: *The teens walked up the hill.* (COCA:NEWS)
                          *The teens walked the hill up
– phrasal verb: *Christine ran over the numbers again.* (COCA:FIC)
                          Christine ran the numbers over again.
– prepositional verb: *The road ran over the tops of hills.* (COCA:FIC)
                          *The road ran the tops of hills over.

The two types of verbs have the following underlying structures:

(5)   (Phrasal)   (Prepositional)

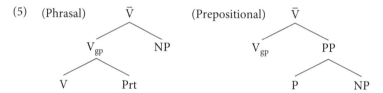

As you can see, the phrasal verb is really a monotransitive verb, with the particle associated with the verb. The particle is generated next to the verb. When it moves, it becomes the sister of the NP, as follows:

(6)

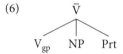

When the NP is a pronoun, this movement is obligatory. That is, one can say *He looked it up*, but not **He looked up it*.

There are a number of syntactic criteria you can use for distinguishing phrasal verbs from prepositional verbs:

1. in transitive phrasal verbs, the particle is movable, but the preposition in a prepositional verb is not;
2. the NP is the object of the verb in phrasal verbs rather than of the preposition;
3. in both transitive and intransitive phrasal verbs, the particle carries stress, as in *She took it óff* or *The plane took óff*, while prepositions are unstressed, as in *We knocked on the dóor.*
4. adverbials cannot intervene between the verb and the particle whereas they can between the verb and the preposition, **looked quickly up the information*, but *looked quickly into the oven.*

(Remember that phrasal verbs can also be intransitive, e.g. *catch on, get by, give in.*)

Self-Testing Exercise: Do Exercises 8.2.

3. Auxiliary

To this point, we have assumed that the verbal element in the $\bar{V}$ consists of the lexical verb in its base form and nothing else. But just as there are specifiers of the noun, there appear to be specifiers of the verb. These are traditionally called "auxiliary verbs", which we saw in Chapter 5 include: the primary auxiliaries (*have* and *be*), the dummy auxiliary *do*, and the modal auxiliaries (*will, can, shall, may,* and *must*) as well as a number of phrasal equivalents and borderline auxiliaries (e.g. *dare, need*). When we considered auxiliaries as a word class, we looked at their special inflectional features (the "defective morphology" of modals in that they do not take -*s* in the 3rd p sg or have nonfinite forms) and their special distribution, e.g. preceding *not* or -*n't*, the subject in a question, or emphatic markers *so, too*. They cannot stand alone in a sentence; instead, there must be a **lexical** or **main verb** present which functions as head of the verb group.

Table 8.1 presents the possible specifiers of the verb with the main verb *bite* (in the active voice only). We note that more than one auxiliary – in fact, up to three auxiliaries – can occur in a single sentence. But these must appear in a certain order and form; there is a complex internal structure to the verb group. And the main verb always comes last in the verb group; that is, unlike the noun, the verb allows no modifiers following it.

Table 8.1. Specifiers of the Verb (Active)

Those dogs				are/were	bite/bit	those cats
	can/could	have/had		been	biting	
	can/could	have/had		be	bitten	
	can/could	have		been	biting	
	can/could	have			bite	
					biting	
					bitten	
					biting	

Let's look at the different elements in the verb group. We begin with Tense (T). Tense is expressed as a bound morph (an inflection) on the first element in the sequence, whether this is an auxiliary or the main verb. Tense is always present; it is an obligatory element. In English the only tense distinctions are past and present (or, more accurately, nonpast; see the discussion of tense in Chapter 5):

> T → {past, pres}

Tense is attached to the first element in the verb group. The verb or auxiliary carrying tense is called **finite**, all other forms (nontensed) are called nonfinite (not restricted in terms of tense, person, and number).

The second element in the verb group is the **modal auxiliary (M)**. The modal auxiliary is the first independent element in the verb group, but it needn't be present. M is optional. If a modal is present, it carries tense.[3] The form of the auxiliary (*have* or *be*) or main verb which follows the modal is the basic stem form, also called the "bare infinitive".

M → {*shall, can, will, may, must*}

The third element in the verb group is Perfect (Perf). Like M, Perf is optional. It contains the auxiliary *have*; the form following *have*, whether it is another auxiliary or the main verb, is in the form of a past (or perfect) participle. We account for this sequence with the following phrase structure rule:

Perf → *have -en*

Here, *-en* is an abstract marker for past participle (realized as *-en, -ed*, and so on), which will later be attached to the form following *have*. If the perfect occurs without a modal, then *have* carries tense (e.g. <u>*had*</u> *broken*); if a modal precedes the perfect, then *have* is in the basic stem form (e.g. *could* <u>*have*</u> *broken*).

The fourth element in the verb group is Progressive (Prog). Prog is also optional. It contains the auxiliary *be*; the form following *be* is in the form of a present participle. In the active voice, the form following *be* is always the main verb. We account for this sequence with the following phrase structure rule:

Prog → *be -ing*

-ing will later be attached to the form following *be*. If progressive is the first element in the verb group, then *be* carries tense (e.g, <u>*is*</u> *swimming*), but if either the perfect or a modal (or both) precede, *be* will be nonfinite (e.g. *has* <u>*been*</u> *swimming, will* <u>*be*</u> *swimming*).

All of the specifiers of the verb are grouped together under the category of **auxiliary (Aux)**, which is expanded as follows:

Aux → T (M) (Perf) (Prog)
T → {past, pres}
M → {*shall, can, will, may, must*}
Perf → *have -en*
Prog → *be -ing*

Thus, the auxiliary in *could have been biting* would have the following tree representation:

(7)

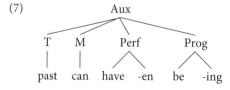

---

3. However, past tense forms of the modals do not usually express past time. For example, *It might* (past) *rain* expresses slightly more uncertainty than *It may* (present) *rain,* though both refer to future time.

To finish accounting for the form of Aux, we need to attach the affixes (past, pres, -*en*, and -*ing*) to the following elements. We do this by means of a rule called **affix hopping**. This rule stipulates that each affix attaches to the <u>verbal</u> element immediately following it and forms the relevant word. In the example above, affix hopping attaches past to *can*, -*en* to *be*, and -*ing* to the main verb (*bite*). The attachment of affixes is written as follows, where # indicates word boundaries:

$$\#can + past\# \ have \ \#be + -en\# \ \#bite \ -ing\#$$

Rules of word formation give *could*, *been*, and *biting*, and thus the "past modal perfect progressive (active)" phrase *could have been biting.*[4]

It remains to determine where Aux is generated in the structure of the sentence. As specifiers, auxiliaries are often thought of as sisters of the V or the V_{gp}, as follows:

$$V_{gp} \rightarrow Aux \ V \ ... \ or \ \bar{V} \rightarrow Aux \ V_{gp}$$

However, Aux would differ from all other specifiers in being obligatory, not optional. An alternate view is to see Aux as sister of the VP and daughter of S, since, in fact, the Aux elements are relevant to the entire sentence.

(8)

$$S$$

$$NP \quad Aux \quad VP$$

Our complete rule for S is then the following:[5]

$$S \rightarrow \begin{cases} NP \ Aux \ VP \\ S \ (\{AdvP, \ PP, \ NP\}) \end{cases}$$

Above, we considered only active forms of Aux. There is a corresponding set of passive forms (see Table 8.2). (Although all of these forms are possible, some are quite rare.)

---

4.   The finite verb is also marked in the present tense for person and number to agree with the subject, but this is very limited in English, only the 3rd p -*s* for most verbs. We will ignore subject-verb agreement.

5.   In X-bar theory (see Chapter 7, Footnote 7), Aux – known as I or INFL (for "inflection") – is seen as head, with the VP as complement, the subject NP as specifier, and S as IP:

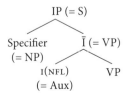

Table 8.2. Specifiers of the Verb (Passive)

Those cats				are/were	bitten	by those dogs
	could	have/had	are/were	being	bitten	
	could	have/had	been	been	bitten	
	could	have	be	being	bitten	
	could	have	been	be	bitten	
				being	bitten	
				been	bitten	
				being	bitten	

These differ from the active forms in having a *be* auxiliary followed by an *-en* form. The *be* auxiliary is always the last auxiliary in the string, and hence the main verb is always in the past participle form. The phrase structure rule for **Passive (Pass)** and the revised rule for Aux would be as follows:

Aux → T (M) (Perf) (Prog) (Pass)
Pass → *be -en*

Note that passive too is optional.

Self-Testing Exercises: Do Exercises 8.3 and 8.4.

4. Passive sentences

Although it is possible to generate a passive sentence directly in the D-structure by simply adding Pass to the phrase structure rule for Aux, as we just did, a passive sentence is typically seen as being directly related to its active counterpart – rather than as a completely different structure – since the choice of the passive, unlike the choice of any other auxiliary, affects the structure of the entire sentence.

Consider this active and passive pair:

The art expert could have detected the forgery. ⇒
The forgery could have been detected by the art expert

This view has the advantage of representing S as having the same structure as all the other phrasal categories (namely XP → Spec $\bar{\bar{X}}$ and $\bar{X}$→ X Complements). If a flat structure of this is given, it looks like our tree:

The passive sentence compares with the active sentence in the following way:

1. the passive verb group contains the *be -en* sequence just before the main verb;
2. the subject of the active sentence (the agent) is the object of the preposition *by* at end of the passive sentence; and
3. the direct object of the active sentence is the subject of the passive sentence.

Passive sentences are thus best understood as deriving from their active counterpart by a syntactic operation involving the following sequence.[6] The passive auxiliary is inserted in the verb specifier position, which causes the agent NP to move to the *by* phrase. The subject position then becomes empty, and since it is not possible in English for the subject to be empty, the object NP moves to fill that position.[7] When it does so, it leaves behind a **trace** (*t*) in its former position. Traces, which encode the base position of a moved constituent, will become more important as we progress.

If NP_1 and NP_2 stand for the active subject (*the art expert*) and object (*the forgery*), respectively, then the two sentences above have the following tree representations on the surface level:

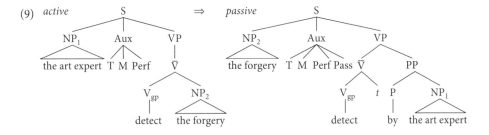

Note that the PP containing the agent phrase becomes the sister of the $\bar{V}$ and hence functions adverbially. We call these **agented passives**.

However, the most frequent kind of passive sentence in English is the **agentless passive** in which the *by* phrase is not present. Its omission is related to the rhetorical functions of the passive (see Chapter 11). However, we will analyze agentless passive sentences as containing an agent in D-structure, an agent which is not specified since it is recoverable from the context or is generally known. This agent will be indicated by Ø (= zero) in the tree in subject position of the D-structure active sentence. You can also think of this Ø as representing an indefinite pronoun such as "someone".

---

6. An alternative account of the passive as base-derived in discussed in Exercise 8.5, Question 3.

7. The movement of the object to subject position is called "NP Movement".

4.1   Verb subcategorization and the passive

Not all active sentences may undergo the passive. In order for a sentence to be passivized, the subject must be an agent (a doer or performer of an action) and the verb must have a direct or prepositional object which can move to the subject position. The subcategorization of the verb is therefore very important in the formation of the passive:

1. Monotransitive verbs may be passivized: the dO of active becomes the Su of the passive sentence:

    A Japanese executive could have done it. (dO).
    It could have been done by a Japanese executive. (COCA:NEWS)

2. Intransitive verbs cannot be passivized since they have no dO. For example, in the case of *The dog barked,* there is no direct object to move into subject position (**__was barked by the dog*).

3. Copulative verbs cannot be passivized since they have no dO (rather a sC) and the subject is not an agent. For example, *She is a good cook* cannot be transformed into **A good cook is been by her.*

4. Ditransitive verbs may be passivized, with either the dO or the iO of the active becoming the Su of the passive sentence:[8]

    My mother gave this recipe (dO) *to me.* ⇒
    This recipe was given to me by my mother. (COCA:FIC)
    A friend gave me (iO) *shelter.* ⇒
    I was given shelter by a friend. (COCA:FIC)

5. Complex transitive verbs (both locative and nonlocative) may be passivized: the dO (but not usually the oC)[9] of the active becomes the Su of the passive sentence:

    The people there elected him (dO) *president.* ⇒
    He was elected president by the people there. (COCA:ACAD)

    but not **President was elected him by the people there.*

    His father placed David (dO) *in an orphanage.* ⇒
    David was placed in an orphanage by his father. (COCA:SPOK)

    but not **An orphanage was placed David in by his father.*

---

8. Note that it is usually the case that it is the NP immediately following the verb which becomes subject, but there can be exceptions, as in the following:

    The missionaries gave them this date (dO). ⇒
    This date was given them by the missionaries [COCA:ACAD]).

9. When the OC is a prepositional phrase, it is often possible to passive the sentence: the OP becomes the Su of the passive sentence: *They were taken good care of* (COCA:NEWS).

6. Prepositional verbs, when they are nonlocative, may usually be passivized: the OP of the active becomes the Su of the passive sentence

   The entire pharmaceutical industry agreed to <u>the same limits</u>. (OP). ⇒
   <u>The same limits</u> were agreed to by the entire pharmaceutical industry. (COCA:NEWS)
   cf. *The picture hung on the wall.* ⇒
      **The wall was hung on by the picture).*

7. Diprepositional verbs may sometimes be passivized: the OP of the first PP in the active becomes the Su of the passive sentence:

   He conferred with the boss about the problem. ⇒
   ?*The boss was conferred with about the problem.*

8. Transitive phrasal verbs may usually be passivized (intransitive phrasal verbs cannot be): the dO of the active becomes the Su of the passive sentence:

   An Oakland newspaper made <u>it</u> (dO) *up.* ⇒
   <u>It</u> was made up by an Oakland newspaper. (COCA:NEWS)

Certain apparently transitive verbs cannot be passivized. These are ones in which the verb is stative in meaning (see Chapter 6), as in the following cases:

Jake resembles his father.	**His father is resembled by Jake.*
Maggie hates chocolates.	**Chocolates are hated by Maggie.*
Florence speaks French fluently.	?*French is spoken fluently by Florence.*
The color suits you.	**You are suited by the color.*
The dress fits me.	**I am fit by the dress.*

The subjects in these cases are not agents performing an action; the grammatical objects are also not affected by the action of the verb and are hence not direct objects.

Self-Testing Exercise: Do Exercise 8.5.

> **HINT:** In Exercise 8.5, remember to turn every passive sentence into an active sentence before giving the D-structure. Thus, if the sentence were *The garbage can was crushed by the car,* the D-structure would be *The car crushed the garbage can*; and if the sentence were *His non-appearance at the party was noticed,* the deep structure would be *(someone) noticed his non-appearance at the party.*

5. *Yes/no* questions and negative sentences

To this point, we have considered only sentences which are declarative and positive. We turn now to negative and interrogative sentences; we will see that these can be treated together because they both make reference to the same sequence of elements in the auxiliary. As with passive sentences, we will consider both types of sentences to be derived via transformations from the corresponding positive and declarative sentences. That is, we are assuming that sentences in D-structure are positive, declarative, and active; we than convert them to negative, interrogative, and passive sentences on the surface by transformations (which permute, add, or delete elements, but do not fundamentally alter the meaning of the sentence). Generating the sentences in this way allows us to show the relationship, for example, between a declarative sentence and the corresponding interrogative – both have the same D-structure.

5.1   *Yes/no questions*

The following examples show the formation of *yes/no* (**or truth**) **questions** from the corresponding declarative sentences:

Richard is leaving soon.	⇒	*Is Richard leaving soon? (COCA:FIC)*
She has really imagined that.	⇒	*Has she really experienced that? (COCA:MAG)*
He has been drinking.	⇒	*Has he been drinking? (COCA:FIC)*
We can afford the costs.	⇒	*Can we afford the costs? (COCA:NEWS)*
It was planned by some higher authority.	⇒	*Was it planned by some higher authority? (COCA:FIC)*

(A second kind of question – the *wh*-question – will be treated in Chapter 9.)

What happens in the formation of each of the questions above is a transformation called **subject-aux(iliary) inversion,** in which the order of the subject of the sentence and the <u>first</u> auxiliary element is reversed, or, more specifically, the first auxiliary moves to a position preceding the subject. The auxiliaries *is, has, can,* and *was* move in front of the subject in the examples above. Since the first auxiliary element carries tense, it is more correct to say that tense and the first auxiliary precedes the subject.

The S-structure tree for the third question takes the following form:

(10)

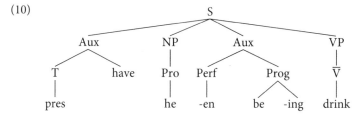

The part of the Aux node containing T and the first independent auxiliary attaches in front of the subject and becomes the daughter of S.[10]

---

10.   It is thought that Aux moves to the complementizer position, as will be discussed in the Chapter 9. For the present, we will not worry about exactly where Aux attaches.

Subject-aux inversion also occurs in some noninterrogative sentences, namely, those beginning with a restricted set of negative adverbs (*never, seldom, rarely, scarcely, no sooner*):

> *Never have we seen so much uproar on immigration.*   (COCA:NEWS)
> *Seldom have I been so terribly wrong.*   (COCA:FIC)
> *Rarely has he seen a leak of this sort involving classified information.* (COCA:SPOK)

5.2 Negative statements and questions

The following sentences show the formation of negative statements from the corresponding positive statements given above:

> ⇒ *Richard is not/isn't leaving soon.*
> ⇒ *She has not/hasn't really experienced that.*
> ⇒ *He has not /hasn't been drinking.*
> ⇒ *We cannot/can't afford the costs.*
> ⇒ *It was not/wasn't planned by some higher authority.*

In this case, the negative element (*not*) is placed after tense and the first auxiliary element. The contraction of *not* to *-n't* is optional and follows insertion of *not* into the string.

The following sentences show the formation of negative questions from the sentences given above:

> ⇒ *Isn't Richard leaving soon?*
> ⇒ *Hasn't she really experienced that?*
> ⇒ *Hasn't he been drinking?*
> ⇒ *Can't we afford the costs?*
> ⇒ *Wasn't it planned by some higher authority?*

In negative questions there is both subject–aux inversion and placement of the negative element after tense and the first auxiliary. Normally the negative element also inverts with the auxiliary; in this case, contraction is obligatory:

> **Is not Richard leaving soon?*
> **Has not he been drinking?*

However, it is possible to leave the negative element behind. Such sentences involve word negation, rather than sentence negation, and the scope of negation is different in them:

> cf.   *Is Richard not leaving soon?*
> *Has he not been drinking?*
> *Can we not afford the costs?*

That is, these sentences involve the negation of an individual word, as in *happy/unhappy/ not happy*. Both kinds of negation can occur in the same sentence:

We didn't not work together. (COCA:NEWS)
I won't not do something, if it is what I think. (COCA:FIC)
I wasn't happy, but I wasn't unhappy either. (COCA:FIC)

5.3   *Do*-support

What happens if you wish to form a negative or interrogative sentence from a sentence that has no auxiliary other than tense:

Bouton wrote that book by himself.
⇒ *Bouton didn't write that book by himself.* (COCA:FIC)
The children stood by their father.
⇒ *Did the children stand by their father?* (COCA:SPOK)

Placing tense before the subject or the negative after tense results in what is called "tense stranding" because by the rule of affix hopping there is nothing for tense to attach to: it must attach to the immediately following element and that element must be verbal, but in the interrogative the subject (NP) follows, and in the negative *not* follows. So a verbal element must be supplied by inserting the **dummy auxiliary *do*.** This serves the function of an auxiliary when there is no other independent auxiliary present. This insertion transformation is called ***do*-support.**[11]

Dummy *do* behaves in all respects like an auxiliary; it is used when an auxiliary is necessary – in questions, tag questions, negatives, contrastive stress – and none is present in the corresponding noninterrogative, positive, nonemphatic sentence. However, dummy *do* is purely structural, a mere tense carrier; since it is empty of lexical meaning, its addition does not change the meaning of the sentence.

The surface tree produced by *do*-support *Did the children stand by their father?* is the following:

(11)

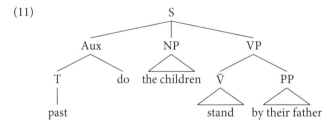

---

11.   An alternative account, *do*-deletion, generates all sentences with *do* in D-structure and deletes it when it is not necessary, that is, when there is a verbal element adjoining to which tense can be affixed.

Do is initially inserted after T in Aux when it stands before V; then this portion of Aux is moved in front of the subject. This leaves a gap in the second portion of Aux. The verbal element following *do* occurs in its basic stem form.[12]

Note that apart from auxiliary dummy *do* there are two other *do*'s in English:

main verb:	*No one does the dishes.* (COCA:NEWS)
	I don't do lunch. (COCA:NEWS)
	We do homework on our laps in the car. (COCA:MAG)
pro-verb:	*He buzzed again, and so did the others.* (COCA:FIC)
	I loved going to those tournaments, and I thought Alex did too. (COCA:MAG)

Lexical verb *do* behaves in all respect like a main verb; it can occur with dummy *do* in the same sentence in negatives and questions when there is no other auxiliary present (as in *I don't do lunch*). Pro-verb *do* functions rather differently. It is like a pronoun, and just as a pronoun replaces the entire NP, the pro-verb replaces an entire VP.

With main verb *be* and *have*, *do*-support works somewhat differently:

1. *The books are in print.*   ⇒   *Are the books in print?* (COCA:SPOK)
2. *Thornton's injury is serious.*   ⇒   *Thornton's injury isn't serious.* (COCA:NEWS)
3. *I have the time for stupid jokes.* ⇒   *I haven't the time for stupid jokes.* (COCA:FIC)
4. *They have the time for training.* ⇒   *They don't have the time for training.* (COCA:ACAD)

---

12.   It is not possible to account for negatives and questions simply by rewriting the phrase structure rules to allow tense and the first auxiliary to be generated optionally before the subject and to allow for the optional placement of the negative element after tense and the first auxiliary element. If we attempted to do so, we would need a rule for the negative something like the following since *not* can follow any of the independent auxiliaries:

Aux → T (M) (*not*) (*have* (*not*) -*en*) (*be* (*not*) -*ing*) (*be* (*not*) -*en*)

The problem with this rule is that we cannot rule out multiple negation since the rule allows us to select all of the negative elements (and there is no mechanism for rewriting the rule to forbid this). It is similarly difficult to write such a phrase structure rule for the interrogative since we need to allow *have* and *be* to either precede or follow the subject:

S → (M) (*have* -*en*) (*be* -*ing*) NP (*have* -*en*) (*be* -*ing*) VP

With this rule, we would be able to select *have* and *be* more than once and to move more than one auxiliary before the subject, which are not permitted by the rules of English.

5. *You have the courage to build the house*   ⇒   *Have you the courage to build the*
    without windows on the street front.   *house without windows on the street*
                                                                          front? (COCA:MAG)

6. *You did not have a good time in France.*   ⇒   *Didn't you have a good time in*
                                                                          France? (COCA:FIC)

When *be* is functioning as a main verb and it is the only verbal element present, it behaves as an auxiliary in respect to subject-aux inversion and negative placement (as in 1 and 2 above); it is not necessary to insert *do*.

When *have* is functioning as a main verb, it behaves either as an auxiliary or a main verb, depending on dialect. In 3 and 5 above, *have* is treated as an auxiliary; in 4 and 6 above, *have* is treated as main verb and takes a dummy-*do*. Most speakers of North American treat *have* as a main verb and insert *do*, except perhaps in some fixed expressions, while most speakers of British English treat *have* an auxiliary.

One way to account for the behavior of *be* and *have* would be to give them the feature [+Aux] in the lexicon.

Self-Testing Exercise: Do Exercise 8.6.

> HINT: Again, you must change questions into statements, passive into active sentences, and negative into positive sentences to arrive at the D-structure. Thus, the interrogative *Is the television too loud?* would be declarative *The television is too loud* in D-structure. Sometimes, you must change more than one feature of a sentence, so the sentence *Isn't the water boiling* would be *The water is boiling* in D-structure (changing interrogative to declarative and negative to positive), and the sentence *The concert date hasn't been announced* would be *(someone) has announced the concert date* (changing passive to active and negative to positive).

5.4   Tag questions

In the sections above, we studied the structure of the *yes/no* question. An additional type of question is the **tag question**:

> *Your three-year-old is healthy, isn't she?* (COCA:MAG)
> *People haven't always driven like this, have they?* (COCA:NEWS)
> *Einstein would have never said that, would he?* (COCA:SPOK)
> *I should have known, shouldn't I?* (COCA:FIC)
> *You worked for Penny Marshall, didn't you?* (COCA:SPOK)

The "tag" follows the comma and consists of the following:

1. tense and the first auxiliary of the main clause (or *do* if there isn't one);
2. a pronoun identical in person, number, and gender with the subject of the main clause; and

3. a marker of negative polarity; that is, if the main clause is positive, *-n't* occurs (note that the negative element is obligatorily contracted), and if the main clause is negative, no negative element occurs.

Point (1) above should remind you of subject-aux inversion. However, in the formation of tag questions, tense plus the first auxiliary are copied rather than reordered. Also, rather than moving the subject, its features of person, number, and gender are duplicated in a pronoun. Note that tag questions are ill-formed if the pronoun does not have the same features as the subject or if a different auxiliary than that in the main clause is used:

> *Alison will be leaving soon, won't {she, *he, *they, *you}?*
> *Alison will be leaving soon, {won't, *can't, *isn't, *doesn't} she?*

Certain modal auxiliaries do not work particularly well in tag questions, so some other auxiliary is sometimes substituted, such as the use of *won't* instead of *mayn't* or *wouldn't* instead of *mightn't*:[13] The phrasal equivalents of the modals and the borderline auxiliaries are particularly awkward in tags:

> *ought to* may have a tag with *do* or *should*
> > *They ought to be censored, shouldn't they?* (COCA:SPOK)
> *used to* often may have a tag with *do*
> > *You used to be a lawyer, didn't you?* (COCA:FIC)
> *have to* may have a tag with *do*
> > *And he has to get water from the fridge, doesn't he?* (COCA:FIC)
> *needn't* and *daren't* may have tags with *do*

Note the behavior of main verb *have* and *be* in tag questions. As in *yes/no* questions, *be* behaves universally as an auxiliary, and *have* (in the meaning of 'possess') behaves as either as an auxiliary or as a main verb.

> *We're all patients these days, aren't we?* (COCA:FIC)
> *He has a bit of a reputation, hasn't he?* (COCA:FIC)
> *She has pretty eyes, doesn't she?* (COCA:NEWS)

However, *do* is required in tags when *have* does not have the meaning of 'possess', as in *They had a party, {didn't, *hadn't} they?* or *She had a long bath this evening, {didn't, *hadn't} she?*:

> *You had a fight that night, didn't you?* (COCA:FIC)

---

13. Some of corpus examples of these forms can be found, but they are not common:

> *I may call you Margaret, mayn't I?* (COCA:FIC)
> *One might even call it the betting track, mightn't one?* (COCA:FIC)

6.   Imperatives

We have so far accounted for the formation of declarative and interrogative sentences, but not for the formation of **imperative** sentences such as the following:

> Pass these out before each class. (COCA:ACAD)
> Take a look at your sales records. (COCA:MAG)
> Don't be a doormat. (COCA:NEWS)

Our rule for S will not account for these because they have no subject. Traditionally, it is said that a *you* subject is "understood", or elliptical. Is there any validity to this? There are a number of tests for *you* in imperatives. First, consider **reflexive pronouns**. These are forms with *-self* or *-selves* attached to a personal pronoun which have the same referent as the subject of the clause; that is, they agree in person, number, and gender with the subject:

> Just do your job, <u>he</u> told <u>himself</u>. (COCA:ACAD)
> <u>This cycle</u> repeats <u>itself</u> until the air pressure is insufficient to start again. (COCA:ACAD)
> <u>They</u> take <u>themselves</u> too seriously, they exaggerate. (COCA:SPOK)
> And all things considered, I think <u>she</u> considers <u>herself</u> a very lucky woman today. (COCA:SPOK)

(The last example shows that the reflexive must agree with the subject of the clause in which it occurs, not with the subject of some higher clause.) In imperatives, only *yourself*, not any other reflexive pronoun, can occur:

> Shoot {yourself, *himself, *myself}!
> Dress {yourself, *themselves, *itself}!

Furthermore, the 2nd person pronoun must be the reflexive, not the nonreflexive form:

> *Shoot you!
> *Dress you!

Second, consider the idiom *lose/find one's way*. Only a possessive pronoun coindexed with the subject can occur:

> Andrew {lost, found} (his, *her, ?their} way.

When this idiom occurs in an imperative, only *your* can occur:

> Don't lose {your, *my, *their} way home!

Third, consider the behavior of tag questions with imperatives:

> Help me, won't {you, *she, *he, *they}?

As discussed in the previous section, the pronoun in a tag question has the same referent as the subject of the main clause. With imperatives, only *you* can occur. These tests all suggest, therefore, that there is an understood, or underlying, *you* in the subject position of imperative sentences.

The last test also suggests that there is an underlying *will* in imperatives, because as you will recall from the previous section, the auxiliary of the main clause is copied in the auxiliary of the tag with reversed polarity:

Help me, {won't, *can't, *isn't} you?

The presence of an underlying *will* accounts for the occurrence of the basic stem form of the verb in imperatives as well. Since tense is copied from the main clause to the tag, the same test also argues for an underlying present tense in imperatives:

Help me, {won't, *wouldn't} you?

In D-structure, therefore, an imperative will have a subject *you*, present tense, and *will* plus the rest of imperative, as in the following D-structure for *Pass the salt!*:

(12)

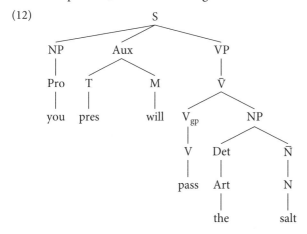

These are deleted in an imperative transformation to produce the appropriate S-structure. Imperatives cannot occur with a modal or auxiliary *have/be* in S-structure:

*Have opened the door!
*Be writing a letter!
*Can pass the salt!

Modals are restricted because the modal position (in D-structure) is already occupied by *will* (there may be semantic reasons for the restriction as well); *have* and *be* are restricted because a command must relate to a future action, not to a past (completed) or present (ongoing) action.[14]

---

14.   If a framing temporal clause is added, the progressive command sounds much better (*Be cleaning your room when I return*). *Have your room cleaned by the time I return* is not a true perfect, but rather a stative with a focus on the actions bringing about the state ('do such things as will bring your room into a cleaned state').

Generally, states cannot occur in the imperative because someone cannot be commanded to be in a state. A state is not a matter of will and hence cannot be brought about volitionally (see Chapter 6):

> *Resemble your father!*
> *Be six feet tall!*
> *Have brown eyes!*

Only if the stative verb, including *have* and *be,* can be given an active reading does the verb appear in the imperative. [15]

> *Know your limits.* (COCA:MAG) = 'Learn your limits, come to know your limits'
> *Be sure to take a sweater or even a jacket.* (COCA:NEWS) = 'Take a sweater or a jacket'
> *Have another person get into the sleeping bag with him.* (COCA:MAG) = 'See to it that another person gets into the sleeping bag with him'

In the formation of negative imperatives, *do*-support is always required, even in the case of *be*:

> *Don't write about what really happened.* (COCA:FIC)
> *Don't be afraid to get up and ask a question.* (COCA:SPOK)
> *Don't have non-singers sing.* (COCA:MAG)

Self-Testing Exercise: Do Exercise 8.7. Remember to convert imperatives into declaratives and to remove tags in D-structure.

7. From D-structure to S-structure

HINT: See Appendix IIa for a complete listing of the phrase structure rules for simple sentences.

As we have now learned all the phrase structure rules except those accounting for complex sentences (See Chapter 9), it is perhaps useful to review what these rules do. They tell us the following:

- the lexical categories of words;
- the order of elements in D-structure; and
- the hierarchical relationships of the categories (what is a constituent of what, what dominates what, and what modifies or is a complement of what).

---

15. Many corpus examples with *be* in the imperative can be found, such as *be happy/be patient/ be careful/be honest.* Such imperatives are not a command to the hearer to be in a particular state, but rather to behave in a way consistent with the being in such a state. The most common structure by far is *be sure to.*

Corpus examples of *have* in the imperative express a 'causative' notion, as in *Have the sales clerk measure your feet.* (COCA:MAG).

The terminal symbols of the phrase structure rules are abstract symbols that need to be filled by particular instances of the category, which we select from the lexicon, a kind of dictionary, which lists the morphemes of the language, along with phonological information, semantic information (selectional restrictions), inherent subcategorization (the lexical category), and strict subcategorization (the syntactic environments in which the word can occur). For example, the entry for the word *bite* might contain the following information (in addition to a feature analysis of the meaning of the word):

> [baɪt] V; _____ NP (PP)
> [baɪt] + {past} → /bɪt/
> takes [+ANIMATE] subject

The lexicon gives all irregular or idiosyncratic information. We also need a set of lexical insertion rules which tell us to insert the appropriate word under the relevant phrase marker, i.e. the word of the proper class with the subcategorization properties required by the phrase marker. Because of the recursive nature of the phrase structure rules as well as the choices allowed by both the phrase structure rules and the lexicon, different applications of the finite set of phrase structure rules can produce an infinite number of surface strings.

The phrase structure rules and the lexicon together form the **base**. The base derives deep or underlying structures, which are unambiguous and contain all meaning. Remember that the same D-structure may have different surface manifestations and the same S-structure (a structurally ambiguous string) will have more than one D-structure. These D-structure sentences are active as opposed to passive, declarative as opposed to interrogative or imperative, and positive as opposed to negative; they are also simple as opposed to complex. Such sentences are known as kernel sentences. Then to produce passive, interrogative or imperative, or negative sentences, what is needed is another kind of rule, a transformation, which converts a D-structure into a S-structure.

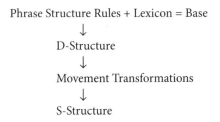

Phrase Structure Rules + Lexicon = Base
↓
D-Structure
↓
Movement Transformations
↓
S-Structure

Below is a listing of all of the grammatical functions, verb subcategories, and phrase structure rules that we have studied so far:

Functions	Verb Types
Subject (Su)	Intransitive
Direct Object (dO)	(Mono)transitive
Indirect Object (iO)	Ditransitive

Subject Complement (sC)
Object Complement (oC)
Adjunct Adverbial (aA)
Disjunct Adverbial (dA)
Conjunct Adverbial (cA)
Modifier (Mod)
Specifier (Spec)
Prepositional Complement (pC)
Object of the Preposition (OP)
Complement of Adjective (Comp of A)

Complex Transitive
Phrasal
Prepositional
Copulative
Diprepositional

Chapter summary

Now that you have completed this chapter, you should be able to:

1. identify adjunct, disjunct, and conjunct adverbials;
2. distinguish between prepositional phrases functioning as verbal complements, as adverbials, and as noun modifiers;
3. name and analyze the structure of the possible auxiliary phrases in English;
4. account for, by means of tree diagrams, the generation of passive sentences, *yes/no* questions, imperatives, and negative sentences from the corresponding active, declarative, and positive sentences;
5. explain the formation of tag questions by a rule of copying; and
6. disambiguate certain English sentences using D-structure tree diagrams.

Recommended additional reading

Treatments of English syntax which are similar in depth and level of formality to the treatment in this chapter include Brown and Miller (1991, Chapters 7 and 10, pp. 125–132), Kaplan (1995, Chapter 8, pp. 306–326), Burton-Roberts (1997, Chapters 5–6), Hopper (1999, Chapters 6–7 and 10–11), Disterheft (2004, Chapter 8), and Tallerman (2005, Chapter 7). Wardhaugh (1995, Chapters 6–7) and Klammer, Schultz, and Della Volpe (2010, Chapter 9) are clear, but less formal treatments.

For more advanced treatments, see the references in Chapter 7.

Chapter 9

Finite and nonfinite clauses

1. Finite clauses
2. Nonfinite clauses
3. Review of complex sentences

Chapter preview

This chapter treats the syntax of complex sentences in English. It begins by looking at the structure, function, and behavior of *that*-clauses. A similar treatment is accorded adverbial clauses. *Wh*-clauses are then discussed, including main clause *wh*-questions and embedded *wh*-clauses. The roles of the *wh*-words are examined, and the internal structure of the clause is accounted for by a rule of *wh*-movement. An analysis is given of the functions and behavior of embedded *wh*-clauses, both relative clauses and indirect questions. Brief attention is paid to the distinction between restrictive and nonrestrictive relative clauses, to "headless", indefinite, and sentential relative clauses, and to cleft and pseudocleft sentences. The final section of the chapter deals with nonfinite clauses: with forms of the nonfinite verb, with omissions from the nonfinite clause, either controlled or indefinite, with complementizers in nonfinite clauses, and with the various functions of nonfinite clauses.

Commentary

We move now from the simple sentence to the complex sentence, that is, to a sentence that consists of more than one clause: a **main clause** (also called a higher S [referring to its position in the tree diagram], a matrix S, or a superordinate clause) and one or more **dependent clauses** (also called lower Ss, embedded Ss, or subordinate clauses). Dependent clauses are related to the main clause by a process of embedding. There are a number of different types of dependent clauses, each serving a variety of functions in respect to the main clause.

(On the teaching of complex sentences by a method called "sentence combining", see Chapter 12.)

1.   Finite clauses

Finite clauses are those clauses containing a subject and finite verb (marked for tense, person, and number). There are three main types of finite dependent clauses: *that*-clauses, adverbial clauses, and *wh*-clauses. *Wh*-clauses may also be independent.

1.1   *That*-clauses

That-clauses are so named because they usually begin with the subordinating conjunction *that*, as in the examples in Table 9.1.

Table 9.1. *That*-Clauses

1.   Subject: <u>That coffee grows in Brazil</u> is well known to all.
2.   Direct Object: I know <u>that coffee grows in Brazil</u>.
3.   Direct Object (after indirect object): He told his mother <u>that coffee grows in Brazil</u>.
4.   Subject Complement: My understanding is <u>that coffee grows in Brazil</u>.
5.   Complement of Adjective: He is certain <u>that coffee grows in Brazil</u>.
6.   Complement of N̄: His claim <u>that coffee grows in Brazil</u> is correct.
7.   Extraposed Subject: It is well known <u>that coffee grows in Brazil</u>.

Form.   We begin with the internal structure of the clause. The subordinating conjunction *that* which begins the clause has no function within the clause, but serves to connect the clauses. We say that it syntactically subordinates the second clause to, makes it dependent on, or embeds it in the first clause. *That* is thus a marker of subordination which we call a **complementizer** (**Comp**). The remainder of the clause after *that* is a fully formed S:

– it has a finite verb;
– it may have any number of auxiliaries: *that coffee might have been growing in Brazil*;
– it may be passive: *that coffee was grown in Brazil*;
– it may be negative: *that coffee doesn't grow in Brazil*; and
– it may itself be complex: *that though coffee tastes good, it is bad for your health*.

> **HINT:** The two restrictions on the form of the *that*-clause are that it may not be a question (**that does coffee grow in Brazil*) and it may not be an imperative (**that buy some Brazilian coffee!*). In other words, there may be no disruption of the normal clausal order.

Function.   In all cases, the *that*-clause has a nominal function; it is functioning as an NP would: it answers the question "what?". In fact, *that*-clauses may serve virtually all of the functions served by NP's, as shown in Table 9.1.

> **HINT:** Note that a *that*-clause cannot serve the nominal function of indirect object because as a clause it denotes an abstract proposition; a clause cannot denote an animate being. A *that*-clause also cannot serve as an object complement.

The functions of Su, dO, and sC (sentences (1)–(4)) are nominal functions with which you are already familiar. Because all of these are obligatory positions, if the *that*-clause is removed, the main clause becomes grammatically incomplete. Thus, in (1), if "that coffee grows in Brazil" is removed, the incomplete fragment "is well known to all" is left over. Note that in (3), when a direct object is clausal, it must follow the indirect object; it cannot precede, as in **He told that coffee grows in Brazil to his mother.*[1] *That*-clauses frequently act as direct objects after a verb of communication: *I {said, stated, thought, believed} that the world is flat*. In these cases, they are reporting the speech or thought of others; these structures are called *indirect speech* (or *indirect discourse*).

You have not before encountered the nominal functions exemplified in (5) and (6):

–   In (5) the *that*-clause functions as Complement of A. Until now you have seen only PPs functioning as complements of adjectives (e.g. *close to the door*); however, *that*-clauses may also serve this function.
–   In (6) the *that*-clause functions as Complement of N̄. The only postnominal function that you have seen so far is the PP as modifier (e.g. *the book on the shelf*); the postnominal *that*-clause in (6) has a different function, namely, as complement. Such *that*-clauses follow abstract nouns such as *claim, fact, idea, hope, notion, proposal,* and *lie* and express the content of the abstract noun. The clause complements the entire N̄, not just the N; e.g. in *his incorrect claim that coffee grows in Brazil*, the clause gives the content of his "incorrect claim", not just of his "claim".

> **HINT:** The clause serving as complement of N̄ bears a relation to the noun which is analogous to the relation a direct object bears to the related verb: *His claim that coffee grows in Brazil* … = *He claimed that coffee grows in Brazil.*

---

1.   This restriction may be due to the tendency in English to put "heavy" elements (such as *that*-clauses) at the end of the sentence (see below).

In order to account for *that*-clauses in our phrase structure rules, we need to modify the rules in various ways. First, we need a rule for the form of embedded S's, which we will term **S-bar (S̄)**:[2]

$$\bar{S} \quad \rightarrow \text{Comp S}$$
$$\text{Comp} \rightarrow \quad that$$

Then we need to account for the different functions of the *that*-clause. To indicate its function as subject NP and as object of P, we add S̄ to the possible expansions of NP:

$$NP \rightarrow \{(\text{Det})\,\bar{N},\, PN,\, Pro,\, \bar{S}\}$$

We also have to allow S̄ to serve as complement of an adjective:

$$AP \rightarrow (\{\text{Deg}, \text{AdvP}\})\, A\, (\{PP, \bar{S}\})$$

In order to account for S̄ as a complement of N̄, we have to create a new syntactic position following N̄:

$$NP \rightarrow (\text{Det})\, \bar{N}\, (\bar{S})$$

What about S̄ as complement of the verb? These revised rules could be seen as accounting for S̄ as direct object and subject complement since they allow S̄ to be generated under NP, and NP is a position following the verb. However, there seems to be little justification for analyzing postverbal clauses as NPs since S̄ figures in verb subcategorization quite separately from NP. That is, certain verbs take both NP and S̄ complements, while others take only one or the other:

V takes both NP and S̄ complements: *We expected <u>bad news</u>.*
We expected <u>that the news would be bad</u>.

---

2.   In X-bar theory (see Chapter 7, Note 7), there is assumed to be a phrasal category CP (= Complement Phrase), with Comp as its head and S as the complement; S̄ is equivalent to C̄, and there is also a Spec position:

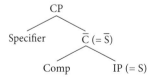

It is further assumed that all Ss, not just dependent clauses, have this structure.

V takes NP but not S̄ complement: *Sally lifted my spirits.*
                                         **Sally lifted that I feel happier.*
V takes S̄ but not NP complement: **Tom hoped good results.*
                                         Tom hoped that he had done well.

Thus, we rewrite our rule for V as follows

$$\bar{V} \rightarrow V_{gp} \left(\left\{ \begin{array}{l} \text{NP}(\{\text{NP, PP, AP}\}) \\ \text{AP} \\ \text{PP (PP)} \\ \text{(NP) } \bar{S} \end{array} \right\} \right)$$

The (generalized) tree diagrams for sentences (1) and (2) differ as follows:

(1)

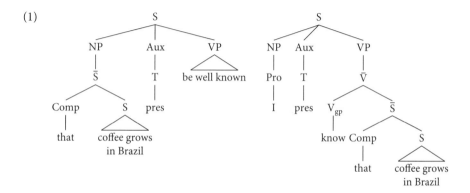

Extraposition.   There is a tendency in English not to like heavy elements, such as clauses, at the beginning of a sentence, but to prefer them at the end. This preference is a result of the basic Su-V-O structure of English, where objects are typically longer than subjects. Thus, in Table 9.1, while sentence (1) *That coffee grows in Brazil is well known to all* above is perfectly grammatical, it is much more natural to use the synonymous sentence (7) *It is well known that coffee grows in Brazil.*

Because sentences (1) and (7) are synonymous and because the *that*-clause is logically functioning as subject in both sentences, we will derive sentence (7) from sentence (1) by a rightward movement transformation called **extraposition**. Such a transformation moves an element to an "extra" or added "position" at the end of the sentence. When the clause is extraposed, the original subject position, which is an obligatory position in the sentence that cannot be deleted, is filled by a "dummy" place-holder, anticipatory *it; it* has no lexical meaning here, but serves merely as a structural device. The moved clause – the **extraposed subject (eSu)** – becomes a daughter of the main S and sister of the VP. We will assume that in D-structure, extraposition has not yet occurred. The sentence *It is false that the world is flat* has the following D-structure and S-structure:

(2)   D-structure

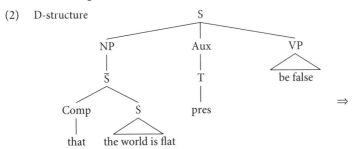

S-structure

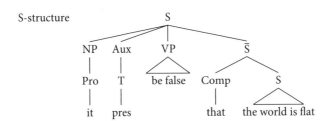

This is extraposition from subject position, which is almost always optional. However, there is a small set of verbs where extraposition is obligatory, including *seem, appear, transpire,* and *happen.* Thus, you cannot say **That the world is flat seems*, but must say *It seems that the world is flat.* Nonetheless, we will generate such surface sentences from a D-structure in which the *that*-clause is in subject position; in other words, the verbs are treated as intransitive.[3]

Extraposition can result in similar S-structures that in fact represent different D-structures:

1.   One is the surface sequence V A S̄:
     You must be careful to distinguish extraposed structures such as (7) (*It is well known that coffee grows in Brazil*) from structures with the *that*-clause as complement of the

---

3.   We also find, much less frequently, extraposition from object position, such as:

> You hear *it* said *that violence is part of human nature.* (COCA:MAG)
> he thinks *it* likely *that she has no brothers or sisters.* (COCA:FIC)

Normally, such extraposition is obligatory and occurs in a number of fixed expressions such as {*break, put*} *it to me that, bring it about that,* and *see to it that.*

A such as (5) (*He is certain that coffee grows in Brazil*) above. Consider the following two sentences:

a.   eSu: *It is regrettable* (A) *that the picnic had to be canceled* ($\bar{\text{S}}$).
b.   complement of A: *Harry is regretful* (A) *that he forgot my birthday* ($\bar{\text{S}}$).

Sentence (a) is an extraposed structures like (7) above. Here the $\bar{\text{S}}$ can be moved back to subject position, replacing the *it* (*That the picnic had to be canceled is regrettable*). In sentence (b) the *that*-clause is complement of the A, as in sentence as (5) above. The $\bar{\text{S}}$ cannot be moved back to subject position (**That he forgot my birthday is regretful*).

2.   Another is the sequence *It* V NP $\bar{\text{S}}$:

a.   eSu: *It is a proven fact that the world is flat.*
b.   complement of $\bar{\text{N}}$: *It contained a recommendation that we cancel the program.*

Sentence (a) contains an extraposed subject and is equivalent to *That the world is flat is a proven fact.* Sentence (b), however, is <u>not</u> equivalent to **That we cancel the program contained a recommendation.* In this sentence the *that*-clause is complement of the $\bar{\text{N}}$ as in (6) above. Note that in the first sentence, *it* is a dummy marker, while in the second *it* is a meaningful pronoun, referring to some previous noun phrase such as *the report*.

> **HINT:** A phenomenon similar to extraposition is right movement, where the *that*-clause moves to an extraposition at the end of the sentence, but it is not necessary to insert *it* in the position vacated since it is not an obligatory position:
>
> > a.   complement of A: *He was certain that the world was flat when I saw him yester-day.* ⇒ *He was certain when I saw him yesterday that the world was flat.*
> > b.   complement of $\bar{\text{N}}$: *His belief that coffee grows in Brazil is correct.* ⇒ *His belief is correct that coffee grows in Brazil.*
>
> Speaker judgments may vary concerning the grammaticality of sentences with right movement.

Deletion of the complementizer.   Sometimes *that* does not appear, as in *He thinks the world is flat.* In these cases, we assume that the Comp position was originally filled and that there was then deletion of the complementizer.

We find that *that* can always be deleted when the clause has the following functions (the numbers here refer to the sentences in Table 9.1, with Ø denoting the deleted *that*):

2.   direct object: *I know Ø coffee grows in Brazil.*
3.   direct object after indirect object: *He told his mother Ø coffee grows in Brazil.*
5.   complement of A: *He is certain Ø coffee grows in Brazil.*

It is perhaps possible to delete *that* in the following cases, though speakers might disagree about the acceptability of these deletions:

4. subject complement: *My understanding is Ø coffee grows in Brazil.*
6. complement of N̄: *His claim Ø coffee grows in Brazil is correct.*
7. extraposed subject: *It is well known to all Ø coffee grows in Brazil.*

However, it is never possible to delete *that* when the clause serves as subject:

1. **Coffee grows in Brazil is well known to all.*

The reason for this restriction relates to sentence processing. Since the first sequence "coffee grows in Brazil" forms a complete clause, when the sentence continues with "is well known to all", the hearer has to go back and adjust his or her reading of the structure, and interpretive difficulties may result.

Passive and interrogative. If one begins with the complex sentence *Everyone believes that the police falsely accused Ramona*, passive can work in the following ways:

– the *that*-clause is passive: *Everyone thinks that Ramona was falsely accused by the police*;
– the main clause is passive: *That the police falsely accused Ramona is believed by everyone*; or
– both clauses can be passive *That Ramona was falsely accused by the police is believed by everyone.*

Extraposition may also apply to the second two sentences, giving *It is believed by everyone that the police falsely accused Ramona* and *It is believed by everyone that Ramona was falsely accused by the police*, respectively.

Interrogative interacts in a more limited way because only the main clause, not the *that*-clause, may be a question. In (a) below the *that*-clause functions as direct object; the corresponding question is (b). In (c) the *that*-clause functions as subject; one would expect to find the corresponding question (d), but this is ungrammatical; in these cases, extraposition is obligatory, as in (e):[4]

---

4. The reason that subject–aux inversion is impossible in cases such as (d) has been explained by seeing the *that*-clause as filling the Comp position rather than the subject position. For the same reason, passive (which moves the subject) is impossible:

> *That Ali had read the book impressed me.* ⇒
> **I was impressed by that Ali had read the book.*

The same explanation may hold for subject clauses which are non-finite.

a. *Jacob said that he had seen the movie already.* ⇒
b. *Did Jacob say that he had seen the movie already?*
c. *That Jacob has seen that movie already is possible.* ⇒
d. **Is that Jacob has seen that movie already possible?*
e. *Is it possible that Jacob has seen that movie already?*

You may also have multiple embedding, of course. Below is the D-structure tree for the sentence *It is possible that Ferdinand could have believed that the world is not flat*:

(3)

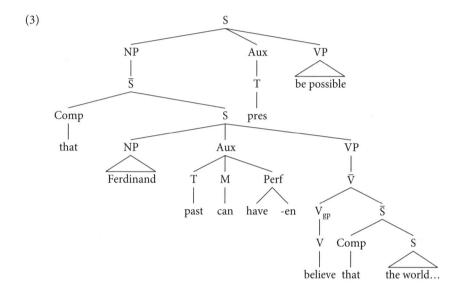

Self-Testing Exercise: Do Exercise 9.1

1.2 Adverbial clauses

Table 9.2. Adjunct Adverbial Clauses

1. The words popped out <u>before I had time to check them</u>. (COCA:FIC)
2. He searched the empty bar <u>as if he were looking for assistance</u>. (COCA:FIC)
3. Meg felt embarrassed <u>because she wore only a thin T-shirt</u>. (COCA:FIC)
4. And there's coffee on the counter <u>if you want it</u>. (COCA:FIC)
5. I frowned, <u>although I wasn't sure why</u>. (COCA:FIC)
6. The bureaucracy is tediously slow, <u>while the legislature works at light speed</u>. (COCA:MAG)
7. I came to England in <u>such</u> a hurry <u>that I only packed one pair of shoes</u>. (COCA:FIC)
8. She earns less and works harder <u>than she did in a corporation</u>. (COCA:NEWS)
9. She wanted to keep talking <u>so that the conversation would not end</u>. (COCA:FIC)

In the previous chapter, we saw PPs, AdvPs, and occasionally NPs functioning adverbially. In this section, we look at clauses which can have an adverbial function; these are called **adverbial clauses**. Table 9.2 provides examples of clauses functioning as adjunct adverbials. These clauses express the adverbial notions of time (1), manner (2), and reason (3) – that is, they answer the questions when?, how?, and why? – and are comparable to PPs and AdvPs such as (1) {*at noon, yesterday*}, (2) {*curiously, with a happy expression*}, and (3) *out of fear*. However, adverbial clauses can express a wider range of adverbial notions, such as condition (4), concession (5), contrast (6), result (7), comparison (8), and purpose (9).

Adverbial clauses may also function as disjunct and conjunct adverbials, e.g.:

if I may speak frankly	(dA)	*although these are important considerations*	(cA)
if I judge accurately	(dA)	*while we're on the subject*	(cA)
unless I am mistaken	(dA)	*in case you don't know*	(cA)

Disjunct adverbial clauses are much more common than conjunct adverbial clauses.

Like the *that*-clause, the adverbial clause includes a fully formed S, with the similar restriction that it cannot be interrogative or imperative. Also like the *that*-clause, it begins with a complementizer, but in adverbial clauses, a much greater variety of lexical items serve as complementizers. We will need to revise our rule for Comp as follows:

Comp → {*while, since, because, although, if, when, so that, as, such, before, after, until, as long as, as soon as, by the time that, now that, once, inasmuch as* ... }[5]

Note that this is not an exhaustive listing of the complementizers. An adverbial clause is thus an $\bar{S}$.

> **HINT:** We call the complementizer *that* in *that*-clauses and the complementizers introducing adverbial clauses "pure complementizers" because they have only one function, namely, to subordinate the clause that follows to the one that precedes. In D-structure, these complementizers appear in Comp position. Below we will see that other complementizers (relatives and interrogatives) are not generated in Comp position in D-structure but are moved there. They have dual functions, as will be explained, and are thus not "pure complementizers".

We need to revise our phrase structure rules for both adjunct adverbials (in the VP) and conjunct/disjunct adverbials (in the S) in the following ways to account for adverbial clauses:

$$VP \rightarrow \bar{V} (\{AdvP, PP, NP, \bar{S}\})$$
$$S \rightarrow \begin{cases} S (\{AdvP, PP, NP \ \bar{S}\}) \\ NP \ Aux \ VP \end{cases}$$

---

5. As discussed in Chapter 5, there is an overlap between many of the forms which function as prepositions and those which function as conjunctions (e.g. *since, before, after, until*). Note that some complementizers are complex forms incorporating *that: except that, given that, provided that, supposing that, assuming that, so that, such that.*

We generate adverbial clauses at the end, but like other adverbials, they move fairly freely to the beginning of the sentence.

Abridgment of adverbial clauses. Consider the following sentences:

1. *When doing this exercise, keep your hands in front.* (COCA:MAG)
2. *Though modest in number, the quotes are well chosen.* (COCA:MAG)
3. *Mark turned into a whirlwind of rage when confronted by dishonesty.* (COCA:FIC)
4. *Check seasoning and adjust if necessary.* (COCA:NEWS)

The underlined sequences express adverbial notions, but they do not seem to be complete clauses. Each sequence begins with a complementizer, but omitted is some form of the verb BE as well as tense:

> in (1) the progressive auxiliary
> in (2) the main verb
> in (3) the passive auxiliary, and
> in (4) the main verb.

The tense omitted is the same as the tense in the main clause.

Each underlined clause is also missing a subject. In (1)–(3), the subject omitted is the same as the subject in main clause: "(you) keep your hands in front", "though the quotes are modest in number", and "when Mark is confronted by dishonesty". In (4), an impersonal "it" must be supplied: "if it is necessary".

We therefore analyze these sequences as elliptical adverbial clauses because the subject, tense, and verbal can be supplied from the context (the main clause). We assume that in D-structure these are complete clauses.

Ambiguity of modification. Consider the following sentence:

> *He said when we met he would help me.*

It is ambiguous, with two possible interpretations:

a. the helping and meeting coincide: *He said that when we met he would help me. He said that he would help me when we met.*
b. the saying and meeting coincide: *He said when we met that he would help me. When we met, he said that he would help me.*

"When we met" is a so-called *squinting modifier* since it can modify either the preceding clause ("he said") or the following clause ("he would help me"). In (a) the adverbial clause ("when we met") is an adjunct adverbial modifying the $\bar{V}$, "would help me"; it is then moved to the beginning of the S which dominates it. In (b) the adverbial clause is an adjunct adverbial modifying the $\bar{V}$, "said that he would help me"; the *that*-clause is then moved to the right following the adverbial clause. Study the following trees, which show the two D-structures and the movement of the adverbial clause (shown by arrows):

(4)

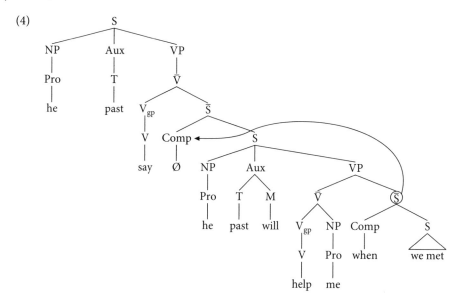

(5)

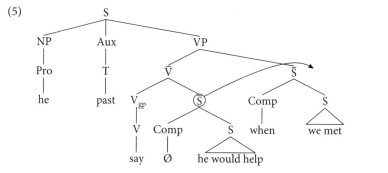

Self-Testing Exercise: Do Exercise 9.2 on nominal and adverbial clauses.

1.3   *Wh*-clauses

In this section, we will study three types of *wh*-clauses:

1.   *wh*-questions;
2.   relative clauses; and
3.   indirect questions.

The first is a type of main clause; the second two are types of subordinate clauses.

Wh-questions.   In the previous chapter, we looked at two types of questions, *yes/no* (or truth) questions and tag questions. A third type of question is the **wh- (or content) question**.

Like an adverbial clause, the *wh*-question always begins with a complementizer, in this case, *who, whom, whose, what, which, why, when, where,* and *how.* Note that with the exception of *how,* all of the complementizers begin with *wh-,* hence the name **wh-words**. However, an important difference between adverbial clauses and *wh*-questions is that the complementizer in the *wh*-clause, the *wh*-word, always has a function in its own clause. If the *wh*-word is removed, the clause usually becomes incomplete.

> **HINT:** To determine the function of the *wh*-word, try putting the question in the form of a statement: e.g. *We did learn <u>what</u> today* (*what* is the dO of *learn*), *You did vote for <u>who</u>* (*who* is the OP *for*), *You did leave early <u>why</u>* (*why* is an adverb modifying *leave*).

Table 9.3. Forms of the Interrogative *Wh*-Complementizer

a. Pronoun

<u>What</u> happened when the cows escaped the ranch? (COCA:MAG) (subject)
<u>Who</u> asked questions? (COCA:SPOK) (subject)
<u>What</u> did we learn today? (COCA:SPOK) (direct object)
<u>Whom</u> did they most admire? (COCA:SPOK) (direct object)
<u>Who</u> did you give that to? (COCA:SPOK) (indirect object)
<u>Who</u> did you vote for? (COCA:SPOK) (object of preposition)
<u>What</u> did you call me? (COCA:FIC) (object complement)

b. Determiner

<u>Whose</u> dog was hurt? (COCA:FIC)
<u>Which</u> country is the biggest threat to U.S. security? (COCA:SPOK)
<u>What</u> role did Britain play? (COCA:NEWS)

c. Adverb

<u>Why</u> didn't I say that? (COCA:NEWS)
<u>When</u> had she become a coward? (COCA:FIC)
<u>Where</u> would you draw the line? (COCA:MAG)
<u>How</u> will women respond? (COCA:MAG)

d. Degree Word

<u>How</u> important has art been to your work? (COCA:SPOK) (modifying A)
<u>How</u> often do you meditate? (COCA:MAG) (modifying Adv)

The form of the *wh*-complementizer depends upon its function:

1. *Who, whom,* and *what* function as interrogative pronouns (Table 9.3a). They are standing for NPs (or clauses functioning nominally) which could serve as answers to the questions:

    > *Who asked questions? The students.*
    > *What did we learn today? The multiplication tables.*

> **HINT:** According to prescriptive rules, the pronoun *who* is the subject form and *whom* is the object form. However, it is common, especially in colloquial English, to use the *who* form for both, as in *Well, who did she see?* (COCA:SPOK).

2. *Whose, which*, and *what* are interrogative determiners (Table 9.3b) since they precede nouns or adjectives, as in:

> *Whose car did you take? Gunter's.*
> *Which car did you buy? The red one.*
> *What dessert do you want? Ice cream.*

The answers provided to questions containing interrogative determiners are usually possessives or NPs containing modifiers, commonly accompanied by the dummy noun *one*.

3. *Why, when, where*, and *how* are interrogative adverbs (Table 9.3c); the answers provided are generally adverbial phrases or clauses:

> *Where did you eat dinner? At home/In a restaurant.*
> *Why did you do is? Because I felt like it.*

> **HINT:** Interrogative adverbs may also stand for an obligatory element in the sentence, as in:
>
> > *Where did you put my glasses?*
> > *Where are my glasses?*
>
> In the first case, *where* stands for the object complement of the complex transitive verb *put* (*You did put my glasses where*); in the second case, it stands for the subject complement of the copula verb *be* (*My glasses are where*).

4. Finally, *how* is also an interrogative degree word (Table 9.3d); like all degree words, these may modify either adverbs or adjectives.

In the formation of questions, the *wh*-word is moved from its D-structure position in the sentence (the "extraction site"), which is determined by its function, to the beginning of the sentence. We will say that the *wh*-word moves into Comp position.[6] The difficulty of introducing the Comp position here is that *wh*-questions are main clauses, and $\bar{S}$ is otherwise always subordinate. While there are good reasons for believing that every S is, in fact, an $\bar{S}$ (see Footnote 1), we will introduce $\bar{S}$ only when it is necessary to account for the presence of a complementizer. This transformation which moves the *wh*-word is called **wh-fronting**

---

6. Current thinking is that the *wh*-word moves to the Spec position of CP (see Footnote 2) and that Aux moves to Comp position. There are a number of reasons for believing this to be the case, not least of which is that it accounts for the order of the *wh*-word and the auxiliary.

or **wh-movement**.[7] When the *wh*-word moves, there is a **trace**, an empty constituent (represented by *t*), left behind.

In *wh*-fronting, different constituents may move to the front, but they always contain the *wh*-word:

1.   When the *wh*-word is a pronoun serving as a direct object, the NP moves:

   You did see $_{NP}$*[whom] last night.* ⇒ *Whom did you see [t] last night?*

2.   When the *wh*-word is a pronoun serving as object of a preposition, either the NP or the PP moves:

   Alexandra went to the movie $_{PP}$*[* $_P$*[with]* $_{NP}$*[whom]] last night.* ⇒
   Whom did Alexandra go to the movie with [t] last night? or
   With whom did Alexandra go to the movie [t]?

   Speakers have a choice whether to move the NP or the entire PP. The former option results in "preposition stranding", a preposition left in place (often at the end of the sentence) without its accompanying object. The latter option is called rather colorfully *pied piping*, but it is usually restricted to more formal style. Sometimes, however, pied piping appears to be obligatory:

   *What classes should we meet between [t]?
   Between what classes should we meet [t]?

   (On the question of preposition stranding and the teaching of usage, see Chapter 12.)

3.   When the *wh*-word is an adverb or degree word, the entire AdvP or AP moves:

   You left early $_{AdvP}$*[* $_{Adv}$*[why]].* ⇒ *Why did you leave early [t.]?*
   You can get here $_{AdvP}$*[* $_{Deg}$*[how]* $_{Adv}$ *[quickly]].* ⇒ *How quickly can you get here [t]?*
   The show was $_{AP}$*[* $_{Deg}$*[how]* $_A$*[expensive]].* ⇒ *How expensive was the show [t]?*

   It is not possible to move Deg alone:

   *How can you get here [t] quickly?
   *How was the show [t] expensive? (However, this can sometimes be interpreted 'in what manner')

4.   When the *wh*-word is a determiner, the entire NP moves:

   You like [$_{Det}$ *[what] fruit].* ⇒ *What fruit do you like [t]?*

   It is not possible to move Det alone:

   *What do you like [t] fruit?

---

7.   *Wh*-movement, subject–auxiliary inversion, and passive (NP movement) are sometimes grouped together as "move α" since they all move an element (unspecified, hence α) to the left.

In addition to *wh*-fronting, there is subject–auxiliary inversion, as there is in *yes/no* questions. *Do*-support applies if necessary. In the following examples, $[t_1]$ denotes the moved Aux and $[t_2]$ denotes the moved *wh*-word:

> *Sean will buy a new computer when. When will Sean $[t_1]$ buy a new computer $[t_2]$?*
> *Joey bought a new computer when. When did Joey $[t_1]$ buy a new computer $[t_2]$?*

Note that the order of the fronted elements is *wh*-word and then Aux. This order can be accounted for if we assume that these elements move into different positions (see Footnote 6), though, for our purposes, it suffices to say that they both move to Comp.

> **HINT:** In *wh*-questions in which the *wh*-word is subject, as in *Who asked questions?*, the D-structure and the S-structure order appear to be the same. One might question, then, whether *wh*-movement and subject–aux inversion have taken place. There are three possible answers to this question:
>
> 1. Neither rule applies.
> 2. *Wh*-fronting occurs but not inversion (because once the *wh*-word is fronted to Comp position, there is nothing in subject position and hence subject–aux inversion cannot occur):[8]
>
> $_{Comp}$[Who] $_S$[[*t*] asked the questions]
>
> 3. Both rules apply; that is, subject–aux inversion occurs first and then *wh*-fronting, which restores the original order:
>
> $_{Comp}$[Who is] $_S$[[t_1] [t_2] asked the questions]
>
> The third solution provides a consistent treatment of all *wh*-questions.

We find in *wh*-questions a phenomenon known as long *wh*-movement, in which a *wh*-word moves out of a dependent clause to the beginning of the main clause; movement in this case is said to be "unbounded" since it crosses clause boundaries. The movement occurs in successive cyclic steps, with the *wh*-word moving first to the Comp position of its own clause and then to the Comp position of the main clause. Below is the D-structure for *What did Fraser say that Elise was doing tonight?*, with the movement of *what* indicated.[9]

---

8. We say that the rule applies "vacuously" because it shows no effects on the surface. In the third solution, both rules apply vacuously.

9. Previously it was argued that the reason that the *wh*-word must move twice is that the Comp position of the dependent clause is already filled by *that*, and two complementizers cannot fill a single Comp position (the so-called "Doubly-filled Comp Constraint"). In the view presented in Footnote 6, where the *wh*-word moves to Spec position, this constraint no longer applies.

(6)

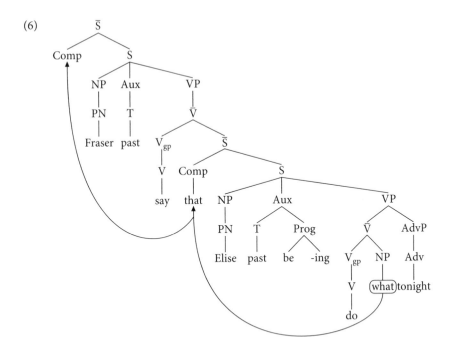

Another kind of question with a *wh*-word, the echo question,[10] has neither *wh*-fronting nor subject–aux inversion. The D-structure and the S-structure orders are the same:

The voice said <u>what</u>? (COCA:FIC)

The echo question involves rising intonation and stress on the *wh*-word. It serves to echo a statement by another speaker, questioning part of the statement.

---

10. There are a number of constraints on *wh*-movement (having to do with a bounding restriction called "subjacency") where only echo questions are possible. *Wh*-movement cannot take place:

a. from an indirect question:
    She wondered whether he said what → **What did she wonder whether he said [t]?*
b. from a complex NP, either one with a complement to Ñ, or a relative clause:
    Tony spread the rumor that Jane said what → **What did Tony spread the rumor that Jane said [t]?*
    Tony spread a rumor that who had been fired → **Who did Tony spread a rumor that [t] had been fired?*
c. from an adverbial clause:
    We will leave when who arrives → **Who will we leave when [t] arrives?*

Wh-movement also cannot occur from coordinated structures: *We like ice cream and what* → **What do we like ice cream and?*

Wh-fronting may also be involved in noninterrogative main clauses, namely in exclamations, which are formed with either *what a* or *how*:

> *What a stupid remark he made!*
> *How happy I am to see you!*   ·

Such clauses do not have subject–aux inversion.

> *Self-Testing Exercise:* Do Exercise 9.3.

Relative clauses.   The second kind of *wh*-clause is the **relative clause** (see Table 9.4).

Table 9.4. Relative Clauses

Relative pronoun (animate)

They have eight *children* <u>who are black belts</u>. (COCA:MAG)
I have three *children* <u>that play sports at the high school and college level</u>. (COCA:SPOK)
This program owes much to several *individuals* <u>who I wish to recognize at this time</u>. (COCA:ACAD)
People <u>whom I hardly knew</u> said hello to us. (COCA:FIC)
The only *person* <u>to whom I will tell the entire story</u> is my sister, Annabel. (COCA:FIC)
The *bum at the corner* <u>whom she gave fifty cents to most days</u> would probably love this life. (COCA:FIC)

Relative pronoun (inanimate)

This gets to be a little bit like a scene in a *movie* <u>which I haven't seen</u>. (COCA:SPOK)
I hope you like a *movie* <u>that isn't about violence or sex</u>. (COCA:NEWS)
This is a *matter* <u>about which many people feel very strongly</u>. (COCA:MAG)
take the defense *cuts* <u>which everybody's already agreed on</u> (COCA:SPOK)

Relative determiner

Angie turned and saw him, coming toward her out of a long *hallway* <u>whose end she could not see</u>. (COCA:FIC)
She was rejected by one *kid* <u>whose mother said she wasn't pretty enough</u>. (COCA:NEWS)
Howard himself, holding a long fishing *rod* <u>from the end of which dangled a fair-sized fish</u>. (COCA:FIC)

Relative adverb

Had it happened last *year* <u>when she hit thirty</u>? (COCA:FIC)
I see no *reason* <u>why we can't all just get along</u>. (COCA:FIC)
I look for a *place* <u>where she can not see me</u>. (COCA:FIC)

The function of relative clauses is different from the functions of the other embedded clauses that we have studied. Relative clauses always serve an adjectival function; they are modifiers which follow the noun, analogous to PPs:

> *The girl <u>with red hair</u>* = *The girl <u>who has red hair</u>*

Relative clauses express a quality or feature of the noun modified. They answer the question "which?" (i.e. *Which girl? The girl who has red hair*). Thus, in Table 9.4 "who are black belts" identifies the "children" that are being discussed, or "when she hit thirty" identifies the "year" that is being discussed.

The noun in the main clause that is modified is called the head noun, or the **antecedent** ('that which goes before'); the head noun can serve any function in the main clause (e.g. subject, object, object of preposition, etc.). We say that the *wh*-word refers back to the head noun. The head noun therefore "goes before" the relative. In Table 9.4, the head noun in each case is italicized. The relative word (the *wh*-word) is "coindexed" with the head noun; that is, it refers to the same person or thing in the real world.

> **HINT:** You can understand the relative clause as deriving from a full clause, as shown below; the relative pronoun then replaces the full NP:
>
> *The girl [the girl has red hair] > The girl [who has red hair]*

We must modify our phrase structure rule for N̄ to account for relative clauses as post-modifiers:

$$\bar{N} \to (AP) \, \bar{N} \, (PP) \, (\bar{S})$$

We show in this revised rule that the relative clause, S̄, is the sister of the other modifiers of N̄, namely AP and PP. Furthermore, the rule shows that it is possible for both PP and S̄ to occur, as in *the girl in the front row who has red hair*.[11]

The internal structure of relative clauses is similar to that of *wh*-question: both begin with a *wh*-word which serves a function in its own clause and which has been fronted. Just as in *wh*-questions, the *wh*-words have different forms depending on the function they serve within their clause:

- relative pronouns: *who(m), which, that*[12]
- relative determiner: *whose*
- relative adverbs: *why, when, where*

Note that the inventory of *wh*-relatives differs somewhat from the inventory of *wh*-interrogatives.

---

11.   In contrast, the S̄ serving as complement of N̄ is the sister of Det, as discussed above.

12.   The relative pronoun *that* is sometimes treated differently from the *wh*-words; it is base-generated directly in Comp position (like the *that* of *that*-clauses). Doing so accounts for certain restrictions on *that*, for example, that it cannot follow a preposition nor occur in nonrestrictive relative clauses (see below). But it then becomes necessary to postulate a null *wh*-phrase (coindexed with the head noun) which moves to Comp. The same must be done for relatives with no overt complementizer. We are adopting a somewhat simpler analysis here.

HINT: What distinguishes *which, who(m), whose,* and *that*?

Which is used to refer back to inanimate head nouns (e.g. *the house which …*), while *who(m)* is used to refer back to animate head nouns (e.g. *the child who(m) …*). Contrary to what students are sometimes taught, *that* may refer to both animate and inanimate head nouns (e.g. *the house that …, the children that*). (*That* cannot be used in non-restrictive clauses, as we will discuss below.)

Whose can refer to both animate and inanimate head nouns as well (e.g. *the kid whose …, the house whose*). On the model of *who(m)* vs. *which*, some prescriptive grammarians have tried to argue that *whose* should <u>not</u> refer to inanimate head nouns, but rather the construction *of which* should be used (e.g. *the backyard of which,* <u>not</u> *the backyard whose*), but *of which* is considered formal and is not frequently used.

Relative pronouns may serve most of the nominal functions:

Su: *that [t] isn't about violence or sex* (< *the movie isn't about violence or sex*)[13]
dO: *which I haven't seen [t]* (< *I haven't seen a scene in a movie*)
OP: *which everybody's already agreed on [t]* (< *everybody's already agreed on the defense cuts*)
iO: *to whom I will tell the entire story [t]* (< *I will tell the entire story to the only person*)

HINT: *Who* and *whom* are distinguished by the use of *who* as the subject form and *whom* as the object form. However, as with interrogatives, though to a lesser extent, it is common for *whom* to be replaced by *who* in all functions. There is no distinction between *that* in subject and object form, and in the types of relative clauses under discussion here, with one exception, it can replace all forms of *who* and *whom*. It cannot replace *who/whom/which* when these forms follow a prepositon (e.g. **a matter about that many people feel very strongly, *the only person to that I will tell the entire story, *a long fishing rod from the end of that dangled a fair-sized fish*).

Moreover, the *wh*-word in a relative clause has a dual function; in addition to its function within its own clause, it functions as a complementizer, subordinating the dependent clause in the main clause. This embedding function is analogous to the function of *that* in *that*-clauses.

Wh-movement operates in relative clauses just as it does in *wh*-questions. The *wh*-word moves to the Comp position.

–   A complete NP or AdvP is fronted.
–   A Det alone cannot be fronted (**a long hallway whose she could not see end*).

---

13.   As noted in the previous section, it is often best to put the *wh*-word back into its D-structure position – to "undo" *wh*-movement – in order to identify its function.

- Optionally either a complete PP or the NP object of the P may be moved (i.e. pied piping occurs): e.g. *about which* many people feel very strongly or *which* everybody's already agreed *on*.
- When the relative pronoun is subject of its clause, *wh*-movement shows no change on the surface, e.g. *who [t] are black belts*.

Unlike *wh*-questions, there is no subject–auxiliary inversion in relative clauses since inversion can only occur in main clauses.

Deletion of the relative pronoun or adverb is permitted in certain cases, similar to the deletion of *that*. The relative pronoun can be deleted when it is serving as direct object, indirect object, or object of the preposition (if pied piping has not occurred). It may also be possible to delete the relative adverb.

dO:	People Ø *I hardly knew* said hello to us.
iO:	The bum at the corner Ø *she gave fifty cents to most days* would probably love this life.
OP:	take the defense cuts Ø *everybody's already agreed on*
aA:	I see no reason Ø *we can't all just get along*.
	I look for a place Ø *she cannot see me*.

But the relative can never be deleted if:

- it is a subject pronoun[14]

    *They have eight children Ø *are black belts*.
    *I hope you like a movie Ø *isn't about violence or sex*.

- it is a determiner

    *She was rejected by one kid Ø *mother said she wasn't pretty enough*.

- pied piping has occurred

    *This is a matter *about* Ø *many people feel very strongly*.

(On the relation between the structure of relative clauses in English and other languages to the teaching of English, see Chapter 12.)

As with *wh*-questions, there can also be long *wh*-movement in the case of relative clauses:

The party which Julian said that Sarah was going to [t] this weekend is at Fred's
< The party [Julian said that Sarah was going to which this weekend] is at Fred's
< The party [Julian said Sarah was going to the party this weekend] is at Fred's

---

14. Deletion of the subject relative pronoun may occur very colloquially, as in: *I know a person Ø [t] can stop anything they choose to.* (COCA:ACAD).

Similar to the extraposition of *that*-clauses, it possible to move relative clauses to an extraposition at the end of the sentence in certain cases. However, since the relative clause is an optional modifier, it is not necessary to fill its original position with a place-holder such as *it*:

> *I met a man in the park Ø yesterday who was walking his dog.* (COCA:SPOK)
> *There was a guy Ø here last week who bought them all.* (COCA:MAG)

This is called "extraposition from NP". Speakers do not always agree on the acceptability of these structures.

There are, in fact, two types of relative clauses, traditionally called **restrictive relative** and **nonrestrictive relative** (or appositive). A restrictive relative clause is necessary to identify which person or thing (denoted by head noun) is being talked about; it "restricts", limits, or picks out the referent(s) from a larger set or referents. In a nonrestrictive relative clause, the head noun is sufficiently restricted or limited in order to be identified; the relative clause simply adds additional (or parenthetical) information. Consider the following examples:

1.   *An appeal was made to the Prime Minister, <u>who turned it down</u>.* (COCA:ACAD)
2.   a.   *People are looking for a leader <u>who gives them a sense of direction</u>.* (COCA:NEWS)
     b.   *I want to start with the leader <u>who's stepping off the stage</u>.* (COCA:SPOK)

The relative clause is (1) is nonrestrictive because the head noun has a unique referent (in the context, which is a discussion of Canada) and is hence identifiable; the relative clause adds only additional information that is not necessary for identifying which leader is being spoken about. The relative clauses in (2) is restrictive because the relative clauses are needed to restrict the referent in each case; without the relative clauses, you would not know which leader or what kind of leader was being discussed. Note that the relative clause following a proper noun is always nonrestrictive (as in 1), and the relative clause following an indefinite or generic NP (with *a*, *any*, as in 2a) is always restrictive. Usually, however, it is the context which determines whether a noun phrase is sufficiently identified (without the relative clause) or not.[15]

There are formal differences between the two types of relative clauses as well:

–   nonrestrictive clauses are set off by commas in writing, by comma intonation (pauses) in speech;

---

15.   Prenominal modifiers (adjectives) are similarly restrictive and nonrestrictive. In the sentence *My rich sister just bought a new house*, if I have only one sister, *rich* must be nonrestrictive, but if I have more than one sister, *rich* is restrictive, for it identifies which of my sisters, namely the rich one, bought the house.

- *that* cannot be used in a nonrestrictive relative clause (e.g. *An appeal was made to the Prime Minister, that turned it down*); and
- nonrestrictive clauses do not allow deletion of the relative pronoun (e.g. *I ran into Erica, ~~who~~ I know from work*).
- nonrestrictive clauses do not allow extraposition from NP (e.g. *?I ran into Erica on my way home from work, who is a friend from my childhood.*)

We are going to analyze the two types of relative clauses differently:

restrictive: $\bar{N} \rightarrow$ (AP) $\bar{N}$ (PP) ($\bar{S}$)
nonrestrictive: NP $\rightarrow$ NP $\bar{S}$ [16]

That is, for the nonrestrictive clause, the noun phrase is complete without the relative clause, which is outside of and independent of the head noun phrase; it is outside the scope of the determiner as well. In contrast, the restrictive clause is part of the noun phrase and is specified by the determiner.

Relative clauses may also be ambiguous between a restrictive reading and a nonrestrictive reading, as in *Children who have vivid imaginations should avoid this program.*[17] Either (a) all children have vivid imaginations (the nonrestrictive reading) or (b) only some children – those who should avoid the program – have vivid imaginations. Below are D-structure trees for the two readings:

(7)   nonrestrictive

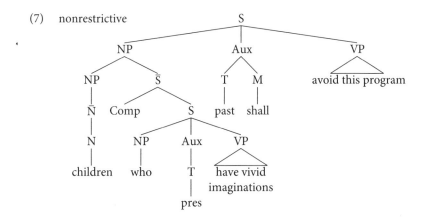

---

16.   The complete rule for NP is as follows:

NP $\rightarrow$ {NP $\bar{S}$, (Det) $\bar{N}$ ($\bar{S}$)}

17.   The punctuation distinguishing the two readings has been omitted.

(8)   restrictive

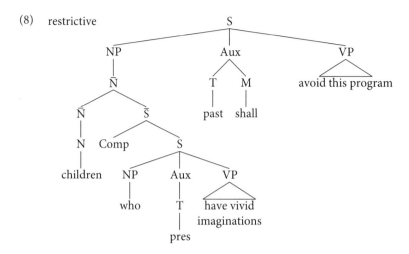

The use of *that* as both a relative pronoun and a pure complementizer can lead to confusion between appositive *that*-clauses and relative clauses:

a.   The suggestion *that he might fail* is disturbing.
b.   The suggestion *that he made* is disturbing.

The subordinate clause in (a) is functioning as a <u>complement</u> of N̄ (equivalent to a direct object of the verb *suggest*: Someone suggested that he might fail). The complementizer *that* has no function in its own clause, and the embedded clause is complete without *that* and can stand alone as a complete sentence *He might fail*. The *that*-clause can also function as an NP (for example, as subject of a sentence): *That he might fail is disturbing*. The subordinate clause in (b) is functioning as a relative clause, as a <u>modifier</u> of N̄. The relative *that* has the function of direct object in its own clause, and hence the embedded clause is not complete without the relative: **He made*. The embedded clause cannot function as an NP: **That he made is disturbing*. Note that *which* can substitute for *that* in this case but not in the other: *The suggestion which he made is disturbing*, **The suggestion which he might fail is disturbing*. Generalized D-structure trees for the sentences are given below:

(9)   complement of N̄

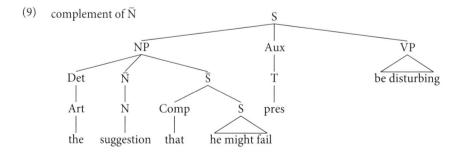

(10)   modiflier of N̄

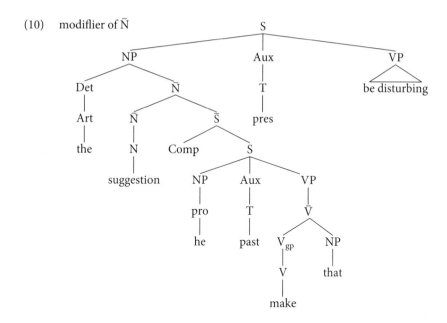

The surface similarity of these two types of clauses can lead to ambiguity. The sentences in (1) and (2) can have two possible readings:

1. *The idea that he proposed made her laugh.*
    that-clause (complement of N̄): his proposing made her laugh (that he proposed made her laugh)
    relative clause (modifier of N̄): his idea made her laugh (he proposed the idea)
2. *The fact that Bill forgot was verified.*
    that-clause (complement of N̄): Bill's forgetting was verified (that Bill forgot was verified)
    relative clause (modifier of N̄) the fact was verified (Bill forgot the fact)

The following embedded clauses resemble relative clauses:

> *they've never discussed <u>what went wrong</u>* (COCA:NEWS)
> *she knew <u>when Laurie's eyes would close in front of the TV</u>* (COCA:FIC)
> *I know <u>what time it is</u>.* (COCA:FIC)

Note that the *wh*-word begins the clause and serves a function in it (in this case, subject, adjunct adverbial, and determiner, respectively). However, the problem is that there is no head noun in the main clause for the underlined clauses to modify; for this reason, such clauses have been called **free** or **headless relatives**. One way to analyze these clauses is to interpret *what* as *that which*; then, the clause can be understood as a relative clause modifying the head noun *that* (*they've never discussed that which went wrong*). But this paraphrase is quite awkward and is even more difficult with the other sentences. A preferable analysis is to understand the free relative clause as filling the direct object position (as a *that*-clause fills the dO position in *I know that he will attend*), rather than a modifying position, and hence as functioning as a nominal clause (for this reason, free relatives are also called "nominal relative clauses"). While the free relatives shown above all occupy the dO position in the main clause, they may also serve any other nominal function – Su, eSu, or OP, respectively, in the examples below:

> *How the disease is transmitted is well-known.* (COCA:MAG)
> *It is clear what he meant.* (COCA:SPOK)
> *Have you thought about why that is?* (COCA:MAG)

In a tree diagram, the free relative should be generated under NP, as is the *that*-clause, e.g.

(11)

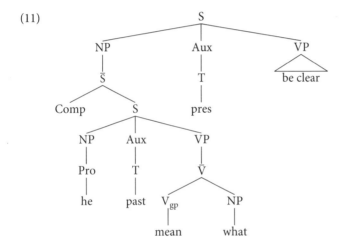

An embedded clause similar to the free relative is the **indefinite relative** clause, beginning with an indefinite pronoun ending with *-ever*:

> *Whatever goes upon four legs or has wings is a friend.* (COCA:FIC)
> *Whoever expects punishment already suffers it.* (COCA:NEWS)
> *I can have fun talking to whomever I want while he's away.* (COCA:FIC)
> *then they write whatever they want* (COCA:MAG)

Again, the entire clause fills a nominal function: Su, Su, OP, and dO of the main clause in the examples above. The *wh*-word itself fills a function in its own clause (Su, Su, dO, dO, above).

> **HINT:** Remember that the word *whenever* can also be a complementizer introducing an adverbial clause: *Whenever he is gone, it is very quiet here.*

Pseudocleft sentences (see Chapter 11) contain a headless relative clause, the verb BE, and a NP, VP, or AP:

> *What I want is an answer.* (COCA:FIC)
> *What we saw was a cuddly ball of red and gold fur.* (COCA:SPOK)
> *What surprised him was the crunch it made against the bone.* (COCA:FIC)
> *What she did was obtain evidence to corroborate her version of the event.* (COCA:SPOK)
> *What I did was write down the truth of my mother's life.* (COCA:FIC)
> *What I did was wrong.* (COCA:SPOK)

Cleft sentences (see Chapter 11), on the other hand, consist of *it*, the verb BE, a NP or PP, and a true relative clause:

> *It was a breakthrough that had taken five months.* (COCA:SPOK)
> *It was the dog that awakened her.* (COCA:FIC)
> *It was after Reuven's birth that she had become such an addict.* (COCA:FIC)

One last problem is posed by sentences such as the following containing nonrestrictive relative clauses:

> *But she also loved pleasing her mother, which wasn't always an easy thing to do.* (COCA:FIC)
> *Last summer, the girls were inseparable, which made the mothers happy.* (COCA:FIC)
> *Most had no rafting experience, which didn't surprise him; but one couldn't swim, which did.* (COCA:FIC)

The trouble here is that the relative pronoun does not refer back to any specific head noun, rather to the entire S. Strict prescriptive grammarians consider these structures wrong, but they are very common in colloquial and even more formal usage. These can be termed **sentential relative** clauses. We could account for these with some modification of our phrase structure rules, making the relative clause the sister of S.

Self-Testing Exercise: Do Exercise 9.4

Indirect questions.   The third kind of *wh*-clause is **indirect questions** (see Table 9.5). The functions of the indirect question clause are the same as those of the *that*-clause. That is, they serve various nominal functions, as shown in Table 9.5. Like the *that*-clause, the indirect question clause cannot function as indirect object nor as object complement and may be extraposed when serving as subject of the main clause, as in *It is often asked why students who take occupational courses … are included in the cohort* (COCA:ACAD).

Indirect questions are a type of indirect speech; in our discussion above, we saw that indirect statements following verbs of communication were expressed by *that*-clauses. Both *yes/no* and *wh*-questions can be reported in a similar fashion:

- direct *yes/no*: *Rosie asked Paul, "Is your sister going to Toronto tomorrow?"*
- indirect: *Rosie asked Paul whether his sister was going to Toronto the next day.*

- direct *wh-*: *Rosie asked Paul, "Why is your sister going to Toronto tomorrow?"*
- indirect: *Rosie asked Paul why his sister was going to Toronto the next day.*

Table 9.5. Indirect Questions

	function	indirect *wh*-question	indirect *yes/no* question
1.	Subject	How he could lose all that music is anyone's guess. (COCA:FIC)	Whether he can succeed in that remains to be seen. (COCA:SPOK)
2.	Direct Object	He asked which beach we would go to. (COCA:NEWS)	I asked whether his zoo had any gators. (COCA:NEWS)
3.	Direct Object after Indirect Object	We asked them why they like this particular book. (COCA:SPOK)	we asked them whether they thought stricter gun control would actually reduce violent crime. (COCA:SPOK)
4.	Subject Complement	The question is what they'll do when they get here. (COCA:NEWS)	The question is whether it is justified. (COCA:NEWS)
5.	Object of Preposition	I whined in my journal about how quickly pens seem to lose their ink. (COCA:ACAD)	there are questions about whether his company can survive (COCA:NEWS)
6.	Complement of Adjective	And people are uncertain what tomorrow is going to bring. (COCA:NEWS)	He was uncertain whether he ought to cry too. (COCA:FIC)
7.	Complement of N̄	I couldn't really answer the question why I wanted a son. (COCA:FIC)	there is serious question whether it will miss us or not. (COCA:FIC)

A number of changes occur when direct questions are shifted to indirect questions, including the shifting of verb tenses, pronouns, and certain adverbs (such as *here* and *now*). For our purposes, the important changes are the following:

- a complementizer – either *if* or *whether* – is supplied for *yes/no* questions.
- *wh*-movement is retained in *wh*-questions
- subject–auxiliary inversion is "undone"

In the indirect *yes/no* question, *if* or *whether* always function as pure complementizers; that is, they have no function other than as markers of subordination. Like *that* in *that*-clauses, they are generated in Comp position in D-structure. In indirect *wh*-questions, the *wh*-words serve a dual role, as they do in relative clauses, serving as complementizers embedding the indirect question into the main clause and as pronouns, determiners, adverbs and degree words within their own clauses. The *wh*-word is generated in D-structure in the position corresponding to its function and then moved to Comp position by *wh*-fronting. In Table 9.5, the *wh*-words (but not *whether*) have the following functions within their own clause:

> in (1), (3), and (7) *how* and *why* are interrogative adverbs,
> in (2) *which* is an interrogative determiner,
> in (5) *how* is an interrogative degree word, and
> in (4) and (6) *what* is an interrogative pronoun

Extraposition is possible with indirect questions:

> *It is anyone's guess <u>how he could lose all that music</u>.*
> *It remains to be seen <u>whether he can succeed in that</u>.*

> **HINT:** We have now studied a number of different dependent clauses which have a surface similarity. Can you identify the type of subordinate clause in each of the following?
>
> > a. *I asked <u>when the meeting would finish</u>.*
> > b. *I don't know the time <u>when the meeting will finish</u>.*
> > c. *I will leave <u>when the meeting is finished</u>.*
>
> The first (a) is an indirect question, functioning as direct object of *asked*, with the interrogative adverb *when*. The second (b) is a relative clause, modifying *the time*, with the relative adverb *when*. The third (c) is an adverbial clause, with the complementizer *when*.

Indirect exclamatory sentences, like their direct counterparts, are formed with *what a* or *how* + A/Adv and *wh*-movement, but no inversion:

> *It's strange <u>how much you can change in just one year</u>.* (COCA:FIC)
> *I'm surprised <u>how heavy it is</u>.* (COCA:FIC)
> *Everyone always says <u>what a nice person you are</u>.* (COCA:MAG)

> *Self-Testing Exercise:* As a review of all *wh*-clauses, do Exercise 9.5.

> **HINT:** When analyzing complex sentences with one or more dependent clauses, your first step should be to identify the main clause. Then bracket all of the dependent clauses and identify their function. Remember that to arrive at the D-structure all passive clauses must be returned to active, interrogative to declarative, and negative to positive; extraposition must be reversed. For example, below is the D-structure tree for *Did Matthew say whether the movie he saw yesterday was interesting?*, which consists of a main clause question containing an indirect question (functioning as direct object) which itself contains an embedded relative clause.

(12)

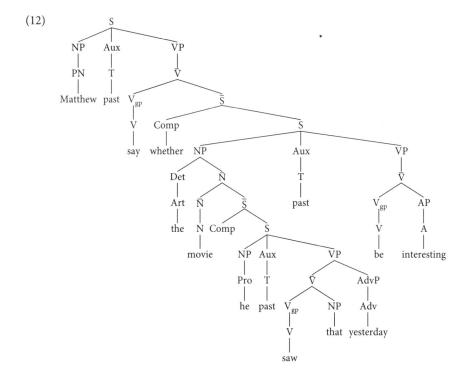

2. Nonfinite clauses

In the first half of the chapter, we treated the various types of finite clauses; we turn now to **nonfinite clauses**, which are formed with a **nonfinite verb**, a verbal element that is not marked for person, number, or tense. By definition, nonfinite clauses are always dependent, or embedded, since a main clause must have a finite verb.

2.1 Forms of nonfinite clauses

The verbal element in nonfinite clauses may take one of four forms, usually determined by the verb in the main clause.

The first nonfinite form is the **bare infinitive** (what we have encountered before as the stem form of the verb), as in the following:

> *The teacher made me <u>do</u> it.*
> *I saw Aaron <u>leave</u>.*

We will denote all nonfinite forms with the feature [–tense] in Aux since the lack of tense is their most salient characteristic.[18] A tree diagram for Aux + V in the second sentence above would be as follows:

(13)   Aux   +   V
        [–tense]
          | |
          Ø   leave

The bare infinitive is, in fact, quite limited, occurring after verbs of causation (e.g. *make*) and of perception (e.g. *see*), as well as modal auxiliaries.

The second nonfinite form is the ***to*-infinitive**. It consists of *to* followed by the stem form of the verb or auxiliary. It can also include the perfect, progressive, and passive in the order and with the endings that you will recognize from our analysis of the finite Aux:

simple active:	*I want <u>to give</u> you a present.*
perfect active:	*He seems <u>to have left</u>.*
progressive active:	*Sally appears <u>to be doing</u> well.*
perfect progressive active:	*He seems <u>to have been doing</u> better recently.*
simple passive:	*She wants <u>to be given</u> more responsibility.*
perfect passive:	*He seems <u>to have been overlooked</u>.*
progressive passive:	*<u>To be being asked</u> stupid questions all the time bothers him.*[19]
perfect progressive passive:	*?<u>To have been being asked</u> stupid questions all the time bothered him.*

The progressive passive and perfect progressive passive are awkward, perhaps because of the presence of two *be* auxiliaries. The Aux of the *to*-infinitive, which like all nonfinites has the feature [–tense], includes *to* and, as necessary, Perf, Prog, or Pass. Thus, *to have been being asked* (admittedly, a rare form) would be represented as follows:

(14)

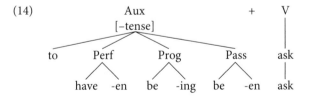

18.   Nonfinite verbs also lack agreement features (hence are [-Agr]), but we are ignoring agreement.

19.   Examples of this construction, though rare, can be found in actual usage, especially spoken English, e.g.: *no one seems <u>to be being held</u> accountable for these failures* (COCA:SPOK).

To arrive at the S-structure form, one has to perform affix hopping. Note that modals cannot occur here because they have no nonfinite forms.

The third nonfinite form is the *-ing* **participle**, or present participle. It too occurs in a number of different forms, always beginning with an *-ing* form:

simple active:	He stopped *working* there a year ago.
perfect active:	*Having arrived* late, she missed much of the concert.
progressive active:	*?being asking*[20]
perfect progressive active:	*Having been writing* for a long time, she took a break.
perfect passive:	He resents *having been asked* to help.
progressive passive:	She doesn't like *being left* out of the plan.
perfect progressive passive:	*Having been being given* so much attention pleases him.

When the *-ing* participle has a nominal function, it is known as a **gerund** (e.g. *Paying taxes is a bit like going to the dentist.* [COCA:NEWS]). The sequence *having been writing* is represented as follows:

(15)

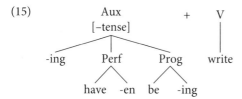

Affix hopping would attach the affixes appropriately here.

The fourth nonfinite form is the *-en* **participle**, consisting of the past participial form of the verb. It has only one form:[21]

simple passive: *The book given to him yesterday is very valuable.*

(16)
```
    Aux    +    V
  [–tense]      |
     |          |
    -en        give
```

> **HINT:** Recall that the past participial verb form differs depending on the type and class of verb: Some end in *-ed* or *-d* (e.g. *worked, created*), some in *-t* (e.g. *spent, crept*), some in *-en* or *-n* (e.g. *written, blown*), some in Ø (e.g. *cut, hurt*), while others have internal vowel changes (e.g. *met* from *meet*, *bled* from *bleed*). The designation *-en* is used here to cover all these cases.

---

20.   This form can also be found in spoken English: *the need to not worry about being conforming with the people around you* (COCA:SPOK). Its rarity has been explained by the "double *-ing* constraint".

21.   In traditional grammar, it is customary to categorize the passive forms of the *-ing* participle with the *-en* participle (as passive or past participles) because they are all passive in meaning.

Note that modals cannot occur in either the *-ing* or *-en* form because they have no participial forms.

2.2   Omissions from nonfinite clauses

A characteristic of nonfinite clauses is that they are often incomplete, missing obligatory elements such as subject or direct object. For this reason, nonfinite clauses are called "phrases" in traditional grammar. But they are better understood as deriving from complete clauses by the omission of obligatory elements. These omissions are called **PRO**, or "big PRO" (PRO for "pronoun"); PRO refers to the phonetically null subject and object NPs of nonfinite clauses. PROs may be of two types: controlled or indefinite (arbitrary). A **controlled PRO** is one in which the missing element in the nonfinite embedded clause is identical to an element in the main clause, such as the subject, object, or indirect object. The omitted element can be supplied from the main clause to reconstitute a complete clause, as follows:

> *I want [PRO to do well]. < I want [I do well]*

In the sentence above, the PRO in the nonfinite clause is said to be "controlled" by the subject of the main clause, and since the PRO is the subject of the nonfinite clause, we call it a "subject PRO". Thus, it is a subject PRO controlled by the subject of the higher S (note that the controller NP needn't be in the main clause, but just in the next higher clause). We can represent this as follows:

> *I want ₛ[PRO to do well]. Leslie said that she wanted ₛ[PRO to do well].*
> └_____↑   └_____↑

The various possibilities of controls and PROs are shown in Table 9.6a. You will note that there may be both subject and object PROs and that the two PROs can occur in the same clause.[22]

The second type of PRO is an **indefinite PRO**. This is one in which the missing element in the nonfinite clause can be filled with the general *you* or *one*, not with any specific element from the higher clause (see Table 9.6b). The two types of PROs can occur in the same clause (see Table 9.6c).

---

22.   In some versions of generative grammar, elliptical adverbial clause (see above) are treated as nonfinite clauses in which there is a subject PRO controlled by the subject of the main clause:

> *When PRO doing her homework, she listens to music*
> *When PRO apprehended by the police, he had the stolen goods on him.*

Sentences such as *If necessary, you may have more time to finish the exam* present difficulties for this analysis.

Table 9.6. Controlled and Indefinite PRO in Nonfinite Clauses

a. Controlled PRO:
  1. subject PRO controlled by subject of higher S:
    The man ₅[PRO sitting at the desk] is the clerk. < the man is sitting at the desk

    I wondered ₅[when PRO to call him]. < I call him

    She demonstrated her determination ₅[PRO to succeed]. < she succeed

    ₅[PRO Faced with an ultimatum], they gave in. < they are faced with an ultimatum

  2. subject PRO controlled by object of higher S:
    We persuaded him ₅[PRO to try again]. < he try again

    ₅[PRO Running five miles] exhausted me. < I run five miles

    I saw a picture ₅[PRO painted by Renoir]. < a picture painted by Renoir

  3. subject PRO controlled by indirect object of higher S:
    I told Karen ₅[when PRO to leave]. < Karen leave when

  4. object PRO controlled by subject of higher S:
    The question is too difficult ₅[for Bill to answer PRO]. < Bill answer the question

  5. object PRO controlled by object of higher S:
    We have a job ₅[for Paul to do PRO]. < Paul do the job

  6. more than one controlled PRO in the same clause:
    She gave John the book ₅[PRO to return PRO]. < John return the book

    subject PRO controlled by indirect object of higher S
    object PRO controlled by object of higher S
    I need a knife ₅[PRO to cut the bread with PRO]. < I cut the bread with a knife

    subject PRO controlled by subject of higher S
    object (of preposition) PRO controlled by object of higher S
b. Indefinite PRO:
    ₅[PRO Running five miles] is exhausting. < you run five miles
    ₅[PRO To leave now] would be wrong. < you leave now
    It's time ₅[PRO to start dinner]. < you start dinner

(Continued)

Table 9.6. Controlled and Indefinite PRO in Nonfinite Clauses (Continued)

c.   Controlled and Indefinite PRO in the same clause:
That question is too difficult $_{\bar{S}}$[PRO to answer PRO]. < you answer that question

object PRO controlled by subject of higher S
indefinite subject PRO
The best answer $_{\bar{S}}$[PRO to give PRO] is no answer. < you give the answer

object PRO controlled by subject of higher S
indefinite subject PRO

2.3   Complementizers in nonfinite clauses

Unlike finite embedded clauses, nonfinite clauses are usually not preceded by a complementizer. However, complementizers are used in two situations.

1.   The complementizer *for* occurs in the so-called *for-to-infinitive*. This is a *to*-infinitive with an explicit subject. *For* is used when such an infinitive has one of the following functions (the functions are discussed below):

> subject: $_{\bar{S}}$[*For him to say that*] *is nonsense.* (COCA:NEWS)
> complement of A: *The mother is anxious* $_{\bar{S}}$[*for her daughter to get home*]*.* (COCA:FIC)
> adverbial: $_{\bar{S}}$[*For us to win this game*]*, we have to play for each other.* (COCA:NEWS)
> postmodifier of N̄: *This was a perfect opportunity* $_{\bar{S}}$[*for him to express his admiration for her*]*.* (COCA:FIC)
> complement of N̄: *She had told their story, and that was a cue* $_{\bar{S}}$[*for them to tell theirs*]*.* (COCA:FIC)

Explicit subjects are not permitted when the infinitive functions as object of P. The only situation in which *for* is almost never used is when the infinitive functions as direct object of the verb, whether it is a *to*-infinitive or a bare infinitive:

> *We wanted (*for) him to return.*
> *We made (*for) him return.*
> cf. *We arranged for him to return.*

For never precedes PRO. The subject of an *-en* or *-ing* participle never takes *for*.[23]

---

23.   The subject of the gerund usually appears in the possessive (either the inflected –'s form or the periphrastic *of* form):

> *The child's crying annoyed me.*
> *The crying of the child annoyed me.*

2.   The second situation in which a complementizer is used is with **wh-infinitives**. These are either nonfinite indirect questions, both *wh*-questions (a) and *yes/no* questions (b), or nonfinite free relatives (c). Like finite indirect questions, nonfinite indirect questions do not have sub-auxiliary inversion. Indirect *wh*-questions and free relatives have *wh*-movement of a *wh*-word serving some function in the embedded clause. The fronted *wh*-word moves to the complementizer position:

a.   nonfinite indirect *wh*-questions

I asked $_{\bar{S}}$[what PRO to tell his friends in Europe [t]]. (COCA:ACAD)
This debate is about $_{\bar{S}}$[where PRO to draw that line [t]]. (COCA:NEWS)
his question is $_{\bar{S}}$[when PRO to pull the plug [t]] (COCA:MAG)

b.   nonfinite indirect *yes/no* questions

she wondered $_{\bar{S}}$[whether PRO to call it hope or fear] (COCA:FIC)
He's uncertain $_{\bar{S}}$[whether PRO to take off his shirt]. (COCA:FIC)
Professional sports organizations question $_{\bar{S}}$[whether PRO to ban athletes for unacceptable behavior off the field]. (COCA:SPOK)

c.   nonfinite free relatives

I know $_{\bar{S}}$[{what PRO to say [t], where PRO to go [t], when PRO to keep my mouth shut [t], who PRO to expect [t]}].

Note that nonfinite indirect questions always contain a subject PRO controlled by the subject of the higher clause.

We will use $\bar{S}$ in all cases of subordinate clauses, but Comp is empty in cases where there is not a pure complementizer (*for, if/whether*).

When the gerund is formed from a transitive verb, a number of variations are possible with the subject:

possessive subject: *The Prince's hunting foxes, the hunting of the Prince ...*
subject in *by* phrase: *The hunting of foxes by the Prince ...*
subject gap: *The hunting of foxes, Ø hunting foxes ...*

In current English, it is common to omit the possessive marker on the subject of the gerund, giving sentences such as *The Prince hunting foxes disturbs me*; this might sound more natural to you.

The object can also be expressed in different ways:

of preceding object: *The Prince's hunting of foxes ...*
possessive object: *the hunting of foxes, foxes' hunting ...*
object gap: *The Prince's hunting Ø ...*

The possibility of both the subject and the object occurring in an *of*-phrase leads to ambiguity, as in the phrase *the shooting of the hunters*, where *hunters* can be either the subject or the object, namely 'the hunters shoot something' or 'someone shoots the hunters'.

Finally, both subject and object can be omitted: *Hunting ...*

2.4   Functions of nonfinite clauses

The grammatical functions of nonfinite clauses are the same as those we identified for finite clauses (nominal, adjectival, and adverbial), but not all nonfinite forms can serve all functions.

Subject and subject complement.   Both *to*-infinitives (including *wh*-infinitives) and *-ing* participles (gerunds) can function as subject of the sentence. Like finite clauses, nonfinite subject clauses freely extrapose to the end of the sentence. Examples are as follows:

Su $_{\bar{S}}$[PRO *To decide what to do] is difficult.*
eSu   *It is difficult* $_{\bar{S}}$[PRO *to decide what to do]. (COCA:NEWS)*
Su $_{\bar{S}}$[for *them to have this positive self-concept] is important.*
eSu   *It is important* $_{\bar{S}}$[for *them to have this positive self-concept]. (COCA:SPOK)*
Su $_{\bar{S}}$[PRO *Learning to shoot] seemed out of the question. (COCA:FIC)*
eSu   *It seemed out of the question* $_{\bar{S}}$[PRO *learning to shoot].*
Su $_{\bar{S}}$[*Their doing so] will require US investors. (COCA:ACAD)*
eSu   *?It will require US investors* $_{\bar{S}}$[*their doing so].*
Su $_{\bar{S}}$[*What PRO to do [t]] is also clear from his account. (COCA:ACAD)*
eSu   *It is also clear from his account* $_{\bar{S}}$[*what PRO to do [t]].*

Extraposition is not always possible when the gerund has an explicit subject (as in *their doing so* above). The same forms (including occasionally bare infinitives) may also function as subject complements:

The fourth task was $_{\bar{S}}$[PRO *making and keeping friends]. (COCA:ACAD)*
What I want to do is $_{\bar{S}}$[PRO *see some fresh new faces]. (COCA:SPOK)*
His task is $_{\bar{S}}$[PRO *to re-envision a timeless classic]. (COCA:NEWS)*
The problem is $_{\bar{S}}$[*what PRO to charge him with [t]]. (COCA:NEWS)*

-en participles may also function as subject complements:

Mont and Han stayed $_{\bar{S}}$[PRO *concealed behind the sail]. (COCA:NEWS)*

> **HINT:** Another type of sentence which should be analyzed as containing a subject nonfinite clause is the following: *The politician seems to be honest.* You will recall that sentences of the type *It seems that the politician is honest* were analyzed above as containing a *that*-clause subject which was obligatorily extraposed. Similarly, we analyze this sentence as having the following D-structure:
>
> $_{NP}$[$_{\bar{S}}$[the politician to be honest]] [seems]
>
> The S-structure results from extraposition of the $\bar{S}$ with "raising" of the subject NP *the politician* to subject of the matrix clause. (Raising is discussed in more detail below.)

Complement of A.   Both *to*-infinitives and *-ing* participles can serve as the complement of an adjective:

> *I've been very happy ₅[PRO doing this film].* (COCA:SPOK)
> *I was determined ₅[PRO to bask in the sunshine].* (COCA:FIC)
> *I'm anxious ₅[for that to happen].* (COCA:FIC)
> *This elegant course is very easy ₅[PRO to make PRO].* (COCA:MAG)
> *the images were really enjoyable ₅[for me to work with PRO].* (COCA:MAG)

There are two classes of adjectives which take such a complement

1.   With adjectives like *determined, anxious, eager, hesitant, unwilling, furious, happy, liable, quick, reluctant, likely, bound, afraid, delighted,* and *able,* the nonfinite clause has a subject PRO controlled by the subject of the upper clause
2.   With adjectives like *difficult, impossible, easy, hard, tough, tiresome, boring, enjoyable,* and *delicious,* the nonfinite clause has an object PRO controlled by the subject of the upper clause.[24]

> **HINT:** A *to*-infinitive clause or *-ing* participle may serve as subject of a sentence with one of these adjectives in the predicate:
>
> ₅[PRO {Answering, To answer} all these questions] is tiresome.
>
> When the subject is then extraposed, the resulting construction resembles the constructions given above, except that the sentences begin with a dummy *it*:
>
> It is tiresome ₅[PRO {answering, to answer} all these questions].

Object of P.   Only *-ing* participles (gerunds) can serve as objects of prepositions. Nonfinites can occur as OPs no matter what the function of the PP as a whole:

PP is complement of V	*I thought [about ₅[PRO going back for a shirt]].* (COCA:FIC)
PP is adjunct adverbial (expressing manner)	*You can change the setting [by ₅[PRO turning the nozzle of your air valve]].* (COCA:FIC)
PP is modifier of N̄	*What are the results [of ₅[PRO being a Christian]]?* (COCA:MAG)
PP is complement of A	*The Blue Jackets have never come close [to ₅[PRO reaching the playoffs]].* (COCA:MAG)

Adverbial.   *To*-infinitives may function as adjunct adverbials (1)–(3), disjunct adverbials (4), and conjunct adverbials (5):

1.   ₅[PRO To get ahead], get a good education. (COCA:NEWS)
2.   ₅[PRO To make the salad], bring a large pot of water to a boil. (COCA:MAG).

---

24.   Sentences with these adjectives have also been analyzed by a type of construction called "*tough*-movement" (see Chapter 11).

3. $_{\bar S}$[For me to win], I have to play really well. (COCA:MAG)
4. $_{\bar S}$[PRO To tell the truth], I don't even know what I'm writing. (COCA:FIC)
5. $_{\bar S}$[PRO To summarize], keep ISO low. (COCA:ACAD)

Both -ing and -en participles may also serve an adverbial function as adjunct adverbials (6–7), disjunct adverbials (8), and conjunct adverbials (9):[25]

6. $_{\bar S}$[PRO Arriving in America], he was literally penniless. (COCA:FIC)
7. $_{\bar S}$[PRO Discouraged by the fence], no one visited at first. (COCA:FIC)
8. $_{\bar S}$[PRO Generally speaking], that doesn't work. (COCA:SPOK)
9. $_{\bar S}$[PRO Speaking of fun], why do you have three flat-screened TVs above your fireplace? (COCA:MAG).

Modifier of N̄ or of NP. Both -ing and -en participles and to-infinitives can function as adjectival modifiers of N̄; that is, they can function like restrictive relative clauses. The -en and -ing participles always have a missing subject (a subject PRO), which is controlled by the immediately preceding noun:

> Our eyes remain glued on the letter $_{\bar S}$[PRO lying on the wooden table]. (COCA:FIC)
> This is a book $_{\bar S}$[PRO written by a very famous golfer]. (COCA:NEWS)

For infinitives, there may be a missing subject or object PRO, or both:

> She need someone $_{\bar S}$[PRO to hold down her sofa]. (COCA:FIC)
> So it's a very hard thing $_{\bar S}$[for them to wiggle out of PRO]. (COCA:NEWS)
> There are more mouths $_{\bar S}$[PRO to feed PRO]. (COCA:SPOK)

---

25. The nonfinite clauses in (a)–(c) have the special name of "absolute constructions":

    a. $_{\bar S}$[The plane arriving late], we missed our connection.
    b. $_{\bar S}$[Their home ruined by fire], they had to seek shelter with relatives.
    c. [With $_{\bar S}$[his parents visiting]], he is too busy to attend class.

They consist of a participle and an explicit subject (not PRO) and sometimes a preposition. Absolute constructions have no real grammatical connection with the rest of the sentence (hence the term "absolute"). They generally express the adverbial notion of "circumstance" (cause or time) and can be understood as adverbial. In certain cases, a *being* participle has been deleted, leaving the complement PP, AP, or NP: *Her eyes (being) wide with astonishment, the child watched the clown.* The causal meaning is not as strong when *being* is omitted (compare *His cap being in his hand, he couldn't hold the box* and *His cap in his hand, he left the room*), nor is it as strong when the absolute is in mid or final position rather than initial position (e.g. *The participants, some elderly, were very eager; The report is divided into sections, each devoted to a different aspect of the problem*). It might be possible to analyze absolute constructions with -en participles as having an elliptical *being*, as in *Their house now (being) ruined, they had to seek shelter with relatives.*

HINT: The function of these nonfinite clauses is identical to that of adjectives (including participles) which precede the noun and of PPs or finite relative clauses which follow the noun. This equivalency can be seen in the following finite relative clause paraphrases of the above nonfinite clauses:

> the letter which is lying on the wooden table
> the book which is written by a very famous golfer
> someone who will hold down her sofa
> a hard thing which they can wiggle out of
> more mouths which you must feed

The only difference between participial relative clauses and the finite relative clauses is the presence of the relative pronoun subject *which* and a form of BE.[26]

Note that the difference between participial clauses which follow the noun and participles functioning as adjectives which precede the noun (as discussed in Chapter 7) is the presence of a complement PP. A simple participle cannot follow the noun, as a complemented participle cannot precede the noun:

> the ripped flag *the flag ripped
> the flag ripped by the wind *the ripped by the wind flag

Nonfinite clauses may also serve as nonrestrictive adjectives, that is, as modifiers of the NP, as in the following examples:

> Then Shelby, ₅[PRO sitting in the co-pilot's seat], saw miles of lights. (COCA:FIC)
> Seattle's stunning public library, ₅[PRO designed by the architect Rem Koolhaas], attracted 2.3 million visitors. (COCA:NEWS)
> Trading places is a way to support the adolescent quest for identity, ₅[PRO to have status]. (COCA:ACAD)

It is sometimes difficult to distinguish adverbial from nonrestrictive adjectival participial clauses since both can be moved to the beginning of the sentence:

– Adverbial: *Disgusted by the movie, we left.* < *We left, disgusted by the movie.*
– Adjectival: *Discussed by everyone in the class, the movie seemed to generate lots of interest.* < *The movie, discussed by everyone in the class, seemed to generate lots of interest.*

But note that the adverbial clause answers the question "why?" while the adjectival one does not; the adverbial clause can be replaced by a *because* clause ("because we were

---

26. In the earliest versions of generative grammar, it was the practice to derive adjectival participial clauses from relative clauses by a process of deletion: e.g. *the book awarded the prize* < *the book which was awarded the prize*. It is also possible to derive appositional phrases from reduced relative clauses: e.g. *my friend, the physicist* < *my friend, who is a physicist*. Among other difficulties, there are certain participial clauses, such as those containing stative verbs, which cannot be so derived: *the student knowing the answer* < **the student who is knowing the answer*.

disgusted by the movie", but not "because the movie was discussed by everyone"). On the other hand, it is possible to replace the adjectival participial clause with a relative clause, but the adverbial clause lends itself less naturally to such a replacement ("the movie, which was discussed by everyone", but not "we, who were disgusted by the movie").

> **HINT:** There appears to be a rule – in writing at least – that the PRO of the fronted participial clause must be controlled by the subject of the matrix clause. If this is not the case, then the participial clause is not immediately linked to the main clause (its subject must be found in the larger discourse) and it can be seen as "dangling". Such structures are quite common in speech, but in writing are considered an "error" known as a *dangling participle*, as in:
>
> 1. *Looking out of the window, there were the flower beds in the front garden* (Butler, *The Way of All Flesh* as cited in Visser, 1972, p. 1144).
> 2. *On pouring some water from the carafe over his forehead he opened his eyes* (Conan Doyle, *Complete Short Stories* as cited in Visser, 1972, pp. 1143–4). Here the "he" subject of the main clause cannot be the one doing the pouring of the water as the grammar of the sentence would suggest.
>
> Dangling participles may sometimes be (unintentionally) funny.[27]

Complement of N̄. Like *that*-clauses, *to*-infinitives may function as complements of N̄ following an abstract noun:

> *Boggs should have heeded Buckley's suggestion [PRO to keep his rhetoric less extreme].* (COCA:NEWS)
> *These researchers conclude with a recommendation [for the military to intensify its efforts].* (COCA:ACAD)

The relationship of the clause to the abstract noun is comparable to that of a direct object to a verb: *They recommended [that the military intensify its efforts].*

> **HINT:** Just as it was important to distinguish *that*-clauses functioning as complement of N̄ from those functioning as modifiers of N̄ (i.e. as relative clauses), it is important to make the same distinction here. If the nonfinite clause is functioning as a complement of N̄, it cannot be replaced by a relative clause: **suggestion which he keep his rhetoric less extreme*. Furthermore, the PRO is not controlled by the head noun: *the suggestion [*the suggestion keep his rhetoric less extreme]*. In contrast, if the clause is functioning as a modifier of N̄, it can be replaced by a relative clause *someone who will hold down her sofa*, and PRO is controlled by the head noun *someone [someone hold down her sofa]*.

Below are generalized trees exemplifying all of the functions discussed.

---

27.   A very informative discussion of "dangling participles" by Arnold Zwicky may be found at http://itre.cis.upenn.edu/~myl/languagelog/archives/001174.html.

a. Subject: *Running a small business is difficult.*

(17)

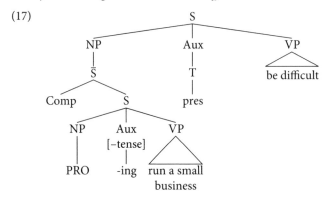

b. Subject Complement: *Her first job was selling computers.*

(18)

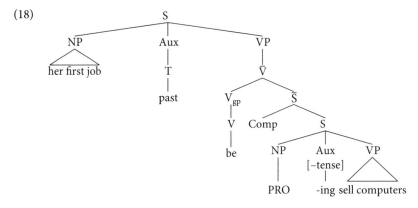

c. Complement of A: *The question is difficult to answer.*

(19)

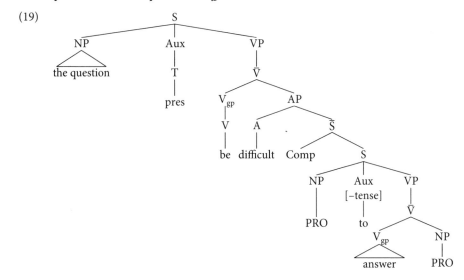

d.   Object of P: *We talked about going to the movies.*

(20)

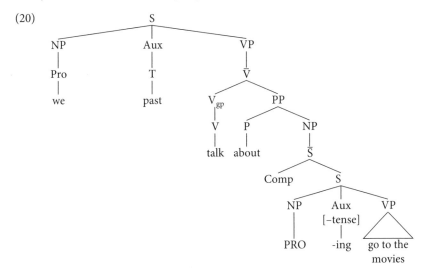

e.   Adjunct Adverbial: *You must work hard to get ahead.*

(21)

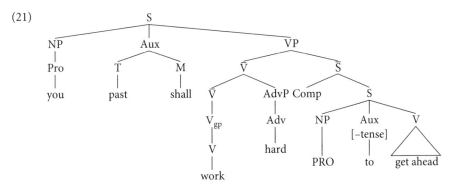

f.   Modifier of N̄: *The tree toppled by the wind was very old.*

(22)

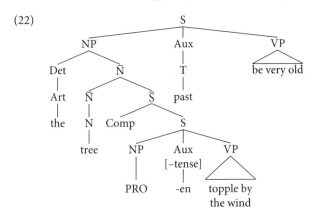

g. Complement of N̄: *The proposal to erect a new building is absurd.*

(23)

```
                              S
            ┌─────────────────┼─────────────────┐
           NP                Aux                VP
     ┌──────┴──────┐          │              (be absurd)
    Det    N̄        S̄         T
     │     │     ┌──┴──┐      │
    Art    N   Comp    S     pres
     │     │      ┌────┴────┐
  the proposal   NP  Aux    VP
                  │  [−tense] (erect a new
                 PRO   to        building)
```

For (f) note that although the *-en* participle is logically passive, we are not changing it to active in D-structure.

2.5 Nonfinite clauses as complements of V

The most important function of nonfinite clauses is as complement of the verb, but a full treatment of it would require several chapters and is beyond the scope of this text. The complement function is the most difficult function to analyze, for a couple of reasons:

1. It is traditional to see clauses as serving as direct objects and object complements, but it is not clear that clauses in these functions are comparable to noun phrases and other phrasal categories that also have these functions. For this reason, clausal verb complements have been seen as directly dominated by V̄, not NP.
2. If clausal complements are included, an entirely new subcategorization system of verbs is required. For example, a preliminary classification of verbs which considers only infinitive and *that*-clause complements yields at least ten different types:

   - verbs taking {*to* V, NP *to* V, *that* S} complements (e.g. *expect*)
   - verbs taking {*to* V, *that* S} complements (e.g. *claim*)
   - verbs taking {NP *to* V, *that* S} complements (e.g. *believe*)
   - verbs taking NP *to* V complements (e.g. *force*)
   - verbs taking *to* V complements (e.g. *try*)
   - verbs taking {NP *to* V, NP *that* S} complements (e.g. *remind*)
   - verbs taking {*for* NP *to* V, *that* S} complements (e.g. *arrange*)
   - verbs taking {NP V, *that* S} complements (e.g. *hear*)
   - verbs taking {NP V} complements (e.g. *make*)
   - verbs taking {NP *to* V} complements (e.g. *cause*)

With non-finite complements, the crucial factor seems to be whether there is an explicit NP between the matrix and embedded clause. Note that some verbs optionally allow such an NP (*expect to go/expect him to go*), others obligatorily require one (**remind to go/remind him to go*), while others do not permit one (*try to go/*try him to go*).

When the NP is absent, the structure can quite easily be analyzed as follows:

Sally forgot ₅[PRO to close the door].
└──────────↑

Patricia expects ₅[PRO to get a good mark].
└──────────↑

Mary practiced ₅[PRO reciting the poem].
└──────────↑

He tried ₅[PRO {to cut, cutting} the rope].
└─────↑

She {hates, likes} ₅[PRO {to vacuum, vacuuming}].
└──────────↑

That is, the nonfinite clause has a subject PRO controlled by the subject of the upper clause. This is semantically quite obvious: if Patricia expects to get a good mark, then it is Patricia's getting a good mark that is expected; another way to look at it is as two main clauses: Patricia expect [Patricia get a good mark].

> **HINT:** There is also a formal test using reflexives that shows us that PRO is controlled by the subject of the upper clause. We know (from Chapter 8) that a reflexive must be co-indexed with the subject of its own clause. Therefore, in the following sentences there must be a deleted subject of the nonfinite clause, namely PRO, which is coindexed to the subject:
>
> *Lucy expects ₅[PRO to improve {herself, *themselves, *yourself}].*
> *Graham said that Mary wanted ₅ [PRO to protect {herself, *himself}].*

Only *to*-infinitives and *-ing* participles may occur in the structure without an intervening NP. Note that some verbs take only *to*-infinitives (e.g. *expect, hope, wish, want*), some verbs take only *-ing* participles (e.g. *admit, keep on, finish, practice, enjoy, give up, avoid, deny, appreciate*), and some verbs may take either (e.g. *begin, start, stop, continue, go on, try, regret, prefer, dread*). In the last case, the different nonfinite forms sometimes convey different meanings, as in:

We stopped to eat. vs. *We stopped eating.*
He remembered to mail the letter. vs. *He remembered mailing the letter.*

When the NP is present, all four types of nonfinites may occur:

1. bare infinitive
   And then I heard the crowd <u>gasp</u> (COCA:ACAD)
   What made the critics <u>change</u> their mind about Hitchcock? (COCA:ACAD)

2. *to*-infinitive

He'd convinced her *to hop* a short flight to Las Vegas. (COCA:FIC)

They all expected her *to fail*. (COCA:FIC)

3. *-ing* participle

They resent the West *telling* them what they should do. (COCA:ACAD)

I saw her lips *moving*. (COCA:FIC)

4. *-en* participle

They had discovered banana phytoliths *dated* to 500 B.C. in Cameroon. (COCA:ACAD)

Queen Victoria kept her castle *filled* with the scent. (COCA:NEWS)

The structure is not easily analyzed because the status of the NP is in question: Is it the subject of the embedded clause or the object of the main clause? That is, which of these two bracketings is correct?

They all expected ₅[her to fail] OR

They all expected her ₅[PRO to fail]?

A complementizer, which would clearly delineate the embedded from the main clause, occurs with only a few verbs in English, such as *prefer* and *wish*:

I'd prefer ₅[for the president to make the announcement]. (COCA:SPOK)

Furthermore, when a pronoun substitutes for the NP, it occurs in the objective form. While this might suggest the second analysis, one can argue that subjects of nonfinites always occur in the objective case (e.g. *for him to leave*) or perhaps the genitive case (e.g. *John's drinking*), but not the nominative case.

To try to decide this issue, let's look at two example sentences (a) and (b):

(1)	(2) Question test	(3) Passive test	(4) Pseudo-cleft test
a. *John wants Mary to accept the job.*	*What did John want?* *For Mary to accept the job.*	*John wants the job to be accepted by Mary.*	*What John wanted was for Mary to accept the job.*
b. *John persuaded Mary to accept the job.*	*Who did John persuade (to accept the job)? Mary.*	**John persuaded the job to be accepted by Mary.*	**What John persuaded was for Mary to accept the job.*

Semantically, in (a) John wants an entire state of affairs, namely Mary's accepting the job; the entire proposition (Mary accept the job) is the object of John's wanting. In (b) John persuades a person to do something (he persuades Mary, Mary accept the job); he does not persuade an entire proposition (Mary accept the job). It is syntactically possible to delete the second NP in the case of *want* (John wants to accept the job) but not in case of *persuade* (*John persuaded to accept the job); rather, we must insert a reflexive pronoun (*John persuaded himself to accept the job*). If we question the nonfinite clauses, the questions and answers take different forms, as shown in the column (2) above. It is not possible to reverse the questions:

a.   *Who did John want? Mary.
b.   *What did John persuade? For Mary to accept the job.

If we passivize the nonfinite clauses, we see a difference, as shown in column (3) above. With *want*, there is synonymy between the active and passive versions: John wants the same state of affairs in both active or passive, namely, the job's acceptance. With *persuade*, however, either the passive is not possible, or there isn't synonymy between active and passive: e.g. in *John persuaded Mary see a doctor/ John persuaded a doctor to seen by Mary* either John acts upon Mary or he acts upon the doctor. In pseudocleft sentences, the two verbs also behave differently, as shown in column (4) above.

There are differences in the type of NP that can follow *expect* or *persuade*:

- The NP following *persuade* must be animate, because only an animate being can be made to do something: *The director wants the play to succeed* but not **The director persuaded the play to succeed.*
- The NP following *want* may be one which is restricted to subject position (namely existential *there* and the dummy *it* in weather expressions), but these forms cannot follow *persuade*: *Bronwyn wants {it to rain, there to be sun} tomorrow.* but not **Gwendolyn persuaded {it to rain, there to be sun} tomorrow.*

Because of these semantic and formal differences, we set up two classes of verbs.

1.   ***want*-type verbs**: the NP is subject of the nonfinite embedded clause: V_{gp} $_{\bar{S}}$[NP VP]. The nonfinite clause functions as direct object of the upper V.
2.   ***persuade*-type verbs**: the NP is object of the main clause verb, but controls the deleted subject of the nonfinite clause: V_{gp} NP $_{\bar{S}}$[PRO VP]. The nonfinite clause functions as object complement, completing the direct object.

There is a problem for our classification, however. Consider the verb *expect*. In most respects, it seems to pattern like *want*:

1.   *Barbara expects Megan to feed the dog.*
2.   question test: *What does Barbara expect? For Megan to feed the dog.*
3.   passive test: *Barbara expects the dog to be fed by Megan.*
4.   pseudo-cleft test: *What Barbara expects is for Megan to feed the dog.*
5.   subject test: *Barbara expects {it to rain, there to be sunshine} tomorrow.*

However, in one important respect, the *expect* case is like the *persuade* case and unlike the *want* case. First, the second NP can be questioned: *Who does Barbara expect to feed the dog? Megan.* Second, note what happens when the matrix clause is passivized:

1.   **Megan was wanted by Barbara to feed the dog.*
2.   *Megan was persuaded by Barbara to feed the dog.*
3.   *Megan was expected by Barbara to feed the dog.*

This evidence suggests that with *expect*, the second NP is object of the matrix clause since it can become the subject of a corresponding passive. Remember that the rule for passive instructs us to move the direct object to subject position. A variant passive, however – *For Megan to feed the dog was expected by Barbara* – moves the entire clause to subject position, treating *Megan* as subject of the embedded clause. Thus, *Megan* seems to behave as both subject of the embedded clause and direct object of the matrix clause. How can this be? To account for this apparently contradictory behavior, we say that the NP there is **raising** of the NP from the position of subject of the lower clause to the position of object of the upper clause ("subject-to-object raising"). Note that this operation does not manifest itself in any difference in the S-structure order of elements, but involves rebracketing of constituent structure.

(24)

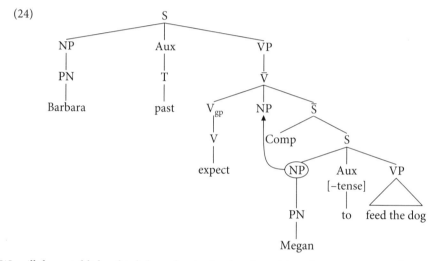

We will thus establish a third class of verbs that involve raising, the ***expect*-type verbs**. It is possible to classify verbs followed by infinitives, but also those followed by *-ing* or *-en* participles into these three categories. Table 9.7 contains a sample of verbs falling into these three classes.

Table 9.7. *Persuade-, Expect-, and Want-*type Verbs in English

	persuade-type verbs
NP *to* V:	*tell, order, ask, dare, forbid, beg, coax, advise, convince, encourage, permit, allow, oblige, force, cause*
NP V:	*make, have*
	expect-type verbs
NP *to* V:	*believe, assume, understand, consider, suppose, know, think, imagine, find, help*
NP V-*ing* or NP V:	*see, hear, witness, observe, notice, feel, taste*
NP V-*ing*:	*discover, catch, send, find, leave*
NP V-*en*:	*keep, make*
	want-type verbs
NP *to* V:	*wish, hope, prefer, like, desire, love, hate, dread, need*
NP V-*ing*:	*resent, regret*
NP V-*en*:	*have, want, get, need, see, hear*

Self-Testing Exercises: Do Exercise 9.7, and then as a review of finite and nonfinite clauses, do Exercise 9.8.

3. Review of complex sentences

In this chapter, we have modified the following phrase structure rules in order to account for embedded clauses:

$$\bar{S} \rightarrow \text{Comp S}$$

$$NP \rightarrow \left[\begin{array}{l} \left\{ \begin{array}{l} \text{(Det) } \bar{N} \text{ ($\bar{S}$)} \\ \text{PN} \\ \text{Pro} \\ \bar{S} \\ \text{(NP) } \bar{S} \end{array} \right\} \end{array} \right]$$

$$\bar{N} \rightarrow \left\{ \begin{array}{l} \text{(AP) } \bar{N} \text{ (PP) ($\bar{S}$)} \\ \text{N} \end{array} \right\}$$

$$AP \rightarrow \left(\left\{ \begin{array}{l} \text{Deg} \\ \text{AdvP} \end{array} \right\} \right) A \left(\left\{ \begin{array}{l} \text{PP} \\ \bar{S} \end{array} \right\} \right)$$

Comp → {*that, although, when, whether* ...}

$$VP \rightarrow \bar{V} \left(\left\{ \begin{array}{l} \text{AdvP} \\ \text{PP} \\ \text{NP} \\ \bar{S} \end{array} \right\} \right)$$

$$\bar{V} \rightarrow \left[\begin{array}{ll} V_{gp} & \left(\left\{ \begin{array}{l} \text{NP ({NP, PP, AP})} \\ \text{AP} \\ \text{PP (PP)} \\ \text{(NP) } \bar{S} \end{array} \right\} \right) \\ \bar{V} & \text{({ AdvP, PP, NP, $\bar{S}$})} \end{array} \right]$$

$$S \rightarrow \left[\begin{array}{l} S \left(\left\{ \begin{array}{l} \text{PP} \\ \text{AdvP} \\ \text{NP} \\ \bar{S} \end{array} \right\} \right) \\ \text{NP Aux VP} \end{array} \right]$$

HINT: See Appendix IIb for a complete listing of the phrase structure rules for simple and complex sentences.

We have examined the following types of finite main clauses:

> *wh*-question

We have examined the following types of finite dependent clauses:

that-clause	free or headless relative clause
adverbial clause	indefinite relative clause
relative clause (restrictive or nonrestrictive)	indirect question
sentential relative clause	

We have examined the following forms of nonfinite dependent clauses:

bare infinitive	*wh*-infinitive
to-infinitive	*-ing* participle or gerund
for-to-infinitive	*-en* participle

We have identified the following functions of dependent clauses:

subject	object of P	complement of A
extraposed subject	disjunct adverbial	modifier of N̄
subject complement	adjunct adverbial	modifier of NP
direct object	conjunct adverbial	complement of N̄
object complement	complement of V	

Finally, we have encountered the following types of complementizers:

> interrogative pronoun, determiner, adverb, degree adverb
> relative pronoun, adverb, determiner
> pure complementizer (base-generated under Comp) (*whether, that, since, because,* etc.)
> *for* subject of infinitive

Chapter summary

Now that you have completed this chapter, you should be able to:

1. identify the embedded finite and nonfinite clauses in a complex sentence;
2. determine the type and function of each embedded finite clause;
3. determine the form and function of each embedded nonfinite clause;
4. determine the type and function of each complementizer; and
5. give a tree diagram for any complex sentence, showing the hierarchical relation of each embedded clause, as well as its D-structure position and form.

Recommended additional reading

Treatments of English syntax which are similar in depth and level of formality to the treatment in this chapter include Brown and Miller (1991, Chapters 9 and 10, pp. 132–140), Kaplan

(1995, Chapter 6, pp. 251–267, Chapter 8, pp. 326–355, and Chapter 9), Burton-Roberts (1997, Chapters 8–10), Hopper (1999, Chapters 13–16), and Disterheft (2004, Chapter 9). Less formal treatments include Delahunty and Garvey (1994, Chapter 10), Morenberg (2002, Chapters 6–9), and Klammer, Schultz, and Della Volpe (2010, Chapters 10–12).

For more advanced treatments, see the references in Chapter 7.

Chapter 10

Sentence semantics

1. Propositions
2. Thematic roles
3. Predications

Chapter preview

The chapter considers the semantic relationships between the verb and the nominal elements within a sentence. We begin by analyzing the core semantic content of sentences as propositions, consisting of nominal arguments and a predicate. We then consider the semantic functions that arguments can serve, using the notion of thematic roles – roles such as Agent, Force, Source, Goal, and so on. The roles are defined, their surface manifestations in English are exemplified, and dual roles are examined. We explore how predicates uniquely select arguments serving particular thematic roles. The chapter next explores the ways in which predicates relate nominal arguments to one another. Using various relational semantic features, different descriptive, cognitive, and locative/possessive predicates are analyzed using semantic features. These include different aspectual types (inchoative, continuative, egressive) and different situation types (stative, causative, agentive).

Commentary

In Chapter 6, we considered the semantics of individual lexical items. We will now consider the semantic relationships between nouns and verbs in a sentence. In the preceding chapters on syntax, we followed the approach of many linguists, who believe that it is possible to treat syntax as autonomous, or syntax and semantics as essentially separate, with semantics treated as purely interpretative. In this chapter, we will follow the approach of other linguists who believe that syntax and semantics are intrinsically linked; in their view, semantics is, in fact, fundamental, and D-structure is a *semantic* representation using semantic features. It is a much more abstract logical representation than we considered in the previous chapters.

Note that just as there are many different ways to approach word meaning, there are alternative approaches to sentence meaning, only a couple of which will be examined in this chapter. Moreover, for many linguists, sentence meaning incorporates many of the concepts that will be treated in Chapter 11.

1. Propositions

Our analysis of sentence semantics begins with the concept of the proposition (prop), the semantic content of a clause minus any particular syntactic structure as well as its intended communicative force (communicative force will be treated in Chapter 11). For example, the proposition [Harriet call the doctor] may be expressed in the following forms, among others:

Did Harriet call the doctor?	*Will Harriet call the doctor?*
Harriet called the doctor.	*for Harriet to call the doctor*
Harriet's calling the doctor	*It was Harriet who called the doctor.*
It was the doctor whom Harriet called.	*The one who called the doctor was Harriet.*

Thus, the proposition may occur in different sentence types, in nonfinite as well as finite form, and in utterances with different focuses. Note that the proposition itself crucially lacks tense, aspect, modality and agreement marking.

A proposition is divided into a **predicate (pred)** and its **arguments (arg)**. An argument is any of the various elements of the sentence that are set in relation to one another by the predicate. Arguments are typically noun phrases. The predicate is the operation carried out on an argument or arguments; it places the arguments in relation to one another. Predicates are typically verbs (including accompanying prepositions and particles), prepositions, and (predicate) adjectives. Predicates differ in respect to valency, the number of arguments that cooccur with a predicate. There are different types of valencies, Ø-, 1-, 2-, and 3-place predicates; these, along with the less common 4-place predicate, are exemplified in Table 10.1. Note the different verb types occurring in each structure:

1. Zero-place predicates consist of a class of impersonal constructions called weather expressions in which the subject is a dummy *it*.
2. One-place predicates consist of what are traditionally known as intransitive verbs (*burn, choke*), intransitive phrasal verbs (*fly away, run out*), and some copula + subject complements (*be Irish, be depressed, be a dancer, become a lawyer*).
3. Two-place predicates consist of transitive verbs (*break, sand, surprise, write, left*), transitive phrasal verbs (*write down, press flat*), prepositional verbs (*belong to, look into, start at*), as well as adjectival structures with *be* (*be similar to, be behind, be upset with*). Elliptical structures such as the following would also be considered 2-place

structures because of the presence of a latent object: *Jack is eating (something). Fiona is jealous (of someone).*

> **HINT:** The "identifying" statement (containing a definite article) *Violet is the lead ballerina* is a 2-place predicate, and the "descriptive" statement (containing an indefinite article) *Violet is a dancer* is 1-place. In the first case two entities (Violet, lead ballerina) are being equated, while in the second case one entity (Violet) is said to belong to an abstract class (dancers).

4.   Three-place predicates include ditransitive (*give*), complex transitive (*put, donate, crawl*), and diprepositonal verbs (*extend*).

Table 10.1. Ø-, 1-, 2-, 3-, and 4-Place Predicates

Ø-place:	
It is sunny.	It is snowing.
It is hot.	It felt chilly.
1-place:	
The house is burning.	The bird flew away.
Frank is Irish.	The child choked.
His time ran out.	Sam is depressed.
There are two answers.	Violet is a dancer.
Janet became a lawyer.	
2-place:	
Mary broke the glasses.	The carpenter sanded the desk.
The book belongs to Peter.	The news surprised us.
Diana left the gym.	The teacher is upset with him.
Gary wrote a paper.	Violet is the lead ballerina.
Frank is similar to John.	The coat is behind the door.
The contest starts at noon.	He pressed the papers flat.
He wrote the address down.	The witch looked into the cauldron.
Alice is my aunt (=is an aunt to me).	

3-place:
  The police officer gave a ticket to the speeder.
  Mary put the keys on the table.
  We donated the clothes to charity.
  The baby crawled from the chair to the sofa.
  Santa Cruz is between Los Angeles and San Francisco.
  The road extends from coast to coast.

4-place:
  He flew from New York to Havana via Miami.

The predicate and argument(s) of a proposition may be represented in tree diagrams, as follows:

(1) 1-place

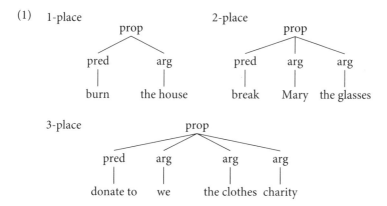

Note that arguments include only the nuclear elements of sentences, not adverbial elements. Thus, in the sentence *Patsy is knitting a sweater in the living room*, "in the living room" is not an argument (because *knit* is a transitive verb), while in the sentence *Patsy put the sweater in the living room*, "in the living room" is an argument (because *put* is a complex transitive verb). The second sentence is a single 3-place predicate:

(2)

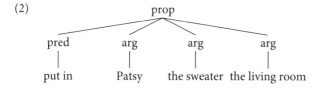

(An analysis of the first sentence is given in the Self-Testing Exercise.)

Now that propositions have been analyzed into the predicate and argument(s), we can examine how these parts are related semantically.

Self-Testing Exercise: Do Exercise 10.1.

2. Thematic roles

The concept of **thematic roles** (or **θ-roles**) is a means of accounting for the functions of arguments in respect to the predicate; thematic roles are the "grammatically relevant semantic relations between predicates and arguments" (Frawley, 1992, p. 201). This approach was first proposed by Charles Fillmore (1968; 1977) and was originally known as "case grammar". To define the roles of arguments, Fillmore borrows the notion of case used in the analysis of grammatical categories, but applies it in a slightly different way.

1. Traditionally, case is understood as a formal marking on nouns (typically expressed by inflection), with a number of these formal markers of case distinguished: nominative, genitive, dative, accusative, and so on. But the meaning of a case ending (the function of the noun carrying a particular case inflection) may be complex. This is perhaps most obvious with the genitive, which can express possessive, subjective, objective, descriptive, partitive, or adverbial meaning (as we discussed in Chapter 5). The nominative case, which denotes the grammatical function of subject of the sentence, would seem to be fairly unified in meaning, but even it expresses a variety of concepts, including agent, cause, recipient, object, or instrument of an action.

2. Traditionally, it is also unclear whether the notion of case should be restricted to case inflections – what is known as *morphological case* – which are used almost exclusively in a synthetic language,[1] or should embrace other formal means to express the same grammatical functions, namely periphrases (using prepositions) and word order, which are the primary means for the expression of case in an analytic language such as English.

Since languages seem to make use of various surface forms for the same grammatical function and to express the same grammatical function with different surface forms, Fillmore decides to use *case* in a new way: to indicate "semantic case" or the underlying semantic-syntactic functional relationships. He conceives of these semantic cases as finite in number and universal, not language specific, much like semantic features. They are a matter of D-structure, while their formal marking is a matter of S-structure.

This approach to the function of noun phrases offers certain advantages over the purely structural approach of syntactic analysis (as we undertook in Chapters 7–9). In this approach, case refers to the position of a noun phrase in D-structure; thus, the "subject" is the NP to the left of the verb or directly dominated by S, while the "direct object" is the NP to the right of V or directly dominated by VP. As is obvious from the terms "right" and "left", these relations are considered for SuVO word order only. While the structural approach could be modified to account for other word orders, such as SuOV, VOSu, and OVSu, where O is adjacent to V, it would be more difficult to account for VSuO or OSuV. Case grammar abandons the idea that noun phrases are ordered in the base; rather, it sees them as assigned a particular surface position according to their thematic role.

---

1. A synthetic language is one such as Latin or Old English, in which grammatical categories are expressed primarily by inflection. In contrast, a synthetic language such as Modern English or French expresses grammatical categories with a few inflections, but primarily through word order and periphrasis.

Another advantage of case grammar is that it is able to recognize a relationship among sentences such as the following:

The chef roasted the meat (over the fire).
The fire roasted the meat.
The meat roasted (over the fire).

In a purely structural approach, we would need to postulate three separate verbs *roast* with similar semantic features but different subcategorization rules:

roast   _____ NP (PP)
           _____ NP
           _____ (PP)

In case grammar, it is possible to see the three instances as a single verb selecting certain thematic roles, which then appear in different surface syntactic positions.

While Fillmore envisages a finite number of universal thematic roles, there is not yet general agreement on the inventory of these roles, on their designations, or on their definitions. Despite the fact that determination of thematic roles is described by one scholar as "intuitionism run wild" (Dillon, 1977, p. 73), we may consider the following as a list of some of the possible thematic roles served by arguments in a sentence:[2]

1. **Agent**: the animate initiator, causer, doer, or instigator of an action who acts by will or volition, takes responsibility for the action, and is its direct cause;
2. **Force**: the inanimate cause of an action, which does not act by will or volition;
3. **Instrument**: the means by which an event is caused, or the tool, generally inanimate, used to carry out an action; an instrument does not act but is acted upon;
   (Agent, Force, and Instrument together could be considered "Cause".)
4. **Experiencer**: the animate being affected inwardly by a state or action;
5. **Source**: the place-from-which or person-from-whom an action emanates;
6. **Goal**: the place-to-which or person-to-whom an action is directed, including indirect objects and directional adverbs;
7. **Path**: the path taken in moving from one place to another in the course of an action;
8. **Location**: the place-at/in-which or the time-at-which an action occurs;
9. **Possessor**: the possessor of a thing, really a special kind of locative, since the thing and the possessor must coincide; there are two kinds of possession, depending on whether the possessor and the thing possessed are inherently connected, such as *Judy's head* (inalienable possession) or not, such as *Judy's car* (alienable possession);

---

2.   Many of these thematic roles have alternative names: Agent and Force are also known as "actor", Instrument is known as "means", Experiencer as "dative" or "affected", Goal as "recipient", Location as "place" or "temporal", Factitive as "result" or "effected", Patient as "affected", "object(ive)", or "theme", Neutral as "theme", and range as "extent".

10. **Benefactive**: the person or thing for which an action is performed or the person who derives something from the actions of another;
11. **Factitive**: the object resulting from an action or state, having no prior existence but coming about by virtue of the action or state;
12. **Patient**: the person or thing affected by an action, or the entity undergoing a change;
13. **Theme**: the person or thing which undergoes an action, or that which is transferred or moved by an event but otherwise unchanged;
14. **Neutral**: the person or thing which is not changed or even acted upon, but simply present at an action:
15. **Range**: the specification or limitation of an action; and
16. **Role**: a person playing a role or part in an action or state.

> HINT: Note the differences between Patient, Theme, Neutral, and Factitive:
>
> *Jane broke the vase.* (Patient)
> *Jane moved the vase.* (Theme)
> *Jane saw the vase.* (Neutral)
> *Jane made a vase.* (Factitive)
>
> A Patient is changed in some way by the action, while a Theme is affected by the action, often by changing location, but is itself unchanged. A Neutral is present at the event but does not undergo an action. A Factitive comes about by virtue of the action itself.

2.1 The expression of thematic roles in English

Each underlying thematic role is expressed in a variety of ways on the surface in English, including case inflection, function word, and word order. In Table 10.2 are examples of the most common ways in which the different cases are expressed syntactically.

Both Agent and Force are generally expressed as the subject of an active sentence or in the *by*-phrase of a passive sentence and only rarely as object. Instrument is most often expressed in a *with* or *by* phrase. Experiencer is normally the subject of a state verb. The roles of Source, Goal, Path, and Location are normally expressed prepositionally: Source typically with *from, out of,* or *off,* Goal with *to,* Path with *via, along,* or *over,* and Location with *on, in, over, behind,* or *under.* However, Goal is a complex role including indirect objects (occurring in three different positions in the sentence) as well as locative goals and directional adverbs.

> HINT: Note that the expression of inalienable possession is more varied than the expression of alienable possession. In fact, the only meaning attributable to *The brown hair belongs to her* or *The brown hair is hers* is one of alienable possession – perhaps one of her hairs has fallen into the soup!

Table 10.2. The Syntactic Expression of Thematic Roles in English

AGENT	The logger felled the tree.
	The tree was felled by the logger.
FORCE	The wind felled the tree.
	The tree was felled by the wind.
	The logger felled the tree with a single blow.
INSTRUMENT	The tree was felled with an axe.
	The sweater was knitted by hand.
	He used an axe to fell the tree.
	Liquor killed him.
	His insights impressed us.
	He impressed us with his insights.
EXPERIENCER	Marianne is lonely/ feels lonely/ is suffering.
	I like the book.
	The news pleases me. The news enraged me.
	The news is pleasing to me.
SOURCE	I got the book from the library.
	I got some money out of the bank.
	The child took the book off the shelf.
	I borrowed the book from my teacher.
	His leaving pleases me
	('is a source of pleasure to').
	The sun gives off heat.
	A caterpillar turns into a butterfly.
	The plane left (from) Boston.
GOAL	I sent a card to my grandmother.
	I sent my grandmother a card.
	My grandmother was sent a card.
	My grandmother got a card from me.
	She reached the coast.
	I sent the package to Europe.
	A new idea came to me.
	We hung the picture on the wall.
	Susy jumped onto the step.
	I sent the child home.
	I walked upstairs.
	She did it {for love, to gain attention}.
PATH	Hannibal traveled over the mountains.
	We walked along the railroad tracks.
	The package came via London.
LOCATION	The dog is in the house/ on the chair/ under the table/behind the couch.
	I will return on Tuesday/ at noon.
	There are many people in the room.

(Continued)

Table 10.2. (Continued)

	The room has many people in it.
	That bottle contains alcohol.
	People filled the room.
	Vancouver is a rainy city.
POSSESSOR	
alienable:	He has/owns/possesses a dog.
	The dog belongs to him. The dog is his.
	The jewels are in his possession.
	That dog of his is a nuisance.
	His dog is a nuisance.
	The man with the dog/ who has the dog …
inalienable:	She has/?owns/?possesses brown hair.
	?The brown hair belongs to her.
	?The brown hair is hers.
	?The brown hair is in her possession.
	That brown hair of hers is beautiful.
	Her brown hair is beautiful.
	The man with the brown hair.
	The man who has brown hair
BENEFACTIVE	Jack answered the phone for José.
	The store special-ordered the book for me.
	The maitre d' reserved a place for our party.
FACTITIVE	They formed a circle.
	Sir Christopher Wren designed St. Paul's.
	The coach turned into a pumpkin.
	He baked a cake.
PATIENT	I baked the chicken.
	The chicken was baked by me.
	The chicken baked in the oven.
THEME	I put the letter on the table.
	The letter flew out of the window
	We read the letter.
NEUTRAL	The house costs a lot.
	The table measures three feet by three feet.
	Richard saw a tree on the horizon.
RANGE	The dress costs a hundred dollars.
	The man weighs 80 kilograms.
	We drove ten miles.
	He hummed a silly tune.
	He lived out his life happily.
ROLE	We made Lise treasurer of the club.
	Hilda is the principal of the school.

Benefactive should not be confused with Goal, though they are both expressed in a *for* phrase: Benefactive is paraphrasable with 'in the place of' or 'in the stead of', and only animate Goal may undergo indirect object movement (note the ungrammaticality of **Jack answered José the phone*). While Factitive, Theme, Patient, and Range are all expressed by the noun phrase immediately following the verb in an active sentence, only Factitive, Patient, and Theme, but not Range, are what are traditionally known as direct objects since they can become the subject in a passive sentence (note the ungrammaticality of **A hundred dollars is cost by the dress*). Neutral is expressed by both subjects and direct objects. Role is denoted by subject and subject or object complements.

There appears to be a hierarchy among thematic roles in their filling of subject position. Fillmore (1968) proposed a "subject hierarchy"[3] of Agent > Instrument > Patient; this says that if Agent is present, it will be subject, then Instrumental will be subject, then Patient will be subject. Choices of subject which violate this hierarchy, such as a Patient in subject position when an Agent is expressed in the same sentence, always represent a marked option, as in the case described, the passive.

2.2   Dual thematic roles

Often an argument may have more than one thematic role. Dual roles occur with arguments of certain classes of verbs:

1.   With verbs of motion, such as *run, walk, swim, wade, climb, stand up, roll over,* or *travel,* an animate subject is both Agent and Theme:

> *Lucille sat down.*   Lucille = Agent and Theme

The subject both performs an intentional action (sitting) and is acted upon, that is, changes location (from standing to sitting). However, some verbs of motion, such as *fall, slip, slide,* or *sink,* may be ambiguous in respect to thematic role:

> *Jack {fell down, slipped over the edge, slid down the slope}.*

Here Jack may have intentionally performed these actions (in which case *Jack* is both Agent and Theme), but another interpretation of the sentences is that these are events that simply befell Jack, without his being responsible (in which case *Jack* is Theme but not Agent). The second reading is obvious if one inserts "accidentally" in the sentences above.

2.   Ditransitive verbs and related verbs such as *give, sell, lend, hire, rent, supply, furnish, award, issue, show,* or *tell* show the following thematic structures:

> *They presented an award to Sam.*   They = Agent and Source
> Sam = Goal
> award = Theme

---

3.   The subject hierarchy has been formulated in different ways by different scholars. Another formulation is Agent > Benefactive > Theme/Patient > Instrument > Location.

They presented Sam with an award.   They = Agent and Source
Sam = Theme and Goal
award = Neutral

In each case, the subject is both an Agent performing the action of presenting and the Source of the award, while the indirect object, Sam, is the Goal of the award in the first sentence. However, since the position immediately following the verb seems to be closely associated with the Theme (or Patient) role, the movement of the indirect object to this position in the second sentence makes it Theme as well, or part of what the sentence is "about", as we will see in the next chapter.

3.   Verbs such as *spray, cram, pile, stack, smear, mark, engrave,* or *plant,* show the following thematic structures:

She sprayed paint on the wall.   She = Agent
paint = Patient
wall = Location
She sprayed the wall with paint.   She = Agent
the wall = Patient and Location
paint = Theme

Again, the position directly following the verb seems to correlate with the Patient role. The second sentence has a strong implication of 'completeness' or 'total affectedness', that is, that the wall is completely covered, since the wall is not only Location but also Patient in this case – the thing affected by the action – whereas in the first sentence the wall is merely Location.[4] Further evidence that the sense of 'total affectedness' is associated with the role of Patient or Theme is provided by sentences such as the following, in which the relevant argument is in subject position:

Bees swarmed in the garden.   the garden = Location
The garden swarmed with bees.   The garden = Location and Patient

The second sentence likewise has the implication of completeness. Note that not all verbs (with similar meanings) permit both variants. For example *cover* or *fill* allow only the first, while *put* allows only the second:

She {covered the wall with a quilt, filled the glass with water}.
**She {covered a quilt on the wall, filled water into the glass}.*
**She put the wall with a quilt.*
She put a quilt on the wall.

---

4.   This sense of completeness seems to hold up even when the sentences are passivized (suggesting that thematic roles are assigned at D-structure, before arguments are moved): *The wall was sprayed with paint* (completive) vs. *Paint was sprayed on the wall* (noncompletive).

4. Verbs like *steal, take, borrow, rent, hire, snatch, grab, get, rob, strip*, and *empty* allow the following thematic structures:

	The thief stole her jewels.	The thief = Agent and Goal
		her = Possessor
		jewels = Theme
	The thief stole the jewels from her.	The thief = Agent and Goal
		her = Source
		jewels = Theme
cf.	*The thief robbed her of the jewels.*	The thief = Agent and Goal
		her = Theme and Source
		jewels = Neutral

While the thief is Agent and Goal in all of these sentences, note that the three structures lead to different focuses, depending on the thematic roles of the other arguments. With all these verbs, then, the effect of moving a word to the position immediately following the verb is to give the noun the role of Patient or Theme, in addition to any other role it may have.[5] A final example of dual roles in simple sentences occurs in object complement constructions:

Howard jumped the horse over the fence.	Howard = Agent
	the horse = Theme and Agent
	the fence = Location
We made Alexandra captain.	We = Agent
	Alexandra = Theme and Experiencer
	captain = Role

In the first sentence, the horse is acted upon by Howard (hence Theme), but itself acts by jumping (hence Agent); this interpretation depends upon a view of horses as beings capable of intentional action. Note that in *Howard drove the car out of the driveway*, "the car" is only Theme, not Agent. In the second sentence, Alexandra is the entity acted upon by us (hence Theme) but is also the being affected inwardly by serving as captain (hence Experiencer).

Dual roles also come about in embedded structures, where a noun phrase has one thematic role by virtue of being the direct object of the higher verb, and another role by virtue of being the subject of the lower verb:

Susan forced Katy to write the letter.	Susan = Agent
	Katy = Theme and Agent
	the letter = Factitive

(Actually, it is PRO in the embedded clause that has the role of Agent, but we ignore this fine point here.) In contrast, the same argument, when it follows an *expect*-type verb, as

---

5. Patient supersedes Neutral. An argument with a Neutral role, when moved to object position, assumes the Patient role and loses its Neutral role.

in *Susan expects Katy to write the letter* has the sole role of Agent since it is the subject of *write*, but not the object of *expect*. In the following sentences, *Stu* is the Goal of her teaching, but in the first sentence he also has – by virtue of his position as direct object of the upper clause – the role of Theme:

> *She taught Stu to cook.*   Stu = Theme and Goal
> *She taught cooking to Stu.*   cooking = Theme, Stu = Goal

Again, the Theme role carries the implication of completeness, so that to say *She taught Stu to cook, but he can't cook a thing* is illogical, while to say *She taught cooking to Stu, but he can't cook a thing* seems acceptable.

> **HINT:** It is important to distinguish dual thematic roles from ambiguous roles, as in the following:
>
> *Crane made a speech for Crawford.*
> *Vanessa drowned in the river.*
> *Bill floated in the lake.*
> *Alex tasted the wine.*
>
> In the first sentence, Crawford is ambiguous between Goal and Benefactive, depending on whether Crane made a speech in support of Crawford or whether he made a speech in his stead. In the second sentence, Vanessa is Agent (and Patient) if she intentionally drowned herself, but only Patient if she accidentally drowned; likewise, Bill is Agent (and Theme) if he made himself float in the lake, but only Theme if through no actions of himself he floated (if it were, for example, his dead body that was being talked about). Finally, Alex may be Agent (and Experiencer) if he deliberately sampled the wine, but Experiencer only if he just happened to detect wine in a dish he was eating.

2.3   Thematic role grids

If we consider again the sentences given above:

> *The chef roasted the meat (over the fire).*
> *The fire roasted the meat.*
> *The meat roasted (over the fire).*

we can see that the verb *roast* (or more specifically the predicate *roast over*) seems to occur with an Agent role (*the chef*), an Instrument role (*the fire*), and a Patient role (*the meat*). It can be said that the predicate *roast* "assigns" thematic roles to its arguments. If we consider predicates more generally, we find that any particular predicate occurs uniquely with its own set of arguments serving particular thematic roles, just as it occurred with its own set of NP/AP/PP complements filling syntactic functions such as direct object, indirect object, etc. Some of these roles will be obligatory and some will be optional. As was the case with complement structures, information concerning the thematic roles of a predicate is given in the lexicon.

The thematic role assignment of a predicate can be specified in what is called a "thematic role grid", which is "the abstract specification of the thematic role possibilities for each predicate" (Frawley, 1992, p. 241). A thematic grid – what used to be called a case frame – is much like the syntactic subcategorization frame of a verb.

Consider the verb *open*, for example:

> *The key* (In) *opened the door* (Th).
> *The intruder* (Ag) *opened the door* (Th) *with the key* (In).
> *The wind* (Fo) *opened the door* (Th).
> *The door* (Th) *opened.*
> **The intruder* (Ag) *opened.* **The wind* (Fo) *opened.* **The key* (In) *opened.*

It assigns only one obligatory role, Theme, and optionally either Agent or Force and optionally Instrument. Note that Agent or Force or Instrument cannot appear alone. We thus represent the thematic grid as follows. It indicates optional case roles by the use of parentheses and mutually exclusive choices by *or*:

> *open*   Theme + (Agent or Force) + (Instrument)

Note that any optional adverbial elements would not be considered here, just as they are not considered in the subcategorization of verbs. Thus, in *The intruder opened the door at midnight*, *at midnight* is a Locative Role, but as an adjunct adverbial, it is ignored in the thematic grid.

Sample thematic grids are given in Table 10.3.

The verbs *melt* and *cook* are similar in both assigning the obligatory role of Patient and an optional Agent, Force, or Instrument. The verb *cook* differs in permitting Patient to be elliptical and also in allowing Factitive to replace Patient[6]. The semantically-related verbs *kill*, *die*, and *murder* differ in their thematic role assignments. While both *kill* and *murder* assign Agent and Patient roles, *kill* allows a nonintentional Force role to replace the Agent; *die* assigns only the Patient role. We are ignoring various circumstantial roles such as Location, which could optionally accompany these predicates, as in *Smithers died in the train station* (Location) or *The gangster murdered Smithers last night* (Location).

---

6.   The thematic grids shown in Table 10.3 for *melt* and *cook* are somewhat simplified. In fact, Instrument may occur either on its own (as shown) or with Agent (but not with Force):

> *Harry melted the butter with a microwave.*
> **The flame melted the butter with a microwave.*
> *Lily cooked the rice with a rice-cooker.*
> **The heat cooked the rice with a rice-cooker.*

Table 10.3. Thematic Grids for English Verbs

melt	Patient + (Agent or Force or Instrument)
	Harry (Ag) melted the butter (Pa).
	The flame (Fo) melted the butter (Pa).
	The microwave (In) melted the butter (Pa).
	The butter (Pa) melted.
	*Harry (Ag) melted. *The heat (Fo) melted.
	*The microwave (In) melted.
cook	Patient or Factitive + (Agent or Force or Instrument)
	Lily (Ag) is cooking rice (Pa).
	Lily (Ag) is cooking. (Patient is elliptical)
	The rice (Pa) is cooking.
	The rice-cooker (In) cooked the rice (Pa).
	The heat (Fo) cooked the rice (Pa).
	Dinner (Pa) is cooking.
kill	Agent (Instrument) or Force + Patient
	The {blow, gunshot, accident} (Fo) killed Smithers (Pa).
	The man (Ag) killed Smithers (Pa) with a knife (I).
	*The knife (In) killed Smithers (Pa).
	*Smithers (Pa) killed. *The {man, blow) (Ag, Fo) killed.
murder	Agent + Patient + (Instrument)
	The gangster (Ag) murdered Smithers (Pa) with a knife (In).
	The gangster (Ag) murdered Smithers (Pa).
	*The gangster (Ag) murdered.
	*Smithers (Pa) murdered.
die	Patient
	Smithers (Pa) died.
	*The man (Ag) died Smithers.
	*The accident (Fo) died Smithers.

Perception verbs fall into sets, depending on whether the subject is Experiencer or Agent, as in:

	hear	Experience + Neutral	*I* (Ex) *heard the noise* (Neu).
vs.	*listen (to)*	Agent + Goal	*I* (Ag) *listened intently to the lecture* (Go).
	see	Experiencer + Neutral	*I* (Ex) *saw a sudden light* (Neu).
vs.	*look (at)*	Agent + Goal	*I* (Ag) *looked at the old book* (Go).

Another use of the verb *look* occurs in *The dog looked happy (to me)*, or *The room looked clean (to me)*, where Neutral or Location is an obligatory role and Experiencer is optional. In the case of visual and auditory perception, there are separate lexical verbs, but in the case of tactile perception (as well as olfactory and gustatory perception), there is only one verb:

_____

Thus, our rules would need to be rewritten as follows:

> *melt* Patient + (Agent (Instrument) or Force or Instrument)
> *cook* Patient or Factitive + (Agent (Instrument) or Force or Instrument)

> *feel*₁ Experiencer + Neutral   *He* (Ex) *felt the presence* (Neu) *of an intruder in the house.*
>
> *feel*₂ Agent + Theme or Location   *He* (Ag) *felt the clothes* (Th) *to see if they were dry.*
> *He* (Ag) *felt under the blanket* (Lo) *to see what was there.*

For *feel*, one would also need to account for *His hands* (Th) *felt moist (to me)* and *The room* (Lo) *felt damp (to me)*; in this case, Theme or Location is obligatory and Experiencer is optional. Thematic grids can also distinguish between other stative and active verbs in the same way:

> *know*   Experiencer + Neutral   *I* (Ex) *know the answer* (Neu).
> vs. *learn*   Agent + Neutral   *I* (Ag) *learned the French vocabulary* (Neu).

Learn can also have an Experiencer subject, as in *I learned a lesson from that experience.*

Thematic grids provide a means for subcategorizing verbs. For example, using the set of arguments that particular verbs assign, Dixon (1991, pp. 102–113) sorts the verbs of English into eleven major classes. His AFFECT class includes verbs assigning an Agent, Patient, and Instrument role. Within this class, he identifies eight subtypes based on the way in which the Patient is affected: (a) TOUCH verbs (*touch, stroke*), (b) HIT verbs (*strike, kick*), (c) STAB verbs (*saw, slice*), (d) RUB verbs (*polish, lick*), (e) WRAP verbs (*cover, butter*), (f) STRETCH verbs (*twist, burn*), (g) BUILD verbs (*knit, cook*), and (h) BREAK verbs (*crush, explode*).

Another use of thematic grids is that they may predict syntactic behavior. For example, consider the sentences discussed above:

> *She* (Ag) *sprayed* <u>*paint*</u> (Pa) *on* <u>*the wall*</u> (Lo).
> *She* (Ag) *sprayed* <u>*the wall*</u> (Pa/Lo) *with* <u>*paint*</u> (Th).

Passive can move only Pa to subject position. Thus, we find:

> *Paint was sprayed on the wall (by her)*
> *The wall was sprayed with paint (by her)*

But we cannot move Lo or Th to subject position:

> *?The wall was sprayed paint on by her*
> **Paint was sprayed the wall with by her*

(In syntactic terms, we explained this constraint by pointing out that passive moves the dO but in most cases not the OP to subject position; see Chapter 8.)

Self-Testing Exercise: Do Exercise 10.2.

3. Predications

Now that we have examined the roles that noun phrases serve in a sentence, we can look at the way that the verbal predicates set the noun phrases in relation to one another; this may be called predication analysis. It is a way of analyzing the relational features of verbs, a method mentioned briefly in Chapter 6. It is useful in analyzing predicates expressing different views of a situation (different aspects: inchoative, continuative, egressive) as well as those belonging to a number of different semantic classes (stative, agentive, causative). We will look at a number of different types of predicates: descriptive predicates, cognitive predicates, and locative/possessive predicates

3.1   Descriptive predicates

The first type of predicate that we will look at is the **descriptive predicate**, which serves to qualify or identify the subject.

Stative and inchoative. Consider the following sets of sentences:

stative

1. *The pages <u>are yellow</u>.*   *The clothes <u>are dry</u>.*
    The water <u>is cool</u>.   *The children <u>are quiet</u>.*

inchoative

2. *The pages <u>yellowed</u>.*   *The clothes <u>dried</u>.*
    The water <u>cooled</u>.   *The children <u>quieted (down)</u>.*

3. *The pages {<u>got</u>, <u>turned</u>, <u>became</u>} yellow.*   *The pages <u>came to be yellow</u>.*
    The clothes {<u>got</u>, ?<u>turned</u>, <u>became</u>} dry.   *The clothes <u>came to be dry</u>.*
    The water {<u>got</u>, <u>turned</u>, <u>became</u>} cool.   *The water <u>came to be cool</u>.*
    The children {<u>got</u>, ?<u>turned</u>, <u>became</u>} quiet. *The children <u>came to be quiet</u>.*

All of these are 1-place predicates. The predicates in (1) are **stative**, denoting an unchanging condition (of yellowness, dryness, coolness, quietness). In the case of inanimates (i.e. *pages, water, clothes*), the subject is a Neutral role; in the case of animates (i.e. *children*), the subject is an Experiencer role. States are assumed to be basic, not further analyzable. Thus, the predicates in the sentences in (1) are analyzed with the stative feature BE (i.e. BE yellow, BE dry, BE cool, or BE quiet).

In contrast, the predicates in (2) and (3) are **inchoative**, denoting a change in state (from not yellow to yellow, wet to dry, not cool to cool, not quiet to quiet), or more precisely, the beginning of a new state. Again, this is a 1-place predicate, with a Patient (inanimate) or Experiencer (animate) subject role. Each set of sentences in (2) and (3) consists of structurally different but semantically synonymous sentences; they would have the same propositional analysis, with only the surface lexical items differing. The predicates in the sentences in (2) and (3) are analyzed with the appropriate stative feature plus an additional inchoative feature, which can be represented as CHANGE, BECOME, or simply COME; remember that semantic features are capitalized to distinguish them from actual words of the language (see Chapter 6). The feature analyses of the sentences is (2) are the following:

the pages (Pa) COME BE yellow
the clothes (Pa) COME BE dry
the water (Pa) COME BE cool
the children (Ex) COME BE quiet

Since we are analyzing the predicate, our feature analysis must include the arguments which are set in relation by the predicate. A kind of primitive paraphrase of our analysis of the first set of sentences is 'it come about that the pages be yellow' or 'the pages come to be yellow'. Another way of understanding relational features is as abstract predicates, each heading a separate proposition, as in the following tree for the first set of sentences in (2) and (3):

(3)

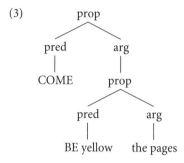

(Note that each proposition is an argument of the proposition above it.)

In (2), *The pages yellowed*, *The clothes dried*, *The water cooled*, and *The children quieted* the inchoative feature and the stative feature are amalgamated, or lexicalized, as a single surface verb *yellow*, *dry*, or *cool* (by a process known as "predicate raising").

In (3), each feature is lexicalized separately, the inchoative element as *turn*, *get*, *become*, or *come* and the stative element as *yellow*, *dry*, *cool*, or *quiet*. We can consider the first option as synthetic and the second option as analytic, as in the following sentences:

Synthetic	Analytic
The sky {cleared, blackened}.	*The sky became {black, clear}.*
	The sky turned {black, clear}.
	The sky came to be {clear, black}.

One reason for the existence of synthetic as well as analytic forms is that the latter avoid bald Su-V sequences and easily allow modification, since adjectival modification, (e.g. *The pages became {slightly, very, more} yellow*) is considered to be easier than adverbial modification, (e.g. *The pages yellowed {slightly, ?very much, ?more}*) As we will see below (Table 10.4), there are a variety of forms in synthetic/analytic sets, and synthetic forms do not always exist.

Causative and agentive.   Now consider the following sets of sentences:

inchoative-causative
4. *The sunlight <u>yellowed</u> the pages.*
    The heat <u>dried</u> the clothes.
    The breeze <u>cooled</u> the water.

5. *The sunlight {<u>made</u>, <u>turned</u>} the pages <u>yellow</u>.*
    The heat {<u>made</u>, ?<u>turned</u>} the clothes <u>dry</u>.
    The breeze {<u>made</u>, <u>turned</u>} the water <u>cool</u>.

6. *The sunlight <u>caused</u> the pages <u>to become yellow</u>.*
   The heat <u>caused</u> the clothes <u>to become dry</u>.
   The breeze <u>caused</u> the water <u>to become cool</u>.

These sentences are all **causative**, denoting something bringing about a change of state in an entity. They involve a 2-place predicate, with a Force role (the causer) and a Patient role (the thing that is altered). We will propose a causative feature CAUSE. Because the predicate involves a change, we must also include the feature of COME in our analysis, thus:

CAUSE COME BE {yellow, dry, cool}

Again, the sets of sentences in (4), (5), and (6) are structurally different yet semantically synonymous, and the predicates in each set are analyzable as follows:

The sunlight (Fo) CAUSE the pages (Pa) COME BE yellow
The heat (Fo) CAUSE the clothes (Pa) COME BE dry
The breeze (Fo) CAUSE the water (Pa) COME BE cool

A rough paraphrase of the first yields 'the sunlight cause the pages to come to be yellow'. Since these sentences are causative (the feature CAUSE) and inchoative (the feature COME) as well as stative, we call them "inchoative-causative". The three features may find expression as a single lexical item, *yellow*, *dry*, or *cool* (as in 4), or the causative and inchoative feature may be lexicalized together as *make* or *turn* separate from the stative feature (as in 5), or each feature may be lexicalized separately (as in 6), where CAUSE surfaces as *cause*, COME as *become*, and the statives as *yellow*, *dry*, and *cool*. An analysis of the three features as separate predicates produces the following tree:

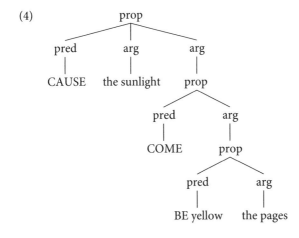

(4)

Finally, consider the following sentence:

inchoative-agentive
7. *?Orlando <u>yellowed</u> the pages.*
   Orlando <u>dried</u> the clothes.
   Orlando <u>cooled</u> the water.

8. *Orlando {made, turned} the pages yellow.* (cf. *Orlando painted the pages yellow.*)
   Orlando {?made, *turned} the clothes dry.
   Orlando {made, ?turned} the water cool.

9. *Orlando caused the pages to become yellow.*
   Orlando caused the clothes to become dry.
   Orlando caused the water to become cool.

These sentences are **agentive**, involving a human agent who intentionally brings about a change in state in an entity. They consist of a 2-place predicate with an Agent and a Patient role. We analyze these sentences with the additional agentive feature DO, thus DO CAUSE COME BE, as follows:

> Orlando (Ag) DO CAUSE the pages (Pa) COME BE yellow
> Orlando (Ag) DO CAUSE the clothes (Pa) COME BE dry
> Orlando (Ag) DO CAUSE the water (Pa) COME BE cool

(While CAUSE always cooccurs with DO and could probably be omitted, we retain it here, since DO does not always cooccur with CAUSE.) These sentences can be termed "inchoative-agentive". Notice that the sentences in (7) lexicalize all of the features in one verb, those in (8) lexicalize the agentive, causative, and inchoative features as a verb and the stative feature separately as an adjective, and those in (9) lexicalize the agentive plus causative features as a verb, the inchoative feature as a second verb, and the stative feature as an adjective. While the agentive forms are almost identical to the causative forms, they are rather more restricted.

The propositional tree for the first set of agentive sentences would be the following:

(5)

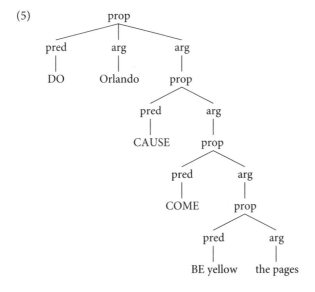

Table 10.4. Stative, Inchoative, and Causative/Agentive Forms

a.	warm – warm – warm	open – open – open
	empty – empty – empty (out)	clear – clear – clear (away)
	slow – slow – slow (down)	thin – thin – thin (out)
	quiet – quiet – quiet (down)	narrow – narrow – narrow
b.	full – fill – fill	hot – heat – heat (up)
c.	torn – tear – tear	rotten – rot – rot
	closed – close – close	melted/molten – melt – melt
	drained – drain – drain	locked -lock – lock
d.	ripe – ripen – ripen	broad – broaden – broaden
	wide – widen – widen	red – redden – redden
	black – blacken – blacken	deep – deepen – deepen
	stiff – stiffen – stiffen	strong – strengthen – strengthen
e.	*-en*	
	moist – become moist – moisten	cheap – become cheap – cheapen
	sharp – become sharp – sharpen	
	-ify	
	beautiful – become beautiful – beautify	
	-ize	
	sterile – become sterile – sterilize	fertile – become fertile – fertilize
	modern – become modern – modernize	passive – become passive – passivize
	en-	
	large – become large – enlarge	rich – become rich – enrich
	Ø	
	dirty – become dirty – dirty	free – become free – free
	hollow – become hollow – hollow	ready – become ready – ready
f.	brushed – become brushed – brush	halved – become halved – halve
	cashed – become cashed – cash	sliced – become sliced – slice
	hammered – become hammered – hammer	plowed – become plowed – plow

The same surface form, *yellow, dry, cool,* or *quiet,* can be stative, inchoative, or inchoative-causative/agentive. Other examples of such sets of forms are given in Table 10.4, where a variety of different formal correspondences can be seen:

1. We see sets in which the three forms are the same, with the possible addition of a particle (Table 10.4a).
2. The stative (or adjectival) form differs from the other two (10.4b).
3. The past participle serves as the stative form, as in (10.4c). The past participle may be a "regular" form such as *closed* or a relic form such as *rotten* which is no longer used as a true past participle: *The food has rotted* not **The food has rotten.*[7]

---

7. *Melt* is an interesting case since the relic form seems to be restricted to describing only certain substances: *The lava is molten* but not **The cheese is molten.*

4. Derivation may also be involved. The suffix -en can form the inchoative and causative/ agentive forms (10.4d). (The form *strengthen* exhibits a minor phonological change which fronts the "o" vowel of *strong*. Can you think of another example of this sort?)
5. In (10.4e) and (10.4f), we find sets in which one of the forms is missing and must be supplied by an analytic form.

   - In many cases, the inchoative form is analytic and the causative/agentive form is the result of adding one of a variety of derivational affixes (10.4e).
   - In other cases, the past participle serves as the stative form with an analytical inchoative form, while a zero-derived "denominal" verb (one derived from the noun) serves as the causative/agentive form (10.4f).

Finally, all three forms may be different, as with *dead – die – kill*, or one may be analytical and the others different, as with *cold – turn cold – chill* or *clean – become clean – cleanse*.

While the sentences that we have examined all involve predicate adjectives, the same analysis also applies to sentences with predicate nominals:

stative:	*Rachel is president of the student body.*
inchoative:	*Rachel became president of the student body.*
inchoative-causative:	*The election made Rachel president of the student body.*
inchoative-agentive:	*A majority elected Rachel president of the student body.*

Continuative and egressive.   Up to this point, we have been considering only the existence of states and the beginning of states, but it is also the case that states may come to an end and that states may continue. In order to provide an analysis of such situations, we need to introduce the feature negative, or NEG. The end or cessation of a state is termed **egressive** ('going out', in contrast to *ingressive* 'going in') and can be analyzed COME NEG, that is, 'to come to not be in a state'. To express the egressive, English does not have simple lexical verbs, as is the case with the inchoative, but must make use of auxiliary-like verbs called aspectualizers, including *cease, stop,* and *quit*.[8] The end of a situation may simply come about, or it may be caused by a force or agent:

egressive:	*The eaves stopped filling with leaves.*
	The clothes stopped drying.
	The water ceased to be cool.

---

8. Another set of aspectualizers, *begin, commence,* and *start,* focus on the initial stages of a state and may be combined with causative and agentive:

   a. *The pages began to yellow. The clothes began to dry. The water began to cool.*
   b. *The heat began to dry the clothes. The breeze started to cool the water.*
   c. *Orlando began to dry the clothes. Orlando started cooling the water.*

These might be analyzed with the additional feature BEGIN. This view of an action is often called *ingressive* (or *inceptive* or *inchoative*), while what we are here calling *inchoative* might be better understood by the traditional aspectual term *perfective*.

egressive-causative:	*The wind stopped filling the eaves with leaves.*
	The heat stopped drying the clothes.
	The refrigerator quit cooling the water.
egressive-agentive:	*We stopped filling the eaves with leaves.*
	We stopped drying the clothes.
	We quit cooling the water.

To express the continuation of a state – the **continuative** – English makes use of the aspectualizers *continue*, *stay*, and *remain* and causative-agentive *keep* or *retain*:

continuative:	*The eaves continued to fill with leaves.*
	The clothes stayed dry.
	The water remained cool.
continuative-causative:	*The wind continued to fill the eaves with leaves*
	The heat kept the clothes dry.
	The refrigerator caused the water to remain cool.
continuative-agentive:	*We continued to fill the eaves with leaves.*
	We kept the clothes dry.
	We caused the water to stay cool.

> **HINT:** Note that the expression of continuation differs from the expression of the simple stative. When we use a form such as *stay*, there is an implication that the situation might have stopped but did not; the stative has no such implication. For example, when we say *The clothes stayed wet*, the expectation is that the clothes might have become dry, but didn't. When we say *The clothes are wet*, there is no such implication.
>
> Thus, we analyze continuative forms as containing the features NEG COME NEG 'to not come to not be in a state' (which is, of course, logically the same as COME, with the two negative "canceling" one another).

Negative. Stative, inchoative, continuative, and egressive may also be negated:

negative-stative:	*The eaves aren't full of leaves.*
	The clothes aren't dry.
	The water isn't cool.
negative-inchoative:	*The eaves didn't fill with leaves.*
	The clothes didn't dry.
	The water didn't cool.
negative-continuative:	*The eaves didn't continue to fill with leaves.*
	The clothes didn't stay dry.
	The water didn't remain cool.
negative-egressive:	*The eaves didn't stop filling with leaves.*
	The clothes didn't stop drying.
	The water didn't cease cooling.

The forms are analyzed as follows:

negative-stative:	NEG BE	(e.g. the water NEG BE cool)
negative-inchoative:	NEG COME BE	(e.g. The water NEG COME BE cool)
negative-: continuative	NEG NEG COME NEG BE which is equivalent to COME NEG BE	(e.g. the water NEG NEG COME NEG BE cool/the water COME NEG BE cool)
negative egressive:	NEG COME NEG BE	(e.g. the water NEG COME NEG BE cool)

> **HINT:** Note that negative-egressive is equivalent to the continuative ('it didn't stop' = 'it continued'); thus, if the clothes didn't stop being dry, they continued to be dry.
> Negative-continuative is equivalent to egressive ('it didn't continue' = 'it stopped'); thus, if the clothes didn't continue being dry, they stopped being dry.

Negative-inchoative, negative-continuative, and negative-egressive can also be combined with causative or agentive, e.g.:

negative-inchoative-causative:	*The refrigerator didn't cool the water.*
negative-inchoative-agentive:	*We didn't cool the water.*
negative-continuative-causative:	*The refrigerator didn't keep the water cool.*
negative-continuative-agentive:	*We didn't keep the water cool.*
negative-egressive-causative:	*The refrigerator didn't stop cooling the water.*
negative-egressive-agentive:	*We didn't stop cooling the water.*

3.2   Cognitive predicates

With the features, COME, CAUSE, and DO, and stative predicates, we can analyze a number of different types of predicates. The first that we will consider are **cognitive predicates**, which denote cognitive states and events within the mind.

1. stative:

    BE

Ex +	*Ryan knows Chinese.*
Neu	*Kristin was aware of the facts of the case.*
	Carol knows Alison.

2. inchoative:

    COME BE

Ex +	*Ryan learned Chinese as his mother tongue.*
Neu	*Kristin became aware of the facts of the case.*
	Carol {got, came} to know Alison. Carol met Alison.

3. inchoative-causative/ agentive:

    DO CAUSE COME BE   Ag +   *Ryan learned Chinese as an adult.*
                       Ex +   *Shihong taught Ryan Chinese.*
                       Neu   *Pete {told, informed} Kristin of the facts of the case.*
                              Beverly introduced Carol to Alison.

> **HINT:** Throughout this section, we are using BE to represent the stative concept, though it would often be more appropriate to use the relevant stative verb. Thus, *Ryan knows Chinese* could be analyzed as:
>
>   Ryan BE knowledgeable Chinese
>
> or more simply as:
>
>   Ryan KNOW Chinese.

Since one learns one's first language apparently effortlessly, it might be possible to view the predicate *learn* as purely inchoative, as in (2). Generally, however, learning a language requires conscious effort by the learner, so in (3), *learn* is seen as agentive. Here, Ryan acts upon himself in order to learn Chinese: Ryan DO CAUSE Ryan COME KNOW Chinese.

4. continuative:

    NEG COME   Ex +   *Ryan remembers Chinese.*
    NEG BE   Neu   *Kristin continues to be aware of the facts of the case.*
                        Carols continues to be acquainted with Alison.
                        Carol remembers Alison.

5. continuative-causative/agentive:

    DO CAUSE NEG   Ag or Fo   *A short stay in China made Ryan remember*
    COME NEG BE   + Ex +   *Chinese.*
                    Neu   *Pete kept Kristin aware of the facts of the case.*
                                Carol kept in touch with Alison.

6. egressive:

    COME NEG BE   Ex + Neu   *Ryan forgot Chinese.*
                               Kristin ceased to be aware of the facts of the case.
                               Carol ceased to know Alison. Carol forgot Alison.

7. egressive-causative/agentive:

    CAUSE COME   Fo +   *Time away from China made Ryan forget his*
    NEG BE   Ex + Neu   *Chinese.*

3.3 Locative and possessive predicates

If we introduce the stative feature COINCIDE, we are able to analyze a large number of locative and possessive predicates. **Locative predicates** express the location of an entity in time or space, while **possessive predicates**, since possession can be treated as a special kind of location, express the location of an entity coincidental with a person.

In the case of statives, the place role is understood as Locative or Possessor.

1. stative-locative:

COINCIDE	Neu +	*Gabriel is {at school, in the house, behind the garage, under*
	Lo	*his bed}.*

    The vase sits on the mantle. The mantle has a vase on it.
    The umbrella is standing in the corner.
    The book is lying on the table.

    stative-possessive:

COINCIDE	Neu +	*Sam {has, owns, possesses} a book.*
	Po	*The book is Sam's.*

    Sam has brown hair.

    > **HINT:** The correct analysis of sentences with predicates such as *lie, sit,* or *stand* depends on the animacy of the subject. An inanimate subject is clearly static and does not "do" anything to remain in a position; thus, the sentence *The umbrella is standing in the corner* would be unambiguously analyzed as umbrella COINCIDE corner. But an animate subject must supply energy, that is, do something, to remain in a position; thus, it seems, *Kate is standing in the corner* is better analyzed as Kate DO CAUSE COINCIDE Kate corner (agentive-locative), not as Kate COINCIDE corner.

In the case of inchoatives, the place role is understood as Goal or Possessor:

2. inchoative-locative:

COME	Th +	*Brigitte {got to, reached, arrived at} the top of the*
COINCIDE	Go	*mountain.*

    The bus ran into the house.
    The ball rolled into the street.
    A fly fell into his drink.

    inchoative-possessive:

COME	Th +	*Joe {got, acquired, obtained, received} a book.*
COINCIDE	Po	

3.　inchoative-causative-locative:

CAUSE COME	Fo +	*The wind blew the dust into the house.*
COINCIDE	Th +	*The waves carried the raft out to sea.*
	Go	*The hurricane flattened his house.*[9]
		Lightening felled the tree.

inchoative-causative-possessive:

CAUSE COME	Fo +	
COINCIDE	Th +	*?His will donated his fortune to the university.*[10]
	Po	

4.　inchoative-agentive-locative:

DO CAUSE	Ag +	*Carol {put, placed, stood, laid, piled} a book on the desk.*
COME	Th +	*Kate {sat down, stood up, lay down, rolled over}.*
COINCIDE	Go	*The mover {pushed, dragged} the box down the ramp.*
		The child rolled the ball to his friend.
		The mad driver drove the car into the building.
		She {ran, skated, skipped} to the end of the block.
		The company {mailed, shipped, couriered} the package to the customer.
		He planted {ideas in her head, roses in the garden}.
		She {painted the wall, watered the plants, saddled the horse, wrapped the package, loaded the car}.
		He {bottled the wine, landed the fish, seated the guests}.

inchoative-agentive-possessive:

DO CAUSE	Ag +	*The teacher {gave, presented, rented, lent, took, sold,*
COME	Th +	*awarded, donated} the book to Maya.*
COINCIDE	Po	

Note that in a sentence such as *Kate sat down*, Kate acts upon herself to cause a change in her position (to an understood goal) – Kate DO CAUSE Kate COME COINCIDE (chair) – in contrast to a sentence such as *Kate is sitting down* (like *Kate is standing in the corner*, discussed above), where Kate acts upon herself to maintain a position.

The predicate often contains the means by which the change in location is effected, e.g.:

> *She skipped to the end of the block.* = She DO CAUSE herself COME COINCIDE the end of the block (by skipping)

9.　In the case of sentences such as *The hurricane flattened his house* and *Lightening felled the tree*, the goal (the ground) is implicit.

10.　It is difficult to think of a force causing someone to come into possession of something.

The company couriered the package to the customer. = The company DO CAUSE the package COME COINCIDE the customer (by couriering)

The verb may also lexicalize the Theme role, e.g. *water*, or the Goal role, e.g. *land*:

She watered the plants. = She DO CAUSE water COME COINCIDE the plants
He landed the fish. = He DO CAUSE the fish COME COINCIDE land

In the continuative, the place role is Location or Possessor (as with statives).

5. continuative-locative:

NEG COME	Neu + Lo	*The papers {remained, stayed} on the table.*
NEG COINCIDE		

continuative-possessive:

NEG COME NEG	Neu + Po	*She continued to own the company.*
COINCIDE		

6. continuative-causative-locative:[11]

CAUSE NEG	Fo + Neu	*The water kept him afloat.*
COME NEG	+ Lo	*The tornado left his house standing.*
COINCIDE		

7. continuative-agentive-locative:

DO CAUSE NEG	Ag + Neu	*She {stayed, remained} on the bucking horse.*
COME NEG	+ Lo	*She (intentionally) left her purse at home.*
COINCIDE		*We keep our motor-home in the back yard.*

continuative-agentive-possessive:

DO CAUSE NEG	Ag + Neu	*She held on to her jewels.*
COME NEG	+ Po	*He didn't sell his stocks.*
COINCIDE		*They didn't give up the family home.*

Finally, with the egressive, the place role is Source or Possessor (cf. the place role with inchoatives, which is Goal or Possessor).

8. egressive-locative:

COME NEG	Th + So	*The leaves fell from the trees.*
COINCIDE		*The ghost vanished from the room.*
		The train departed from the station.
		The child disappeared.

---

11. Again, possessive meanings are difficult to imagine.

| | | *The fog cleared.*[12] |
| | | *The bird molted.*[13] |

egressive-possessive:

| COME NEG | Th + Po | *She lost her keys.* |
| COINCIDE | | *He dropped a few pounds.* |

9. egressive-causative-locative:

| CAUSE COME | Fo + Th | *The wind blew the leaves from the trees.* |
| NEG COINCIDE | + So | |

egressive-causative-possessive:

| CAUSE COME | Fo + Th | *?The cave gave up its secrets.* |
| NEG COINCIDE | + Po | |

10. egressive-agentive-locative:

DO CAUSE	Ag + Th	*The sheriff {left, departed from} town.*
COME NEG	+ So	*Joanne stripped the wallpaper from the wall.*
COINCIDE		*Amanda {took, removed, pulled, dragged} the box from the cupboard.*
		He dropped the ball from the roof.
		Felicity drove the car out of the garage.
		She {peeled the apple, dusted the furniture}.
		She removed the spot from the shirt.
		They {unearthed the treasure, mined the diamonds}.

egressive-agentive-possessive:

DO CAUSE	Ag +	*Sam {rented, took, bought, borrowed} the*
COME NEG	Th + Po	*book from Maya.*
COINCIDE		*Janice gave up her apartment.*

For a number of verbs, whether the predicate is inchoative or egressive depends on whether a Goal or a Source role cooccurs, e.g. *He dropped the ball {into the pool, from the roof}.* The verb may lexicalize the Theme role, as in the case of *dust*, or the Source role, as in *unearth*:

> *She dusted the furniture.* = She DO CAUSE dust COME NEG COINCIDE the furniture
> *He unearthed the treasure.* = He DO CAUSE the treasure COME NEG COINCIDE the earth

---

12. The Source may be implicit, as in *The fog cleared (from the sky).*

13. A sentence such as *The bird molted* could be understood as Feathers COME NEG COINCIDE the bird.

The oppositeness of inchoative and egressive can be seen clearly in the morphology of English, as the privative marker *un-* attaches to many inchoative forms to create egressive forms, e.g. *wrap – unwrap, saddle – unsaddle, cork – uncork, cover – uncover, load – unload.* The verb lexicalizes the Theme role in both cases.

Self-Testing Exercise: Do Exercise 10.3.

One of the things that this approach to predicates and arguments does is to cast doubt on the traditional categories, N, A, V, etc., because in D-structure, there are no lexical categories, only thematic roles and relational features. Lexical categories seem to be just a surface structure phenomenon, added after transformations. They are an idiosyncratic aspect of language, unpredictable and accidental. D-structures may then be universal, while lexical categories and lexicalization are language specific.

Chapter summary

Now that you have completed this chapter, you should be able to:

1. determine the propositional structure of utterances;
2. identify the thematic roles of the noun phrases in a proposition; and
3. analyze different types of predicates using a set of semantic features, or abstract predicates.

Recommended additional reading

The primary source on thematic roles is Fillmore's (1968, 1977) work on case grammar. Good secondary discussions can be found in Frawley (1992, Chapter 5), Palmer (1994, especially Chapters 1 and 2), Kearns (2000, Sections 8.3 and 10.1–10.2), and Saaed (2009, Chapter 6). For a different view of thematic roles, see Dixon (1991).

A rather old, but very clear discussion of predication analysis is Parisi and Antinucci (1976, Chapter 4). Brown and Miller (1991, Chapter 18) and Kreidler (1998, Chapters 4 and 10) are good textbook discussions of both thematic roles and predication analysis; Hurford, Heasley, and Smith (2007, Chapters 19–20) contains exercises treating both topics.

Chapter 11

Information structuring and speech acts

1. Pragmatics and syntax
2. Speech act theory
3. The cooperative principle and conversational implicature

Chapter preview

The first half of the chapter introduces certain functional concepts such as topic/ comment and given/new and then explores how the options provided by the syntax of English have pragmatic consequences in how information is organized and presented in a text – what is known as "information structuring". The second half of the chapter then accounts for the functions of language in context using the framework of speech act theory. Direct speech acts and indirect speech acts are examined in detail, considering both their communicative force and the conditions on their appropriate use. Relevant to this discussion is the treatment of politeness in indirect speech acts. The chapter ends with a brief discussion of the cooperative principle and the pragmatic maxims that control conversation.

Commentary

To this point in the text, we have been treating traditional concerns of phonology, morphology, syntax, and semantics, but have not considered language above the level of the sentence. As we have discussed, pragmatics is the study of how language is used, how the forms of language are matched with or adapted to the functions that it is serving in context, and how language is used to create **discourse** – the sequence of two or more sentences, either written or spoken, that cohere in some way.

Another important part of pragmatics is the study of how contextual conditions influence the form of language used; contextual factors include such things as the social

positions or roles of the participants in discourse and their interpersonal relations of intimacy and power, the psychological states of the speaker (Sp) and hearer (H), the intentions,
beliefs, attitudes of Sp and H, and even the circumstances (physical and social) of speech.

As competent communicators, we almost instinctively know how to adapt our speech
to all of these many diverse conditions. This knowledge is known as **communicative competence**, the knowledge which enables Sp and H to understand and produce utterances in
relation to communicative purposes and the speech context. Our study of pragmatics, then,
will have two parts: the study of how language is used to create cohesive texts and the study of
how language use is determined by social interactions between individuals. We will attempt
to determine to what extent these aspects of language use follow identifiable principles.

1. Pragmatics and syntax

The conscious choice of one linguistic formulation over another is not restricted to literary
language. In everyday language use, we are always making choices about how to express
ourselves. The syntax of the language provides alternate ways of saying the same thing. We
have already seen, for example, how syntax may change thematic roles, and how such roles
may be determined (in part) by syntax. Why do we choose one way of saying something
over another? The choice often depends on contextual factors, especially the context of
the immediate discourse. We organize our discourse in a particular way in order to create cohesive and coherent texts, for example, to emphasize (foreground) or deemphasize
(background) aspects of our discourse or to fit our contribution into an ongoing discourse.
This process is called **information structuring**; the language provides a variety of means
for achieving our ends of arranging material for specific effects in discourse.

1.1 Basic distinctions

Before we look at the various options provided by English syntax for structuring information, we must define a number of key terms. These terms represent basic semantic distinctions which are universal, not language-specific.

Given and new information.   **Given** (or **old**) **information** is already known to the participants, having been "given" in the preceding discourse, while **new information** is not
known to the hearer, being introduced into the discourse for first time. Given information
may be evoked either textually or situationally or it may be inferrable (Prince, 1981). That
is, it may be mentioned explicitly in the previous discourse; it may be part of the communicative context (e.g. the 1st and 2nd persons participating in the discourse are always
given); or it may be information shared privately by the participants in the discourse,
information assumed to be culturally known, or information implied by something already

introduced into the discourse, for example by being part of the thing or in close association with it. Given information may be introduced by the same or another speaker. If assumed, it need not be overtly referred to at all. The subject of the sentence is typically given information. Given information is expressed in abbreviated ways, by, for example, pronouns or unstressed nouns. In contrast, new information is either brand new or unused for some period (Prince, 1981). It must be expressed fully and explicitly, in full noun phrases, with more stress, and with modifiers spelled out in full. The predicate of the sentence is typically new information. Table 11.1 summarizes what constitutes given versus old information.

Table 11.1. Given versus New Information

Given Information	New Information
already known to the participants (i.e. part of the communicative context or assumed to be culturally known)	not known to the hearer
a. explicitly mentioned in the preceding discourse; or	introduced into discourse for the first time or unused for some period
b. part of the communicative context (e.g. the interlocutors *I* and *you*); or	
c. implied by something already introduced into the discourse (e.g. by being part of the thing or in close association with it); or	
d. not overtly referred to but assumed knowledge or information shared privately by the discourse participants	
expressed in abbreviated ways (e.g. by pronouns or unstressed nouns)	expressed fully and explicitly (e.g. by full noun phrases, with more stress, and with modifiers spelled out in full)

Consider the following short discourse:

(1) *I must tell you about my move.* (2) *First, the movers arrived two hours late.* (3) *Then, they damaged my new couch.* (4) *The upholstery on the back is badly ripped.* (5) *And they dropped two boxes of dishes.* (6) *What a nightmare!*

In (1), the first person *I* (the speaker) and the telling are old information being given in the communicative context but the "move" is new information. In (2), though they are appearing for the first time, the "movers" are given information, since they can be assumed from the context of the move. The movers continue to be given information in (3) and again in (5) and are referred to pronominally; the "new couch" is new information and set out in a full NP. In (4), the "upholstery" is given information because it can be assumed from the context of the couch (almost all couches are upholstered); furthermore, the back is a subpart of the couch itself, so it too is given information and it is not necessary to specify "the back (of the couch)". Sentence (5) shows the usual pattern of given information ("they") and then new information ("dropped two boxes of dishes"). Finally, the subject (the move) can be omitted altogether in (6), since it is given information.

Topic and comment.[1]   The **topic** is what an utterance is about, its starting point, its center of attention, or the perspective from which it is viewed. It is usually the subject of the sentence. The **comment** is what is said about the topic; it is usually the predicate of a sentence. The usual situation is for the topic to be given and the comment to be new information, as in *They damaged my new couch.* This is a sentence about the movers (the topic); it says of the movers that they damaged the new couch (the comment). A less typical, but possible, situation is for the topic to be new and the comment to be old information, as in the following: *As for my chair, it got ripped too.* Here, the chair is new information, introduced for the first time; it is the topic of the sentence. "getting ripped too" is in the context of the discourse old information, but it functions as a comment about the couch. *As for* and *speaking of* are special linguistic means for marking topic.

> **HINT:** A test for topic is that it answers the question "Tell me something about X [i.e. the topic]"; in this case, "Tell me something about your move" or, less likely, "Tell me what happened yesterday".

Although the examples given have all equated the topic with the subject of the sentence, which is a simple NP, we will see below that there are many structures in which the topic is not the grammatical subject; furthermore, the topic may be an entire clause (e.g. *That my furniture was damaged was upsetting*) or another type of element moved to the front of the sentence.

Contrast.   Information is in **contrast** if it is in opposition to another entity or is selected from a larger set of entities. Noun phrases in contrast may be linguistically marked by *only* and are typically expressed with stress. In the following "Phyllis" contrasts with "most of my high school friends":

> *Most of my high school friends have moved away; only Phyllis still lives in town.*

Note that "Phyllis" would not be in contrast if the discourse were *(even) Phyllis has now left town.* The noun phrase to which a noun phrase stands in contrast may follow *rather than* (e.g. *Phyllis rather than Amanda still lives in town*), or it may not be expressed, but just implied or part of the context. Furthermore, both the subject and the predicate may be contrastive, as would be the case if the above discourse continued *and Phyllis has died.*

Contrastive information bears some resemblance to new information; however, new information picks out one entity from an unlimited set of possibilities, whereas

---

1.   Other terms used for topic and comment are *theme* and *rheme*, although sometimes these designate structural positions in the sentence, as opposed to conceptual notions.

contrastive information picks out one entity as opposed to another entity or a limited set of other entities.

Definite and indefinite.   Information is **definite** if the referent of the noun phrase is familiar to the hearer, while it is **indefinite** if the referent is novel, or unfamiliar to the hearer.

> **HINT:** Proper nouns, pronouns, and nouns preceded by the definite article or demonstratives are usually definite; the speaker assumes that the hearer will be able to identify the referent.
>   Nouns preceded by the indefinite article or *any* are usually indefinite; the speaker assumes that the hearer cannot identify the referent.

The combination of the notion of definiteness with the notion of givenness provides four possibilities:

1.   indefinite + new   *A couple I know just returned from a vacation in Africa.*
2.   indefinite + given   *They visited four countries – a vacation they'll never forget.*
3.   definite + given   *They went on a photographic safari in Tanzania.*
4.   definite + new   *The guide on their trip was excellent.*

While it is usual for new information to be indefinite and given information to be definite (as in cases 1 and 3), given information may be indefinite if it is not necessary for the hearer to identify the referent (case 2) or new information may be definite if it can have only one possible referent (case 4).

Specific, nonspecific, and generic.   Information is **specific** if it denotes a particular entity in the real world, while it is **nonspecific** if it denotes no particular entity in the real world.

> **HINT:** Pronouns and proper nouns are usually specific, though some pronouns, such as general *you, one,* or *they,* are nonspecific, as in *You never can tell, One must consider all options, They never tell you anything,* where no person is being referred to.
>   A test for specific is whether the noun can fit in the slot: *There is a certain _____.*

Combining specificity with definiteness yields the following possibilities:

1.   specific + definite   *Tomorrow I'm going to polish the car.*
2.   nonspecific + indefinite   *I dream of buying an expensive car.*
3.   specific + indefinite   *I saw a car I liked yesterday.*
4.   nonspecific + definite   *I'm going to buy the first car off the production line.*

The underlined expression in (1) refers to a particular car in the real world which the hearer can identify; in (2) it refers to no particular car, and thus the hearer cannot identify it; and in (3) it refers to a particular car but the hearer cannot identify it. Note that it is rather odd to refer to no particular entity which the hearer can identify, though it can occur, as shown in (4).

Generic refers to a set, whereas specific refers to particular members of the set. Generic nouns refer to the class or category ("genus") of an entity. They can be either definite or indefinite:

1. generic + indefinite   *Houses* are expensive.   *A house* is expensive.
2. generic + definite   *The house* is the largest purchase you will make in your lifetime.

Contrast a specific reference such as *The house is beautiful* (the particular house that I am looking at). Note the use of the so-called "bare plural" *houses* with generic reference.

Self-Testing Exercise: Do Exercise 11.1

1.2 Syntactic options and pragmatic considerations

We will now analyze the different syntactic possibilities that can be exploited in order to manipulate the semantic distinctions we have been considering. These syntactic structures provide means to structure information in different ways; we will find that discourse functions are to some extent matched with syntactic form.

Fronting. **Fronting** consists of the movement of a word, phrase, or clause to the beginning of the sentence, as in the underlined NPs in each set below:

> *Which holiday do you like best?*
>   *Christmas I like best; Thanksgiving I like least.*
> *Do you swim or run for exercise?*
>   *Swimming I do everyday, but running very seldom.*

Fronting the information results in its becoming the topic of the utterance. Fronting is thus a means of echoing topically what has been contextually given. The fronted element must be given information in the context; it must also be definite:

> **A movie I want to see.*
> *That movie I want to see.*

Note that the fronted element may be contrastive (as in the example of preferring Christmas to Thanksgiving above). In the first sentence below, what is most important or salient is that the assignment is "for tomorrow's class" and hence it must be part of the structure that is fronted:

> *?That assignment I finally finished for tomorrow's class.*
> *That assignment for tomorrow's class I finally finished.*

Fronting may serve to put in end-focus the most important part of the sentence: *A very short run I can handle*. Note that fronting does not change the grammatical subject of the sentence, nor does it alter any of the functional relations within the sentence, but the fronted element necessarily becomes the new topic of the utterance.

In addition to the fronting of obligatory NPs, it is also common to front optional adverbial elements. **Adverb fronting** may move adverbial words, phrases, or clauses to the front of the sentence and topicalize them:

> *Suddenly the car careered across the road.*
> *The day after tomorrow/on Tuesday I hope to return home.*
> *Working late, I missed my train.*
> *If you don't stop playing that loud music, I'll go crazy.*
> *Because Rosa's leaving next week, we're planning a party.*
> *When we get home, let's watch a video.*

The fronting of adverbial subordinate clauses, especially conditional and causal clauses, is particularly common. Another phenomenon is adverb fronting + inversion (of subject and verb/auxiliary), which can occur with some locative and negative adverbs:

> *Out popped a clown.*
> *On the porch sat a fierce dog.*
> *Never have I seen such a sight.*
> *Here comes my brother.*
> *There is the book I was looking for.*

Inversion has the effect of end-focusing the subject (see below).

Left-dislocation. Like fronting, **left-dislocation** moves a word, phrase, or clause to the beginning of the sentence, but it has the additional feature that it leaves a pronominal copy of the fronted element in its original place:

> *Annette, she'll be home late tonight.*

Left-dislocation serves to reintroduce given information that has not been talked about for a while; this information becomes topic. It is frequently contrastive and usually definite. Left-dislocation is typically used when going through a list:

> *There are several interesting people we have met here, Mary, Sue, or Sarah. Sarah, we met her the first day we arrived.*

Note that a NP can be left-dislocated from any position in the sentence; it may even be dislocated from an embedded sentence:

> *That party, Alison said that Susie had organized it for Dean.*

Cleft sentence. A **cleft sentence** consists of a dummy *it* subject, a form of BE, an item in "cleft" position (underlined below), and a relative clause. Beginning with the standard declarative sentence *Jane gave this book to Bill on Saturday because it was his birthday*, cleft-ing yields the following possible transformations:

> *It was <u>this book</u> [NP] that Jane gave to Bill.*
> *It was <u>Bill</u> [NP] who Jane gave this book to.*
> *It was <u>Jane</u> [NP] who gave this book to Bill.*
> *It was <u>on Saturday</u> [PP] that Jane gave this book to Bill.*
> *It was because it was his birthday [S̄] that Jane gave this book to Bill.*

Note that a NP, a PP, or an S̄ (aA) may be clefted.

The clefted element is new information and comment, while the relative clause is given information and topic. The clefted element is frequently contrastive: e.g. *It was <u>Jane</u> (not Sally) who gave this book to Bill.* Cleft sentences have the effect not only of isolating the new information but also of putting the main focus towards the end of the sentence.

Though the information in the relative clause of a cleft is given information, the speaker does not assume that the hearer is thinking about it at the moment, merely that the hearer can readily deduce or recall it. For this reason, cleft sentences may begin a narrative.

> *It was in these neighborhoods that I received the best education I ever had.* (COCA: NEWS)

Occasionally, the information in cleft position is not new, as in the following short discourse:

> *His ego knew no bounds. It was his egoism* (given) *that I despised, but it was his brilliance* (new) *that I admired.*

Finally, note that although the cleft sentence alters the syntactic form of the sentence, it does not alter the functional relations within the sentence (apart from moving an element into cleft position).

Pseudocleft sentence.   A **pseudocleft sentence** consists of a free relative clause, a form of BE, and either a NP or a VP (underlined below). Beginning with the standard declarative sentence *Henry studied linguistics at university*, pseudoclefting involves the following transformations:

> *What Henry studied at university was <u>linguistics</u> [NP].*
> *What Henry did was <u>study linguistics at university</u> [VP].*

The new information is expressed in the NP or VP following BE. The pseudocleft structure thus postpones the sentence focus (the new information) to the end. The new information may also be contrastive, as in *What Henry studied at university was linguistics (not mathematics).* The free relative is given information, which the reader or hearer must be thinking about; hence, pseudocleft sentences cannot begin narratives. It is also the topic of the sentence.

Note that reversing the order of the NP/VP and the free relative changes the topic: <u>Linguistics</u> (topic and given) *was what Henry studied at university.*[2] A structure similar to the pseudocleft is what can be called a *one*-cleft sentence, which permits the same reversal of order:

> *The one who studied linguistics at university was <u>Henry</u>* (comment and new).
> <u>*Henry*</u> (topic and new) *was the one who studied linguistics at university.*

Stress.   Both new information and contrastive information receive phonological stress (as well as higher pitch):

> *Sálly (not Júne) will help.*
> *I sent it to Sálly (not Júne).*

In neutral cases, the last major element (noun, verb, or adjective) in a sentence is stressed:

> *I ate a piece of cáke.*
> *He's is the next róom.*
> *I stóod there. We sáw them.*

In these cases, either the stressed element is new or the entire sentence is:

> *Fido got bitten by a snáke.*

But stress can move elsewhere in a sentence to mark information that is new or contrastive:[3]

> *The ców jumped over the moon.*   (as opposed to the horse)[4]
> *The cow júmped over the moon.*   (as opposed to stepped)
> *The cow jumped óver the moon.*   (as opposed to around)
> *The cow jumped over the móon.*   (neutral/unmarked case; or as opposed to the sun)

Note that the topic would also differ in these cases.

Passive.   Unlike the constructions discussed so far, an agented passive alters the functional relations within the sentence: the agent of the active sentence is expressed in a *by*-phrase in the passive sentence and the direct or indirect object of the active sentence becomes its subject. Compare:

> <u>*The jury*</u> *awarded <u>Jim</u> first prize.*   <u>*Jim*</u> *was awarded first prize <u>by the jury</u>.*

---

2. This interpretation depends upon the stress falling within the free relative (on *Henry* or *university*). If *linguistics* is stressed, it becomes the new information and comment.

3. Stress is discussed in further detail in Chapter 3.

4. Compare the alternative strategy of using a cleft sentence: *It was the ców that jumped over the moon.*

This has the effect of making the passive subject given information and the topic of the sentence. Look at the following exchange:

a.   *Did you hear the news about Adele?*
b.   <u>*She*</u> *was given a commendation by the council.*
b'.   *?*<u>*The council*</u> *gave her a commendation.*

It would be odd to respond to the above question, which introduces "Adele" and makes her topic of the discourse, with (b'), since this suggests that the council is the topic and given information. Subjects of agented passives tend to be definite: *?A cake was baked by Adelaide* (cf. *The cake was baked by Adelaide*).

While agentless passives make the passive subject topic, they are used in additional contexts:[5]

1.	when the agent is unknown	*The bakery was broken into last night.* (COCA:FIC) *Our garage was vandalized a few days ago.* (COCA:NEWS)
2.	when the speaker does not wish to specify the agent	*I was threatened the first day I got here.* (COCA:NEWS) *I was falsely accused of something that I did not do.* (COCA:SPOK)
3.	when the agent is general, nonspecific, or obvious from context	*I was thrown out of New York University in my first year there.* (COCA:SPOK) *Initially the contestants were told that the show would be broadcast nationally on the ION Network.* (COCA:SPOK)
4.	when an NP other than the agent is topic	*Some security measures were agreed to verbally.* (COCA:NEWS) *"Evening News" anchor, Katie Couric, was altered to make her to appear 20 pounds thinner.* (COCA:SPOK) *It was given a standing ovation at a Lincoln Center screening.* (COCA:NEWS) *Atlanta's two principal downtown depots – Terminal Station and Union Station – were demolished in the 1970s.* (COCA:NEWS)

The passive is also used to create cohesion in a text by beginning a sentence with the NP which ended the previous sentence (e.g. *Tanya walked up behind Harry. He was startled* vs. *?She startled him*). Moreover, the passive is characteristic of certain styles of writing,

---

5.   Despite prescriptive prohibitions against the passive, it has many legitimate uses in all types of discourse.

such as instructions or technical/scientific writing where the intended agent is general or understood. In scientific writing the use of the passive is connected with the replicability of results.[6]

Note the alteration of topic in the following, as well as the effect of deleting the agent:

> *You can buy a good computer for $1500.*
> *$1500 can get you a good computer.*
> *A good computer can be bought for $1500.*

Another passive form is the so-called "passive of experience", which uses *have*:

> *She had her hopes dashed by the news.* (< The news dashed her hopes.)
> *He had his reputation tarnished by the rumors.* (< The rumors tarnished his reputation.)

Rather than making the active object the topic (as in *Her hopes were dashed by the news*), the passive of experience makes the experiencer "she" the topic.[7] The construction of BE plus past participle has the same effect of making the experiencer the topic:

> *We were amused by the movie.* (< The movie amused us.)
> *I am frightened by the prospect of tackling that job.* (< The prospect of tackling that job frightens me.)

The past participles of *confuse, bore, disgust, amaze, puzzle,* and *worry* behave in the same way.

Other topicalizing transformations.   English does not have as many options here as other languages, but it still provides a number of permutations of word order which move elements leftwards into topic position or make them part of the topic. This process is called **topicalization**. In the following cases, the underlined segment is part of the topic:

1. *tough*-movement: So called because it may occur with the adjective *tough* (as well as *difficult, hard, easy,* and *impossible*), *tough*-movement moves the object of an infinitive to the subject (and hence topic) position of the matrix clause:

    <u>*The right answer*</u> *is difficult to find.* (< To find the right answer is difficult. It's difficult to find the right answer.)

2. subject-to-subject raising: This transformation moves, or "promotes", the subject of the *that*-clause occurring with *likely, certain, happen,* and *seem* to the subject position in the matrix clause:

---

6.   On the teaching of the passive to second-language learners, see Chapter 12.

7.   The passive of experience should not be confused with causative *have* + past participle, e.g. *She had her suit dry-cleaned* (= 'caused her suit to be dry-cleaned').

Sam is certain to foot the bill. (< That Sam will foot the bill is certain. It is certain that Sam will foot the bill.)

3. subject selection: Certain verbs in English permit "lexical packaging variants" (Foley & Van Valin, 1985) in which a different NP is placed in subject, or topic, position. These may exist as matched pairs of verbs (e.g. *buy/sell, imply/infer*):[8]

> *John bought a computer from Bill. Bill sold a computer to John.*
> *The news {pleased, amused} me. I liked the news.*
> *The volcano emitted poisonous fumes. Poisonous fumes emanated from the volcano.*
> *The newspaper account implied that the drive was drunk. I inferred from the newspaper account that the driver was drunk.*

Sometimes the same verb may permit the selection of different subjects, perhaps with a change in accompanying preposition (e.g. *rent from* vs. *rent to*) or in the voice of the following infinitive (e.g. *need to V/need to be V-en*):

> *Canada grows a lot of wheat. A lot of wheat grows in Canada.*
> *The Smiths rented the cabin from Henry. Henry rented the cabin to the Smiths.*
> *I need to tune my bike. My bike needs to be tuned.*
> *The new regulations will benefit the entire community. The entire community will benefit from the new regulations.*

Finally, *there*-insertion (see below) also leads to a change in subject:

> *The tent has a hole in it. There's a hole in the tent.*

A variety of other transformations, although they do not move elements to subject position, allow some degree of leftward movement, altering the topical structure of the sentence:

1. dative (or indirect object) movement:
    As discussed in Chapter 7, ditransitive verbs allow variant orders, V dO *to/for* iO or V iO dO:

> *I gave the report to George.*
> *I gave George the report.*

Assuming unmarked sentence stress, the topic in the first instance might be considered "my giving the report to someone", with "George" being the comment, whereas the topic in the second instance might be considered "my giving George something", with "the report" being the comment. Contrastive stress could alter this topic/comment structure, as in the sentence *Í gave the report to George* (i.e. Jerry didn't give it to him), in which case "giving the report to George" can be considered the topic and "I" can be considered the new information and comment.

---

8. Other matched pairs of verbs include *give/take, teach/learn, borrow/lend, rob/steal, regard/strike.*

Similar to dative movement are the types of sentences discussed in Chapter 10, where again the leftward movement of an NP alters the topic:

Sentence	Topic	Comment
They loaded the cart with hay.	"their loading the cart"	"with hay"
They loaded hay onto the cart.	"their loading hay"	"onto the cart"
We sprayed the wall with paint.	"our spraying the wall"	"with paint"
We sprayed paint on the wall.	"our spraying paint"	"on the wall"

2. particle movement:

As discussed in Chapter 8, phrasal verbs allow placement of the particle before or after the direct object:

Sentence	Topic	Comment
He wore <u>out</u> the brakes.	"his wearing out (something)"	"the brakes"
He wore the brakes <u>out</u>.	"his wearing the brakes"	"out"

The second sentence also conveys a completive sense resulting from the final placement of the particle *out*, which carries heavy stress.

Note the completive sense – captured by the converted verbs *down* and *out*[9] – in the second sentence in each set below:

> *He cut down the tree.*   *He cut the tree down.*
> = He downed the tree by cutting.
> *She rubbed out the error.*   *She rubbed the error out.*
> = She "outed" the error by rubbing.

Focusing transformations. There are two important positions in the sentence, the beginning and the end. We have just seen that by moving an element to the beginning, we can make it the topic. We can also choose to move an element to the end of the sentence, the second prominent position. This has the effect of **focusing**, thus emphasizing, that element. Two such focusing transformations – *it*-extraposition and extraposition from NP – have been previously discussed in Chapter 9. Focusing operations include those exemplified in Table 11.2.

Table 11.2. Focusing Operations in English

1. *it*-extraposition:
   <u>It</u> has been confirmed <u>that Boris won the election</u>.
   < <u>That Boris won the election</u> has been confirmed.
   It happens <u>that I'm related to the Russian royal family</u>.
   < *<u>That I'm related to the Russian royal family</u> happens.
2. extraposition from NP:
   A new course will be offered <u>which explores the influence of global warming</u>.
   < A new course <u>which explores the influence of global warming</u> will be offered.

(Continued)

---

9. See Chapter 5 on the conversion of particles to verbs.

Table 11.2. (Continued)

3. subject–verb inversion:
   In the room were several people I knew.
   < Several people I knew were in the room.
   Down the hill careened an out-of-control car.
   < An out-of-control car careened down the hill.

4. *there*-insertion:
   There were two children killed in the fire.
   < Two children were killed in the fire. The fire killed two children.
   There was a (*the) beautiful Ming vase on the mantelpiece.
   <?A beautiful Ming vase was on the mantelpiece.
   There seems to be no solution.
   < *No solution seems to be.

5. heavy NP shift:
   You should see before it leaves <u>the show at the art gallery</u>.
   < You should see <u>the show at the art gallery</u> before it leaves.

6. quantifier postposing:
   The ships in the harbor <u>all</u> suffered damage in the storm.
   < <u>All</u> the ships in the harbor suffered damage in the storm.

7. right-dislocation:
   <u>She</u>'s gone out shopping, <u>your mother</u>.
   We want <u>him</u> caught, <u>that criminal</u>.
   <u>He</u>'s amazing, <u>that man is</u>.
   <u>He</u>'s jilted her, <u>Jack has</u>.

1. *It*-extraposition: This operation involves the movement of a *that*-clause to the end of the sentence. In the second example of *it*-extraposition given above (*it happens that …*), extraposition is obligatory.

2. Extraposition from NP: This operation involves the movement of a relative clause or other modifying element out of the NP to the end of the sentence (see Chapter 9).

3. Subject–verb inversion: This operation is similar to subject–auxiliary inversion discussed in Chapter 8, but involves a main verb; it occurs in cases where there is a sentence-initial locative or directional adverbial, or, less commonly, where there is an adjectival phrase (e.g. *Near the entrance stood a solemn-looking man*) or a participial phrase (e.g. *Destroyed in the fire were two large warehouses, Lying by the fire was a large dog*).

4. *There*-insertion: This operation occurs with copula verbs and definite noun phrases; note that in cases of heavy subjects, *there*-insertion is the preferred structure while in other cases, it may be obligatory.

5. Heavy NP shift: This is the shifting of a heavily modified NP to the end.

6. Quantifier postposing: This entails the movement of a quantifier such as *each* or *all* from its position before the NP to after the NP.

7. Right-dislocation is the reverse of left dislocation (see above); however, right-dislocation differs from left-dislocation in that both a noun phrase and an auxiliary can right dislocate, as in the second example given in Table 11.2.

Relative clauses.   Finally, we consider the differences between restrictive and nonrestrictive relative clauses in terms of information structuring. Nonrestrictive relative clauses modify only specific nouns, which may be either definite or indefinite:

specific, definite	*I am going to remodel <u>the kitchen</u>, which is fifty years old.*
specific, indefinite	*Yesterday I saw <u>a beautiful kitchen</u>, which had granite counters.*
nonspecific, indefinite	**I dream of having <u>a new kitchen</u>, which has a gas stove.*
nonspecific, definite	**<u>The biggest kitchen</u>, which I can afford, costs $10,000.*

Restrictive relative clauses modify either specific or nonspecific nouns, both definite and indefinite:

specific, definite	*I'm going to buy <u>the cabinets</u> that I looked at yesterday.*
specific, indefinite	*Yesterday I saw <u>a model kitchen</u> that I can afford.*
nonspecific, definite	*I'm going to build <u>the biggest kitchen</u> that I can afford.*
nonspecific, indefinite	*I dream of having <u>a kitchen</u> that has sufficient storage space.*

> **HINT:** Another way to view this restriction is to see the function of a restrictive relative clause as that of turning a nonspecific noun into a specific one.

1.3   Information structuring in a passage

One way of seeing the effects of syntactic differences on information structuring is to compare a "normal" passage (Text A) with an "odd" passage (Text B) (taken from Brown & Yule, 1983, p. 128):

Text A	Text B
1. *The sun's shining, it's a perfect day.*	1. *It's the sun that's shining, the day that's perfect.*
2. *Here come the astronauts.*	2. *The astronauts come here.*
3. *They're just passing the Great Hall;*	3. *The Great Hall they're just passing;*
4. *perhaps the President will come out to greet them.*	4. *he'll perhaps come out to greet them, the President.*
5. *No, it's the admiral who's taking the ceremony.*	5. *No, it's the ceremony that the admiral's taking.*

In sentence (1), the cleft sentence in Text B treats the facts that something is shining and that something is perfect as given and topic, as well as in the forefront of the hearer's consciousness; furthermore, the sun and the day are possibly contrastive. In contrast, the corresponding sentence in Text A treats only the sun as given (in the sociophysical context).

Sentence (2) of Text B treats the astronauts as given and topic, though they are obviously new information; the inverted sentence (2) of Text A has the advantage of end-focusing this new information.

The fronting in sentence (3) of Text B topicalizes the Great Hall, which is treated as old information, whereas the unmarked structure in Text A rightly presents the astronauts as old information (expressed pronominally)/topic and the Great Hall as new information/comment.

In the right-dislocated structure in sentence (4) in Text B, the President is end-focused; he is initially presented as given information (expressed pronominally), though he is in fact new information. The effect of adverb fronting in sentence (4) in Text A is to topicalize the notion of doubt and to make the rest of the sentence new information.

Sentence (5) in both texts is a cleft sentence, but in Text B the cleft position is occupied by the wrong word; the new (and contrastive) information here is not the ceremony (ceremony can be inferred from the context), but the admiral, as in the version in Text A.

While this is an obviously concocted example, you should be able to see the importance of effective information structuring in the construction of cohesive and coherent texts.

Self-Testing Exercises: Do Exercises 11.2 and 11.3.

2. Speech act theory

An important means of accounting for the function of language in context, developed within the philosophy of language, is **speech act theory**. The first writer on this topic was the British philosopher J.L. Austin, whose Harvard lectures were published in a book entitled *How to Do Things with Words* (1962). Austin's student, the American philosopher John Searle, has carried on his work, first in a book entitled *Speech Acts* (1969) and in subsequent work. Linguists have utilized speech act theory in the area of pragmatic analysis; but it has also been applied to literary texts (see, e.g. Pratt, 1977).

Austin observes that – contrary to the position of logicians – not all utterances have "truth value". He thus makes a fundamental distinction between "constatives", which are assertions which are either true or false, and "performatives", which cannot be characterized as either true or false, but are, in Austin's terms, "felicitous" (happy) or "infelicitous" (unhappy). These are utterances by which the speaker carries out an action, hence the term *speech act*. Examples of performatives are utterances such as the following:

> *Today I name a new chairman of the Joint Chiefs…* (COCA:SPOK)
> *I refuse to believe that my father would make such a deal with you.* (COCA:FIC)
> *… we authorize the use of force for certain specified purposes…* (COCA:SPOK)
> *I promise you that America will get stronger and more united, more prosperous, more secure.* (COCA:SPOK)
> *I congratulate you for a fine campaign.* (COCA:SPOK)
> *I bet you a million dollars they're on auto pilot.* (COCA:SPOK)
> *I swear it wasn't me.* (COCA:FIC)

Simply by uttering each of these statements, the speaker performs an action, such as naming, authorizing, promising, congratulating, and betting, These actions require no further action other than the linguistic action in order to be what they are. As in the examples given, speech acts may contain an explicit **performative verb**, which is normally first person and simple present tense (i.e. *I name, I congratulate, I promise, I bet*, and so on). Performatives can occur with "hereby", as in the sentence *We hereby promise that we shall accomplish the task entrusted to our care to the utmost of our abilities* (COCA: FIC). Searle rejects Austin's distinction between constative and performative, interpreting all utterances as performatives, even those which we might understand as representing a state of affairs and hence true or false, for example, *It is raining*. He categorizes such a speech act as a representative (see below). Before looking at his categorization, however, we will consider how he analyzes speech acts and the bases he uses for his taxonomy.

2.1 Components of speech acts

Austin argues that every utterance can be understood as consisting of three parts:

1. a locutionary act, including both an utterance act and a propositional act; a locutionary act is the recognizable grammatical utterance (its form and meaning);
2. an illocutionary act, such as stating, promising, or commanding; an illocutionary act is the communicative purpose of an utterance, the use to which language is being put, or what the speaker is trying to do with his locutionary act, and
3. a perlocutionary act, such as persuading, annoying, consoling, or alarming; the perlocutionary act is the intended or actual effects of a locutionary act, the consequences these acts have on hearers' attitudes, beliefs, or behavior. The effects of a speech act are not conventional but depend upon the context.

The same locutionary act, such as *It's raining*, may be a statement of fact about the weather, advice to carry an umbrella, or a warning that one shouldn't go outside.

The semantic structure of a speech act consists of its **illocutionary force** (abbreviated **IF**), and its **propositional content** (abbreviated **prop**). Illocutionary force is the way in which the propositional content (the state of affairs expressed in a given sentence) is to be taken (i.e. as a statement, a question, etc.). Illocutionary force is expressed by performative verbs, but also by a variety of other means, including sentence type, word order, stress, intonation, punctuation, or mood or modal auxiliaries. The same proposition [He not smoke] may have different illocutionary forces:

He doesn't smoke.   *Doesn't he smoke?*   *Would that he didn't smoke.*

An utterance is thus analyzable as IF(prop). Either the illocutionary force or the proposition can be negated, represented ~IF(prop) and IF(~prop) (using the logical symbol for negation ~), for example *I do not promise to be there on time* (negating the illocutionary force) and *I promise not to hurt you* (negating the propositional content).

Every illocutionary act, Searle postulates, can be understood in respect to three features:

1. its illocutionary point or force;
2. its direction of fit; and
3. its expressed psychological state.

Direction of fit refers to the way in which language relates to the external world: it may be word-to-world, where the speaker intends what he says to match things in the world, to be true or false statements about the world, or it may be world-to-word, where the speaker intends the world to come to match what he says, to bring about or effect a change by saying something. The British philosopher G.E.M. Anscombe (1957, p. 56) exemplifies these directions of fit with a story of a detective following a shopper in the food market. The shopper's list of things to buy has a world-to-word fit, but the detective's list of what the shopper has selected has a word-to-world fit. (The shopper may not get everything on his or her list, but note that we could not say that his or her list is "false" in this case. If the detective misses out an item, however, we could say that his or her list is wrong.)

> **HINT:** To better understand this, consider the following analogy. In the nonlinguistic domain, the word-to-world fit would be analogous to a drawing of a house, which is meant to be a true representation of an existing structure, whereas the world-to-word fit would be analogous to an architect's blueprint of a house, which is meant to lead to the construction of such a structure. If the house departs from the plans as construction proceeds, we would not say that the original blueprints were "false", but if the drawing does not depict the house as it is, we would say that it is "inaccurate" or "misleading" (i.e. "false").

The **expressed psychological state** of a speaker of a speech act, also known as the **sincerity condition** of a speech act, consists of the beliefs and attitudes of the speaker, the psychological state of the speaker towards the propositional content of the speech act. If you say something and do not have the corresponding state of mind, then your speech act is insincere (what Austin called "infelicitous"), for example, promising to do something without intending to do so. If you say something and deny the corresponding psychological state, then your utterance is absurd, for example, promising to do something and then denying that you intend to do it.

2.2   Taxonomy of speech acts

In an article entitled "A Taxonomy of Illocutionary Acts" (1979), Searle uses the three factors – illocutionary force, direction of fit, and expressed psychological state – as the basis for classifying all speech acts. He identifies six classes:[10]

---

10.   A number of different taxonomies have been proposed (see Hancher, 1979).

1. **Directives**: A directive speech act is an attempt by Sp to get H to do something. Examples of directives are ordering, commanding, requesting, pleading, begging, entreating, daring, inviting, insisting, suggesting, permitting, and challenging. Questioning also constitutes a type of directive because it is an attempt to get H to perform the speech act of answering. Any action requested must be future and voluntary, because it is impossible to ask someone to perform an action in the past or to do something which is not a matter of human will. For example, *I command you to leave yesterday* or *I order you to grow taller* are "infelicitous" commands. Note that volition here does not refer to one's liking to do what is commanded, but merely to its being humanly possible. The expressed psychological state of a directive is that Sp must want or wish for H to do something; to say *Turn on the t.v., but I don't want you to* is contradictory. The direction of fit is world-to-word, for S is attempting to get the world to resemble his or her words. With directives, as all speech acts, either the proposition or the illocutionary force can be negated. And we have names for these different negated forms:

Command	IF(prop)	*I command you to close the door.*
Forbid, Prohibit	IF(~prop)	*I command you not to close the door. I forbid you to close the door.*
Permit	~IF(prop)	*I don't command you to close the door.*
	~IF(~prop)	*I don't command you not to close the door = you may close the door.*

2. **Commissives**: With a commissive speech act, Sp commits himself or herself to the performance of an action. Examples of commissives are promising, vowing, pledging, threatening, guaranteeing, agreeing, consenting, and refusing. Again, the promised action must be future and voluntary; note the infelicitousness of *I promise to leave yesterday* or *I promise to grow taller*. The expressed psychological state is that Sp intends to do something. The direction of fit is world-to-word.

3. **Representatives**: Here Sp represents a state of affairs. Examples of representatives are affirming, declaring, describing, claiming, stating, explaining, classifying, insisting, telling, hypothesizing, recalling, mentioning, attesting, confiding, emphasizing, and predicting. A representative commits Sp to the truth of the proposition. The expressed psychological state is one of belief, though Sp's state of belief can be more or less strong, ranging from conviction (as in affirming) to tentativeness (as in predicting). The direction of fit of a representative is word-to-world in that the description is meant to match the situation in the world.

4. **Expressives**: In an expressive speech act, Sp expresses a psychological state about the situation or state of affairs denoted by the proposition. Examples of expressives are thanking, apologizing, consoling, congratulating, greeting, welcoming, and deploring. The propositional content is something which affects Sp or H; note that it would be odd to say *I console you on the war in Afghanistan* or *I congratulate you on the Queen's eighty-fifth birthday* unless these events somehow affected H. As you are aware, however, many, if not most, expressives are highly conventionalized; Sp may say *Congratulations*

on your promotion even when he or she is intensely envious or *Thank you for the beautiful gift* even when he or she thinks the gift tasteless or useless. What is most important in these cases is that the utterance <u>counts as</u> an expressive, not that the psychological state is deeply felt. Expressives have no direction of fit, since the proposition is presupposed rather than asserted. For example, if Sp says *I am sorry about your car accident*, the occurrence of the car accident is being assumed, or presupposed, and this utterance would be infelicitous if a car accident had not occurred. The only exception is the optative mood (expressing a wish), which has a world-to-word direction-of-fit, for example *Would that it would rain, If only Noel would come.*

5. **Verdictives**: Sp expresses a value judgment or rates something. Examples of verdictives are assessing, ranking, rating, estimating, grading, diagnosing, calculating, and measuring. Verdictives may be a subcategory of representatives since the expressed psychological state of the speaker is belief in the value judgment, and the direction of fit is word-to-world.

6. **Declaratives**: Declaratives are the prototypical speech act. Here the Sp brings about a change in the world by uttering a locutionary act. Examples of declaratives are declaring war, seconding a motion, adjourning a meeting, firing, nominating, christening, finding guilty/innocent, betting, passing (in a game), divorcing, baptizing, arresting, and resigning. Generally Sp must hold some position in an extralinguistic institution in order for the speech act to be effective. However, there are two exceptions:

    a. in supernatural cases, as when God says *Let there be light*, or
    b. for ordinary speakers, when making statements about language, for example, defining, abbreviating, naming, calling, and dubbing.

    The direction of fit of a declarative is in both directions since the speaker is both representing a state of affairs and bringing it about at the same time. There is no psychological state expressed; the president can declare war or the prime minister can disband parliament no matter what his or her feelings about the action.

There may be hybrid speech acts which combine two different types of speech acts. For example, inviting is both a directive (Sp tries to get H to do something) and a commissive (Sp is committed to accepting H's actions) or a referee's declaring a foul is both a representative (Sp believes that a fouling action has occurred) and a declarative (by virtue of Sp saying that a foul has occurred, it is a foul, with the consequences that entail).

2.3   Appropriateness conditions on speech acts

The conditions under which a speech act can successfully be performed are called its **appropriateness conditions** (Austin's "felicity conditions"). They are the "unspoken rules" by which a speech act is governed, or its pragmatic presuppositions. They dictate how, when, where, and by whom a speech act can be performed felicitously, such as the circumstances of speech, the relationship of Sp and H, the beliefs and attitudes of the participants, and even the form of the speech act itself. Generally, the speaker believes that all the appropriateness conditions are met and presupposes that the hearer takes this for granted.

General appropriateness conditions on speech acts.   While each kind of speech act is subject to its own set of conditions, a number of general appropriateness conditions apply to all speech acts:

- propositional content condition: the content of the proposition of the speech act must be appropriate to its illocutionary force; for example, a prediction must concern a future event, and a report a present or past event.
- preparatory conditions: Sp and/or H must hold certain beliefs before a particular speech act can appropriately be performed, and the speech act must occur in a conventionally recognized context or the appropriate circumstances. Also, Sp must be in an appropriate position to perform the speech act.
- nonobvious condition: it must not be obvious that in the normal course of events the proposition of the speech act is occurring or will occur. (For example, if I command you to hand in your exam as you are putting your exam in my hand, my speech act would be inappropriate.)
- essential condition: the utterance counts as, or must be recognized by H as counting as, the performance of a particular type of speech act.
- sincerity condition: Sp is responsible for what he or she is saying and is sincere. H will assume Sp is being sincere.
- the relation of Sp to H must be correct; the speaker must have the right to speak as he or she does. For example, a different relation of the speaker in respect to the hearer is necessary to perform the speech acts of commanding (Sp superior to H), pleading (Sp inferior to H), or urging (Sp and H equals).
- the interests of Sp and/or H in respect to the propositional content must be appropriate. Note the very different interests of Sp in boasting or complaining, and the very different interests of H who receives a warning or advice, or congratulations or condolences:

  Let me {boast/complain} for a moment about what just happened to me.
  I {congratulate/console} you on your marriage.
  I {warn, advise} you not to speak to him. I {advise, *warn} you to speak to him.

- the strength or commitment of Sp to the speech act must be appropriate. For example, Sp has different degrees of commitment to the proposition when suggesting and insisting:

  I suggest that we go to a movie tonight. Why don't we go to a movie tonight?
  I insist that we go to a movie tonight.

- the speech act must relate to the previous discourse in an appropriate way. For example, answers and replies cannot begin a segment of discourse, though they may end it; conclusions must necessarily end a segment of discourse; and interjections or interruptions cannot either begin or end a segment of discourse:

  I {begin, end, interrupt} by pointing out …

-   the style or formality of the performance must be appropriate to the speech act. For example, one can announce on television, but generally not confide (daytime talk shows may be an exception); one can assert, report, or inform explicitly, but one can hint, insinuate, or intimate only indirectly.
-   an extralinguistic institution may be required for some speech acts, with Sp and/or H occupying certain positions within that institution, as is the case in excommunicating, arresting, convicting, or declaring man and wife.

> **HINT:** It is important to distinguish the appropriateness conditions on speech acts from general rules of conversational politeness, or social decorum since violations of either set of rules have quite different results. If appropriateness conditions are violated, the speech act is not or cannot be performed; if rules of conversational politeness are violated, the speech act is performed – it would count as the speech act – but it would be judged as rude. In other words, appropriateness conditions are constitutive rules, while rules of conversational politeness are regulatory rules (see Chapter 1). Remember that regulatory rules control already existing behavior (e.g. *When cutting food, hold the knife in the right hand*), while constitutive rules create or define new forms of behavior (e.g. *Checkmate is made when the king is attacked in such a way that no move will leave it unattacked*).

Appropriateness conditions on promising.   The appropriateness conditions on promising will serve as an example of the specific conditions relevant to one kind of speech act. The performer of the speech act of promising says the essential condition, expresses the sincerity condition, and presupposes the other appropriateness conditions:

-   propositional content condition: the proposition denotes a future act committed or performed by Sp.
-   preparatory conditions: Sp is able to do what he or she promises; H would prefer Sp's doing what is promised; and Sp believes H would prefer his doing it. Note the oddness of *I promise to kill you* as a promise, though it would work as a threat or warning.
-   nonobvious condition: it is not obvious to both Sp and H that Sp will perform the action in the normal course of events.
-   sincerity condition (expressed psychological state): Sp intends to do what he or she promises (and thinks it is possible to do it). If Sp meets the sincerity condition, the promise is sincere; if Sp does not have the proper intention, but purports to, the promise is insincere.
-   essential condition: Sp intends that the utterance will place him or her under an obligation to do what is promised; and Sp intends H to recognize that his utterance counts as a promise.

Note that "I promise" is one of strongest devices for indicating commitment, so it is often used not only when promising but also when uttering a forceful representative, as in: *Believe me, you'll quit before me, I promise you.* (COCA:NEWS)

Now consider Table 11.3. It gives a list of the appropriateness conditions on two directives (*request*, *question*), three representatives (*assert*, *advise*, *warn*), and three expressives (*thank*, *greet*, *congratulate*). The following abbreviations are used: Ac = action and E = event.

Table 11.3. Types of Speech Acts and their Appropriateness Conditions

Type of condition

Request
Propositional Content: Future Ac of H.
Preparatory: 1. H is able to do Ac. Sp believes H is able to do Ac.
          2. It is not obvious to both Sp and H that H will do Ac in the normal course of events of his or her own accord.
Sincerity: Sp wants H to do Ac.
Essential: Counts as an attempt to get H to do Ac.
Comment: Order and command have the additional preparatory rule that Sp must be in a position of authority over H. Command probably does not have the pragmatic condition requiring nonobviousness. Furthermore, in both the authority relationship infects the essential condition because the utterance counts as an attempt to get H to do Ac in virtue of the authority of Sp over H.

Assert, state (that), affirm
Propositional Content: Any proposition (prop).
Preparatory: 1. Sp has evidence (reasons, etc.) for the truth of prop.
          2. It is not obvious to both Sp and H that H knows (does not need to be reminded of, etc.) prop.
Sincerity: Sp believes prop.
Essential: Counts as an undertaking to the effect that prop represents an actual state of affairs.
Comment: Unlike argue these do not seem to be essentially tied to attempting to convince. Thus "I am simply stating that prop and not attempting to convince you" is acceptable, but "I am arguing that prop and not attempting to convince you" sounds inconsistent.

*Question**
Propositional Content: Any proposition or propositional function.
Preparatory: 1. Sp does not know 'the answer', i.e., does not know if the proposition is true, or, in the case of the propositional function, does not know the information needed to complete the proposition truly (but see comment below).
          2. It is not obvious to both Sp and H that H will provide the information at the time without being asked.
Sincerity: Sp wants this information.
Essential: Counts as an attempt to elicit this information from H.
Comment: There are two kinds of questions, (a) real questions, (b) exam questions. In real questions Sp wants to know (find out) the answer; in exam questions, Sp wants to know if H knows.

Thank (for)
Propositional Content: Past Ac done by H.
Preparatory: Ac benefits Sp and Sp believes Ac benefits Sp.

*In the sense of "ask a question" not in the sense of "doubt".

(*Continued*)

Table 11.3. (Continued)

Sincerity: Sp feels grateful or appreciative for Ac.

Essential: Counts as an expression of gratitude or appreciation.

Comment: Sincerity and essential rules overlap. Thanking is just expressing gratitude in a way that, e.g., promising is not just expressing an intention.

Advise

Propositional Content: Future act Ac of H.

Preparatory: 1. Sp has some reason to believe Ac will benefit H.

2. It is not obvious to both Sp and H that H will do Ac in the normal course of events.

Sincerity: Sp believes Ac will benefit H.

Essential: Counts as an undertaking to the effect that Ac is in H's best interest.

Comment: Contrary to what one might suppose advice is not a species of requesting. It is interesting to compare "advise" with "urge", "advocate" and "recommend". Advising you is not trying to get you to do something in the sense that requesting is. Advising is more like telling you what is best for you.

Warn

Propositional Content: Future event or state, etc., E.

Preparatory: 1. Sp has reason to believe E will occur and is not in H's interest.

2. It is not obvious to both Sp and H that E will occur.

Sincerity: Sp believes E is not in H's best interest.

Essential: Counts as an undertaking to the effect that E is not in H's best interest.

Comment: Warning is like advising, rather than requesting. It is not, I think necessarily an attempt to get you to take evasive action, Notice that the above account is of categorical not hypothetical warnings. Most warnings are probably hypothetical: "If you do not do X then Y will occur".

Greet

Propositional Content: None.

Preparatory: Sp has just encountered (or been introduced to, etc.) H.

Sincerity: None.

Essential: Counts as courteous recognition of H by Sp.

Congratulate

Propositional Content: Some event, act, etc., E related to H.

Preparatory: E is in H's interest and Sp believes E is in H's interest.

Sincerity: Sp is pleased at E.

Essential: Counts as an expression of pleasure at E.

Comment: "Congratulate" is similar to "thank" in that it is an expression of its sincerity condition.

(From John Searle, *Speech Acts: an Essay in the Philosophy of Language*, 66-67. © Cambridge University Press, 1969. Reprinted with the permission of Cambridge University Press.)

Self-Testing Exercise: Do Exercise 11.4.

2.4   Indirect speech acts

We often perform speech acts indirectly rather than directly, especially in spoken discourse. That is, by means of one explicit speech act, we actually perform another implicit one. But for such **indirect speech acts** to be successful, there must be some principle underlying them. How they work is that we give expression to one of the appropriateness conditions of the speech act we want to perform. This expression itself is the explicit speech act, a type of speech act such as a statement (representative), expressive, or question (directive), but it has the illocutionary force of the intended speech act. It "functions as" the implicit speech act. The clearest example of an indirect speech act is the indirect directive, because in polite social behavior, there is a tendency to avoid the direct imperative. In fact, in spoken discourse, there is a tendency to use no performatives at all, except as emphasis, often as parentheticals, "I tell you", "I promise", or "I declare".

Consider the directive *(I command you to) pass the salt*, expressed explicitly with a performative verb or imperative sentence. Appropriateness conditions on this directive are the sincerity condition (1) and the preparatory conditions (2). A speaker may perform this directive indirectly, then, by giving expression to either of these appropriateness conditions in the following ways:

1.   Sp has a wish or desire for salt/for H to pass the salt:
     I {would like, want} the salt.
     I {would like, want} you to pass the salt.
     It would be nice if you passed the salt.

2.   the action to be performed is a future, voluntary (able and willing) action of H:
     {Can, could, would} you pass the salt?
     Can you reach the salt?
     Would you mind passing the salt?
     Is it possible for you to pass the salt?
     Would it be possible for you to pass the salt?
     Would it be too much trouble for you to pass the salt?
     Do you think you can manage to pass the salt? (sarcasm)
     Why don't you pass the salt?
     Why not pass the salt? (there is nothing stopping you)

A test that these are all used as directives is the fact that they all take *please*, and negative responses to them could all include a phrase such as *I'm sorry*. Note the asymmetry here: it is usual to state Sp's desire and to question H's ability or willingness; the sincerity condition is related to the speaker, while the preparatory condition is related to the hearer:

     ?Do I want the salt?
     The salt is in front of you, Bill (so it is possible for you to pass it)
     You can pass the salt now.

It would also be possible to perform the directive indirectly by expressing the fact that Sp doesn't have what he wants, as in:

     The cook forgot the salt in this dish.
     This dish {needs, could use} salt.
     A little salt would help this dish.

(Note that these do not take final *please*, though they might be able to take initial *please*).

Indirect speech acts are idiomatic English, so they are not always translatable into other languages. However, indirect speech acts are not idioms. That is, it is not the case that there is one speech act with idiomatic meaning, that "Can you pass the salt" has the idiomatic meaning "Pass the salt!", just as "kick the bucket" has the idiomatic meaning "die". The words in indirect speech acts have their literal meaning; they are not a case of "noncompositionality" (see Chapter 5 on idioms). It is also not the case that the explicit speech act is somehow "defective". The question "Can you pass the salt?" is not defective in the way that "Can you eat Mt. Everest?" is. The former functions as a request and the latter does not. Finally, we should not understand the indirect speech as ambiguous; rather, the explicit speech act is being used in two ways.

When performing a speech act indirectly, we are actually performing two speech acts at the same time:

1. the literal, or explicit speech act, which is secondary, and
2. the nonliteral, or implicit speech act, which is primary.

In some contexts, both speech acts are functional. A person could acknowledge a literal speech act by responding, for example:

Literal speech act	Response to literal speech act
Can you reach the salt?	*No, it's too far away.*
Do you have the time?	*No, I don't wear a watch.*
Do you have a match?	*No, I don't smoke.*

In fact, all of the indirect forms of *Pass the salt* given above have uses where they are not directives, except those with *Why not*, *Why don't you*, and *How about*. Note also that in some contexts a speaker may want to deny the indirect speech act: *I'd like some salt, but I'm not asking you to pass it.* So the explicit speech act still has literal meaning and is used with literal meaning.

2.5   Politeness

Requests and orders tend to be especially threatening, since the speaker expects the hearer to comply with his/her wishes. To "soften" these speech acts, and simultaneously to enhance the chance of the hearer's compliance, speakers often employ politeness strategies. These may be of two types:

1. **Positive politeness** strategies: These strategies involve the speaker's catering to "positive face" (i.e. one's desire to be liked and/or approved of). They include the speaker's complimenting the hearer, using close or affectionate terms of address, and thanking the hearer or offering reciprocal kindness in exchange for a favor.

2.   **Negative politeness** strategies: These strategies involve the speaker's catering to "negative face" (one's desire not to be imposed upon). They include the speaker's using expressions of deference, apologizing, and making use of indirect speech acts.

Table 11.4 illustrates both positive and negative politeness strategies.[11]

Table 11.4. Positive and Negative Politeness

	Positive Politeness
Complimenting	Well, first of all, this is so *gracious of you* to do. (COCA:SPOK)
	I mean, it's very *generous of you* to have me. (COCA:FIC)
Using "close" terms of address	Please, *dear*, sit up. (COCA:ACAD)
	Honey, it's the last game of the season. (COCA:FIC)
Thanking	I *really appreciate* your joining us tonight. (COCA:SPOK)
	I am *extremely grateful* to the American people for the support they have given me over the last three years. (COCA:ACAD)
Offering reciprocal kindness	But remember, we are always ready to *return the favor*. (COCA:FIC)
	I could buy you a cappuccino, *in exchange for* the cigarette. (COCA:FIC)
	Negative Politeness
Using expressions of deference	We still need a partner for the member-guest, but you're *probably too busy* playing in the U.S. Open. (COCA:MAG)
	I know I'm *asking a lot*, but it doesn't have to be a permanent move. (COCA:FIC)
Apologizing	Dad, I wrecked your car, I'm *so sorry*. (COCA:SPOK)
	I *truly apologize* for how long it took us to activate emergency energies. (COCA:FIC)
Using indirect speech acts with orders or requests	Yes, *if you could* use the microphone, please. (COCA:SPOK)
	As a courtesy, *I was wondering if you could* upgrade my room. (COCA:MAG)

It should be stressed here that rules for politeness vary tremendously from one culture to another (and within a given culture, from one speech community to another). Other factors that play a role in the use of politeness strategies include the social distance of the interlocutors (i.e. is one of higher status than the other?), the formality of the context, the closeness of the conversational participants, their age, and their gender.

Look now at Table 11.5. It gives numerous examples of indirect directives, which are based on the appropriateness conditions of that type of speech act: Group 1 concerns the preparatory conditions on directives, Group 2 the sincerity conditions, Group 3 the

---

11.   This table draws on Curzan and Adams (2009).

propositional content, Group 4 the preparatory conditions, and Group 5 the reasonableness conditions.

Table 11.5. Sentences Conventionally Used in the Performance of Indirect Directives

GROUP 1:	Sentences concerning H's ability to perform Ac:
	Can/Could you be a little more quiet?
	You could be a little more quiet.
	You can go now (this may also be a permission = you may go now).
	Are you able to reach the book on the top shelf?
	Have you got change for a dollar?
GROUP 2:	Sentences concerning Sp's wish or want that H will do Ac:
	I would like you to go now.
	I want you to do this for me, Henry.
	I would/should be most grateful if you would/could do it for me.
	I would/should be most grateful if you would/could help us out.
	I'd rather you didn't do that any more.
	I'd be very much obliged if you would pay me the money back soon.
	I hope you'll do it. I wish you wouldn't do that.
GROUP 3:	Sentences concerning H's doing Ac:
	Officers will henceforth wear ties at dinner.
	Will you quit making that awful racket?
	Would you kindly get off my foot?
	Won't you stop making that noise soon?
	Aren't you going to eat your cereal?
GROUP 4:	Sentences concerning H's desire or willingness to do Ac:
	Would you be willing to write a letter of recommendation for me?
	Do you want to hand me that hammer over there on the table?
	Would you mind not making so much noise?
	Would it be convenient for you to come on Wednesday?
	Would it be too much (trouble) for you to pay me the money next Wednesday?
GROUP 5:	Sentences concerning reasons for doing Ac:
	You ought to be more polite to your mother.
	You should leave immediately.
	Must you continue hammering that way?
	Ought you to eat quite so much spaghetti?
	Should you be wearing John's tie?
	You had better go now. Hadn't you better go now?
	Why not stop here?
	Why don't you try it just once? Why don't you be quiet?
	It would be better for you (for us all) if you would leave the room.
	It wouldn't hurt if you left now.
	It might help if you shut up.
	It would be better if you gave me the money now.
	It would be a good idea if you left town.
	We'd all be better off if you'd just pipe down a bit.

(Continued)

Table 11.5. Sentences Conventionally Used in the Performance of Indirect Directives (Continued)

This class also contains many examples that have no generality of form but obviously, in an appropriate context, would be uttered as indirect requests, e.g.:

> You're standing on my foot.
>
> I can't see the movie screen while you have that hat on.

Also in this class belong, possibly:

> How many times have I told you (must I tell you) not to eat with your fingers?
>
> I must have told you a dozen times not to eat with your mouth open.
>
> If I have told you once I have told you a thousand times not to wear your hat in the house.

GROUP 6:   Sentences embedding one of these elements inside another; also, sentences embedding an explicit directive illocutionary verb inside one of these contexts. Would you mind awfully if I asked you if you could write me a letter of recommendation?

> Would it be too much if I suggested that you could possibly make a little less noise?
>
> Might I ask you to take off your hat?

(From John R. Searle, Expression and Meaning: *Studies in the Theory of Speech Acts*. Cambridge: Cambridge University Press, 1979.)

Self-Testing Exercise: Do Exercise 11.5.

3.   The cooperative principle and conversational implicature

How does the hearer recognize the presence of an implicit speech act? First, there are some conventional forms for performing various indirect speech acts. Second, the propositional content may make a difference, as in:

> *Can you reach the salt?*   vs.   *Can you reach the ceiling?*

Most importantly, there is an appropriateness condition on language use in general which is in force. This condition was identified by the philosopher Paul Grice (1989a, 1989b) and termed the **cooperative principle**: "Make your conversational contribution such as is required, at the stage at which it occurs, by the accepted purpose or direction of the talk exchange in which you are engaged" (1989a, p. 26). It is the principle that Sp has a communicative (or other) purpose in speaking and makes this purpose clear to H; likewise, H trusts that Sp has a purpose and will do his or her best to discern it. In order to ensure that hearers recognize their intent, speakers should make their conversational contribution such as is required at the stage at which it occurs in the discourse; it should adhere to the the accepted purpose or direction of the talk exchange in which the participants are engaged. According to Grice (1989a), certain maxims should be followed by the speaker:

1. the maxim of quantity: be as informative as necessary but not more informative than necessary;
2. the maxim of quality: do not say what you believe is false, do not say what you don't have evidence for;
3. the maxim of manner: avoid obscurity and ambiguity, be brief, be orderly;
4. the maxim of relation: be relevant.

When the maxim seems to be intentionally "flouted" or violated, H will attempt to understand the utterance by taking contextual information into account and making certain inferences – called **conversational implicatures** – which conform to the cooperative principle (that Sp is trying to make his or her communicative purpose clear to H) and the maxims of conversation. For example, consider the following short conversations:

1. Speaker A: *Do you have any money?*
    Speaker B: *I have a ten-dollar bill.*
2. Speaker A: *What color is her jacket?*
    Speaker B: *It's white.*
3. Speaker A: *Is Jim coming to the party tonight?*
    Speaker B: *His parents are visiting for the weekend.*
4. Speaker A: *Is Ellen at home?*
    Speaker B: *Her light is on.*
5. Speaker A: *What on earth has happened to the roast beef?*
    Speaker B: *The dog is looking very happy* (Levinson, 1983, p. 126).

In (1) Speaker A would make the implicature that Speaker B has only ten dollars. However, if B has more than ten dollars, he or she is not uttering a false statement, but one that flouts the maxim of quantity. Likewise in (2) Speaker A would make the implicature that the jacket is entirely white. However, if it is white and black, then B has again flouted the maxim of quantity, without uttering a false statement. In (3), (4), and (5), Speaker B's response does not on the surface address Speaker A's question. But A will assume that it follows the maxim of relevance and attempt to interpret it, in (3) making the implicature that because Jim's parents are in town he will not be coming to the party and in (4) making the implicature that Ellen's light being on is an indication that she is at home. In (5), the maxim of relevance would lead A to the implicature that the dog has eaten the roast beef.

Conversational implicatures have the feature that they are "defeasible" or cancelable; for example, in (1) above, Speaker B could continue by saying *I have a ten-dollar bill, in fact three ten-dollar bills*, thus canceling the implicature that he or she has only ten dollars, or in (3) above, Speaker B could continue by saying *His parents are visiting for the weekend, but he will be able to come to the party.*[12]

Indirect speech acts function much like examples (3) and (4), where the maxim of relevance is apparently flouted. The hearer must make certain implicatures, determining that some implicit speech act, rather than the explicit speech act, is relevant in context. This is known as the principle of **conversational relevance**. Of course, there are still cases where both direct and indirect speech acts are not recognized, and not communicated, where there are breakdowns in the communicative process. These may be either intentional (when Sp is lying, obscuring, purposely confusing, or disguising his or her illocutionary intent) and unintentional (when Sp's illocutionary intent is misunderstood or H fails to understand).

One way in which the relevance of one utterance to another is indicated is by means of forms called **discourse markers**. These are short words or phrases, such as *well, so, y'know, actually, anyway, then,* and *I mean,* which are hard to classify in terms of part of speech. They are seemingly devoid of meaning, but are of high frequency in speech, usually occurring at the beginning of utterances. Discourse markers were traditionally seen as empty fillers, but they are now understood as signaling the relevance of the utterance they introduce to the ongoing discourse (among other functions). Look again at example (3) above with the discourse marker *well* added:

3'.   Speaker A: *Is Jim coming to the party tonight?*
      Speaker B: <u>*Well,*</u> *his parents are visiting for the weekend.*

Well here indicates that the most immediately accessible context may not be the most relevant one for interpretation of the following utterance. Or consider a version of example (4) above with *so* or *then* added:

4'.   Speaker A: *Ellen's lights are on.*
      Speaker B: {<u>*So, Then*</u>} *she must be at home.*

The discourse marker here indicates that the following statement is a conversational implicature of the preceding statement. Note that the discourse marker *so* differs from the *so* expressing causal or result (e.g. *Ellen was hungry so she ate some potato chips*), just as the discourse marker *then* differs from the temporal *then* (e.g. *Ellen went home, then went to bed*).

---

12. It is common to distinguish between "conventional implicatures" and "conversational implicatures". Conversational implicatures are "nondetachable" (not attached to any one word in a sentence, paraphrases carrying the same implicatures) and nonconventional (not part of the conventional meaning of words), whereas conventional implicatures may be part of the conventional meaning of individual words. This distinction is being ignored here.

Chapter summary

Now that you have completed this chapter, you should be able to:

1. define concepts of information structuring;
2. analyze the effects of a variety of syntactic possibilities in English upon information structuring;
3. determine the illocutionary force, expressed psychological state, direction of fit, and speech act type of an utterance;
4. discuss the appropriateness conditions of different speech act types;
5. explain the operation of an indirect speech act in relation to the corresponding direct speech act;
6. recognize the importance of politeness in indirect speech acts and be able to differentiate between positive and negative politeness strategies;
7. identify conversational implicatures in respect to Gricean maxims and the principle of conversational relevance; and
8. distinguish between positive and negative politeness strategies.

Recommended additional reading

The classic treatment of the concepts of information structuring is Chafe (1976); a general exploration of the topic is Brown and Yule (1983, Chapters 3, 4, and 5) and a cross-linguistic approach is Foley and Van Valin (1985). A thorough discussion of the given-new contrast can be found in Prince (1981). A good textbook treatment of information structuring is Finegan (2008, Chapter 8).

The primary discussions of speech act theory are Austin (1962) and Searle (1969, 1975, 1976). Conversational maxims are discussed in Grice (1989c). Secondary treatments of speech act theory are Levinson (1983, Chapter 5), Allan (1986, Vol. 2, Chapter 8), Saaed (2009, Chapter 8). Kreidler (1998, Chapter 9), Griffiths (2009, Chapter 8), Plag, Braun, Lappe, and Schramm (2009, Chapter 6), and Finegan (2008, Chapter 9, pp. 281–312) contain coverage of speech acts, and Hurford, Heasley, and Smith (2007, Chapters 6) contains practice exercises on speech acts. Interesting articles on indirect speech acts are included in Cole and Morgan (1975). The classic treatment of politeness is Brown and Levinson (1987); for a shorter treatment of the topic see Holmes (2008, Chapter 11). Conversational implicature is well treated in Levinson (1983, Chapter 3), Kearns (2000, Chapter 11), and Saaed (2009, Section 7.7). The concept of conversational relevance is the subject of Sperber and Wilson (1995) and is well summarized in Blakemore (1988), who also discusses discourse markers.

Chapter 12

Linguistics in language teaching

Howard Williams

1. Linguistics and native-language teaching
2. Linguistics and second-language teaching
3. Conclusion

Chapter preview

While this textbook is primarily concerned with the analysis of language and use, it is in the language classroom that this knowledge is actually applied. In this chapter, we examine some of these classroom applications. The chapter is divided into two parts. The first is addressed to teachers of students whose native language is English. The second is addressed to teachers of English as a second or foreign language (ESL/EFL). In the first section, we will review the role of the study of language structure – its nature and its rationale – over the years, and some changes in that role. We will ask how the study of structure might be useful in the study of composition and literature in the typical English classroom. We will also address the role of linguistics in informing the often acrimonious instruction in second-language study and again ask how knowledge of linguistics might inform the second-language teacher in the task of instructing developing speakers and writers. Some parallels in the history of these two types of instruction will soon become apparent: in both cases, the study of grammar has had strong advocates as well as detractors.

Commentary

The idea that there is something tangible to be gained from a detailed knowledge of language structure has a long history in the English-speaking world. This is so nowadays more than before, since grammar study has now been applied in ways that no one would have dreamed of fifty years ago. According to the website of the Linguistic Society of America,[1] areas in which linguists can and do work include computer programming, speech therapy, dialect coaching and accent improvement, lexicography, criminology (linguistic forensics), business, language policy and planning, publishing, machine translation, and language testing. The role of linguistic training involved in each of these areas varies greatly and no doubt merits long discussion. However, surely the applications which most people think of first are connected to the teaching and studying of languages; that will be the concern of this chapter. We will identify two distinct areas of application. One concerns what a language teacher might know and impart to students whose first language is English; the second concerns the role of explicit linguistic instruction, especially grammar instruction, in the teaching of English as a second language.[2]

1. Linguistics and native-language teaching

1.1 Pedagogical grammar

We have seen various categorizations of grammar in this text: structuralist vs. generative, formal vs. functional, descriptive vs. prescriptive, among others. To these we now add a distinction between descriptive and **pedagogical grammar**. The latter is the sort of presentation of grammar meant to be useful either to a native-language classroom teacher in an elementary or secondary school or to a teacher of a second language – especially the sort of grammar that either teacher would find useful in the classroom. The term is also used to refer to a book which contains such a presentation. Pedagogical grammars do not typically aim at a theory of language or an exhaustive list of facts about a language; they are normally intended for a certain audience of nonlinguists who, for some purpose, are learning something about language structure. Thus, the analysis stops at a certain level of detail and the topics selected for discussion are quite selective, as deemed appropriate for the purpose.

Pedagogical grammar texts have a long history in the English-speaking world and in continental Europe. Even until the beginning of the twentieth century, the study of Latin was considered vital to a well-rounded education in England and North America, although its utility was probably questioned long before it was finally abandoned as a requirement in most schools. Up to a certain point in European history, there was good justification

---

1. See http://lsadc.org/info/ling-fields.cfm.

2. While classrooms are not always exclusively of one sort or the other, the distinction made here follows a typical distinction made in school curricula.

for a Latin requirement: Latin was the language of the Church, and until the Renaissance the educated class was church-educated. The revival of Greek and Latin classical literature necessitated the study of these languages, which came eventually to be seen as somehow purer and superior to the modern tongues. By the Renaissance, English had lost most of the inflections which were characteristic of the old language. Latin and Ancient Greek, by contrast, were replete with markings for case, gender, and number such that it was possible to detect grammatical relations among elements of the sentence regardless of the actual order of words. Perhaps partly for such reasons, and because of a certain reverence for classical writers, Latin and Greek were thought of as somehow more "logical" than English and held up as models of near-perfection. Since Latin had long lost currency as a spoken language, it was not generally studied to develop spoken fluency; rather, it was useful mainly for reading (and, to an extent, composition). One therefore did not become "fluent" in Latin as one might learn a modern language through exposure to input from native speakers; the road to mastery was through long study of ancient texts and through **sentence parsing** – taking sentences apart, identifying their components, and recognizing the relations among these components.

Eventually, the parsing approach came to be applied to English as well – though interestingly, this came rather late. As England became economically powerful in the sixteenth century and after, English itself came to be felt as a legitimate object of study. The rise of the middle class is often held to have been a catalyst for such study since those whose station in life was felt to be rising developed an interest in proprieties of speech – proprieties which were defined by more affluent economic classes. Soon, prescriptive grammar – the study of grammar for the purpose of changing native-language speech habits – was born. From that point on, the study of grammar developed an association which survives to this day and which is not present in any other traditional school subject – an association with a corrective function which lent it a moralistic tone. This function is no doubt largely responsible for the fact that the study of grammar has often been held in especially low esteem among generations of students who have found it stultifying, boring, and unrelated to anything interesting in their lives.

An early application – sentence diagramming. In 1875, Reed and Kellogg's book *Higher Lessons in English* appeared in the United States. It introduced a system of **sentence diagramming** which proved durable enough to last for generations in secondary schools as the primary formal language instruction tool. It survives today in somewhat modified form as part of descriptive grammars such as Kolln and Funk (2005).

Reed and Kellogg's diagrams, sometimes called *stick* or *line diagrams*, are a rough and simplified form of phrase structure grammar. The authors employed a base line which in a general way represented the argument structure of the sentence; modifiers were placed on additional lines branching from the base line. The sentence below would be represented as in Figure 12.1:

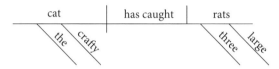

The crafty cat has caught three large rats.

Figure 12.1. Diagram of a simple sentence

The diagram is read as follows. The subject of the sentence always occurs in the leftmost slot on the main line; the verb complex (usually just treated as a unit) is written to the right of it, divided from the subject by a perpendicular line passing through the main line, and the direct object lies to the right of a line also perpendicular to the main line but not passing through it.[3] Determiners like *the* and modifiers like *crafty* and *large* are written below the main line to illustrate that these words are less important to understanding the main thrust of meaning in the sentence than are the words on the main line. Treated as adjectives, they are said to answer the questions *What kind? Which one? How many?* When sentences contain more than one finite clause, two main lines are drawn, but the main line for the dependent clause is shown to branch from the main line of the independent clause, thus depending on it:

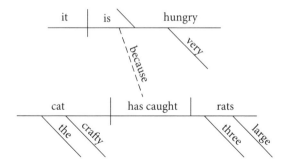

The crafty cat has caught three large rats because it is very hungry.

Figure 12.2. Diagram of a complex sentence

As illustrated in Figure 12.2, a slanting line is drawn to illustrate that in the dependent clause, the predicate consists not of a verb plus an object, but a verb plus a subject complement. The word *very* then modifies this complement. The logic of the dotted-line connection between the two clauses is that the *because*-clause is adverbial (answering the adverbial question *why?*); hence it should be represented as a modifier of the verb complex.

---

3. The intuition here seems to parallel the modern linguistic idea that [V + object NP] forms a unit in English, while [subject NP + V] does not; thus the leftmost perpendicular appears orthographically "stronger".

Illustrating the dependent nature of certain clauses in this way should assist students in avoiding sentence fragments (in this case, the writing of dependent clauses beginning with a capital letter and ending with a period).

That the Reed and Kellogg system of representing constituent structure is inadequate for a linguist's understanding of syntax is easily seen even with these two relatively simple examples. Determiners, adjective modifiers, and the word *very* are drawn to look as if they were of the same class of unit, yet they are not, as Chapter 5 has made evident. It is also not at all clear that a *because*-clause in any real sense modifies the verb(s) in the main clause, and it is important to note that neither Reed and Kellogg nor many of their descendants provide actual arguments to support their analysis over other possible analyses. This lends such grammars a didactic tone rather than the inductive, exploratory, invitational tone typical of scientific investigation. Moreover, representations of certain problematic structures – idioms, raising constructions (e.g. *easy-to-please/eager-to-please*) – are simply glossed over in the system. However, it can charitably be argued that descriptive adequacy was never a goal of this type of analysis; rather, diagramming was used for graphic illustration of the basic structure of the most common sentence types in the language so that a secondary-school student could grasp the basic notion of constituent structure.

Implicit or explicit in the teaching of diagramming was the notion that, by engaging in this activity, students could somehow improve their language-use skills, particularly those in writing. Exactly what was thought to be in need of improvement, and how diagramming was to serve as catalyst, was not always made clear. According to Sherwin (1969), Reed and Kellogg's method, and variants thereof, had their first heyday in secondary-school classrooms in America prior to the 1920s, declined for a time in the 1920s, and reappeared in the 1930s, remaining strong until a number of controlled studies questioned their value. The most important of these studies were done at the University of Iowa in the early 1940s. A controlled study by Stewart (1942), for example, compared student groups on language-use-accuracy test scores; half of the students had studied diagramming and half had studied grammar in a less rigorous and formal way (through, for example, sentence correction activities in composition classes) prior to the tests. Stewart reported that the teaching of diagramming led to no more significant improvement in writing than did other methods of promoting metalinguistic awareness.

A decade later Tovatt (1952), skeptical of the near-universal approval accorded sentence diagramming as an alleged means to improving writing, performed a small experiment of his own: he assembled test subjects, largely advanced college students and professionals, who were presumed likely to possess good writing skills, and tested them on their current ability to diagram. The idea was that if diagramming sentences had really helped them to "visualize" sentence structure in secondary school and in the process improve and maintain quality in their writing, then they ought to have retained much or most of their original skill at diagramming. As it turned out, fully 96 percent of the subjects were unable to reproduce a diagram of a simple stimulus sentence! In view of the fact that a majority of these subjects still maintained that, when they wrote, they visualized sentence elements as they would diagram them and that they endorsed the continuation of diagramming in schools, Tovatt seemed to sense a strange psychology at work: if the subjects advocate the teaching of a skill which they themselves obviously no longer control, how useful could the skill actually have been? Yet at the time of writing, Tovatt's survey of teachers indicated that almost three-quarters of all high-school English teachers made use of diagramming in their teaching.

> **NOTE:** None of these studies went without reply by advocates of diagramming. In the case of Tovatt, one might object that there are many cases in life of explicit knowledge serving as catalyst to the development of procedural skills (such as writing), the explicit knowledge later passing out of accessible memory. If such a chain of events is possible in learning to ride a bicycle or speak a foreign language, why should it not be possible in the process of developing effective native-language writing skills as well? Others defended the activity as a variety of mental discipline, valid irrespective of any other uses it might have.

Other varieties of pedagogical grammar.   Though diagramming continues to be taught in some schools, it has never been the only way of teaching young students about the elements of language. Methods which simply rely on drilling students in terminology largely drawn from Latin grammar, much of which survives in modern linguistics – *subject, predicate, modify, subordinate*, and so on – have also been widely used. Here, too, controlled studies have been done to test the purported connection between improved command of grammar and improvement in students' writing skills. Some, like Frogner (1939), have attempted to compare writing improvements in equivalent groups of students using two different approaches to sentence-level problems. In Frogner's case, an approach relying on drill in grammatical terminology was compared with an approach based "entirely from the standpoint of the adequate expression of thought" (1939, p. 519) – that is, based on whether successful communication has taken place. In fact, the level of improvement in writing skills reported on in these studies generally depends on the extent to which students' writing problems are presented not as structural problems per se, but as communication problems. In other words, teaching grammar outside the context of meaning has been claimed to have little direct, positive effect on writing skills (though there may be effects in other areas such as general analytical skills).

Another facet of traditional school grammar, one which survives today, concerns **usage rules**. Certain common habits of speech and writing have long been disapproved of and continue to attract the attention of educators, despite being in common usage in both spoken (and oftentimes even written) English. These include the comma splice (a variety of run-on or run-together sentence), clauses ending with prepositions, split infinitives, misplaced modifiers, shifts in tense and person, sentence fragments, lack of number and person agreement between subject and verb, and various spelling demons (e.g. *accommodate, dependent, existence, grammar, proceed, capital/capitol, effect/affect, principle/principal*).[4] The following examples from the COCA corpus illustrate the ways in which usage conventions are often disregarded:

comma splice	*Our money was stolen, we can't afford a ticket back to the village.*	COCA:ACAD
	Originally I never used to watch the news, I never kept up with any type of politics what so ever.	COCA:NEWS
clauses ending with prepositions	*Make sure that you tell us which story your poem is taken <u>from</u>.*	COCA:NEWS
	Shoshana turned around to see what Hobo was looking <u>at</u>.	COCA:FIC
split infinitives	*Children who are gifted are said <u>to often</u> <u>have</u> intense expressions in these domains and these expressions are thought to indicate advanced development.*	COCA:ACAD
	<u>To fully accept</u> aging, we must become comfortable with our own aging.	COCA:MAG
misplaced modifiers	*I've always known you can <u>only</u> skate for so many years.*	COCA:MAG
	The world eating champion took home $3,200 for finishing her burger first and for keeping it down <u>barely</u>.	COCA:SPOK
shifts in tense and person	*I thought that just <u>happened</u> when you <u>get</u> older.*	COCA:MAG
	But upon investigation, <u>we</u> discovered that <u>you</u> had to buy them!	COCA:NEWS
sentence fragments	*Great breads, muffins and the baked goods that supply Myriad's restaurants.*	COCA:MAG
	Because we let ourselves be dragged into their feud.	COCA:FIC
lack of agreement between subject and verb	*There <u>is</u> a lot of <u>things</u> they want to do.*	COCA:SPOK
	One concern that the election <u>results</u> <u>has</u> raised for me is the willingness of some to dichotomize regions of the countries as being made up of entirely yokels or the enlightened.	COCA:ACAD
spelling demons	*This has been perhaps the <u>principle</u> cause of the social and political tension in Ethiopia today*	COCA:ACAD
	The discharges would have the <u>affect</u> of inundating many.	COCA:ACAD

---

4.   Often, the use of mnemonic devices is employed to help students learn the correct spelling – e.g. "<u>Emma</u> has a dil<u>emma</u>", "<u>Jealousy</u> is <u>lousy</u>" and "The princip<u>al</u> is my <u>pal</u>".

If such features did not regularly appear in student writing, they would no doubt not arise as issues to be addressed. Often, language curricula center around such prescriptive issues; every bookstore and library has a section containing works on correct usage.

As has been mentioned, the advocacy of correct English usage has a long history. If a person in the twenty-first century were magically transformed back to the eighteenth century, much would seem familiar, but much would not. On the one hand, official disapproval of the use of *It's me* (for *It is I*) and *Who did you want?* (for *Whom did you want?*) – both modeled after case usage in Latin – remains in force in formal speech. On the other hand, resistance to the increasing use of the progressive passive in the early 1800s seems strange today. Prior to that time, the passive had not generalized to the progressive: rather than saying *The house is being built*, one said *The house is building*. The passive form was attacked by one writer as "an outrage upon English idiom to be detested, abhorred, execrated" (quoted in Baugh & Cable, 2002, p. 293). Today, many of the above historical objections seem unfounded and certain practices (such as splitting infinitives and ending sentences with prepositions) are common among even educated writers. Studies of actual usage (e.g. Peters, 2004) show that some prescriptive rules are no longer being followed, and as a result are now being abandoned.[5]

What can a teacher learn and make use of from these facts? We will consider this question in the following section.

1.2 A role for linguistics in first-language instruction

The scientific study of language in secondary schools.   In reviewing the debate over the pros and cons of formal grammar instruction in schools, it is important to bear in mind that the historical focus of that debate has been on the value of grammar instruction for a certain practical purpose – namely, the improvement of students' language-use skills, especially in writing. Studies of the effect of grammar instruction on writing improvement, particularly the early studies, have not considered that syntax or phonology might be studied simply for what they reveal about the structure of human language – in short, that this area of study might be approached with enthusiasm as a topic of inquiry and analysis in its own right. Thus, many of the participants on both sides of the debate have often seemed stuck in an older frame of reference in which grammar study was seen essentially as a corrective mechanism. Yet language is a human attribute – some have called it the one truly unique human attribute – and its nature is as deserving of attention as anything in the traditional life sciences.

---

5. *Webster's Dictionary of English Usage* (1989) is an excellent discussion of the history of many usage issues.

HINT: Consider, as an analogy, the idea that we justify the study of anatomy in the belief that it will improve students' posture. If students continue to slouch in their chairs, should schools abandon the study of anatomy?

A genuinely linguistic approach to language study in the schools is possible, where the study of verbal behavior is treated in a scientific rather than a prescriptive spirit. What is unique about the study of linguistics in the classroom is that students have usable data – in the form of intuitions about possible and impossible sounds and word sequences – at their immediate disposal. Far from viewing themselves as "grammar-deficient", students can gradually come to recognize their own *expertise* in grammar, as reflected in their ability to make these judgments. For example, Kolln and Funk (2005) show how the topic of modification of nouns, a traditional point in school grammar, can be studied in a spirit of discovery. After showing how the referent of a noun can be delimited using modifiers inside a larger noun phrase (*the college student in our class* vs. simply *the student*), the teacher can then bring students' attention to the fact that modifiers seem to follow a certain ordering pattern. That is, we can say *the Penn State student, the blonde student, the blonde Penn State student*, but not *the Penn State blonde student. What accounts for the unacceptability of the last example? By coming up with additional examples using their own mental resources, students may eventually reach a conclusion like the following: "when a lexical noun is pressed into service as a *modifier* of another noun, it immediately precedes the noun that it modifies". Thus we get *an expensive carpet cleaner, a big house party*, and so on.

HINT: Consider what happens as we attempt to insert more and more modifiers into the noun phrase, for example

Modifiers: *a, lacquer, old, lovely, black, large, painted*
Head noun: *box*

How would these words be arranged in a noun phrase? Is there more than a single ordering possibility? In general, students' intuitions will supply them with fairly uniform judgments; a teacher can then lead the class in asking what these judgments are based on. Does it matter, for example, whether the modifier has to do with color, with shape, with location?

By introducing additional examples, the teacher can engage students in a session of hypothesis-testing which will contribute in its own way to their critical thinking skills. In the process, such explicit attention to language may have the additional benefit of calling attention to the descriptive possibilities inherent to the noun phrase; it may thus serve a rhetorical purpose. Additional ways in which introductory grammar can be presented in a scientific spirit can be found in Yoder (1996) and Tchudi and Thomas (1996).

Linguistics and the teaching of composition and literature. Composition pedagogy has undergone considerable changes in recent years. Traditional composition classes tended to present idealized essays to students as models to which all coherent writing must conform. These models typically consisted of an introduction with a thesis statement, a body in which the thesis was developed into discrete points, and a conclusion in which the thesis was either repeated or commented on. Students were then encouraged to use these models as guideposts in their own writing – from conceptual content, to concept organization, to the language in which the concepts are expressed. It was thought that by writing an outline or essay plan first, students would be able to work linearly from the first word to the last, while paying attention to structural hierarchy. Grammar and usage rules were to be kept in mind and applied every step of the way.

This **product approach** mode of teaching has been seen in the past several decades as inadequate to the extent that it ignores the process by which successful writers actually compose their work. Writers are highly idiosyncratic, and it is unreasonable to suppose that they all operate in a lockstep fashion, from introduction to conclusion, when producing drafts.

> **HINT:** Readers might consider their own history of writing papers for classes. As an author, my writing process is typically quite complicated and not as "logical" as the description given above. It involves writing some kind of provisional thesis statement followed by an attempt at organizing some support for the thesis. Often, the support does not come easily, with the result that I then somewhat revise the thesis. I next make an attempt at a conclusion. Then, I return to the thesis statement for further revision. It then seems possible for me to write a fairly coherent body. On rereading the paper, I typically notice that the discrete divisions of the paper's body do not seem discrete enough for comfort. I thus reconstitute and rewrite the paper's body. Finally, I am able to write the entire introduction. Note that this description of the process of my writing may seem familiar to you, or it may seem bizarre. This is due to the fact that the writing process is highly individualized.[6]

The current **process approach** to teaching composition might emphasize a multiple drafting process, with conceptual development placed first. Concept development is followed by careful organization and reorganization of these ideas into parts to make them as fully comprehensible to the reader as possible, then followed again by a careful third-draft editing of the language in which they are couched. In this last step, attention to issues of grammar, style, punctuation, and spelling is thought to be most useful. As is often pointed

---

6. As an interesting side note, the well-known author John Irving reports that he always writes the last sentence of his novels first.

out nowadays, it makes little sense to ask students to pay special attention to sentence-level issues in a draft which is about to undergo major revisions in conceptual (and hence textual) content. A typically professional, multi-step approach to writing is masked in the earlier product approach, which tends only to hold up ideal forms as guideposts to developing writers. In a composition class in which several drafts are submitted, teachers might not pay close attention to sentence form until relatively late in the drafting process. By way of responding to actual student papers, teachers may then address – either individually or as a whole-class activity – matters of syntax and usage that arise, introducing just enough unfamiliar structural terminology to convey what needs to be conveyed.

This is an approach favored, for instance, by Constance Weaver (1996a, 1996b), who describes her philosophy as teaching "a minimum of grammar for maximum benefits" (1996b, p. 15). Apart from being more attuned to the way that seasoned writers actually work, an approach like Weaver's is appealing in several other ways:

1. First, the sentences which will be subject to grammatical attention are "naturalistic" ones; that is, they have been produced by the students themselves, not invented by a grammarian for the purpose of illustrating a point.
2. Second, specific grammatical issues can be attended to in an economical, piecemeal way as the need arises.
3. Third and most importantly, students are more likely to feel a concrete stake in learning since they are attempting to improve a product of their own self-expression.

The use of linguistics in the teaching of composition need not center on emphasizing, as traditional usage instruction did, what students should avoid in their writing; nor need it involve memorization of long lists of grammatical terminology. It is entirely possible to emphasize the *possibilities* of available structures for self-expression without even using traditional terms such as *relative clause*, *participial*, and so on. From a series of research studies in the 1960s and 1970s (Hunt, 1965; Bateman & Zidonis, 1966; Mellon, 1969; O'Hare, 1973) that were partially inspired by the mechanics of early transformational grammar, a technique called **sentence combining** emerged. O'Hare believed student writing could be improved through focused attention to structure without prior instruction in traditional parsing or grammatical terminology.

A sentence-combining technique provides students initially with a simple or kernel sentence and then encourages them to develop it in a semi-creative way through cues provided by capitalized "combining signals", most often accompanied by additional phrases or clauses. Consider some examples from O'Hare (1973, pp. 91ff.). Given the sentence in (1) below, students are then instructed to rewrite it by inserting the word *there* and making other necessary changes – changes which will in general fall within the range of comprehension of developing native writers. This type of sentence transformation is later made more complex by additional signal cues (whose meaning is explained as part of the exercise), as in (2). Eventually, this technique encourages transformations which developing writers would be much less likely to make in their writing, as in (3) below:

1. Given sentence and cue: *A garbage dump is behind the restaurant. (THERE – INS)*
    Transformed sentence: *There is a garbage dump behind the restaurant.*
2. Given sentence and cues: *Some telephones are nearby. (THERE – INS + NEG*
                                  + QUES)
    Transformed sentence: *Aren't there some telephones nearby?*
3. Given sentences and cue: *It would be impossible to ignore the fact that*
                                  SOMETHING caused a great deal of controversy.
                                  Simmons published the experiment.
    Transformed sentence: *It would be impossible to ignore the fact that Sim-*
                                  mons' publication of the experiment caused a great deal
                                  of controversy.

By utilizing a set of signals which can combine with one another in numerous ways, teachers can stimulate the generation of a wide variety of sentence types that students would normally not produce in their writing and a heightened awareness of their rhetorical effects.

There is considerable empirical support for the value of a sentence-combining approach. In a well-controlled classroom study, O'Hare had two skill-equivalent groups of seventh-grade students produce writing samples twice over the course of a school year, once in October, once in May. One group was then exposed to almost two hours per week of sentence-combining activities during the year, while the other group followed a more traditional language-arts curriculum. The spring writing samples were then compared to the fall set and rated according to six criteria of "syntactic maturity" (including, for instance, relative length of clauses and relative frequency of dependent clause types). After exposure to sentence-combining for most of the school year, the experimental group's syntax had matured greatly, while the gains of the control group were only slight by comparison. In addition, independent raters strongly judged the *overall* quality of the compositions of the experimental group to be higher than that of the control group.

O'Hare also reports a high level of student enthusiasm for combining activities. While he demonstrates that it is not necessary for a teacher to teach linguistics directly in the sense of having students do explicit grammatical analysis, he does show the value for teachers of being able to bring their explicit knowledge of English structural options into the classroom for a practical purpose.

Where students do become familiar with traditional structural terminology, grammar study lends itself easily to the analysis of literary works. For example, students may recognize the effectiveness of much of William Faulkner's descriptive prose in his frequent use of appositive, participial, and absolute constructions:

> *He crossed the gap between house and kitchen, the gap of iron earth beneath the brilliant and rigid night where the stove glowed, fogging the windows, and where Boon already sat at the table at breakfast, hunched over his plate, almost in his plate, his working jaws blue with stubble and his face innocent of water and his coarse, horse-mane hair innocent of comb – the quarter-Indian, grandson of a Chickasaw squaw … (Faulkner, Go Down Moses, 1942, p. 227).*

While Faulkner's style of extended description has had its critics, its utility for effecting a certain economy of expression cannot be disputed: had each subordinate construction been made independent, the resulting repetition of nouns and verbs would have lengthened the passage considerably.

In the study of literary style, linguistics has many potential uses. Traugott and Pratt (1980), in a linguistics textbook designed especially for such study, draw many fruitful connections in this area. They discuss the value of phonology to the study of rhyme and meter pointing out, for instance, that Old English poetry made more use of alliteration ("Over breaking billows, with bellying sail … ") than did later English and suggesting that the change was at least partially a result of the loss of predominant first-syllable stress in later Middle English. They discuss ways in which verb tense/aspect configurations are juxtaposed in narrative to effect backgrounding and foregrounding, how deictic expressions like *here/there, this/that* establish speaker perspective, and how the juxtaposition of lexical items of certain types is thought to establish a sense of cohesion in texts. They also provide a sketch of the formal characteristics of regional varieties of English evidenced in literary dialogue. Gleason (1965) also suggests that a study of historical syntax may serve as an aid to the understanding of older literary texts in English. The syntax of Shakespeare, for example, may be quite daunting in a first-year literature course. Of course, all of these features of literature may be and have been studied independently of linguistics, but an explicit knowledge of language structure adds a vital dimension to the inquiry and may facilitate the understanding of texts.

Linguistics and the teaching of usage.   On matters of usage, linguistics can be of help to the language teacher, but not necessarily for the reason one might expect. Linguistics begins as a descriptive science: it aims, at the very least, at an accurate description of what people actually say when they speak. Linguists have in general been less than charitable about the existence of prescriptive rules, which are most often seen as based more on sociopolitical concerns than anything else. Still, there is no reason to assume out of hand that all prescriptive rules are arbitrary, and a linguist's view of language can help separate the two types of issue. Consider the matter of stranding prepositions. A highly formal register would approve the sentence *In which box did he put the tools?* Ordinary spoken English would approve *Which box did he put the tools in?* In general, despite the traditional prescriptive rule, very few native speakers would utter the first sentence except in an extremely self-conscious manner.

Linguists have no great difficulty in formulating a descriptive rule to account for the alternation between the two sentences above: in one case there is leftward pied piping[7] of the preposition, in the other not. The alternation is thus rule-governed, exhibiting the typical characteristics of language. From the point of view of communication, nothing is lost when a preposition is stranded: the two sentences do not differ in meaning, and neither is ambiguous. Wholesale objections to the stranding of prepositions should, as a result, be viewed with considerable suspicion – much like the earlier objections to *The house is being built*. In fact, as often happens, the culprit is partially the eighteenth-century habit of holding Latin up as a model of optimal usage: Latin did not strand prepositions, nor do many other languages which have a similar construction; it was asserted that there was something "illogical" about the separation of a preposition from its object. Though few study Latin nowadays, the prescriptive rule continues to appear in some manuals of usage. A teacher will want to bear these facts in mind in dealing with the issue.

On the other hand, a sentence such as *John told Peter that he had won the lottery*, which contains a vague pronoun reference, might present a real communication problem if uttered or written. Context might already have made it clear whose lottery ticket was in question, but if our mutual understanding of prior context does not reveal this information, we are left with an ambiguity which needs to be resolved. The issue here seems a pragmatic one, though a description of the problem makes reference to a grammatical category (i.e. pronouns). Likewise, the use of commas is a convention which serves (among other things) to reflect spoken intonation: a valid objection to the run-on sentence *It's late, we need to leave* would be that commas are commonly read as markers of rising intonation (as an oral reading of *We had beans, rice, vegetables, and coffee* will illustrate), and that intonation does not rise after the word *late* above. Here, the issue is at least partially a phonological one. In both cases, the student writer knows what he or she intends to say, but there is a likely mismatch between the student's intentions and the message conveyed to readers. To the extent that such a mismatch exists, communication is not optimal.

---

7. See Chapter 9.

HINT: Recall that in Chapter 9, we discussed the ambiguity that arises with restrictive vs. non-restrictive relative clauses. Consider the following two sentences:

1.   *The climbers who reached the summit had a beautiful view.*
2.   *The climbers, who reached the summit, had a beautiful view.*

In these sentences, commas serve to disambiguate the meaning. It is therefore clear that in sentence (1), only some members of the climbing team reached the summit whereas in sentence (2), all members reached the top.[8] Another case where communication can be impeded concerns the so-called squinting modifiers, in sentences such as *He said when we met he would help me*. In such cases, commas cannot serve to disambiguate the meaning. Instead, convention dictates that the sentence be rewritten as either (1) *When we met, he said he would help me* or (2) *He said that he would help me when we met*. Finally, consider the case of (often unintentionally humorous) dangling modifiers, as in the sentence *Slamming on the brakes, the car skidded into the opposing lane of traffic*. Again here, convention suggests rewriting this sentence as *When she slammed on the brakes, her car skidded into the opposing lane of traffic*. In all the above cases, the need for precise meaning dictates that we conform to usage rules.

Clear justification for a particular rule of usage is not always easy to find; in the puzzling cases, often knowledge of the history of English language and society will reveal the original source of disapproval. What is clear is that native-language students will not willingly obey these rules in their writing unless the rules make current sense. Insistence on certain usages which no longer have much currency in speech (or in fact may never have had much currency at all) may contribute to student contempt for language study itself, just as it has contributed to a number of books[9] which seem to reject prescriptivism altogether.

Self-Testing Exercise: As we've discussed previously, in the writing classroom, teachers typically require students to learn prescriptive rules of grammar. Read the brief discussion and do self-testing exercise 12.1.

Linguistics and issues of dialect and register.   A background in linguistics can also help contribute to clearer thinking about questions of nonstandard **dialects** and variant **registers** (the stylistic variations of language used in different social contexts).[10]

---

8.   In spoken discourse, both the division into tone units (two vs. three, respectively) and the location of non-terminal falling intonation (after *summit* in the first sentence and after both *climbers* and *summit* in the second) would serve this same purpose of disambiguating meaning.

9.   Jim Quinn's *American Tongue in Cheek* (1980) is an example.

10.   As an example of variant registers, consider a student at university deciding which course s/he should take to satisfy degree requirements. In conversation with an academic counselor, the student might ask "Is it advisable to take The History of English?" whereas in conversation with other students, s/he might ask "Is History of English worth taking?"

What is a dialect in the first place? In linguistic science, the term is not always used in a completely uniform way. Definitions of "dialect" tend to fall into three categories:

1. One sense of "dialect" has often been interchangeable with idiolect, which is the language system of an individual speaker, including those ways of speaking that the speaker finds "normal" or "acceptable". If that speaker is willing to accept the use of the progressive *-ing* participle in utterances such as *Being working on a project at the moment, she was unwilling to be disturbed*, it is difficult to argue with the judgment without risk of offense.

2. More commonly, however, "dialect" is used by linguists to refer to (a) a set of lexical items and (b) a set of rules, which together generate a (potentially infinite) set of possible sentences, all of which are perceived as acceptable and "normal" to native speakers within a certain fairly well-defined speech-community (and some of which distinguish that community perceptibly from adjacent communities who are, however, still generally thought to be "speaking the same language"). Thus, the sentence *I didn't do it, but I should have done* is commonly heard in Britain, but seldom in North America, where it would likely be considered outside the norm of the language community. Speech communities are often defined by the region in which a given dialect is spoken (such as Appalachian English spoken in the Southern Midland area of the U.S.) However, even within a given region, individuals belonging to different social strata (e.g. as represented by class, ethnicity, gender, age, or social situation) may speak different dialects. This is the case with African American Vernacular English or the "upper crust" dialect of Boston.

3. A third sense of "dialect" is its more popular, everyday sense, in which the term is fully distinguishable from "language". This sense is a heavily political one: dialects are seen to be deviations from some *standard* language – a language which is itself *not* a dialect. In Britain, the standard is referred to as Received Pronunciation or RP, the prestige dialect used by British Broadcasting Corporation and spoken in the privileged public schools of England.[11] In the U.S. and Canada, the standard might be defined as the absence of a regional "accent" – i.e. not the regional English of the South of the U.S., its eastern seaboard, the Maritime provinces and Newfoundland in Canada – or in general the various regional Englishes spoken in rural areas of North America. This sense of "languagehood" is not rooted in human biology but rather in judgments about the relative status of a range of existing communities. These communities speak in ways that are in general mutually intelligible but somehow distinctively "different". Depending

---

11. Today, only a very small percentage of the British population speaks the codified version of RP described by Daniel Jones in the first edition of his *Cambridge English Pronouncing Dictionary*, and Estuary English, the urban-influenced dialect spoken in the greater London area, along the estuary of the Thames River and in surrounding areas, is gradually exerting its influence on RP.

on the sociopolitical relationships among these groups, this conception of dialect may easily lead speakers of the dominant variety to see certain dialects as charming linguistic variations; it may alternatively lead them to believe that a dialect is somehow "lesser" in nature than the dominant language.

Linguists stress that each dialect in the second sense above constitutes a language in its own right. In particular, when language ability is seen as a part of our biological inheritance and languages are seen to be more or less equally complex in a structural sense, it is a misplaced criticism to speak of "lesser" or "substandard" speech communities: from the point of view of structure, speech communities are equal. The everyday concept of dialect is largely a political construction born of language dominance: had the capital of England come to be located in the far northern part of the country, the Northumbrian dialect would have become the standard in Britain and the sort of British English now considered as prestigious would have been labeled as "dialect". Had happenstance made the speakers of the dialect in Boston in which *car* is typically pronounced as [ka:] rather than [ka:r] the most influential economic class in the United States, then the current standard in the U.S. might now sound different. Notions of "substandard" or "nonstandard" arise primarily in connection with social class and political dominance.

What effect might awareness of these facts have on language teaching? There are many speech communities in North America which are, for one or another reason, isolated from the mainstream, where by "mainstream" is meant that part of society which is most highly educated, which wields the greatest economic power, which publishes most of the books and periodicals, which broadcasts the television news, and which sets most of the standards of linguistic behavior. This isolation may or may not reflect elements of historical exclusion. If it does so reflect exclusion, a red flag should go up in the minds of a teacher who wishes to pass judgment, or who has heard judgment passed, on the propriety of speech patterns in the community in question. In the late 1990s in the United States, a controversy arose over the decision of a school board in Oakland, California – a largely poor and heavily black district – to recognize local patterns of speech, termed "Ebonics", as constituting a language in its own right (see e.g. Leland & Joseph, 1997). The issues are complicated, but some of the objection seemed to center around the claim that what had formerly been seen by the mainstream as a nonstandard "dialect" was now being recognized as a "language".

How would a linguist speak to this issue? The almost uncontested view among linguists is that every human speaks a language in the truest sense and that the common notion of dialect has relatively little to do with linguistic facts and much to do with sociopolitical ones. While few citizens of the United States would find the English speech patterns of Scotland anything but charming, opinions may change drastically when considering dialects spoken in certain parts of their own country – dialects commonly associated with uneducated speech. A language teacher must understand that dialects are not substandard, but simply different; that dialects may have their own ways of making subtle distinctions among (for instance) tense and aspect that do not exist in the standard language; that dialects are systemic; that the existence of an extensive technical vocabulary in the standard language reflects the size of the lexicon, not essential structure; and that students who speak one of these dialects may have problems of adjustment not wholly unlike (nor wholly like) those of the speakers of what we call foreign languages. For this last reason especially, it is wise for teachers themselves to understand something about the structure of the dialect in order to aid students in acquiring the standard.[12]

2.   Linguistics and second-language teaching

The teaching of second languages has never followed a single, lockstep course of development with one set of operating principles. Rather, over the last century a host of methods claiming to be new and revolutionary have appeared, much like new brands of products entering the market; we cannot cover them all here. Despite the welter of new methods, one may trace certain lines of change in recent years in English as a Second or Foreign Language (ESL/EFL) teaching; the view of the role of explicit grammar instruction in the process of effortful learning has changed accordingly. In certain ways, the course of development will appear strikingly similar to what we have seen for native-language instruction. But it must be kept in mind that the goals of teaching foreign languages are far different from the traditional goals of native-language instruction and prescriptive grammar. In the former case, the student begins with virtually no skills at all in a certain language and moves toward linguistic behavior approximating that of the average native speaker of a language; in the latter, a student who has already mastered the essentials of a native language is made cognizant of what he or she has already mastered and is then, retroactively, asked to focus on those areas which he or she is held not yet to have mastered. Second-language errors are not the "errors" of a coherent speech-community – as the use of *should have saw* (for *should have seen*) among certain English-speaking populations is thought to be an error; they are rather the result of a student's not having completely become a part of any speech-community particular to the language being learned.

2.1   The rise and fall of audiolingualism

An influential early attempt to make language teaching respectable by tying it to a theory of psychology and, ipso facto, to scientific linguistics was the **audiolingual method (ALM)**,

---

12.   Teachers may go further by integrating a discussion of dialect into their own syllabi; examples are found in Weaver (1996a).

the goal of which was to get students to mimic native speaker speech as closely as possible and to treat deviations from this standard rather seriously as cases of mislearned habits. ALM enjoyed a vogue, mostly in North America, from the 1940s through the 1960s. For most of that time the dominant model in linguistics was structuralism (see Chapter 1). The structuralism of that time was indebted to behaviorism in psychology, which held that human learning is essentially a result of conditioned responses to stimuli, and rejected the idea of innate, bioprogrammed mental faculties. Linguistic structures were thought to be of the first sort: when one learns a language as a child, one learns habits of speech which lead to desired results if the habits correspond more or less to what is heard and expected by adults – nativelike pronunciation, syntax, and so on. An instance of **negative transfer** from the first language – where, for example, a German speaker produces uvular rather than nonuvular *r*'s when speaking English – was seen as an ingrained habit in need of unlearning in the context of English acquisition. With this stress on habits, relatively little attention was paid to actual communication; learning a language the ALM way involved seemingly endless mechanical drills which placed heavy emphasis on correct pronunciation but concerned meaning only in an incidental way. For the student, *conscious* rule-learning – the ability to state rules – played no role or only a marginal one; the goal was to ensure accurate production through mimicry and analogy. For the teacher, in contrast, it was considered quite important to know the relevant facts of both the target (taught) language and the students' native languages, especially their phonology. By doing what was known as a **contrastive analysis** of the native and target language, the teacher would be able to identify potential problem areas and adjust lesson plans accordingly. In the heyday of ALM, many such contrastive accounts comparing English with some other language were written for the purpose of helping teachers to fine-tune their classroom syllabi to the specific needs of their students.

The behaviorist model of language learning was severely shaken and eventually practically abandoned in the wake of Chomsky's work in the late 1950s and 1960s. The idea that language learning commences on a "blank slate" purely as a result of habit-formation and analogizing came to be seen as inadequate for something as complex and as quickly acquired as a native language; the belief that the human organism is preprogrammed with certain basic features of linguistic structure eventually came to prevail, and with it the value of contrastive analysis declined. It seemed no longer necessary to assume that the study of native-language features could account completely for students' difficulty in learning second languages; while persistent negative transfer of these features did occur, especially in pronunciation for older learners, the process of learning could no longer be seen essentially as a process of simultaneous unlearning. Rather, the picture came to be somewhat different: learners were seen as organisms capable of drawing on an innate capacity for language learning who were learning a new tongue not different in essentials from the one they had learned as infants. To be sure, this advantage did not extend to the lexicon: the vocabulary of Chinese differs almost entirely from that of English. However, the structure of Chinese is held subject to the same essential universal constraints as English, and a learner's strategies for learning ought somehow to assume these constraints. Moreover, student errors may have many sources; only partially stemming from transfer. The practice of **error analysis** came into vogue as a way of identifying these sources, soon to be replaced by **interlanguage analysis,** which held that nonnative speakers have something characterizable as genuine competence, but of a special sort: it is a fleeting sort of competence in an idiosyncratic language which redefines itself constantly in the direction of a more stable native-speaker-like competence.

It is well known that after a certain age, learning a new language is quite difficult. A student who begins study of a second language after puberty will only rarely come to exhibit the skills of a native speaker of that language. However, an older learner comes to the task of second-language learning with certain advantages, chief among them analytical skills. And with these skills, it is possible to shortcut time-consuming inductive learning by means of explicit rule-learning which can be applied deductively to new situations. The influence of the new mentalism in linguistics that began with Chomsky came to support a return to deliberate grammar instruction; an influential new pedagogical school of thought was called the **cognitive-code approach.** Often, the grammar taught included much of the machinery of 1960s-style transformational grammar although, as soon became clear, generative grammar was often not very useful as a pedagogical model, especially because generative theory was constantly undergoing revisions which made it difficult for teachers to keep current on how the rules of English were presently formulated in the theory. Many second-language materials writers borrowed what was teachable and relatively straightforward from the new theory and depended on more traditionally reliable descriptive "rules of thumb" in other areas.

2.2   Krashen and the Natural Approach

Another highly influential group of second-language pedagogues took a different view with radical consequences for grammar instruction. In the early 1970s, studies of the production of grammatical morphemes in populations of second-language learners (most particularly the work of Dulay and Burt; see Dulay and Burt, 1974, for example) led many to the belief that there was something like an invariant **natural order of acquisition** of grammatical structures in second languages which was similar to that which appeared from the work of Roger Brown (1973) to hold for learners of first languages. One effect of this research was that some asked whether it made any appreciable difference whether grammar was taught at all to second-language learners: if accuracy of production in the use of the possessive -s morpheme (as in *the cat's tail*) lags behind accurate production of the *-ing* morpheme (as in *We are leaving*), and if both morphemes are eventually acquired for most speakers anyway, it does not seem to matter much whether a teacher drills students in the possessive form: the student will acquire it when the student is at an optimal stage of development (i.e. "ready") for the acquisition of *-s* and has had sufficient exposure to the morpheme in use. From this standpoint, the teaching of structure is somewhat futile.

Later in the 1970s Stephen Krashen made use of this data, in part, to elaborate a view of acquisition which he called the "Monitor Model". Language teachers often feel frustrated to find students who are perfectly capable of scoring high on written tests of structure – say, multiple-choice tests which instruct a student to choose the proper form of a verb in a given sentence – but who, in their actual spontaneous spoken language, consistently exhibit a failure to produce these forms. A frequent case in point is the third person singular -s ending in English: *The dog runs*, not **The dog run*. The correct form is taught at an early stage in most ESL syllabi, yet highly proficient nonnative speakers of English continue to utter the ungrammatical form after years of study, even though they can select the proper form when given time and the opportunity to focus on correctness. This phenomenon, said Krashen, is due to the fact the there is a crucial difference between "learning" and "acquisition". "Acquisition" is an unconscious process similar or identical to the way in which children pick up a mother tongue, and is identified with the discrete mental faculty assumed in generative grammar to constitute the locus of linguistic ability (often called by Chomsky the "Language Acquisition Device"). "Learning", by contrast, is "conscious knowledge of a second language, knowing the rules, being aware of them, and being able to talk about them" (Krashen, 1982, p. 10). Despite the alleged existence of a natural order of acquisition or structures, it was noticed that when second-language students of English took multiple-choice-type tests in which they were quizzed on the correctness of particular structures, students were likely to choose correct test options which they did not yet produce in spontaneous speech. Krashen claimed that the seeming disruption of the natural order of acquisition on such tests is due to test takers' being forced to bring this conscious element to the task. The proper function of learning is as **monitor**, or editor of production after the fact of speaking. But as with proofreading a written composition, monitoring, in Krashen's view, requires time and close focus on something other than the message itself; it does not reflect what a learner has actually acquired and is capable of producing in normal, everyday, unmonitored speech.

If learning is not a key to acquisition, then, what is? Krashen has long espoused the view that the key element is **comprehensible input**: that "we acquire by understanding language that contains structure a bit beyond our current level of comprehension, called (i+1). This is done with the help of context or extra-linguistic information. When communication is successful, when the input is understood and there is enough of it, i+1 will be provided automatically" (Krashen, 1982, pp. 21ff.).

Note that this view of acquisition runs counter to a long-held assumption held by lay people and language teaching professionals alike – that when one studies a second language, progress is facilitated by means of graded practice of structures leading to their automatization and mastery. While earlier approaches differed somewhat in the importance given to actual consciousness of rules in this process, none considered that grammar study could be dispensed with in classes. Krashen has claimed that it can: even if grammar could play a significant role, it is difficult in the average classroom of second-language learners to find all students at exactly the same stage of grammatical development, so that spending much time on drills would mean a scattershot teaching syllabus in which some students are bored by the elementary nature of the material, others are alienated by its difficulty, and still others find it somewhat beneficial. While the majority of students were thought to find grammar for its own sake uninteresting, focusing on real-world situations tends to stimulate general classroom interest, and Krashen and his colleague Tracy Terrell became exponents of what the latter called the **Natural Approach** to second-language learning (Krashen & Terrell, 1983). In this approach, the focus is on creating a classroom that "conforms to the naturalistic principles found in successful second language acquisition" (Richards & Rodgers, 2001, p. 179) and on creating an environment in which students are devoid of anxiety and therefore open to acquiring the second language (see e.g. Terrell, 1982).

Such a view of the proper manner in which to instruct students makes it somewhat difficult to see what purpose an explicit knowledge of structure would serve for the language *teacher*, other than to satisfy personal curiosity about language itself. While Krashen has nowhere said that teachers should not bother to study the structure of the language they are teaching, many have been led to the impression that his approach to grammar study is "anti-pedagogical" (Marton, 1994) and that it suggests that "you do not have to know very much to be a good language teacher" (Gregg, 1986, p. 121). Yet many critics have also embraced much of Krashen's *overall* message in reaction to the methods which preceded it – methods which were long on pattern drills and pronunciation practice but short on giving students opportunities to use language in everyday situations to solve problems. Such opportunities would naturally feed a motivation to say things, to pay attention to what others say, and to feel eager and confident about learning more. When language learning as a whole tends toward decontextualized drill, it tends also to be bloodless and uninteresting. This was not a new observation with Krashen; what was new was the extent to which his program took the idea and dictated that everything inconsistent with it be expurgated from the curriculum. Krashen has since had great influence, particularly in the U.S., on elementary and secondary school curricula.

2.3   A new role for grammar

For a time in the late 1970s and early 1980s, Krashen's way of thinking saw its high tide in the United States. This was true partially because there was no competing account of second-language acquisition which claimed to constitute a theory. Many thought the complexity of the Monitor Model impressive. Yet reaction soon arose to counter many of its claims. It seemed quite a jump of inference to assert, from rank order acquisition data on a small number of English morphemes, that *all* grammatical structures are internalized in a particular, invariant order. Indeed, it was never made clear exactly what a "structure" was supposed to be: can the suffix *-ing* really be placed on a scale with (and thus be somehow comparable to) pseudocleft sentences? VanPatten (1984) argued that closer attention to the semantics of the morphemes could reveal something about why they were acquired in the order that they are – that it was not structure per se which was relevant. Gregg (1984), in a many-faceted critique, said that the mere fact that learning does not always lead to acquisition (as in the third person -*s* example) does not entail that it *cannot* do so; there is plenty of anecdotal evidence that focused study of grammar at least sometimes yields results, and some studies have pointed to this conclusion. Gregg also asks why the uttering of sentences which are both understood *and* part of focused grammar practice cannot constitute cases of comprehensible output rechanneled as comprehensible input; in other words, the idea that grammar practice and meaningful input are mutually exclusive is simply false so long as one pays attention to what one is practicing.

Moreover, what does it mean for a teacher to "call attention to form" in the first place? Rutherford and Sharwood-Smith (1988) and Sharwood-Smith (1988) ask whether a Krashen-type program is not lumping all strategies for teaching grammatical structure into one undifferentiated mass. The study of form need not necessarily take the road of endless drills as in an audiolingual syllabus. It is possible that a teacher can call attention to certain problematic aspects of structure by providing intensive examples of the structure in the input. Thus, a teacher might teach the semantics of the present perfect progressive (*We have been staying here for a week*) by close focused discussion of real-world situations which have manifestly begun in the past and continue directly to the moment of student discussion. If the discussion itself is relevant to the students' lives in some way, then it is clear that the teacher is "stacking the deck" in favor of a certain point of grammar and thereby drawing attention to form in some sense. If at the same time, the teacher merely highlights without further comment the relevant affixes and lexical collocations associated with the structure (by writing, for example, *We ha<u>ve</u> be<u>en</u> sta<u>ying</u> here <u>for</u> a wee*k on the blackboard), the teacher is again subtly but decisively indicating the importance of these details while downplaying overt explanations. There is absolutely no evidence, in the authors' view, that such **consciousness-raising (CR)** activities in any way hinder communication or fail to contribute to emerging language competence. And several studies seem to vindicate some form of CR. Yip (1994), in a controlled pretest-posttest study, shows improvement on the production of students' active-passive verb morphology following explicit discussion of subcategorization frames for certain verbs in English. In many other languages, verbs such as *happen, occur*, and *roll* (usually called "ergative" verbs, whose case-markings pattern in a fairly uniform way distinct from other verbs) occur with passive markings, as in *The event was occurred*. Master (1994) shows performance improvement on the English article system following systematic focus on the contexts of article use. In addition, the claim that comprehensible input is a sufficient condition for achieving near-native fluency is disputed in Harley and Swain (1984).[13]

---

13.   An updated and very thorough treatment of studies on the efficacy of enhanced input on second-language acquisition (e.g. via input flooding, boldfacing, etc.) is found in Ellis (2008).

2.4   A role for linguistics in second-language instruction

A typical beginning teacher of English as a second language is confronted from the first day in the classroom with student language which may depart significantly from that which a native speaker would produce. At practically every turn, the teacher is faced with decisions about how best to deal with such deviations from the norm. Contrary to what one might assume, it would be virtually impossible to call students' attention to all of their production errors, for the cost would be wasted time, student and teacher frustration, and ultimately little production at all. The current view of second-language acquisition holds that it is certainly *not* necessary to treat errors in a one-by-one way as serious problems. As long as we do not regard every error in a student's **interlanguage** – the term used for linguistic competence at any stage short of native-speaker competence – as a manifestation of a bad habit to be unlearned, many errors may be passed over as evidence of transitional stages of development. Yet it is still valuable to ascertain the nature and source of these errors, for this will in part determine how to address them.

It is often wise to know something about the structure of the native languages of second-language students – if only a thumbnail sketch – as a reasonably high number of errors do appear to involve negative transfer. Let us consider *wh*-fronting as an extended example. As Chapter 9 has illustrated, English *wh*-expressions originate in various positions in the sentence and are fronted to first position in a sentence, in each case leaving behind a gap or trace (a gap, as noted, that is not visible on the surface for subjects). Thus, we get *Who(m) did you see [t] last night?* Yet not all languages work in quite this way. Many languages employ what are referred to as resumptive pronouns, where the fronted NP is repeated in the position from which it would be moved in English; the result is something like *Who(m) did you see him last night?* Such a sentence, if uttered in English, borders on the uninterpretable. Exactly what operations are involved in forming such a structure in the languages (such as Farsi) in which resumptive pronouns occur is a matter for theoretical discussion. However, resumptive pronouns regularly occur in the English "interlanguage" of speakers of these languages, and the teacher will find it useful to have a rough idea of the facts of both English and the student's native language, and to make a teaching decision accordingly.

Likewise, it is worthwhile to know something about the overall *typology* of relative clauses across the world's languages. As Chapter 9 has shown, English has quite a few options for relativizing. The possibilities include relatives functioning as subjects (*The people who arrived*), direct objects (*The paper which I wrote*), prepositional objects (*The firm to which she applied*), possessive determiners (*The man whose car broke down*), and several adverbial words (*The place where we went, The time when she broke the vase, The reason why we did that*). For a learner of English, not all of these will likely be acquired at an equal pace. As Keenan and Comrie (1977) and Keenan (1985) show, not all languages make use of relatives in each of these positions. They sketch what they call an "accessibility hierarchy" along which the likelihood of occurrence of true relative pronouns decreases: *subject*

> *direct object > indirect object > object of preposition or postposition > possessor.* Thus, a language which has the rough equivalent to *The man <u>who</u> arrived yesterday,* a subject relative, may use a personal rather than a relative pronoun to mark prepositional object relatives: *The man I gave the book to <u>him</u> arrived yesterday* (where *man* and *him* are coreferential).[14]

Current ESL grammar materials tend toward communicative or **contextual grammars** which seek to adopt the best part of Krashen's message without abandoning completely a certain amount of abstract rule presentation. Some of these take an eclectic approach with an eye to catering both to those students who seem to respond well to more formal work and to those who do not. Some writers, like Raimes (1998), approach the teaching of structure in the context of actual texts drawn from books and periodicals; others, like the authors of the *Grammar Dimensions* series (Larsen-Freeman, 2007), take a discourse-functional approach in which students are taught not only the formal aspects of individual structures but the uses to which they are put in discourse. The rationale of a series like *Grammar Dimensions* is that there is no sense in teaching, for example, passivization without a clear explanation of what native speakers actually *do* with the passive voice.[15] Beyond merely explaining the rules and discourse contexts for use of the passive, such an approach will typically embed class activities and exercises into situations, real or imagined, where passivization is most likely to occur. For example, students might be asked to describe an event (such as a crime) where the identity of the agent (the criminal) is unknown.

Where grammar instruction forms part of a larger school program in second-language reading and writing, contextualization of grammar may profitably take place while students investigate a specific subject area in some depth – say, the issue "heredity vs. environment" or "the effect of deforestation on the earth's atmosphere". Such **content-based instruction** is predicated on the belief that the discussion of real-world issues in the classroom will result in a more congenial learning atmosphere and serve as a natural springboard to valuable class discussions needed for language practice. As grammar issues arise in the course of discussions and composition-writing, they are treated as a natural part of the composing process. For example, suppose that a class is focusing on the role of folk objects in cultures and that each student's assignment is to bring in a folk object and explain its purpose. As

---

14.   Exactly why the accessibility hierarchy holds as a generalization across languages is not clear; however, the point is that the option of using relative determiners as in English (*The person* whose *number you gave me wasn't home*) is a marked one in the languages of the world. It is likely that second-language students will experience difficulty with this use of *wh*-relatives, and it will be helpful for the teacher to have clues as to the source of the difficulty.

15.   For example, when one passivizes, one may wish to place strong focus on the logical object for some reason; by omitting a *by*-phrase in passive sentences, one may be deliberately concealing the fact that one does not know the identity of this subject, or that one knows the identity the subject but does not want to divulge it; perhaps most commonly, it may not matter who or what the subject is (see Chapter 11).

soon as the student is put in the position of saying or writing, *My folk object is an object which* … a possible context for a study of relative clauses exists. Since students will likely find reason to use several types of relatives in writing their essay, it seems appropriate for a class to review at least the major types.

In another approach to composition called **mode-based instruction**, the writing curriculum is structured according to typical (if often idealized) rhetorical modes such as "comparison-contrast", "cause and effect", "description of a process", "interview report", and so on. Such structuring lends itself even more directly to a focus on specific grammatical areas. For example, the complexities of comparatives may be presented in a unit on comparison and contrast; passives are usefully covered in connection with process descriptions (such as formal written instructions, where sentences like *The screw should not be over-tightened* (frequently occur); indirect speech fits well with interview reports; apposition is common in extended definitions (e.g. *The opossum, a variety of marsupial, is found widely across North America*); a discussion of most types of subordination and coordination seems appropriate to all modes. While there is certainly no natural congruence between content or rhetorical mode and every imaginable grammatical point, it seems worthwhile to exploit the connections where they exist, provided student writing stands to benefit from attention to these points.

No matter what one may discover in magazine advertisements for schools claiming that their methods can teach native speaker competence practically overnight, it remains true that there are no panaceas in second-language learning. Professionals in the field have not yet uncovered "the secret" to quick and accurate mastery of a foreign language. It is generally held that when people reach puberty, language acquisition becomes difficult. For most people, becoming a highly competent speaker of a second language involves time, effort, and concentration. Along the road to acquisition, a knowledge of linguistics can be useful for both teacher and student in two ways.

First is the obvious role that knowledge of phonology, morphology, syntax, and the lexicon can play in instruction. There is a wealth of published materials that a teacher or a student may draw on for assistance and insights in teaching or learning these areas of language, many of which incorporate pragmatics as well. While systematic teaching of language structure is not always the best focus at all times for every student in developing linguistic competence, while it may seldom be the best focus for certain students, and while it is never adequate by itself in second-language teaching, it remains true that many second-language students – especially older ones – respond well to such teaching and expect their instructor to be able to provide answers and explanations. It will not do for the instructor to tell the student that conscious knowledge of the mechanics of the second language is irrelevant to mastery of the language (though certain students may indeed have an inflated notion of the role that conscious learning has played in their own language acquisition).

The second role is more indirect: it is the role that a good knowledge of linguistic theory and acquisition studies may play in informing teachers about the nature of language learning. The decline of behaviorism in American linguistics and the concomitant rise of the mentalistic generative grammar of Chomsky have had profound and abiding effects on language teaching. Generative grammar has since undergone many changes which have made its direct applicability to pedagogy even more difficult now than in the 1960s. At the same time, functional approaches to grammar have influenced grammar class syllabi, which now frequently exploit connections between grammar and discourse. Where extensive mechanical pattern drills in a particular grammatical structure once existed as a means to internalize that structure, ESL students today may be given the statement of a rule together with several examples and a few practice exercises, followed by exposure to a text taken from a newspaper article showing multiple instances of that structure in context, followed again by a writing assignment designed to elicit use of the structure. Teachers may then reinforce their teaching by making an effort to include numerous examples of the structure in their own speech and in further class texts even after they have moved the conscious attention of students to new topics.

3. Conclusion

We may tie together the discussions of native-language and ESL grammar instruction by noticing a common historical thread. In both cases, the centrality of grammar in the curriculum once went unquestioned. Then for a number of reasons this focus came to be seen as mistaken, with the result that attention to language form came into disrepute. In both cases, the dethroning of grammar met with mixed reactions. Many felt a sense of liberation from curricula that seemed to have drained the life out of their subject and to have missed the point of language study. Yet the complete elimination of grammar from the curriculum flouted the intuitions of others who valued the role of grammar study in their own language learning and attested to its value in their students' experience.

Since the mid-1980s grammar has made a comeback, the consensus having moved toward a more refined and balanced approach. A knowledge of the particulars of linguistics is surely not the only sort of knowledge relevant for a teacher – neither for an ESL instructor nor for a secondary-school teacher whose students are mainly native speakers of English. However, it is surely essential knowledge, and applied in an intelligent way, it has in important role to play in fostering language development.

Self-Testing Exercise: A basic understanding of the interlanguage of English language learners is useful to those who have nonnative speakers of English in their classroom. Read the brief discussion and do self-testing exercise 12.2

Chapter summary

Now that you have completed this chapter, you should be able to:

1. identify the key questions involved in the teaching of English structure to native speakers of English;
2. identify the key questions involved in the teaching of English structure to nonnative speakers of English;
3. sketch the recent history of grammar teaching; and
4. make preliminary reasoned judgements about the possible benefits and drawbacks to the use of linguistics in the teaching of structure.

Recommended additional reading

The references below are intended to supplement those given throughout the text of this chapter.

A thorough review of the history of sentence diagramming and the uses of grammar in the teaching of writing is found in Sherwin (1969). Discussions of process vs. product approaches to composition may be found in Berlin (1982), Hairston (1982), and Coe (1987), among others. In addition to satiric treatments such as Quinn (1980), an excellent analysis of prescriptivism in general appears in Nunberg (1983) and Battistella (2005). Brinton (1988) discusses the application of prescriptivist rules to student writing. Weaver with Bush (2008) contains a thorough discussion of the role of grammar in writing.

Professional journals for college and secondary-school language arts teachers have given considerable space to articles on pedagogical grammar over the years. An entire issue of *English Journal* (85(7), November 1996) is devoted to articles (some quite amusing) on the use and misuse of grammar instruction in the classroom and includes some interesting classroom-tested lesson plans. For two book-length treatments of the subject and descriptions of sample lessons, see Noguchi (1991) and Weaver (1996a).

Capsule descriptions of second-language teaching methods over the years appear in Diller (1971), Ellis (1990), Larsen-Freeman (2000), and Richards and Rodgers (2001). For experimental evidence that the explicit teaching of structure yields positive results, see Long (1983), Master (1994), Yip (1994), and Yorio (1994). The standard text on the facts of English structure of potential use to second-language teachers, which also provides strategies for teaching structure to students, is Celce-Murcia and Larsen-Freeman (1999). This book incorporates a certain amount of cross-linguistic comparison and contrast. Also very useful for ESL/EFL teachers seeking to understand the sources of their students' errors is Swan and Smith (2001), which provides useful contrastive analyses of English and many of the languages commonly spoken by students in the second-language classroom. A rationale for content-based instruction is given in Brinton, Snow, and Wesche (2003); a useful example of a thematically oriented content-based ESL textbook series with attention to grammar issues is Brinton et al. (1997). There are many mode-based composition textbooks, some designed primarily for native speakers and others for nonnatives; for an example of the latter see Oshima and Hogue (2006). Among the more useful "communicatively-oriented" grammar textbook series for ESL students are Elbaum (2011) and Larsen-Freeman (2007). The volumes in both series are graded according to proficiency level.

Finally, an excellent antidote to any and all schools of thought which claim to have found "the answer" on issues of language pedagogy is Clarke (1982).

References

Allan, Keith. (1986). *Linguistic meaning* (Vols. 1–2). London: Routledge.

Anscombe, Gertrude E.M. (1957). *Intention*. Oxford: Clarendon Press.

Armstrong, Sharon Lee, Gleitman, Lila R., & Gleitman, Henry. (1983). What some concepts might not be. *Cognition, 13*, 263–308.

Atwood, Margaret. (2000). *The blind assassin*. New York: Doubleday (Nan A. Talese).

Austin, John L. (1962). *How to do things with words*. Cambridge, MA: Harvard University Press.

Bateman, Donald, & Zidonis, Frank. (1966). *The effect of a study of transformational grammar on the writing of ninth and tenth graders*. Champaign, IL: National Council of Teachers of English.

Battistella, Edwin L. (2005). *Bad language: Are some words better than others?* Oxford: Oxford University Press.

Bauer, Laurie. (1983). *English word formation*. Cambridge: Cambridge University Press.

Bauer, Laurie. (2003). *Introducing linguistic morphology* (2nd ed.). Washington, DC: Georgetown University Press.

Baugh, Albert C., & Cable, Thomas. (2002). *A history of the English language* (5th ed.). Englewood Cliffs, NJ: Prentice-Hall.

Berlin, James A. (1982). Contemporary composition: The major pedagogical theories. *College English, 44*, 765–777.

Biber, Douglas, Conrad, Susan, & Leech, Geoffrey. (2002). *Longman student grammar of spoken and written English*. White Plains, NY: Pearson.

Biber, Douglas, Johansson, Stig, Leech, Geoffrey, Conrad, Susan, & Finegan, Edward. (1999). *Longman grammar of spoken and written English*. Harlow, UK: Pearson.

Biber, Douglas. (1992). *Variation across speech and writing*. Cambridge: Cambridge University Press.

Bickford, Anita C., & Floyd, Rick. (2006). *Articulatory phonetics: Tools for analyzing the world's languages* (4th ed.). Dallas, TX: SIL International.

Blakemore, Diane. (1988). The organization of discourse. In Frederick J. Newmeyer (Ed.), *Linguistics: The Cambridge survey: Vol. 4. Language: The socio-cultural context* (pp. 229–250). Cambridge: Cambridge University Press.

Bloomfield, Leonard. (1933). *Language*. New York: Holt, Rinehart & Winston.

Bolinger, Dwight. (1986). *Intonation and its parts: Melody in spoken English*. Stanford, CA: Stanford University Press.

Brinton, Donna M., Frodesen, Jan, Holten, Christine, Jensen, Linda, & Repath-Martos, Lyn. (1997). *Insights: A content-based ESL text for academic preparation* (Vols. 1–2).White Plains, NY: Addison Wesley Longman.

Brinton, Donna M., Snow, Marguerite Ann, & Wesche, Majorie Bingham. (2003). *Content-based second language instruction (classics ed.)*. Ann Arbor: University of Michigan.

Brinton, Laurel J. (1988). Grammar, usage, or style? Rule violations in student writing. *Technostyle, 7*, 37–46.

Brinton, Laurel J. (2009 [1988]). *The development of aspectual English systems: Aspectualizers and post-verbal particles*. Cambridge: Cambridge University Press.

Brown, Gillian, & Yule, George. (1983). *Discourse analysis*. Cambridge: Cambridge University Press.

Brown, Keith, & Miller, Jim. (1991). *Syntax: A linguistic introduction to sentence structure* (2nd ed.). London: Harper Collins.

Brown, Penelope, & Levinson, Stephen C. (1987). *Politeness: Some universals in language use*. Cambridge: Cambridge University Press.

Brown, Roger. (1973). *A first language*. Cambridge, MA: Harvard University Press.

Burton-Roberts, Noel. (1997). *Analysing sentences: An introduction to English syntax* (2nd ed.). London: Longman.

Carnie, Andrew. (2002). *Syntax: A generative introduction*. Malden, MA: Blackwell.

Carr, Philip. (1999). *English phonetics and phonology: An introduction*. Cambridge, MA: Blackwell.

Carstairs-McCarthy, Andrew. (2002). *An introduction to English morphology*. Edinburgh: Edinburgh University Press.

Catford, John C. (2002). *A practical introduction to phonetics*. New York: Oxford University Press.

Celce-Murcia, Marianne, & Larsen-Freeman, Diane. (1999). *The grammar book: An ESL/EFL teacher's course* (2nd ed). Boston: Heinle and Heinle.

Celce-Murcia, Marianne, Brinton, Donna M., & Goodwin, Janet M. (with Griner, Barry D.). (2010). *Teaching pronunciation: A reference and course text* (2nd ed.). New York: Cambridge University Press.

Chafe, Wallace L. (1976). Givenness, contrastiveness, definiteness, subjects, topics, and point of view. In Charles Li (Ed.), *Subject and topic* (pp. 25–55). New York: Academic Press.

Chomsky, Noam. (2002). *Syntactic structures* (2nd ed.). Berlin: Mouton de Gruyter.

Clark, John, Yallop, Colin, & Fletcher, Janet. (2007). *An introduction to phonetics and phonology*. Malden, MA: Blackwell.

Clarke, Mark A. (1982). On bandwagons, tyranny, and common sense. *TESOL Quarterly, 16*, 437–48.

Coates, Richard. (1999). *Word structure*. London: Routledge.

Coe, Richard M. (1987). An apology for form; or, who took the form out of the process? *College English, 49*, 13–28.

Cole, Peter, & Morgan, Jerry L. (Eds.). (1975). *Syntax and semantics: Vol. 3. Speech acts*. New York: Academic Press.

Cruse, Alan. (2006). *A glossary of semantics and pragmatics*. Edinburgh: Edinburgh University Press.

Cruse, D.A. (1986). *Lexical semantics*. Cambridge: Cambridge University Press.

Crystal, David. (2008). *A dictionary of linguistics and phonetics* (6th ed.). New York: Wiley Blackwell.

Crystal, David. (2010). *The Cambridge encyclopedia of language* (3rd ed.). Cambridge: Cambridge University Press.

Curme, George O. (1931, 1935). *A grammar of the English language* (Vols. 1–2). Boston: Heath.

Curme, George O. (1947). *English grammar*. New York: Barnes & Noble.

Curzan, Anne, & Adams, Michael. (2009). *How English works: A linguistic introduction* (2nd ed.). New York: Pearson.

Davis, Joel. (1994). *Mother tongue: How humans create language*. Secaucus, NJ: Carol Publishing.

Delahunty, Gerald P., & Garvey, James J. (1994). *Language, grammar and communication: A course for teachers of English*. New York: McGraw Hill.

Diller, Karl. (1971). *Language teaching controversy*. Rowley, MA: Newbury House.

Dillon, George L. (1977). *Introduction to contemporary linguistic semantics*. Englewood Cliffs, NJ: Prentice Hall.

Disterheft, Dorothy. (2004). *Advanced grammar: A manual for students*. Upper Saddle River, NJ: Pearson Prentice Hall.

Dixon, R.M.W. (1991). *A new approach to English grammar, on semantic principles*. Oxford: Clarendon Press.

Dulay, Heidi, & Burt, Marina. (1974). Natural sequences in child second language acquisition. *Language Learning, 24*, 37–53.

Elbaum, Sandra. (2010–11). *Grammar in context* (5th ed., Vols. 1–3). Boston: Heinle and Heinle.

Ellis, Rod. (1990). *Instructed second language acquisition*. Oxford: Blackwell.

Ellis, Rod. (2008). *The study of second language acquisition* (2nd ed.). Oxford: Oxford University Press.

Evans, Vyvyan, & Green, Melanie. (2006). *Cognitive linguistics: An introduction*. Edinburgh: Edinburgh University Press.

Facchinetti, Roberta, Krug, Manfred, & Palmer, Frank (Eds.). (2003). *Modality in contemporary English*. Berlin: Mouton de Gruyter.

Fauconnier, Giles. (1994). *Mental spaces: Aspects of meaning construction in natural language* (2nd ed.). Cambridge: Cambridge University Press.

Faulkner, William. (1942). *Go down, Moses*. New York: Random House.

Fillmore, Charles J. (1968). The case for case. In Emmon Bach & Robert T. Harms (Eds.), *Universals in linguistic theory* (pp. 1–88). New York: Rinehart & Winston.

Fillmore, Charles J. (1977). The case for case reopened. In Peter Cole & Jerrold M. Sadock (Eds.), *Syntax and semantics: Vol. 8. Grammatical relations* (pp. 59–81). New York: Academic Press.

Finegan, Edward. (2008). *Language: Its structure and use* (5th ed.). Boston: Thompson.

Foley, William A., & Van Valin, Robert D. Jr. (1985). Information packaging in the clause. In Timothy Shopen (Ed.), *Language typology and syntactic description: Vol. 1. Clause structure* (pp. 282–364). Cambridge: Cambridge University Press.

Fowler, Henry W. (1965). *A dictionary of modern English usage* (2nd ed. revised and edited by Sir Ernest Gower). New York: Oxford University Press. (Original work published in 1926)

Francis, W. Nelson. (1958). *The structure of American English*. New York: Ronald.

Frawley, William. (1992). *Linguistic semantics*. Hillsdale, NJ: Lawrence Erlbaum.

Fries, Charles Carpenter. (1952). *The structure of English: An introduction to the construction of English sentences*. New York: Harcourt Brace.

Frogner, Ellen. (1939). Grammar approach versus thought approach in teaching sentence structure. *English Journal, 28*, 518–526.

Fromkin, Victoria, Rodman, Robert, & Hyams, Nina. (2007). *An introduction to language* (8th ed). Boston: Thomson.

Giegerich, Heinz J. (1992). *English phonology: An introduction*. Cambridge: Cambridge University Press.

Gleason, Henry A., Jr. (1965). *Linguistics and English grammar*. New York: Holt, Rinehart, & Winston.

Greenbaum, Sidney, & Quirk, Randolph. (1990). *A student's grammar of the English language*. London: Longman.

Gregg, Kevin. (1984). Krashen's monitor and Occam's razor. *Applied Linguistics, 5*, 79–100.

Gregg, Kevin. (1986). [Review of the book *The input hypothesis*]. *TESOL Quarterly, 20*, 116–122.

Grice, H. Paul. (1989a). Logic and conversation. In *Studies in the ways of words* (pp. 22–40). Cambridge, MA: Harvard University Press. (Originally published in Peter Cole & Jerry L. Morgan (Eds.), *Syntax and semantics: Vol. 3. Speech acts* (pp. 41–58). New York: Academic Press, 1975.)

Grice, H. Paul. (1989b). Presupposition and conversational implicature. In *Studies in the ways of words* (pp. 269–282). Cambridge, MA: Harvard University Press. (Originally published in Peter Cole & Jerry L. Morgan (Eds.), *Syntax and semantics: Vol. 3. Speech acts* (pp. 183–198). New York: Academic Press, 1975.)

Grice, H. Paul. (1989c). *Studies in the way of words*. Cambridge, MA: Harvard University Press.

Griffiths, Patrick. (2006). *An introduction to English semantics and pragmatics*. Edinburgh: Edinburgh University Press.

Haegeman, Liliane. (2006). *Thinking syntactically: A guide to argumentation and analysis.* Malden, MA: Blackwell.

Haegeman, Liliane, & Guéron, Jacqueline. (1999). *English grammar: A generative perspective.* Oxford: Blackwell.

Hairston, Maxine. (1982). The einds of vhange: Thomas Kuhn and the revolution in the teaching of writing. *College Composition and Communication, 33,* 76–88.

Hancher, Michael. (1979). The classification of cooperative illocutionary acts. *Language in Society, 8,* 1–14.

Harley, Birgit, & Swain, Merrill. (1984). The interlanguage of immersion students and its implications for second language teaching. In Alan Davies (Ed.), *Interlanguage* (pp. 291–311). Edinburgh: Edinburgh University Press.

Harley, Heidi. (2006). *English words: A linguistic introduction.* Malden, MA: Blackwell.

Hillix, William A., & Rumbaugh, Duane. (2004). *Animal bodies, human minds: Ape, dolphin, and parrot language skills.* New York: Kluwer Academic/Plenum Publishers.

Holmes, Janet (2008). *An introduction to sociolinguistics* (3rd ed.). New York: Pearson Longman.

Hopper, Paul J. (1999). *A short course in grammar: A course in the grammar of standard written English.* New York: W.W. Norton.

Huddleston, Rodney D., & Pullum, Geoffrey K. (2005). *A student's introduction to English grammar.* Cambridge: Cambridge University Press.

Huddleston, Rodney D., & Pullum, Geoffrey K. (with Bauer, Laurie et al.). (2002). *The Cambridge grammar of the English language.* New York: Cambridge University Press.

Hughes, Arthur, Trudgill, Peter, & Watt, Dominic. (2005). *English accents and dialects: An introduction to social and regional varieties of English in the British Isles* (4th ed.). London: Hodder Arnold.

Hunt, Kellogg W. (1965). *Grammatical structures written at three grade levels.* Champaign, IL: National Council of Teachers of English.

Hurford, James R. (1994). *Grammar: A student's guide.* Cambridge: Cambridge University Press.

Hurford, James R., Heasley, Brendan, & Smith, Michael S. (2007). *Semantics: A coursebook* (2nd ed.). Cambridge: Cambridge University Press.

Jeffries, Lesley. (2006). *Discovering language: The structure of Modern English.* New York: Palgrave Macmillan.

Jespersen, Otto. (1909-49). *A modern English grammar on historical principles* (Vols. 1–7). London: Allen & Unwin.

Jespersen, Otto. (1933). *Essentials of English grammar.* London: George Allen and Unwin.

Johnson, Mark. (1987). *The body in the mind: The bodily basis of meaning, imagination, and reason.* Chicago: University of Chicago Press.

Jones, Daniel. (2006). *Cambridge English pronouncing dictionary* (17th ed.). (Peter Roach, James Hartman, & Jane Setter, Eds.). Cambridge: Cambridge University Press.

Justice, David. (1987, December). *The lexicography of recent semantic change.* Paper presented at the annual meeting of the Modern Language Association, San Francisco, CA.

Kaplan, Jeffrey P. (1995). *English grammar: Principles and facts* (2nd ed.). Englewood Cliffs, NJ: Prentice Hall.

Katamba, Francis. (1989). *An introduction to phonology.* London: Longman.

Katz, Jerrold J., & Fodor, Jerry. (1963). The structure of a semantic theory. *Language, 39,* 170–210.

Kearns, Kate. (2000). *Semantics.* New York: Palgrave Macmillan.

Keenan, Edward, & Comrie, Bernard. (1977). NP accessibility and universal grammar. *Linguistic Inquiry 8,* 63–100.

Keenan, Edward. (1985). Relative clauses. In Timothy Shopen (Ed.), *Language typology and syntactic description: Vol. 2. Complex constructions* (pp. 141–170). Cambridge: Cambridge University Press.

Kiparsky, Paul, & Kiparsky, Carol. (1971). Fact. In Danny D. Steinberg & Leon A. Jakobvits (Eds.), *Semantics: An interdisciplinary reader in philosophy, linguistics and psychology* (pp. 345–369). Cambridge: Cambridge University Press.

Klammer, Thomas P., Schulz, Muriel R., & Della Volpe, Angela. (2010). *Analyzing English grammar* (6th ed.). New York: Pearson Longman.

Kolln, Martha, & Funk, Robert. (2005). *Understanding English grammar* (7th ed.). New York: Pearson Longman.

Krashen, Stephen D. (1982). *Principles and practice in second language acquisition.* Oxford: Pergamon.

Krashen, Stephen D., & Terrell, Tracy D. (1983). *The natural approach: Language acquisition in the classroom.* Oxford: Pergamon Press.

Kreidler, Charles W. (1998). *Introducing English semantics.* New York: Routledge.

Kreidler, Charles W. (2004). *The pronunciation of English: A course book* (2nd ed). New York: Wiley-Blackwell.

Ladefoged, Peter. (2005). *Vowels and consonants: An introduction to the sounds of languages* (2nd ed). Malden, MA: Blackwell.

Ladefoged, Peter. (2006). *A course in phonetics* (5th ed.). Boston: Thomson.

Lakoff, George, & Johnson, Mark. (1980). *Metaphors we live by.* Chicago: University of Chicago Press.

Larsen-Freeman, Diane. (2000). *Techniques and principles in language teaching* (2nd ed.). New York: Oxford University Press.

Larsen-Freeman, Diane. (Ed.). (2007). *Grammar dimensions: Form, meaning, and use* (4th ed., Vols. 1–4). Boston: Heinle and Heinle.

Lee, David. (2001). *Cognitive Linguistics: An introduction.* New York: Oxford University Press.

Leech, Geoffrey N. (2004). *Meaning and the English verb* (3rd ed.). London: Longman.

Leech, Geoffrey, Deuchar, Margaret, & Hoogenraad, Robert. (2006). *English grammar for today* (2nd ed.). New York: Palgrave Macmillan.

Leland, John, & Joseph, Nadine. (1997, January 13). Hooked on ebonics. *Newsweek,* 78–80.

Levinson, Stephen C. (1983). *Pragmatics.* Cambridge: Cambridge University Press.

Long, Michael. (1983). Does second language instruction make a difference? A review of research. *TESOL Quarterly, 17,* 359–382.

Lyons, John. (1995). *Linguistic semantics: An introduction.* Cambridge: Cambridge University Press.

Marchand, Hans. (1969). *The categories and types of present-day English word-formation: A synchronic-diachronic approach* (2nd ed.). Munich: C.H. Beck.

Marton, Waldemar. (1994). The anti-pedagogical aspects of Krashen's theory of second language acquisition. In Ronald M. Barasch & C. Vaughan James (Eds.), *Beyond the monitor model: Comments on current theory and practice in second language acquisition* (pp. 57–70). Boston: Heinle and Heinle.

Master, Peter. (1994). The effect of systematic instruction on learning the English article system. In Terence Odlin (Ed.), *Perspectives on pedagogical grammar* (pp. 229–252). Cambridge: Cambridge University Press.

Matthews, Peter H. (1991). *Morphology: An introduction to the theory of word structure* (2nd ed.). Cambridge: Cambridge University Press.

McMahon, April. (2002). *An introduction to English phonology.* Edinburgh: Edinburgh University Press.

Mellon, John C. (1969). *Transformational sentence-combining: A method for enhancing the development of syntactic fluency in English composition*. Urbana, IL: National Council of Teachers of English.

Miller, Jim. (2009). *An introduction to English syntax* (2nd ed.). Edinburgh: Edinburgh University Press.

Minkova, Donka, & Stockwell, Robert. (2009). *English words: History and structure* (2nd ed.). Cambridge: Cambridge University Press.

Morenberg, Max. (2002). *Doing grammar* (3rd ed.). New York: Oxford University Press.

Murray, Thomas E. (1995). *The structure of English: Phonetics, phonology, morphology*. Boston: Allyn & Bacon.

Noguchi, Rei. (1991). *Grammar and the teaching of writing*. Urbana, IL: National Council of Teachers of English.

Nunberg, Geoffrey. (1983, December). The decline of grammar. *Atlantic Monthly*, 31–46.

O'Grady, William, & Archibald, John. (Eds). (2009). *Contemporary linguistic analysis: An introduction* (6th ed.). Toronto: Pearson Longman.

O'Hare, Frank. (1973). *Sentence combining: Improving student writing without formal grammar instruction*. Urbana, IL: National Council of Teachers of English.

Odden, David. (2005). *Introducing phonology*. Cambridge: Cambridge University Press.

Orwell, George. (1946). *A collection of essays*. New York: Harcourt Brace Jovanovich.

Oshima, Alice, & Hogue, Ann. (2006). *Writing academic English* (2nd ed.). New York: Pearson Longman.

Ouhalla, Jamal. (1999). *Introducing transformational grammar: From principles and parameters to minimalism* (2nd ed.). New York: Oxford University Press.

Palmer, Frank R. (1981). *Semantics: A new outline* (2nd ed.). Cambridge: Cambridge University Press.

Palmer, Frank R. (1990). *Modality and the English modals* (2nd ed.). New York: Longman.

Palmer, Frank R. (1994). *Grammatical roles and relations*. Cambridge: Cambridge University Press.

Parisi, Domenico, & Antinucci, Francesco. (1976). *Essentials of grammar* (Elizabeth Bates, Trans.). New York: Academic Press. (Original work published in 1973)

Peters, Pam. (2004). *The Cambridge guide to English usage*. Cambridge: Cambridge University Press.

Pinker, Steven. (1994). *The language instinct: How the mind creates language*. New York: William Morrow.

Pinker, Steven. (2007). *The stuff of thought: Language as a window into human nature*. New York: Penguin.

Plag, Ingo, Braun, Maria, Lappe, Sabine, & Schramm, Mareile. (2009). *Introduction to English linguistics* (2nd ed.). New York: Mouton de Gruyter.

Poutsma, Hendrik. (1904–26). *A grammar of late modern English* (Vols. 1–4). Groningen, The Netherlands: Noordhoff.

Pratt, Mary Louise. (1977). *Toward a speech act theory of literary discourse*. Bloomington: Indiana University Press.

Prince, Ellen F. (1981). Toward a taxonomy of given-new information. In Peter Cole (Ed.), *Radical pragmatics* (pp. 223–255). New York: Academic Press.

Pullum, Geoffrey K., & Ladusaw, William A. (1996). *Phonetic symbol guide* (2nd ed.). Chicago: University of Chicago Press.

Quinn, Jim. (1980). *American tongue and cheek*. New York: Pantheon.

Quirk, Randolph, Greenbaum, Sidney, Leech, Geoffrey, & Svartvik, Jan. (1985). *A comprehensive grammar of the English language*. London: Longman.

Radford, Andrew. (2004). *English syntax: An introduction*. Cambridge: Cambridge University Press.

Raimes, Ann. (1998). *How English works*. New York: Cambridge University Press.

Reed, Alonzo, & Kellogg, Brainerd. (1875). *Higher lessons in English*. New York: Maynard, Merrill.

Reinhart, Tanya. (1980). On understanding poetic metaphor. In Marvin K.L. Ching, Michael C. Haley, & Ronald F. Lunsford (Eds.), *Linguistic perspectives on literature* (pp. 91–114). Boston: Routledge.

Richards, Jack C., & Rodgers, Theodore S. (2001). *Approaches and methods in language teaching* (2nd ed.). Cambridge: Cambridge University Press.

Rosch, Eleanor H. (1973). Natural categories. *Cognitive Psychology, 4*, 328–350.

Rutherford, William, & Sharwood-Smith, Michael. (1988). Consciousness raising and universal grammar. In William Rutherford & Michael Sharwood-Smith (Eds.), *Grammar and second language teaching* (pp. 107–166). New York: Newbury House.

Saeed, John I. (2009). *Semantics* (3rd ed.). Malden, MA: Wiley-Blackwell.

Sapir, Edward. (1921). *Language: An introduction to the study of speech*. New York: Harcourt, Brace & World.

Saussure, Ferdinand de. (1986). *Course in general linguistics* (Charles Bally & Albert Sechehaye in collaboration with Albert Riedlinger, Eds.; Roy Harris, Trans.). La Salle, IL: Open Court. (Original work published in 1983)

Searle, John R. (1969). *Speech acts: An essay in the philosophy of language*. Cambridge: Cambridge University Press.

Searle, John R. (1975). Indirect speech acts. In Peter Cole & Jerry L. Morgan (Eds.), *Syntax and semantics: Vol. 3. Speech acts* (pp. 59–82). New York: Academic Press.

Searle, John R. (1976). A classification of illocutionary acts. *Language in Society, 5,* 1–23.

Sharwood-Smith, Michael. (1988). Consciousness raising and the second language learner. In William Rutherford & Michael Sharwood-Smith (Eds.), *Grammar and second language teaching* (pp. 51–60). New York: Newbury House.

Sherwin, J. Stephen. (1969). *Four problems in teaching English: A critique of research*. Scranton, PA: International Textbook.

Smith, Carlota S. (1997). *The parameter of aspect* (2nd ed.). Dordrecht: Kluwer.

Spencer, Andrew. (1991). *Morphological theory: An introduction to word structure in generative grammar*. Malden, MA: Blackwell.

Sperber, Dan, & Wilson, Deidre. (1995). *Relevance: Communication and cognition* (2nd ed.). Cambridge, MA: Blackwell.

Stegner, Wallace. (1955). *Wolf willow: A history, a story, and a memory of the last plains frontier*. Lincoln: University of Nebraska Press.

Stewart, James R. (1942). The effect of diagraming on certain skills in English composition. *Journal of Experimental Education, 11,* 1–8.

Strang, Barbara M.H. (1968). *Modern English structure* (2nd ed.). London: Arnold.

Swan, Michael, & Smith, Bernard. (2001). *Learner English: A teacher's guide to interference and other problems* (2nd ed.). Cambridge: Cambridge University Press.

Swan, Michael. (2005). *Practical English usage* (3rd ed.). New York: Oxford University Press.

Sweetser, Eve. (1990). *From etymology to pragmatics: Metaphorical and cultural aspects of semantic structure*. Cambridge: Cambridge University Press.

Tallerman, Maggie. (2005). *Understanding syntax* (2nd ed.). London: Hodder Arnold.

Taylor, John R. (2003). *Linguistic categorization: Prototypes in linguistic theory* (3rd ed.). New York: Oxford University Press.

Tchudi, Stephen, & Thomas, Lee. (1996). Taking the g-r-r out of grammar. *English Journal, 85,* 46–54.

Terrell, Tracy. (1982). The natural approach to language teaching: An update. *Modern Language Journal, 66*, 121–132.

Thurber, James. (1931). Ladies' and gentlemen's guide to modern English usage. In *The owl in the attic and other perplexities* (pp. 73–113). New York: Harper & Row.

Tovatt, Anthony L. (1952). Diagramming: A sterile skill. *English Journal, 41*, 91–93.

Trask, Robert L. (1993). *A dictionary of grammatical terms in English*. London: Routledge.

Traugott, Elizabeth Closs, & Pratt, Mary Louise. (1980). *Linguistics for students of literature*. New York: Harper Brace Jovanovich.

Truss, Lynne. (2003). *Eats, shoots & leaves: The zero tolerance approach to punctuation*. New York: Gotham.

Ungerer, Friedrich, & Schmid, Hans-Jörg. (2006). *An introduction to cognitive linguistics* (2nd ed.). Harlow: Pearson Longman.

VanPatten, Bill. (1984). Processing strategies and morpheme acquisition. In Fred R. Eckman, Lawrence H. Bell, & Diane Nelson (Eds.), *Universals of second language acquisition* (pp. 88–98). Rowley, MA: Newbury House.

Vendler, Zeno. (1967). *Linguistics in philosophy*. New York: Cornell University Press.

Visser, F. Th. (1972). *An historical syntax of the English language*. Part Two: *Syntactical units with one verb (concluded)*. Leiden, The Netherlands: E.J. Brill

Wardhaugh, Ronald. (1995). *Understanding English grammar: A linguistic approach*. Cambridge, MA: Blackwell.

Weaver, Constance (with Bush, Jonathan). (2008). *Grammar to enrich and enhance writing*. Portsmouth, NH: Heinemann.

Weaver, Constance. (1996a). *Teaching grammar in context*. Portsmouth, NH: Heinemann.

Weaver, Constance. (1996b). Teaching grammar in the context of writing. *English Journal, 85*(7), 15–24.

Webster's dictionary of English usage. (1989). Springfield, MA: Merriam-Webster.

Wells, John C. (1982). *Accents of English* (Vols. 1–3). Cambridge: Cambridge University Press.

Wells, John C. (2005). *English intonation: An introduction*. Cambridge: Cambridge University Press.

White, Elwyn B. (1934). *Essays of E.B. White*. New York: Harper & Row.

Wolfram, Walt, & Schilling-Estes, Natalie. (2005). *American English: Dialects and variation* (2nd ed.). New York: Wiley-Blackwell.

Yavaş, Mehmet. (2006). *Applied English phonology*. Malden, MA: Blackwell.

Yip, Virginia. (1994). Grammatical consciousness-raising and universal grammar. In Terence Odlin (Ed.), *Perspectives on pedagogical grammar* (pp. 123–139). Cambridge: Cambridge University Press.

Yoder, Rhoda Byler. (1996). Of fake verbs and kid words: Developing a useful grammar. *English Journal, 85*, 82–87.

Yorio, Carlos. (1994). The case for learning. In Ronald M. Barasch & C. Vaughan James (Eds.), *Beyond the monitor model: Comments on current theory and practice in second language acquisition* (pp. 125–137). Boston: Heinle and Heinle.

Glossary

abstract   a class of nouns having the feature of denoting referents which are not tangible and cannot be known through the senses
Example: *honesty, kindness, divinity*

abstract predicate   a small set of semantic features constituting the meaning of predicates: COME, CAUSE, DO, NEG, COINCIDE, and BE statives
Example: *be rich* = BE rich; *become rich* = COME BE rich; *make rich* = CAUSE COME BE rich

accomplishment   a dynamic situation with a terminal point or "climax" which is logically necessary for it to be what it is
Example: the verb *write up* denotes an accomplishment

achievement   a dynamic situation which is conceived of as occurring instantaneously
Example: the verb *trip* denotes an achievement

acoustic phonetics   the study of the speech sounds of human language with respect to their physical properties

acronym   a word formed by combining the initial letters of words in a phrase; pronounced as a word
Example: *REM* (< *Rapid Eye Movement*)

active articulator   the moving speech organ used in the production of speech sounds
Example: the tongue and lower lip

active voice   a structure indicating that the subject is performing the action of the verb or being something
Example: *The police dispersed the crowd. Jane is a dancer.*

activity   a dynamic situation which goes on in time (potentially indefinitely)
Example: the verb *brush* denotes an activity

adjectivalizer   a derivational affix creating an adjective
Example: *-ful* in *hopeful* (changing a N to a V)

adjective (A)   in English, a word which meets certain inflectional tests (e.g. takes comparative *-er* or superlative *-est*) and distributional tests (e.g. precedes a noun, follows a degree word); typically functions to qualify or quantify a noun
Example: *slender, happy, original*

adjective phrase (AP)   a phrasal category that has an adjective as its head
Example: *The instructions are very detailed.*

adjunct adverbial (aA)   optional modifiers of $\bar{V}$ (AdvP, PP, NP, $\bar{S}$) typically expressing manner, place, time, or reason
Example: *He spoke loudly in the theater last night because he is rude.*

adverb (Adv)   in English, a word that is sometimes inflected for degree, may be modified by a degree word, and functions to modify all parts of speech except nouns
English: *fast, smoothly, happily, consequently*

adverb fronting   the movement of adverbial words, phrases, or clauses to the front of the sentence in order to topicalize them
Example: *Working late, I missed my train.*

adverb phrase (AdvP)   a phrasal category which has an adverb as its head
Example: *We proceeded very cautiously.*

adverbial clause   a clause that functions as an adjunct, disjunct, or conjunct
Example: *when you see him; if I may be honest with you; while we're on the subject*

adverbializer   a derivational affix creating an adverb
Example: *-ward* in *skyward* (changing a N to an Adv)

affix   a morphological unit that does not carry the core meaning and is always bound to a root, in English either to the beginning or the end of the root
Example: *under-* and *-ed* in *underrated*

affix hopping   a syntactic operation by which bound elements in Aux are attached to the immediately following verbal element
Example: past + play $\Rightarrow$ #play + past#

affricate   a sound involving a stop released into a fricative
Example: the sound /dʒ/ in *jump*

Agent (Ag)   thematic role expressing the animate doer or instigator of an action who acts by will or volition, and is the direct cause of the action
Example: *Rafael* (Ag) *sliced up the apple.*

agented passive a passive sentence that includes the *by*-phrase expressing the agent performing the action
Example: *Adele was given a commendation <u>by the council</u>.*

agentive a verbal predicate denoting a change of state in an entity brought about by a human agent acting intentionally; analyzable with the abstract predicates DO CAUSE
Example: *She <u>salted the water</u>* = She DO CAUSE the water COME BE salty

agentless passive a passive sentence without the *by*-phrase expressing the agent performing the action
Example: *The car was driven into a wall.*

allomorph semantically similar (but not necessarily phonologically similar) variants of a morpheme that are in complementary distribution
Example: /d/, /t/, and /ə d/ are allomorphs of the morpheme {past} in verbs, as are zero and vowel alternations.

allophone a predictable variant of a phoneme
Example: aspirated [tʰ] vs. unreleased [t˺]

alveolar a sound articulated by the tip of the tongue making contact with or being in close approximation with the alveolar ridge
Example: the sound of /t/ in *rate*

alveolar ridge the area on the roof of the mouth just behind the upper front teeth

alveolopalatal a sound articulated by raising the tongue in the area between the alveolar ridge and the palate
Example: the sound /ʃ/ in *mesh*

amalgamated compound a word which in origin is a compound, but which in the course of time has become fused and is no longer separable into two distinct parts
Example: *marshal* < *mearh* 'horse' + *scealc* 'servant'

ambisyllabic a sound belonging to two adjacent syllables
Example: the *d* in *read.y/rea.dy*

anaphoric the quality of 'pointing back' in the discourse to something already introduced, as in the case of definite articles and pronouns
Example: *The girl ... she, A car ... the car.*

anomaly the lack of literal meaning in the everyday word
Example: *The tree greeted me.*

antecedent the noun in the upper clause that is modified by a relative clause and "referred back to" (coreferential with) the relative word
Example: *I complained about <u>the dog</u> which was barking*

antonymy in structural semantics a semantic relation of oppositeness expressing gradable concepts
Example: *light* and *dark* are antonyms

apparent tautology tautologous language in which the two uses of the same word (or two synonyms) have different meanings
Example: *War is war* focuses on different aspects of this complex human activity ('battles/fighting is ruthless/deadly/painful, etc.')

appropriateness condition the "unspoken rules" by which a speech act is governed; its pragmatic presuppositions
Example: appropriateness conditions govern how, when, where, and by whom a speech act can be performed felicitously

approximant a class of sounds involving the articulators approaching each other but not producing friction
Example: laterals, retroflex sounds, and glides (semivowels)

arbitrary the connection between the sequence of sounds constituting a word and the thing in the real world which it names
Example: the word *apple* bears no natural, necessary, logical, or inevitable connection to the fruit it names

argument any of the various elements of the sentence that are set in relation to one another by the predicate, typically noun phrases
Example: *<u>Margot</u> wrote <u>the phone number</u> on <u>the wall</u>.*

articulator the speech organs used in the production of speech sounds
Example: the lips, the tongue, the teeth, the roof of the mouth

articulatory phonetics the study of the speech sounds of human language with respect to their production

aspect indication of whether an action is complete or incomplete, see *imperfective aspect, perfective aspect*

aspirated   a speech sound involving the release of a small puff of air following articulation of the sound
Example: the [tʰ] in *top*

assimilation   the process whereby two neighboring (usually adjacent) sounds become more like one another in respect to one or more phonetic features
Example: the /s/ in *horse* pronounced as /ʃ/ in the compound *horse shoe* in anticipation of the /ʃ/ in *shoe*

audiolingual method   a method of language teaching that viewed language errors as bad habits needing to be eradicated through error correction and repetition of correct utterances; see also *cognitive-code approach*

auditory phonetics   the study of the speech sounds of human language with respect to their perception

auxiliary (Aux)   the specifiers of the verb, represented Aux → T (M) (Perf) (Prog) in phrase structure rules
Example: *He should have been planning the party*

back   the position of the tongue within the rear of the oral cavity (in the velar area)
Example: the sound /ʊ/ in *book*

back formation   the derivation of a morphologically simple word from a word which is, or is analyzed as, a morphologically complex word
Example: *jell < jelly, surveille < surveillance*

bare infinitive   nonfinite verb form consisting of the base form of the verb
Example: *I made him bathe.*

basic level term   the level at which people normally conceptualize and name things
Example: *tree* is a basic level term; *eucalyptus* and *ash* are not

Benefactive (Ben)   thematic role expressing the person or thing for which an action is performed or the person who derives something from the actions of another
Example: *He set up her computer for her* (Ben).

bilabial   a sound articulated by bringing the lower lip against the upper lip
Example: the sound of /b/ in *baby*

blend   a process of word formation involving two types of change, compounding and clipping. Two free words are combined and blended.
Example: *cineplex < cine(ma) + (multi)plex, guestimate < guess + (est)imate*

bound morph   a morphological unit that may not stand alone as a word
Example: *-ify* (in *ratify*)

bound root   a morphological unit that carries the principal meaning but may not stand alone as an independent word
Example: *kempt* in *unkempt*

broad transcription   transcription which records the basic features of speech sounds
Example: the phoneme /t/

case   indication of the function of a noun or pronoun in a sentence, either by inflection, periphrase, or word order
Example: *I* (= subject: inflection) *gave the book* (direct object: word order) *to the student* (indirect object: periphrase)

causative   a verbal predicate denoting a change of state in an entity brought about by some force; analyzable with the abstract predicate CAUSE
Example: *The dog's tail tipped over the vase* = The dog's tail CAUSE the vase COME BE tipped over

central   the position of the tongue within the central area of the oral cavity (midway between the palate and velum)
Example: the sound /ʌ/ in *come*

clause   a grammatically complete sequence of words that minimally contains a subject and a predicate; either finite or nonfinite
Example: *She opened the door; (it was difficult) for her to open the door*

cleft sentence   a sentence consisting of a dummy *it* subject, a form of BE, an item in "cleft" position (underlined below), and a relative clause; compare *pseudocleft sentence*
Example: *It was on Saturday that Jane gave the book to Bill.*

clipping   the production of a new word by deliberately dropping part of a word, while retaining the meaning and word class of the original
Example: *ad < advertisement, flu < influenza*

coda (Co)   the sequence of one to four consonants that can close a syllable
Example: /fθs/ in *fifths*

cognitive-code approach   a pedagogical approach holding that language acquisition – rather than involving a set of habits – involves conscious mental processes; see also *audiolingual method*

cognitive predicate a class of verbal predicates that express mental or emotional states of mind
Example: She _hates romantic comedies_.

cohyponym within the relation of hyponymy, the terms which are entailed by the higher level term
Example: _cup, saucer, plate_ are entailed by _dish_

collective a class of nouns having the feature of denoting groups of individuals perceived as a unit
Example: _herd, flock, committee, cutlery_

comment what is said about the topic; usually the predicate of a sentence
Example: They _damaged my new couch_.

commissive a speech act in which the speaker commits himself or herself to the performance of an action
Example: promising, vowing, pledging, etc.

common a class of nouns having the feature of denoting a nonunique referent
Example: _city, newspaper, country_

common case any nongenitive case in English, generally unmarked on nouns
Example: My neighbor's _dog_ chased my _cat_ into the _street_

common gender the expression of masculine and feminine gender in the same form
Example: -er, as in _singer_

commonization the process by which a proper noun is converted into a common word
Example: _Bikini (Islands) > bikini_

communicative competence the knowledge enabling the speaker and hearer to understand and produce utterances in relation to communicative purposes and the speech context

comparative degree (compr) expression of a greater degree or intensity of the quality in one of two items, expressed by inflection or periphrase
Example: _smarter, more intelligent_

competence the implicit knowledge that speakers have about the grammar of their native language, as contrasted with their actual performance
Example: a native speaker knowing the difference between _go_ versus _went_

complement the obligatory element within a phrasal constituent that "completes" the governing element
Example: see _a movie_, on _the television_, similar _to me_

complement of A the obligatory element, usually a prepositional phrase or clause, which completes certain adjectives,
Example: close _to the door_, happy _that I am done_

complementarity in structural semantics, a relation of oppositeness expressing contradiction, in which the denial of one term is the assertion of its complementary term
Example: _asleep_ and _awake_ are complementary terms

complementary distribution the situation in which positional variants of a phoneme each occur in different, predictable phonetic environments
Example: [pʰ], [p˺], and [p] are all allophones of /p/ and occur in complementary distribution

complementizer (Comp) a marker of subordination serving to attach one clause (the dependent clause) to another clause (the main clause)
Example: The noise _that_ the machine is making is horrible

complex transitive verb (complex trans) a class of verbs which is complemented by a direct object and an object complement
Example: The artist _molded_ the clay into a ball.

components the conventional divisions of language
Example: phonology, syntax

compound the combination of two or more free roots
Example: _homework, artist's loft, sewing machine, blow-dry_

comprehensible input Krashen's theory that second language learners most readily acquire language that contains structures which are just above their current level of comprehension (a level that he terms _i+1_)

concrete a class of nouns having the feature of denoting referents which are knowable by the senses
Example: _book, plum, skyscraper_

conjunct adverbial (cA) an optional sentence modifier (AdvP, PP, S̄) serving to link clauses and expressing a logical connection such as addition or contrast; also called a "conjunctive adverb"
Example: _Nevertheless_, she is content.

connotation   the feelings, attitudes, or opinions (personal or societal) evoked by a word; may be positive, neutral, or negative
Example: *economical* is neutral, *thrifty* is positive, and *miserly* is negative

consciousness-raising   the classroom practice of calling student attention to certain problematic aspects of structures but downplaying overt explanation with the goal of raising learner consciousness and assisting the process of acquisition
Example: teaching the semantics of the present perfect progressive via close focused discussion of real-world situations

consonant   a sound which can occur at the beginning or end of a syllable and which is articulated with some degree of closure of the articulators
Example: /b/ /s/ /r/

consonant cluster   combinations of two or more consonants that can occur at the beginning and/or end of a syllable
Example: *stride*, *ba<u>ts</u>*, *<u>tw</u>ig<u>s</u>*

constituent   the proper subpart of a sentence, identified by a number of different constituency tests; in a tree diagram, all and only the nodes dominated by a single node
Example: In *The teacher handed out the exams*, the constituents are *the teacher/the exams/handed out/ handed out the exams*. (*Teacher handed/ out the exams/out the* are NOT constituents.)

constitutive rule   a rule that determines how something works
Example: The sentence *Cat the the dog chased* violates the constitutive rules of English word order.

content word   a word that carries the primary communicative force of an utterance, belongs to an open or productive class, and is variable in form (inflected); see also *lexical morpheme*
Example: noun, verb, adjective

content-based instruction   an approach to second language instruction that embeds the learning of language within real-world content
Example: teaching the various language skills using the content of "heredity vs. environment" or "the effect of deforestation on the earth's atmosphere"

contextual grammar   an approach to the teaching of structure which relies on the context of actual texts drawn from books and periodicals

continuative   a verbal predicate denoting the continuation of a situation; analyzable with the abstract predicates NEG COME NEG
Example: *The ship <u>remained afloat</u>* = The ship NEG COME NEG BE floating

contradiction   the quality of being logically incompatible (i.e. if one statement is true, the other must be false)
Example: *The king was accidentally assassinated.*

contrast   information that is in opposition to another entity or is selected from a larger set of entities
Example: *Phyllis* in *Most of my high school friends have moved away; only Phyllis still lives in town.*

contrastive analysis   in structural linguistics, research conducted into differences between languages with the goal of identifying potential problem areas and adjusting the lesson plan accordingly; see also *error analysis* and *interlanguage analysis*

controlled PRO   a PRO in which the missing element in the nonfinite embedded clause is identical to an element in the main clause; see *PRO*
Example: *We hoped* [PRO *to see you*], where PRO = *we*

conversational implicature   the attempt by the hearer, when the speaker violates the cooperative principle, to understand the utterance by taking contextual information into account and making certain inferences; see also *cooperative principle*

conversational relevance   the need for the hearer to make certain implicatures, determining that some implicit speech act, rather than the explicit speech act, is relevant in the context
Example: In the conversational exchange:
A: *Are you coming to the party?* B: *My car is out of gas.*
B's response is only conversationally relevant if A makes the implicature that B requires his/her car to come to the party.

converseness   in structural semantics, a semantic relation of oppositeness expressing reversal
Example: *host/guest* (*Mary is Fay's guest; Fay is Mary's host*)

conversion   see *functional shift*

cooperative principle   A principle first identified by Paul Grice by which the speaker makes his/her communicative purpose in speaking clear to the hearer and likewise, the hearer does his/her best to discern this purpose

copula(tive) verb (cop) a class of verbs which is complemented by a subject complement
Example: *became* in *The children at the party became very noisy.*

core member cognitively most central members of a semantic category (most frequent, most readily and quickly identified as members of the category)
Example: *milk, yoghurt, cottage cheese* are core members of the category "dairy product"

count a class of nouns having the feature that they are individuated and can be counted (or pluralized)
Example: *button* is a count noun

creative the quality of language that allows humans to create and understand novel sentences of infinite length and even new words
Example: We can understand a lengthy sentences such as *This is the dog that worried the cat that killed the rat that ate the malt that lay in the house that Jack built*

dative case the case of the indirect object, expressed by periphrasis with *to/for* or by word order
Example: *She sold the car to her sister* (dative case). *He sold her sister* (dative case) *the car.*

declarative a speech act in which the speaker brings about a change in the world by uttering a locutionary act
Example: declaring war, seconding a motion, adjourning a meeting

deep (D-) structure the abstract syntactic level in which all meaning resides; D-structure is generated by the phrase structure rules of the grammar. D-structures are simple (as opposed to complex), active (as opposed to passive), declarative (as opposed to interrogative or imperative), and positive (as opposed to negative) sentences.
Example: *The cat caught the mouse*

definite article the determiner that denotes definiteness; see *definite information*
Example: *Yesterday I bought a car. The car is silver.*

definite information information where the referent is known, familiar, or identified to the speaker and hearer, for example, because it is previously mentioned in the discourse
Example: "Mary and Joe" in *Mary and Joe just returned from a vacation in Africa.*

definiteness see *definite article, indefinite article*

degree see *comparative degree, positive degree, superlative degree*

degree word (Deg) a word that intensifies the meaning of the following adjective or adverb, including forms such as *so, too, very, somewhat, rather, quite, more, most, slightly, highly, moderately, completely, awfully, incredibly,* or *unbelievably*
Example: *slightly imperfect, quite slowly*

denotation the literal or referential meaning of a word; compare *connotation*
Example: *economical, thrifty,* and *miserly* all have the denotation 'careful financial management'

dental a sound articulated by the tip of the tongue touching the back of the upper front teeth or protruding between the teeth
Example: the sound of /t/ in Spanish or the sound /ð/ in English

deontic modal meaning based on what is required, necessary, or compulsory
Example: In *We had to buy a new car, have to* expresses obligation imposed upon the speaker to buy a new car

dependent clause a clause, either finite or nonfinite, that cannot stand alone as a complete utterance but must be attached to a main clause
Example: *He said that he ran in the morning. He enjoys running in the morning.*

derivation the addition of a word-forming affix (a prefix or a suffix)
Example: *re-* + *turn* > *return, sign* + *-age* > *signage*

derivational affix an affix that converts one part of speech to another (class changing) and/or changes the meaning of the root (class maintaining).
Example: *-able* in *washable* changes a V to a N and adds the meaning 'capable of being washed'

descriptive grammar a grammar that explains or analyzes how language works and how it is used, without regulating usage
Example: adjectives in English typically precede the noun (*blue car,* not *car blue*)

descriptive predicate a class of verbal predicates which qualify or identify the subject
Example: *The paper is wrinkled.*

determiner (Det) a class of words occupying a particular syntactic slot, including articles (such as *a, the*), demonstratives (such as *this, that*), possessives (such as *my, her*), wh-words (such as *which, whose*), and quantifiers (such as *many, several*)

diacritic a mark added to a phonetic symbol to represent allophonic variation
Example: the superscript ʰ in [pʰ] to represent aspirated /p/ in *party*

dialect variations of the standard language (e.g. standard North American English or British Received Pronunciation), often as spoken regionally or in various social classes
Example: the dialectal English of the Canadian Maritime Provinces

diphthong a sound produced with the tongue gliding from one position to another within the single syllable
Example: the sound /ɔɪ/ in *soil*

diprepositional verb (diprep) a class of verbs which is complemented by two prepositional phrases
Example: *confer* in *We conferred with him about the plans.*

direct object (dO) the complement of a (di)transitive, complex transitive, or transitive phrasal verb; a NP immediately following the verb (or sister of V$_{gp}$) which denotes the person or thing affected by the action of the verb
Example: *her glasses* in *She broke her glasses. She rubbed her glasses clean. She pulled out her glasses.*

direct speech act see *performative verb*

direction of fit the way in which language relates to the external world; in a "word to world" fit the speaker expects what s/he says to match things in the physical world; in a "world to word" fit the speaker intends the world to match what s/he says (i.e. for a change to come about)
Example: a declarative such as *it's raining* has a "world to word" direction of fit since the words match or correspond to the external world

directive a speech act in which the speaker attempts to get the hearer to do something
Example: ordering, commanding, requesting, etc.

discourse the sequence of two or more sentences, either written or spoken, that cohere in some way

discourse (utterance) semantics the meaning of extended discourse (spoken or written), or the semantic relationships among utterances used in context
Example: speech act theory and information structuring

discourse marker short words or phrases that are traditionally seen as empty fillers, but are now understood as signaling the relevance of the utterance they introduce to the ongoing discourse
Example: A: *Do you want to come to the party?* B: *Well, my parents are visiting.* (With the discourse marker *well* B implies that his/her parents' visiting poses some impediment to attending the party.)

disjunct adverbial (dA) optional sentence modifier (AdvP, PP, S̄) denoting the speaker's attitude toward or judgment of the proposition; also called a *sentence adverb*
Example: *Honestly I have no explanation for their strange behavior* ('I am being honest when I say that …')

distributional test means of subclassifying words in which words which may fill the same syntactic slot are said to belong to the same class
Example: The words *table, garage, candy*, all of which fill the slot Det A ___, can be classified as nouns

ditransitive verb (ditrans) a class of verbs which is complemented by a direct object and an indirect object
Example: *Lily lent her book to Rose*

do-support Operation which inserts *do* when required (in negatives and questions) when no other independent auxiliary element is present
Example: *Helen arrived on time* → *Did Helen arrive on time? Helen did not arrive on time.*

double genitive use of both the inflectional and the periphrastic genitive in the same expression, generally with a partitive sense
Example: *a quirk of Susan's* (= 'one of Susan's (many/several) quirks')

dummy auxiliary *do* structural (and meaningless) element that occurs in Aux when necessary; see *do*-support
Example: *Did you do a search of the neighborhood for your lost cat?*

durative a feature characteristic of a situation that goes on in time or lasts for a certain period
Example: the verb *love* denotes a situation that can be analyzed with the feature [+DURATIVE]

egressive a verbal predicate denoting the end or cessation of a situation; analyzable with the abstract predicates COME NEG
Example: *The siren finished wailing* = The siren COME NEG BE wailing

egressive pulmonic system the prevalent system for producing speech sounds which involves air exiting from the lungs

-en participle nonfinite form of the verb formed with the past participial form of the verb; represented with the abstract marker -en
Example: *broken, potted, spent, cut* (as in *broken record, potted plant, spent bank account, cut flowers*)

enclitic a bound form that typically derives from an independent word but must be attached to the preceding word
Example *-n't* in *isn't*

entailment an utterance that is the logical consequence, or implication, of another.
Example: *My husband just called me* entails *I am a married woman.*

epistemic modal meaning based on knowledge or belief (possibility, probability, certainty, etc.)
Example: In *Careful, the gun may be loaded, may* expresses possibility, the speaker's belief that the gun is loaded.

error analysis the practice of analyzing actual student errors based on the belief that student errors have many sources; see also *contrastive analysis* and *interlanguage analysis*

expect-type verbs class of verbs taking NP + nonfinite verbal complements where the NP is subject of the lower clause but is raised to the object position in the upper clause:
$V_{gp\ \bar{5}}[NP\ VP] \rightarrow V_{gp\ \bar{5}}\ NP_{\bar{5}}[PRO\ VP]$.
Example: *We want you to help us.*

Experiencer (Ex) thematic role expressing the animate being affected inwardly by a state or action
Example: *The mother* (Ex) *was concerned when her daughter did not come home on time.*

expressed psychological state in speech act theory, the beliefs and attitudes of the speaker; the speaker's attitude towards the propositional content of the speech act
Example: a speaker's promising to do something without intending to do so represents an insincere speech act

expressive a speech act in which the speaker expresses a psychological state about the situation or state of affairs denoted by the proposition
Example: thanking, apologizing, consoling, etc.

extension the entities (referents) in the real world that are denoted by a word
Example: *pants* refers to capri pants, bermuda shorts, dress slacks, jeans, chinos, etc.

extraposed subject (eSu) a clausal subject that has been moved to an "extra" position at the end of the sentence; see *extraposition*

extraposition movement of a clause rightward to an added position at the end of the sentence
Example *That he offered to help is encouraging → It is encouraging that he offered to help*

Factitive (Fa) thematic role expressing the object resulting from, or coming about by virtue of, an action or state; having no prior existence
Example: *She gave an account* (Fa) *of the events.*

factive a main clause that presupposes its complement clause
Example: *I'm sorry that I forgot your birthday* presupposes that the speaker did in fact forget the hearer's birthday

falling intonation one of two possible intonation contours in English, where the pitch contour falls at the end of the tone unit
Example: the pitch contour in the statement *I'm ready.*

finite clause a grammatically complete sequence of words that minimally contains a subject and a predicate with a finite verb
Example: "the dog ate my homework" is a finite clause in *The dog ate my homework* and in *I claimed that the dog ate my homework*

finite verb form of the verb or auxiliary restricted in person, number, tense
Example: *helped* (but not *do*) in *She helped him do the dishes*

flap a sound involving the active articulator striking the passive articulator once only
Example: the medial consonant sound /ɾ/ in *butter*

focusing the movement of elements to the end of the clause or sentence in order to emphasize the given element
Example: *That Boris won the election* has been confirmed. ⇒ It has been confirmed *that Boris won the election*

Force (Fo) thematic role expressing the inanimate cause of an action, which does not act by will or volition
Example: *The mud slide* (Fo) *buried the city*

free (or headless) relative   a clause which in form resembles a relative clause (with a relative word and *wh*-fronting) but which functions as a noun phrase
Example: *She always knows what I like.*
free morph   a morphological unit that may stand alone as a word
Example: *chair*
fricative   a sound involving the close approximation of two articulators producing turbulent air flow (a hissing sound)
Example: the sound /v/ in *value*
front   the position of the tongue within the most forward area of the oral cavity (in the palatal area)
Example: the sound /i/ in *meet*
fronting   the movement of a word, phrase, or clause to the beginning of the sentence
Example: *Tennis I like but jogging I avoid.*
function   the grammatical role of a constituent (word or phrase), see *direct object, subject, modifier, specifier,* etc.
function word   a word that expresses grammatical meaning, belongs to a closed or unproductive class, and is generally invariable in form; its distribution is definable by the grammar; see also *grammatical morpheme*
Example: article, preposition, conjunction
functional shift   the conversion of one part of speech to another without the addition of a suffix, or the addition of a zero (Ø) derivational suffix
Example: *to commute* (V) > *a commute* (N)
future tense   verbal distinction which in English is expressed by a variety of noninflectional means
Example: *The package will arrive tomorrow.*
gender   See *grammatical gender, natural gender*
generative   the characteristic of syntactic rules of English that they are able to produce (or "generate") any possible sentence of English (and no impossible sentences of English).
generic noun   a noun that refers to the class or category ("genus") of an entity; generic nouns can be either definite or indefinite
Example: *A house is a major purchase.*
generic number   the expression of both singular and plural at the same time
Example: *A dog makes a good pet.*

generic person   the expression of all persons in the same form
Example: *You can never win.* (meaning 'I, you, they can never win')
genitive case   the case of the possessor; also used for many other relations between two nouns, expressed by inflection or periphrase
Example: *Bill's* (genitive case) *car is in the garage. The door of the garage* (genitive case) *is closed.*
gerund   form identical with the *-ing*-participle that functions as a nominal
Example: *Smoking is harmful to your health, I objected to his smoking.*
given information   information that is already known to the participants in a variety of ways (e.g. mentioned in the preceding discourse, part of the communicative context, culturally known, etc.); also called *old information*
Example: *I saw a movie last night. The movie was depressing.* (*The movie* has been previously mentioned in the discourse.)
glide   a sound involving the tongue moving to or from a vowel; also known as *semivowel*
Example: the sound /w/ in *was*
glottal   a sound articulated by making a brief closure of the vocal cords
Example: the sound /ʔ/ in *battle* (in some dialects)
glottis   the space between the vocal cords
Goal (Go)   thematic role expressing the place-to-which or person-to-whom an action is directed, including indirect objects and directional adverbs
Example: *He ran to the bus stop* (Go).
governor   the element within a phrasal constituent that controls ("governs") the presence of another element. Its lexical category determines the type of phrase
Example: *on the telephone*
grammatical category   a semantic distinction often expressed by inflectional morphology or periphrasis (function words)
Example: number (singular vs. plural), tense (present vs. past)
grammatical gender   a linguistic system in which nouns have a gender that is unrelated to the sex of the item in the real world; often a means of classifying nouns
Example: Old English *lār* 'learning' is feminine gender

grammatical morpheme   a morpheme that expresses one of a limited number of very common meanings, such as tense or number, or expresses relations within the sentence
Example: *the legs of the table*

grapheme   an alphabet letter used to spell a word
Example: *b, e, x*

head   the essential and obligatory part of a phrasal constituent; its lexical category determines the type of phrase
Example: In *the bright light* the noun *light* is the head of the NP

high   the relative height of the tongue within the highest area of the oral cavity
Example: the sound /i/ in *feet* or /u/ in *tomb*

homonymy   two words which are identical in form (orthographic/phonetic form) but different in meaning
Example: *pine₁* means 'species of evergreen tree' and *pine₂* means 'to waste away'

homorganic   two sounds articulated in the same position
Example: the stops /p, b/ and the nasal /m/

hyponymy   in structural semantics, a relation of inclusion or entailment. A superordinate includes its cohyponyms, while a cohyponym entails its superordinate
Example: *organ* and *liver/kidney/heart/pancreas, etc.* bear a relation of hyponymy

iconic sign   a thing that resembles what it represents
Example: a photograph

idiom   a sequence of words which is syntactically fixed and semantically conventionalized and functions as a single unit
Example: *call it a day, be under the weather,*

illocutionary force (IF)   the way in which the proposition is to be taken (e.g. as a statement, a command, or a question)
Example: *It's cold outside* could have the illocutionary force of a statement (a simple description of the weather) or of a suggestion (to put on a coat).

imperative   sentence form in English without an explicit subject; derived from a D-structure containing *you* and *will*
Example: *Answer the door!*

imperative mood   a verbal distinction denoting a direct 2nd p command (expressed by a special syntactic form in English) or 1st or 3rd person commands
Example: *Stop making all that noise! Let's go to the mall. Let him do the dishes.*

imperfective aspect   verbal distinction which denotes an action as incomplete and ongoing
Example: *We are planning our vacation.*

inchoative   a verbal predicate denoting a change in state; analyzable with the abstract predicate COME
Example: *She turned pink* = She COME BE pink

inclusion   one utterance that encompasses another
Example: *I am a professor* includes *I teach classes, I do research, I perform university service.*

indefinite article   the determiner used to express indefiniteness; see *indefinite information*.
Example: *Yesterday I bought a car. The car is silver.*

indefinite information   information in which the referent of the noun phrase is novel, unfamiliar, or not known to the hearer; for example, because it is being mentioned for the first time in the discourse
Example: "a couple" in the sentence *A couple I know just returned from a vacation in Africa.*

indefinite relative   a clause containing an indefinite relative (a form with *-ever* that undergoes *wh*-movement) which functions as a noun phrase
Example: *I will be happy with whatever you cook*

indexical sign   a thing that points to or has a necessary connection with what it represents
Example: smoke (representing fire)

indefinite PRO   a PRO in which the missing element in the nonfinite clause can be filled with the general *you* or *one*, not with any specific element from the higher clause
Example: *It is easy [PRO to bake bread] < [you bake bread]*

indicative mood   a verbal distinction indicating that the situation is viewed as fact, expressed by the simple and compound tenses of the verb in English
Example: *The door slammed shut. The sun is shining. The weather has cleared.*

indirect object (iO)   the complement of a ditransitive verb (in combination a direct object); an NP denoting the animate goal or benefactive of the action
Example: *He showed Felix the flowers/He showed the flowers to Felix.*

indirect object movement   syntactic operation which allows the indirect object following *to* or *for* to move to a position before the direct object (V NP$_2$ *to/for* NP$_1$ $\Rightarrow$ V NP$_1$ NP$_2$)
Example: *The child told a lie to his mother* $\Rightarrow$ *The child told his mother a lie*

indirect question   a *yes/no* or *wh*-question expressed as a dependent clause, usually in indirect speech; contains *wh*-fronting but no subject-auxiliary inversion
Example: *She asked when I was leaving for New York; She asked whether/if I liked New York.*

indirect speech act   a speech act the force of which is that of the implicit act rather than of the explicit act
Example: *Can you hand me the book* is an explicit question about the hearer's abilities but functions as a request for the hearer to hand the speaker the book.

infinitive   see *bare infinitive*, *to-infinitive*, *wh-infinitive*

inflectional affix   an affix that indicates grammatical meaning, such as tense or number; in English always a suffix.
Example: *computers*

inflectional test   means of subclassifying words in which words taking the same inflection are said to belong to the same class
Example: The words *table, garage, candy*, all of which take the *-s* plural inflection, can be classified as nouns

information structuring   the way in which discourse is organized to create cohesive and coherent texts, for example, to emphasize (foreground) or deemphasize (background) aspects of the discourse or to fit the contribution into an ongoing discourse

-*ing* participle   nonfinite form of the verb beginning with an *-ing* (present participial) verbal form
Example: *singing, having coughed, having been running*

initialism   word formed by combining the initial letters of words in a phrase; pronounced as letters
Example: *UFO* (<*unidentified flying object*)

innate   the inborn capacity or genetic predisposition of humans to acquire language
Example: children are able learn their first language despite the fact that they are seldom explicitly "taught" or corrected

Instrument (I)   thematic role expressing the means by which an event is caused, or the tool, generally inanimate, used to carry out an action
Example: *He rubbed out his mistake with an eraser* (I).

intension   the set of defining or characteristic properties shared by all of the referents of a word
Example: the intension of *table* is any piece of furniture with one or more legs and a flat top surface, used for writing, dining, etc.

interlanguage   the nonnative speaker's linguistic competence at any stage short of native-speaker competence

interlanguage analysis   the analysis of nonnative speaker production which is based on the belief that the language of nonnative speakers is constantly redefining itself in the direction of a more stable, native-speaker-like competence as learners are increasingly exposed to the target language; see also *contrastive analysis* and *error analysis*

International Phonetic Alphabet (IPA)   an internationally-used system of recording sounds in which there is a one-to-one relationship between sound and symbol
Example: the IPA symbol /i/ represents the vowel sound in the words *meat, meet, key, niece*, and *be*

intonation   the rises and falls (or movement) of pitch that extend over a given phrase
Example: a rise in pitch over the phrase *He said he would help* signals a question

intransitive verb (intrans)   a class of verbs which takes no complement
Example: *Anthony spoke slowly.*

labialization   rounding of the lips during the articulation of a sound
Example: the alveolopalatal consonants /ʃ/ and /ʒ/

labiodental   a sound articulated by bringing the lower lip against the upper front teeth
Example: the sound /f/ in *fancy*

lateral   a sound involving the air passing around the sides of the tongue
Example: the sound /l/ in *loan*

lax vowel   vowels that are produced with less tension and cannot occur in a stressed, open syllables
Example: the vowel /ʊ/ in *took*

left-dislocation   the movement of a word, phrase, or clause to the beginning of the sentence, leaving a pronominal copy of the fronted element in its original place; see also *fronting*
Example: *Annette, she'll be home late tonight.*
lexeme   all inflected forms of a word, conventionally represented with small caps
Example: the lexeme WRITE included *write, writes, wrote, written, writing*
lexical (main) verb   the verb functioning as head of the VP, carrying the primary verbal meaning and immediately following AUX
Example: *We will have <u>eaten</u> dinner by that time.*
lexical ambiguity   a word or phrase allowing more than one meaning in context
Example: *The food is hot* can mean either 'the food is hot' or 'the food is spicy'
lexical category   the categories noun, verb, adjective, adverb, and preposition; these form the head or the governor of a phrasal category, see *phrasal category*
Example: *happy* belongs to the lexical category A, and forms the head of the phrasal category AP
lexical field   A set of terms that divides up, or partitions, a conceptual field
Example: the field of body part terms, including *arm, head, neck, leg,* etc.
lexical morpheme   a morpheme which expresses lexical or dictionary meaning
Example: *the <u>legs</u> of the <u>table</u>*
lexical semantics   the meaning properties of individual words (lexical items) in isolation
Example: sense relations such as hyponomy, synonymy, and antonymy as well as selectional restrictions and figurative language
linguistic sign   a sequence of sounds that represents concrete objects and events as well as abstractions
Example: any word (e.g. *apple*)
literary coinage   a new word formation which is attributed to a particular author
Example: *blasé* (Byron), *malapropism* (Sheridan)
Location (Lo)   thematic role expressing the place-at/in-which or the time-at-which an action occurs
Example: *The concert begins at <u>8:00</u> (Lo) in <u>the main auditorium</u> (Lo).*

locative predicate   a class of verbal predicates that express the location of an entity in time or space
Example: *Mary <u>is in her office</u>.*
loudness   increased volume of the voice related to the pressure and volume of air expelled
low   the relative height of the tongue within the lowest area of the oral cavity
Example: the sound /æ/ in *mat*
main clause   A finite clause that can stand alone as a complete utterance
Example: *My omelette was overcooked.*
manner of articulation   the amount of constriction of the air flow (i.e. whether it is complete, partial, or relatively open)
Example: the stop /b/ involves complete constriction; /f/ involves partial constriction; /æ/ is relatively open (i.e. involves no constriction)
meronymy   the relationship of part to whole
Example: *roof* to *building, torso* to *human being*
metaphor   figurative language which involves a sense transfer from one domain to another, often from the concrete to the abstract or the physical to the cognitive
Example: *<u>head</u> of foam, traffic <u>jam</u>*
metonymy   figurative language which denotes something by naming a thing or characteristic associated with it
Example: *the stage* refers to the theatrical profession
mid   the relative height of the tongue within the middle area of the oral cavity
Example: the sound /ɛ/ in *set*
minimal pair   a set of different words consisting of all the same sounds except for one
Example: *<u>c</u>at* vs. *<u>b</u>at; <u>pi</u>n* vs. *<u>pe</u>n*
modal auxiliary (M)   the class of auxiliaries occupying the first position in AUX following tense and expressing mood
Example: *shall, can, may, will, must*
mode-based instruction   an approach to teaching writing where the writing curriculum is structured according to typical (if often idealized) rhetorical modes
Example: "comparison-contrast", "cause and effect", "description of a process", and so on

modifier (Mod)   an optional element within a phrasal constituent that depends upon the head and cannot occur without it; expresses some quality or aspect of the head.
Example: *ask politely; speak in a low voice*
modifier of N   an optional element modifying the noun, either in pre-position (an adjective) or post-position (a prepositional phrase or relative clause).
Example: In *green apple,* "green" is a pre-modifier of the N; in *apple on the tree,* "on the tree" is a post-modifier of the N
monitor   the notion that learners can consciously edit or "monitor" their production but typically are not able to do so during spontaneous speech
Example: the learner may omit the 3rd person -s on a present tense verb when speaking (e.g. *She need_ a piece of paper.*) but on a multiple choice test would be able to provide the correct response *needs.*
monophthong   a single or simple vowel sound produced with the tongue in a constant position
Example: the sound /i/ in *treat*
mood   indication of whether the verbal situation is seen as fact or non-fact; see *indicative mood, subjunctive mood, imperative mood*
morph   the concrete realization of a morpheme, or the actual segment of a word.
Example: the morpheme {past} may be realized as the morph /t/ in *hoped* or as the morph /d/ in *jumped*
morpheme   the smallest meaningful unit in a language
Example: *re-bound-s* has three morphemes
morphemic rule   a rule accounting for the allomorphs of a morpheme, giving their conditioning environments
Example: rule setting out the phonological conditioning of the allomorphs /d/, /t/, and /əd/ of the morpheme {past}
morphological realization rule   the process by which (abstract) morphemes combine to produce a concrete word
Example: {FOOD} + {pl} > *foods* (agglutinative); {FOOD} + {past} > *feed* (fusional); {FOOD} + {sg} > *food* (null); {PUT} + {past} > *put* (zero)
morphology   the study of the structure and classification of words

Example: *freedom* consists of the root *free* and the suffix *-dom* and is classified as a noun
N-bar (N̄)   an intermediate category consisting of the noun and its pre- and post-modifiers
Example: *There were large stones in the middle of the road*
narrow transcription   transcription which records all the nuances and finer aspects of speech sounds
Example: allophones of /t/, e.g. aspirated [tʰ], unreleased [t̚]
nasal   a sound involving complete closure of two articulators with the velum lowered
Example: the sound /m/ in *marry*
nasal cavity   the nose, which serves as a resonator of speech sounds
nasal sound   a sound produced with air passing out only through the nasal cavity
Example: /m/, /n/ /ŋ/
nasalized sound   a sound produced with air passing out through both the oral and nasal cavities
Example: the allophone [ĩ] in *sin*
Natural Approach   an approach to second language learning which stresses the need to respond to learners' affective needs and focus on real-world situations in order to stimulate general classroom interest
natural gender   a linguistic system in which the sex of the item in the real world is denoted, for example, by pronoun forms
Example: *The boy cleaned his room.*
natural order of acquisition   the belief that there is an invariant order of acquisition of grammatical structures regardless or the learner's first language and that this order
is the same or similar to that of first language acquisition
negative politeness   linguistic strategies that cater to one's desire not be imposed upon
Example: using expressions of deference, apologizing
negative transfer   in language acquisition, the transfer of patterns from the learner's first language to the target language
Example: a German speaker pronouncing /r/ in English using his/her native uvular variety of the consonant

Neutral (Neu) thematic role expressing the person or thing which is not changed or even acted upon, but simply present at an action
Example: *We saw many cathedrals* (Neu) *in Europe*.

new information information that is not known to the hearer, being introduced into the discourse by the speaker for the first time
Example: *Let me tell you about my move*.

nominalizer a derivational affix which creates a noun
Example: *-ment* in *judgment* (changing a V to a N)

nominative case (nomn) the case of the subject and subject complement
Example: *She* (nominative case) *opened the door*.

noncount (mass) a class of nouns having the feature of denoting a referent that exists in bulk or is otherwise not countable
Example: *concrete, grass, reliability*

nonfactive a main clause that does not presuppose its complement clause
Example: *I suppose he is rich* does not presuppose that 'he is rich' but merely expresses some degree of certainty concerning his being rich

nonfinite clause a sequence of words that minimally contains a nonfinite verb and is always dependent
Example: *Here is a book for you to read*

nonfinite verb a verb form that is not restricted for person, number, and tense, including infinitives, gerunds, and participles

nonrestrictive relative a relative clause that is not necessary to limit the reference of the noun it modifiers, adds additional information; typically modifies a unique or specific noun; in writing it is set off by commas
Example: *I visited Los Angeles, which is the second largest city in the United States*.

nonspecific information information that denotes no particular entity in the real world
Example: *One must consider all options*.

notional passive an expression which is active in form but must be interpreted as passive in meaning
Example: *The dog trains easily* (= 'the dog is easily trained')

noun (N) in English, a word which meets certain inflectional tests (e.g. takes plural *-s*, genitive *-'s*) and distributional tests (e.g. follows determiner or adjective)

Example: *stapler* (count), *soil* (mass/noncount), *emotion* (abstract), *bowl* (concrete), *flock* (collective), *Guatemala* (proper), *country* (common)

noun phrase (NP) a phrasal category which has a noun or pronoun as its head
Example: In *The morning newspaper arrived late today*, the NP is "the morning newspaper"

nucleus (Nu) the acoustic peak of the syllable consisting of a vowel or syllabic consonant which can potentially carry stress
Example: /ɛ/ in *threat*

number a grammatical category with two terms in English, singular ('one') and plural ('more than one')
Example: *this* is the singular demonstrative; *these* is the plural demonstrative

object complement (oC) the complement of a complex transitive verb (along with a direct object); a NP, AP, or PP describing, identifying or locating the object, either in its current or resultant state
Example: *We deemed the project successful*.

object of the preposition (OP) an NP which serves as a complement of a preposition
Example: *on the highest shelf*

objective case the case of the object (direct or indirect)
Example: *She sold the car* (objective case) *to her sister*

obstruent the natural class of sounds consisting of affricates, fricatives, and stops which involve obstruction of the air through the oral cavity
Example: the sounds /p, f, ð, dʒ/

old information see *given information*

onset the sequence of one to three consonants that can begin a syllable
Example: /str/ in *string*

oral cavity the mouth, which serves as a resonator and generator of speech sounds

oral sound a sound produced with air passing out only through the oral cavity
Example: /b/, /p/, /t/

orthography the graphic symbols or letters used in writing
Example: the orthographic symbols "th" represent the phonemes /θ/ or /ð/

oxymoron figurative language involving explicitly contradictory terms
Example: *cruel kindness*: "I must be cruel only to be kind" (Shakespeare, *Hamlet*)

palatal   a sound articulated by bringing the tongue up against the palate
Example: the sound /j/ in English
palatalization   the process whereby alveolar obstruents become alveolopalatal obstruents before an original /y/ in the following syllable, either word internally or between words
Example: /dʒ/ in *educate* (word internal); /tʃ/ in *didn't you* (between words)
palate   the domed roof of the mouth consisting of a bony plate
paradox   see *oxymoron*
parallel distribution   the situation in which phonemes can occur in the same phonetic environments
Example: the phonemes /p/, /t/, and /k/ occur in parallel distribution in the phonetic environment /_æd/: pad, tad, cad
paraphrase   two (or more) utterances which have the same meaning but use different words
Example: *The boy watched a film* is a paraphrase of *The young man viewed a movie.*
particle (Prt)   in English, small indeclinable forms, including prepositions, conjunctions, post-verbal particles, and some adverbs
Example: *since, up*
passive articulator   the stationary speech organ used in the production of speech sounds
Example: the teeth, the roof of the mouth, and the back of the throat
passive voice (Pass)   a periphrase (and associated sentence form) indicating that the subject is being affected by the action or being acted upon; accounted for by a syntactic operation converting an active sentence into a passive sentence
Example: *The crowd was dispersed by the police.*
past tense   a verbal distinction which in English indicates past events and states, expressed inflectionally
Example: *She saw a movie last week. She liked movies when she was young.*
Path (Pa)   thematic role expressing the path taken in moving from one place to another in the course of an action
Example: *The fire burned up the mountain* (Path)
Patient (Pa)   thematic role expressing the person or thing affected by an action, or the entity undergoing a change
Example: *We emptied the wine bottle* (Pa).

pedagogical grammar   grammar meant to be useful either to a native-language classroom teacher or to a teacher of a second language
perfect (Perf)   verbal periphrase in English consisting of HAVE plus the past participle that denotes past events as relevant either by their continuation into the present (and beyond) or by their results in the present. Represented as Perf → have -en in phrase structure rules
Example: *It has rained all day.*
perfective aspect   verbal distinction which denotes an action or state as complete and whole; in English expressed by the simple past
Example: *He ate an apple.*
performance   native speakers' actual use of language; as contrasted with their linguistic competence
Example: a native speaker saying *There's two possible solutions to this problem,* despite knowing the construction *there is* should be followed by a singular noun
performative verb   According to Austin, a type of verb (typically 1st person, simple present tense) which allows the speaker to carry out an action
Example: *I hereby name this ship the "Queen Elizabeth".*
peripheral member   cognitively less central members of a semantic category (less frequent, less readily and quickly identified as members of the category)
Example: *Manx* and *cougar* are peripheral members of the category "cat" (the former is tailless, the latter is not domesticated)
periphrasis (periphrastic form)   a phrase containing a function word, which is functionally equivalent to an inflection
Example: *the population of the city = the city's population*
person   an indication of the person speaking (1st person), the person spoken to (2nd person), or the person or thing spoken about (3rd person)
Example: *I* denotes the speaker; *you* denotes the addressee
personification   figurative language attributing human-like qualities to inanimate objects or abstract concepts
Example: *Time marches on.*

***persuade*-type verbs**   class of verbs taking NP + nonfinite verbal complements where the NP is object of the main clause verb, but controls the missing subject of the nonfinite clause (V$_{gp}$ NP$_{\bar{s}}$ [PRO VP]) and the nonfinite clause functions as object complement.
Example: *We coaxed the kitten to come out from under the house.*

phoneme   a distinctive or contrastive sound in a language
Example: /t/ vs. /f/; /ɛ/ vs. /æ/

phonemic rule   a rule stipulating the different environments in which each allophone is found
Example: /t/ at the end of a word is realized as unreleased [t̚] as in *but* or *pat*; /t/ at the beginning of a word or stressed syllable is realized as aspirated [t^h]

phonetics   the study of the speech sounds of human language in general, either from the perspective of their production, perception, or physical properties
Example: the phoneme /r/ has different possible articulations in different languages (e.g. retroflex in North American English, trilled in Spanish, etc.)

phonological rule   a rule that describes the general processes of phonological change in allophonic variation, often as they apply to classes of sounds
Example: all alveolar sounds are dentalized before the dentals /θ/ and /ð/

phonology   the study of the speech sounds of a particular language
Example: /r/ in North American English is retroflex

phonotactics   the constraints on positions and sequences of sounds in a language
Example: /ŋ/ does not occur at the beginning of a syllable in English; in initial position in English, the only clusters with three consonants begin with /s/

phrasal category   a category that always occurs on the left side of a phrase structure rule and is composed of other categories (lexical and phrasal). The lexical category of the head or governor determines the type of phrasal category, see *lexical category*
Example: the phrasal category AdvP is expanded as (Deg) Adv. The head of this phrasal category is Adv.

phrasal verb   a verb consisting of a verb and a post-verbal particle that is moveable before or after the direct object: V$_{gp}$ → V Prt

Example: transitive, as in *He cleaned out the garage/ cleaned the garage out* or intransitive, as in *The plane took off*.

phrase   sequences of words – or a single word – having syntactic significance (forming a constituent), see *constituent, noun phrase, adjective phrase, adverb phrase, verb phrase, prepositional phrase*

phrase compound   a phrase that functions as a semantically unified morphological unit (a compound) but may be internally modified
Example: *pins and needles, son-in-law* (cf. *sons-in-law*)

phrase structure rules   rules which account for the form of D-structures, specifying what is a constituent of what and revealing the hierarchical structures of sentences.
Example: S → NP + VP

pitch   the quality and range of sounds emitted as a consequence of the frequency of the sound wave

place of articulation   for consonants, the point at which the articulators meet or are in closest contact; for vowels, the position of the highest part of the tongue
Example: /b/ involves the lower lip touching the upper lip; /i/ involves the high point of the tongue in the high front quadrant of the oral cavity

polysemy   the existence of more than one meaning for a word out of context; the meanings are related to one another in some way
Example: The word *barb* can mean either 'backwards projection of an arrow' or 'hurtful remark'

positive degree (pos)   expression of a quality, denoted by the root of an adjective or adverb
Example: *smart, intelligent, fast*

positive politeness   linguistic strategies that cater to one's desire to be liked and/or approved of
Example: complimenting the hearer, using close or affectionate terms of address

possessive predicate   a class of verbal predicates that express the location of an entity coincidental with a person
Example: *We own a large house*.

Possessor (Po)   thematic role expressing the possessor of a thing; Possessor is a special kind of locative, since the thing and the possessor must coincide
Example: *They have a dog* (alienable Po), *which has a curly coat* (inalienable Po).

pragmatics the study of the functions of language and its use in context
Example: The phrase *The light is green* uttered by a passenger to the driver of a car stopped at an intersection signals the driver to begin driving.

predicate in syntactic analysis, a VP (containing a finite verb) that expresses what is being said about the subject (e.g. the action or state of the subject)
Example: *She ran a marathon*.

predicate (pred) in semantic analysis, the part of a proposition (typically the verb and accompanying prepositions) which operates on arguments, placing them in relation to one another; "place" refers to the number of arguments
Example: *It is cold* (Ø-place), *She is tall* (1-place), *He watched television* (2-place), and *The dog ran from the yard into the street* (3-place).

prefix an affix that attaches to the beginnings of a root
Example *bio-* in *biodiversity*

preposition (P) an indeclinable word which governs an object
Example: *in the morning, after the movie, of the book*

prepositional complement (pC) a PP which serves as a complement of a prepositional verb or an adjective
Example: "for a refund" in *They asked for a refund*.

prepositional phrase (PP) a phrasal category which has a preposition as governor
Example: *We watched television after dinner*.

prepositional specifier (PSpec) a determining element occurring before (to the left of) a preposition, including *right, straight*, and measure phrases
Example: In *He left right after the lecture*.

prepositional verb (prep) a class of verbs which is complemented by a prepositional complement
Example: *The pen fell into the crack*.

prescriptive grammar a grammar that prescribes (dictates) and proscribes (forbids) certain ways of speaking and writing in an attempt to establish and maintain a standard of correctness
Example: infinitives should not be split (*to comprehend fully*, not *to fully comprehend*)

present tense (pres) a verbal distinction which in English indicates a variety of nonpast distinctions such as habits or states
Example: *She sees a movie every week. She loves movies*.

presupposition what is assumed beforehand by a proposition
Example: *I resumed working* presupposes that I was working in the past.

primary stress the strongest of the three levels of word stress
Example: the stress on the underlined syllable in the word *rèlatívity*

PRO phonetically null subject and/or object NPs of nonfinite clauses
Example: *I bought a book* [PRO *to read* PRO] < [*I read a book*]

process approach the current approach to teaching composition which emphasizes the multiple drafting process, with conceptual development placed first; compare *product approach*

product approach the approach to teaching composition in which idealized essays are presented as models and students are encouraged to conform to these models; compare *process approach*

progressive (Prog) verbal periphrase in English consisting of BE plus the present participle that denotes events as in progress, ongoing, and incomplete (not yet ended). Represented Prog → be *-ing* in phrase structure rules
Example: *The tide is coming in*.

proper a class of nouns having the feature of denoting a unique referent
Example: *Chicago, The New York Times, Afghanistan*

proposition the semantic content of a clause minus any particular syntactic structure or grammatical marking (e.g. tense); any semantic ambiguity or vagueness is eliminated, as is the intended communicative force
Example: The proposition underlying both *Did you feed the birds?* (a question) and *Would you feed the birds* (a request) is [you feed the birds].

propositional content the state of affairs expressed in a given sentence; see *proposition*

prototype a good, clear exemplar of a semantic category
Example: a *robin* is a prototypical bird, an *emu* is not

pseudocleft sentence a sentence consisting of a headless relative clause (underlined below), a form of BE, and either a NP or a VP, thus postponing the sentence focus to the end; compare *cleft sentence*
Example: *What Henry studied at university* was linguistics.

raising movement of an NP from a syntactic position in the lower sentence to a syntactic position in the upper sentence
Example: "subject-to-object" raising: *I need [you to be on time]* ⇒ *I need you [to be on time]*
"object-to-subject" raising (also known as *"tough"*-movement": *It is easy [to read this book]* ⇒ *This book is easy to read*
"subject-to-subject" raising: *It is certain [that Betsy will win]* ⇒ *Betsy is certain to win*

Range (Ra) thematic role expressing the specification or limitation of an action
Example: *The concert lasted two hours* (Ra)

recategorization shifting of a part of speech from one subclass to another or from one class to another
Example: *set* (V) > *set* (N), *tea* (mass) > *tea(s)* (count)

recursive quality of grammatical rules in which a category introduces itself or introduces another category which introduces it; recursion is the main formal means of accounting for the infinite and creative nature of language
Example: NP is recursive in the following set of rules:
NP → (Det) N (PP)
PP → P NP

reduplication a process of word formation in which the initial syllable or the entire word is doubled, exactly or with a slight phonological change
Example: *fifty-fifty, tip-top, helter-skelter*

referent see *extension* or *intension*

reflexive pronoun form consisting of the objective form of the personal pronoun plus *-self* or *-selves*; used when the object of the sentence is coreferential with the subject
Example: *They congratulated themselves on a job well done.*

register the stylistic variations of language used in different social contexts
Example: *Chem 10 is a killer course.* (spoken to a close friend) vs. *I found the curriculum of Chemistry 10 to be extremely challenging.* (spoken to the professor of the course).

regulatory rules rules that control behavior; see also *prescriptive grammar*
Example: The sentence *He did good on the exam* would be understood by a native speaker although it violates the regulatory rules of English.

relative clause an adjective clause which functions as a post-modifier of the N̄ or NP
Example: *The porch which they built is huge.*

representative a speech act in which the speaker represents a state of affairs
Example: affirming, declaring, describing, etc.

restrictive relative relative clause that "restricts" or limits the reference of the noun it modifiers
Example: *The cup that I broke was very expensive.*

retracted the allophonic variation of a vowel that is articulated with the tongue further back in the mouth
Example: the sound [i̠] in *seal*

retroflex a sound involving the tongue curling up and back behind the alveolar ridge
Example: the sound /r/ in North American English

rising intonation one of two possible intonation contours in English, where the pitch contour rises at the end of the tone unit
Example: the pitch contour in the question *Are you ready?*

Role (Ro) thematic role expressing a person playing a role or part in an action or state
Example: *She is the CEO* (Ro) *of a computer company.*

root a morphological unit that carries the principal lexical or grammatical meaning of a word
Example: *crime* in *criminalize*

root allomorphy the existence of two predictable variants of a root
Example: [haʊs] and [haʊz] (in the context of {pl})
for *house*

root creation the invention of an entirely new root morpheme
Example: *quark*

rounded the pursing or rounding of the lips in vowel production
Example: the sound /u/ in *boot*

S-bar (S̄) a S preceded by a complementizer position, typically a dependent clause
Example: *Before work begins, the land must be cleared.*

scalar adjectives sets of antonymous adjectives which are understood in respect to a norm
Example: *deep/shallow, fancy/plain*

secondary stress the second or next strongest level of the three levels of word stress
Example: the stress on the underlined syllable in the word *relatívity*

selectional restriction   a restriction on the inherent semantic features of adjacent words with in a grammatical construction
Example: the word *crawl* has the selectional restriction that its subject must be [+QUADRUPED]

semantic feature (component)   a basic and universal component of meaning, generally conceived of as binary. Features are the shared semantic characteristics of words. Each word can be analyzed into a unique combination of features.
Example: [+HUMAN] is a feature of *boy, girl, woman, waitress, professor*, etc.

semantics   the study of how meaning is conveyed by linguistic units (e.g. words, phrases, clauses); see also *lexical semantics, sentence semantics*
Example: the meaning of *film* and *movie* are synonymous; the meaning of *legal* and *illegal* are antonymous

semivowel   see *glide*

sense   concepts existing in the mind of the speaker by which he or she refers to things denoted by a word, often existing in relation to other meanings in the language
Example: *glass* has the sense 'a vessel for holding liquid, used for drinking'; this sense is distinguished from, and stands in relation to, the other senses of glass, such as 'hard, brittle, transparent substance'

sentence (S)   a syntactic category consisting of NP + VP
Example: *The comic told a joke, The play lasted three hours, He gave her a lift* are sentences. *The comic* is a not a sentence, nor is *told a joke.*

sentence combining   a teaching technique in which students are initially provided with a kernel sentence and then encouraged to develop it in a semi-creative way through combining signals (most frequently additional phrases or clauses)
Example: Given sentence and cue: *A garbage dump is behind the restaurant. (THERE – INS)*
Student rewrite: *There is a garbage dump behind the restaurant.*

sentence diagramming   an earlier, simplified form of phrase structure grammar employing stick or line diagrams to identify the various sentence components and their relationships; see also *sentence parsing*

Example:

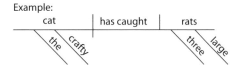

The crafty cat has caught three large rats.

sentence parsing   taking sentences apart, identifying their components, and recognizing the relations among these components; see also *sentence diagramming*

sentence semantics   the study of the meaning properties of a sentence, meaning determined by the grammatical form of a sentence
Example: predication analysis and theta roles

sentential relative   a relative clause that modifies the entire clause rather than a specific head noun in the main clause
Example: *Jack helped me move, which was very kind of him.*

sibilant   the class of fricatives and affricates that involve a high degree of hissing (produced by directing the air over the teeth)
Example: /s, z, ʃ, ʒ, tʃ, dʒ/

sign   a thing that stands for or represents something else
Example: a nation's flag

sincerity condition   see *expressed psychological state*

sonorant   the class of sounds consisting of approximants, nasals, vowels, and glides which involve a certain degree of resonance in their articulation
Example: /a, æ, y, w, r, l, m, n, ŋ/

Source (So)   thematic role expressing the place-from-which or person-from-whom an action emanates
Example: *Crowds ran from the burning building* (So).

specific information   Information that denotes a particular entity in the real world
Example: "the car" in *Tomorrow I'm going to polish the car.*

specifier   elements that limit or quantify the elements which follow, including determiners, auxiliaries, and prepositional specifiers
Example: *that* barking dog; *will* retire; *straight* after class

specifier of N   a determiner serving as specifier of the noun
Example: *that* worker, *his* opinion

specifier of P (PSpec)   a small set of words (including *right, straight,* measure terms) that can limit prepositions
Example: <u>*right*</u> *before lunch,* <u>*two hours*</u> *after lunch*
speech act theory   an important theory, first proposed by J.L. Austin and further developed by John Searle, which attempts to account for the function of language within context
state   a nondynamic situation, such as emotional, cognitive, and physical states, conditions, or qualities
Example: the verb *love* denotes a state
stative   a semantic feature characteristic of a situation that does not involve change or is not dynamic or a verbal predicate denoting such a situation; analyzable with the abstract predicate BE
Example: the stative verb *love* denotes a situation that can be analyzed with the feature [+STATIVE]; *The wall* <u>*is green*</u> = The wall BE green
stop   a sound involving complete closure of two articulators with the velum raised
Example: the sound /g/ in *green*
stress   an increase in the activity of the respiratory muscles forcing more air out of the lungs during the articulation of a particular syllable
Example: the second syllable in *abóve*
strong form   a function word pronounced with the full (stressed) version of the vowel
Example: *Yes I* <u>*ám!*</u> /æm/ (emphatic statement)
subject (Su)   the NP immediately dominated by S, typically the topic, the actor, or thing which is talked about in a sentence
Example: In *On Tuesday,* <u>*the locksmith*</u> *came to our house.*
subject complement (sC)   the complement of a copula verb; a NP, AP, or PP describing, identifying or locating the subject, either in its current or resultant state
Example: *The question is* <u>*complicated*</u>.
subject-auxiliary inversion   syntactic operation in which tense plus the <u>first</u> independent auxiliary element moves to a position preceding the subject
Example: *She has cleaned her room* ⇒ *Has she cleaned her room?*
subjunctive mood   indication that the verbal situation is non-fact (possibility, probability, prediction, ability, etc.), expressed by remnant inflections or by periphrase
Example: *If I* <u>*were*</u> *smart, I* <u>*could answer*</u> *the question.*

suffix   an affix that attaches to the end of roots
Example: *-ency* in *transparency*
superlative degree (supl)   expression of the greatest degree or intensity of the quality in one of three or more items, expressed by inflection or periphrase
Example: *smartest, most intelligent*
superordinate term   within the relation of hyponymy, the term which includes all of the other terms
Example: *professional* is the superordinate term including *doctor, lawyer, accountant, executive, CEO,* and so on
suppletion   an instance in which the inflected forms of a word are constructed from different roots
Example: *bad/worse/worst; go/went*
suprasegmental feature   an articulatory feature that is superimposed over more than one segment
Example: stress and intonation
surface (S-) structure   the actual linear order of words in a sentence, the concrete realization of a D-structure; S-structure is generated by applying transformations to D-structure
Example: *The mouse was caught by the cat* (the D-structure is *The cat caught the mouse*).
syllabic   the ability of all vowels (and certain "syllabic" consonants) to stand alone in a syllable
Example: the sound /aɪ/ in the personal pronoun *I* or the syllabic "n" in the second syllable of *button*
syllable (Sy)   a phonological unit which consists minimally of a vowel and optionally of consonants at the beginning and/or end of the unit
Example: the three-syllable word *paranoid*: par.a.noid
symbolic sign   a thing that is only conventionally related to what it represents
Example: a rose (representing love)
symmetry   in structural semantics, a special relation of converseness allowing a conjoined syntactic construction
Example: *Line A is parallel to line B; Lines A and B are parallel.*
synecdoche   figurative language in which the whole is referred to by naming the part (or the substance from which something is made)
Example: *grass* (= lawn), *iron, wood* (=golf clubs)
synesthesia   figurative language in which a term from one sense domain is used to refer to a different sense domain
Example: *a sweet song* (*sweetness* – taste; *song* – sound), *a flat note* (*flat* – vision/touch; *note* – sound)

synonymy   a semantic relationship of sameness in meaning
Example: *garbage* and *trash* are synonyms

syntax   the study of the order and arrangement of words into hierarchical units (e.g. phrases, clauses) and the relationship among words within these units
Example: *into the woods* is a prepositional phrase in which *into* governs the object
the woods

tag question   question "tag" attached to a main clause declarative sentence; consisting of subject-auxiliary inversion, a pronominal copy of the subject, and reversed polarity from the main clause
Example: *He is studying to become an opera singer, isn't he?* or *He isn't driving his car anymore, is he?*

tautology   language which is "true by definition"
Example: *unmarried bachelor*

telic   a semantic feature characteristic of a situation that has an endpoint or goal that is necessary for the situation to be what it is
Example: the verb *mature* denotes a situation that can be analyzed with the feature [+TELIC]

tense (T)   the verbal indication of the time of an action in respect to the moment of speaking, conceptually past, present, or future but morphologically past or present in English
Example: *We arrived* home yesterday (past relative to the moment of speaking)

tense vowel   a vowel that is produced with more tension and can occur in stressed, open syllables
Example: the vowel /u/ in *loon*

***that*-clause**   a finite dependent clause introduced by the complementizer *that* (*that* may be deleted)
Example: *I realized that I needed more money.*
I realized I needed more money.

thematic role (θ-role)   the semantic function or role of arguments in respect to the predicate, including Agent, Force, Instrument, etc.
Example: *She* (Ag) *mowed the lawn* (Pa).

Theme (Th)   thematic role expressing the person or thing which undergoes an action, or that which is transferred or moved by an event but otherwise unchanged
Example: *She put the paper* (Th) *in the recycling box.*

***to*-infitive**   nonfinite form of the verb consisting of *to* plus the base form of the verb
Example: *I wanted to succeed.*

tone group   the division of longer sequences of discourse into discrete units of information, each of which has an accompanying tone pattern or intonation contour
Example: *She sat by the window in the late afternoon,// reading a letter.* (2 tone units, each with falling intonation contours)

tonic syllable   the syllable within a tone group that carries the major shift in intonation and emphasizes new or unknown information; usually the last stressed syllable in the tone group
Example: the first syllable of *accident* in *She had an accident.*

topic   what an utterance is about, its starting point, its center of attention, or the perspective from which it is viewed
Example: *they* in the sentence *They damaged my new couch.*

topicalization   the alteration of word order which moves elements into topic position or makes them part of the topic
Example: *The right answer is difficult to find.*

trace   an empty constituent in a position from which a *wh*-word has been moved; represented by [*t*]
Example: He asked I want <u>what</u> for dinner ⇒ *He asked what I wanted [t] for dinner*

transformation   a syntactic operation which applies to the output of the phrase structure rules to produce an S-structure; transformations may move, transpose, add, and delete elements, but not change meaning.
Example: "passive" applies to *The cat chased the mouse* to produce *The mouse was chased by the cat.*

transitive verb (trans)   a class of verbs which is complemented by a direct object
Example: *Marion opened the door slowly.*

tree diagram   the graphic representation of the linear order and hierarchical structure of a phrase or clause
Example:

PP

P   NP

trill a sound involving rapid vibration of the active against the passive articulator
Example: the Scottish "r"
underlying structure see *deep structure*
universals the general set of constraints on language which are not language-specific but are found in all languages of the world
Example: there are only three basic word orders that occur with any frequency among world languages, namely, SuVO, SuOV, and VSuO
unreleased a stop sound where the articulators do not open and release air
Example: the [t̚] in *but*
unrounded the spreading of the lips in vowel production
Example: the sound /i/ in *heat*
unstressed vowel the central vowels which occur only in unstressed syllables
Example: the /ə / vowel in the first syllable of *about*; the /ɨ/ vowel in *spinach*
usage rules rules concerning common habits of speech and writing that are disapproved of by language educators; see also *prescriptive grammar*
Example: a clause should not end with a preposition
V-bar ($\bar{V}$) an intermediate category consisting of the verb and its complements
Example: *He took the dog on a walk last night*
velar a sound articulated by bringing the tongue into contact with the velum
Example: the sound /k/ in *conch*
velum the muscular flap at the rear of the roof of the mouth which can be raised (velic closure) or lowered (velic opening)
verb (V) in English, a word which meets certain inflectional tests (e.g. takes present participle *-ing*, 3rd p sg *-s*) and distributional tests (e.g. follows auxiliary)
Example: *be, run, swim, laugh*
verb group (V_{gp}) the lexical verb with or without a particle
Example: The verb *read* is a verb group in *He read the names*; the verb and particle *read* and *out* is a verb group in *He read out the names.*
verb phrase (VP) a phrasal category which consists of the verb and its complement
Example: *we cooked a soufflé*
verb subcategorization the classification of verbs based on the type of complement structures that they require, see *transitive verb, ditransitive verb, prepositional verb*, etc.
verbalizer derivational affix creating a verb
Example: *-ize* in *categorize* (changing an N to a V)
verdictive a speech act in which the speaker expresses a value judgment or rates something
Example: assessing, ranking, rating, etc.
vocal cords the two small flaps in the larynx which can be set into vibration
voice See *active voice, passive voice*
voiced a speech sound produced with vibration of the vocal cords
Example: the sound /z/ in *zone*
voiceless a speech sound produced with the vocal cords open and not vibrating
Example: the sound /s/ in *soon*
voluntary a semantic feature characteristic of a situation that comes about through an agent's voluntary or willfull action
Example: the verb *walk* denotes a situation that can be analyzed with the feature [+VOLUNTARY]
vowel a sound which occurs in the nucleus of a syllable and which is articulated with no closure
Example: /ə / /æ/ /ɔ/
vowel length the relative time spent in articulating a vowel
Example: the vowel in *seat* takes longer to articulate than the vowel in *seed*
***want*-type verbs** a class of verbs taking NP + nonfinite verbal complements where the NP is subject of the nonfinite embedded clause ($V_{gp\bar{S}}$[NP VP]) and the nonfinite clause functions as direct object of the *want*-type verb
Example: *I found him to be a helpful person.*
weak form a function word pronounced with the weak (unstressed) version of the vowel
Example: *I am so sleepy.* /ə m/
***wh*- (or content) question** a question formed with subject-auxiliary inversion and containing a *wh*-word in initial position
Example: *When is dinner?*
***wh*-fronting (or *wh*-movement)** movement of the *wh*-word from the position it occupies in D-structure (according to its function) to complementizer position; occurs in *wh*-questions and relative clauses

Example: She asked what question ⇒ *What question did she ask?*

***wh*-infinitive**   nonfinite form of the verb consisting of a *wh*-word plus a *to*-infinitive
Example: *I wondered <u>what to say</u>.*

***wh*-word**   a complementizer introducing direct and indirect *wh*-questions and relative clauses; may function as a pronoun, a determiner, an adverb, or a degree word
Example: *Here is the book <u>which</u> you wanted.I asked <u>what</u> time he would be home. <u>Where</u> is the remote?*

word class   category to which a word belongs based on its semantic, formal, and syntactic characteristics, traditionally known as "part of speech"
Example: noun, verb, adjective, adverb

***yes/no* (or truth) question**   question formed by subject-auxiliary inversion in the main clause; answerable with *yes* or *no*
Example: *Have you seen Harjit today?*

zero morph   a morph which has no phonetic or overt realization
Example: the {pl} morpheme in *fish* (as in *The fish are very colorful*) is realized by a zero morph

Appendices

Appendix I: Abbreviations

The following abbreviations are used in this textbook and accompanying website:

A	adjective	Lo	Location (thematic role)
aA	adjunct adverbial	m	masculine gender
Ac	action	M	modal auxiliary
Adv	adverb	Mod	modifier
AdvP	adverb phrase	n	neuter gender
Ag	Agent (thematic role)	N	noun
AP	adjective phrase	N̄	N-bar
arg	argument	Neu	Neutral (thematic role)
Art	article	Nom	nominal
Aux	auxiliary	nomn	nominative case
Ben	Benefactive (thematic role)	Nu	nucleus
C	consonant	obj	objective case
cA	conjunct adverbial	oC	object complement
Co	coda	On	onset
Comp	complementizer	OP	object of the preposition
complex trans	complex transitive verb	p	person
		P	preposition
compr	comparative degree	Pa	patient (thematic role)
cop	copula(tive) verb	Pass	passive
dA	disjunct adverbial	pC	prepositional complement
Deg	degree word	Perf	perfect aspect
Dem	demonstrative	pl	plural number
Det	determiner	PN	proper noun
ditrans	ditransitive verb	pos	positive degree
dO	direct object	poss	possessive
D-structure	deep structure	Po	Possessor (thematic role)
eSu	extraposed subject	PP	prepositional phrase
Ex	Experiencer (thematic role)	pred	predicate
f	feminine gender	prep	prepositional verb
Fa	Factitive (thematic role)	pres	present tense
Fo	Force (thematic role)	Pro	pronoun
Go	Goal (thematic role)	PRO	gap in nonfinite clause
H	hearer	Prog	progressive aspect
I	Instrument (thematic role)	prop	proposition(al context)
IF	illocutionary force	prsprt	present participle
intrans	intransitive verb	Prt	particle
iO	indirect object	PSpec	prepositional specifier
IPA	International Phonetic Alphabet	pstprt	past participle
		Q	quantifier

Ra	Range (thematic role)	Vo	vowel
Rh	rhyme	VP	verb phrase
Ro	Role (thematic role)	W	word
S	sentence	*wh-*	*wh-*word
S̄	S-bar	*	ungrammatical
sC	subject complement	?	questionable grammaticality
sg	singular number	{ }	mutually exclusive choice
So	Source (thematic role)	( )	optional
Sp	speaker	1st	first person
S-structure	surface structure	2nd	second person
Su	subject	3rd	third person
Sy	syllable	#	word or syllable boundary
supl	superlative degree	→	is realized as, has as its allophones/allomorphs OR is rewritten/expanded as
T	tense		
Th	Theme (thematic role)		
trans	transitive (monotransitive) verb	⇒	is transformed into
		>	becomes
V	verb	<	comes from
V̄	V-bar	Ø	zero-realized
vd	voiced	[ ]	narrow transcription
V$_{gp}$	verb group	/ /	broad transcription
vl	voiceless	~	(logical) negation

Appendix IIa: Phrase structure rules (simple sentences)

$$S \rightarrow \begin{bmatrix} S \left(\begin{Bmatrix} PP \\ AdvP \\ NP \end{Bmatrix} \right) \\ NP \; Aux \; VP \end{bmatrix}$$

$$NP \rightarrow \begin{bmatrix} (Det) \; \overline{N} \\ PN \\ Pro \end{bmatrix}$$

$$\overline{N} \rightarrow \begin{Bmatrix} (AP) \; \overline{N} \; (PP) \\ N \end{Bmatrix}$$

$$AP \rightarrow \left(\begin{Bmatrix} Deg \\ AdvP \end{Bmatrix} \right) A \; (PP)$$

$$AdvP \rightarrow (Deg) \; Adv$$

$$PP \rightarrow (PSpec) \; P \begin{Bmatrix} NP \\ PP \end{Bmatrix}$$

$$Det \rightarrow \begin{bmatrix} Art \\ Dem \\ Poss \\ Q \\ Wh\text{-} \end{bmatrix}$$

$$Poss \rightarrow \begin{Bmatrix} NP\text{-'s} \\ my, your, his\ldots \end{Bmatrix}$$

$$VP \rightarrow \overline{V} \left(\begin{Bmatrix} AdvP \\ PP \\ NP \end{Bmatrix} \right)$$

$$\overline{V} \rightarrow \begin{bmatrix} V_{gp} \left(\begin{Bmatrix} NP \; (\{NP, PP, AP\}) \\ AP \\ PP \; (PP) \end{Bmatrix} \right) \\ \overline{V} \left(\begin{Bmatrix} Advp \\ PP \\ NP \end{Bmatrix} \right) \end{bmatrix}$$

$$V_{gp} \rightarrow V \; (Prt)$$

$$Aux \rightarrow T \; (M) \; (Perf) \; (Prog)$$

$$T \rightarrow \begin{Bmatrix} past \\ pres \end{Bmatrix}$$

$$Perf \rightarrow have\text{-}en$$

$$Prog \rightarrow be\text{-}ing$$

Appendix IIb: Phrase structure rules (complete set)

$\bar{S} \rightarrow \text{Comp } S$

$\text{Comp} \rightarrow \{that, although, when, whether \ldots\}$

$S \rightarrow \begin{bmatrix} \text{NP Aux VP} \\ S(\{\text{PP, AdvP, NP, } \bar{S}\}) \end{bmatrix}$

$\text{NP} \rightarrow \begin{bmatrix} (\text{Det}) \, \bar{N} \, (\bar{S}) \\ \text{PN} \\ \text{Pro} \\ \bar{S} \\ (\text{NP}) \, \bar{S} \end{bmatrix}$

$\bar{N} \rightarrow \begin{bmatrix} (\text{AP}) \, \bar{N} \, (\text{PP}) \, (\bar{S}) \\ \text{N} \end{bmatrix}$

$\text{Det} \rightarrow \{\text{Art, Dem, Poss, Q, } Wh\text{-}\}$

$\text{Dem} \rightarrow \{this, that, these, those\}$

$\text{Art} \rightarrow \{a, an, the\}$

$Wh\text{-} \rightarrow \{which, what, whose\}$

$\text{Poss} \rightarrow \{\text{NP } \text{-'s}, my, our, their \ldots\}$

$Q \rightarrow \{some, any, every, each, neither, more \ldots\}$

$\text{AP} \rightarrow \left(\begin{bmatrix} \text{Deg} \\ \text{AdvP} \end{bmatrix} \right) A \left(\begin{bmatrix} \text{PP} \\ \bar{S} \end{bmatrix} \right)$

$\text{VP} \rightarrow \bar{V} \ (\{\text{AdvP, PP, NP, } \bar{S}\})$

$\bar{V} \rightarrow \begin{bmatrix} V_{gp} \left(\begin{bmatrix} \text{NP} (\{\text{NP, PP, AP}\}) \\ \text{AP} \\ \text{PP (PP)} \\ (\text{NP}) \, \bar{S} \end{bmatrix} \right) \\ \bar{V} \ (\{\text{AdvP, PP, NP, } \bar{S}\}) \end{bmatrix}$

$V_{gp} \rightarrow V \ (\text{Prt})$

$\text{Aux} \rightarrow T \, (M) \, (\text{Perf}) \, (\text{Prog})$

$T \rightarrow \{past, pres\}$

$M \rightarrow \{shall, can, will, may, must\}$

$\text{Perf} \rightarrow have \text{-} en$

$\text{Prog} \rightarrow be \text{-} ing$

$\text{AdvP} \rightarrow (\text{Deg}) \, \text{Adv}$

$\text{PP} \rightarrow (\text{PSpec}) \, P \, \{\text{NP, PP}\}$

Index